SPIKING NEURON MODELS
Single Neurons, Populations, Plasticity

Neurons in the brain communicate by short electrical pulses, the so-called action potentials or spikes. How can we understand the process of spike generation? How can we understand information transmission by neurons? What happens if thousands of neurons are coupled together in a seemingly random network? How does the network connectivity determine the activity patterns? And, vice versa, how does the spike activity influence the connectivity pattern? These questions are addressed in this introductory text aimed at those taking courses in computational neuroscience, theoretical biology, neuronal modeling, biophysics, or neural networks. The authors focus on phenomenological approaches so that beginners can get to grips with the theoretical concepts before confronting the wealth of detail in biological systems. The book is in three Parts dealing, in order, with neurons and connections, collective behavior in networks, and synaptic plasticity and its role in learning, memory, and development. Each chapter ends with a literature survey, and a comprehensive bibliography is included. As such the book will also introduce readers to current research.

The approach will be suitable for students of physics, mathematics, or computer science with an interest in biology; but it will also be useful for biologists who are interested in mathematical modeling. A large number of worked examples are embedded in the text, which is profusely illustrated. There are no mathematical prerequisites beyond what the audience would meet as undergraduates: more advanced techniques are introduced in an elementary, concrete fashion when needed.

SPIKING NEURON MODELS

Single Neurons, Populations, Plasticity

Wulfram Gerstner

Swiss Federal Institute of Technology, Lausanne

Werner M. Kistler

Erasmus University, Rotterdam

CAMBRIDGE UNIVERSITY PRESS

CAMBRIDGE UNIVERSITY PRESS
Cambridge, New York, Melbourne, Madrid, Cape Town,
Singapore, São Paulo, Delhi, Tokyo, Mexico City

Cambridge University Press
The Edinburgh Building, Cambridge CB2 8RU, UK

Published in the United States of America by Cambridge University Press, New York

www.cambridge.org
Information on this title: www.cambridge.org/9780521890793

© Cambridge University Press 2002

First published 2002
Fourth printing 2008

A catalogue record for this publication is available from the British Library

ISBN 978-0-521-81384-6 Hardback
ISBN 978-0-521-89079-3 Paperback

Contents

Preface

The task of understanding the principles of information processing in the brain poses, apart from numerous experimental questions, challenging theoretical problems on all levels from molecules to behavior. This books concentrates on modeling approaches at the level of neurons and small populations of neurons, since we think that this is an appropriate level to address fundamental questions of neuronal coding, signal transmission, or synaptic plasticity. In this text we concentrate on theoretical concepts and phenomenological models derived from them. We think of a neuron primarily as a dynamic element that emits output pulses whenever the excitation exceeds some threshold. The resulting sequence of pulses or "spikes" contains all the information that is transmitted from one neuron to the next. In order to understand signal transmission and signal processing in neuronal systems, we need an understanding of their basic elements, i.e., the neurons, which is the topic of Part I. New phenomena emerge when several neurons are coupled. Part II introduces network concepts, in particular pattern formation, collective excitations, and rapid signal transmission between neuronal populations. Learning concepts presented in Part III are based on spike-time-dependent synaptic plasticity.

We wrote this book as an introduction to spiking neuron models for advanced undergraduate or graduate students. It can be used either as the main text for a course that focuses on neuronal dynamics, or as part of a larger course in computational neuroscience, theoretical biology, neuronal modeling, biophysics, or neural networks. For a one-semester course on neuronal modeling, we usually teach one chapter per week focusing on the first sections of each chapter for lectures and give the remainder as reading assignments. Many of the examples can be adapted to become exercises or projects for students. While writing the book we had in mind students of physics, mathematics, or computer science with an interest in biology; but it might also be useful for students of biology who are interested in mathematical modeling. All the necessary mathematical concepts are introduced in an elementary fashion and we have provided many illustrative figures which complement the mathematical analysis and help the reader picture what is going on. No prior knowledge beyond undergraduate mathematics should be necessary to read the book. An asterisk (*) marks those sections that have a more mathematical focus. These sections can be skipped at a first reading.

We have also tried to keep the book self-contained with respect to the underlying neurobiology. The fundamentals of neuronal excitation and synaptic signal transmission are briefly introduced in Chapter 1 together with an outlook on the principal topics of the book, viz., formal spiking neuron models and the problem of neuronal coding. In Chapter 2 we review biophysical models (such as Hodgkin–Huxley) of neuronal dynamics and models of dendritic integration based on the cable equation. These are the starting point for a systematic reduction to neuronal models with a reduced complexity that are open to an analytical treatment. Whereas Chapter 3 is dedicated to two-dimensional differential equations as a description of neuronal dynamics, Chapter 4 introduces formal spiking neuron models, namely the integrate-and-fire model and the Spike Response Model. These formal neuron models are the foundation for all the following chapters. Part I on "Single Neuron Models" is rounded off by Chapter 5 which gives an overview of spike-train statistics and illustrates how noise can be implemented in spiking neuron models.

The step from single-neuron models to networks of neurons is taken in Chapter 6 where equations for the macroscopic dynamics of large populations of neurons are derived. Based on these equations phenomena such as signal transmission and coding (Chapter 7), oscillations and synchrony (Chapter 8), and pattern formation in spatially structured networks (Chapter 9) can be investigated. Up to this point, only networks with a fixed synaptic connectivity have been discussed. The third part of the book, finally, deals with synaptic plasticity and its role in development, learning, and memory. In Chapter 10, principles of Hebbian plasticity are presented and various models of synaptic plasticity are described that are more or less directly inspired by neurobiological findings. Equations that relate the synaptic weight dynamics to the statistical properties of neuronal spike activity are derived in Chapter 11. Last but not least, Chapter 12 presents an – admittedly personal – choice of illustrative applications of spike-timing-dependent synaptic plasticity to fundamental problems of neuronal coding.

While the book contains material which is now considered as standard for courses of the type mentioned earlier, it also provides a bridge to current research which has developed over the last few years. In most chapters, the reader will find some sections which either report recent results or shed new light on well-known models. The viewpoint taken in the presentation of the material is of course highly subjective and a bias towards our own research is obvious. Nevertheless, we hope that the book will find the interest of students and researchers in the field.

Werner M. Kistler
Wulfram Gerstner
Lausanne, November 2001

Acknowledgments

This book would not have been possible without the help of our friends and colleagues who made many valuable comments and spotted numerous mistakes. In particular, we would like to thank Silvio Borer, Nicolas Brunel, Stefano Fusi, Evan Haskell, Andreas Herz, Renaud Jolivet, Maurizio Mattia, Jean-Pascal Pfister, Hans-Ekkehard Plesser, Marc van Rossum, Walter Senn, and Arnaud Tonnelier for a careful reading of the text. We owe special thanks to Leo van Hemmen who encouraged us to write a book on our joint work. Even though the scope of the text has changed over the years, the original initiative is due to him. Finally, we thank all the students who attended tutorials or classes taught by us and whose critical comments helped us to organize our thoughts.

W.G. and W.K.

1

Introduction

The aim of this chapter is to introduce several elementary notions of neuroscience, in particular the concepts of action potentials, postsynaptic potentials, firing thresholds, and refractoriness. Based on these notions, a first phenomenological model of neuronal dynamics is built that will be used as a starting point for a discussion of neuronal coding. Due to the limitations of space we cannot – and do not want to – give a comprehensive introduction into such a complex field as neurobiology. The presentation of the biological background in this chapter is therefore highly selective and simplistic. For an in-depth discussion of neurobiology we refer the reader to the literature mentioned at the end of this chapter. Nevertheless, we try to provide the reader with a minimum of information necessary to appreciate the biological background of the theoretical work presented in this book.

1.1 Elements of neuronal systems

Over the past hundred years, biological research has accumulated an enormous amount of detailed knowledge about the structure and function of the brain. The elementary processing units in the central nervous system are neurons which are connected to each other in an intricate pattern. A tiny portion of such a network of neurons is sketched in Fig. 1.1 which shows a drawing by Ramón y Cajal, one of the pioneers of neuroscience around 1900. We can distinguish several neurons with triangular or circular cell bodies and long wire-like extensions. This picture can only give a glimpse of the network of neurons in the cortex. In reality, cortical neurons and their connections are packed into a dense network with more than 10^4 cell bodies and several kilometers of "wires" per cubic millimeter. In other areas of the brain the wiring pattern may look different. In all areas, however, neurons of different sizes and shapes form the basic elements.

The cortex does not consist exclusively of neurons. Beside the various types of neuron there is a large number of "supporter" cells, so-called glia cells, that are

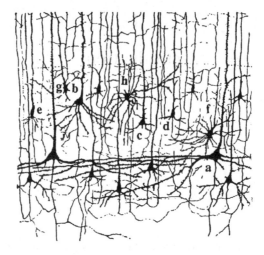

Fig. 1.1. This reproduction of a drawing of Ramón y Cajal shows a few neurons in the mammalian cortex that he observed under the microscope. Only a small portion of the neurons contained in the sample of cortical tissue have been made visible by the staining procedure; the density of neurons is in reality much higher. Cell b is a nice example of a pyramidal cell with a triangularly shaped cell body. Dendrites, which leave the cell laterally and upwards, can be recognized by their rough surface. The axons are recognizable as thin, smooth lines which extend downwards with a few branches to the left and right. From Ramón y Cajal (1909).

required for energy supply and structural stabilization of brain tissue. Since glia cells are not directly involved in information processing, we will not discuss them any further. We will also neglect a few rare subtypes of neuron, such as analog neurons in the mammalian retina. Throughout this book we concentrate on spiking neurons only.

1.1.1 The ideal spiking neuron

A typical neuron can be divided into three functionally distinct parts, called dendrites, soma, and axon; see Fig. 1.2. Roughly speaking, the dendrites play the role of the "input device" that collects signals from other neurons and transmits them to the soma. The soma is the "central processing unit" that performs an important nonlinear processing step. If the total input exceeds a certain threshold, then an output signal is generated. The output signal is taken over by the "output device", the axon, which delivers the signal to other neurons.

The junction between two neurons is called a synapse. Let us suppose that a neuron sends a signal across a synapse. It is common to refer to the sending neuron as the presynaptic cell and to the receiving neuron as the postsynaptic cell. A single neuron in vertebrate cortex often connects to more than 10^4 postsynaptic neurons.

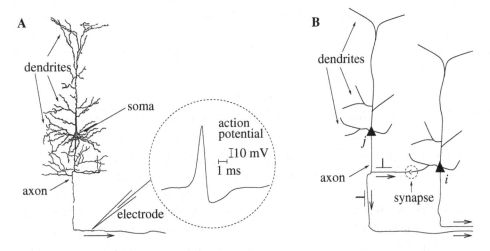

Fig. 1.2. **A**. Single neuron in a drawing by Ramón y Cajal. Dendrite, soma, and axon can be clearly distinguished. The inset shows an example of a neuronal action potential (schematic). The action potential is a short voltage pulse of 1–2 ms duration and an amplitude of about 100 mV. **B**. Signal transmission from a presynaptic neuron j to a postsynaptic neuron i. The synapse is marked by the dashed circle. The axons at the lower right end lead to other neurons (schematic figure).

Many of its axonal branches end in the direct neighborhood of the neuron, but the axon can also stretch over several centimeters so as to reach to neurons in other areas of the brain.

1.1.2 Spike trains

The neuronal signals consist of short electrical pulses and can be observed by placing a fine electrode close to the soma or axon of a neuron; see Fig. 1.2. The pulses, so-called action potentials or spikes, have an amplitude of about 100 mV and typically a duration of 1–2 ms. The form of the pulse does not change as the action potential propagates along the axon. A chain of action potentials emitted by a single neuron is called a spike train – a sequence of stereotyped events which occur at regular or irregular intervals. Since all spikes of a given neuron look alike, the form of the action potential does not carry any information. Rather, it is the number and the timing of spikes which matter. The action potential is the elementary unit of signal transmission.

Action potentials in a spike train are usually well separated. Even with very strong input, it is impossible to excite a second spike during or immediately after a first one. The minimal distance between two spikes defines the absolute refractory period of the neuron. The absolute refractory period is followed by a phase of relative refractoriness where it is difficult, but not impossible, to excite an action potential.

1.1.3 Synapses

The site where the axon of a presynaptic neuron makes contact with the dendrite (or soma) of a postsynaptic cell is the synapse. The most common type of synapse in the vertebrate brain is a chemical synapse. At a chemical synapse, the axon terminal comes very close to the postsynaptic neuron, leaving only a tiny gap between pre- and postsynaptic cell membranes, called the synaptic cleft. When an action potential arrives at a synapse, it triggers a complex chain of biochemical processing steps that lead to the release of neurotransmitter from the presynaptic terminal into the synaptic cleft. As soon as transmitter molecules have reached the postsynaptic side, they will be detected by specialized receptors in the postsynaptic cell membrane and open (either directly or via a biochemical signaling chain) specific channels so that ions from the extracellular fluid flow into the cell. The ion influx, in turn, leads to a change of the membrane potential at the postsynaptic site so that, in the end, the chemical signal is translated into an electrical response. The voltage response of the postsynaptic neuron to a presynaptic action potential is called the postsynaptic potential.

Apart from chemical synapses neurons can also be coupled by electrical synapses, so-called gap junctions. Specialized membrane proteins make a direct electrical connection between the two neurons. Not very much is known about the functional aspects of gap junctions, but they are thought to be involved in the synchronization of neurons.

1.2 Elements of neuronal dynamics

The effect of a spike on the postsynaptic neuron can be recorded with an intracellular electrode which measures the potential difference $u(t)$ between the interior of the cell and its surroundings. This potential difference is called the membrane potential. Without any spike input, the neuron is at rest corresponding to a constant membrane potential. After the arrival of a spike, the potential changes and finally decays back to the resting potential, cf. Fig. 1.3A. If the change is positive, the synapse is said to be excitatory. If the change is negative, the synapse is inhibitory.

At rest, the cell membrane already has a strong negative polarization of about -65 mV. An input at an excitatory synapse reduces the negative polarization of the membrane and is therefore called depolarizing. An input that increases the negative polarization of the membrane even further is called hyperpolarizing.

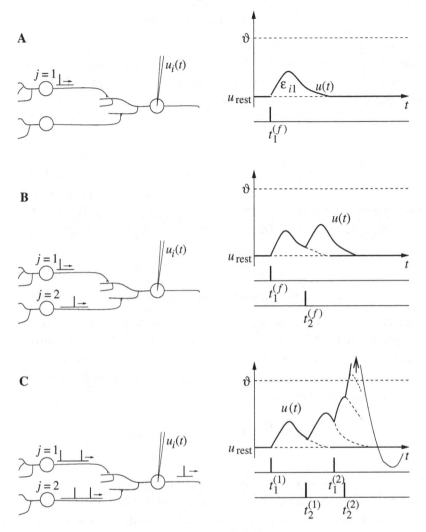

Fig. 1.3. A postsynaptic neuron i receives input from two presynaptic neurons $j = 1, 2$. **A.** Each presynaptic spike evokes an excitatory postsynaptic potential (EPSP) that can be measured with an electrode as a potential difference $u_i(t) - u_{rest}$. The time course of the EPSP caused by the spike of neuron $j = 1$ is $\epsilon_{i1}(t - t_1^{(f)})$. **B.** An input spike from a second presynaptic neuron $j = 2$ that arrives shortly after the spike from neuron $j = 1$ causes a second postsynaptic potential that adds to the first one. **C.** If $u_i(t)$ reaches the threshold ϑ, an action potential is triggered. As a consequence, the membrane potential starts a large positive pulse-like excursion (arrow). On the voltage scale of the graph, the peak of the pulse is out of bounds. After the pulse the voltage returns to a value below the resting potential.

1.2.1 Postsynaptic potentials

Let us formalize the above observation. We study the time course $u_i(t)$ of the membrane potential of neuron i. Before the input spike has arrived, we have $u_i(t) = u_{\text{rest}}$. At $t = 0$ the presynaptic neuron j fires its spike. For $t > 0$, we see at the electrode a response of neuron i

$$u_i(t) - u_{\text{rest}} = \epsilon_{ij}(t) \,. \tag{1.1}$$

The right-hand side of Eq. (1.1) defines the postsynaptic potential (PSP). If the voltage difference $u_i(t) - u_{\text{rest}}$ is positive (negative) we have an excitatory (inhibitory) PSP or short EPSP (IPSP). In Fig. 1.3A we have sketched the EPSP caused by the arrival of a spike from neuron j at an excitatory synapse of neuron i.

1.2.2 Firing threshold and action potential

Consider two presynaptic neurons $j = 1, 2$, which both send spikes to the postsynaptic neuron i. Neuron $j = 1$ fires spikes at $t_1^{(1)}, t_1^{(2)}, \ldots$, similarly neuron $j = 2$ fires at $t_2^{(1)}, t_2^{(2)}, \ldots$. Each spike evokes a PSP ϵ_{i1} or ϵ_{i2}, respectively. As long as there are only few input spikes, the total change of the potential is approximately the sum of the individual PSPs,

$$u_i(t) = \sum_j \sum_f \epsilon_{ij}(t - t_j^{(f)}) + u_{\text{rest}} \,, \tag{1.2}$$

i.e., the membrane potential responds linearly to input spikes; see Fig. 1.3B.

However, linearity breaks down if too many input spikes arrive during a short interval. As soon as the membrane potential reaches a critical value ϑ, its trajectory shows a behavior that is quite different from a simple summation of PSPs: the membrane potential exhibits a pulse-like excursion with an amplitude of about 100 mV, viz., an action potential. This action potential will propagate along the axon of neuron i to the synapses of other neurons. After the pulse the membrane potential does not directly return to the resting potential, but passes through a phase of hyperpolarization below the resting value. This hyperpolarization is called "spike-afterpotential".

Single EPSPs have amplitudes in the range of 1 mV. The critical value for spike initiation is about 20–30 mV above the resting potential. In most neurons, four spikes – as shown schematically in Fig. 1.3C – are thus not sufficient to trigger an action potential. Instead, about 20–50 presynaptic spikes have to arrive within a short time window before postsynaptic action potentials are triggered.

1.3 A phenomenological neuron model

In order to build a phenomenological model of neuronal dynamics, we describe the critical voltage for spike initiation by a formal threshold ϑ. If $u_i(t)$ reaches ϑ from below we say that neuron i fires a spike. The moment of threshold crossing defines the firing time $t_i^{(f)}$. The model makes use of the fact that action potentials always have roughly the same form. The trajectory of the membrane potential during a spike can hence be described by a certain standard time course denoted by $\eta(t - t_i^{(f)})$.

1.3.1 Definition of the model SRM$_0$

Putting all elements together we have the following description of neuronal dynamics. The variable u_i describes the momentary value of the membrane potential of neuron i. It is given by

$$u_i(t) = \eta(t - \hat{t}_i) + \sum_j \sum_f \epsilon_{ij}(t - t_j^{(f)}) + u_{\text{rest}}, \tag{1.3}$$

where $\hat{t}_i$ is the last firing time of neuron i, i.e., $\hat{t}_i = \max\{t_i^{(f)} \mid t_i^{(f)} < t\}$. Firing occurs whenever u_i reaches the threshold ϑ from below,

$$u_i(t) = \vartheta \text{ and } \frac{\mathrm{d}}{\mathrm{d}t}u_i(t) > 0 \implies t = t_i^{(f)}. \tag{1.4}$$

The term ϵ_{ij} in Eq. (1.3) describes the response of neuron i to spikes of a presynaptic neuron j. The term η in Eq. (1.3) describes the form of the spike and the spike-afterpotential.

Note that we are only interested in the potential *difference*, viz., the distance from the resting potential. By an appropriate shift of the voltage scale, we can always set $u_{\text{rest}} = 0$. The value of $u(t)$ is then directly the distance from the resting potential. This is implicitly assumed in most neuron models discussed in this book.

The model defined in Eqs. (1.3) and (1.4) is called SRM$_0$ where SRM is short for Spike Response Model (Gerstner, 1995). The subscript zero is intended to remind the reader that it is a particularly simple "zero order" version of the full model that will be introduced in Chapter 4. Phenomenological models of spiking neurons similar to the models SRM$_0$ have a long tradition in theoretical neuroscience (Hill, 1936; Stein, 1965; Geisler and Goldberg, 1966; Weiss, 1966). Some important limitations of the model SRM$_0$ are discussed below in Section 1.3.2. Despite the limitations, we hope to be able to show in the course of this book that spiking neuron models such as the SR Model are a useful conceptual framework for the analysis of neuronal dynamics and neuronal coding.

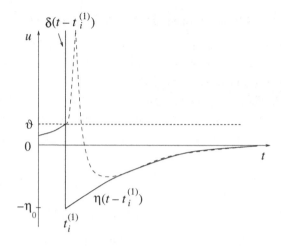

Fig. 1.4. In formal models of spiking neurons the shape of an action potential (dashed line) is usually replaced by a δ pulse (vertical line). The negative overshoot (spike-afterpotential) after the pulse is included in the kernel $\eta(t - t_i^{(1)})$ (thick line) which takes care of "reset" and "refractoriness". The pulse is triggered by the threshold crossing at $t_i^{(1)}$. Note that we have set $u_{\text{rest}} = 0$.

Example: formal pulses

In a simple model, we may replace the exact form of the trajectory η during an action potential by, e.g., a square pulse, followed by a negative spike-afterpotential,

$$\eta(t - t_i^{(f)}) = \begin{cases} 1/\Delta t & \text{for } 0 < t - t_i^{(f)} < \Delta t \\ -\eta_0 \exp\left(-\dfrac{t - t_i^{(f)}}{\tau}\right) & \text{for } \Delta t < t - t_i^{(f)} \end{cases} \qquad (1.5)$$

with parameters $\eta_0, \tau, \Delta t > 0$. In the limit of $\Delta t \to 0$ the square pulse approaches a Dirac δ function; see Fig. 1.4.

The positive pulse marks the moment of spike firing. For the purpose of the model, it has no real significance, since the spikes are recorded explicitly in the set of firing times $t_i^{(1)}, t_i^{(2)}, \ldots$. The negative spike-afterpotential, however, has an important implication. It leads after the pulse to a "reset" of the membrane potential to a value below threshold. The idea of a simple reset of the variable u_i after each spike is one of the essential components of the integrate-and-fire model that will be discussed in detail in Chapter 4.

If $\eta_0 \gg \vartheta$ then the membrane potential after the pulse is significantly lower than the resting potential. The emission of a second pulse immediately after the first one is therefore more difficult, since many input spikes are needed to reach the threshold. The negative spike-afterpotential in Eq. (1.5) is thus a simple model of neuronal refractoriness.

Example: formal spike trains

Throughout this book, we will refer to the moment when a given neuron emits an action potential as the firing time of that neuron. In models, the firing time is usually defined as the moment of threshold crossing. Similarly, in experiments firing times are recorded when the membrane potential reaches some threshold value ϑ from below. We denote firing times of neuron i by $t_i^{(f)}$ where $f = 1, 2, \ldots$ is the label of the spike. Formally, we may denote the spike train of a neuron i as the sequence of firing times

$$S_i(t) = \sum_f \delta(t - t_i^{(f)}), \qquad (1.6)$$

where $\delta(x)$ is the Dirac δ function with $\delta(x) = 0$ for $x \neq 0$ and $\int_{-\infty}^{\infty} \delta(x) \, dx = 1$. Spikes are thus reduced to points in time.

1.3.2 Limitations of the model

The model presented in Section 1.3.1 is highly simplified and neglects many aspects of neuronal dynamics. In particular, all postsynaptic potentials are assumed to have the same shape, independently of the state of the neuron. Furthermore, the dynamics of neuron i depends only on its most recent firing time $\hat{t}_i$. Let us list the major limitations of this approach.

(i) Adaptation, bursting, and inhibitory rebound

To study neuronal dynamics experimentally, neurons can be isolated and stimulated by current injection through an intracellular electrode. In a standard experimental protocol we could, for example, impose a stimulating current that is switched at time t_0 from a value I_1 to a new value I_2. Let us suppose that $I_1 = 0$ so that the neuron is quiescent for $t < t_0$. If the current I_2 is sufficiently large, it will evoke spikes for $t > t_0$. Most neurons will respond to the current step with a spike train where intervals between spikes increase successively until a steady state of periodic firing is reached; cf. Fig. 1.5A. Neurons that show this type of adaptation are called regularly firing neurons (Connors and Gutnick, 1990). Adaptation is a slow process that builds up over several spikes. Since the model SRM$_0$ takes only the most recent spike into account, it cannot capture adaptation. Detailed neuron models which will be discussed in Chapter 2 describe the slow processes that lead to adaptation explicitly. To mimic adaptation with formal spiking neuron models we would have to add up the contributions to refractoriness of several spikes back in the past; cf. Chapter 4.

Fast-spiking neurons form a second class of neurons. These neurons show no adaptation and can therefore be well approximated by the model SRM$_0$ introduced

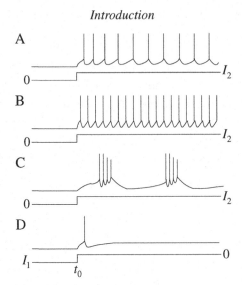

Fig. 1.5. Response to a current step. In **A–C**, the current is switched on at $t = t_0$ to a value $I_2 > 0$. Regular-spiking neurons (**A**) exhibit adaptation of the interspike intervals whereas fast-spiking neurons (**B**) show no adaptation. An example of a bursting neuron is shown in **C**. Many neurons emit an inhibitory rebound spike (**D**) after an inhibitory current $I_1 < 0$ is switched off. Schematic figure.

in Section 1.3.1. Many inhibitory neurons are fast-spiking neurons. Apart from regular-spiking and fast-spiking neurons, there are also bursting neurons which form a separate group (Connors and Gutnick, 1990). These neurons respond to constant stimulation by a sequence of spikes that is periodically interrupted by rather long intervals; cf. Fig. 1.5C. Again, a neuron model that takes only the most recent spike into account cannot describe bursting. For a review of bursting neuron models, the reader is referred to Izhikevich (2000).

Another frequently observed behavior is postinhibitory rebound. Consider a step current with $I_1 < 0$ and $I_2 = 0$, i.e., an inhibitory input that is switched off at time t_0; cf. Fig. 1.5D. Many neurons respond to such a change with one or more "rebound spikes": even the release of inhibition can trigger action potentials. We will return to inhibitory rebound in Chapter 2.

(ii) Saturating excitation and shunting inhibition

In the model SRM_0 introduced in Section 1.3.1, the form of a postsynaptic potential generated by a presynaptic spike at time $t_j^{(f)}$ does not depend on the state of the postsynaptic neuron i. This is of course a simplification and reality is somewhat more complicated. In Chapter 2 we will discuss detailed neuron models that describe synaptic input as a change of the membrane conductance. Here we simply summarize the major phenomena.

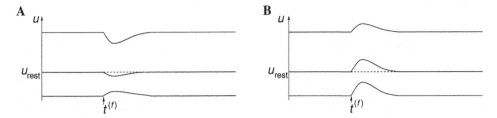

Fig. 1.6. The shape of postsynaptic potentials depends on the momentary level of depolarization. **A**. A presynaptic spike that arrives at time $t^{(f)}$ at an inhibitory synapse has hardly any effect on the membrane potential when the neuron is at rest, but a large effect if the membrane potential u is above the resting potential. If the membrane is hyperpolarized below the reversal potential of the inhibitory synapse, the response to the presynaptic input changes sign. **B**. A spike at an excitatory synapse evokes a postsynaptic potential with an amplitude that depends only slightly on the momentary voltage u. For large depolarizations the amplitude becomes smaller (saturation). Schematic figure.

In Fig. 1.6 we have sketched schematically an experiment where the neuron is driven by a constant current I_0. We assume that I_0 is too weak to evoke firing so that, after some relaxation time, the membrane potential settles at a constant value u_0. At $t = t^{(f)}$ a presynaptic spike is triggered. The spike generates a current pulse at the postsynaptic neuron (postsynaptic current, PSC) with amplitude

$$\text{PSC} \propto u_0 - E_{\text{syn}} \tag{1.7}$$

where u_0 is the membrane potential and E_{syn} is the "reversal potential" of the synapse. Since the amplitude of the current input depends on u_0, the response of the postsynaptic potential does so as well. Reversal potentials are systematically introduced in Section 2.2; models of synaptic input are discussed in Chapter 2.4.

Example: shunting inhibition and reversal potential

The dependence of the postsynaptic response upon the momentary state of the neuron is most pronounced for inhibitory synapses. The reversal potential of inhibitory synapses E_{syn} is below, but usually close to, the resting potential. Input spikes thus have hardly any effect on the membrane potential if the neuron is at rest; cf. Fig. 1.6A. However, if the membrane is depolarized to a value substantially above rest, the very same input spikes evoke a pronounced inhibitory potential. If the membrane is already hyperpolarized, the input spike can even produce a depolarizing effect. There is an intermediate value $u_0 = E_{\text{syn}}$ – the reversal potential – at which the response to inhibitory input "reverses" from hyperpolarizing to depolarizing.

Though inhibitory input usually has only a small impact on the membrane potential, the local conductivity of the cell membrane can be significantly increased.

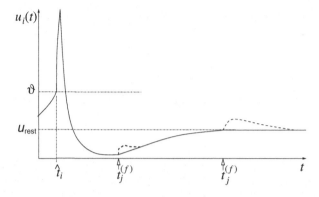

Fig. 1.7. The shape of postsynaptic potentials (dashed lines) depends on the time $t - \hat{t}_i$ that has passed since the last output spike current of neuron i. The postsynaptic spike has been triggered at time $\hat{t}_i$. A presynaptic spike that arrives at time $t_j^{(f)}$ shortly after the spike of the postsynaptic neuron has a smaller effect than a spike that arrives much later. The spike arrival time is indicated by an arrow. Schematic figure.

Inhibitory synapses are often located on the soma or on the shaft of the dendritic tree. Due to their strategic position a few inhibitory input spikes can "shunt" the whole input that is gathered by the dendritic tree from hundreds of excitatory synapses. This phenomenon is called "shunting inhibition".

The reversal potential for excitatory synapses is usually significantly above the resting potential. If the membrane is depolarized $u_0 \gg u_{rest}$ the amplitude of an excitatory postsynaptic potential is reduced, but the effect is not as pronounced as for inhibition. For very high levels of depolarization a saturation of the EPSPs can be observed; cf. Fig. 1.6B.

Example: conductance changes after a spike

The shape of the postsynaptic potentials does not only depend on the level of depolarization but, more generally, on the internal state of the neuron, e.g., on the timing relative to previous action potentials.

Suppose that an action potential has occurred at time $\hat{t}_i$ and that a presynaptic spike arrives at a time $t_j^{(f)} > \hat{t}_i$. The form of the postsynaptic potential depends now on the time $t_j^{(f)} - \hat{t}_i$; cf. Fig. 1.7. If the presynaptic spike arrives during or shortly after a postsynaptic action potential it has little effect because some of the ion channels that were involved in firing the action potential are still open. If the input spike arrives much later it generates a postsynaptic potential of the usual size. We will return to this effect in Section 2.2.

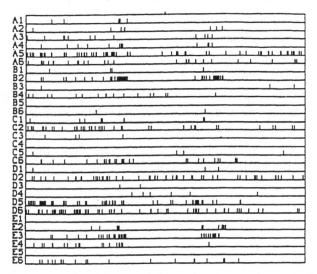

Fig. 1.8. Spatio-temporal pulse pattern. The spikes of 30 neurons (A1–E6, plotted along the vertical axes) are shown as a function of time (horizontal axis, total time is 4000 ms). The firing times are marked by short vertical bars. From Krüger and Aiple (1988).

Example: spatial structure

The form of postsynaptic potentials also depends on the location of the synapse on the dendritic tree. Synapses that are located at the distal end of the dendrite are expected to evoke a smaller postsynaptic response at the soma than a synapse that is located directly on the soma; cf. Chapter 2. If several inputs occur on the same dendritic branch within a few milliseconds, the first input will cause local changes of the membrane potential that influence the amplitude of the response to the input spikes that arrive slightly later. This may lead to saturation or, in the case of so-called active currents, to an enhancement of the response. Such nonlinear interactions between different presynaptic spikes are neglected in the model SRM_0. A purely linear dendrite, on the other hand, can be incorporated in the model as we will see in Chapter 4.

1.4 The problem of neuronal coding

The mammalian brain contains more than 10^{10} densely packed neurons that are connected to an intricate network. In every small volume of cortex, thousands of spikes are emitted each millisecond. An example of a spike train recording from 30 neurons is shown in Fig. 1.8. What is the information contained in such a spatio-temporal pattern of pulses? What is the code used by the neurons to transmit that information? How might other neurons decode the signal? As external observers, can we read the code and understand the message of the neuronal activity pattern?

The above questions point to the problem of neuronal coding, one of the fundamental issues in neuroscience. At present, a definite answer to these questions is not known. Traditionally it has been thought that most, if not all, of the relevant information was contained in the mean firing rate of the neuron. The firing rate is usually defined by a temporal average; see Fig. 1.9. The experimentalist sets a time window of, say, $T = 100$ ms or $T = 500$ ms and counts the number of spikes $n_{sp}(T)$ that occur in this time window. Division by the length of the time window gives the mean firing rate

$$v = \frac{n_{sp}(T)}{T} \tag{1.8}$$

usually reported in units of s^{-1} or Hz.

The concept of mean firing rates has been successfully applied during the last 80 years. It dates back to the pioneering work of Adrian (Adrian, 1926, 1928) who showed that the firing rate of stretch receptor neurons in the muscles is related to the force applied to the muscle. In the following decades, measurement of firing rates became a standard tool for describing the properties of all types of sensory or cortical neurons (Mountcastle, 1957; Hubel and Wiesel, 1959), partly due to the relative ease of measuring rates experimentally. It is clear, however, that an approach based on a temporal average neglects all the information possibly contained in the exact timing of the spikes. It is therefore no surprise that the firing rate concept has been repeatedly criticized and is the subject of an ongoing debate (Bialek et al., 1991; Abeles, 1994; Shadlen and Newsome, 1994; Hopfield, 1995; Softky, 1995; Rieke et al., 1996; Oram et al., 1999).

During recent years, more and more experimental evidence has accumulated which suggests that a straightforward firing rate concept based on temporal averaging may be too simplistic to describe brain activity. One of the main arguments is that reaction times in behavioral experiments are often too short to allow long temporal averages. Humans can recognize and respond to visual scenes in less than 400 ms (Thorpe et al., 1996). Recognition and reaction involve several processing steps from the retinal input to the finger movement at the output. If, at each processing step, neurons had to wait and perform a temporal average in order to read the message of the presynaptic neurons, the reaction time would be much longer.

In experiments on a visual neuron in the fly, it was possible to "read the neural code" and reconstruct the time-dependent stimulus based on the neuron's firing times (Bialek et al., 1991). There is evidence of precise temporal correlations between pulses of different neurons (Abeles, 1994; Lestienne, 1996) and stimulus-

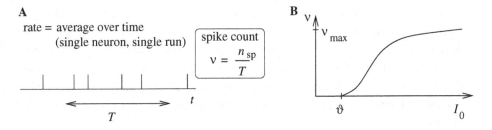

Fig. 1.9. **A**. Definition of the mean firing rate via a temporal average. **B**. Gain function, schematic. The output rate v is given as a function of the total input I_0.

dependent synchronization of the activity in populations of neurons (Eckhorn et al., 1988; Gray and Singer, 1989; Gray et al., 1989; Engel et al., 1991a; Singer, 1994). Most of these data are inconsistent with a naïve concept of coding by mean firing rates where the exact timing of spikes should play no role.

In the following sections, we review some potential coding schemes and ask: what exactly is a pulse code – and what is a rate code? The question of neuronal coding has important implications for modeling, because pulse codes require a more detailed description of neuronal dynamics than rate codes. Models of neurons at different levels of detail will be the topic of Part I of the book.

1.5 Rate codes

A quick glance at the experimental literature reveals that there is no unique and well-defined concept of "mean firing rate". In fact, there are at least three different notions of rate which are often confused and used simultaneously. The three definitions refer to three different averaging procedures: an average over time, an average over several repetitions of the experiment, or an average over a population of neurons. The following three subsections will reconsider the three concepts. An excellent discussion of rate codes is given elsewhere (Rieke et al., 1996).

1.5.1 Rate as a spike count (average over time)

The first and most commonly used definition of a firing rate refers to a temporal average. As discussed in the preceding section, this is essentially the spike count in an interval of duration T divided by T; see Fig. 1.9. The length T of the time window is set by the experimenter and depends on the type of neuron recorded from and the stimulus. In practice, to get sensible averages, several spikes should occur within the time window. Typical values are $T = 100$ ms or $T = 500$ ms, but the duration may also be longer or shorter.

This definition of rate has been successfully used in many preparations, particularly in experiments on sensory or motor systems. A classic example is the stretch receptor in a muscle spindle (Adrian, 1926). The number of spikes emitted by the receptor neuron increases with the force applied to the muscle. Another textbook example is the touch receptor in the leech (Kandel and Schwartz, 1991). The stronger the touch stimulus, the more spikes occur during a stimulation period of 500 ms.

These classic results show that the experimenter as an external observer can evaluate and classify neuronal firing by a spike count measure – but is this really the code used by neurons in the brain? In other words, is a neuron that receives signals from a sensory neuron only looking at and reacting to the number of spikes it receives in a time window of, say, 500 ms? We will approach this question from a modeling point of view later on in the book. Here we discuss some critical experimental evidence.

From behavioral experiments it is known that reaction times are often rather short. A fly can react to new stimuli and change the direction of flight within 30–40 ms; see the discussion in Rieke et al. (1996). This is not long enough for counting spikes and averaging over some long time window. The fly has to respond after a postsynaptic neuron has received one or two spikes. Humans can recognize visual scenes in just a few hundred milliseconds (Thorpe et al., 1996), even though recognition is believed to involve several processing steps. Again, this does not leave enough time to perform temporal averages on each level. In fact, humans can detect images in a sequence of unrelated pictures even if each image is shown for only 14–100 ms (Keysers et al., 2001).

Temporal averaging can work well in cases where the stimulus is constant or slowly varying and does not require a fast reaction of the organism – and this is the situation usually encountered in experimental protocols. Real-world input, however, is hardly stationary, but often changing on a fast time scale. For example, even when viewing a static image, humans perform saccades, rapid changes of the direction of gaze. The image projected onto the retinal photoreceptors changes therefore every few hundred milliseconds.

Despite its shortcomings, the concept of a firing rate code is widely used not only in experiments, but also in models of neural networks. It has led to the idea that a neuron transforms information about a single input variable (the stimulus strength) into a single continuous output variable (the firing rate); cf. Fig. 1.9B. The output rate ν increases with the stimulus strength and saturates for large input I_0 towards a maximum value ν_{max}. In experiments, a single neuron can be stimulated by injecting with an intracellular electrode a constant current I_0. The relation between the measured firing frequency ν and the applied input current I_0 is sometimes called the frequency–current curve of the neuron. In models, we

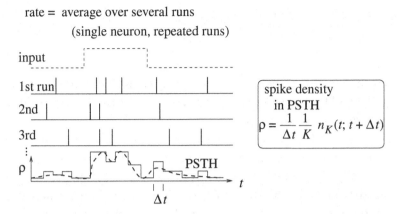

Fig. 1.10. Definition of the spike density in the peri-stimulus-time histogram (PSTH) as an average over several runs of the experiment. Taken from Gerstner (1998) with permission.

formalize the relation between firing frequency (rate) and input current and write $\nu = g(I_0)$. We refer to g as the neuronal gain function or transfer function.

From the point of view of rate coding, spikes are just a convenient way to transmit the analog output variable ν over long distances. In fact, the best coding scheme to transmit the value of the rate ν would be by a regular spike train with intervals $1/\nu$. In this case, the rate could be reliably measured after only two spikes. From the point of view of rate coding, the irregularities encountered in real spike trains of neurons in the cortex must therefore be considered as noise. In order to get rid of the noise and arrive at a reliable estimate of the rate, the experimenter (or the postsynaptic neuron) has to average over a larger number of spikes. A critical discussion of the temporal averaging concept can be found elsewhere (Shadlen and Newsome, 1994; Softky, 1995; Rieke et al., 1996).

1.5.2 Rate as a spike density (average over several runs)

There is a second definition of rate which works for stationary as well as for time-dependent stimuli. The experimenter records from a neuron while stimulating with some input sequence. The same stimulation sequence is repeated several times and the neuronal response is reported in a peri-stimulus-time histogram (PSTH); see Fig. 1.10. The time t is measured with respect to the start of the stimulation sequence and Δt is typically in the range of one or a few milliseconds. The number of occurences of spikes $n_K(t; t+\Delta t)$ summed over all repetitions of the experiment divided by the number K of repetitions is a measure of the typical activity of the neuron between time t and $t + \Delta t$. A further division by the interval length Δt

yields the spike density of the PSTH

$$\rho(t) = \frac{1}{\Delta t} \frac{n_K(t; t + \Delta t)}{K}. \tag{1.9}$$

Sometimes the result is smoothed to get a continuous "rate" variable. The spike density of the PSTH is usually reported in units of Hz and often called the (time-dependent) firing rate of the neuron.

As an experimental procedure, the spike density measure is a useful method for evaluating neuronal activity, in particular in the case of time-dependent stimuli. The obvious problem with this approach is that it cannot be the decoding scheme used by neurons in the brain. Consider for example a frog which wants to catch a fly. It cannot wait for the insect to fly repeatedly along exactly the same trajectory. The frog has to base its decision on a single "run" – each fly and each trajectory is different.

Nevertheless, the experimental spike density measure can make sense, if there are large populations of independent neurons that receive the same stimulus. Instead of recording from a population of N neurons in a single run, it is experimentally easier to record from a single neuron and average over N repeated runs. Thus, the spike density coding relies on the implicit assumption that there are always populations of neurons and therefore leads us to the third notion of a firing rate, viz., a rate defined as a population average.

1.5.3 *Rate as a population activity (average over several neurons)*

The number of neurons in the brain is huge. Often many neurons have similar properties and respond to the same stimuli. For example, neurons in the primary visual cortex of cats and monkeys are arranged in columns of cells with similar properties (Hubel and Wiesel, 1962, 1977; Hubel, 1988). Let us idealize the situation and consider a population of neurons with identical properties. In particular, all neurons in the population should have the same pattern of input and output connections. The spikes of the neurons in a population m are sent off to another population n. In our idealized picture, each neuron in population n receives input from all neurons in population m. The relevant quantity, from the point of view of the receiving neuron, is the proportion of active neurons in the presynaptic population m; see Fig. 1.11A. Formally, we define the population activity

$$A(t) = \frac{1}{\Delta t} \frac{n_{\text{act}}(t; t + \Delta t)}{N} = \frac{1}{\Delta t} \frac{\int_t^{t+\Delta t} \sum_j \sum_f \delta(t - t_j^{(f)}) \, dt}{N} \tag{1.10}$$

where N is the size of the population, $n_{\text{act}}(t; t + \Delta t)$ the number of spikes (summed over all neurons in the population) that occur between t and $t + \Delta t$, and Δt a small

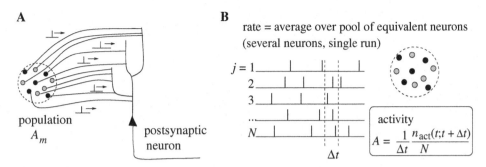

Fig. 1.11. **A**. A postsynpatic neuron receives spike input from the population m with activity A_m. **B**. The population activity is defined as the fraction of neurons that are active in a short interval $[t, t + \Delta t]$ divided by Δt.

time interval; see Fig. 1.11. Eq. (1.10) defines a variable with units s^{-1} – in other words, a rate.

The population activity may vary rapidly and can reflect changes in the stimulus conditions nearly instantaneously (Gerstner, 2000; Brunel et al., 2001). Thus the population activity does not suffer from the disadvantages of a firing rate defined by temporal averaging at the single-unit level. A potential problem with the definition (1.10) is that we have formally required a homogeneous population of neurons with identical connections, which is hardly realistic. Real populations will always have a certain degree of heterogeneity both in their internal parameters and in their connectivity pattern. Nevertheless, rate as a population activity (of suitably defined pools of neurons) may be a useful coding principle in many areas of the brain. For inhomogeneous populations, the definition (1.10) may be replaced by a weighted average over the population.

Example: population vector coding

We give an example of a weighted average in an inhomogeneous population. Let us suppose that we are studying a population of neurons which respond to a stimulus **x**. We may think of **x** as the location of the stimulus in input space. Neuron i responds best to stimulus $\mathbf{x}_i$, another neuron j responds best to stimulus $\mathbf{x}_j$. In other words, we may say that the spikes for a neuron i "represent" an input vector $\mathbf{x}_i$ and those of j an input vector $\mathbf{x}_j$. In a large population, many neurons will be active simultaneously when a new stimulus **x** is represented. The location of this stimulus can then be estimated from the weighted population average

$$\mathbf{x}^{\mathrm{est}}(t) = \frac{\int_t^{t+\Delta t} \sum_j \sum_f \mathbf{x}_j \, \delta(t - t_j^{(f)}) \, \mathrm{d}t}{\int_t^{t+\Delta t} \sum_j \sum_f \delta(t - t_j^{(f)}) \, \mathrm{d}t}. \tag{1.11}$$

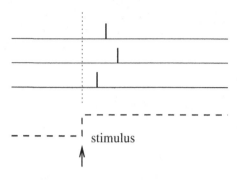

Fig. 1.12. Time-to-first spike. The spike train of three neurons are shown. The third neuron from the top is the first one to fire a spike after the stimulus onset (arrow). The dashed line indicates the time course of the stimulus.

Both numerator and denominator are closely related to the population activity (1.10). The estimate (1.11) has been successfully used for an interpretation of neuronal activity in primate motor cortex (Georgopoulos et al., 1986; Wilson and McNaughton, 1993). It is, however, not completely clear whether postsynaptic neurons really evaluate the fraction (1.11). In any case, Eq. (1.11) can be applied by external observers to "decode" neuronal signals, if the spike trains of a large number of neurons are accessible.

1.6 Spike codes

In this section, we will briefly introduce some potential coding strategies based on spike timing.

1.6.1 Time-to-first-spike

Let us study a neuron which abruptly receives a "new" input at time t_0. For example, a neuron might be driven by an external stimulus which is suddenly switched on at time t_0. This seems to be somewhat academic, but even in a realistic situation abrupt changes in the input are quite common. When we look at a picture, our gaze jumps from one point to the next. After each saccade, the photoreceptors in the retina receive a new visual input. Information about the onset of a saccade would easily be available in the brain and could serve as an internal reference signal. We can then imagine a code where for each neuron the timing of the *first* spike after the reference signal contains all information about the new stimulus. A neuron which fires shortly after the reference signal could signal a strong stimulation; firing somewhat later would signal a weaker stimulation; see Fig. 1.12.

In a pure version of this coding scheme, each neuron only needs to fire a single spike to transmit information. (If it emits several spikes, only the first spike after the reference signal counts. All following spikes would be irrelevant.) To implement a clean version of such a coding scheme, we imagine that each neuron is shut off by inhibition as soon as it has fired a spike. Inhibition ends with the onset of the next stimulus (e.g., after the next saccade). After the release from inhibition the neuron is ready to emit its next spike that now transmits information about the new stimulus. Since each neuron in such a scenario transmits exactly one spike per stimulus, it is clear that only the timing conveys information and not the number of spikes.

A coding scheme based on the time-to-first-spike is certainly an idealization. In a slightly different context coding by first spikes has been discussed by S. Thorpe (Thorpe et al., 1996). Thorpe argues that the brain does not have time to evaluate more than one spike from each neuron per processing step. Therefore the first spike should contain most of the relevant information. Using information-theoretic measures on their experimental data, several groups have shown that most of the information about a new stimulus is indeed conveyed during the first 20 or 50 ms after the onset of the neuronal response (Optican and Richmond, 1987; Tovee et al., 1993; Kjaer et al., 1994; Tovee and Rolls, 1995). Rapid computation during the transients after a new stimulus has also been discussed in model studies (Hopfield and Herz, 1995; Tsodyks and Sejnowski, 1995; van Vreeswijk and Sompolinsky, 1997; Treves et al., 1997). Since time-to-first spike is a highly simplified coding scheme, analytical studies are possible (Maass, 1998).

1.6.2 Phase

We can apply a code by "time-to-first-spike" also in the situation where the reference signal is not a single event, but a periodic signal. In the hippocampus, in the olfactory system, and also in other areas of the brain, oscillations of some global variable (for example, the population activity) are quite common. These oscillations could serve as an internal reference signal. Neuronal spike trains could then encode information in the phase of a pulse with respect to the background oscillation. If the input does not change between one cycle and the next, then the same pattern of phases repeats periodically; see Fig. 1.13.

The concept of coding by phases has been studied by several different groups, not only in model studies (Hopfield, 1995; Jensen and Lisman, 1996; Maass, 1996), but also experimentally (O'Keefe and Recce, 1993). There is, for example, evidence that the phase of a spike during an oscillation in the hippocampus of the rat conveys information on the spatial location of the animal which is not fully accounted for by the firing rate of the neuron (O'Keefe and Recce, 1993).

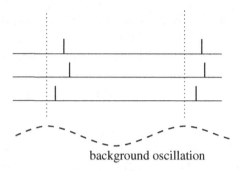

background oscillation

Fig. 1.13. Phase. The neurons fire at different phases with respect to the background oscillation (dashed). The phase could code relevant information.

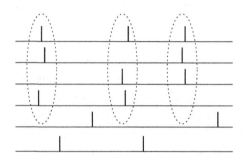

Fig. 1.14. Synchrony. The upper four neurons are nearly synchronous, two other neurons at the bottom are not synchronized with the others. Taken from Gerstner (1998) with permission.

1.6.3 Correlations and synchrony

We can also use spikes from other neurons as the reference signal for a spike code. For example, synchrony between a pair or many neurons could signify special events and convey information which is not contained in the firing rate of the neurons; see Fig. 1.14. One famous idea is that synchrony could mean "belonging together" (Milner, 1974; von der Malsburg, 1981). Consider for example a complex scene consisting of several objects. It is represented in the brain by the activity of a large number of neurons. Neurons which represent the same object could be "labeled" by the fact that they fire synchronously (von der Malsburg, 1981; Eckhorn et al., 1988; Gray and Singer, 1989; von der Malsburg and Buhmann, 1992). Coding by synchrony has been studied extensively both experimentally (Eckhorn et al., 1988; Gray and Singer, 1989; Gray et al., 1989; Engel et al., 1991a,b; Kreiter and Singer, 1992; Singer, 1994) and in models (Eckhorn et al., 1990; Wang et al., 1990; König and Schillen, 1991; Schillen and König, 1991; von der Malsburg and Buhmann, 1992; Aertsen and Arndt, 1993; Gerstner et al.,

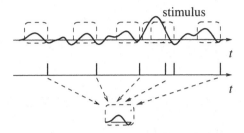

Fig. 1.15. Reverse correlation technique (schematic). The stimulus in the top trace has caused the spike train shown immediately below. The time course of the stimulus just before the spikes (dashed boxes) has been averaged to yield the typical time course (bottom).

1993a; Ritz et al., 1994; Terman and Wang, 1995; Wang, 1995). For a review of potential mechanism, see Ritz and Sejnowski (1997).

More generally, not only synchrony but any precise spatio-temporal pulse pattern could be a meaningful event. For example, a spike pattern of three neurons, where neuron 1 fires at some arbitrary time t_1 followed by neuron 2 at time $t_1 + \delta_{12}$ and by neuron 3 at $t_1 + \delta_{13}$, might represent a certain stimulus condition. The same three neurons firing with different relative delays might signify a different stimulus. The relevance of precise spatio-temporal spike patterns has been studied intensively by Abeles (Abeles, 1991; Abeles et al., 1993; Abeles, 1994). Similarly, but on a somewhat coarse time scale, correlations of auditory and visual neurons are found to be stimulus dependent and might convey information beyond that contained in the firing rate alone (deCharms and Merzenich, 1996; Steinmetz et al., 2000).

1.6.4 Stimulus reconstruction and reverse correlation

Let us consider a neuron which is driven by a time-dependent stimulus $s(t)$. Every time a spike occurs, we note the time course of the stimulus in a time window of about 100 ms immediately before the spike. Averaging the results over several spikes yields the typical time course of the stimulus just before a spike (de Boer and Kuyper, 1968). Such a procedure is called a "reverse correlation" approach; see Fig. 1.15. In contrast to the PSTH experiment sketched in Section 1.5.2 where the experimenter averages the neuron's response over several trials with the same stimulus, reverse correlation means that the experimenter averages the input under the condition of an identical response, viz., a spike. In other words, it is a spike-triggered average; see, e.g., de Ruyter van Stevenick and Bialek (1988); Rieke et al. (1996). The results of the reverse correlation, i.e., the typical time course of the stimulus which has triggered the spike, can be interpreted as the "meaning" of a single spike. Reverse correlation techniques have made it possible to measure,

A

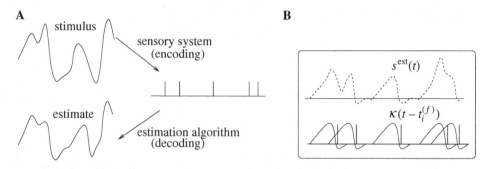

B

Fig. 1.16. Reconstruction of a stimulus (schematic). **A.** A stimulus evokes a spike train of a neuron. The time course of the stimulus may be estimated from the spike train; redrawn after Rieke et al. (1996). **B.** In the framework of linear stimulus reconstruction, the estimation $s^{est}(t)$ (dashed) is the sum of the contributions κ (solid lines) of all spikes.

for example, the spatio-temporal characteristics of neurons in the visual cortex (Eckhorn et al., 1993; DeAngelis et al., 1995).

With a somewhat more elaborate version of this approach, W. Bialek and his co-workers have been able to "read" the neural code of the H1 neuron in the fly and to reconstruct a time-dependent stimulus (Bialek et al., 1991; Rieke et al., 1996). Here we give a simplified version of their argument.

Results from reverse correlation analysis suggest that each spike signifies the time course of the stimulus preceding the spike. If this is correct, a reconstruction of the complete time course of the stimulus $s(t)$ from the set of firing times $\mathcal{F} = \{t^{(1)}, \ldots, t^{(n)}\}$ should be possible; see Fig. 1.16.

As a simple test of this hypothesis, Bialek and co-workers have studied a linear reconstruction. A spike at time $t^{(f)}$ gives a contribution $\kappa(t - t^{(f)})$ to the estimation $s^{est}(t)$ of the time course of the stimulus. Here, $t^{(f)} \in \mathcal{F}$ is one of the firing times and $\kappa(t - t^{(f)})$ is a kernel which is nonzero during some time before and around $t^{(f)}$; cf. Fig. 1.16B. A linear estimate of the stimulus is

$$s^{est}(t) = \sum_{f=1}^{n} \kappa(t - t^{(f)}). \qquad (1.12)$$

The form of the kernel κ was determined through optimization so that the average reconstruction error $\int dt \, [s(t) - s^{est}(t)]^2$ was minimal. The quality of the reconstruction was then tested on additional data which were not used for the optimization. Surprisingly enough, the simple linear reconstruction (1.12) gave a fair estimate of the time course of the stimulus even though the stimulus varied on a time scale comparable to the typical interspike interval (Bialek et al., 1991; Bialek and Rieke, 1992; Rieke et al., 1996). This reconstruction method shows nicely that information about a time-dependent input can indeed be conveyed by spike timing.

1.7 Discussion: spikes or rates?

The dividing line between spike codes and firing rates is not always as clearly drawn as it may seem at first sight. Some codes that were first proposed as pure examples of pulse codes have later been interpreted as variations of rate codes. For example, the stimulus reconstruction with kernels as in Eq. (1.12) seems to be a clear example of a spike code. Nevertheless, it is not so far from a rate code based on spike counts either (Abbott, 1994; Theunissen and Miller, 1995). To see this, consider a spike count measure with a running time window K. We can estimate the rate ν at time t by

$$\nu(t) = \frac{\int K(\tau)\, S(t - \tau)\, d\tau}{\int K(\tau)\, d\tau}, \tag{1.13}$$

where $S(t) = \sum_{f=1}^{n} \delta(t - t^{(f)})$ is the spike train under consideration. The integrals run from minus to plus infinity. For a rectangular time window $K(\tau) = 1$ for $-T/2 < \tau < T/2$ and zero otherwise, Eq. (1.13) reduces exactly to our definition (1.8) of a rate as a spike count measure.

The time window in Eq. (1.13) can be made rather short so that at most a few spikes fall into the interval T. Furthermore, there is no need for the window $K(\cdot)$ be symmetric and rectangular. We may just as well take an asymmetric time window with smooth borders. Moreover, we can perform the integration over the δ function, which yields

$$\nu(t) = c \sum_{f=1}^{n} K(t - t^{(f)}), \tag{1.14}$$

where $c = [\int K(s)\, ds]^{-1}$ is a constant. Except for the constant c (which sets the overall scale to units of one over time), the generalized rate formula (1.14) is now identical to the reconstruction formula (1.12). In other words, the linear reconstruction is just the firing rate measured with a cleverly optimized time window.

Similarly, a code based on the "time-to-first-spike" is also consistent with a rate code. If, for example, the mean firing rate of a neuron is high for a given stimulus, then the first spike is expected to occur early. If the rate is low, the first spike is expected to occur later. Thus the timing of the first spike contains a lot of information about the underlying rate.

Finally, a code based on population activities introduced above as an example of a rate code may be used for very fast temporal coding schemes. As discussed later in Chapter 6, the population activity reacts quickly to any change in the stimulus. Thus rate coding in the sense of a population average is consistent with fast temporal information processing, whereas rate coding in the sense of a naïve spike count measure is not.

The discussion of whether or not to call a given code a rate code is still ongoing, even though precise definitions have been proposed (Theunissen and Miller, 1995). What is important, in our opinion, is to have a coding scheme which allows neurons to quickly respond to stimulus changes. A naïve spike count code with a long time window is unable to do this, but many of the other codes are. The name of such a code, whether it is deemed a rate code or not, is of minor importance.

Example: towards a definition of rate codes

We have seen above in Eq. (1.14) that stimulus reconstruction with a linear kernel can be seen as a special instance of a rate code. This suggests a formal definition of a rate code via the reconstruction procedure. If all information contained in a spike train can be recovered by the linear reconstruction procedure of Eq. (1.12), then the neuron is, by definition, using a rate code. Spike codes would then be codes where a linear reconstruction is not successful. Theunissen and Miller have proposed a definition of rate coding that makes the above ideas more precise (Theunissen and Miller, 1995).

To see how their definition works, we have to return to the reconstruction formula (1.12). It is, in fact, the first term of a systematic Volterra expansion for the estimation of the stimulus from the spikes (Bialek et al., 1991)

$$s^{\text{est}}(t) = \sum_f \kappa_1(t - t^{(f)}) + \sum_{f,f'} \kappa_2(t - t^{(f)}, t - t^{(f')}) + \cdots . \qquad (1.15)$$

For a specific neuron, inclusion of higher-order terms $\kappa_2, \kappa_3, \ldots$ may or may not improve the quality of the estimation. For most neurons where the reconstruction has been carried through it seems that the higher-order terms do not contribute a large amount of information (Rieke et al., 1996). The neurons would then be classified as rate coding.

Let us now suppose that the reconstruction procedure indicates a significant contribution of the second-order term. Does this exclude rate coding? Unfortunately this is not the case. We have to exclude two other possibilities. Firstly, we might have chosen a suboptimal stimulus. A neuron might for example encode the variable x by a rate code, so that a nearly perfect linear reconstruction of x would be possible,

$$x(t) \approx x^{\text{est}} = \sum_{f=1}^{n} \kappa_{1;x}(t - t^{(f)}) . \qquad (1.16)$$

But if we chose a stimulus $s = x^2$ instead of x, then the reconstruction for s^{est} would involve second-order terms, even though the neuron is really using rate code.

Secondly, according to Theunissen and Miller (1995) a spike code should show a temporal structure that is more precise than the temporal structure of the stimulus.

The fact that neurons show precise and reliable spike timing as such is, for them, not sufficient to classify the neuron as a temporal encoder, since the neuronal precision could just be the image of precise temporal input. Let us consider a stimulus with cut-off frequency ω. In order to exclude the possibility that the timing is induced by the stimulus, Theunissen and Miller propose to consider the Fourier spectrum of the higher-order reconstruction kernels. If the Fourier transform of the higher-order kernels contains frequencies less than ω only, then the code is a rate code. If higher-order kernels are significant and contain frequencies above ω, then the information is encoded temporally. A positive example of a spike code (or of "temporal encoding") according to this definition would be the code by correlation and synchrony introduced above. Another example would be the phase code, in particular if the number of spikes per cycle is independent of the stimulus strength. For the exact mathematical definition of a temporal code according to Theunissen and Miller, the reader is refered to the original literature (Theunissen and Miller, 1995).

1.8 Summary

The neuronal signal consists of short voltage pulses called action potentials or spikes. These pulses travel along the axon and are distributed to several postsynaptic neurons where they evoke postsynaptic potentials. If a postsynaptic neuron receives several spikes from several presynaptic neurons within a short time window, its membrane potential may reach a critical value and an action potential is triggered. This action potential is the output signal which is, in turn, transmitted to other neurons.

The sequence of action potentials contains the information that is conveyed from one neuron to the next – but what is the code used by the neurons? Even though it is a question of fundamental importance, the problem of neuronal coding is still not fully resolved. We have reviewed three concepts of rate codes, viz. spike count over some time window, spike density in a histogram, and population activity in an ensemble of neurons. All three concepts have been successfully used in experimental data analysis. All of these concepts are, however, problematic when they are interpreted as the actual code used for neuronal information transmission. A constructive criticism of rate codes may come from a presentation of potential spike codes, if their usefulness in terms of computational power or ease of implementation in biological hardware can be shown. It should be clear that modeling cannot give definite answers to the problem of neuronal coding. The final answers have to come from experiments. One task of modeling may be to discuss possible coding schemes, study their computational potential, exemplify their utility, and point out their limitations.

It is difficult to draw a clear borderline between pulse and rate codes. Whatever the name of the code, it should offer a neural system the possibility to react quickly to changes in the input. This seems to be a minimum requirement if fast behavioral reaction times are to be accounted for.

If pulse coding is relevant, a description of information processing in the brain must be based on spiking neuron models. If all information is contained in the mean firing rate, then models on the level of rates suffice. Since we do not want to take any decision *a priori* about the neuronal code, we concentrate in this book on models of spiking neurons. In some cases, for example for stationary input, it will turn out that the spiking neuron models can be strictly reduced to rate models; in other cases such a reduction is not possible. By modeling on the level of spiking neurons, the question of neuronal coding can thus be kept open.

Literature

An elementary, nontechnical introduction to neurons and synapses can be found in the book by Thompson (1993). At an intermediate level is *From neuron to brain* by Kuffler et al. (1984). A standard textbook on neuroscience covering a wealth of experimental results is *Principles of neural science* by Kandel and Schwartz (1991).

Phenomenological spiking neuron models similar to the model discussed in Section 1.3.1 have a long tradition in theoretical neuroscience (e.g., Lapicque 1907; Hill 1936; McCulloch and Pitts 1943; Stein 1965; Geisler and Goldberg 1966; Weiss 1966; Stein 1967b). They are reviewed in Holden (1976), Tuckwell (1988), and Maass and Bishop (1998).

An excellent discussion of the problem of neuronal coding can be found in the book *Spikes – exploring the neural code* by Rieke et al. (1996). The debate of spikes versus rates is also highlighted in several papers (Abbott, 1994; Abeles, 1994; Shadlen and Newsome, 1994; Softky, 1995; Theunissen and Miller, 1995; Maass and Bishop, 1998).

Part one

Single neuron models

2

Detailed neuron models

From a biophysical point of view, action potentials are the result of currents that pass through ion channels in the cell membrane. In an extensive series of experiments on the giant axon of the squid, Hodgkin and Huxley succeeded in measuring these currents and describing their dynamics in terms of differential equations. In Section 2.2, the Hodgkin–Huxley model is reviewed and its behavior illustrated by several examples.

The Hodgkin–Huxley equations are the starting point for detailed neuron models which account for numerous ion channels, different types of synapse, and the specific spatial geometry of an individual neuron. Ion channels, synaptic dynamics, and the spatial structure of dendrites are the topics of Sections 2.3–2.5. The Hodgkin–Huxley model is also an important reference model for the derivation of simplified neuron models in Chapters 3 and 4. Before we can turn to the Hodgkin–Huxley equations, we need to give some additional information on the equilibrium potential of ion channels.

2.1 Equilibrium potential

Neurons are, just as other cells, enclosed by a membrane which separates the interior of the cell from the extracellular space. Inside the cell the concentration of ions is different from that in the surrounding liquid. The difference in concentration generates an electrical potential which plays an important role in neuronal dynamics. In this section, we want to provide some background information and give an intuitive explanation of the equilibrium potential.

2.1.1 Nernst potential

From the theory of thermodynamics, it is known that the probability that a molecule takes a state of energy E is proportional to the Boltzmann factor, $p(E) \propto$

A

B

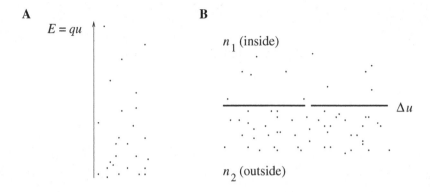

$E = qu$

n_1 (inside)

Δu

n_2 (outside)

Fig. 2.1. **A**. At thermal equilibrium, positive ions in an electric field will be distributed so that fewer ions are in a state of high energy and more at low energy. Thus a voltage difference generates a gradient in concentration. **B**. Similarly, a difference in ion concentration generates an electrical potential. The concentration n_2 inside the neuron is different from the concentration n_1 of the surround. The resulting potential is called the Nernst potential. The solid line indicates the cell membrane. Ions can pass through the gap.

$\exp(-E/kT)$, where k is the Boltzmann constant and T the temperature. Let us consider positive ions with charge q in a static electrical field. Their energy at location x is $E(x) = q\,u(x)$ where $u(x)$ is the potential at x. The probability of finding an ion in the region around x is therefore proportional to $\exp[-q\,u(x)/kT]$. Since the number of ions is huge, we may interpret the probability as an ion density. For ions with positive charge $q > 0$, the ion density is therefore higher in regions with low potential u. Let us write $n(x)$ for the ion density at point x. The relation between the density at point x_1 and point x_2 is

$$\frac{n(x_1)}{n(x_2)} = \exp\left[-\frac{q\,u(x_1) - q\,u(x_2)}{k\,T}\right]. \tag{2.1}$$

A difference in the electrical potential $\Delta u = u(x_1) - u(x_2)$ generates therefore a difference in ion density; cf. Fig. 2.1.

Since this is a statement about an equilibrium state, the reverse must also be true. A difference in ion density generates a difference Δu in the electrical potential. We consider two regions of ions with concentration n_1 and n_2, respectively. Solving Eq. (2.1) for Δu we find that, at equilibrium, the concentration difference generates a voltage

$$\Delta u = \frac{k\,T}{q} \ln \frac{n_2}{n_1} \tag{2.2}$$

which is called the Nernst potential (Hille, 1992).

2.1.2 Reversal potential

The cell membrane consists of a thin bilayer of lipids and is a nearly perfect electrical insulator. Embedded in the cell membrane are, however, specific proteins which act as ion gates. A first type of gate are the ion pumps, a second one are ion channels. Ion pumps actively transport ions from one side to the other. As a result, ion concentrations in the intracellular liquid differ from those of the surround. For example, the sodium concentration inside the cell ($\approx$ 60 mM) is lower than that in the extracellular liquid ($\approx$ 440 mM). On the other hand, the potassium concentration inside is higher ($\approx$ 400 mM) than in the surround ($\approx$ 20 mM).

Let us concentrate for the moment on sodium ions. At equilibrium the difference in concentration causes a Nernst potential E_{Na} of about +50 mV. That is, at equilibrium the interior of the cell has a positive potential with respect to the surround. The interior of the cell and the surrounding liquid are in contact through ion channels where Na^+ ions can pass from one side of the membrane to the other. If the voltage difference Δu is smaller than the value of the Nernst potential E_{Na}, more Na^+ ions flow into the cell so as to decrease the concentration difference. If the voltage is larger than the Nernst potential ions would flow out of the cell. Thus the direction of the current is reversed when the voltage Δu passes E_{Na}. For this reason, E_{Na} is called the reversal potential.

Example: reversal potential for potassium

As mentioned above, the ion concentration of potassium is higher inside the cell ($\approx$ 400 mM) than in the extracellular liquid ($\approx$ 20 mM). Potassium ions have a single positive charge $q = 1.6 \times 10^{-19}$ C. Application of the Nernst equation with the Boltzmann constant $k = 1.4 \times 10^{-23}$ J/K yields $E_K \approx -77$ mV at room temperature. The reversal potential for K^+ ions is therefore negative.

Example: resting potential

So far we have considered either sodium or potassium. In real cells, these and other ion types are simultaneously present and contribute to the voltage across the membrane. It is found experimentally that the resting potential of the membrane is about $u_{rest} \approx -65$ mV. Since $E_K < u_{rest} < E_{Na}$, potassium ions will, at the resting potential, flow out of the cell while sodium ions flow into the cell. The active ion pumps balance this flow and transport just as many ions back as pass through the channels. The value of u_{rest} is determined by the dynamic equilibrium between the ion flow through the channels (permeability of the membrane) and active ion transport (efficiency of the ion pumps).

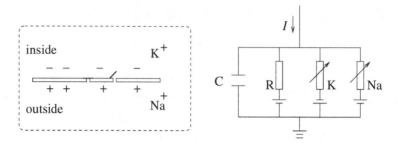

Fig. 2.2. Schematic diagram of the Hodgkin–Huxley model. The passive electrical properties of the cell membrane are described by a capacity C and a resistor R. The nonlinear properties are attributed to voltage-independent ion channels for sodium (Na) and potassium (K).

2.2 Hodgkin–Huxley model

Hodgkin and Huxley (1952) performed experiments on the giant axon of the squid and found three different types of ion current, viz., sodium, potassium, and a leak current that consists mainly of Cl^- ions. Specific voltage-dependent ion channels, one for sodium and another one for potassium, control the flow of those ions through the cell membrane. The leak current takes care of other channel types which are not described explicitly.

2.2.1 Definition of the model

The Hodgkin–Huxley model can be understood with the help of Fig. 2.2. The semipermeable cell membrane separates the interior of the cell from the extracellular liquid and acts as a capacitor. If an input current $I(t)$ is injected into the cell, it may add further charge on the capacitor, or leak through the channels in the cell membrane. Because of active ion transport through the cell membrane, the ion concentration inside the cell is different from that in the extracellular liquid. The Nernst potential generated by the difference in ion concentration is represented by a battery.

Let us now translate the above considerations into mathematical equations. The conservation of electric charge on a piece of membrane implies that the applied current $I(t)$ may be split in a capacitive current I_{cap} which charges the capacitor C and further components I_k which pass through the ion channels. Thus

$$I(t) = I_{cap}(t) + \sum_k I_k(t), \tag{2.3}$$

where the sum runs over all ion channels. In the standard Hodgkin–Huxley model there are only three types of channel: a sodium channel with index Na, a potassium channel with index K and an unspecific leakage channel with resistance R; cf. Fig. 2.2. From the definition of a capacity $C = Q/u$ where Q is a charge and u the voltage across the capacitor, we find the charging current $I_{cap} = C\, du/dt$. Hence from (2.3)

$$C\frac{du}{dt} = -\sum_k I_k(t) + I(t).\qquad(2.4)$$

In biological terms, u is the voltage across the membrane and $\sum_k I_k$ is the sum of the ionic currents that pass through the cell membrane.

As mentioned above, the Hodgkin–Huxley model describes three types of channel. All channels may be characterized by their resistance or, equivalently, by their conductance. The leakage channel is described by a voltage-independent conductance $g_L = 1/R$; the conductance of the other ion channels is voltage and time dependent. If all channels are open, they transmit currents with a maximum conductance g_{Na} or g_K, respectively. Normally, however, some of the channels are blocked. The probability that a channel is open is described by additional variables m, n, and h. The combined action of m and h controls the Na^+ channels. The K^+ gates are controlled by n. Specifically, Hodgkin and Huxley formulated the three current components as

$$\sum_k I_k = g_{Na}\, m^3 h\, (u - E_{Na}) + g_K\, n^4\, (u - E_K) + g_L\, (u - E_L).\qquad(2.5)$$

The parameters E_{Na}, E_K, and E_L are the reversal potentials. Reversal potentials and conductances are empirical parameters. In Table 2.1 we have summarized the original values reported by Hodgkin and Huxley (1952). These values are based on a voltage scale where the resting potential is zero. To get the values accepted today, the voltage scale has to be shifted by -65 mV. For example, the corrected value of the sodium reversal potential is $E_{Na} = 50$ mV that of the potassium ions is $E_K = -77$ mV.

The three variables m, n, and h are called gating variables. They evolve according to the differential equations

$$\dot{m} = \alpha_m(u)\,(1 - m) - \beta_m(u)\,m$$
$$\dot{n} = \alpha_n(u)\,(1 - n) - \beta_n(u)\,n$$
$$\dot{h} = \alpha_h(u)\,(1 - h) - \beta_h(u)\,h\qquad(2.6)$$

with $\dot{m} = dm/dt$, and so on. The various functions α and β, given in Table 2.1, are empirical functions of u that have been adjusted by Hodgkin and Huxley to fit the data of the giant axon of the squid. Equations (2.4)–(2.6) with the values given in Table 2.1 define the Hodgkin–Huxley model.

Table 2.1. *The parameters of the Hodgkin–Huxley equations. The membrane capacity is $C = 1 \ \mu F/cm^2$. The voltage scale is shifted so that the resting potential vanishes.*

x	E_x (mV)	g_x (mS/cm^2)
Na	115	120
K	−12	36
L	10.6	0.3

x	$\alpha_x(u/mV)$	$\beta_x(u/mV)$
n	$(0.1 - 0.01u)/[\exp(1 - 0.1u) - 1]$	$0.125 \exp(-u/80)$
m	$(2.5 - 0.1u)/[\exp(2.5 - 0.1u) - 1]$	$4 \exp(-u/18)$
h	$0.07 \exp(-u/20)$	$1/[\exp(3 - 0.1u) + 1]$

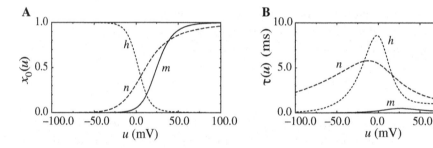

Fig. 2.3. Equilibrium function (**A**) and time constant (**B**) for the three variables m, n, h in the Hodgkin–Huxley model. The resting potential is at $u = 0$.

In order to getter a better understanding of the three equations (2.6), it is convenient to rewrite each of the equations in the form

$$\dot{x} = -\frac{1}{\tau_x(u)}[x - x_0(u)], \tag{2.7}$$

where x stands for m, n, or h. For fixed voltage u, the variable x approaches the value $x_0(u)$ with a time constant $\tau_x(u)$. The asymptotic value $x_0(u)$ and the time constant $\tau_x(u)$ are given by the transformation $x_0(u) = \alpha_x(u)/[\alpha_x(u) + \beta_x(u)]$ and $\tau_x(u) = [\alpha_x(u) + \beta_x(u)]^{-1}$. Using the parameters given by Hodgkin and Huxley (1952), we have plotted in Fig. 2.3 the functions $x_0(u)$ and $\tau_x(u)$.

2.2.2 Dynamics

In this subsection we study the dynamics of the Hodgkin–Huxley model for different types of input. Pulse input, constant input, step current input, and time-dependent input are considered in turn. These input scenarios have been chosen so as to provide an intuitive understanding of the dynamics of the Hodgkin–Huxley model.

Example: spike generation

We see from Fig. 2.3A that m_0 and n_0 increase with u whereas h_0 decreases. Thus, if some external input causes the membrane voltage to rise, the conductance of sodium channels increases due to increasing m. As a result, positive sodium ions flow into the cell and raise the membrane potential even further. If this positive feedback is large enough, an action potential is initiated.

At high values of u the sodium conductance is shut off due to the factor h. As indicated in Fig. 2.3B, the "time constant" τ_h is always larger than τ_m. Thus the variable h which closes the channels reacts more slowly to the voltage increase than the variable m which opens the channel. On a similar slow time scale, the potassium (K^+) current sets in. Since it is a current in outward direction, it lowers the potential. The overall effect of the sodium and potassium currents is a short action potential followed by a negative overshoot; cf. Fig. 2.4A. The amplitude of the spike is about 100 mV.

In Fig. 2.4A, the spike has been initiated by a short current pulse of 1 ms duration applied at $t < 0$. If the amplitude of the stimulating current pulse is reduced below some critical value, the membrane potential returns to the rest value without a large spike-like excursion; cf. Fig. 2.4B. Thus we have a threshold-type behavior.

Example: mean firing rates and gain function

The Hodgkin–Huxley equations (2.4)–(2.6) may also be studied for constant input $I(t) = I_0$ for $t > 0$. (The input is zero for $t \leq 0$.) If the value I_0 is larger than a critical value $I_\theta \approx 6\ \mu\text{A/cm}^2$, we observe regular spiking; Fig. 2.5A. We may define a firing rate $\nu = 1/T$ where T is the interspike interval. The firing rate as a function of the constant input I_0 defines the gain function plotted in Fig. 2.5B.

Example: step current input

In the previous example we have seen that a constant input current $I_0 > I_\theta$ generates regular firing. In this paragraph we study the response of the Hodgkin–Huxley model to a step current of the form

$$I(t) = I_1 + \Delta I\ \Theta(t). \qquad (2.8)$$

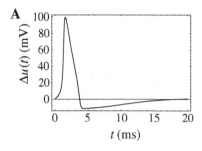

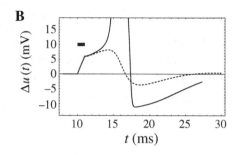

Fig. 2.4. **A**. Action potential. The Hodgkin–Huxley model has been stimulated by a short, but strong, current pulse before $t = 0$. The time course of the membrane potential $\Delta u(t) = u(t) - u_{rest}$ for $t > 0$ shows the action potential (positive peak) followed by a relative refractory period where the potential is below the resting potential. In the spike response framework, the time course $u(t) - u_{rest}$ of the action potential for $t > 0$ defines the kernel $\eta(t)$. **B**. Threshold effect in the initiation of an action potential. A current pulse of 1 ms duration has been applied at $t = 10$ ms. For a current amplitude of 7.0 μA/cm^2, an action potential with an amplitude of about 100 mV as in **A** is initiated (solid line, the peak of the action potential is off scale). If the stimulating current pulse is slightly weaker (6.9 μA/cm^2) no action potential is emitted (dashed line) and the voltage $\Delta u(t) = u(t) - u_{rest}$ always stays below 10 mV. Note that the voltage scale in **B** is different from that in **A**.

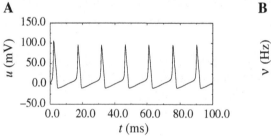

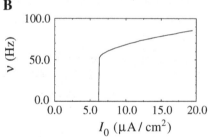

Fig. 2.5. **A** Spike train of the Hodgkin–Huxley model for constant input current I_0. **B**. Gain function. The mean firing rate ν is plotted as a function of I_0.

Here $\Theta(t)$ denotes the Heaviside step function, which is defined by $\Theta(t) = 0$ for $t \leq 0$ and $\Theta(t) = 1$ for $t > 0$. At $t = 0$ the input jumps from a fixed value I_1 to a new value $I_2 = I_1 + \Delta I$; see Fig. 2.6A. We may wonder whether spiking for $t > 0$ depends only on the final value I_2 or also on the step size ΔI.

The answer to this question is given by Fig. 2.6B. A large step ΔI facilitates the spike initiation. Even for a target value $I_2 = 0$ (i.e., no stimulation for $t > 0$) a spike is possible, provided that the step size is large enough. This is an example of inhibitory rebound: a single spike is fired, if an inhibitory current $I_1 < 0$ is released. The letter S in Fig. 2.6B denotes the regime where only a single spike is

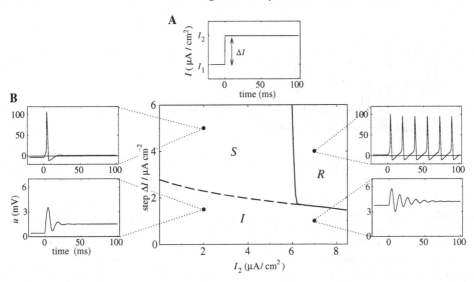

Fig. 2.6. Phase diagram for stimulation with a step current. **A.** The input current $I(t)$ changes at $t = 0$ from I_1 to I_2. **B.** Response of the Hodgkin–Huxley model to step current input. Three regimes denoted by S, R, and I may be distinguished. In I no action potential is initiated (inactive regime). In S, a single spike is initiated by the current step (single spike regime). In R, periodic spike trains are triggered by the current step (repetitive firing). Examples of voltage traces in the different regimes are presented in the smaller graphs to the left and right of the phase diagram in the center. Taken from Kistler et al. (1997) with permission.

initiated. Repetitive firing (regime R) is possible for $I_2 > 6\ \mu\text{A}/\text{cm}^2$, but must be triggered by sufficiently large current steps.

We may conclude from Fig. 2.6B that there is no unique current threshold for spike initiation: the trigger mechanism for action potentials depends not only on I_2 but also on the size of the current step ΔI. More generally, it can be shown that the concept of a threshold itself is questionable from a mathematical point of view (Rinzel and Ermentrout, 1998; Koch et al., 1995). In a mathematical sense, the transition in Fig. 2.4B, that "looks" like a threshold is, in fact, smooth. If we carefully tuned the input current in the regime between 6.9 and 7.0 $\mu\text{A}/\text{cm}^2$, we would find a family of response amplitudes in between the curves shown in Fig. 2.4B. For practical purposes, however, the transition can be treated as a threshold effect. A mathematical discussion of the threshold phenomenon can be found in Chapter 3.

Example: stimulation by time-dependent input

In order to explore a more realistic input scenario, we stimulate the Hodgkin–Huxley model by a time-dependent input current $I(t)$ that is generated by the

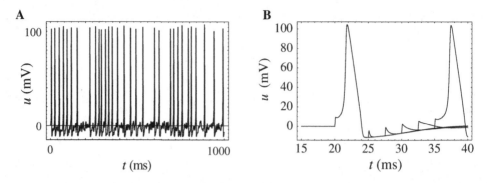

Fig. 2.7. **A.** Spike train of the Hodgkin–Huxley model driven by a time-dependent input current. The action potentials occur irregularly. The figure shows the voltage u as a function of time. **B.** Refractoriness of the Hodgkin–Huxley model. At $t = 20$ ms the model is stimulated by a short current pulse so as to trigger an action potential. A second current pulse of the same amplitude applied at $t = 25, 27.5, 30$, or 32.5 ms is not sufficient to trigger a second action potential.

following procedure. Every 2 ms, a random number is drawn from a Gaussian distribution with zero mean and standard deviation $\sigma = 3$ $\mu\text{A}/\text{cm}^2$. To get a continuous input current, a linear interpolation was used between the target values. The resulting time-dependent input current was then applied to the Hodgkin–Huxley model (2.4)–(2.6). The response to the current is the voltage trace shown in Fig. 2.7. Note that action potentials occur at irregular intervals.

Example: refractoriness

In order to study neuronal refractoriness, we stimulate the Hodgkin–Huxley model by a first current pulse that is sufficiently strong to excite a spike. A second current pulse of the *same* amplitude as the first one is used to probe the responsiveness of the neuron during the phase of hyperpolarization that follows the action potential. If the second stimulus is not sufficient to trigger another action potential, we have a clear signature of neuronal refractoriness. In the simulation shown in Fig. 2.7B, a second spike is possible if we wait at least 15 ms after the first stimulation. It would, of course, be possible to trigger a second spike after a shorter interval if a significantly stronger stimulation pulse was used; for classic experiments along those lines, see, e.g., Fuortes and Mantegazzini (1962).

If we look more closely at the voltage trajectory of Fig. 2.7B, we see that neuronal refractoriness manifests itself in two different forms. Firstly, due to the hyperpolarizing spike-afterpotential the voltage is lower. More stimulation is therefore needed to reach the firing threshold. Secondly, since a large portion of channels is open immediately after a spike, the resistance of the membrane is reduced compared to the situation at rest. The depolarizing effect of a stimulating current pulse decays therefore faster immediately after the spike than 10 ms later. An efficient description of refractoriness plays a major role in simplified neuron models discussed in Chapter 4.

2.3 The zoo of ion channels

The equations of Hodgkin and Huxley provide a good description of the electro-physiological properties of the giant axon of the squid. These equations capture the essence of spike generation by sodium and potassium ion channels. The basic mechanism of generating action potentials is a short influx of sodium ions that is followed by an efflux of potassium ions. This mechanism is essentially preserved in higher organisms. Cortical neurons in vertebrates, however, exhibit a much richer repertoire of electrophysiological properties than the squid axon studied by Hodgkin and Huxley. These properties are mostly due to a large variety of different ion channels (Llinás, 1988; Hille, 1992; Koch, 1999).

In this section we give an overview of some of the ion channels encountered in different neurons. The basic equation of detailed neuron models is more or less the same as that of the Hodgkin–Huxley model (Hodgkin and Huxley, 1952) except that it contains more types of ion channels. The membrane potential u of the neuron is given by

$$C \frac{\mathrm{d}}{\mathrm{d}t} u(t) = I_{\mathrm{syn}}(t) + \sum_k I_k(t). \tag{2.9}$$

Here, C is the membrane capacity, I_{syn} the synaptic input current, and I_k is the current through ion channel k. As in the Hodgkin–Huxley model, sodium and potassium currents are described by equations of the form

$$I_k = \bar{g}_k \, m^{p_k} \, h^{q_k} \, (u - E_k), \tag{2.10}$$

with $\bar{g}_k$ being the maximum conductance of ion channel k, E_k is the reversal potential, and m and h are activation and inactivation variables, respectively. The exponents p_k and q_k are parameters. The potassium current of the Hodgkin–Huxley model, for example, has $p_k = 4$ and $q_k = 0$ so that the variable h can be omitted. Figures 2.8 and 2.9 give an overview of equilibrium values and time constants of the activation and inactivation variables for various types of ion channel.

2.3.1 Sodium channels

Apart from fast sodium ion channels, which are qualitatively similar to those of the Hodgkin–Huxley model and denoted by I_{Na}, some neurons contain a "persistent" or "noninactivating" sodium current I_{NaP}. "Noninactivating" means that this current

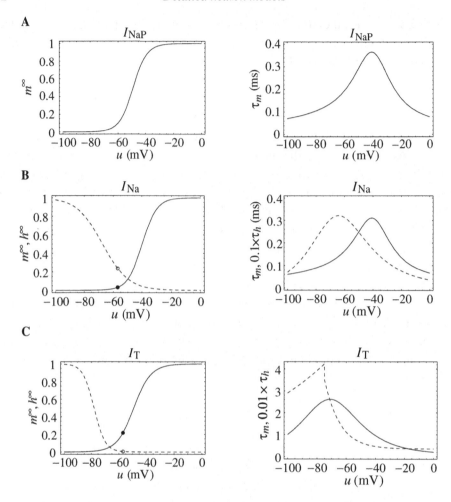

Fig. 2.8. Stationary values (left) and time constants (right) of the activation variable m (solid line) and the inactivation variable h (dashed line) of various ion currents. **A.** Persistent sodium current I_{NaP}. **B.** Transient sodium current I_{Na}. **C.** Low-threshold calcium current I_T. Small circles indicate the equilibrium values of m and h at the resting potential. Note that the activation and inactivation curves for the low-threshold calcium current are shifted towards a more hyperpolarized level of the membrane potential as compared to those of the transient sodium current. Note also that different scales have been used for τ_m and τ_h since the dynamics of the inactivation variable h is slower by a factor of 10–100 than that of the activation variable m. Numerical values of parameters correspond to a model of neurons in the deep cerebellar nuclei (Kistler et al., 2000).

has $q_{NaP} = 0$. In other words, it is described by an activation variable m only and does not have a separate inactivation variable h,

$$I_{NaP} = \bar{g}_{NaP}\, m\, (u - E_{Na})\,. \tag{2.11}$$

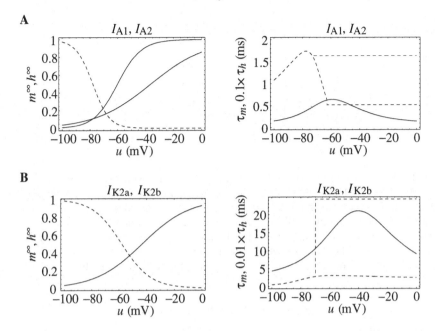

Fig. 2.9. Stationary values (left) and time constants (right) of the activation (solid line) and inactivation (dashed line) variables of the rapidly inactivating potassium currents I_{A1} and I_{A2} (**A**) and the slowly inactivating potassium currents I_{K2a} and I_{K2b} (**B**).

The current I_{NaP} increases the overall excitability of the neuron because the corresponding channels open when the membrane is depolarized so that an influx of positive sodium ions then leads to an even larger depolarization. Typical equilibrium values and time constants of the noninactivating sodium current I_{NaP} are presented in Fig. 2.8A and may be compared with that of the fast sodium current I_{Na} in Fig. 2.8B.

2.3.2 Potassium channels

Voltage-clamp experiments on various neurons have revealed that there is more than just one type of potassium channel. In thalamic relay neurons, for example, two different types of potassium channels are present, viz. a rapidly inactivating potassium current I_A (inactivation time constant $\tau_h \approx 10$ ms) and a slowly inactivating potassium current I_{K2} (time constant $\tau_h \approx 200\ldots2000$ ms); cf. Fig. 2.9. Both classes can even be further subdivided into two different subtypes I_{A1}, I_{A2}, and I_{K2a}, I_{K2b}, respectively, in order to fit activation and inactivation curves that contain more than a single time constant (Huguenard and McCormick, 1992).

A   **B**

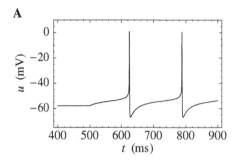
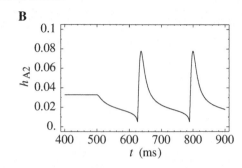

Fig. 2.10. Slowly firing neuron and long-latency response to a sudden onset of an excitatory stimulus. **A**. Membrane potential of a neuron with a pronounced A-type potassium conductance. Repetitive firing at a very low frequency is started by a depolarizing current step at $t = 500$ ms. The first spike occurs with a delay of about 120 ms after the onset of the input current. **B**. Time course of the inactivation variable h of the A current in the same simulation as in **A**. The delay between stimulus onset and the first action potential is due to the slowly inactivating A current which is apparent here by the smooth decay of $h_{A2}(t)$.

Example: slowly firing neurons

The aforementioned A current I_A is just one member of a large class of transient potassium currents. These currents have in common an inactivation time constant of a few tens of milliseconds, which is rather long compared to the sodium dynamics. Since potassium currents are outward currents, the current I_A tends to hyperpolarize the membrane potential and therefore slows down the firing of action potentials. For weak sustained stimulation, new action potentials only occur after the A current has become sufficiently inactivated (Connor et al., 1977).

In a similar way, A currents are responsible for a long delay between the sudden onset of an excitatory stimulus and the very first action potential; cf. Fig. 2.10. The onset of a depolarizing current will quickly lead to an activation of the A current, which in turn counteracts a depolarization of the membrane potential. Following the slow inactivation of the A current, the membrane potential finally rises to the firing threshold and an action potential is released.

Example: model of a neocortical interneuron

The gain function of the Hodgkin–Huxley model is discontinuous at the firing threshold which means that it cannot produce low-frequency spike trains with a constant input current. Nevertheless, low firing rates can also be achieved without the inactivating current I_A provided that the potassium currents have suitable characteristics. In a model of neocortical interneurons (Erisir et al., 1999), there are two noninactivating potassium channels and an inactivating sodium channel of the Hodgkin–Huxley type. With a suitable choice of parameters, the gain function is continuous, i.e., repetitive firing is possible in the full range of frequencies between

A

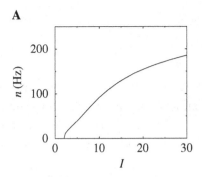

B

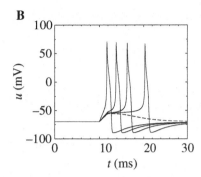

Fig. 2.11. **A.** Gain function of a neocortical interneuron model. The firing rate ν is shown as a function of a constant input current I. **B.** Delayed spike initiation. A short current pulse of 2 ms duration is applied at $t = 10$ ms. The action potential that is elicited in response to the current pulse is shown for different pulse amplitudes. Note that the action potential for weak superthreshold stimulation can occur 10 ms *after* the end of the current pulse.

zero and a few hundred hertz; cf. Fig. 2.11B. A short current pulse from rest can elicit action potentials if a critical threshold voltage is exceeded. In contrast to the Hodgkin–Huxley model, stimulation that is only slightly above threshold leads to delayed pulse generation; cf. Fig. 2.11B. Neurons with continuous gain function and delayed pulse generation are called type I whereas neurons with discontinuous gain function are called type II. The distinction between type I and type II plays an important role in Chapter 3.

2.3.3 *Low-threshold calcium current*

Apart from channels for sodium and potassium ions, many central neurons also contain channels for calcium ions. Similarly to the common sodium and potassium currents, calcium currents are described in terms of a maximum permeability $\bar{p}_k$ times a combination of activation m and inactivation h variables. In contrast to sodium and potassium the intracellular calcium concentration is very low and can be significantly affected by the calcium influx during an action potential. The current that passes through open channels thus depends on the actual calcium concentrations $[Ca^{2+}]_{i,e}$ inside and outside the cell, and on the voltage u across the membrane. The conductivity of a calcium channel is described by the Goldman–Hodgkin–Katz equation which accounts for a small nonlinearity in the voltage-current relationship of the *open* channel that is caused by the large concentration gradient across the membrane (Hille, 1992, chapter 13). Altogether, the current through calcium channel x is given by

$$I_x = \bar{p}_x \, m^{p_x} \, h_x^q \, \frac{u \, z^2 \, F^2}{RT} \, \frac{[Ca^{2+}]_e \, e^{-u \, z \, F/RT} - [Ca^{2+}]_i}{1 - e^{-u \, z \, F/RT}}, \tag{2.12}$$

with $z = 2$ for Ca^{2+}, Faraday's constant $F = 9.648 \cdot 10^4 \, C \, mol^{-1}$, and the gas constant $R = 8.314 \, V \, C \, K^{-1} \, mol^{-1}$. The extracellular calcium concentration is usually assumed to be constant at $[Ca^{2+}]_e = 2.0$ mM, whereas the intracellular calcium concentration, $[Ca^{2+}]_i$, may depend on the amount of Ca^{2+} influx in the recent past.

Neurons of the deep cerebellar nuclei, for example, contain two different types of calcium channels that give rise to a so-called *high-threshold calcium current* (I_L) and a *low-threshold calcium current* (I_T), respectively (Jahnsen, 1986; Llinás and Mühlethaler, 1988). From a functional point of view, the low-threshold calcium current is particularly interesting, because it is responsible for a phenomenon called *postinhibitory rebound*. Postinhibitory rebound means that a hyperpolarizing current, which is suddenly switched off, results in an overshoot of the membrane potential or even in the triggering of one or more action potentials. Through this mechanism, action potentials can be triggered by *inhibitory* input. These action potentials, however, occur with a certain delay after the arrival of the inhibitory input, viz., after the end of the inhibitory postsynaptic potential (IPSP) (Aizenman and Linden, 1999).

The low-threshold calcium current is "inactivating", i.e., the corresponding ion channel is shutting down after the membrane has become depolarized ($q_x = 1$). In this respect, the I_T current is similar to the fast sodium current of the Hodgkin–Huxley model. The discerning feature of the I_T current, however, is the fact that the activation and inactivation curves are shifted significantly towards a hyperpolarized membrane potential so that the channel is completely *inactivated* ($h \approx 0$) at the resting potential; see Fig. 2.8C. This is qualitatively different from the situation of the sodium channels of the Hodgkin–Huxley model. These channels are also closed at rest; the reason, however, is different. In the Hodgkin–Huxley model the sodium channels are *not activated* ($m \approx 0$) whereas the T-type calcium current is *inactivated* ($h \approx 0$); cf. Fig. 2.8B and C.

Example: postinhibitory rebound

The basic mechanism of postinhibitory rebound can be easily understood by means of Fig. 2.8C which shows the stationary values of the activation and the inactivation variables, together with their time constants as a function of the membrane potential. In order to open the T-type calcium channels it is first of all necessary to remove its inactivation by *hyperpolarizing* the membrane. The time constant of the inactivation variable h is rather high (dashed line in the right panel

A

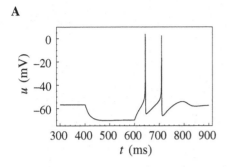

B

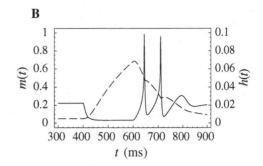

Fig. 2.12. Postinhibitory rebound. **A**. Membrane potential as a function of time. Injection of a hyperpolarizing current pulse (100 pA for 200 ms from $t = 400$ ms to $t = 600$ ms) results in a low-threshold calcium spike when the current is turned off, which in turn triggers two sodium action potentials. **B**. Time course of activation (solid line, left scale) and inactivation (dashed line, right scale) variables of the I_T current that is responsible for this phenomenon.

of Fig. 2.8C) and it thus takes a while until h has reached a value sufficiently above zero. But even if the channels have been successfully "de-inactivated" they remain in a closed state, because the activation variable m is zero as long as the membrane is hyperpolarized; cf. left panel of Fig. 2.8C. However, the channels will be transiently opened if the membrane potential is rapidly relaxed from the hyperpolarized level to the resting potential, because activation is faster than inactivation and, thus, there is a short period when both m and h are nonzero. The current that passes through the channels is terminated ("inactivated") as soon as the inactivation variable h has dropped to zero again. The resulting current pulse is called a *low-threshold calcium spike*.

The increase in the membrane potential caused by the low-threshold calcium spike may be sufficient to trigger ordinary sodium action potentials. We will refer to action potentials generated by this mechanism as *rebound spikes*. Figure 2.12A shows an example of rebound spikes that are triggered by an inhibitory current pulse. The time course of the activation and inactivation variables of the low-threshold calcium current are plotted in Fig. 2.12B.

2.3.4 High-threshold calcium current and calcium-activated potassium channels

In addition to the low-threshold calcium current, some neurons, e.g., cortical pyramidal cells, contain a second type of calcium current, called *high-threshold calcium current*, or I_L current for short. Similar to the persistent sodium current this current is noninactivating (or "long-lasting" – hence the index L), but it is activated

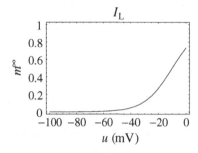
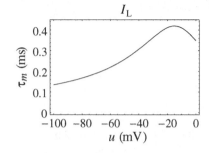

Fig. 2.13. Stationary values (left) and time constants (right) of the activation variable m of the high-threshold calcium current I_L. It is called "high-threshold" because the equilibrium value $m^\infty(u)$ is close to zero for $u \leq -50$ mV.

only at rather high levels of depolarization; cf. Fig. 2.13A. The I_L channels are thus open during action potentials, but otherwise closed. The current through these channels is described by the Goldman–Hodgkin–Katz equation (2.12) with $p_x = 2$ and $q_x = 0$, i.e., the inactivation variable h is absent.

The role of calcium in generating spikes is twofold. On the one hand, calcium ions carry a positive electrical charge and contribute to the depolarization of the membrane. On the other hand, calcium ions are an important second messenger that is involved in all kinds of intracellular signaling. An example of the latter role of calcium ions is provided by calcium-*activated* potassium channels. The potassium current I_C that passes through these channels is described by the familiar equation

$$I_C = \bar{g}_C\, m\, (u - E_K),\qquad(2.13)$$

with $\bar{g}_C$ being the maximum conductance, m the activation variable, and $E_K = -85$ mV the potassium reversal potential. In contrast to previous equations of this form, the differential equation for m depends explicitly on the intracellular calcium concentration. A typical parameterization is

$$\frac{dm}{dt} = \alpha\, m - \beta\, (1 - m),\qquad(2.14)$$

with

$$\alpha = 2.5{\cdot}10^5\, [Ca^{2+}]_i\, \exp(u/24) \quad\text{and}\quad \beta = 0.1\, \exp(-u/24).\qquad(2.15)$$

Here, $[Ca^{2+}]_i$ is the intracellular calcium concentration in mol/l; u is the membrane potential in mV. The stationary value of the activation variable, $m^\infty = \alpha/(\alpha + \beta)$, and its time constant, $\tau = (\alpha + \beta)^{-1}$, are shown in Fig. 2.14.

The plot in Fig. 2.14 shows that the stationary value of m rises as the calcium concentration increases. Similarly, the relaxation towards the stationary value becomes faster since the time constant τ_m decreases with increasing calcium

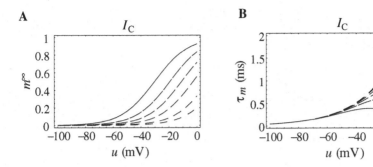

Fig. 2.14. Calcium-activated potassium channels. **A**. Stationary values of the activation variable for the calcium-dependent potassium channel current I_C as a function of membrane potential. Different traces correspond to different concentrations of intracellular calcium $[Ca^{2+}]_i = 0.1$ (dashed line), 0.2, 0.5, 1.0, 2.0, 5.0 µmol/l (solid line). **B**. Corresponding time constants for various calcium concentrations as in **A**.

concentration; cf. Fig. 2.14B. The I_C current is thus *activated* by intracellular calcium, as indicated by its name. Due to the short time constant of its activation variable the maximum of this potassium current is reached during or immediately after an action potential. If present, the calcium-activated potassium channels can provide a major contribution to the repolarization of the membrane after an action potential.

Example: adaptation

Closely related to the I_C current is another calcium-activated potassium current, the so-called I_{AHP} current (AHP is short for afterhyperpolarization). In contrast to its C-type sibling the activation of this current is much slower and purely $[Ca^{2+}]_i$ dependent, i.e., *voltage independent*. This current is activated by calcium ions that enter through (voltage-gated) L-type channels during an action potential (Tanabe et al., 1998a). More precisely, we have

$$I_{AHP} = \bar{g}_{AHP} \, m \, (u - E_K) \,, \qquad (2.16)$$

with

$$\frac{dm}{dt} = \alpha \, m - \beta \, (1 - m) \,, \qquad (2.17)$$

as usual, and, in the case of hippocampal pyramidal neurons, $\beta = 0.001$, $\alpha = \min\left(c\,[Ca^{2+}]_i, 0.01\right)$, with c an appropriate constant (Traub et al., 1991).

Because AHP channels are not inactivating and because of their low time constant at rest, each action potential simply increases the activation m by a more or less fixed amount. If the neuron is stimulated by a constant depolarizing current each action potential increases the amount of open AHP channels and the

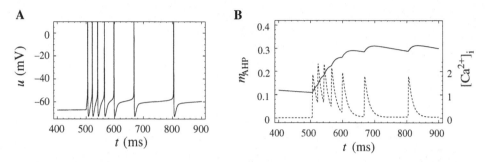

Fig. 2.15. Firing frequency adaptation as it is produced by the calcium-activated potassium current I_{AHP}. **A.** Membrane potential of a neuron equipped with AHP-type ion channels. In this simulation a constant depolarizing input current is switched on at time $t = 500$ ms. **B.** Time course of the activation m of the AHP channels (solid line) and intracellular calcium concentration (dashed line, arbitrary units) in the same simulation as in **A.** Note that the activation of the I_{AHP} current is increased stepwise by each Ca^{2+} transient that occurs in the wake of an action potential.

corresponding potassium current subtracts from the applied stimulus. The firing frequency is thus decreasing, a phenomenon that is known as *firing frequency adaptation*; cf. Fig. 2.15.

2.3.5 Calcium dynamics

Among all ions of the intra- and extracellular fluid calcium ions are particularly interesting. On the one hand, they contribute to the ionic current across the membrane; see Section 2.3.3. On the other hand, some potassium channels are controlled by the intracellular calcium concentration; see Section 2.3.4. These channels are not present in the model of Hodgkin and Huxley, but they are responsible for interesting electrophysiological properties of neurons in different brain areas.

Whereas sodium and potassium concentrations are large as compared to the ionic influx or efflux during an action potential, the intracellular calcium concentration is not and, hence, it cannot be treated as a constant. Since both the influx through calcium channels and the state of the aforementioned potassium channels depend on the intracellular calcium concentration we have to describe this concentration explicitly by a variable $[\mathrm{Ca}^{2+}]_i$.

Modeling the calcium concentration, however, is no trivial task because both diffusion and chemical calcium buffers ought to be taken into account. To avoid these difficulties a purely phenomenological approach can be adopted. The intracellular calcium concentration $[Ca^{2+}]_i$ is described by a linear differential equation,

$$\frac{d[Ca^{2+}]_i}{dt} = -\tau_{Ca}^{-1} [Ca^{2+}]_i + \phi_{Ca} I_{Ca} \,, \tag{2.18}$$

where I_{Ca} is the calcium current across the membrane, τ_{Ca} is the time constant that governs the decay of a calcium transient, and ϕ_{Ca} is a constant that scales the amplitude of the calcium transient as it is produced during an action potential. Both τ_{Ca} and ϕ_{Ca} are adjusted so as to fit experimental results.

2.4 Synapses

So far we have encountered two classes of ion channel, namely *voltage*-activated and *calcium*-activated ion channels. The third type of ion channels we have to deal with are the *transmitter*-activated ion channels involved in synaptic transmission. Activation of a presynaptic neuron results in a release of neurotransmitters into the synaptic cleft. The transmitter molecules diffuse to the other side of the cleft and activate receptors that are located in the postsynaptic membrane. So-called *ionotropic receptors* have a direct influence on the state of an associated ion channel whereas *metabotropic receptors* control the state of the ion channel by means of a biochemical cascade of g-proteins and second messengers. In any case the activation of the receptor results in the opening of certain ion channels and, thus, in an excitatory or inhibitory postsynaptic current (EPSC or IPSC).

Instead of developing a mathematical model of the transmitter concentration in the synaptic cleft we try to keep things simple and describe transmitter-activated ion channels as an explicitly time-dependent conductivity $g_{syn}(t)$ that will open whenever a presynaptic spike arrives. The current that passes through these channels depends, as usual, on the difference between its reversal potential E_{syn} and the actual value of the membrane potential,

$$I_{syn}(t) = g_{syn}(t) \, (u - E_{syn}) \,. \tag{2.19}$$

The parameter E_{syn} and the function $g_{syn}(t)$ can be used to characterize different types of synapse. Typically, a superposition of exponentials is used for $g_{syn}(t)$. For inhibitory synapses E_{syn} equals the reversal potential of potassium ions (about -75 mV), whereas for excitatory synapses $E_{syn} \approx 0$.

2.4.1 Inhibitory synapses

The effect of fast inhibitory neurons in the central nervous system of higher vertebrates is almost exclusively conveyed by a neurotransmitter called γ-aminobutyric acid, or GABA for short. In addition to many different types of inhibitory interneurons, cerebellar Purkinje cells form a prominent example of projecting neurons that use GABA as their neurotransmitter. These neurons synapse onto neurons in the deep cerebellar nuclei (DCN) and are particularly important for an understanding of cerebellar function.

The parameters that describe the conductivity of transmitter-activated ion channels at a certain synapse are chosen so as to mimic the time course and the amplitude of experimentally observed spontaneous postsynaptic currents. For example, the conductance $\bar{g}_{\text{syn}}(t)$ of inhibitory synapses in DCN neurons can be described by a simple exponential decay with a time constant of $\tau = 5$ ms and an amplitude of $\bar{g}_{\text{syn}} = 40$ pS,

$$g_{\text{syn}}(t) = \sum_f \bar{g}_{\text{syn}}\, e^{-(t-t^{(f)})/\tau}\, \Theta(t - t^{(f)}) . \tag{2.20}$$

Here, $t^{(f)}$ denotes the arrival time of a presynaptic action potential. The reversal potential is given by that of potassium ions, viz. $E_{\text{syn}} = -75$ mV.

Of course, more attention can be paid to account for the details of synaptic transmission. In cerebellar granule cells, for example, inhibitory synapses are also GABAergic, but their postsynaptic current is made up of two different components. There is a fast component that decays with a time constant of about 5 ms, and there is a component that is ten times slower. The underlying postsynaptic conductance is thus of the form

$$g_{\text{syn}}(t) = \sum_f \left(\bar{g}_{\text{fast}}\, e^{-(t-t^{(f)})/\tau_{\text{fast}}} + \bar{g}_{\text{slow}}\, e^{-(t-t^{(f)})/\tau_{\text{slow}}} \right) \Theta(t - t^{(f)}) . \tag{2.21}$$

2.4.2 Excitatory synapses

Most, if not all, excitatory synapses in the vertebrate central nervous system rely on glutamate as their neurotransmitter. The postsynaptic receptors, however, can have very different pharmacological properties and often different types of glutamate receptors are present in a single synapse. These receptors can be classified by certain amino acids that may be selective agonists. Usually, NMDA (*N*-methyl-D-aspartate) and nonNMDA receptors are distinguished. The most prominent among the nonNMDA receptors are AMPA receptors.[1] Ion channels controlled by AMPA receptors are characterized by a fast response to presynaptic spikes and a quickly decaying postsynaptic current. NMDA-receptor-controlled channels are significantly slower and have additional interesting properties that are due to a voltage-dependent blocking by magnesium ions (Hille, 1992).

Excitatory synapses in cerebellar granule cells, for example, contain two different types of glutamate receptors, viz. AMPA and NMDA receptors. The time

---

[1] AMPA is short for α-amino-3-hydroxy-5-methyl-4-isoxalone propionic acid.

course of the postsynaptic conductivity caused by an activation of AMPA receptors at time $t = t^{(f)}$ can be described as follows

$$g_{\text{AMPA}}(t) = \bar{g}_{\text{AMPA}} \cdot \mathcal{N} \cdot \left[e^{-(t-t^{(f)})/\tau_{\text{decay}}} - e^{-(t-t^{(f)})/\tau_{\text{rise}}} \right] \Theta(t - t^{(f)}), \quad (2.22)$$

with rise time $\tau_{\text{rise}} = 0.09$ ms, decay time $\tau_{\text{decay}} = 1.5$ ms, and maximum conductance $\bar{g}_{\text{AMPA}} = 720$ pS; cf. (Gabbiani et al., 1994). The numerical constant $\mathcal{N} = 1.273$ normalizes the maximum of the braced term to unity.

NMDA-receptor-controlled channels exhibit a significantly richer repertoire of dynamic behavior because their state is not only controlled by the presence or absence of their agonist, but also by the membrane potential. The voltage dependence itself arises from the *blocking* of the channel by a common extracellular ion, Mg^{2+} (Hille, 1992). Unless Mg^{2+} is removed from the extracellular medium, the channels remain closed at the resting potential even in the presence of NMDA. If the membrane is depolarized beyond -50 mV, then the Mg^{2+}-block is removed, the channel opens, and, in contrast to AMPA-controlled channels, stays open for 10–100 ms. A simple description that accounts for this additional voltage dependence of NMDA-controlled channels in cerebellar granule cells is

$$g_{\text{NMDA}}(t) = \bar{g}_{\text{NMDA}} \cdot \mathcal{N} \cdot \left[e^{-(t-t^{(f)})/\tau_{\text{decay}}} - e^{-(t-t^{(f)})/\tau_{\text{rise}}} \right] g_{\infty} \Theta(t - t^{(f)}),$$

$$\text{with } g_{\infty} = \left(1 + e^{\alpha u} [Mg^{2+}]_o/\beta \right)^{-1}, \quad (2.23)$$

with $\tau_{\text{rise}} = 3$ ms, $\tau_{\text{decay}} = 40$ ms, $\mathcal{N} = 1.358$, $\bar{g}_{\text{NMDA}} = 1.2$ nS, $\alpha = 0.062 \, \text{mV}^{-1}$, $\beta = 3.57$ mM, and the extracellular magnesium concentration $[Mg^{2+}]_o = 1.2$ mM (Gabbiani et al., 1994).

A final remark on the role of NMDA receptors in learning is in order. Though NMDA-controlled ion channels are permeable to sodium and potassium ions, their permeability to calcium is even five or ten times larger. Calcium ions are known to play an important role in intracellular signaling and are probably also involved in long-term modifications of synaptic efficacy. Calcium influx through NMDA-controlled ion channels, however, is bound to the coincidence of presynaptic (NMDA release from presynaptic sites) and postsynaptic (removal of the Mg^{2+}-block) activity. Hence, NMDA receptors operate as a kind of molecular coincidence detector as they are required for a biochemical implementation of Hebb's learning rule; cf. Chapter 10.

2.5 Spatial structure: the dendritic tree

Neurons in the cortex and other areas of the brain often exhibit highly developed dendritic trees that may extend over several hundreds of micrometers. Synaptic input to a neuron is mostly located on its dendritic tree; however, spikes are

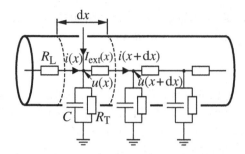

Fig. 2.16. Part of a dendrite and the corresponding circuit diagram. Longitudinal and transversal resistors are denoted by R_L and R_T, respectively. The electrical capacity of each small piece of dendrite is symbolized by capacitors C.

generated at the soma near the axon hillock. What are the consequences of the spatial separation of input and output? Up to now we have discussed point neurons only, i.e., neurons without any spatial structure. The electrical properties of point neurons have been described as a capacitor that is charged by synaptic currents and other *transversal* ion currents across the membrane. A nonuniform distribution of the membrane potential on the dendritic tree and the soma induces additional *longitudinal* current along the dendrite. We are now going to derive the cable equation that describes the membrane potential along a passive dendrite as a function of time *and* space. In Section 2.6 we will see how geometrical and electrophysiologic properties of a certain type of neuron can be integrated in a comprehensive biophysical model.

2.5.1 Derivation of the cable equation

Consider a piece of a dendrite decomposed in short cylindrical segments of length dx each. The schematic drawing in Fig. 2.16 shows the corresponding circuit diagram. Using Kirchhoff's laws we find equations that relate the voltage $u(x)$ across the membrane at location x with longitudinal and transversal currents. Firstly, a longitudinal current $i(x)$ passing through the dendrite causes a voltage drop across the longitudinal resistor R_L according to Ohm's law,

$$u(t, x + dx) - u(t, x) = R_L\, i(t, x), \tag{2.24}$$

where $u(t, x + dx)$ is the membrane potential at the neighboring point $x + dx$. Secondly, the transversal current that passes through the RC-circuit is given by $C\, \partial u(t, x)/\partial t + u(t, x)/R_T$. Kirchhoff's law regarding the conservation of current at each node leads to

$$i(t, x + dx) - i(t, x) = C \frac{\partial}{\partial t} u(t, x) + \frac{u(t, x)}{R_T} - I_{ext}(t, x).$$ (2.25)

The values of the longitudinal resistance R_L, the transversal conductivity R_T^{-1}, the capacity C, and the externally applied current can be expressed in terms of specific quantities per unit length r_L, r_T^{-1}, c, and i_{ext}, respectively, viz.

$$R_L = r_L \, dx, \quad R_T^{-1} = r_T^{-1} dx, \quad C = c \, dx, \quad I_{ext}(t, x) = i_{ext}(t, x) \, dx.$$ (2.26)

These scaling relations express the fact that the longitudinal resistance and the capacity increase with the length of the cylinder, whereas the transversal resistance is decreasing, simply because the surface through which the current can pass is increasing. Substituting these expressions in Eqs. (2.24) and (2.25), dividing by dx, and taking the limit $dx \to 0$ leads to

$$\frac{\partial}{\partial x} u(t, x) = r_L \, i(t, x)$$ (2.27a)

$$\frac{\partial}{\partial x} i(t, x) = c \frac{\partial}{\partial t} u(t, x) + \frac{u(t, x)}{r_T} - i_{ext}(t, x).$$ (2.27b)

Taking the derivative of these equations with respect to x and crosswise substitution yields

$$\frac{\partial^2}{\partial x^2} u(t, x) = c \, r_L \frac{\partial}{\partial t} u(t, x) + \frac{r_L}{r_T} u(t, x) - r_L \, i_{ext}(t, x)$$ (2.28a)

$$\frac{\partial^2}{\partial x^2} i(t, x) = c \, r_L \frac{\partial}{\partial t} i(t, x) + \frac{r_L}{r_T} i(t, x) - \frac{\partial}{\partial x} i_{ext}(t, x).$$ (2.28b)

We introduce the characteristic length scale $\lambda^2 = r_T/r_L$ ("electrotonic length scale") and the membrane time constant $\tau = r_T c$. If we multiply Eq. (2.28) by λ^2 we get

$$\lambda^2 \frac{\partial^2}{\partial x^2} u(t, x) = \tau \frac{\partial}{\partial t} u(t, x) + u(t, x) - r_T \, i_{ext}(t, x)$$ (2.29a)

$$\lambda^2 \frac{\partial^2}{\partial x^2} i(t, x) = \tau \frac{\partial}{\partial t} i(t, x) + i(t, x) - \frac{r_T}{r_L} \frac{\partial}{\partial x} i_{ext}(t, x).$$ (2.29b)

After a transformation to unit-free coordinates,

$$x \to \hat{x} = x/\lambda, \quad t \to \hat{t} = t/\tau,$$ (2.30)

and rescaling the current variables,

$$i \to \hat{i} = \sqrt{r_T \, r_L} \, i, \quad i_{ext} \to \hat{i}_{ext} = r_T \, i_{ext},$$ (2.31)

we obtain the cable equations (where we have dropped the hats)

$$\frac{\partial}{\partial t} u(t, x) = \frac{\partial^2}{\partial x^2} u(t, x) - u(t, x) + i_{\text{ext}}(t, x), \tag{2.32a}$$

$$\frac{\partial}{\partial t} i(t, x) = \frac{\partial^2}{\partial x^2} i(t, x) - i(t, x) + \frac{\partial}{\partial x} i_{\text{ext}}(t, x), \tag{2.32b}$$

in a symmetric, unit-free form. Note that it suffices to solve one of these equations due to the simple relation between u and i given in Eq. (2.27a).

The cable equations can be easily interpreted. These equations describe the change in time of voltage and longitudinal current. Both equations contain three different contributions. The first term on the right-hand side of Eq. (2.32) is a diffusion term that is positive if the voltage (or current) is a convex function of x. The voltage at x thus tends to decrease if the values of u are lower in a neighborhood of x than at x itself. The second term on the right-hand side of Eq. (2.32) is a simple decay term that causes the voltage to decay exponentially towards zero. The third term, finally, is a source term that acts as an inhomogeneity in the otherwise autonomous differential equation. This source can be due to an externally applied current, to synaptic input, or to other (nonlinear) ion channels; cf. Section 2.5.3.

Example: stationary solutions of the cable equation

In order to get an intuitive understanding of the behavior of the cable equation we look for stationary solutions of Eq. (2.32a), i.e., for solutions with $\partial u(t, x)/\partial t = 0$. In that case, the partial differential equation reduces to an ordinary differential equation in x, viz.

$$\frac{\partial^2}{\partial x^2} u(t, x) - u(t, x) = -i_{\text{ext}}(t, x). \tag{2.33}$$

The general solution to the homogeneous equation with $i_{\text{ext}}(t, x) \equiv 0$ is

$$u(t, x) = c_1 \sinh(x) + c_2 \cosh(x), \tag{2.34}$$

as can easily be checked by taking the second derivative with respect to x. Here, c_1 and c_2 are constants that are determined by the boundary conditions.

Solutions for nonvanishing input current can be found by standard techniques. For a stationary input current $i_{\text{ext}}(t, x) = \delta(x)$ localized at $x = 0$ and boundary conditions $u(\pm\infty) = 0$ we find

$$u(t, x) = \frac{1}{2} e^{-|x|}, \tag{2.35}$$

cf. Fig. 2.17. This solution is given in units of the intrinsic length scale $\lambda = (r_{\text{T}}/r_{\text{L}})^{1/2}$. If we re-substitute the physical units we see that λ is the length over

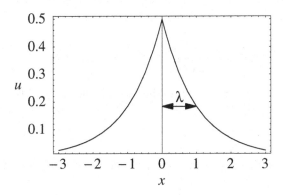

Fig. 2.17. Stationary solution of the cable equation with a constant current of unit strength being injected at $x = 0$, i.e., $i_{ext}(t, x) = \delta(x)$. The electrotonic length scale λ is the distance over which the membrane potential drops to $1/e$ of its initial value.

which the stationary membrane potential drops by a factor $1/e$. In the literature λ is refered to as the electrotonic length scale (Rall, 1989). Typical values for the specific resistance of intracellular medium and the cell membrane are $100\,\Omega\,cm$ and $30\,k\Omega\,cm^2$, respectively. In a dendrite with radius $\rho = 1\,\mu m$ this amounts to a transversal and a longitudinal resistance of $r_L = 100\,\Omega\,cm/(\pi\rho^2) = 3\cdot10^5\,\Omega\,\mu m^{-1}$ and $r_T = 30\,k\Omega\,cm^2/(2\pi\rho) = 5\cdot10^{11}\,\Omega\,\mu m$. The corresponding electrotonic length scale is $\lambda = 1.2\,mm$. Note that the electrotonic length can be significantly smaller if the transversal conductivity is increased, e.g., due to open ion channels.

For arbitrary stationary input current $i_{ext}(x)$ the solution of Eq. (2.32a) can be found by a superposition of translated fundamental solutions (2.35), viz.,

$$u(t, x) = \int dx'\, \frac{1}{2}\, e^{-|x-x'|}\, i_{ext}(x')\,. \tag{2.36}$$

This is an example of the Green's function approach applied here to the stationary case. The general time-dependent case will be treated in the next section.

2.5.2 Green's function (*)

In the following we will concentrate on the equation for the voltage and start our analysis by deriving the Green's function for a cable extending to infinity in both directions. The Green's function is defined as the solution of a linear equation such as Eq. (2.32) with a Dirac δ-pulse as its input. It can be seen as an elementary solution of the differential equation because – due to linearity – the solution for any given input can be constructed as a superposition of these Green's functions.

In order to find the Green's function for the cable equation we thus have to solve

Eq. (2.32a) with $i_{ext}(t, x)$ replaced by a δ impulse at $x = 0$ and $t = 0$,

$$\frac{\partial}{\partial t} u(t, x) - \frac{\partial^2}{\partial x^2} u(t, x) + u(t, x) = \delta(t)\,\delta(x)\,. \tag{2.37}$$

Fourier transformation with respect to the spatial variable yields

$$\frac{\partial}{\partial t} u(t, k) + k^2\, u(t, k) + u(t, k) = \delta(t)/\sqrt{2\pi}\,. \tag{2.38}$$

This is an ordinary differential equation in t and has a solution of the form

$$u(t, k) = \exp\left[-\left(1 + k^2\right) t\right]/\sqrt{2\pi}\,\Theta(t) \tag{2.39}$$

with $\Theta(t)$ denoting the Heaviside function. After an inverse Fourier transform we obtain the desired Green's function $G_\infty(t, x)$,

$$u(t, x) = \frac{\Theta(t)}{\sqrt{4\pi\, t}} \exp\left[-t - \frac{x^2}{4\,t}\right] \equiv G_\infty(t, x)\,. \tag{2.40}$$

The general solution for an infinitely long cable is therewith given through

$$u(t, x) = \int_{-\infty}^{t} dt' \int_{-\infty}^{\infty} dx'\, G_\infty(t - t', x - x')\, i_{ext}(t', x')\,. \tag{2.41}$$

Example: checking the Green's property

We can check the validity of Eq. (2.40) by substituting $G_\infty(t, x)$ into the left-hand side of Eq. (2.37). After a short calculation we find

$$\left[\frac{\partial}{\partial t} - \frac{\partial^2}{\partial x^2} + 1\right] G_\infty(t, x) = \frac{1}{\sqrt{4\pi\, t}} \exp\left(-t - \frac{x^2}{4t}\right) \delta(t)\,, \tag{2.42}$$

where we have used $\partial\Theta(t)/\partial t = \delta(t)$. As long as $t \neq 0$ the right-hand side of Eq. (2.42) vanishes, as required by Eq. (2.37). For $t \to 0$ we find

$$\lim_{t \to 0} \frac{1}{\sqrt{4\pi\, t}} \exp\left(-t - \frac{x^2}{4t}\right) = \delta(x)\,, \tag{2.43}$$

which proves that the right-hand side of Eq. (2.42) is indeed equivalent to the right-hand side of Eq. (2.37).

Having established that

$$\left[\frac{\partial}{\partial t} - \frac{\partial^2}{\partial x^2} + 1\right] G_\infty(t, x) = \delta(x)\,\delta(t)\,, \tag{2.44}$$

we can readily show that Eq. (2.41) is the general solution of the cable equation for arbitrary input currents $i_{ext}(t_0, x_0)$. We substitute Eq. (2.41) into the cable equation, exchange the order of integration and differentiation, and find

$$
\left[\frac{\partial}{\partial t} - \frac{\partial^2}{\partial x^2} + 1 \right] u(t, x)
$$

$$
= \int_{-\infty}^{t} dt' \int_{-\infty}^{\infty} dx' \left[\frac{\partial}{\partial t} - \frac{\partial^2}{\partial x^2} + 1 \right] G_\infty(t - t', x - x') \, i_{ext}(t', x')
$$

$$
= \int_{-\infty}^{t} dt' \int_{-\infty}^{\infty} dx' \, \delta(x - x') \delta(t - t') \, i_{ext}(t', x') = i_{ext}(t, x). \quad (2.45)
$$

Example: finite cable

Real cables do not extend from $-\infty$ to $+\infty$ and we have to take extra care to correctly include boundary conditions at the ends. We consider a finite cable extending from $x = 0$ to $x = L$ with sealed ends, i.e., $i(t, x = 0) = i(t, x = L) = 0$ or, equivalently, $\frac{\partial}{\partial x} u(t, x = 0) = \frac{\partial}{\partial x} u(t, x = L) = 0$.

The Green's function $G_{0,L}$ for a cable with sealed ends can be constructed from G_∞ by applying a trick from electrostatics called "mirror charges" (Jackson, 1962). Similar techniques can also be applied to treat branching points in a dendritic tree (Abbott, 1991). The cable equation is linear and, therefore, a superposition of two solutions is also a solution. Consider a δ current pulse at time t_0 and position x_0 somewhere along the cable. The boundary condition $\frac{\partial}{\partial x} u(t, x = 0) = 0$ can be satisfied if we add a second, virtual current pulse at a position $x = -x_0$ *outside* the interval $[0, L]$. Adding a current pulse outside the interval $[0, L]$ comes for free since the result is still a solution of the cable equation on that interval. Similarly, we can fulfill the boundary condition at $x = L$ by adding a mirror pulse at $x = 2L - x_0$. In order to account for both boundary conditions simultaneously, we have to compensate for the mirror pulse at $-x_0$ by adding another mirror pulse at $2L + x_0$ and for the mirror pulse at $x = 2L - x_0$ by adding a fourth pulse at $-2L + x_0$ and so forth. Altogether we have

$$
G_{0,L}(t_0, x_0; t, x) =
$$

$$
\sum_{n=-\infty}^{\infty} G_\infty(t - t_0, x - 2nL - x_0) + G_\infty(t - t_0, x - 2nL + x_0). \quad (2.46)
$$

We emphasize that in the above Green's function we have to specify both (t_0, x_0) and (t, x) because the setup is no longer translation invariant. The general solution on the interval $[0, L]$ is given by

$$
u(t, x) = \int_{-\infty}^{t} dt_0 \int_{0}^{L} dx_0 \, G_{0,L}(t_0, x_0; t, x) \, i_{ext}(t_0, x_0). \quad (2.47)
$$

An example of the spatial distribution of the membrane potential along the cable

A

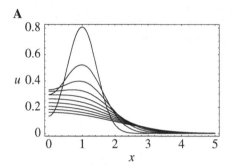

B

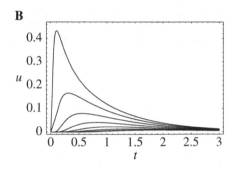

Fig. 2.18. Spatial distribution (**A**) and temporal evolution (**B**) of the membrane potential along a dendrite ($L = 5$) with sealed ends ($\frac{\partial}{\partial x} u\big|_{x \in \{0,L\}} = 0$) after injection of a unit current pulse at $x = 1$ and $t = 0$. The various traces in **A** show snapshots for time $t = 0.1, 0.2, \ldots, 1.0$, respectively (top to bottom). The traces in **B** give the membrane potential as a function of time for different locations $x = 1.5, 2.0, 2.5, \ldots, 5.0$ (top to bottom) along the cable.

is shown in Fig. 2.18A, where a current pulse has been injected at location $x = 1$. In addition to Fig. 2.18A, subfigure B exhibits the *time course* of the membrane potential measured at various distances from the point of injection. It is clearly visible that the peak of the membrane potential measured at, e.g., $x = 3$ is more delayed than at, e.g., $x = 2$. Also the amplitude of the membrane potential decreases significantly with the distance from the injection point. This is a well-known phenomenon that is also present in neurons. In the absence of active amplification mechanisms, synaptic input at distal dendrites produces a broader and weaker response at the soma as compared to synaptic input at proximal dendrites.

2.5.3 Nonlinear extensions to the cable equation

In the context of a realistic modeling of "biological" neurons two nonlinear extensions of the cable equation have to be discussed. The obvious one is the inclusion of nonlinear elements in the circuit diagram of Fig. 2.16 that account for specialized ion channels. As we have seen in the Hodgkin–Huxley model, ion channels can exhibit complex dynamics that is in itself governed by a system of (ordinary) differential equations. The current through one of these channels is thus not simply a (nonlinear) function of the actual value of the membrane potential but may also depend on the time course of the membrane potential in the past. Using the symbolic notation $i_{\text{ion}}[u](t, x)$ for this functional dependence the extended cable equation takes the form

$$\frac{\partial}{\partial t} u(t, x) = \frac{\partial^2}{\partial x^2} u(t, x) - u(t, x) - i_{\text{ion}}[u](t, x) + i_{\text{ext}}(t, x). \tag{2.48}$$

A more subtle complication arises because a synapse cannot be treated as an ideal current source. The effect of an incoming action potential is the opening of ion channels. The resulting current is proportional to the difference between the membrane potential and the corresponding ionic reversal potential. Hence, a time-dependent conductivity as in Eq. (2.19) provides a more realistic description of synaptic input than an ideal current source with a fixed time course.

If we replace in Eq. (2.32a) the external input current $i_{ext}(t, x)$ by an appropriate synaptic input current $-i_{syn}(t, x) = -g_{syn}(t, x)[u(t, x) - E_{syn}]$, with g_{syn} being the synaptic conductivity and E_{syn} the corresponding reversal potential, we obtain[2]

$$\frac{\partial}{\partial t} u(t, x) = \frac{\partial^2}{\partial x^2} u(t, x) - u(t, x) - g_{syn}(t, x)[u(t, x) - E_{syn}]. \qquad (2.49)$$

This is still a linear differential equation but its coefficients are now time dependent. If the time course of the synaptic conductivity can be written as a solution of a differential equation then the cable equation can be re-formulated so that synaptic input reappears as an inhomogeneity to an autonomous equation. For example, if the synaptic conductivity is simply given by an exponential decay with time constant τ_{syn} we have

$$\frac{\partial}{\partial t} u(t, x) - \frac{\partial^2}{\partial x^2} u(t, x) + u(t, x) + g_{syn}(t, x)[u(t, x) - E_{syn}] = 0, \qquad (2.50a)$$

$$\frac{\partial}{\partial t} g_{syn}(t, x) - \tau_{syn}^{-1} g_{syn}(t, x) = S(t, x). \qquad (2.50b)$$

Here, $S(t, x)$ is a sum of Dirac δ functions which describe the presynaptic spike train that arrives at a synapse located at position x. Note that this equation is *non*linear because it contains a product of g_{syn} and u, which are both unknown functions of the differential equation. Consequently, the formalism based on Green's functions cannot be applied.

2.6 Compartmental models

We have seen that analytical solutions can be given for the voltage along a passive cable with uniform geometrical and electrical properties. If we want to apply the above results in order to describe the membrane potential along the dendritic tree of a neuron we face several problems. Even if we neglect "active" conductances formed by nonlinear ion channels a dendritic tree is at most *locally* equivalent to a uniform cable. Numerous bifurcations and variations in diameter and electrical

---

[2] We want outward currents to be positive, hence the change in the sign of i_{ext} and i_{syn}.

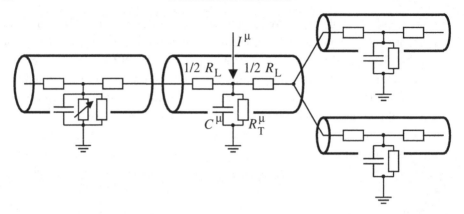

Fig. 2.19. Multicompartment neuron model. Dendritic compartments with membrane capacitance C^μ and transversal resistance R_T^μ are coupled by a longitudinal resistance $r^{\nu\mu} = (R_L^\nu + R_L^\mu)/2$. External input to compartment μ is denoted by I^μ. Some or all compartments may also contain nonlinear ion channels (variable resistor in leftmost compartment).

properties along the dendrite render it difficult to find a solution for the membrane potential analytically (Abbott et al., 1991).

Numerical treatment of partial differential equations such as the cable equation requires a discretization of the spatial variable. Hence, all derivatives with respect to spatial variables are approximated by the corresponding quotient of differences. Essentially we are led back to the discretized model of Fig. 2.16, that has been used as the starting point for the derivation of the cable equation. After the discretization we have a large system of ordinary differential equations for the membrane potential at the chosen discretization points as a function of time. This system of ordinary differential equations can be treated by standard numerical methods.

In order to solve for the membrane potential of a complex dendritic tree numerically, compartmental models are used that are the result of the abovementioned discretization (Yamada et al., 1989; Ekeberg et al., 1991; Bower and Beeman, 1995). The dendritic tree is divided into small cylindrical compartments with an approximately uniform membrane potential. Each compartment is characterized by its capacity and transversal conductivity. Adjacent compartments are coupled by the longitudinal resistance that are determined by the geometrical properties of the dendrite (cf. Fig. 2.19).

Once numerical methods are used to solve for the membrane potential along the dendritic tree, some or all compartments can be equipped with nonlinear ion channels as well. In this way, effects of nonlinear integration of synaptic input can be studied (Mel, 1994). Apart from practical problems that arise from a

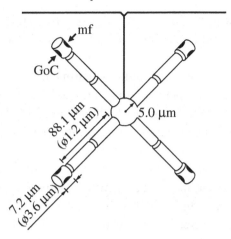

Fig. 2.20. Schematic representation of the granule cell model (not to scale). The model consists of a spherical soma (radius 5.0 μm) and four cylindrical dendrites (diameter 1.2 μm, length 88.1 μm) made up of two compartments each. There is a third compartment at the end of each dendrite, the dendritic bulb, that contains synapses with mossy fibers (mf) and Golgi cells (GoC). The active ion channels are located at the soma. The dendrites are passive. The axon of the granule cell, which rises vertically towards the surface of the cerebellar cortex before it undergoes a T-shaped bifurcation, is not included in the model.

growing complexity of the underlying differential equations, conceptual problems are related to a drastically increasing number of free parameters. The more so, since almost no experimental data regarding the distribution of any specific type of ion channel along the dendritic tree are available. To avoid these problems, all nonlinear ion channels responsible for generating spikes are usually lumped together at the soma and the dendritic tree is treated as a passive cable. For a review of the compartmental approach we refer the reader to the book of Bower and Beeman (1995). In the following we illustrate the compartmental approach by a model of a cerebellar granule cell.

Example: a multicompartment model of cerebellar granule cells

As an example of a realistic neuron model we discuss a model for cerebellar granule cells in the turtle developed by Gabbiani and co-workers (Gabbiani et al., 1994). Granule cells are extremely numerous tiny neurons located in the lowest layer of the cerebellar cortex. These neurons are particularly interesting because they form the sole type of excitatory neuron of the whole cerebellar cortex (Ito, 1984).

Figure 2.20 shows a schematic representation of the granule cell model. It consists of a spherical soma and four cylindrical dendrites that are made up of two compartments each. There is a third compartment at the end of each dendrite, the dendritic bulb, that contains synapses with mossy fibers and Golgi cells.

One of the major problems with multicompartment models is the fact that the *spatial distribution* of ion channels along the surface of the neuron is almost completely unknown. In the present model it is therefore assumed for the sake of simplicity that all active ion channels are concentrated at the soma. The dendrites, on the other hand, are described as a passive cable.

The granule cell model contains a fast sodium current I_{Na} and a calcium-activated potassium current that makes a major contribution to the generation of action potentials. There is also a high-voltage-activated calcium current $I_{Ca(HVA)}$ similar to the I_L current discussed in Section 2.3.4. Finally, there is a so-called delayed rectifying potassium current I_{KDR} that also contributes to the rapid repolarization of the membrane after an action potential (Hille, 1992).

Cerebellar granule cells receive excitatory input from mossy fibers and inhibitory input from Golgi cells. Inhibitory input is conveyed by fast GABA-controlled ion channels with a conductance that is characterized by a bi-exponential decay; cf. Section 2.4. Excitatory synapses contain both fast AMPA and voltage-dependent NMDA receptors. How these different types of synapse can be handled in the context of conductance-based neuron models is explained in Section 2.4.

Figure 2.21 shows a simulation of the response of a granule cell to a series of excitatory and inhibitory spikes. The plots show the membrane potential measured at the soma as a function of time. The arrows indicate the arrival time of excitatory and inhibitory spikes. Figure 2.21A shows nicely how subsequent EPSPs add up almost linearly until the firing threshold is finally reached and an action potential is triggered. The response of the granule cell to inhibitory spikes is somewhat different. In Fig. 2.21B a similar scenario as in subfigure A is shown, but the excitatory input has been replaced by inhibitory spikes. It can be seen that the activation of inhibitory synapses does not have a huge impact on the membrane potential. The reason is that the reversal potential of the inhibitory postsynaptic current of about -75 mV is close to the resting potential of -68 mV. The major effect of inhibitory input therefore is a modification of the membrane conductivity and not so much of the membrane potential. This form of inhibition is also called "silent inhibition".

A final example shows explicitly how the spatial structure of the neuron can influence the integration of synaptic input. Figure 2.22 shows the simulated response of the granule cell to an inhibitory action potential that is followed by a short burst of excitatory spikes. In Fig. 2.22A both excitation and inhibition arrive on the same dendrite. The delay between the arrival time of inhibitory and excitatory input is chosen so that inhibition is just strong enough to prevent

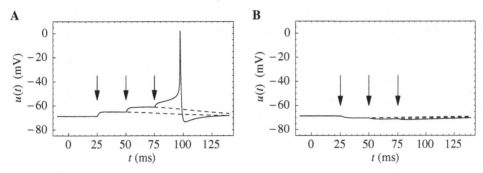

Fig. 2.21. Simulation of the response of a cerebellar granule cell to three subsequent excitatory (**A**) and inhibitory (**B**) spikes. The arrival time of each spike is indicated by an arrow. **A**. Excitatory postsynaptic potentials nicely sum up almost linearly until the firing threshold is reached and an action potential is fired. **B**. In granule cells the reversal potential of the inhibitory postsynaptic current is close to the resting potential. The effect of inhibitory spikes on the membrane potential is therefore almost negligible, though there is a significant modification of the membrane conductivity ("silent inhibition").

the firing of an action potential. If, however, excitation and inhibition arrive on two different dendrites, then there will be an action potential although the timing of the input is precisely the same; cf. Fig. 2.22B. Hence, excitatory input can be suppressed more efficiently by inhibitory input if excitatory and inhibitory synapses are closely packed together.

This effect can be easily understood if we recall that the major effect of inhibitory input is an increase in the conductivity of the postsynaptic membrane. If the activated excitatory and inhibitory synapses are located close to each other on the same dendrite (cf. Fig. 2.22A), then the excitatory postsynaptic current is "shunted" by nearby ion channels that have been opened by the inhibitory input. If excitatory and inhibitory synapses, however, are located on opposite dendrites (cf. Fig. 2.22B), then the whole neuron acts as a "voltage divider". The activation of an inhibitory synapse "clamps" the corresponding dendrite to the potassium reversal potential, which is approximately equal to the resting potential. The excitatory input to the other dendrite results in a local depolarization of the membrane. The soma is located at the center of this voltage divider and its membrane potential is accordingly increased through the excitatory input.

The difference in the somatic membrane potential between the activation of excitatory and inhibitory synapses located on the same or on two different dendrites may decide whether a spike is triggered or not. In cerebellar granule cells this effect is not very prominent because these cells are small and electrotonically compact. Nevertheless, the influence of geometry on synaptic integration can be quite substantial in neurons with a large dendritic tree. Effects based on the geometry

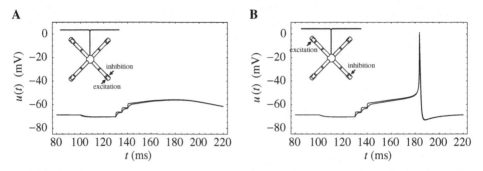

Fig. 2.22. Effect of geometry on the neuronal integration of synaptic input demonstrated in the granule cell model. The cell receives an inhibitory action potential at time $t = 100$ ms followed by three excitatory spikes at $t = 130$ ms, 135 ms, and 140 ms. The plots show the membrane potential measured at the soma (lower trace) and at the dendritic bulb that receives the excitatory input (upper trace). **A.** If excitation and inhibition arrive at the same dendritic bulb (see inset) the inhibitory input is strong enough to "shunt" the excitatory input so that no action potential can be triggered. **B.** If, however, excitation and inhibition arrive at two different dendrites, then an action potential occurs.

of the dendritic tree may even have important implications for the computational "power" of a single neuron (Koch and Segev, 2000).

2.7 Summary

"Real" neurons are extremely complex biophysical and biochemical entities. Before designing a model it is therefore necessary to develop an intuition for what is important and what can be safely neglected. The Hodgkin–Huxley model describes the generation of action potentials at the level of ion channels and ion current flow. It is the starting point for detailed neuron models which in general include more than the three types of currents considered by Hodgkin and Huxley.

Electrophysiologists have described an overwhelming richness of different ion channels. The set of ion channels is different from one neuron to the next. The precise channel configuration in each individual neuron determines a good deal of its overall electrical properties. Synapses are usually modeled as specific ion channels that open for a certain time after presynaptic spike arrival.

The geometry of the neuron can play an important role in synaptic integration because the effect of synaptic input on the somatic membrane potential depends on the location of the synapses on the dendritic tree. Though some analytical results can be obtained for *passive* dendrites, it is usually necessary to resort to numerical methods and multicompartment models in order to account for complex geometry and active ion channels.

Literature

A nice review of the Hodgkin–Huxley model including some historical remarks can be found in Nelson and Rinzel (1995). Mathematical aspects of the Hodgkin–Huxley equations are discussed in the Monograph of Cronin (1987).

A comprehensive and readable introduction to the biophysics of single neurons is provided by the book of Christof Koch (Koch, 1999). Even more detailed information on ion channels and nonlinear effects of the nervous membrane can be found in B. Hille's book on *Ionic channels of excitable membranes* (Hille, 1992). A practical guideline for do-it-yourself experiments with computer simulations of detailed neuron models is the book by Bower and Beeman (1995).

3

Two-dimensional neuron models

The behavior of high-dimensional nonlinear differential equations is difficult to visualize – and even more difficult to analyze. Two-dimensional differential equations, however, can be studied in a transparent manner by means of a phase plane analysis. A reduction of the four-dimensional equation of Hodgkin and Huxley to a two-variable neuron model is thus highly desirable. In the first section of this chapter we exploit the temporal properties of the gating variables of the Hodgkin–Huxley model so as to approximate the four-dimensional differential equation by a two-dimensional one. Section 3.2 is devoted to the phase plane analysis of generic neuron models consisting of two coupled differential equations, one for the membrane potential and the other one for the so-called relaxation variable. One of the questions to which we will return repeatedly throughout this chapter is the problem of the firing threshold. Section 3.3 summarizes some results on threshold and excitability in two-dimensional models. As a first step, however, we have to go through the approximations that are necessary for a reduction of the Hodgkin–Huxley model to two dimensions.

3.1 Reduction to two dimensions

In this section we perform a systematic reduction of the four-dimensional Hodgkin–Huxley model to two dimensions. To do so, we have to eliminate two of the four variables. The essential ideas of the reduction can also be applied to detailed neuron models that may contain many different ion channels. In this case, more than two variables would have to be eliminated, but the procedure would be completely analogous (Kepler et al., 1992).

3.1.1 General approach

We focus on the Hodgkin–Huxley model discussed in Section 2.2 and start with two qualitative observations. Firstly, we see from Fig. 2.3B that the time scale of the dynamics of the gating variable m is much faster than that of the variables n, h, and u. This suggests that we may treat m as an instantaneous variable. The variable m in the ion current Eq. (2.5) of the Hodgkin–Huxley model can therefore be replaced by its steady-state value, $m(t) \to m_0[u(t)]$. This is what we call a *quasi steady-state approximation*.

Secondly, we see from Fig. 2.3B that the time constants $\tau_n(u)$ and $\tau_h(u)$ are roughly the same, whatever the voltage u. Moreover, the graphs of $n_0(u)$ and $1 - h_0(u)$ in Fig. 2.3A are rather similar. This suggests that we may approximate the two variables n and $(1 - h)$ by a single effective variable w. To keep the formalism slightly more general we use a linear approximation $(b - h) \approx a\,n$ with some constants a, b and set $w = b - h = a\,n$. With $h = b - w$, $n = w/a$, and $m = m_0(u)$, Eqs. (2.4) and (2.5) become

$$C\frac{du}{dt} = -g_{\mathrm{Na}}[m_0(u)]^3\,(b - w)\,(u - E_{\mathrm{Na}}) - g_{\mathrm{K}}\left(\frac{w}{a}\right)^4 (u - E_{\mathrm{K}}) - g_L\,(u - E_L) + I\,,$$

$$\tag{3.1}$$

or

$$\frac{du}{dt} = \frac{1}{\tau}\,[F(u, w) + R\,I]\,,\tag{3.2}$$

with $R = g_L^{-1}$, $\tau = R\,C$ and some function F. We now turn to the three equations (2.6). The m equation has disappeared since m is treated as instantaneous. Instead of the two Eqs. (2.6) for n and h, we are left with a single effective equation

$$\frac{dw}{dt} = \frac{1}{\tau_w}G(u, w)\,,\tag{3.3}$$

where τ_w is a parameter and G a function that has to be specified. Eqs. (3.2) and (3.3) define a general two-dimensional neuron model. The mathematical details of the reduction of the four-dimensional Hodgkin–Huxley model to the two equations (3.2) and (3.3) are given below. Before we go through the mathematical step, we will present two examples of two-dimensional neuron dynamics. We will return to these examples repeatedly throughout this chapter.

Example: Morris–Lecar model

Morris and Lecar (1981) proposed a two-dimensional description of neuronal spike dynamics. A first equation describes the evolution of the membrane potential u, the second equation the evolution of a slow "recovery" variable $\hat{w}$. In dimensionless variables, the Morris–Lecar equations read

$$\frac{du}{dt} = -g_1 \, \hat{m}_0(u) \, (u - 1) - g_2 \, \hat{w} \, (u - V_2) - g_L \, (u - V_L) + I \,, \quad (3.4)$$

$$\frac{d\hat{w}}{dt} = -\frac{1}{\tau(u)} \left[\hat{w} - w_0(u) \right] \,. \quad (3.5)$$

The voltage has been scaled so that one of the reversal potentials is unity. Time is measured in units of $\tau = RC$. If we compare Eq. (3.4) with Eq. (3.1), we note that the first current term on the right-hand side of Eq. (3.1) has a factor $(b - w)$ which closes the channel for high voltage and which is absent in (3.4). Another difference is that neither $\hat{m}_0$ nor $\hat{w}$ in Eq. (3.4) has exponents. To clarify the relation between the two models, we could set $\hat{m}_0(u) = [m_0(u)]^3$ and $\hat{w} = (w/a)^4$. In the following we consider Eqs. (3.4) and (3.5) as a model in its own right and drop the hats over m_0 and w.

The equilibrium functions shown in Fig. 2.3A typically have a sigmoidal shape. It is reasonable to approximate the voltage dependence by

$$m_0(u) = \frac{1}{2} \left[1 + \tanh\left(\frac{u - u_1}{u_2} \right) \right] \quad (3.6)$$

$$w_0(u) = \frac{1}{2} \left[1 + \tanh\left(\frac{u - u_3}{u_4} \right) \right] \quad (3.7)$$

with parameters $u_1, \ldots, u_4$, and to approximate the time constant by

$$\tau(u) = \frac{\tau_w}{\cosh\left(\frac{u - u_3}{u_4} \right)} \quad (3.8)$$

with a further parameter τ_w.

The Morris–Lecar model (3.4)–(3.8) gives a phenomenological description of action potentials. Action potentials occur if the current I is sufficiently strong. We will see later on that the firing threshold in the Morris–Lecar model can be discussed by phase plane analysis.

Example: FitzHugh–Nagumo model

FitzHugh and Nagumo were probably the first to propose that, for a discussion of action potential generation, the four equations of Hodgkin and Huxley can be replaced by two, i.e., Eqs. (3.2) and (3.3). They obtained sharp pulse-like oscillations reminiscent of trains of action potentials by defining the functions $F(u, w)$ and $G(u, w)$ as

$$F(u, w) = u - \frac{1}{3}u^3 - w$$

$$G(u, w) = b_0 + b_1 u - w \,, \quad (3.9)$$

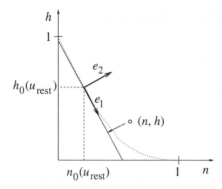

Fig. 3.1. Arbitrary points (n, h) are projected onto the line in direction of e_1 and passing through the point $(n_0(u_{\rm rest}), h_0(u_{\rm rest}))$. The dotted line gives the curve $(n_0(u), h_0(u))$.

where u is the membrane voltage and w is a recovery variable (FitzHugh, 1961; Nagumo et al., 1962). Note that both F and G are linear in w; the sole nonlinearity is the cubic term in u. The FitzHugh–Nagumo model is one of the simplest model with nontrivial behavior lending itself to a phase plane analysis, which will be discussed below in Sections 3.2 and 3.3.

3.1.2 Mathematical steps (*)

The reduction of the Hodgkin–Huxley model to Eqs. (3.2) and (3.3) presented in this paragraph is inspired by the geometrical treatment of Rinzel (1985); see also the slightly more general method of Abbott and Kepler (1990) and Kepler et al. (1992).

The overall aim of the approach is to replace the variables n and h in the Hodgkin–Huxley model by a single effective variable w. At each moment of time, the values $(n(t), h(t))$ can be visualized as points in the two-dimensional plane spanned by n and h; cf. Fig. 3.1. We have argued above that the time course of the variable n is expected to be similar to that of $1 - h$. If, at each time, n was equal to $1-h$, then all possible points (n, h) would lie on the straight line $h = 1-n$ passing through the points $(0, 1)$ and $(1, 0)$ of the plane. To keep the model slightly more general we allow for an arbitrary line $h = b - a\,n$ which passes through $(0, b)$ and $(1, b - a)$. It would be unreasonable to expect that all points $(n(t), h(t))$ that occur during the temporal evolution of the Hodgkin–Huxley model fall exactly on that line. The reduction of the number of variables is achieved by a projection of those points onto the line. The position along the line $h = b - a\,n$ gives the new variable w; cf. Fig. 3.1. The projection is the essential approximation during the reduction.

To perform the projection, we will proceed in three steps. A minimal condition for the projection is that the approximation introduces no error while the neuron is at rest. As a first step, we therefore shift the origin of the coordinate system to the rest state and introduce new variables

$$x = n - n_0(u_{rest}) \tag{3.10}$$
$$y = h - h_0(u_{rest}). \tag{3.11}$$

At rest, we have $x = y = 0$.

Secondly, we turn the coordinate system by an angle α which is determined as follows. For a given constant voltage u, the dynamics of the gating variables n and h approaches the equilibrium values $(n_0(u), h_0(u))$. The points $(n_0(u), h_0(u))$ as a function of u define a curve in the two-dimensional plane. The slope of the curve at $u = u_{rest}$ yields the turning angle α via

$$\tan \alpha = \frac{\frac{dh_0}{du}\big|_{u_{rest}}}{\frac{dn_0}{du}\big|_{u_{rest}}}. \tag{3.12}$$

Turning the coordinate system by α moves the abscissa e_1 of the new coordinate system in a direction tangential to the curve. The coordinates (z_1, z_2) in the new system are

$$\begin{pmatrix} z_1 \\ z_2 \end{pmatrix} = \begin{pmatrix} \cos \alpha & \sin \alpha \\ -\sin \alpha & \cos \alpha \end{pmatrix} \begin{pmatrix} x \\ y \end{pmatrix}. \tag{3.13}$$

Thirdly, we set $z_2 = 0$ and retain only the coordinate z_1 along e_1. The inverse transform,

$$\begin{pmatrix} x \\ y \end{pmatrix} = \begin{pmatrix} \cos \alpha & -\sin \alpha \\ \sin \alpha & \cos \alpha \end{pmatrix} \begin{pmatrix} z_1 \\ z_2 \end{pmatrix}, \tag{3.14}$$

yields $x = z_1 \cos \alpha$ and $y = z_1 \sin \alpha$ since $z_2 = 0$. Hence, after the projection, the new values of the variables n and h are

$$n' = n_0(u_{rest}) + z_1 \cos \alpha, \tag{3.15}$$
$$h' = h_0(u_{rest}) + z_1 \sin \alpha. \tag{3.16}$$

In principle, z_1 can directly be used as the new effective variable. From (3.13) we find the differential equation

$$\frac{dz_1}{dt} = \cos \alpha \frac{dn}{dt} + \sin \alpha \frac{dh}{dt}. \tag{3.17}$$

We use Eq. (2.7) and replace, on the right-hand side, $n(t)$ and $h(t)$ by Eq. (3.15) and Eq. (3.16). The result is

$$\frac{dz_1}{dt} = -\cos \alpha \frac{z_1 \cos \alpha + n_0(u_{rest}) - n_0(u)}{\tau_n(u)} - \sin \alpha \frac{z_1 \sin \alpha + h_0(u_{rest}) - h_0(u)}{\tau_h(u)}, \tag{3.18}$$

which is of the form $dz_1/dt = G(u, z_1)$, as desired.

To see the relation to Eqs. (3.1) and (3.3), it is convenient to rescale z_1 and define

$$w = -\tan\alpha\, n_0(u_{\text{rest}}) - z_1\sin\alpha . \tag{3.19}$$

If we introduce $a = -\tan\alpha$, we find from Eq. (3.15) $n' = w/a$ and from Eq. (3.16) $h' = b - w$ which are the approximations that we have used in Eq. (3.1). The differential equation for the variable w is of the desired form $\mathrm{d}w/\mathrm{d}t = G(u, w)$ and can be found from Eq. (3.18). If we approximate the time constants τ_n and τ_h by a common function $\tau(u)$, the dynamics of w is

$$\frac{\mathrm{d}w}{\mathrm{d}t} = -\frac{1}{\tau(u)}\,[w - w_0(u)] . \tag{3.20}$$

with a new equilibrium function $w_0(u)$ that is a linear combination of the functions h_0 and n_0. From Eqs. (3.18) and (3.19) we find

$$w_0(u) = -\sin\alpha\,[\cos\alpha\, n_0(u) + \sin\alpha\, h_0(u) - c] \tag{3.21}$$

with a parameter c that is determined by direct calculation. In practice, both $w_0(u)$ and $\tau(u)$ are fitted by the expressions (3.7) and (3.8).

3.2 Phase plane analysis

In two-dimensional models, the temporal evolution of the variables $u(t)$ and $w(t)$ can be visualized as a point $(u(t), w(t))^{\mathrm{T}}$ that moves in the so-called phase plane. From a starting point $(u(t), w(t))^{\mathrm{T}}$ the system will move in a time Δt to a new state $(u(t + \Delta t), w(t + \Delta t))^{\mathrm{T}}$ which has to be determined by integration of the differential equations (3.2) and (3.3). For Δt sufficiently small, the displacement $(\Delta u, \Delta w)^{\mathrm{T}}$ is in the direction of the flow $(\dot{u}, \dot{w})^{\mathrm{T}}$, i.e.,

$$\begin{pmatrix} \Delta u \\ \Delta w \end{pmatrix} = \begin{pmatrix} \dot{u} \\ \dot{w} \end{pmatrix} \Delta t , \tag{3.22}$$

which can be plotted as a vector field in the phase plane. Here $\dot{u} = \mathrm{d}u/\mathrm{d}t$ is given by Eq. (3.2) and $\dot{w} = \mathrm{d}w/\mathrm{d}t$ by Eq. (3.3). The flow field is also called the phase portrait of the system. Important tools in the construction of the phase portrait are the nullclines which are introduced now.

3.2.1 Nullclines

Let us consider the set of points with $\dot{u} = 0$, called the u-nullcline. The direction of flow on the u-nullcline is in direction of $(0, \dot{w})^{\mathrm{T}}$, since $\dot{u} = 0$. Hence arrows in the phase portrait are vertical on the u-nullcline. Similarly, the w-nullcline is defined by the condition $\dot{w} = 0$ and arrows are horizontal. The fixed points of the

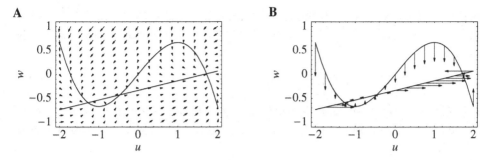

Fig. 3.2. **A.** Phase portrait of the FitzHugh–Nagumo model. The u-nullcline (curved line) and the w-nullcline (straight line) intersect at the three fixed points. The direction of the arrows indicates the flow $(\dot{u}, \dot{w})^T$. **B.** Arrows on the u-nullcline point vertically upward or downward, on the w-nullcline arrows are horizontal. In the neighborhood of the fixed points arrows have short length indicating slow movement. At the fixed point, the direction of arrows changes.

dynamics, defined by $\dot{u} = \dot{w} = 0$ are given by the intersection of the u-nullcline with the w-nullcline. In Fig. 3.2 we have three fixed points.

So far we have argued that arrows on the u-nullcline are vertical, but we do not know yet whether they point up or down. To get the extra information needed, let us return to the w-nullcline. By definition, it separates the region with $\dot{w} > 0$ from the area with $\dot{w} < 0$. Suppose we evaluate $G(u, w)$ on the right-hand side of Eq. (3.3) at a single point, e.g, at $(0, 1)$. If $G(0, 1) > 0$, then the whole area on that side of the w-nullcline has $\dot{w} > 0$. Hence, all arrows along the u-nullcline that lie on the same side of the w-nullcline as the point $(0, 1)$ point upwards. The direction of arrows normally[1] changes where the nullclines intersect; cf. Fig. 3.2B.

3.2.2 Stability of fixed points

In Fig. 3.2 there are three fixed points, but which of these are stable? The local stability of a fixed point (u_{FP}, w_{FP}) is determined by linearization of the dynamics at the intersection. With $x = (u - u_{FP}, w - w_{FP})^T$, we have after the linearization

$$\frac{d}{dt}x = \begin{pmatrix} F_u & F_w \\ G_u & G_w \end{pmatrix} x, \tag{3.23}$$

where $F_u = \partial F/\partial u$, $F_w = \partial F/\partial w, \ldots$, are evaluated at the fixed point. Bold face indicates a two-dimensional vector. To study the stability we set $x(t) = e \exp(\lambda t)$ and solve the resulting eigenvalue problem. There are two solutions with eigenvalues λ_+ and λ_- and eigenvectors e_+ and e_-, respectively. Stability of the fixed point $x = 0$ in Eq. (3.23) requires that the real part of both eigenvalues be

---

[1] Exceptions are the rare cases where the function F or G is degenerate; e.g., $F(u, w) = w^2$.

negative. The solution of the eigenvalue problem yields $\lambda_+ + \lambda_- = F_u + G_w$ and $\lambda_+ \lambda_- = F_u G_w - F_w G_u$. The necessary and sufficient condition for stability is therefore

$$F_u + G_w < 0 \quad \text{and} \quad F_u G_w - F_w G_u > 0. \tag{3.24}$$

If $F_u G_w - F_w G_u < 0$, then the imaginary part of both eigenvalues vanishes. One of the eigenvalues is positive, the other one negative. The fixed point is then called a saddle point.

Equation (3.23) is obtained by Taylor expansion of Eqs. (3.2) and (3.3) to first order in x. If the real part of one or both eigenvalues of the matrix in Eq. (3.23) vanishes, the complete characterization of the stability properties of the fixed point requires an extension of the Taylor expansion to higher order.

Example: linear model

Let us consider the linear dynamics

$$\dot{u} = au - w$$
$$\dot{w} = \epsilon(bu - w), \tag{3.25}$$

with positive constants $b, \epsilon > 0$. The u-nullcline is $w = au$, the w-nullcline is $w = bu$. For the moment we assume $a < 0$. The phase diagram is that of Fig. 3.3A. Note that by decreasing the parameter ϵ, we may slow down the w dynamics in Eq. (3.25) without changing the nullclines.

Because $F_u + G_w = a - \epsilon < 0$ for $a < 0$ and $F_u G_w - F_w G_u = \epsilon(b - a) > 0$, it follows from (3.23) that the fixed point is stable. Note that the phase portrait around the left fixed point in Fig. 3.2 has locally the same structure as the portrait in Fig. 3.3A. We conclude that the left fixed point in Fig. 3.2 is stable.

Let us now keep the w-nullcline fixed and turn the u-nullcline by increasing a to positive values; cf. Fig. 3.3B and C. Stability is lost if $a > \min\{\epsilon, b\}$. Stability of the fixed point in Fig. 3.3B can therefore not be decided without knowing the value of ϵ. On the other hand, in Fig. 3.3C we have $a > b$ and hence $F_u G_w - F_w G_u = \epsilon(b - a) < 0$. In this case one of the eigenvalues is positive ($\lambda_+ > 0$) and the other one negative ($\lambda_- < 0$), hence we have a saddle point. The imaginary part of the eigenvalues vanishes. The eigenvectors e_- and e_+ are therefore real and can be visualized in the phase space. A trajectory through the fixed point in direction of e_- is attracted towards the fixed point. This is, however, the only direction by which a trajectory may reach the fixed point. Any small perturbation around the fixed point that is not strictly in the direction of e_2 grows exponentially. A saddle point as in Fig. 3.3C plays an important role in so-called type I neuron models that are introduced in Section 3.2.4.

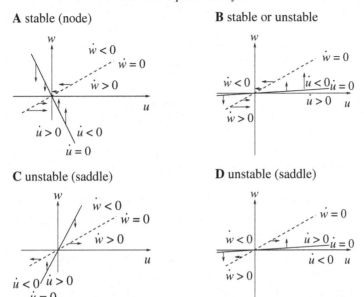

Fig. 3.3. Four examples of phase portraits around a fixed point. Case **A** is stable, cases **C** and **D** are unstable. Stability in case **B** cannot be decided with the information available from the picture alone. **C** and **D** are saddle points.

For the sake of completeness we also study the linear system

$$\dot{u} = -a\,u + w$$
$$\dot{w} = \epsilon\,(b\,u - w)\,, \text{ with } 0 < a < b, \tag{3.26}$$

with positive constants a, b, and ϵ. This system is identical to Eq. (3.26) except that the sign of the first equation is flipped. As before we have nullclines $w = a\,u$ and $w = b\,u$; cf. Fig. 3.3D. Note that the nullclines are identical to those in Fig. 3.3B, only the direction of the horizontal arrows on the w-nullcline has changed.

Since $F_u G_w - F_w G_u = \epsilon\,(a - b) < 0$, the fixed point is unstable if $a < b$. In this case, the imaginary part of the eigenvalues vanishes and one of the eigenvalues is positive ($\lambda_+ > 0$) while the other one is negative ($\lambda_- < 0$). This is the definition of a saddle point.

3.2.3 Limit cycles

One of the attractive features of phase plane analysis is that there is a direct method to show the existence of limit cycles. The theorem of Poincaré–Bendixson (Hale and Koçak, 1991; Verhulst, 1996) tells us that if (i) we can construct a bounding surface around a fixed point so that all flux arrows on the surface are pointing towards the interior, and (ii) the fixed point in the interior is repulsive (real part

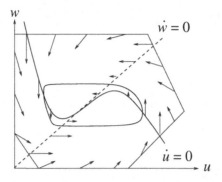

Fig. 3.4. Bounding surface around an unstable fixed point and the limit cycle (schematic figure).

of both eigenvalues positive), then a stable limit cycle must exist around that fixed point.

The proof follows from the uniqueness of solutions of differential equations which implies that trajectories cannot cross each other. If all trajectories are pushed away from the fixed point, but cannot leave the bounded surface, then they must finally settle on a limit cycle; cf. Fig. 3.4. Note that this argument holds only in two dimensions.

Example: FitzHugh–Nagumo model

In dimensionless variables the FitzHugh–Nagumo model is

$$\frac{du}{dt} = u - \frac{1}{3}u^3 - w + I \tag{3.27}$$

$$\frac{dw}{dt} = \epsilon\,(b_0 + b_1\,u - w)\,. \tag{3.28}$$

Time is measured in units of τ and $\epsilon = \tau/\tau_w$ is the ratio of the two time scales. The u-nullcline is $w = u - u^3/3 + I$ with maxima at $u = \pm 1$. The maximal slope of the u-nullcline is $dw/du = 1$ at $u = 0$; for $I = 0$ the u-nullcline has zeros at 0 and $\pm\sqrt{3}$. For $I \neq 0$ the u-nullcline is shifted vertically. The w-nullcline is a straight line $w = b_0 + b_1\,u$. For $b_1 > 1$, there is always exactly one intersection, whatever I. The two nullclines are shown in Fig. 3.5.

A comparison of Fig. 3.5A with the phase portrait of Fig. 3.3A, shows that the fixed point is stable for $I = 0$. If we increase I the intersection of the nullclines moves to the right; cf. Fig. 3.5C. According to the calculation associated with Fig. 3.3B, the fixed point loses stability as soon as the slope of the u-nullcline becomes larger than ϵ. It is possible to construct a bounding surface around the unstable fixed point so that we know from the Poincaré–Bendixson theorem that a limit cycle must exist. Figures 3.5A and C show two trajectories, one for $I = 0$

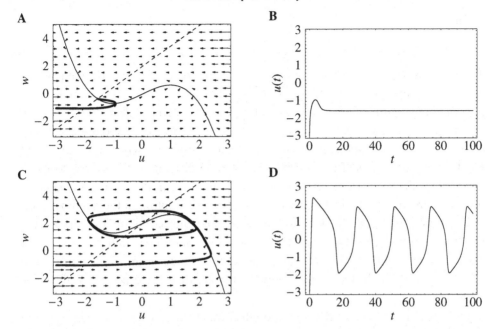

Fig. 3.5. **A**. The nullclines of the FitzHugh–Nagumo model for zero input. The thin solid line is the u-nullcline; the w-nullcline is the straight dashed line, $w = b_0 + b_1 u$, with $b_0 = 2, b_1 = 1.5$. The fat line is a trajectory that starts at $(-3, -1)$ and converges to the fixed point at $(-1.5, -0.3)$. **B**. Time course of the membrane potential of the trajectory shown in **A**. **C**. Same as in **A** but with positive input $I = 2$ so that the fixed point in **A** is replaced by a limit cycle (fat line). **D**. Voltage time course of the trajectory shown in **C**. Trajectories are the result of numerical integration of Eqs. (3.27) and (3.28) with $\epsilon = 0.1$.

converging to the fixed point and another one for $I = 2$ converging towards the limit cycle. The horizontal phases of the limit cycle correspond to a rapid change of the voltage, which results in voltage pulses similar to a train of action potentials; cf. Fig. 3.5D.

Hopf bifurcation (*)

We have seen in the previous example that while I is increased the behavior of the system changes qualitatively from a stable fixed point to a limit cycle. The point where the transition occurs is called a bifurcation point, and I is the bifurcation parameter. Note that the fixed point $(u(t), w(t)) = (u_{FP}, w_{FP})$ remains a solution of the dynamics whatever the value of I. At some point, however, the fixed point loses its stability, which implies that the real part of at least one of the eigenvalues changes from negative to positive. In other words, the real part passes through zero. From the solution of the stability problem Eq. (3.23) we find that at this point, the eigenvalues are

$$\lambda_\pm = \pm i \sqrt{F_u G_w - G_u F_w} \, . \qquad (3.29)$$

These eigenvalues correspond to an oscillatory solution (of the linearized equation) with a frequency given by $\sqrt{F_u G_w - G_u F_w}$. The above scenario of stability loss in combination with an emerging oscillation is called a Hopf bifurcation.

Unfortunately, the discussion so far does not tell us anything about the stability of the oscillatory solution. If the new oscillatory solution, which appears at the Hopf bifurcation, is itself unstable (which is more difficult to show), the scenario is called a subcritical Hopf bifurcation. This is the case in the FitzHugh–Nagumo model where, due to the instability of the oscillatory solution in the neighborhood of the Hopf bifurcation, the dynamics blows up and approaches another limit cycle of large amplitude; cf. Fig. 3.5. The stable large-amplitude limit cycle solution exists in fact slightly before I reaches the critical value of the Hopf bifurcation. Thus there is a small regime of bistability between the fixed point and the limit cycle.

In a supercritical Hopf bifurcation, on the other hand, the new periodic solution is stable. In this case, the limit cycle would have a small amplitude if I is just above the bifurcation point. The amplitude of the oscillation grows with the stimulation I.

Whenever we have a Hopf bifurcation, be it subcritical or supercritical, the limit cycle starts with finite frequency. Thus if we plot the frequency of the oscillation in the limit cycle as a function of the (constant) input I, we find a discontinuity at the bifurcation point. Models where the onset of oscillations occurs with nonzero frequency are called type II excitable membrane models. Type I models have an onset of oscillations with zero frequency is discussed in the next subsection.

3.2.4 Type I and type II models

In the previous example, there was exactly one fixed point whatever I. If I is slowly increased, the neuronal dynamics changes from stationary to oscillatory at a critical value of I where the fixed point changes from stable to unstable via a (subcritical) Hopf bifurcation. In this case, the onset occurs with nonzero frequency and the model is classified as type II.

A different situation is shown in Fig. 3.6. For zero input, there are three fixed points: a stable fixed point to the left, a saddle point in the middle, and an unstable fixed point to the right. If I is increased, the u-nullcline moves upwards and the stable fixed point merges with the saddle and disappears. We are left with the unstable fixed point around which there must be a limit cycle provided the flux is bounded. At the transition point the limit cycle has zero frequency because it

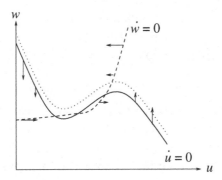

Fig. 3.6. The nullclines of a type I model. For zero input, the u-nullcline (solid line) has three intersections with the w-nullcline (dashed). For input $I > 0$, the u-nullcline is shifted vertically (dotted line) and, if I is sufficiently large, only one fixed point remains which is unstable.

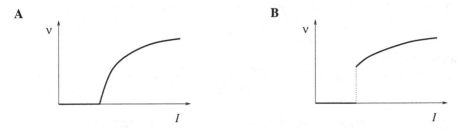

Fig. 3.7. **A.** Gain function for models of type I. The frequency ν during a limit cycle oscillation is a continuous function of the applied current I. **B.** The gain function of type II models has a discontinuity.

passes through the two merging fixed points where the velocity of the trajectory is zero. If I is increased a little, the limit cycle still "feels" the disappeared fixed points in the sense that the velocity of the trajectory in that region is very low. Thus the onset of oscillation is continuous and occurs with zero frequency. Models which fall into this class are called type I; cf. Fig. 3.7.

From the above discussion it should be clear that if we increase I we encounter a transition point where two fixed points disappear, viz., the saddle and the stable fixed point (node). At the same time a limit cycle appears. If we come from the other side, we have first a limit cycle which disappears at the moment when the saddle-node pair shows up. The transition is therefore called a saddle-node bifurcation on a limit cycle.

Example: FitzHugh–Nagumo model

The appearance of oscillations in the FitzHugh–Nagumo model discussed above is of type II. If the slope of the w-nullcline is larger than one, there is only one fixed point, whatever I. This fixed point loses stability via a Hopf bifurcation.

However, if the slope of the w-nullcline is smaller than one, it is possible to have three fixed points, one of them unstable the other two stable; cf. Fig. 3.2. The system is then bistable and no oscillation occurs.

Example: Morris–Lecar model

Depending on the choice of parameters, the Morris–Lecar model is either type I or type II. In contrast to the FitzHugh–Nagumo model the w-nullcline is not a straight line but has positive curvature. It is therefore possible to have three fixed points so that two of them lie in the unstable region where u has large positive slope as indicated schematically in Fig. 3.6. Comparison of the phase portrait of Fig. 3.6 with that of Fig. 3.3 shows that the left fixed point is stable as in Fig. 3.3A, the middle one is a saddle point as in Fig. 3.3C, and the right one is unstable as in Fig. 3.3B provided that the slope of the u-nullcline is sufficiently positive. Thus we have the sequence of three fixed points necessary for a type I model.

Example: canonical type I model

Consider the one-dimensional model

$$\frac{d\phi}{dt} = q\,(1 - \cos\phi) + I\,(1 + \cos\phi) \tag{3.30}$$

where $q > 0$ is a parameter and I with $0 < |I| < q$ the applied current. The variable ϕ is the phase along the limit cycle trajectory. For all currents $I > 0$, we have $d\phi/dt > 0$, so that the system is circling along the limit cycle. The minimal velocity is $d\phi/dt = I$ for $\phi = 0$. Formally, a spike is said to occur whenever $\phi = \pi$. The period of the limit cycle can be found by integration of (3.30) around a full cycle.

Let us now reduce the amplitude of the applied current I. For $I \rightarrow 0$, the velocity along the trajectory around $\phi = 0$ tends to zero. The period of one cycle $T(I)$ therefore tends to infinity. In other words, for $I \rightarrow 0$, the frequency of the oscillation $\nu = 1/T(I)$ decreases (continuously) to zero. For $I < 0$, Eq. (3.30) has a stable fixed point at $\phi = 0$; see Fig. 3.8.

The model (3.30) is a canonical model in the sense that all type I neuron models close to the bifurcation point can be mapped onto (3.30) (Ermentrout, 1996).

3.3 Threshold and excitability

We have seen in the previous chapter that the Hodgkin–Huxley model does not have a clear-cut firing threshold. Nevertheless, there is a critical regime where the sensitivity to input current pulses is so high that it can be fairly well approximated by a threshold. For weak stimuli, the voltage trace returns more or less directly to the resting potentials. For stronger stimuli it makes a large detour, that is, emits

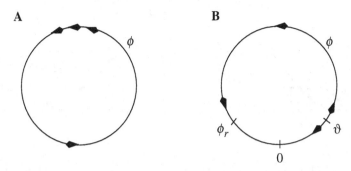

Fig. 3.8. Type I model as a phase model. **A**. For $I > 0$, the system is on a limit cycle. The phase velocity $d\phi/dt$ is positive everywhere. **B**. For $I < 0$, the phase has a stable fixed point at $\phi = \phi_r$ and an unstable fixed point at $\phi = \vartheta$.

a spike; see Fig. 3.10B. This property is characteristic of a large class of systems collectively termed *excitable systems*.

For two-dimensional models, excitability can be discussed in phase space in a transparent manner. We will pose the following questions. What are the conditions for a threshold behavior? If there is no sharp threshold, what are the conditions for a regime of high (threshold-like) sensitivity? We will see that type I models indeed have a threshold whereas type II models do not. On the other hand, even type II models can show threshold-like behavior if the dynamics of w is considerably slower than that of u.

Throughout this section we use the following stimulation paradigm. We assume that the neuron is at rest (or in a known state) and apply a short current pulse $I(t) = q\,\delta(t)$ of amplitude $q > 0$. The input pulse influences the neuronal dynamics via Eq. (3.2). As a consequence, the voltage u jumps at $t = 0$ by an amount $\Delta u = q\,R/\tau$; the time course of the recovery variable w, on the other hand, is continuous. In the phase plane, the current pulse therefore shifts the state (u, w) of the system horizontally to a new value $(u + \Delta u, w)$. How does the system return to equilibrium? How does the behavior depend on the amplitude q of the current pulse?

We will see that the behavior can depend on q in two qualitatively distinct ways. In type I models, the response to the input shows an "all-or-nothing" behavior and consists either of a significant pulse (that is, an action potential) or a simple decay back to rest. In this sense, type I models exhibit threshold behavior. If the action potential occurs, it has always roughly the same amplitude but occurs at different delays depending on the strength q of the stimulating current pulse. In type II models, on the other hand, the amplitude of the response depends continuously on the amplitude q. Therefore, type II models do not have a sharp threshold.

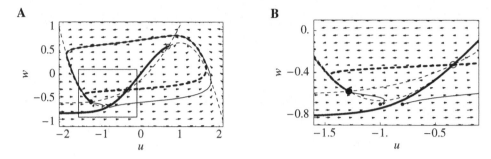

Fig. 3.9. Threshold in a type I model. **A**. The stable manifold (fat solid line) of the saddle point (open circle at about $(u, w) = (-0.4, -0.3)$) acts as a threshold. Trajectories (thin solid lines) that start to the right of the stable manifold cannot return directly to the stable fixed point (filled circle) but have to take a detour around the repulsive fixed point (open circle at $(u, w) = (0.7, 0.6)$). The result is a spike-like excursion of the u-variable. Thin dashed lines are the nullclines; the fat dashed line is the unstable manifold of the saddle point. **B**. Blow-up of the rectangular region in **A**. The starting points of the two sample trajectories are marked by small dots.

Note that even in a model with threshold, a first input pulse that lifts the state of the system above the threshold can be counterbalanced by a second negative input which pulls the state of the system back. Thus, even in models with a threshold, the threshold is only "seen" for the specific input scenario considered here, viz., one isolated short current pulse.

3.3.1 Type I models

As discussed above, type I models are characterized by a set of three fixed points, a stable one to the right, a saddle point in the middle, and an unstable one to the left. The linear stability analysis at the saddle point reveals, by definition of a saddle, one positive and one negative eigenvalue, λ_+ and λ_-, respectively. The imaginary part of the eigenvalues vanishes. Associated with λ_- is the (real) eigenvector e_-. A trajectory which approaches the saddle in direction of e_- from either side will eventually converge towards the fixed point. There are two of these trajectories. The first one starts at infinity and approaches the saddle from below. The second one starts at the unstable fixed point and approaches the saddle from above. The two together define the stable manifold of the fixed point (Hale and Koçak, 1991; Verhulst, 1996). A perturbation around the fixed point that lies on the stable manifold returns to the fixed point. All other perturbations will grow exponentially.

The stable manifold plays an important role in the excitability of the system. Due to the uniqueness of solutions of differential equations, trajectories cannot cross. This implies that all trajectories with initial conditions to the right of the stable manifold must make a detour around the unstable fixed point before they can reach the stable fixed point. Trajectories with initial conditions to the left of the stable manifold return immediately towards the stable fixed point; cf. Fig. 3.9.

Let us now apply these considerations to models of neurons. At rest, the neuron model is at the stable fixed point. A short input current pulse moves the state of the system to the right. If the current pulse is small, the new state of the system is to the left of the stable manifold. Hence the membrane potential u decays back to rest. If the current pulse is sufficiently strong, it will shift the state of the system to the right of the stable manifold. Since the resting point is the only stable fixed point, the neuron model will eventually return to the resting potential. To do so, it has, however, to take a large detour which is seen as a pulse in the voltage variable u. The stable manifold thus acts as a threshold for spike initiation.

Example: canonical type I model

For $I < 0$ on the right-hand side of Eq. (3.30), the phase equation $d\phi/dt$ has two fixed points. The resting state is at the stable fixed point $\phi = \phi_r$. The unstable fixed point at $\phi = \vartheta$ acts as a threshold; cf. Fig. 3.8.

Let us now assume initial conditions slightly above threshold, viz., $\phi_0 = \vartheta + \delta\phi$. Since $d\phi/dt > 0$ for $\phi = \phi_0$ the system starts to fire an action potential but for $\delta\phi \ll 1$ the phase velocity is still close to zero and the maximum of the spike (corresponding to $\phi = \pi$) is reached only after a long delay. This delay depends critically on the initial condition.

3.3.2 Type II models

In contrast to type I models, Type II models do not have a stable manifold and, hence, there is no "forbidden line" that acts as a sharp threshold. Instead of the typical all-or-nothing behavior of type I models there is a continuum of trajectories; see Fig. 3.10A.

Nevertheless, if the time scale of the u dynamics is much faster than that of the w dynamics, then there is a critical regime where the sensitivity to the amplitude of the input current pulse can be extremely high. If the amplitude of the input pulse is increased by a tiny amount, the amplitude of the response increases a lot ("soft" threshold).

In practice, the consequences of a sharp and a "soft" threshold are similar. There is, however, a subtle difference in the timing of the response between type I and type II models. In type II models, the peak of the response is always reached with roughly the same delay, independently of the size of the input pulse. It is the amplitude of the response that increases rapidly but continuously; see Fig. 3.10B. On the other hand, in type I model the amplitude of the response

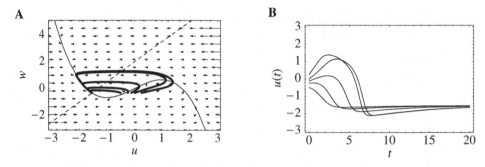

Fig. 3.10. Threshold behavior in a type II model. **A**. Trajectories in the phase starting with initial conditions (u_0, w_{rest}) where $u_0 = -0.5, -0.25, -0.125, 0$, and 0.25. **B**. Projection of the trajectories on the voltage axis. For $u_0 \leq -0.25$, the trajectories return rapidly to rest. The trajectories with $u_0 \geq -0.1$ develop a voltage pulse. Parameters as in Fig. 3.5 with $I = 0$.

is rather stereotyped: either there is an action potential or there is not. For input currents which are just above threshold, the action potential occurs, however, with an extremely long delay. The long delay is because the trajectory starts in the region where the two fixed points (saddle and node) have just disappeared, i.e., in a region where the velocity in phase space is very low.

3.3.3 Separation of time scales

Consider the generic two-dimensional neuron model given by Eqs. (3.2) and (3.3). We measure time in units of τ and take $R = 1$. Equations (3.2) and (3.3) are then

$$\frac{du}{dt} = F(u, w) + I \tag{3.31}$$

$$\frac{dw}{dt} = \epsilon\, G(u, w) \tag{3.32}$$

where $\epsilon = \tau/\tau_w$. If $\tau_w \gg \tau$, then $\epsilon \ll 1$. In this situation the time scale that governs the evolution of u is much faster than that of w. This observation can be exploited for the analysis of the system. The general idea is that of a "separation of time scales"; in the mathematical literature the limit of $\epsilon \to 0$ is called "singular perturbation". Oscillatory behavior for small ϵ is called a "relaxation oscillation".

What are the consequences of the large difference of time scales for the phase portrait of the system? Recall that the flow is in direction of $(\dot{u}, \dot{w})$. In the limit of $\epsilon \to 0$, all arrows in the flow field are therefore horizontal, except those in the neighborhood of the u-nullcline. On the u-nullcline, $\dot{u} = 0$ and arrows are vertical as usual. Their length, however, is only of order ϵ. Intuitively speaking,

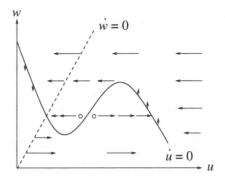

Fig. 3.11. Excitability in a type II model with separated time scales. The u dynamics is much faster than the w dynamics. The flux is therefore close to horizontal, except in the neighborhood of the u-nullcline (schematic figure). Initial conditions (circle) to the left of the middle branch of the u-nullcline return directly to the stable fixed point; a trajectory starting to the right of the middle branch develops a voltage pulse.

the horizontal arrows rapidly push the trajectory towards the u-nullcline. Only close to the u-nullcline are directions of movement other than horizontal possible. Therefore, trajectories slowly follow the u-nullcline, except at the knees of the nullcline where they jump to a different branch.

Excitability can now be discussed with the help of Fig. 3.11. A current pulse shifts the state of the system horizontally away from the stable fixed point. If the current pulse is small, the system returns immediately (i.e., on the fast time scale) to the stable fixed point. If the current pulse is large enough so as to put the system beyond the middle branch of the u-nullcline, then the trajectory is pushed towards the right branch of the u-nullcline. The trajectory follows the u-nullcline slowly upwards until it jumps back (on the fast time scale) to the left branch of the u-nullcline. The "jump" between the branches of the nullcline correspond to a rapid voltage change. In terms of neuronal modeling, the jump from the right to the left branch corresponds to the downstroke of the action potential. The middle branch of the u-nullcline (where $\dot{u} > 0$) acts as a threshold for spike initiation. This is shown in the simulation of the FitzHugh–Nagumo model in Fig. 3.12.

Example: piecewise linear nullclines I

Let us study the piecewise linear model shown in Fig. 3.13,

$$\frac{du}{dt} = f(u) - w + I \tag{3.33}$$

$$\frac{dw}{dt} = \epsilon(bu - w) \tag{3.34}$$

A

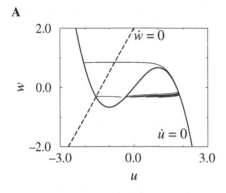

B

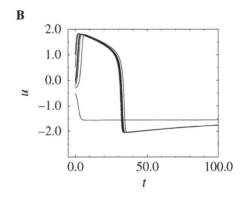

Fig. 3.12. FitzHugh–Nagumo model with separated time scales. All parameters are identical to those of Fig. 3.10 except for ϵ which has been reduced by a factor of 10. **A.** A trajectory which starts to the left-hand side of the middle branch of the u-nullcline returns directly to the rest state; all other trajectories develop a pulse. **B.** Due to slow w dynamics pulses are much broader than in Fig. 3.10.

with $f(u) = a\,u$ for $u < 0.5$, $f(u) = a\,(1 - u)$ for $0.5 < u < 1.5$ and $f(u) = c_0 + c_1\,u$ for $u > 1.5$ where $a, c_1 < 0$ are parameters and $c_0 = -0.5a - 1.5c_1$. Furthermore, $b > 0$ and $0 < \epsilon \ll 1$.

The rest state is at $u = w = 0$. Suppose that the system is stimulated by a short current pulse that shifts the state of the system horizontally. As long as $u < 1$, we have $f(u) < 0$. According to Eq. (3.33), $\dot{u} < 0$ and u returns to the rest state. For $u < 0.5$ the relaxation to rest is exponential with $u(t) = \exp(a\,t)$ in the limit of $\epsilon \to 0$. Thus, the return to rest after a small perturbation is governed by the *fast* time scale.

If the current pulse moves u to a value larger than unity, we have $\dot{u} = f(u) > 0$. Hence the voltage u increases and a pulse is emitted. That is to say, $u = 1$ acts as a threshold.

Let us now assume that an input spike from a presynaptic neuron j arrives at time $t_j^{(f)}$. Spike reception at the neuron generates a subthreshold current pulse $I(t) = c\,\delta(t - t_j^{(f)})$, where $0 < c \ll 1$ is the amplitude of the pulse. The perturbation causes for $t_j^{(f)}$ a voltage response κ with time course,

$$\kappa(t - t_j^{(f)}) = c\,\exp\left(-\frac{t - t_j^{(f)}}{\tau_a}\right), \tag{3.35}$$

where $\tau_a = -1/a$. If several input pulses arrive in a interval shorter than τ_a, then the responses are summed up and move the neuronal state beyond the middle branch of the u-nullcline. At this point a spike is triggered.

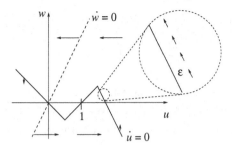

Fig. 3.13. Piecewise linear model. The inset shows the trajectory (arrows) which follows the u-nullcline at a distance of order ϵ.

Trajectory during a pulse (*)

We have argued above that, during the pulse, the trajectory is always pushed towards the u-nullcline. We will show in this paragraph that the trajectory $(u(t), w(t))$ of the piecewise linear system Eqs. (3.33)–(3.34) follows the u-nullcline $w = f(u) + I$ at a distance of order ϵ. We set

$$w(t) = f[u(t)] + I + \epsilon\, x[u(t)] + \mathcal{O}(\epsilon^2) \tag{3.36}$$

where $x(u)$ is the momentary distance at location u. The symbol $\mathcal{O}(\epsilon^2)$ indicates that the next term is of order ϵ^2. We show that Eq. (3.36) gives a consistent solution.

To do so we use Eq. (3.36) on the right-hand side of Eqs. (3.33) and (3.34). Thus, along the trajectory

$$\frac{du}{dt} = -\epsilon\, x(u) + \cdots \tag{3.37}$$

$$\frac{dw}{dt} = \epsilon\, [b\, u - f(u) - I + \cdots], \tag{3.38}$$

where we have neglected terms of order ϵ^2. On the other hand, the derivative of Eq. (3.36) is

$$\frac{dw}{dt} = \frac{df}{du}\frac{du}{dt} + \epsilon\, \frac{dx}{du}\frac{du}{dt} + \cdots . \tag{3.39}$$

We solve Eqs. (3.38) and (3.39) for du/dt. The result to order ϵ is

$$\frac{du}{dt} = \frac{\epsilon}{df/du}\, [b\, u - f(u) - I] . \tag{3.40}$$

Comparison with Eq. (3.37) shows that the distance x is indeed of order one.

Example: piecewise linear nullcline II

Let us study the relaxation to the stable fixed point after a pulse in the piecewise linear model. We use $f' = a$ for the slope of the u-nullcline and b for the slope of the w-nullcline. Evaluation of Eq. (3.40) gives

$$\frac{du}{dt} = -\epsilon \left(1 - \frac{b}{a}\right) u. \tag{3.41}$$

The decay is exponential with a time constant of recovery $\epsilon^{-1}[1-(b/a)]^{-1}$. Hence the relaxation to the resting potential is governed by the slow recovery dynamics with a time scale of order ϵ. The slow relaxation is one of the causes of neuronal refractoriness.

Similarly, the voltage during the spike is given by integrating

$$\frac{du}{dt} = -\epsilon \left(1 - \frac{b}{c_1}\right) u - \epsilon \frac{c_0 + I}{c_1} \qquad \text{for } u > 1.5. \tag{3.42}$$

Let us denote by $\hat{t}$ the time when the spike was triggered (i.e., when u crossed the middle branch of the u-nullcline). After the voltage increase during the initial phase of the limit cycle, the state of the system is on the right branch of the u-nullcline. There it evolves according to Eq. (3.42). When it reaches the knee of the nullcline, it jumps to the left branch where it arrives at time t_{left}. On the left branch, the relaxation to the resting potential is governed by Eq. (3.41). If we neglect the time needed for the jumps, the voltage during the limit cycle is therefore

$$\eta(t - \hat{t}) = \begin{cases} (u_{\text{right}} - \overline{u}) \exp\left(-\dfrac{t - \hat{t}}{\tau_{\text{spike}}}\right) + \overline{u} & \text{for } \hat{t} < t < t_{\text{left}} \\[4mm] (u_{\text{left}} - u_r) \exp\left(-\dfrac{t - \hat{t}}{\tau_{\text{recov}}}\right) + u_r & \text{for } \qquad t_{\text{left}} < t \end{cases} \tag{3.43}$$

with $\tau_{\text{spike}} = \epsilon^{-1}[1-(b/c_1)]^{-1}$, $\tau_{\text{recov}} = \epsilon^{-1}[1-(b/a)]^{-1}$ and parameters $u_{\text{right}} = 1.5 + a/c_1$, $u_{\text{left}} = -0.5$, $\overline{u} = (c_0 + I)/(b - c_1)$, and $u_r = I/(b - a)$. The representation of neuronal dynamics in terms of a response function as in Eq. (3.35) and a recovery function as in Eq. (3.43) plays a key role in formal spiking neuron models discussed in the following chapter.

3.4 Summary

The four-dimensional model of Hodgkin–Huxley can be reduced to two dimensions under the assumption that the m dynamics is fast as compared to u, h, and n, and that the latter two evolve on the same time scale. Two-dimensional models can readily be visualized and studied in the phase plane. In type II models oscillation onset for increasing input starts with nonzero frequency, as is typical for Hopf bifurcations. Type I models exhibit oscillation onset with zero frequency. This behavior can be obtained in two-dimensional models with three fixed points, a stable one, an unstable one, and a saddle point. Oscillations arise through a saddle-node bifurcation when the stable fixed point merges with the saddle. Type I models have a sharp voltage threshold whereas type II models do not. Nevertheless, type II models exhibit a threshold-like behavior if the u dynamics is much faster than that of the recovery variable w.

Literature

An in-depth introduction to dynamical systems, stability of fixed points, and (un)stable manifolds can be found, for example, in the books of Hale and Koçak (1991) and Verhulst (1996). The book of Strogatz (1994) presents the theory of dynamical systems in the context of various problems of physics, chemistry, biology, and engineering. A wealth of applications of dynamical systems to various (mostly nonneuronal) biological systems can be found in the comprehensive book of Murray (1993) which also contains a thorough discussion of the FitzHugh–Nagumo model. Phase plane methods applied to neuronal dynamics are discussed in the clearly written review paper of Rinzel and Ermentrout (1998). A systematic approach to reduction of dimensionality is presented in Kepler et al. (1992). For a further reduction of the two-dimensional model to an integrate-and-fire model, see the article of Abbott and Kepler (1990). The classification of neuron models as type I and type II can be found in Rinzel and Ermentrout (1998) and in Ermentrout (1996). For a systematic discussion of canonical neuron models based on their bifurcation behavior see the monograph of Hoppensteadt and Izhikevich (1997).

4

Formal spiking neuron models

Detailed conductance-based neuron models can reproduce electrophysiological measurements to a high degree of accuracy, but because of their intrinsic complexity these models are difficult to analyze. For this reason, simple phenomenological spiking neuron models are highly popular for studies of neural coding, memory, and network dynamics. In this chapter we discuss formal threshold models of neuronal firing. Spikes are generated whenever the membrane potential u crosses some threshold ϑ from below. The moment of threshold crossing defines the firing time $t^{(f)}$,

$$t^{(f)}: \quad u(t^{(f)}) = \vartheta \quad \text{and} \quad \left. \frac{du(t)}{dt} \right|_{t=t^{(f)}} > 0. \tag{4.1}$$

Since spikes are stereotyped events they are fully characterized by their firing time. We focus on models that are based on a single variable u. Some well-known instances of spiking neuron models differ in the specific way the dynamics of the variable u is defined. We start our discussion with the integrate-and-fire neuron (Section 4.1) and turn then to the Spike Response Model (Section 4.2). In Section 4.3 we illustrate the relation of spiking neuron models to conductance-based models. Section 4.4 outlines an analytical approach for a study of integrate-and-fire neurons with passive dendrites. As a first application of spiking neuron models we reconsider in Section 4.5 the problem of neuronal coding. The spiking neuron models introduced in this chapter form the basis for the analysis of network dynamics and learning in the following chapters.

4.1 Integrate-and-fire model

In this section, we give an overview of integrate-and-fire models. The leaky integrate-and-fire neuron introduced in Section 4.1.1 is probably the best-known example of a formal spiking neuron model. Generalizations of the leaky integrate-

93

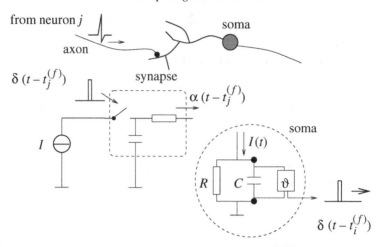

Fig. 4.1. Schematic diagram of the integrate-and-fire model. The basic circuit is the module inside the dashed circle on the right-hand side. A current $I(t)$ charges the RC circuit. The voltage $u(t)$ across the capacitance (points) is compared to a threshold ϑ. If $u(t) = \vartheta$ at time $t_i^{(f)}$ an output pulse $\delta(t - t_i^{(f)})$ is generated. Left part: a presynaptic spike $\delta(t - t_j^{(f)})$ is low-pass filtered at the synapse and generates an input current pulse $\alpha(t - t_j^{(f)})$.

and-fire model include the nonlinear integrate-and-fire model that is discussed in Section 4.1.2. All integrate-and-fire neurons can be stimulated either by external current or by synaptic input from presynaptic neurons. Standard formulations of synaptic input are given in Section 4.1.3.

4.1.1 Leaky integrate-and-fire model

The basic circuit of an integrate-and-fire model consists of a capacitor C in parallel with a resistor R driven by a current $I(t)$; see Fig. 4.1. The driving current can be split into two components, $I(t) = I_R + I_{\text{cap}}$. The first component is the resistive current I_R which passes through the linear resistor R. It can be calculated from Ohm's law as $I_R = u/R$ where u is the voltage across the resistor. The second component I_{cap} charges the capacitor C. From the definition of the capacity as $C = q/u$ (where q is the charge and u the voltage), we find a capacitive current $I_{\text{cap}} = C\,du/dt$. Thus

$$I(t) = \frac{u(t)}{R} + C\frac{du}{dt}. \tag{4.2}$$

We multiply Eq. (4.2) by R and introduce the time constant $\tau_m = R\,C$ of the "leaky integrator". This yields the standard form

$$\tau_m \frac{du}{dt} = -u(t) + R\,I(t)\,. \tag{4.3}$$

We refer to u as the membrane potential and to τ_m as the membrane time constant of the neuron.

In integrate-and-fire models the form of an action potential is not described explicitly. Spikes are formal events characterized by a "firing time" $t^{(f)}$. The firing time $t^{(f)}$ is defined by a threshold criterion

$$t^{(f)}\,: \quad u(t^{(f)}) = \vartheta\,. \tag{4.4}$$

Immediately after $t^{(f)}$, the potential is reset to a new value $u_r < \vartheta$,

$$\lim_{t \to t^{(f)}; t > t^{(f)}} u(t) = u_r\,. \tag{4.5}$$

For $t > t^{(f)}$ the dynamics is again given by Eq. (4.3) until the next threshold crossing occurs. The combination of leaky integration and reset defines the basic integrate-and-fire model (Stein, 1967b). We note that, since the membrane potential is never above threshold, the threshold condition of Eq. (4.1) reduces to the criterion in Eq. (4.4), i.e., the condition on the slope du/dt can be dropped.

In its general version, the leaky integrate-and-fire neuron may also incorporate an absolute refractory period, in which case we proceed as follows. If u reaches the threshold at time $t = t^{(f)}$, we interrupt the dynamics (4.3) during an absolute refractory time Δ^{abs} and restart the integration at time $t^{(f)} + \Delta^{\mathrm{abs}}$ with the new initial condition u_r.

Example: constant stimulation and firing rates

Before we continue with the definition of the integrate-and-fire model and its variants, let us study a simple example. Suppose that the integrate-and-fire neuron defined by Eqs. (4.3)–(4.5) is stimulated by a constant input current $I(t) = I_0$. For the sake of simplicity we take the reset potential to be $u_r = 0$.

As a first step, let us calculate the time course of the membrane potential. We assume that a spike has occurred at $t = t^{(1)}$. The trajectory of the membrane potential can be found by integrating Eq. (4.3) with the initial condition $u(t^{(1)}) = u_r = 0$. The solution is

$$u(t) = R\,I_0\left[1 - \exp\left(-\frac{t - t^{(1)}}{\tau_m}\right)\right]\,. \tag{4.6}$$

The membrane potential approaches for $t \to \infty$ the asymptotic value $u(\infty) = R\,I_0$. For $R\,I_0 < \vartheta$ no further spike can occur. For $R\,I_0 > \vartheta$, the membrane

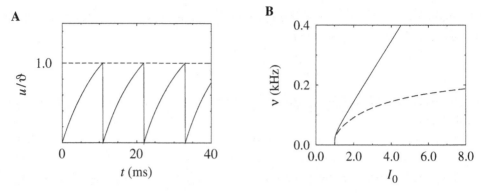

Fig. 4.2. **A**. Time course of the membrane potential of an integrate-and-fire neuron driven by constant input current $I_0 = 1.5$. The membrane potential $u(t)$ is given in units of the firing threshold ϑ. **B**. Gain function. The firing rate ν of an integrate-and-fire neuron without (solid line) and with absolute refractoriness of $\delta_{abs} = 4$ ms (dashed line) as a function of a constant driving current I_0. Current units are normalized so that the onset of repetitive firing is at $I_0 = 1$. Other parameters are $R = 1$, $\tau_m = 10$ ms, and $u_r = 0$.

potential reaches the threshold ϑ at time $t^{(2)}$, which can be found from the threshold condition $u(t^{(2)}) = \vartheta$ or

$$\vartheta = R I_0 \left[1 - \exp\left(-\frac{t^{(2)} - t^{(1)}}{\tau_m} \right) \right]. \tag{4.7}$$

Solving Eq. (4.7) for the time interval $T = t^{(2)} - t^{(1)}$ yields

$$T = \tau_m \ln \frac{R I_0}{R I_0 - \vartheta}. \tag{4.8}$$

After the spike at $t^{(2)}$ the membrane potential is again reset to $u_r = 0$ and the integration process starts again. If the stimulus I_0 remains constant, the following spike will occur after another interval of duration T. We conclude that for a constant input current I_0, the integrate-and-fire neuron fires regularly with period T given by Eq. (4.8). For a neuron with absolute refractory period the firing period T' is given by $T' = T + \Delta^{abs}$ with T defined by Eq. (4.8). In other words, the interspike interval is longer by an amount Δ^{abs} compared to that of a neuron without an absolute refractory period.

The mean firing rate of a noiseless neuron is defined as $\nu = 1/T$. The firing rate of an integrate-and-fire model with absolute refractory period Δ^{abs} stimulated by a current I_0 is therefore

$$\nu = \left[\Delta^{abs} + \tau_m \ln \frac{R I_0}{R I_0 - \vartheta} \right]^{-1}. \tag{4.9}$$

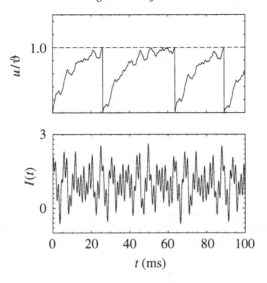

Fig. 4.3. Voltage $u(t)$ of an integrate-and-fire model (top) driven by the input current $I(t)$ shown at the bottom. The input $I(t)$ consists of a superposition of four sinusoidal components at randomly chosen frequencies plus a positive bias current $I_0 = 1.2$ which drives the membrane potential towards the threshold.

In Fig. 4.2B the firing rate is plotted as a function of the constant input I_0 for neurons with and without absolute refractory period.

Example: time-dependent stimulus $I(t)$

The results of the preceding example can be generalized to arbitrary stimulation conditions and an arbitrary reset value $u_r < \vartheta$. Let us suppose that a spike has occurred at $\hat{t}$. For $t > \hat{t}$ the stimulating current is $I(t)$. The value u_r will be treated as an initial condition for the integration of Eq. (4.3), i.e.,

$$u(t) = u_r \exp\left(-\frac{t - \hat{t}}{\tau_m}\right) + \frac{1}{C} \int_0^{t-\hat{t}} \exp\left(-\frac{s}{\tau_m}\right) I(t-s)\, \mathrm{d}s\,. \qquad (4.10)$$

This expression describes the membrane potential for $t > \hat{t}$ and is valid up to the moment of the next threshold crossing. If $u(t) = \vartheta$, the membrane potential is reset to u_r and integration restarts; see Fig. 4.3.

4.1.2 Nonlinear integrate-and-fire model

In a general *nonlinear* integrate-and-fire model, Eq. (4.3) is replaced by

$$\tau \frac{\mathrm{d}u}{\mathrm{d}t} = F(u) + G(u)\, I\,; \qquad (4.11)$$

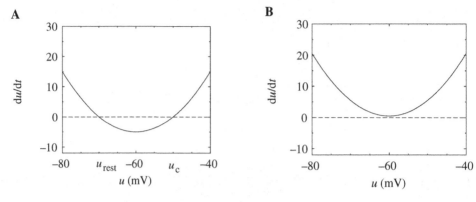

Fig. 4.4. Quadratic integrate-and-fire model. **A.** Without external current $I = 0$, the membrane potential relaxes for all initial condition $u < u_c$ to the resting potential u_{rest}. If the membrane potential is moved above the critical voltage u_c, the potential increases further since $du/dt > 0$. The neuron is said to fire if u reaches the threshold $\vartheta = -40$ mV. **B.** A constant super-threshold current I is characterized by the fact that $du/dt > 0$ for all u. If u reaches the firing threshold of -40 mV, it is reset to -80 mV. This results in repetitive firing.

cf. Abbott and van Vreeswijk (1993). As before, the dynamics is stopped if u reaches the threshold ϑ and reinitialized at $u = u_r$. A comparison with Eq. (4.3) shows that $G(u)$ can be interpreted as a voltage-dependent input resistance while $-F(u)/(u - u_{rest})$ corresponds to a voltage-dependent decay constant. A specific instance of a nonlinear integrate-and-fire model is the *quadratic* model (Latham et al., 2000; Feng, 2001; Hansel and Mato, 2001),

$$\tau \frac{du}{dt} = a_0 (u - u_{rest})(u - u_c) + RI , \qquad (4.12)$$

with parameters $a_0 > 0$ and $u_c > u_{rest}$; cf. Fig. 4.4. For $I = 0$ and initial conditions $u < u_c$, the voltage decays to the resting potential u_{rest}. For $u > u_c$ it increases so that an action potential is triggered. The parameter u_c can therefore be interpreted as the critical voltage for spike initiation by a short current pulse. We will see in the next example that the quadratic integrate-and-fire model is closely related to the so-called Θ-neuron, a canonical type I neuron model (Ermentrout, 1996; Latham et al., 2000).

Rescaling and standard forms (*)

It is always possible to rescale the variables so that threshold and membrane time constant are equal to unity and that the resting potential vanishes. Furthermore, there is no need to interpret the variable u as the membrane potential. For example, starting from the nonlinear integrate-and-fire model Eq. (4.11), we can introduce a new variable $\tilde{u}$ by the transformation

$$u(t) \longrightarrow \tilde{u}(t) = \tau \int_0^{u(t)} \frac{\mathrm{d}x}{G(x)}, \qquad (4.13)$$

which is possible if $G(x) \neq 0$ for all x in the integration range. In terms of $\tilde{u}$ we have a new nonlinear integrate-and-fire model of the form

$$\frac{\mathrm{d}\tilde{u}}{\mathrm{d}t} = \gamma(\tilde{u}) + I(t) \qquad (4.14)$$

with $\gamma(\tilde{u}) = \tau F(u)/G(u)$. In other words, a general integrate-and-fire model (4.11) can always be reduced to the standard form (4.14). By a completely analogous transformation, we could eliminate the function F in Eq. (4.11) and move all the dependence into a new voltage-dependent G (Abbott and van Vreeswijk, 1993).

Example: relation to a canonical type I model (*)

In this section, we show that there is a close relation between the quadratic integrate-and-fire model (4.12) and the canonical type I phase model,

$$\frac{\mathrm{d}\phi}{\mathrm{d}t} = [1 - \cos\phi] + \Delta I [1 + \cos\phi]; \qquad (4.15)$$

cf. Section 3.2.4 (Ermentrout and Kopell, 1986; Strogatz, 1994; Ermentrout, 1996; Hoppensteadt and Izhikevich, 1997; Latham et al., 2000).

Let us denote by I_θ the minimal current necessary for repetitive firing of the quadratic integrate-and-fire neuron. With a suitable shift of the voltage scale and constant current $I = I_\theta + \Delta I$ the equation of the quadratic neuron model can then be cast into the form

$$\frac{\mathrm{d}u}{\mathrm{d}t} = u^2 + \Delta I . \qquad (4.16)$$

For $\Delta I > 0$ the voltage increases until it reaches the firing threshold $\vartheta \gg 1$ where it is reset to a value $u_r \ll -1$. Note that the firing times are insensitive to the actual values of firing threshold and reset value because the solution of Eq. (4.16) grows faster than exponentially and diverges for finite time (hyperbolic growth). The difference in the firing times for a finite threshold of, say, $\vartheta = 10$ and $\vartheta = 10\,000$ is thus negligible.

We want to show that the differential equation (4.16) can be transformed into the canonical phase model (4.15) by the transformation

$$u(t) = \tan\left(\frac{\phi(t)}{2}\right) . \qquad (4.17)$$

To do so, we take the derivative of Eq. (4.17) and use the differential equation (4.15) of the generic phase model. With help of the trigonometric relations $d \tan x/dx = 1/\cos^2(x)$ and $1 + \cos x = \cos^2(x/2)$ we find

$$
\begin{aligned}
\frac{du}{dt} &= \frac{1}{\cos^2(\phi/2)} \frac{1}{2} \frac{d\phi}{dt} \\
&= \tan^2(\phi/2) + \Delta I = u^2 + \Delta I .
\end{aligned} \tag{4.18}
$$

Thus Eq. (4.17) with $\phi(t)$ given by Eq. (4.15) is a solution to the differential equation of the quadratic integrate-and-fire neuron. The quadratic integrate-and-fire neuron is therefore (in the limit $\vartheta \to \infty$ and $u_r \to -\infty$) equivalent to the generic type I neuron (4.15).

4.1.3 Stimulation by synaptic currents

So far we have considered an isolated neuron that is stimulated by an external current $I(t)$. In a more realistic situation, the integrate-and-fire model is part of a larger network and the input current $I(t)$ is generated by the activity of presynaptic neurons.

In the framework of the integrate-and-fire model, each presynaptic spike generates a postsynaptic current pulse. More precisely, if the presynaptic neuron j has fired a spike at $t_j^{(f)}$, a postsynaptic neuron i "feels" a current with time course $\alpha(t - t_j^{(f)})$. The total input current to neuron i is the sum over all current pulses,

$$
I_i(t) = \sum_j w_{ij} \sum_f \alpha(t - t_j^{(f)}) . \tag{4.19}
$$

The factor w_{ij} is a measure of the efficacy of the synapse from neuron j to neuron i.

Though Eq. (4.19) is a reasonable model of synaptic interaction, reality is somewhat more complicated, because the amplitude of the postsynaptic current pulse depends on the actual value of the membrane potential u_i. As we have seen in Chapter 2, each presynaptic action potential evokes a change in the *conductance* of the postsynaptic membrane with a certain time course $g(t - t^{(f)})$. The postsynaptic current generated by a spike at time $t_j^{(f)}$ is thus

$$
\alpha(t - t_j^{(f)}) = -g(t - t_j^{(f)}) \left[u_i(t) - E_{syn} \right] . \tag{4.20}
$$

The parameter E_{syn} is the reversal potential of the synapse.

The level of the reversal potential depends on the type of synapse. For excitatory synapses, E_{syn} is much larger than the resting potential. For a voltage $u_i(t)$ close to the resting potential, we have $u_i(t) < E_{syn}$. Hence the current I_i induced by a presynaptic spike at an excitatory synapse is positive and *increases* the membrane potential.[1] The higher the voltage, the smaller the amplitude of the input current. Note that a positive voltage $u_i > u_{rest}$ is itself the result of input spikes which have arrived at other excitatory synapses. Hence, there is a saturation of the postsynaptic current and the total input current is not just the sum of independent contributions. Nevertheless, since the reversal potential of excitatory synapses is usually significantly above the firing threshold, the factor $(u_i - E_{syn})$ is almost constant and saturation can be neglected.

For inhibitory synapses, the reversal potential is close to the resting potential. An action potential arriving at an inhibitory synapse pulls the membrane potential towards the reversal potential E_{syn}. Thus, if the neuron is at rest, inhibitory input hardly has any effect on the membrane potential. If the membrane potential is instead considerably above the resting potential, then the same input has a strong inhibitory effect. This is sometimes described as silent inhibition: inhibition is only seen if the membrane potential is above the resting potential. Strong silent inhibition is also called "shunting" inhibition, because a significantly reduced resistance of the membrane potential forms a short circuit that literally shunts excitatory input the neuron might receive from other synapses.

Example: pulse-coupling and α-function

The time course of the postsynaptic current $\alpha(s)$ introduced in Eq. (4.19) can be defined in various ways. The simplest choice is a Dirac δ-pulse, $\alpha(s) = q\,\delta(s)$, where q is the total charge that is injected in a postsynaptic neuron via a synapse with efficacy $w_{ij} = 1$. More realistically, the postsynaptic current α should have a finite duration, e.g., as in the case of an exponential decay with time constant τ_s,

$$\alpha(s) = \frac{q}{\tau_s} \exp\left(-\frac{s}{\tau_s}\right) \Theta(s). \tag{4.21}$$

As usual, Θ is the Heaviside step function with $\Theta(s) = 1$ for $s > 0$ and $\Theta(s) = 0$ else. Equation (4.21) is a simple way to account for the low-pass characteristics of synaptic transmission; cf. Fig. 4.1.

An even more sophisticated version of α includes a finite rise time τ_r of the postsynaptic current and a transmission delay Δ^{ax},

$$\alpha(s) = \frac{q}{\tau_s - \tau_r} \left[\exp\left(-\frac{s - \Delta^{ax}}{\tau_s}\right) - \exp\left(-\frac{s - \Delta^{ax}}{\tau_r}\right) \right] \Theta(s - \Delta^{ax}). \tag{4.22}$$

In the limit of $\tau_r \to \tau_s$, Eq. (4.22) yields

$$\alpha(s) = q\,\frac{s - \Delta^{ax}}{\tau_s^2} \exp\left(-\frac{s - \Delta^{ax}}{\tau_s}\right) \Theta(s - \Delta^{ax}). \tag{4.23}$$

---

[1] Note that in Eq. (4.20) we consider the synaptic current as an *external* current whereas in Chapter 2 we have considered it as a membrane current and therefore used a different sign convention. In both cases, an excitatory input increases the membrane potential.

In the literature, a function of the form $x \exp(-x)$ such as in Eq. (4.23) is often called an α-function. While this has motivated our choice of the symbol α for the synaptic input current, α may stand for any form of an input current pulse.

4.2 Spike Response Model (SRM)

The Spike Response Model (SRM) is – just like the nonlinear integrate-and-fire model – a generalization of the leaky integrate-and-fire model. The direction of the generalization is, however, somewhat different. In the nonlinear integrate-and-fire model, parameters are made *voltage* dependent whereas in the SRM they depend on the time since the last output spike. Another difference between integrate-and-fire models and the SRM concerns the formulation of the equations. While integrate-and-fire models are usually defined in terms of differential equations, the SRM expresses the membrane potential at time t as an integral over the past.

The explicit dependence of the membrane potential upon the last output spike allows us to model refractoriness as a combination of three components, viz., (i) a reduced responsiveness after an output spike; (ii) an increase in threshold after firing; and (iii) a hyperpolarizing spike-afterpotential. In Section 4.2.1 the SRM is introduced and its properties illustrated. Its relation to the integrate-and-fire model is the topic of Section 4.2.2. An important special case of the SRM is the simplified model SRM_0 that we have already encountered in Chapter 1. Section 4.2.3 will discuss it in more detail.

4.2.1 Definition of the SRM

In the framework of the SRM the state of a neuron i is described by a single variable u_i. In the absence of spikes, the variable u_i is at its resting value, $u_{\text{rest}} = 0$. Each incoming spike will perturb u_i and it takes some time before u_i returns to zero. The function ϵ describes the time course of the response to an incoming spike. If, after summing the effects of several incoming spikes, u_i reaches the threshold ϑ an output spike is triggered. The form of the action potential and the afterpotential is described by a function η. Let us suppose neuron i has fired its last spike at time $\hat{t}_i$. After firing the evolution of u_i is given by

$$u_i(t) \;=\; \eta(t - \hat{t}_i) + \sum_j w_{ij} \sum_f \epsilon_{ij}(t - \hat{t}_i, t - t_j^{(f)})$$

$$+ \int_0^\infty \kappa(t - \hat{t}_i, s)\, I^{\text{ext}}(t - s)\, \mathrm{d}s, \qquad (4.24)$$

where $t_j^{(f)}$ are spikes of presynaptic neurons j and w_{ij} is the synaptic efficacy. The last term accounts for an external driving current I^{ext}. The two sums run over all presynaptic neurons j and all firing times $t_j^{(f)} < t$ of neuron j. We emphasize that all terms depend on $t - \hat{t}_i$, i.e., the time since the last output spike.

In contrast to the integrate-and-fire neuron discussed in Section 4.1 the threshold ϑ is not fixed but may also depend on $t - \hat{t}_i$

$$\vartheta \quad \longrightarrow \quad \vartheta(t - \hat{t}_i). \tag{4.25}$$

During an absolute refractory period Δ^{abs}, we may for example set ϑ to a large and positive value to avoid firing and let it relax back to its equilibrium value for $t > \hat{t}_i + \Delta^{\text{abs}}$. Firing occurs whenever the membrane potential u_i reaches the dynamic threshold $\vartheta(t - \hat{t}_i)$ from below

$$t = t_i^{(f)} \quad \Leftrightarrow \quad u_i(t) = \vartheta(t - \hat{t}_i) \text{ and } \frac{du_i(t)}{dt} > 0. \tag{4.26}$$

As mentioned before $\hat{t}_i$ is the *last* firing time,

$$\hat{t}_i = \max\left\{t_i^{(f)} < t\right\}. \tag{4.27}$$

Dynamic thresholds are a standard feature of phenomenological neuron models (Fuortes and Mantegazzini, 1962; Geisler and Goldberg, 1966; Weiss, 1966; Stein, 1967b; MacGregor and Oliver, 1974; Horn and Usher, 1989; Eckhorn et al., 1990; Abeles, 1991). Models similar to Eqs. (4.24)–(4.26) can be traced back much further; see, e.g., Hill (1936).

Interpretation

So far Eqs. (4.1) and (4.24) define a mathematical model. Can we give a biological interpretation of the terms? Let us identify the variable u_i with the membrane potential of neuron i. The functions η, κ, and ϵ_{ij} are *response kernels* that describe the effect of spike emission and spike reception on the variable u_i. This interpretation has motivated the name "Spike Response Model", SRM for short (Gerstner, 1995; Kistler et al., 1997). Let us discuss the meaning of the response kernels.

The kernel η describes the standard form of an action potential of neuron i including the negative overshoot which typically follows a spike (afterpotential). Graphically speaking, a contribution η is "pasted in" each time the membrane potential reaches the threshold ϑ; cf. Fig. 4.5. Since the form of the spike is always the same, the exact time course of the action potential carries no information. What matters is whether there is the event "spike" or not. The event is fully characterized by the firing time $t_i^{(f)}$. In a simplified model, the *form* of the action potential may therefore be neglected as long as we keep track of the firing times $t_i^{(f)}$. The kernel η describes then simply the "reset" of the membrane potential to a lower value after

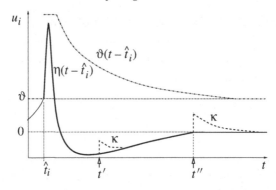

Fig. 4.5. Schematic interpretation of the Spike Response Model. The figure shows the time course $u_i(t)$ of the membrane potential of neuron i as a function of time t. A spike of neuron i has been initiated at $\hat{t}_i$. The kernel $\eta(t - \hat{t}_i)$ for $t > \hat{t}_i$ describes the form of the action potential (positive pulse) and the (negative) spike-afterpotential that follows the pulse (thick solid line). If an input current pulse is applied at a time t'' a long time after the firing at $\hat{t}_i$, it evokes a standard response described by the function $\kappa(\infty, t - t'')$ and indicated by the dashed line starting at t'' (arrow). An input current pulse at t' (arrow) which arrives shortly after the postsynaptic spike at $\hat{t}_i$ evokes, due to refractoriness of the neuron, a response of significantly shorter duration. Its time course is described by the response kernel $\kappa(t - \hat{t}_i, t - t')$; see the dashed line after t'. Immediately after firing at $\hat{t}_i$, the threshold is increased (dot-dashed line).

the spike at $\hat{t}_i$ just as in the integrate-and-fire model. The leaky integrate-and-fire model is in fact a special case of the SRM as we will see below in Section 4.2.2.

The kernel $\kappa(t - \hat{t}_i, s)$ is the *linear response* of the membrane potential to an input current. It describes the time course of a deviation of the membrane potential from its resting value that is caused by a short current pulse ("impulse response"). We have already seen in Section 2.2 and Chapter 3 that the response depends, in general, on the time that has passed since the last output spike at $\hat{t}_i$. Immediately after $\hat{t}_i$ many ion channels are open so that the resistance of the membrane is reduced. The voltage response to an input current pulse decays therefore more rapidly back to zero than in a neuron that has been inactive. A reduced or shorter response is one of the signatures of neuronal refractoriness. This form of refractory effect is taken care of by making the kernel κ depend, via its first argument, on the time difference $t - \hat{t}_i$. We illustrate the idea in Fig. 4.5. The response to a first input pulse at t' is shorter and less pronounced than that to a second one at t'', an effect which is well-known experimentally (Fuortes and Mantegazzini, 1962; Powers and Binder, 1996; Stevens and Zador, 1998).

The kernel $\epsilon_{ij}(t - \hat{t}_i, s)$ as a function of $s = t - t_j^{(f)}$ can be interpreted as the time course of a *postsynaptic potential* evoked by the firing of a presynaptic neuron j at time $t_j^{(f)}$. Depending on the sign of the synapse from j to i, ϵ_{ij} models either an excitatory or inhibitory postsynaptic potential (EPSP or IPSP). Similarly as for the kernel κ, the exact shape of the postsynaptic potential depends on the time $t - \hat{t}_i$ that has passed since the last spike of the postsynaptic neuron i. In particular, if neuron i has been active immediately before the arrival of a presynaptic action potential, the postsynaptic neuron is in a state of refractoriness. In this case, the response to an input spike is smaller than that of an "unprimed" neuron. The first argument of $\epsilon_{ij}(t - \hat{t}_i, s)$ accounts for the dependence upon the last firing time of the postsynaptic neuron.

Total postsynaptic potential

In order to simplify the notation for later use, it is convenient to introduce the *total postsynaptic potential*,

$$h(t|\hat{t}_i) = \sum_j w_{ij} \sum_{t_j^{(f)}} \epsilon_{ij}(t - \hat{t}_i, t - t_j^{(f)}) + \int_0^\infty \kappa(t - \hat{t}_i, s)\, I_i^{\text{ext}}(t - s)\, \mathrm{d}s \,. \quad (4.28)$$

Equation (4.24) can then be written in compact form,

$$u_i(t) = \eta(t - \hat{t}_i) + h(t|\hat{t}_i)\,. \quad (4.29)$$

Refractoriness

Refractoriness may be characterized experimentally by the observation that immediately after a first action potential it is impossible (absolute refractoriness) or more difficult (relative refractoriness) to excite a second spike (Fuortes and Mantegazzini, 1962).

Absolute refractoriness can be incorporated in the SRM by setting the dynamic threshold during a time Δ^{abs} to an extremely high value that cannot be attained.

Relative refractoriness can be mimicked in various ways; see Fig. 4.5. Firstly, after the spike the membrane potential, and hence η, passes through a regime of hyperpolarization (afterpotential) where the voltage is *below* the resting potential. During this phase, more stimulation than usual is needed to drive the membrane potential above threshold. This is equivalent to a transient increase of the firing threshold (see below). Secondly, ϵ and κ contribute to relative refractoriness because, immediately after an action potential, the response to incoming spikes is shorter and, possibly, of reduced amplitude (Fuortes and Mantegazzini, 1962). Thus more input spikes are needed to evoke the same depolarization of the membrane potential as in an "unprimed" neuron. The first argument of the ϵ function (or κ function) allows us to incorporate this effect.

Removing the dynamic threshold

From a formal point of view, there is no need to interpret the variable u as the membrane potential. It is, for example, often convenient to transform the variable u so as to remove the time dependence of the threshold. In fact, a general SRM with arbitrary time-dependent threshold $\vartheta(t - \hat{t}) = \vartheta_0 + \Delta(t - \hat{t})$, can always be transformed into a SRM with fixed threshold ϑ_0 by a change of variables

$$u(t) \longrightarrow \tilde{u}(t) = u(t) - \Delta(t - \hat{t}). \tag{4.30}$$

The function $\Delta(t - \hat{t})$ can easily be absorbed in the definition of the η kernel.

Example: impulse response of the FitzHugh–Nagumo model

In Chapter 3 we have studied the FitzHugh–Nagumo model as an example of a two-dimensional neuron model. Here we want to show that the response of the FitzHugh–Nagumo model to a short input current pulse depends on the time since the last spike. Let us trigger, in a simulation of the model, an action potential at $t = 0$. This can be done by applying a short, but strong current pulse. The result is a voltage trajectory of large amplitude which we identify with the kernel $\eta(t)$. Figure 4.6 shows the hyperpolarizing spike-afterpotential which decays slowly back to the resting level. To test the responsiveness of the FitzHugh–Nagumo model during the recovery phase after the action potential, we apply, at a time $t^{(f)} > 0$, a second short input current pulse of low amplitude. The response to this test pulse is compared with the unperturbed trajectory. The difference between the two trajectories defines the kernel $\kappa(t - \hat{t}, t - t^{(f)})$. In Fig. 4.6 several trajectories are overlayed showing the response to stimulation at $t = 10, 15, 20, 30$ or 40. The shape and duration of the response curve depends on the time that has passed since the initiation of the action potential. Note that the time constant of the response kernel κ is always less than that of the hyperpolarizing spike-afterpotential. Analogous results for the Hodgkin–Huxley model are discussed below in Section 4.3.1.

Example: a motoneuron model

Motoneurons exhibit a rather slow return to the resting potential after an action potential (Powers and Binder, 1996). The time constant of the decay of the hyperpolarizing spike-afterpotential can be in the range of 100 ms or more and is therefore much slower than the membrane time constant that characterizes the response to a short current input. On the other hand, it is found that if motoneurons are stimulated by a constant super-threshold current, their membrane potential has a roughly linear trajectory when approaching threshold. To qualitatively describe

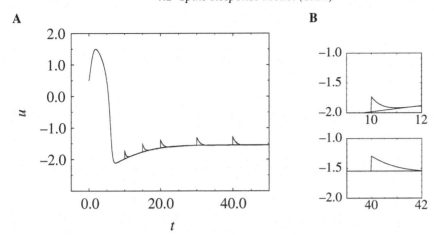

Fig. 4.6. FitzHugh–Nagumo model. An action potential has been triggered at $t = 0$. After the action potential additional pulse input occurs at $t = 10, 15, 20, 30$, or 40 (arbitrary units). In **A** the trajectories of all runs are plotted on top of each other. Part **B** shows a zoomed-in section of two trajectories. A pulse input at time $t = 10$ after the onset of the action potential has a short lasting effect (top right) compared to a pulse at $t = 40$ (bottom right). All parameters as in Fig. 3.5. There is no constant bias current.

these observations, we can use a SRM with the following kernels:

$$\eta(t - \hat{t}) = -\eta_0\, e^{-(t-\hat{t})/\tau_{\text{refr}}}\, \Theta(t - \hat{t}) \tag{4.31}$$

$$\kappa(t - \hat{t}, s) = \frac{R}{\tau_m}\left[1 - e^{-(t-\hat{t})/\tau_{\text{rec}}}\right] e^{-s/\tau_m}\, \Theta(s)\, \Theta(t - \hat{t} - s) \tag{4.32}$$

where τ_m is an effective passive membrane time constant, R is the input resistance, τ_{refr} is the "refractory" time constant, τ_{rec} is the "response recovery" time constant, η_0 is a scale factor for the refractory function. The passive membrane time constant τ_m and input resistance R characterize the membrane response to small current pulses. The refractory function η describes the return of the membrane potential to baseline after an action potential. It is characterized by a slow time constant τ_{refr}. For the κ-kernel we use a decaying exponential in s with time constant τ_m, modulated by the "recovery" factor $\{1 - \exp[-(t-\hat{t})/\tau_{\text{rec}}]\}$. This results in a spike-time-dependent scaling of the amplitude of postsynaptic potentials. The recovery time τ_{rec} is much longer than τ_m.

The effect of modulating of the input conductance as a function of $t - \hat{t}$ is depicted in Fig. 4.7. An input current pulse shortly after the reset at time $\hat{t}$ evokes a postsynaptic potential of much lower amplitude than an input current pulse that arrives much later. Figure 4.7 qualitatively reproduces the membrane trajectory of motoneurons when stimulated by the same input pattern (Poliakov et al., 1996; Powers and Binder, 1996).

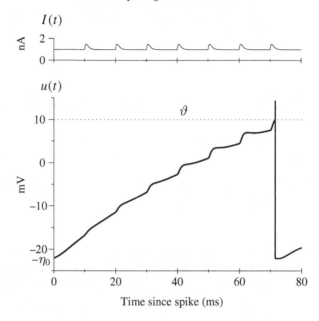

Fig. 4.7. Effect of recovery time constant τ_{rec}. Top: input current consisting of a sequence of pulses superimposed on a constant bias. Bottom: the membrane potential response (thick line) to the input pulses clearly shows that the response amplitude increases as a function of the time since the last spike. Parameters: $\tau_{\text{rec}} = \tau_{\text{refr}} = 100$ ms; $\tau_m = 4$ ms; taken from Herrmann and Gerstner (2001b).

4.2.2 Mapping the integrate-and-fire model to the SRM

In this section, we show that the leaky integrate-and-fire neuron defined in Section 4.1 is a special case of the Spike Response Model (SRM). We consider an integrate-and-fire neuron driven by external current I^{ext} and postsynaptic current pulses $\alpha(t - t_j^{(f)})$. The potential u_i is thus given by

$$\tau_m \frac{du_i}{dt} = -u_i(t) + R \sum_j w_{ij} \sum_f \alpha(t - t_j^{(f)}) + R\, I_i^{\text{ext}}(t)\,. \tag{4.33}$$

In order to construct a mapping of the integrate-and-fire model to the SRM we integrate Eq. (4.33) with $u(\hat{t}_i) = u_r$ as its initial condition. The result is in analogy to Eq. (4.10)

$$u(t) = u_r \exp\left(-\frac{t - \hat{t}_i}{\tau_m}\right) \tag{4.34}$$

$$+ \sum_j w_{ij} \sum_f \frac{1}{C} \int_0^{t - \hat{t}_i} \exp\left(-\frac{s}{\tau_m}\right) \alpha(t - t_j^{(f)} - s)\, ds$$

$$+\frac{1}{C}\int_0^{t-\hat{t}_i}\exp\left(-\frac{s}{\tau_m}\right)I_i^{\text{ext}}(t-s)\,\mathrm{d}s$$

$$=\eta(t-\hat{t}_i)+\sum_j w_{ij}\sum_f \epsilon(t-\hat{t}_i,t-t_j^{(f)})+\int_0^\infty \kappa(t-\hat{t}_i,s)\,I_i^{\text{ext}}(t-s)\,\mathrm{d}s\,,$$

with

$$\eta(s)=u_r\,\exp\left(-\frac{s}{\tau_m}\right),\qquad\qquad (4.35)$$

$$\epsilon(s,t)=\frac{1}{C}\int_0^s \exp\left(-\frac{t'}{\tau_m}\right)\alpha(t-t')\,\mathrm{d}t'\,,\qquad\qquad (4.36)$$

$$\kappa(s,t)=\frac{1}{C}\exp\left(-\frac{t}{\tau_m}\right)\Theta(s-t)\,\Theta(t)\,.\qquad\qquad (4.37)$$

As usual, $\Theta(x)$ denotes the Heaviside step function. The kernels (4.35)–(4.37) allow us to map the integrate-and-fire neuron exactly to the SRM, as desired; cf. Eq. (4.24).

In order obtain an explicit expression for the ϵ kernel (4.36) we have to specify the time course of the postsynaptic current $\alpha(s)$. Here, we take $\alpha(s)$ as defined in (4.21), viz.,

$$\alpha(s)=\frac{q}{\tau_s}\exp\left(-s/\tau_s\right)\Theta(s)\,.\qquad\qquad (4.38)$$

With $q=C=1$, the integration of Eq. (4.36) yields

$$\epsilon(s,t)=\frac{\exp\left(-\max(t-s,0)/\tau_s\right)}{1-\tau_s/\tau_m}$$
$$\times\left[\exp\left(-\frac{\min(s,t)}{\tau_m}\right)-\exp\left(-\frac{\min(s,t)}{\tau_s}\right)\right]\Theta(s)\,\Theta(t)\,;\qquad (4.39)$$

cf. Fig. 4.8. If presynaptic spikes arrive before the last postsynaptic spike, then they have only a small effect on the actual value of the membrane potential because only that part of the postsynaptic current that arrives after $\hat{t}_i$ contributes to the postsynaptic potential. Spikes that arrive after $\hat{t}_i$ produce a full postsynaptic potential. Note that causality implies that the ϵ kernel has to vanishes for negative arguments.

Example: spike-time-dependent time constant

We have seen above that the SRM contains the integrate-and-fire model as a special case. In this example, we show in addition that even a generalization of the integrate-and-fire model that has a time-dependent membrane time constant can be described within the SRM framework.

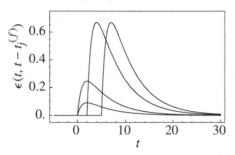

Fig. 4.8. The kernel $\epsilon(t, t - t_j^{(f)})$ as a function of t for various presynaptic firing times $t_j^{(f)} = -2, -1, 2, 5$; cf. Eq. (4.39) with $\tau_s = 1$ and $\tau_m = 5$. The last postsynaptic spike was at $t = 0$. If presynaptic spikes arrive before the last postsynaptic spike, then they have only a small effect on the membrane potential; cf. the two small EPSPs that correspond to $t_j^{(f)} = -2$ and $t_j^{(f)} = -1$. If presynaptic spikes arrive after the last postsynaptic spike then they evoke a full-blown EPSP; cf. the two large EPSPs that correspond to $t_j^{(f)} = 2$ and $t_j^{(f)} = 5$.

To be specific, we consider an integrate-and-fire model with a spike-time-dependent time constant, i.e., with a membrane time constant τ that is a function of the time since the last postsynaptic spike,

$$\frac{du}{dt} = -\frac{u}{\tau(t - \hat{t})} + \frac{1}{C} I^{\text{ext}}(t) ; \qquad (4.40)$$

cf. Wehmeier et al. (1989); Stevens and Zador (1998). As usual, $\hat{t}$ denotes the last firing time of the neuron. The neuron is insensitive to input during an absolute refractory period of duration Δ^{abs}. After the refractory period, the membrane potential is reset to a value u_r. Starting the integration of Eq. (4.40) at $u(\hat{t} + \Delta^{\text{abs}}) = u_r$, we find for $t > \hat{t} + \Delta^{\text{abs}}$

$$
\begin{aligned}
u(t) \;=\; & u_r \exp\left[-\int_{\hat{t}+\Delta^{\text{abs}}}^{t} \frac{dt'}{\tau(t' - \hat{t})} \right] \\
& + \frac{1}{C} \int_0^{\infty} \Theta(t - \hat{t} - \Delta^{\text{abs}} - s) \exp\left[-\int_{t-s}^{t} \frac{dt'}{\tau(t' - \hat{t})} \right] I^{\text{ext}}(t - s)\, ds ,
\end{aligned}
\qquad (4.41)
$$

which is a special case of Eq. (4.24). As we have seen above in Fig. 4.6, the effective membrane time constant of many standard neuron models is reduced immediately after a spike. The reason is that, after a spike, many ion channels are open so that conductance is increased. Since the time constant is inversely proportional to the conductance, the time constant is decreased. The relation between ion channels and spike-time-dependent time constant is discussed in more detail in Section 4.3.2.

4.2.3 Simplified model SRM$_0$

The phenomenological neuron model SRM$_0$ introduced in Section 1.3.1 is a special case of the SRM. In this section we review its relation to the SRM and the integrate-and-fire model.

Relation to the SRM

A simplified version of the SRM can be constructed by neglecting the dependence of κ and ϵ upon the first argument. We set

$$\epsilon_0(s) = \epsilon_{ij}(\infty, s)$$
$$\kappa_0(s) = \kappa_{ij}(\infty, s)$$

and use (4.24) in the form

$$u_i(t) = \eta(t - \hat{t}_i) + \sum_j w_{ij} \sum_{t_j^{(f)}} \epsilon_0(t - t_j^{(f)}) + \int_0^\infty \kappa_0(s)\, I^{\text{ext}}(t - s)\, ds. \quad (4.42)$$

Each presynaptic spike thus evokes a postsynaptic potential with the same time course, independent of the index j of the presynaptic neuron and independent of the last firing time $\hat{t}_i$ of the postsynaptic neuron. The amplitude of the response is scaled with the synaptic efficacy w_{ij}. The postsynaptic potentials are summed until the firing threshold ϑ is reached. In Fig. 4.9 we have assumed a constant threshold. Each output spike is approximated by a δ pulse, followed by a reset to a value below resting potential so as to account for a hyperpolarizing spike-afterpotential,

$$\eta(t - \hat{t}) = \delta(t - \hat{t}) - \eta_0 \exp\left(-\frac{t - \hat{t}}{\tau_{\text{recov}}}\right), \quad (4.43)$$

with a parameter $\eta_0 > 0$. The spike-afterpotential decays back to zero with a recovery time constant τ_{recov}. This simple version of the SRM (SRM$_0$ for short) has been used in the analysis of the computational power of spiking neurons (Maass, 1996, 1998), of network synchronization (Gerstner et al., 1996b), and collective phenomena in locally coupled networks (Kistler et al., 1998; Kistler, 2000). The model defined in Eq. (4.42) can also be fitted to experimental data (Brillinger and Segundo, 1979; Brillinger, 1988, 1992).

Dynamic threshold interpretation

The simplified model SRM$_0$ defined in Eq. (4.42) with the η kernel defined in Eq. (4.43) can be reinterpreted as a model with a dynamic threshold,

$$\vartheta(t - \hat{t}) = \vartheta - \eta_0(t - \hat{t}), \quad (4.44)$$

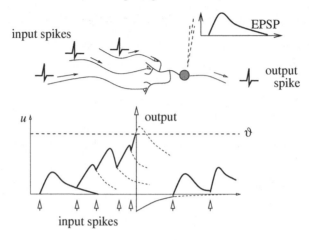

Fig. 4.9. Spike Response Model SRM_0 with constant threshold (schematic). Each input pulse causes an excitatory postsynaptic potential (EPSP) $\epsilon_0(s)$. All EPSPs are added. If the threshold is reached an output spike is emitted (arrow) and a negative kernel $\eta(s)$ is added so that the voltage is reset.

that is increased after each spike. Firing occurs if

$$h_i(t) = \vartheta(t - \hat{t}), \qquad (4.45)$$

where h_i is the input potential,

$$h_i(t) = \sum_j w_{ij} \sum_{t_j^{(f)}} \epsilon_0(t - t_j^{(f)}) + \int_0^\infty \kappa_0(s)\, I^{\text{ext}}(t - s)\, ds. \qquad (4.46)$$

We emphasize that h_i depends on the input only. In particular, there is no dependence upon $\hat{t}_i$. The next spike occurs if the input potential $h_i(t)$ reaches the dynamic threshold $\vartheta(t - \hat{t})$; cf. Fig. 4.10.

Relation to the integrate-and-fire model

The basic equation of the leaky integrate-and-fire model, Eq. (4.3), is a *linear* differential equation. However, because of the reset of the membrane potential after firing, the integration is not completely trivial. In fact, there are two different ways of proceeding with the integration of Eq. (4.3). In Section 4.2.2 we have treated the reset as a new initial condition and thereby constructed an exact mapping of the integrate-and-fire model to the SRM. We now turn to the second method and describe the reset as a current pulse. As we will see, the result is an approximate mapping to the simplified model SRM_0.

Let us consider a short current pulse $I_i^{\text{out}} = -q\,\delta(t)$ applied to the RC circuit of Fig. 4.1. It removes a charge q from the capacitor C and lowers the potential

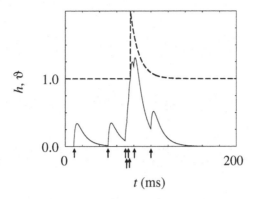

Fig. 4.10. Dynamic threshold interpretation. The input potential $h(t)$ (solid line) is generated by the superposition of the EPSPs (solid line) caused by presynaptic spikes. Each spike arrival is denoted by an arrow. An output spike occurs, if h hits the dynamic threshold ϑ (dashed line). At the moment of spiking the value of the threshold is increased by one. After the spike, the threshold decays exponentially back to its resting value $\vartheta = 1$.

by an amount $\Delta u = -q/C$. Thus, a reset of the membrane potential from a value of $u = \vartheta$ to a new value $u = u_r$ corresponds to an "output" current pulse which removes a charge $q = C(\vartheta - u_r)$. The reset takes place every time the neuron fires. The total reset current is therefore

$$I_i^{\text{out}}(t) = -C(\vartheta - u_r) \sum_f \delta(t - t_i^{(f)}),\qquad(4.47)$$

where the sum runs over all firing times $t_i^{(f)}$. We add the output current (4.47) on the right-hand side of (4.3),

$$\tau_m \frac{du_i}{dt} = -u_i(t) + R\,I_i(t) + R\,I_i^{\text{out}}(t).\qquad(4.48)$$

Here, I_i is the total input current to neuron i, generated by presynaptic spike arrival and by external stimulation $I_i^{\text{ext}}(t)$. Let us assume that each presynaptic pulse evokes a postsynaptic current with time course $\alpha(t - t_j^{(f)})$. The total input current is then

$$I_i(t) = \sum_j w_{ij} \sum_f \alpha(t - t_j^{(f)}) + I_i^{\text{ext}}(t).\qquad(4.49)$$

Since Eq. (4.48) is a linear equation, we can integrate each term separately and superimpose the result at the end. The output pulse I_i^{out} yields a refractory kernel η_0 while each postsynaptic current pulse α generates a postsynaptic potential ϵ_0. More

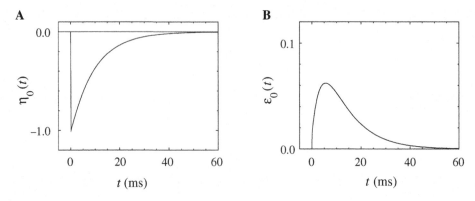

Fig. 4.11. **A.** The refractory kernel η_0 of the integrate-and-fire model with membrane time constant $\tau_m = 10$ ms. **B.** The postsynaptic potential $\epsilon_0(t)$ generated by an exponential current pulse $\alpha(t) \propto \exp(-t/\tau_s)$.

specifically, we have after integration with initial condition $\lim_{t_0 \to -\infty} u_i(t_0) = 0$

$$u_i(t) \;\; = \;\; \sum_f \eta_0(t - t_i^{(f)}) + \sum_j w_{ij} \sum_f \epsilon_0(t - t_j^{(f)})$$

$$+ \int_0^\infty \kappa_0(s)\, I_i^{\text{ext}}(t - s)\, \mathrm{d}s \,, \tag{4.50}$$

with kernels

$$\eta_0(s) \;\; = \;\; -(\vartheta - u_r) \exp\left(-\frac{s}{\tau_m}\right) \Theta(s) \,, \tag{4.51}$$

$$\epsilon_0(s) \;\; = \;\; \frac{1}{C} \int_0^\infty \exp\left(-\frac{s'}{\tau_m}\right) \alpha(s - s')\, \mathrm{d}s'\, \Theta(s) \,, \tag{4.52}$$

$$\kappa_0(s) \;\; = \;\; \frac{1}{C} \exp\left(-\frac{s}{\tau_m}\right) \Theta(s) \,. \tag{4.53}$$

The refractory kernel $\eta_0(s)$ and the postsynaptic potential ϵ_0 are shown in Fig. 4.11.

We note that, in contrast to Eq. (4.42), we still have on the right-hand side of Eq. (4.50) a sum over past spikes of neuron i. According to Eq. (4.51) the effect of the η_0 kernel decays with a time constant τ_m. In realistic spike trains, the interval between two spikes is typically much longer than the membrane time constant τ_m. Hence the sum over the η_0 terms is usually dominated by the *most recent* firing time of neuron i. We therefore truncate the sum over f and neglect the effect of earlier spikes,

$$\sum_f \eta_0(t - t_i^{(f)}) \;\longrightarrow\; \eta_0(t - \hat{t}_i) \,, \tag{4.54}$$

where $\hat{t}_i = \max\{t_i^{(f)} < t\}$ is the last firing time of neuron i. The approximation

(4.54) is good if the mean firing rate of the neuron is low, i.e., if the intervals between two spikes are much longer than τ_m. Loosely speaking, the neuron remembers only its most recent firing. Equation (4.54) is therefore called "short-term memory approximation" (Gerstner et al., 1996b). The final equation is

$$u_i(t) = \eta_0(t - \hat{t}_i) + \sum_j w_{ij} \sum_f \epsilon_0(t - t_j^{(f)}) + \int_0^\infty \kappa(s)\, I^{\text{ext}}(t - s)\, ds \,. \quad (4.55)$$

This is exactly the equation for the model SRM$_0$, defined in (4.42). Note that we have kept, on the right-hand side of (4.55), the sum over all *presynaptic* firing times $t_j^{(f)}$. Only the sum over the η_0's has been truncated.

A careful comparison of Eq. (4.51) with Eq. (4.35) shows that the kernel η_0 is different from the kernel η derived previously for the *exact* mapping of the integrate-and-fire model to the full SRM. The difference is most easily seen if we set the reset potential to $u_r = 0$. While the kernel η in Eq. (4.35) vanishes in this case, the kernel η_0 is nonzero. In fact, whereas in the full SRM the reset is taken care of by the definition of $\epsilon(t - \hat{t}, s)$ and $\kappa(t - \hat{t}, s)$, the reset in the simplified model SRM$_0$ is included in the kernel η_0. The relation between the kernels of the simplified model SRM$_0$ to that of the full model are discussed below in more detail.

Example: postsynaptic potential ϵ_0

If $\alpha(s)$ is given by Eq. (4.21), then the integral on the right-hand side of Eq. (4.52) can be done and yields

$$\epsilon_0(s) = \frac{1}{1 - (\tau_s/\tau_m)} \left[\exp\left(-\frac{s}{\tau_m}\right) - \exp\left(-\frac{s}{\tau_s}\right) \right] \Theta(s) \,, \quad (4.56)$$

where we have set $q = C = 1$. This is the postsynaptic potential ϵ_0 illustrated in Fig. 4.11B. We note that ϵ_0 defined in Eq. (4.56) is closely related, but not identical to the kernel ϵ introduced in Eq. (4.39).

Relation between the kernels ϵ_0 and ϵ (*)

What is the relation between the ϵ kernel derived in Eq. (4.36) and the ϵ_0 introduced in Eq. (4.52)? We will show in this paragraph that

$$\epsilon(s, t) = \epsilon_0(t) - \exp\left(-\frac{s}{\tau_m}\right) \epsilon_0(t - s) \quad (4.57)$$

holds. To this end we rewrite Eq. (4.36) as

$$\epsilon(s,t) = \frac{1}{C} \int_0^\infty \exp\left(-\frac{t'}{\tau_m}\right) \alpha(t-t')\,dt' - \frac{1}{C} \int_s^\infty \exp\left(-\frac{t'}{\tau_m}\right) \alpha(t-t')\,dt'$$

$$= \frac{1}{C} \int_0^\infty \exp\left(-\frac{t'}{\tau_m}\right) \alpha(t-t')\,dt'$$

$$- \exp\left(-\frac{s}{\tau_m}\right) \frac{1}{C} \int_0^\infty \exp\left(-\frac{t'}{\tau_m}\right) \alpha(t-t'-s)\,dt'. \tag{4.58}$$

Using the definition (4.52) of ϵ_0 yields Eq. (4.57).

By a completely analogous sequence of transformations it is possible to show that

$$\kappa(x,s) = \kappa_0(s) - \exp\left(-\frac{x}{\tau_m}\right) \kappa_0(s-x). \tag{4.59}$$

The total postsynaptic potential $h(t|\hat{t}_i)$ defined in Eq. (4.28) can therefore be expressed via the input potential $h_i(t)$ (Gerstner, 2000)

$$h(t|\hat{t}_i) = h_i(t) - \exp\left(-\frac{t-\hat{t}_i}{\tau_m}\right) h_i(\hat{t}_i) \tag{4.60}$$

As expected, the reset at $\hat{t}_i$ has an influence on the total postsynaptic potential. We emphasize that the expressions (4.58)–(4.60) hold only for the integrate-and-fire model.

Similarly we can compare the η kernel in Eq. (4.35) and the η_0 kernel defined in Eq. (4.51),

$$\eta(s) = \eta_0(s) + \vartheta \exp\left(-\frac{s}{\tau_m}\right). \tag{4.61}$$

We can thus write the potential in the form

$$u_i(t) = \eta(t-\hat{t}_i) + h(t|\hat{t}_i)$$

$$= \eta_0(t-\hat{t}_i) + h(t) - [h(\hat{t}_i) - \vartheta] \exp\left(-\frac{t-\hat{t}_i}{\tau_m}\right). \tag{4.62}$$

The truncation in (4.54) is therefore equivalent to a neglection of the last term in Eq. (4.62).

4.3 From detailed models to formal spiking neurons

In this section we study the relation between detailed conductance-based neuron models and formal spiking neurons as introduced above. In Section 4.3.1, we discuss how an approximate mapping between the Spike Response Model (SRM) and the Hodgkin–Huxley model can be established. While the Hodgkin–Huxley model is of type II, cortical neurons are usually described by type I models. In Section 4.3.2 we focus on a type-I model of cortical interneurons and reduce it systematically to different variants of spiking neuron models, in particular to a nonlinear integrate-and-fire model and a SRM. In all sections, the performance of the reduced models is compared to that of the full model. To do so we test the models with a constant or fluctuating input current.

4.3.1 Reduction of the Hodgkin–Huxley model

The system of equations proposed by Hodgkin and Huxley (see Section 2.2) is rather complicated. It consists of four coupled nonlinear differential equations and as such is difficult to analyze mathematically. For this reason, several simplifications of the Hodgkin–Huxley equations have been proposed. The most common approach reduces the set of four differential equations to a two-dimensional problem as discussed in Chapter 3. In this section, we will take a somewhat different approach to reduce the four Hodgkin–Huxley equations to a single variable $u(t)$, the membrane potential of the neuron (Kistler et al., 1997). As we have seen in Fig. 2.4B, the Hodgkin–Huxley model shows a sharp, threshold-like transition between an action potential (spike) for a strong stimulus and a graded response (no spike) for a slightly weaker stimulus. This suggests the idea that emission of an action potential can be described by a threshold process. We therefore aim for a reduction towards a spiking neuron model where spikes are triggered by a voltage threshold. Specifically, we will establish an approximate mapping between the SRM and the Hodgkin–Huxley model.

Action potentials in the Hodgkin–Huxley model have the stereotyped time course shown in Fig. 2.4A. Whatever the stimulating current that has triggered the spike, the form of the action potential is always roughly the same (as long as the current stays in a biologically realistic regime). This is the major observation that we will exploit in the following. Let us consider the spike that has been triggered at time $\hat{t}$. If no further input is applied for $t > \hat{t}$, the voltage trajectory will have a pulse-like excursion before it eventually returns to the resting potential. For $t > \hat{t}$, we may therefore set $u(t) = \eta(t - \hat{t}) + u_{\text{rest}}$ where η is the standard shape of the pulse and u_{rest} is the resting potential. We have $\eta(t - \hat{t}) \to 0$ for $t - \hat{t} \to \infty$, because, without further input, the voltage will eventually approach the resting value.

Let us now consider an additional small input current pulse I which is applied at $t > \hat{t}$. Due to the input, the membrane potential will be slightly perturbed from its trajectory. If the input current is sufficiently small, the perturbation can be described by a linear impulse response function κ. The response to an input pulse, and therewith the response kernel κ, can depend on the arrival time of the input relative to the last spike at $\hat{t}$. For an input with arbitrary time course $I(t)$ we therefore set

$$u(t) = \eta(t - \hat{t}) + \int_0^{t-\hat{t}} \kappa(t - \hat{t}, s) I(t - s) \, ds + u_{rest}. \tag{4.63}$$

Equation (4.63) is a special case of the SRM introduced in Section 4.2. Note that after an appropriate shift of the voltage scale the resting potential can always be set to zero, $u_{rest} = 0$.

To construct an approximate mapping between the SRM and the Hodgkin–Huxley equations, we have to determine the following three terms in Eq. (4.63): (i) the kernel η which describes the response to spike emission, (ii) the kernel κ which describes the response to incoming current, and (iii) the value of the threshold ϑ.

The η kernel

In the absence of input the membrane potential u is at its resting value u_{rest}. If we apply a strong current pulse, an action potential will be triggered. The time course of the action potential determines the kernel η.

To find the kernel η we use the following procedure. We take a square current pulse of the form

$$I(t) = c \frac{q_0}{\Delta} \Theta(t) \Theta(\Delta - t) \tag{4.64}$$

with duration $\Delta = 1$ ms, a unit charge q_0, and c a parameter chosen large enough to evoke a spike. The kernel η allows us to describe the standard form of the spike and the spike-afterpotential. We set

$$\eta(t - \hat{t}) = [u(t) - u_{rest}] \Theta(t - \hat{t}). \tag{4.65}$$

Here, $u(t)$ is the voltage trajectory caused by the supra-threshold current pulse. The firing time $\hat{t}$ is defined by the moment when u crosses the threshold ϑ from below. The kernel $\eta(s)$ with its pronounced hyperpolarizing spike-afterpotential that extends over more than 15 ms is shown in Fig. 4.12A.

The κ kernel

The kernel κ characterizes the linear response of the neuron to a weak input current pulse. To measure κ we use a first strong pulse to initiate a spike at a time $\hat{t} < 0$ and then apply a second weak pulse at $t = 0$. The second pulse is a short stimulus as in Eq. (4.64), but with a small amplitude so that nonlinear effects in the response can be neglected. The result is a membrane potential with time course $u(t)$. Without the second pulse the time course of the potential would be $u_0(t) = \eta(t - \hat{t}) + u_{rest}$

A

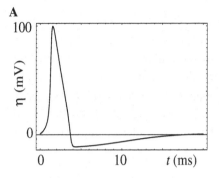

B

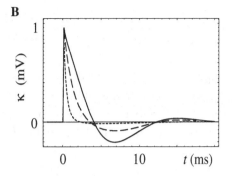

Fig. 4.12. **A**. The action potential of the Hodgkin–Huxley model defines the kernel η. The spike has been triggered at $t = 0$. **B**. The voltage response of the Hodgkin–Huxley model to a short subthreshold current pulse defines the kernel κ. The input pulse was applied at $t = 0$. The last output spike occurred at $\hat{t} = -\Delta t$. We plot the time course $\kappa(\Delta t + t, t)$. For $\Delta t \to \infty$ we get the response shown by the solid line. For finite Δt (dashed line, output spike $\Delta t = 10.5$ ms before the input spike; dotted line $\Delta t = 6.5$ ms), the duration of the response is reduced due to refractoriness; cf. Fig. 2.7B. Taken from Kistler et al. (1997).

for $t > \hat{t}$. The net effect of the second pulse is $u(t) - u_0(t)$, hence

$$\kappa(t - \hat{t}, t) = \frac{1}{c} \left[u(t) - \eta(t - \hat{t}) - u_{\text{rest}} \right]. \tag{4.66}$$

We repeat the above procedure for various spike times $\hat{t}$.

The result is shown in Fig. 4.12. Since the input current pulse delivers its charge during a very short amount of time, the κ-kernel jumps instantaneously at time $t = 0$ to a value of 1 mV. Afterwards it decays, with a slight oscillation, back to zero. The oscillatory behavior is characteristic of type-II neuron models (Izhikevich, 2001). The decay of the oscillation is faster if there has been a spike in the recent past. This is easy to understand intuitively. During and immediately after an action potential many ion channels are open. The resistance of the cell membrane is therefore reduced and the effective membrane time constant is shorter; cf. Fig. 2.7B.

The threshold ϑ

The third term to be determined is the threshold ϑ which we will take as fixed. Even though Fig. 2.4B suggests that the Hodgkin–Huxley equations exhibit a certain form of threshold behavior, the threshold is not well defined (Koch et al., 1995; Rinzel and Ermentrout, 1998) and it is fairly difficult to estimate a voltage threshold directly from a single series of simulations. We therefore take the threshold as a free parameter which will be adjusted by a procedure discussed below.

Input scenarios

In order to test the fidelity of the SRM we use the same input scenarios as in Section 2.2 for the Hodgkin–Huxley model. In particular, we consider constant input current, step current, and fluctuating input current. We start with the time-dependent fluctuating input, since this is probably the most realistic scenario. We will see that the SRM with the kernels that have been derived above can approximate the spike train of the Hodgkin–Huxley model to a high degree of accuracy.

Example: stimulation by time-dependent input

To test the quality of the SRM approximation we compare the spike trains generated by the SRM with that of the full Hodgkin–Huxley model defined in Eqs. (2.4)–(2.6). We study the case of a time-dependent input current $I(t)$ generated by the procedure discussed in Section 2.2.2; cf. Fig. 2.7. The same current is applied to both the Hodgkin–Huxley and the SRM. The threshold ϑ of the SRM has been adjusted so that the total number of spikes was about the same as in the Hodgkin–Huxley model; see Kistler et al. (1997) for details. In Fig. 4.13 the voltage trace of the Hodgkin–Huxley model is compared to that of the SRM with the kernels η and κ derived above. We see that the approximation is excellent both in the absence of spikes and during spiking. As an aside we note that it is indeed important to include the dependence of the kernel κ upon the last output spike time $\hat{t}$. If we neglected that dependence and used $\kappa(\infty, s)$ instead of $\kappa(t - \hat{t}, s)$, then the approximation during and immediately after a spike would be significantly worse; see the dotted line in the lower right graph of Fig. 4.13.

To check whether both models generated spikes at the same time we introduce the coincidence rate

$$\Gamma = \frac{N_{\text{coinc}} - \langle N_{\text{coinc}} \rangle}{\frac{1}{2}(N_{\text{SRM}} + N_{\text{full}})} \frac{1}{\mathcal{N}}, \tag{4.67}$$

where N_{SRM} is the number of spikes of the SRM, N_{full} is the number of spikes of the full Hodgkin–Huxley model, N_{coinc} is the number of coincidences with precision Δ, and $\langle N_{\text{coinc}} \rangle = 2\nu \Delta N_{\text{full}}$ is the expected number of coincidences generated by a homogeneous Poisson process with the same rate ν as the SRM. The factor $\mathcal{N} = 1 - 2\nu \Delta$ normalizes Γ to a maximum value of one which is reached if the spike train of the SRM reproduces exactly that of the full model. A homogeneous Poisson process with the same number of spikes as the SRM would yield $\Gamma = 0$.

We find that the SRM reproduces the firing times and the voltage time course of the Hodgkin–Huxley model to a high degree of accuracy; cf. Fig. 4.13. More precisely, the SRM achieves with a fluctuating input current a coincidence rate Γ of about 0.85 (Kistler et al., 1997). On the other hand, a leaky integrate-and-

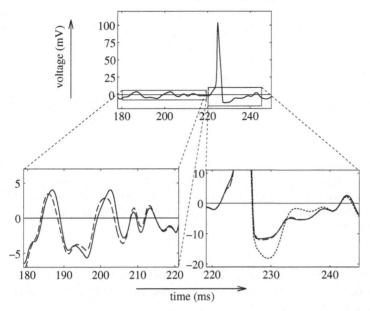

Fig. 4.13. A segment of the spike train of Fig. 2.7. The inset in the lower left corner shows the voltage of the Hodgkin–Huxley model (solid) together with the approximation of the SRM defined by Eq. (4.63) (long-dashed line) during a period where no spike occurs. The approximation is excellent. The inset on the lower right shows the situation during and after a spike. Again the approximation by the long-dashed line is excellent. For comparison, we also show the approximation by the SRM_0 model which is significantly worse (dotted line). Taken from Kistler et al. (1997).

fire model with optimized time constant and fixed threshold yields coincidence rates in the range of only 0.45. The difference in the performance of the SRM and integrate-and-fire models is not too surprising because the SRM accounts for the hyperpolarizing spike-afterpotential; cf. Fig 4.12A. In fact, an integrate-and-fire model with spike-afterpotential (or equivalently a dynamic threshold) achieves coincidence rates in the range of $\Gamma \approx 0.7$ (Kistler et al., 1997). Furthermore, the κ kernel of the SRM describes the reduced responsiveness of the Hodgkin–Huxley model immediately after a spike; cf. Fig 4.12B. The model SRM_0 (with a kernel κ that does not depend on $t - \hat{t}$) yields a coincidence rate Γ that is significantly lower than that of the full SRM.

Example: constant input and mean firing rates

We study the response of the SRM to constant stimulation using the kernels derived by the procedure described above. The result is shown in Fig. 4.14. As mentioned above, we take the threshold ϑ as a free parameter. If ϑ is optimized for stationary input, the frequency plots of the Hodgkin–Huxley model and the SRM are rather

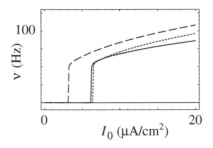

Fig. 4.14. The firing rate ν as a function of the input current I_0 of the Hodgkin–Huxley model (solid line) is compared to that of the SRM. Two cases are shown. If the threshold ϑ is optimized for the constant-input scenario, we get the dotted line. If we take the same value of the threshold as in the dynamic-input scenario of the previous figure, we find the long-dashed line. Taken from Kistler et al. (1997).

similar. On the other hand, if we took the value of the threshold that was found for time-dependent input, the current threshold for the SRM would be quite different as shown by the long-dashed line in Fig. 4.14.

Example: step current input

As a third input paradigm, we test the SRM with step current input. For ϑ we take the value found for the scenario with time-dependent input. The result is shown in Fig. 4.15. The SRM shows the same three regimes as the Hodgkin–Huxley model. In particular, the effect of inhibitory rebound is present in the SRM. The location of the phase boundaries depends on the choice of ϑ.

Example: spike input

In the Hodgkin–Huxley model (2.4), input is formulated as an explicit driving current $I(t)$. In networks of neurons, input typically consists of the spikes of presynaptic neurons. Let us, for the sake of simplicity, assume that a spike of a presynaptic neuron j which was emitted at time $t_j^{(f)}$ generates in the postsynaptic neuron i a current $I(t) = w_{ij}\,\alpha(t - t_j^{(f)})$. Here, α describes the time course of the postsynaptic current and w_{ij} scales the amplitude of the current. The voltage of the postsynaptic neuron i changes, according to Eq. (4.63), by an amount $\Delta u_i(t) = w_{ij} \int_0^{t-\hat{t}_i} \kappa(t-\hat{t}_i, s)\,\alpha(t - t_j^{(f)} - s)\,ds$, where $\hat{t}_i$ is the last output spike of neuron i. The voltage response Δu_i to an input current of unit amplitude ($w_{ij} = 1$) defines the postsynaptic potential ϵ, hence

$$\epsilon(t - \hat{t}_i, t - t_j^{(f)}) = \int_0^{t-\hat{t}_i} \kappa(t - \hat{t}_i, s)\,\alpha(t - t_j^{(f)} - s)\,ds. \qquad (4.68)$$

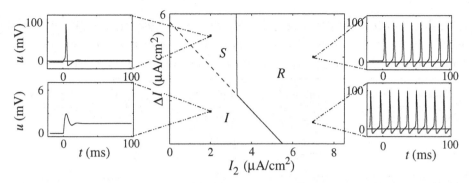

Fig. 4.15. Phase diagram of the SRM for stimulation with a step current. Kernels ϵ and η are adapted to the Hodgkin–Huxley model. The current I is switched at $t = 0$ from I_1 to I_2. The y-axis is the step size ΔI. Three regimes denoted by S, R, and I may be distinguished. In I no action potential is initiated (inactive regime). In S, a single spike is initiated by the current step (single spike regime). In R, periodic spike trains are triggered by the current step (repetitive firing). Examples of voltage traces in the different regimes are presented in the smaller graphs to the left and right of the phase diagram in the center. The phase diagram should be compared to that of the Hodgkin–Huxley model in Fig. 2.6. Taken from Kistler et al. (1997).

What is the meaning of the definition in Eq. (4.68)? If several presynaptic neurons j transmit spikes to neuron i, then the total membrane potential of the postsynaptic neuron is in analogy to Eq. (4.63)

$$u_i(t) = \eta(t - \hat{t}_i) + \sum_j w_{ij} \sum_f \epsilon(t - \hat{t}_i, t - t_j^{(f)}) + u_{\text{rest}} . \qquad (4.69)$$

Equation (4.69) is the standard equation of the SRM. We emphasize that the time course of the postsynaptic potential depends on $t - \hat{t}_i$; the first argument of ϵ takes care of this dependence.

4.3.2 Reduction of a cortical neuron model

We have seen in the previous section that the Spike Response Model (SRM) can provide a good quantitative approximation of the Hodgkin–Huxley model. Though the Hodgkin–Huxley equation captures the essence of spike generation it is "only" a model of the giant axon of the squid which has electrical properties that are quite different from those of cortical neurons we are mostly interested in. The natural question is thus whether the SRM can also be used as a quantitative model of cortical neurons. In the following we discuss a conductance-based neuron model for a cortical interneuron and show how such a model can be reduced to a (nonlinear) integrate-and-fire model or to a SRM.

Table 4.1. *Cortical neuron model. The equilibrium value $x_0(u) = \alpha/(\alpha + \beta)$ is reached with a time constant $\tau_x(u) = 1/(\alpha + \beta)$ where x stands for one of the gating variables $m, h, n_{\text{slow}}, n_{\text{fast}}$. Membrane capacity $C = 1.0\ \mu F/cm^2$.*

Channel	Variable	α (u in mV)	β (u in mV)	g_x (mS/cm^2)	E_x (mV)
Na	m	$\dfrac{-3020+40\,u}{1-\exp\left(-\frac{u-75.5}{13.5}\right)}$	$\dfrac{1.2262}{\exp\left(\frac{u}{42.248}\right)}$	112.5	74
	h	$\dfrac{0.0035}{\exp\left(\frac{u}{24.186}\right)}$	$\dfrac{0.8712+0.017\,u}{1-\exp\left(-\frac{51.25+u}{5.2}\right)}$		
K_{slow}	n_{slow}	$\dfrac{0.014\,(44+u)}{1-\exp\left(-\frac{44+u}{2.3}\right)}$	$\dfrac{0.0043}{\exp\left(\frac{44+u}{34}\right)}$	0.225	-90
K_{fast}	n_{fast}	$\dfrac{u-95}{1-\exp\left(-\frac{u-95}{11.8}\right)}$	$\dfrac{0.025}{\exp\left(\frac{u}{22.22}\right)}$	225	-90
Leak				0.25	-70

The starting point is a conductance-based model that was originally proposed as a model of fast-spiking neocortical interneurons (Erisir et al., 1999). We have chosen this specific model for two reasons. Firstly, just as most other cortical neuron models, this model has – after a minor modification – a continuous gain function (Lewis and Gerstner, 2001) and can hence be classified as a type I model (Ermentrout, 1996). This is in contrast to the Hodgkin–Huxley model which exhibits a discontinuity in the gain function and is hence type II. Secondly, this is a model for interneurons that show little adaptation, so that we avoid most of the complications caused by slow ionic processes that cannot be captured by the class of spiking neuron models reviewed above. Furthermore, the model is comparatively simple, so that we can hope to illustrate the steps necessary for a reduction to formal spiking neuron models in a transparent manner.

The model neuron consists of a single compartment with a nonspecific leak current and three types of ion current, i.e., a Hodgkin–Huxley type sodium current $I_{\text{Na}} = g_{\text{Na}}\, m^3\, h\, (u - E_{\text{Na}})$, a slow potassium current $I_{\text{slow}} = g_{K_{\text{slow}}}\, n_{\text{slow}}^4\, (u - E_K)$, and a fast potassium current $I_{\text{fast}} = g_{K_{\text{fast}}}\, n_{\text{fast}}^2\, (u - E_K)$. The response properties of the cortical neuron model to pulse input and constant current have already been discussed in Section 2.3; cf. Fig. 2.11. We now want to reduce the model to a nonlinear integrate-and fire model or, alternatively, to a SRM. We start with the reduction to an integrate-and-fire model.

Reduction to a nonlinear integrate-and-fire model

In order to reduce the dynamics of the full cortical neuron model to that of an integrate-and-fire model we proceed in two steps. As a first step, we keep all

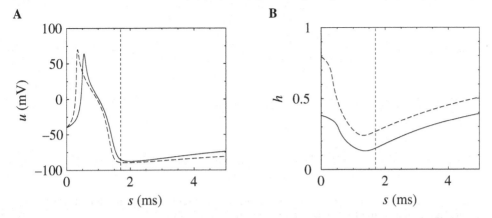

Fig. 4.16. Dynamics during a spike. **A**. Action potentials have roughly the same shape, whether they are triggered by a constant current of 5 μA/cm^2 (solid line) or by a single 2-ms current pulse of amplitude 20 μA/cm^2 (dashed line). **B**. The time course of the gating variable h is, however, significantly different. The time $s = 0$ marks the moment when the voltage rises above −40 mV. The vertical dotted line indicates the absolute refractory period $\Delta^{\text{abs}} = 1.7$ ms.

variables, but introduce a threshold for spike initiation. We call this the multicurrent integrate-and-fire model. In the second step, we separate gating variables into fast and slow ones. "Fast" variables are replaced by their steady-state values, while "slow" variables are replaced by constants. The result is the desired nonlinear integrate-and-fire model with a single dynamical variable.

In step (i), we make use of the observation that the shape of an action potential of the cortical neuron model is always roughly the same, independently of the way the spike is initiated; cf. Fig. 4.16. Instead of calculating the shape of an action potential again and again, we can therefore simply stop the costly numerical integration of the nonlinear differential equations as soon as a spike is triggered and restart the integration after the downstroke of the spike about 1.5–2 ms later. We call such a scheme a multicurrent integrate-and-fire model. The interval between the spike trigger time $\hat{t}$ and the restart of the integration corresponds to an absolute refractory period Δ^{abs}.

In order to transform the cortical neuron model into a multicurrent integrate-and-fire model we have to define a voltage threshold ϑ, a refractory time Δ^{abs}, and the reset values from which the integration is restarted. We fix the threshold at $\vartheta = -40$ mV; the exact value is not critical and we could take values of −20 mV or −45 mV without changing the results. For $\vartheta = -40$ mV, a refractory time $\Delta^{\text{abs}} = 1.7$ ms and a reset voltage $u_r = -85$ mV is suitable; cf. Fig. 4.16.

To restart the integration of the differential equation we also have to specify initial conditions for the gating variables m, h, n_{slow}, and n_{fast}. This, however,

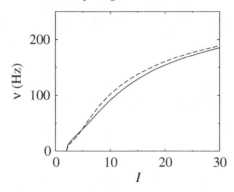

Fig. 4.17. The gain function of the multicurrent integrate-and-fire model (dashed line) compared to that of the full model (solid line).

involves a severe simplification, because their time course is not as stereotyped as that of the membrane potential, but depends on the choice of the input scenario; cf. Fig. 4.16B. In the following we optimize the reset values for a scenario with a constant input current $I^{\text{ext}} = 5\ \mu\text{A/cm}^2$ that leads to repetitive firing at about 40 Hz. The reset values are $m_r = 0.0$; $h_r = 0.16$; $n_{\text{slow},r} = 0.874$; $n_{\text{fast},r} = 0.2$; and $u_r = -85$ mV. This set of parameters yields a near-perfect fit of the time course of the membrane potential during repetitive firing at 40 Hz and approximates the gain function of the full cortical neuron model to a high degree of accuracy; cf. Fig. 4.17.

So far the model contains four gating variables, m, h, n_{slow}, and n_{fast} as well as the membrane potential, u. To eliminate the differential equations that describe the dynamics of the gating variables we have two options. Firstly, if a certain gating variable x is fast as compared to u, then we can replace x by its steady-state value $x_0(u)$. Secondly, if x is evolving much slower than u then we replace x by a constant. Here, m is the only fast variable and we replace $m(t)$ by its steady-state value $m_0[u(t)]$. The treatment of the other gating variables deserves some extra discussion.

A thorough inspection of the time course of $n_{\text{fast}}(t)$ shows that for most of the time n_{fast} is close to its resting value, except for a 2-ms interval during and immediately after the downstroke of an action potential. If we take a refractory time of $\Delta^{\text{abs}} = 4$ ms, most of the excursion trajectory of n_{fast} falls within the refractory period. Between spikes we can therefore replace n_{fast} by its equilibrium value at rest $n_{\text{fast,rest}} = n_{0,\text{fast}}(u_{\text{rest}})$.

The gating variables h and n_{slow} vary slowly, so that the variables may be replaced by averaged values h_{av} and $n_{\text{slow,av}}$. The average, however, depends on the input scenario. We stick to a regime with repetitive firing at 40 Hz where $h_{\text{av}} = 0.7$ and $n_{\text{slow,av}} = 0.8$.

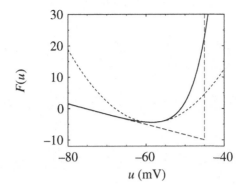

Fig. 4.18. The function $F(u)$ of a nonlinear integrate-and-fire neuron (solid line) derived from a cortical neuron model is compared to a quadratic (dotted line) and a linear (long-dashed line) approximation. The linear approximation stops at the threshold $\vartheta = -45$ mV (vertical line).

With $m = m_0(u)$ and constant values for h, n_{slow}, and n_{fast}, the dynamics of the full cortical neuron model reduces to

$$C \frac{du}{dt} = g_{\text{Na}} [m_0(u)]^3 h_{\text{av}} (u - E_{\text{Na}}) + g_{\text{Kslow}} n^2_{\text{slow,av}} (u - E_{\text{K}})$$

$$+ g_{\text{Kfast}} n^4_{\text{fast,rest}} (u - E_{\text{K}}) + g_l (u - E_l) + I^{\text{ext}}(t). \qquad (4.70)$$

After division by C, we arrive at a single nonlinear equation

$$\frac{du}{dt} = F(u) + \frac{1}{C} I^{\text{ext}}(t). \qquad (4.71)$$

The passive membrane time constant of the model is inversely proportional to the slope of F at rest: $\tau = |dF/du|^{-1}_{u=u_{\text{rest}}}$. In principle the function F could be further approximated by a linear function with slope $-1/\tau$ and then combined with a threshold at, e.g., $\vartheta = -45$ mV. This would yield a linear integrate-and-fire model. Alternatively, F can be approximated by a quadratic function which leads us to a quadratic integrate-and-fire neuron; cf. Fig. 4.18.

To test the fidelity of the reduction to a nonlinear integrate-and-fire model, we compare its behavior to that of the full cortical neuron model for various input scenarios. It turns out that the behavior of the model is good as long as the mean firing rate is in the range of 40 Hz, which is not too surprising given the optimization of the parameters for this firing rate. Outside the range of 40 ± 10 Hz there are substantial discrepancies between the reduced and the full model.

Example: constant input

Let us focus on constant input first. With our set of parameters we get a fair approximation of the gain function, except that the threshold for repetitive firing is

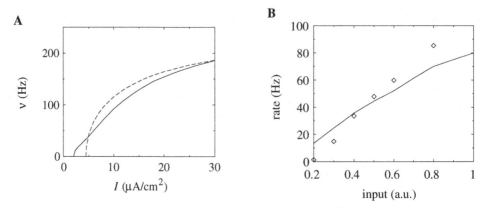

Fig. 4.19. **A** Gain function for stationary input. The firing rate versus the input current of the full cortical neuron model (solid line) compared to that of a nonlinear integrate-and-fire model (long-dashed line). **B**. Fluctuating input. The mean firing rate of the full cortical neuron model (solid line) compared to that of the nonlinear integrate-and-fire model (diamonds) as a function of the amplitude of the input fluctuations. At an amplitude of 0.4 (arbitrary units) both the full and the integrate-and-fire models fire at about 40 Hz.

not reproduced correctly; cf. Fig. 4.19A. We note that the firing rate at a stimulation of 5 μA/cm^2 is reproduced correctly which is no surprise since our choice of parameters has been based on this input amplitude.

Example: fluctuating input

For a critical test of the nonlinear integrate-and-fire model, we use a fluctuating input current with zero mean. The amplitude of the fluctuations determines the mean firing rate. The nonlinear integrate-and-fire model, however, does not reproduce the firing rate as a function of the fluctuation amplitude of the full model, except at $\nu \approx 40$ Hz; cf. Figure 4.19B.

For a more detailed comparison of the nonlinear integrate-and-fire with the full model, we stimulate both models with the same fluctuating current. From Fig. 4.20A, we see that the voltage time course of the two models is indistinguishable most of the time. Occasionally, the nonlinear integrate-and-fire model misses a spike, or adds an extra spike. For this specific input scenario (where the mean firing rate is about 40 Hz), a coincidence rate of about $\Gamma = 0.85$ is achieved (based on a precision of $\Delta = \pm 2$ ms). Outside the regime of $\nu \approx 40$ Hz, the coincidence rate Γ breaks down drastically; cf. Fig. 4.20B.

Reduction to a Spike Response Model

As a second approximation scheme, we consider the reduction of the conductance-based neuron model to a SRM. We thus have to determine the kernels $\eta(t - \hat{t})$, $\kappa(t - \hat{t}, s)$, and adjust the (time-dependent) threshold $\vartheta(t - \hat{t})$. We proceed in

A

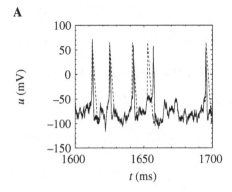

B

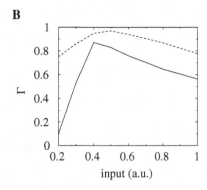

Fig. 4.20. **A**. The spike train of the nonlinear integrate-and-fire model (dashed line) compared to that of the full cortical neuron model (solid line). The integrate-and-fire model fires an extra spike at about $t = 1652$ ms but misses the spike that occurs about 4 ms later. Spikes are replaced by triangular pulses that span the refractory period of $\Delta^{\text{abs}} = 4$ ms. For this input scenario (viz. fluctuation amplitude 0.4), a coincidence rate of about 0.85 is achieved ($\Delta = 2$ ms). **B**. Comparison of the coincidence rates Γ for the multicurrent integrate-and-fire model (dotted line) and the nonlinear integrate-and-fire model (solid line). A value of $\Gamma = 1$ implies perfectly coincident spike trains, while a value of $\Gamma = 0$ implies that coincidences can be explained by chance. For the definition of Γ, see Eq. (4.67).

three steps. As a first step we reduce the model to an integrate-and-fire model with spike-time-dependent time constant. As a second step, we integrate the model so as to derive the kernels η and κ. As a final step, we choose an appropriate spike-time-dependent threshold.

In step (i), we stimulate the full model by a short super-threshold current pulse in order to determine the time course of the action potential and its hyperpolarizing spike-afterpotential. Let us define $\hat{t}$ as the time when the membrane potential crosses an (arbitrarily fixed) threshold ϑ, e.g., $\vartheta = -50$ mV. The time course of the membrane potential for $t > \hat{t}$, i.e., during and after the action potential, defines the kernel $\eta(t-\hat{t})$. If we were interested in a purely phenomenological model, we could simply record the numerical time course $u(t)$ and define $\eta(t - \hat{t}) = u(t) - u_{\text{rest}}$ for $t > \hat{t}$; cf. Section 4.3.1. It is, however, instructive to take a semi-analytical approach and study the four gating variables m, h, n_{slow}, and n_{fast}. About 2 ms after initiation of the spike, all four variables have passed their maximum or minimal values and are on their way back to equilibrium. We set $\Delta^{\text{abs}} = 2$ ms. For $t \geq \hat{t} + \Delta^{\text{abs}}$, we fit the approach to equilibrium by an exponential

$$x(t) = [x_r - x_{\text{rest}}] \exp\left(-\frac{t - \hat{t} - \Delta^{\text{abs}}}{\tau_x}\right) + x_{\text{rest}}, \qquad (4.72)$$

where $x = m, h, n_{\text{slow}}, n_{\text{fast}}$ stands for the four gating variables, τ_x is a fixed time constant, x_r is the initial condition at $t = \hat{t} + \Delta^{abs}$, and $x_{rest} = x_0(u_{rest})$ is the equilibrium value of the gating variable at the resting potential.

Given the time course of the gating variables, we know the conductance of each ion channel as a function of time. For example, the potassium current $I_{K_{fast}}$ is

$$I_{K_{fast}} = g_{K_{fast}} n_{fast}^2 (u - E_K) = g_{fast}(t - \hat{t}) (u - E_K) \tag{4.73}$$

where $g_{fast}(t - \hat{t})$ is an exponential function with time constant $\tau_{n_{fast}}/2$. We insert the time-dependent conductance into the current equation and find for $t \geq \hat{t} + \Delta^{abs}$

$$C \frac{du}{dt} = -\sum_j g_j(t - \hat{t}) (u - E_j) + I^{ext} . \tag{4.74}$$

Here, the sum runs over the four ion channels I_{Na}, $I_{K_{slow}}$, $I_{K_{fast}}$, and I_l. With the definition of an effective time constant, $\tau(t - \hat{t}) = C/\sum_j g_j(t - \hat{t})$, and with $I^{ion} = \sum_j g_j(t - \hat{t}) E_j$ we arrive at

$$\frac{du}{dt} = -\frac{u}{\tau(t - \hat{t})} + \frac{1}{C} I^{ion}(t - \hat{t}) + \frac{1}{C} I^{ext}(t) , \tag{4.75}$$

which is a linear differential equation with spike-time-dependent time constant; cf. Eq. (4.40). The effective time constant is shown in Fig. 4.21.

In step (ii) we integrate Eq. (4.75) with the initial condition

$$u(\hat{t} + \Delta^{abs}) = I^{ion}(\Delta^{abs}) \tau(\Delta^{abs})/C \tag{4.76}$$

and obtain

$$u(t) = \eta(t - \hat{t}) + \int_0^{t - \hat{t} - \Delta^{abs}} \kappa(t - \hat{t}, s) I^{ext}(t - s) \, ds , \tag{4.77}$$

with

$$\kappa(s, t) = \frac{1}{C} \exp\left[-\int_{s-t}^s \frac{dt'}{\tau(t')}\right] \Theta(s - \Delta^{abs} - t) \Theta(t) , \tag{4.78}$$

$$\eta(s) = \frac{1}{C} \int_0^{s-\Delta^{abs}} \exp\left[-\int_{s-t}^s \frac{dt'}{\tau(t')}\right] I^{ion}(s - t) \, dt \, \Theta(s - \Delta^{abs}) . \tag{4.79}$$

Finally, in step (iii) we introduce a dynamical threshold

$$\vartheta(s) = \begin{cases} \vartheta^{refr} & \text{for} \quad 0 < s < \Delta^{abs} \\ \vartheta_0 \left[1 - \exp\left(-\frac{s - \Delta^{abs}}{\tau_\vartheta}\right)\right] & \text{for} \quad s \geq \Delta^{abs} \end{cases} \tag{4.80}$$

in order to fit the gain function for stationary input. During the absolute refractory period Δ^{abs} the threshold has been set to a value $\vartheta^{refr} = 100 \, mV$ that is sufficiently high to prevent the neuron from firing. After refractoriness, the threshold starts at zero and relaxes with a time constant of $\tau_\vartheta = 6 \, ms$ to an asymptotic value of

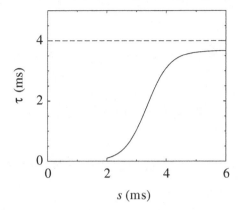

Fig. 4.21. Variable time constant. The Spike Response Model with kernels (4.78) and (4.79) can be interpreted as an integrate-and-fire model with a time constant τ that depends on the time s since the last spike. Integration restarts after an absolute refractory period of 2 ms with a time constant of 0.1 ms. The time constant (solid line) relaxes first rapidly and then more slowly towards its equilibrium value of $\tau \approx 4$ ms (dashed line).

$\vartheta_0 = -50$ mV. With this set of parameters, we get a fair approximation of the gain function of the full cortical neuron model. The approximation for currents that are just super-threshold is bad, but for $I^{\mathrm{ext}} \geq 5$ μA/cm^2 the rates are not too far off, cf. Fig. 4.22A.

Example: fluctuating input

We now test the SRM with the above set of parameters on a scenario with fluctuating input current. The mean firing rate of the full cortical neuron model and the SRM as a function of the fluctuation amplitude are similar; cf. Fig. 4.22B. Moreover, there is a high percentage of firing times of the SRM that coincide with those of the full model with a precision of $\Delta = \pm 2$ ms [coincidence rate $\Gamma = 0.75$; cf. Eq. (4.67)]. A sample spike train is shown in Fig. 4.23A. Figure 4.23B exhibits a plot of the coincidence measure Γ defined in Eq. (4.67) as a function of the fluctuation amplitude. In contrast to the nonlinear integrate-and-fire neuron, the coincidence rate is fairly constant over a broad range of stimulus amplitudes. At low rates, however, the coincidence rate drops off rapidly.

4.3.3 Limitations

Not surprisingly, each approximation scheme is only valid in a limited regime. The natural question is thus whether this is the biologically relevant regime. Since a fluctuating input is probably the most realistic scenario, we have focused our discussion on this form of stimulation. We have seen that in the case of a

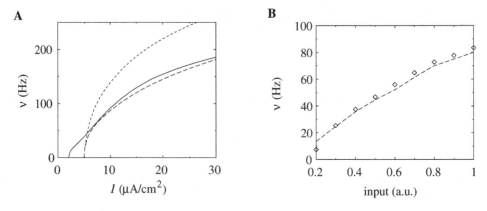

Fig. 4.22. **A**. Stationary input. Gain function of the full model (solid line) and the Spike Response Model with constant (dotted line) and dynamic threshold (long-dashed line). **B**. Fluctuating input. The mean rate of the Spike Response Model (symbols) stimulated by random input is compared with that of the full model for the same input. The amplitude of the random input changes along the horizontal axis.

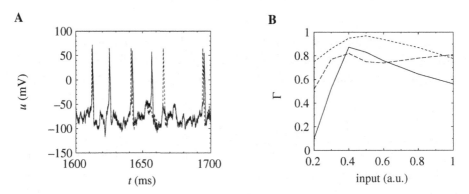

Fig. 4.23. **A**. The spike train of the full model (solid line) is compared to that of the reduced model (dashed line). At about $t = 1655$ ms the reduced model misses a spike while it adds an extra spike about 10 ms later. For this scenario about 80% of the spike times are correct within ± 2 ms. **B**. Comparison of the coincidence rates Γ for the multicurrent integrate-and-fire model (dotted line), the nonlinear integrate-and-fire model (solid line), and the SRM (long-dashed line); cf. Fig. 4.20B.

fluctuating input current, integrate-and-fire and SRM reproduce – to a certain extent – not only the mean firing rate, but also the firing times of the corresponding detailed neuron model. In this discipline, the multicurrent integrate-and-fire model clearly yields the best performance. While it is easy to implement and rapid to simulate, it is difficult to analyze mathematically. Strictly speaking, it does not fall in the class of spiking neuron models reviewed in this chapter. It is interesting to see, however, that even the multicurrent integrate-and-fire model which is based on a seemingly innocent approximation exhibits, for time-dependent input, a coincidence rate Γ significantly below one. On the fluctuating-input task, we find that the single-variable (nonlinear) integrate-and-fire model exhibits a pronounced peak of Γ at the optimal input, but does badly outside this regime. A SRM *without* adapting threshold yields coincidence rates that are not significantly different from the results for the nonlinear integrate-and-fire model. This indicates that the time-dependent threshold that has been included the definition of the SRM is an important component to achieve generalization over a broad range of different inputs. Moreover, the time-dependent threshold seems to be more important for the random-input task than the nonlinearity of the function $F(u)$ in (4.71).

On the other hand, in the immediate neighborhood of the firing threshold, the nonlinear integrate-and-fire model performs better than the SRM. In fact, the SRM systematically fails to reproduce delayed action potentials triggered by an input that is just slightly super-threshold. As we have seen, the nonlinear integrate-and-fire model is related to a canonical type I model and, therefore, exhibits the "correct" behavior in the neighborhood of the firing threshold.

In summary, it is always possible to design an input scenario where formal spiking neuron models fail. For example, none of the models discussed in this chapter is capable of reproducing the effects of a slow adaptation to changes in the input.

4.4 Multicompartment integrate-and-fire model

The models discussed in this chapter are point neurons, i.e., models that do not take into account the spatial structure of a real neuron. In Chapter 2 we have already seen that the electrical properties of dendritic trees can be described by compartmental models. In this section, we want to show that neurons with a linear dendritic tree and a voltage threshold for spike firing at the soma can be mapped, at least approximately, to the Spike Response Model, SRM.

4.4.1 Definition of the model

We study an integrate-and-fire model with a passive dendritic tree described by n compartments. Membrane resistance, core resistance, and capacity of compartment μ are denoted by R_T^μ, R_L^μ, and C^μ, respectively. The longitudinal core resistance between compartment μ and a neighboring compartment ν is $r^{\mu\nu} = (R_L^\mu + R_L^\nu)/2$; cf. Fig. 2.19. Compartment $\mu = 1$ represents the soma and is equipped with a simple mechanism for spike generation, i.e., with a threshold criterion as in the standard integrate-and-fire model. The remaining dendritic compartments ($2 \leq \mu \leq n$) are passive.

Each compartment $1 \leq \mu \leq n$ of neuron i may receive input $I_i^\mu(t)$ from presynaptic neurons. As a result of spike generation, there is an additional reset current $\Omega_i(t)$ at the soma. The membrane potential V_i^μ of compartment μ is given by

$$\frac{d}{dt} V_i^\mu = \frac{1}{C_i^\mu} \left[-\frac{V_i^\mu}{R_{T,i}^\mu} + \sum_\nu \frac{V_i^\mu - V_i^\nu}{r_i^{\mu\nu}} + I_i^\mu(t) - \delta^{\mu 1} \Omega_i(t) \right], \qquad (4.81)$$

where the sum runs over all neighbors of compartment μ. The Kronecker symbol $\delta^{\mu\nu}$ equals unity if the upper indices are equal; otherwise, it is zero. The subscript i is the index of the neuron; the upper indices μ or ν refer to compartments. Below we will identify the somatic voltage V_i^1 with the potential u_i of the SRM.

Equation (4.81) is a system of linear differential equations if the external input current is independent of the membrane potential. The solution of Eq. (4.81) can thus be formulated by means of Green's functions $G_i^{\mu\nu}(s)$ that describe the impact of a current pulse injected in compartment ν on the membrane potential of compartment μ. The solution is of the form

$$V_i^\mu(t) = \sum_\nu \frac{1}{C_i^\nu} \int_0^\infty G_i^{\mu\nu}(s) \left[I_i^\nu(t-s) - \delta^{\nu 1} \Omega_i(t-s) \right] ds. \qquad (4.82)$$

Explicit expressions for the Green's function $G_i^{\mu\nu}(s)$ for arbitrary geometry have been derived by Abbott et al. (1991) and Bressloff and Taylor (1994).

We consider a network made up of a set of neurons described by Eq. (4.81) and a simple threshold criterion for generating spikes. We assume that each spike $t_j^{(f)}$ of a presynaptic neuron j evokes, for $t > t_j^{(f)}$, a synaptic current pulse $\alpha(t - t_j^{(f)})$ into the postsynaptic neuron i; cf. Eq. (4.19). The voltage dependence of the synaptic input is thus neglected and the term $(u_i - E_{\text{syn}})$ in Eq. (4.20) is replaced by a constant. The actual amplitude of the current pulse depends on the strength w_{ij} of the synapse that connects neuron j to neuron i. The total input to compartment μ of neuron i is thus

$$I_i^\mu(t) = \sum_{j \in \Gamma_i^\mu} w_{ij} \sum_f \alpha(t - t_j^{(f)}). \qquad (4.83)$$

Here, Γ_i^μ denotes the set of all neurons that have a synapse with compartment μ of neuron i. The firing times of neuron j are denoted by $t_j^{(f)}$.

In the following we assume that spikes are generated at the soma in the manner of the integrate-and-fire model. That is to say, a spike is triggered as soon as the somatic membrane potential reaches the firing threshold, ϑ. After each spike the somatic membrane potential is reset to $V_i^1 = u_r < \vartheta$. This is equivalent to a current pulse

$$\gamma_i(s) = C_i^1 (\vartheta - u_r) \delta(s), \qquad (4.84)$$

so that the overall current due to the firing of action potentials at the soma of neuron i amounts to

$$\Omega_i(t) = \sum_f \gamma_i(t - t_i^{(f)}).$$ (4.85)

We will refer to Eqs. (4.82)–(4.85) together with the threshold criterion for generating spikes as the multicompartment integrate-and-fire model.

4.4.2 Relation to the model SRM₀

Using the above specializations for the synaptic input current and the somatic reset current the membrane potential of compartment μ in Eq. (4.82) can be rewritten as

$$V_i^\mu(t) = \sum_f \eta_i^\mu(t - t_i^{(f)}) + \sum_\nu \sum_{j \in \Gamma_i^\nu} w_{ij} \sum_f \epsilon_i^{\mu\nu}(t - t_j^{(f)}).$$ (4.86)

with

$$\epsilon_i^{\mu\nu}(s) = \frac{1}{C_i^\nu} \int_0^\infty G_i^{\mu\nu}(s') \alpha(s - s') \, ds',$$ (4.87)

$$\eta_i^\mu(s) = \frac{1}{C_i^1} \int_0^\infty G_i^{\mu 1}(s') \gamma_i(s - s') \, ds'.$$ (4.88)

The kernel $\epsilon_i^{\mu\nu}(s)$ describes the effect of a presynaptic action potential arriving at compartment ν on the membrane potential of compartment μ. Similarly, $\eta_i^\mu(s)$ describes the response of compartment μ to an action potential generated at the soma.

The triggering of action potentials depends on the *somatic* membrane potential only. We define $u_i = V_i^1$, $\eta_i(s) = \eta_i^1(s)$ and, for $j \in \Gamma_i^\nu$, we set $\epsilon_{ij} = \epsilon_i^{1\nu}$. This yields

$$u_i(t) = \sum_f \eta_i(t - t_i^{(f)}) + \sum_j w_{ij} \sum_f \epsilon_{ij}(t - t_j^{(f)}).$$ (4.89)

As in Eq. (4.54), we use a short-term memory approximation and truncate the sum over the η_i-terms. The result is

$$u_i(t) = \eta_i(t - \hat{t}_i) + \sum_j w_{ij} \sum_f \epsilon_{ij}(t - t_j^{(f)}),$$ (4.90)

where $\hat{t}_i$ is the last firing time of neuron i. Thus, the multicompartment model has been reduced to the single-variable model of Eq. (4.42). The approximation is good if the typical interspike interval is long compared to the neuronal time constants.

A

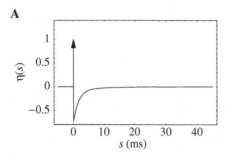

B

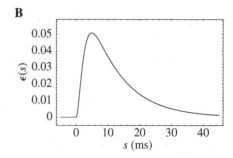

Fig. 4.24. Two-compartment integrate-and-fire model. **A.** Response kernel $\eta_0(s)$ of a neuron with two compartments and fire-and-reset threshold dynamics. The response kernel is a double exponential with time constants $\tau_{12} = 2$ ms and $\tau_0 = 10$ ms. The spike at $s = 0$ is indicated by a vertical arrow. **B.** Response kernel $\epsilon_0(s)$ for excitatory synaptic input at the dendritic compartment with a synaptic time constant $\tau_s = 1$ ms. The response kernel is a superposition of three exponentials and exhibits the typical time course of an excitatory postsynaptic potential.

Example: two-compartment integrate-and-fire model

We illustrate the Spike Response method by a simple model with two compartments and a reset mechanism at the soma (Rospars and Lansky, 1993). The two compartments are characterized by a somatic capacitance C^1 and a dendritic capacitance $C^2 = a\,C^1$. The membrane time constant is $\tau_0 = R^1 C^1 = R^2 C^2$ and the longitudinal time constant $\tau_{12} = r^{12} C^1 C^2 / (C^1 + C^2)$. The neuron fires if $V^1(t) = \vartheta$. After each firing the somatic potential is reset to u_r. This is equivalent to a current pulse

$$\gamma(s) = q\,\delta(s)\,, \tag{4.91}$$

where $q = C^1\,[\vartheta - u_r]$ is the charge lost during the spike. The dendrite receives spike trains from other neurons j and we assume that each spike evokes a current pulse with time course

$$\alpha(s) = \frac{1}{\tau_s} \exp\left(-\frac{s}{\tau_s}\right) \Theta(s)\,. \tag{4.92}$$

For the two-compartment model it is straightforward to integrate the equations and derive the Green's function. With the Green's function we can calculate the response kernels $\epsilon_0(s) = \epsilon_i^{12}$ and $\eta_0(s) = \eta_i^{(1)}$ as defined in Eqs. (4.87) and (4.88); cf. Tuckwell (1988), Bressloff and Taylor (1994). We find

$$\eta_0(s) = -\frac{\vartheta - u_r}{(1+a)} \exp\left(-\frac{s}{\tau_0}\right) \left[1 + a \exp\left(-\frac{s}{\tau_{12}}\right)\right], \tag{4.93}$$

$$\epsilon_0(s) = \frac{1}{(1+a)} \exp\left(-\frac{s}{\tau_0}\right) \left[\frac{1 - e^{-\delta_1 s}}{\tau_s\,\delta_1} - \exp\left(-\frac{s}{\tau_{12}}\right) \frac{1 - e^{-\delta_2 s}}{\tau_s\,\delta_2}\right],$$

with $\delta_1 = \tau_s^{-1} - \tau_0^{-1}$ and $\delta_2 = \tau_s^{-1} - \tau_0^{-1} - \tau_{12}^{-1}$. Figure 4.24 shows the two response kernels with parameters $\tau_0 = 10$ ms, $\tau_{12} = 2$ ms, and $a = 10$. The synaptic time constant is $\tau_s = 1$ ms. The kernel $\epsilon_0(s)$ describes the voltage response of the soma to an input at the dendrite. It shows the typical time course of an excitatory or inhibitory postsynaptic potential. The time course of the kernel $\eta_0(s)$ is a double exponential and reflects the dynamics of the reset in a two-compartment model.

4.4.3 Relation to the full Spike Response Model (*)

In the previous subsection we had to neglect the effect of spikes $t_i^{(f)}$ (except that of the most recent one) on the somatic membrane potential of the neuron i itself in order to map Eq. (4.82) to the SRM. We can do better if we allow for the response kernels ϵ to depend explicitly on the last firing time of the presynaptic neuron. This alternative treatment is an extension of the approach that has already been discussed in Section 4.2.2 in the context of a single-compartment integrate-and-fire model.

In order to account for the renewal property of the SRM we should solve Eq. (4.81) with initial conditions stated at the last presynaptic firing time $\hat{t}_i$. Unfortunately, the set of available initial conditions at $\hat{t}_i$ is incomplete because only the *somatic* membrane potential equals u_r immediately after $t = \hat{t}_i$. For the membrane potential of the remaining compartments we have to use initial conditions at $t = -\infty$, but we can use a short-term memory approximation and neglect *indirect* effects from earlier spikes on the present value of the somatic membrane potential.

We start with Eq. (4.82) and split the integration over s at $s = \hat{t}_i$ into two parts,

$$V_i^1(t) = \sum_\nu \frac{1}{C_i^\nu} \int_{-\infty}^{\hat{t}_i+0} ds\; G_i^{1\nu}(t-s) \left[I_i^\nu(s) - \delta^{1\nu}\,\Omega_i(s) \right]$$

$$+ \sum_\nu \frac{1}{C_i^\nu} \int_{\hat{t}_i+0}^{t} ds\; G_i^{1\nu}(t-s)\, I_i^\nu(s)\,. \tag{4.94}$$

The limits of the integration have been chosen to be at $\hat{t}_i + 0$ in order to ensure that the Dirac δ-pulse for the reset of the membrane potential is included in the first term.

With $G_i^{1\nu}(t-s) = \sum_\mu G_i^{1\mu}(t-\hat{t})\, G_i^{\mu\nu}(\hat{t}-s)$, which is a general property of

Green's functions, we obtain

$$V_i^1(t) = \sum_\mu G_i^{1\mu}(t - \hat{t}_i) \sum_\nu \frac{1}{C_i^\nu} \int_{-\infty}^{\hat{t}_i+0} ds\, G_i^{\mu\nu}(\hat{t}_i - s)\left[I_i^\nu(s) - \delta^{1\nu}\Omega_i(s)\right]$$

$$+ \sum_\nu \frac{1}{C_i^\nu} \int_{\hat{t}_i+0}^{t} ds\, G_i^{1\nu}(t - s)\, I_i^\nu(s)\,. \tag{4.95}$$

With the known initial condition at the soma,

$$V_i^1(\hat{t}_i + 0) = \sum_\nu \frac{1}{C_i^\nu} \int_{-\infty}^{\hat{t}_i+0} ds\, G_i^{1\nu}(\hat{t}_i - s)\left[I_i^\nu(s) - \delta^{1\nu}\Omega_i(s)\right] = u_r\,, \tag{4.96}$$

we find

$$V_i^1(t) = G_i^{11}(t - \hat{t}_i)\, u_r$$

$$+ \sum_{\mu\geq 2}\sum_\nu \frac{1}{C_i^\nu} G_i^{1\mu}(t - \hat{t}_i) \int_{-\infty}^{\hat{t}_i+0} ds\, G_i^{\mu\nu}(\hat{t}_i - s)\left[I_i^\nu(s) - \delta^{1\nu}\Omega_i(s)\right]$$

$$+ \sum_\nu \frac{1}{C_i^\nu} \int_{\hat{t}_i+0}^{t} ds\, G_i^{1\nu}(t - s)\, I_i^\nu(s)\,. \tag{4.97}$$

The voltage reset at the soma is described by $\Omega_i(t) = C_i^1\,(\vartheta - u_r)\sum_f \delta(t - t_i^{(f)})$; cf. Eqs. (4.84) and (4.85). After shifting the terms with Ω to the end and substituting its definition, we obtain

$$V_i^1(t) = G_i^{11}(t - \hat{t}_i)\, u_r$$

$$+ \sum_{\mu\geq 2}\sum_\nu \frac{1}{C_i^\nu} G_i^{1\mu}(t - \hat{t}_i) \int_{-\infty}^{\hat{t}_i+0} ds\, G_i^{\mu\nu}(\hat{t}_i - s)\, I_i^\nu(s)$$

$$+ \sum_\nu \frac{1}{C_i^\nu} \int_{\hat{t}_i+0}^{t} ds\, G_i^{1\nu}(t - s)\, I_i^\nu(s)$$

$$+ (\vartheta - u_r)\sum_{\mu\geq 2}\sum_f G_i^{1\mu}(t - \hat{t}_i)\, G_i^{\mu 1}(\hat{t}_i - t_i^{(f)})\,. \tag{4.98}$$

If we introduce

$$\tilde{G}_i^{1\nu}(r, s) = \begin{cases} \dfrac{1}{C_i^\nu} G_i^{1\nu}(s) & r > s \\[2ex] \dfrac{1}{C_i^\nu} \displaystyle\sum_{\mu\geq 2} G_i^{1\mu}(r)\, G_i^{\mu\nu}(s - r) & r < s \end{cases} \tag{4.99}$$

we can collect the integrals in Eq. (4.98) and obtain

$$
\begin{aligned}
V_i^1(t) = {}& G_i^{11}(t - \hat{t}_i)\, u_r \\
& + \sum_v \int_{-\infty}^{t} ds\, \tilde{G}_i^{1v}(t - \hat{t}_i, t - s)\, I_i^v(s) \\
& + (\vartheta - u_r) \sum_{\mu \geq 2} \sum_f G_i^{1\mu}(t - \hat{t}_i)\, G_i^{\mu 1}(\hat{t}_i - t_i^{(f)}) .
\end{aligned}
\tag{4.100}
$$

This expression has a clear interpretation. The first term describes the relaxation of the somatic membrane potential in the absence of further input. The second term accounts for external input to any of the compartments integrated up to time t. Finally, the last term reflects an indirect influence of previous spikes on the somatic membrane potential via other compartments that are not reset during an action potential. In fact, the sum over the firing times in the last term stops at the last but one action potential since $G_i^{\mu 1}(\hat{t}_i - t_i^{(f)})$, $\mu > 1$, is zero if $\hat{t}_i = t_i^{(f)}$.

If we neglect the last term in Eq. (4.100), that is, if we neglect any *indirect* effects of previous action potentials on the somatic membrane potential, then Eq. (4.100) can be mapped on the SRM (4.24) by introducing kernels

$$
\epsilon_i^v(r, s) = \int_0^{\infty} dt'\, \tilde{G}_i^{1v}(r, t')\, \alpha(t' - s),
\tag{4.101}
$$

and

$$
\eta_i(s) = G_i^{11}(s)\, u_r .
\tag{4.102}
$$

Here, $\alpha(s)$ describes the form of an elementary postsynaptic current; cf. Eq. (4.83). With these definitions the somatic membrane potential $u_i(t) \equiv V_i^1(t)$ of neuron i is

$$
u_i(t) = \eta_i(t - \hat{t}_i) + \sum_v \sum_{j \in \Gamma_i^v} w_{ij} \sum_f \epsilon_i^v(t - \hat{t}_i, t - t_j^{(f)}),
\tag{4.103}
$$

which is the equation of the SRM.

4.5 Application: coding by spikes

Formal spiking neuron models allow a transparent graphical discussion of various coding principles. In this section we illustrate some elementary examples.

Time-to-first-spike

We have seen in Section 1.4 that the time of the first spike can convey information about the stimulus. In order to construct a simple example, we consider a single neuron i described by the Spike Response Model SRM$_0$. The neuron receives spikes from N presynaptic neurons j via synaptic connections that have all the

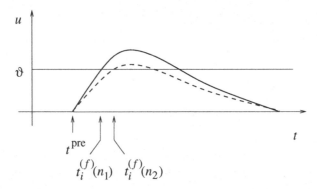

Fig. 4.25. Time-to-first-spike. The firing time t^f encodes the number n_1 or n_2 of presynpatic spikes that have been fired synchronously at t^{pre}. If there are fewer presynaptic spikes, the potential u rises more slowly (dashed) and the firing occurs later. For the sake of simplicity, the axonal delay has been set to zero; taken from Gerstner (1998).

same weight $w_{ij} = w$. There is no external input. We assume that the last spike of neuron i occurred long ago so that the spike-afterpotential η in Eq. (4.42) can be neglected.

At $t = t^{\mathrm{pre}}$, $n < N$ presynaptic spikes are simultaneously generated and produce a postsynaptic potential,

$$u_i(t) = n \, w \, \epsilon(t - t^{\mathrm{pre}}) . \qquad (4.104)$$

A postsynaptic spike occurs whenever u_i reaches the threshold ϑ. We consider the firing time $t_i^{(f)}$ of the first output spike,

$$t_i^{(f)} = \min\{t > t^{\mathrm{pre}} \mid u_i(t) = \vartheta\}, \qquad (4.105)$$

which is a function of n. A larger number of presynaptic spikes n results in a postsynaptic potential with a larger amplitude so that the firing threshold is reached earlier. The time difference $t_i^{(f)} - t^{\mathrm{pre}}$ is hence a measure of the number of presynaptic pulses. To put it differently, the timing of the first spike encodes the strength of the input; cf. Fig. 4.25.

Phase coding

Phase coding is possible if there is a periodic background signal that can serve as a reference. We want to show that the phase of a spike contains information about a static stimulus h_0. As before we take the model SRM_0 as a simple description of neuronal dynamics. The periodic background signal is included in the external input. Thus we use an input potential

$$h(t) = h_0 + h_1 \cos\left(2\pi \, \frac{t}{T}\right), \qquad (4.106)$$

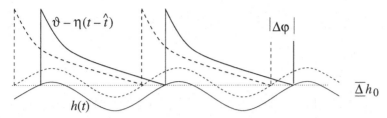

Fig. 4.26. Phase coding. Firing occurs whenever the total input potential $h(t) = h_0 + h_1 \cos(2\pi t/T)$ hits the dynamic threshold $\vartheta - \eta(t - \hat{t})$ where $\hat{t}$ is the most recent firing time. In the presence of a periodic modulation $h_1 \neq 0$, a change Δh_0 in the level of (constant) stimulation results in a change $\Delta \varphi$ in the phase of firing; taken from Gerstner (1998).

where h_0 is the constant stimulus and h_1 is the amplitude of the T-periodic background; cf. Eq. (4.46).

Let us consider a single neuron driven by Eq. (4.106). The membrane potential of a SRM$_0$ neuron is, according to Eqs. (4.42) and (4.46),

$$u(t) = \eta(t - \hat{t}) + h(t),\qquad(4.107)$$

As usual $\hat{t}$ denotes the time of the most recent spike. To find the next firing time, Eq. (4.107) has to be combined with the threshold condition $u(t) = \vartheta$. We are interested in a solution where the neuron fires regularly and with the same period as the background signal. In this case the threshold condition reads

$$\vartheta - \eta(T) = h_0 + h_1 \cos\left(2\pi \frac{\hat{t}}{T}\right).\qquad(4.108)$$

For a given period T, the left-hand side has a fixed value and we can solve for $\varphi = 2\pi \hat{t}/T$. There are two solutions but only one of them is stable. Thus the neuron has to fire at a certain phase φ with respect to the external signal. The value of φ depends on the level of the constant stimulation h_0. In other words, the strength h_0 of the stimulation is encoded in the phase of the spike. In Eq. (4.108) we have moved η to the left-hand side in order to suggest a dynamic threshold interpretation. A graphical interpretation of Eq. (4.108) is given in Fig. 4.26.

Correlation coding

Let us consider two uncoupled neurons. Both receive the same constant external stimulus $h(t) = h_0$. As a result, they fire regularly with period T given by $\eta(T) = h_0$ as can be seen directly from Eq. (4.108) with $h_1 = 0$. Since the neurons are not coupled, they need not fire simultaneously. Let us assume that the spikes of neuron 2 are shifted by an amount δ with respect to neuron 1.

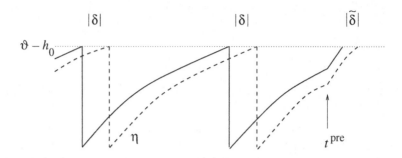

Fig. 4.27. The firing time difference δ between two independent neurons is decreased to $\tilde{\delta} < \delta$, after both neurons receive a common excitatory input at time t^{pre}; taken from Gerstner (1998).

Suppose that, at a given moment t^{pre}, both neurons receive input from a common presynaptic neuron j. This causes an additional contribution $\epsilon(t - t^{\text{pre}})$ to the membrane potential. If the synapse is excitatory, the two neurons will fire slightly sooner. More importantly, the spikes will also be closer together. In the situation sketched in Fig. 4.27 the new firing time difference $\tilde{\delta}$ is reduced, $\tilde{\delta} < \delta$. In later chapters, we will analyze this phenomenon in more detail. Here we just note that this effect would allow us to encode information using the time interval between the firings of two or more neurons.

Decoding: synchronous versus asynchronous input

In the previous paragraphs we have studied how a neuron can encode information in spike timing, phase, or correlations. We now ask the inverse question, viz., how can a neuron read out temporal information? We consider the simplest example and study whether a neuron can distinguish synchronous from asynchronous input. As above we make use of the simplified neuron model SRM_0 defined by Eqs. (4.42) and (4.43). We will show that synchronous input is more efficient than asynchronous input in driving a postsynaptic neuron.

To illustrate this point, let us consider an ϵ kernel of the form

$$\epsilon_0(s) = J \frac{s}{\tau} \exp\left(-\frac{s}{\tau}\right) \Theta(s). \tag{4.109}$$

With parameters $J = 1$ mV and $\tau = 10$ ms. The function (4.109) has a maximum value of J/e at $s = \tau$. The integral over s is normalized to $J\tau$.

Let us consider a neuron i which receives input from 100 presynaptic neurons j. Each presynaptic neuron fires at a rate of 10 Hz. All synapses have the same efficacy $w = 1$. Let us first study the case of asynchronous input. Different neurons fire at different times so that, on average, spikes arrive at intervals of

$\Delta t = 1$ ms. Each spike evokes a postsynaptic potential defined by Eq. (4.109). The total membrane potential of neuron i is

$$u_i(t) = \eta(t - \hat{t}_i) + \sum_j \sum_{t_j^{(f)}} w \, \epsilon_0(t - t_j^{(f)})$$

$$\approx \eta(t - \hat{t}_i) + w \sum_{n=0}^{\infty} \epsilon_0(t - n \, \Delta t). \qquad (4.110)$$

If neuron i has been quiescent in the recent past ($t - \hat{t}_i \to \infty$), then the first term on the right-hand side of Eq. (4.110) can be neglected. The second term can be approximated by an integral over s, hence

$$u_i(t) \approx \frac{w}{\Delta t} \int_0^{\infty} \epsilon_0(s) \, \mathrm{d}s = \frac{w \, J \, \tau}{\Delta t} = 10 \text{ mV}. \qquad (4.111)$$

If the firing threshold of the neuron is at $\vartheta = 20$ mV the neuron stays quiescent.

Now let us consider the same amount of input, but fired synchronously at $t_j^{(f)} = 0, 100, 200, \ldots$ ms. Thus each presynaptic neuron fires as before at 10 Hz but all presynaptic neurons emit their spikes synchronously. Let us study what happens after the first volley of spikes has arrived at $t = 0$. The membrane potential of the postsynaptic neuron is

$$u_i(t) = \eta(t - \hat{t}_i) + N \, w \, \epsilon_0(t) \qquad (4.112)$$

where $N = 100$ is the number of presynaptic neurons. If the postsynaptic neuron has not been active in the recent past, we can neglect the refractory term η on the right-hand side of Eq. (4.112). The maximum of Eq. (4.112) occurs at $t = \tau = 10$ ms and has a value of $wNJ/e \approx 37$ mV which is above threshold. Thus the postsynaptic neuron fires before $t = 10$ ms. We conclude that the same number of input spikes can have different effects depending on their level of synchrony; cf. Fig. 4.28.

We will return to the question of coincidence detection, i.e., the distinction between synchronous and asynchronous input, in the following chapter. For a classic experimental study exploring the relevance of temporal structure in the input, see Segundo et al. (1963).

Example: spatio-temporal summation

In neurons with a spatially extended dendritic tree the form of the postsynaptic potential depends not only on the type, but also on the location of the synapse; cf. Chapter 2. To be specific, let us consider a multicompartment integrate-and-fire model. As we have seen above in Section 4.4, the membrane potential $u_i(t)$ can be described by the formalism of the Spike Response Model. If the last output spike

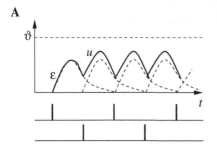
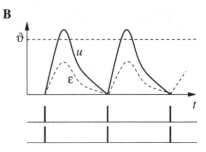

Fig. 4.28. Potential u of a postsynaptic neuron which receives input from two groups of presynaptic neurons. **A**. Spike trains of the two groups are phase shifted with respect to each other. The total potential u does not reach the threshold. There are no output spikes. **B**. Spikes from two presynaptic groups arrive synchronously. The summed excitatory postsynaptic potentials reach the threshold ϑ and cause the generation of an output spike.

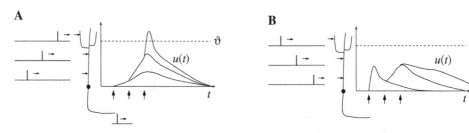

Fig. 4.29. Sensitivity to temporal order of synaptic inputs on a dendrite. **A**. A neuron is stimulated by three synaptic inputs in a sequence that starts at the distal part of the dendrite and ends with an input close to the soma. Since the excitatory postsynaptic potential (EPSP) caused by the distal input has a longer rise time than that generated by the proximal input, the EPSPs add up coherently and the membrane potential reaches the firing threshold ϑ. **B**. If the temporal sequence of spike inputs is reversed, the same number of input spikes does not trigger an action potential (schematic figure).

$\hat{t}_i$ is long ago, we can neglect the refractory kernel η_i and the membrane potential is given by

$$u_i(t) = \sum_j w_{ij} \sum_f \epsilon_{ij}(t - t_j^{(f)}). \qquad (4.113)$$

cf. Eq. (4.90). The subscript ij at the ϵ kernel takes care of the fact that the postsynaptic potential depends on the location of the synapse on the dendrite. Due to the low-pass characteristics of the dendrite, synaptic input at the tip of the dendrite causes postsynaptic potentials with a longer rise time and lower amplitude than input directly into the soma. The total potential $u_i(t)$ depends therefore on the temporal order of the stimulation of the synapses. An input sequence starting at the far end of the dendrite and approaching the soma is more effective in triggering an output spike than the same number of input spikes in reverse order; cf. Fig. 4.29.

4.6 Summary

In formal spiking neuron models, spikes are fully characterized by their firing time $t^{(f)}$ defined by a threshold criterion. Integrate-and-fire and the Spike Response Model are typical examples of spiking neuron models. Leaky integrate-and-fire point neurons with current input can be mapped exactly to the Spike Response Model. Even multicompartment integrate-and-fire models can be mapped to the Spike Response Model, if indirect effects due to previous output spikes are neglected. An integrate-and-fire model with *spike-time*-dependent parameters, which is a generalization of the leaky integrate-and-fire model, can be seen as a special case of the Spike Response Model. The nonlinear integrate-and-fire model, i.e., a model where parameters are *voltage* dependent, is a different generalization. The quadratic integrate-and-fire model is particularly interesting since it is a generic example of a type I neuron model.

Detailed conductance-based neuron models can be approximately mapped to formal spiking neuron models. With the help of formal spiking neuron models, problems of pulse coding can be studied in a transparent graphical manner. The Spike Response Model, defined in this chapter, will be reconsidered in Part II where systems of spiking neurons are analyzed.

Literature

Formal neuron models where spikes are triggered by a threshold process were popular in the 1960s (Stein, 1965, 1967b; Geisler and Goldberg, 1966; Weiss, 1966), but the ideas can be traced back much further (Lapicque, 1907; Hill, 1936). It was recognized early on that these models lend themselves to hardware implementations (French and Stein, 1970) and mathematical analysis (Stein, 1965, 1967a), and can be fitted to experimental data (Brillinger, 1988, 1992). Recent developments in computation and coding with formal spiking neurons is reviewed in the book *Pulsed Neural Networks* edited by Maass and Bishop (1998).

5

Noise in spiking neuron models

In vivo recordings of neuronal activity are characterized by a high degree of irregularity. The spike train of individual neurons is far from being periodic and relations between the firing patterns of several neurons seem to be random. If the electrical activity picked up by an extracellular electrode is made audible by a loudspeaker then we basically hear – noise. The question of whether this is indeed just noise or rather a highly efficient way of coding information cannot easily be answered. Listening to a computer modem or a fax machine might also leave the impression that this is just noise. Being able to decide whether we are witnessing the neuronal activity that is underlying the composition of a poem (or the electronic transmission of a love letter) and not just meaningless noise is one of the most burning problems in neuroscience.

Several experiments have been undertaken to tackle this problem. It seems as if neurons can react in a very reliable and reproducible manner to fluctuating currents that are injected via intracellular electrodes. As long as the same time course of the injected current is used the action potentials occur with precisely the same timing relative to the stimulation (Bryant and Segundo, 1976; Mainen and Sejnowski, 1995). A related phenomenon can be observed by using nonstationary sensory stimulation. Spatially uniform random flicker, for example, elicits more or less the same spike train in retinal ganglion cells if the same flicker sequence is presented again (Berry et al., 1997). A similar behavior has been reported for motion-sensitive neurons of the visual system in flies (de Ruyter van Steveninck et al., 1997) and monkey cortex (Bair and Koch, 1996). On the other hand, neurons produce irregular spike trains in the absence of any temporally structured stimuli. Irregular spontaneous activity, i.e., activity that is not related in any obvious way to external stimulation, and trial-to-trial variations in neuronal responses are often considered as noise (Softky and Koch, 1993; Shadlen and Newsome, 1994).

The origin of the irregularity in the electrical activity of cortical neurons *in vivo* is poorly understood. In spiking neuron models such as the integrate-and-fire or

Spike Response Model (SRM), noise is therefore often added explicitly to neuronal dynamics so as to mimic the unpredictability of neuronal recordings. In this chapter we present three different ways to implement noise in models of neuronal networks, viz. escape noise (Section 5.3), slow noise in the parameters (Section 5.4), and diffusive noise (Section 5.5). In Section 5.6 we discuss the differences between subthreshold and superthreshold stimulation and explain its consequences for spike train variability. In the subthreshold regime, it is possible to relate the diffusive noise model to the escape noise model. Section 5.7 illustrates this relation. The noise models are finally applied to the phenomenon of stochastic resonance in Section 5.8 and compared with rate models in Section 5.9. Before we start with the discussion of the noise models, we review in Section 5.1 some experimental evidence for noise in neurons and introduce in Section 5.2 a statistical framework of spike train analysis.

5.1 Spike train variability

If neuron models such as the Hodgkin–Huxley or the integrate-and-fire model are driven by a sufficiently strong constant current, they generate a regular sequence of spikes. In neuronal models with adaptation currents[1] there might be a short transient phase at the beginning, but then all interspike intervals are constant. Spike trains of typical neurons *in vivo* show a much more irregular behavior. Whether the irregularity is the sign of noise or of a rich code is at present an open question (Softky and Koch, 1993; Shadlen and Newsome, 1994; Bair and Koch, 1996). In the first subsection we review some evidence for neuronal variability and spike train irregularity. We then discuss potential sources of noise.

5.1.1 Are neurons noisy?

Many *in vivo* experiments show noisy behavior of central neurons. The activity of neurons from the visual cortex, for example, can be recorded while a slowly moving bar is presented on a screen within the visual field of the animal (Hubel and Wiesel, 1959, 1977). As soon as the bar enters the neuron's receptive field the firing rate goes up until the bar leaves the receptive field at the opposite border. The spike train, however, varies considerably from trial to trial if the same experiment is repeated several times. Furthermore, the very same neuron is spontaneously active even if the screen is blank and no external stimulus is applied. During spontaneous activity, the intervals between one spike and the next exhibit a large variability resulting in a broad distribution of interspike intervals; see e.g., Softky and Koch (1993).

---

[1] We neglect here intrinsically bursting and chaotic neurons.

Are these experiments convincing evidence for ubiquitous noise in the central nervous system? The above two observations refer to experiments on the neural system as a whole. The cortical neuron that is recorded from does not only receive input from the retina, but also from many other neurons in the brain. The effective input to this neuron is basically unknown. It is thus possible that there is a substantial fluctuation in the input current to cortical neurons, even though the external (visual) stimulus is only slowly changing.

In fact, when neurons are driven by a known time-dependent intracellular input current, neurons seem to behave more or less deterministically (Bryant and Segundo, 1976; Mainen and Sejnowski, 1995; Zador, 1998). Moreover, if the external visual stimulus changes rapidly, neurons in the visual system react much more reliably than for constant or slowly moving stimuli (Bialek et al., 1991; Bair and Koch, 1996; Berry et al., 1997; Maršálek et al., 1997; de Ruyter van Steveninck et al., 1997). Whether a neuron behaves nearly deterministically or rather randomly thus depends, at least to a certain extent, on the stimulus.

5.1.2 Noise sources

We distinguish between intrinsic noise sources that generate stochastic behavior on the level of the *neuronal* dynamics, and extrinsic sources that arise from network effects and synaptic transmission (Manwani and Koch, 1999).

A source of noise, which is literally omnipresent, is thermal noise. Due to the discrete nature of electric charge carriers, the voltage u across any electrical resistor R fluctuates at finite temperature (Johnson noise). The variance of the fluctuations at rest is[2] $\langle \Delta u^2 \rangle \propto R\, k\, T\, B$ where k is the Boltzmann constant, T the temperature and B the bandwidth of the system (Manwani and Koch, 1999). Since neuronal dynamics is described by an equivalent electrical circuit containing resistors (cf. Section 2.2), the neuronal membrane potential fluctuates as well. Fluctuations due to Johnson noise are, however, of minor importance compared to other noise sources in neurons (Manwani and Koch, 1999).

Another source of noise that is specific to neurons arises from the finite number of ion channels in a patch of neuronal membrane (Schneidman et al., 1998; White et al., 2000). Most ion channels have only two states: they are either open or closed. The electrical conductivity of a patch of membrane for ion type i is proportional to the number of open ion channels. For a given constant membrane potential u, a fraction $P_i(u)$ of ion channels of type i is open *on average*. The actual number of open channels fluctuates around $N_i\, P_i(u)$ where N_i is the total number of ion channels of type i in that patch of membrane. The formulation

---

[2] Unless otherwise noted, angled brackets denote an expectation value, e.g., $\langle x \rangle$ is the expected value of the variable x.

of the Hodgkin–Huxley equations in terms of ion channel conductivities (see Section 2.2) is implicitly based on the assumption of a large number of ion channels so that fluctuations can be neglected. Since, in reality, N_i is finite, the conductivity fluctuates and so does the potential. If the membrane potential is close to the threshold, channel noise can be critical for the generation of action potentials. Models that take the finite number of ion channels into account can reproduce the observed variability of real neurons with intracellular stimulation (Chow and White, 1996; Schneidman et al., 1998). In particular, they show little spike jitter if the input current is rapidly changing, but are less reliable if the input current is constant.

Apart from intrinsic noise sources at the level of an individual neuron there are also sources of noise that are due to signal transmission and network effects (extrinsic noise). Synaptic transmission failures, for instance, seem to impose a substantial limitation to signal transmission within a neuronal network. Experiments with double electrode recordings from two synaptically connected neurons suggest that only 10–30% of presynaptic spikes generate a postsynaptic response (Hessler et al., 1993; Markram and Tsodyks, 1996).

Finally, an important part of the irregularity of neuronal spiking during spontaneous activity seems to be due to the properties of the network as a whole rather than to individual neurons. In model studies it has been shown that networks of excitatory and inhibitory neurons with fixed random connectivity can produce highly irregular spike trains – even in the absence of any source of noise (Nützel et al., 1994; van Vreeswijk and Sompolinsky, 1996; Brunel and Hakim, 1999; Fusi et al., 2000a; Kistler and De Zeeuw, 2002). We will discuss the underlying mechanisms in Sections 6.4.3 and 8.3. As a result of the network activity, each neuron receives as input an irregular spike sequence that can be described as stochastic spike arrival; cf. Section 5.5. The difference between the large variability of neurons *in vivo* compared to that during intracellular stimulation *in vitro* can therefore be, at least partially, attributed to network effects.

5.2 Statistics of spike trains

In this section, we introduce some important concepts for the statistical description of neuronal spike trains. A central notion will be the interspike interval distribution which is discussed in the framework of a generalized input-dependent renewal theory. We start in Section 5.2.1 with the definition of renewal systems and turn then in Section 5.2.2 to interval distributions. The relation between interval distributions and neuronal models will be the topic of Sections 5.3 and 5.5.

5.2.1 Input-dependent renewal systems

We consider a single neuron such as an integrate-and-fire or SRM unit. Let us suppose that we know the last firing time $\hat{t} < t$ of the neuron and its input current I. In formal spiking neuron models such as the SRM, the membrane potential u is then completely determined, i.e.,

$$u(t|\hat{t}) = \eta(t - \hat{t}) + \int_0^\infty \kappa(t - \hat{t}, s)\, I(t - s)\, ds\,, \tag{5.1}$$

cf. Eq. (4.24). In particular, for the integrate-and-fire model with membrane time constant τ_m and capacity C we have

$$u(t|\hat{t}) = u_r\, \exp\left(-\frac{t - \hat{t}}{\tau}\right) + \frac{1}{C} \int_0^{t - \hat{t}} \exp\left(-\frac{s}{\tau}\right) I(t - s)\, ds\,, \tag{5.2}$$

cf. Eq. (4.10). In general, part or all of the input current I could arise from presynaptic spikes. Here we simply assume that the input current I is a known function of time.

Given the input and the firing time $\hat{t}$ we would like to predict the next action potential. In the absence of noise, the next firing time $t^{(f)}$ of a neuron with membrane potential (5.1) is determined by the threshold condition $u = \vartheta$. The first threshold crossing occurs at

$$t^{(f)} = \min\{t > \hat{t} \,|\, u(t|\hat{t}) \geq \vartheta\}\,. \tag{5.3}$$

In the presence of noise, however, we are no longer able to predict the exact firing time of the next spike, but only the probability that a spike occurs. The calculation of the probability distribution of the next firing time for arbitrary time-dependent input I is one of the major goals in the theory of noisy spiking neurons.

Equations (5.1) and (5.2) combined with a (stochastic) spike generation procedure are examples of input-dependent renewal systems. Renewal processes are a class of stochastic point processes that describe a sequence of events (spikes) in time (Cox, 1962; Papoulis, 1991). Renewal systems in the *narrow* sense (stationary renewal processes), presuppose stationary input and are defined by the fact that the state of the system, and hence the probability of generating the next event, depends only on the "age" $t - \hat{t}$ of the system, i.e., the time that has passed since the last event (last spike). The central assumption of renewal theory is that the state does not depend on earlier events (i.e., earlier spikes of the same neuron). The aim of renewal theory is to predict the probability of the next event given the age of the system.

Here we use the renewal concept in a broader sense and define a renewal process as a system where the state at time t (and hence the probability of generating an event at t) depends both on the time that has passed since the last event (i.e., the firing time $\hat{t}$) *and* the input $I(t')$, $\hat{t} < t' < t$, that the system received since the last event. Input-dependent renewal systems are also called modulated renewal processes (Reich et al., 1998), nonstationary renewal systems (Gerstner, 1995, 2000), or inhomogeneous Markov interval processes (Kass and Ventura, 2001). The aim of a theory of input-dependent renewal systems is to predict the probability of the next event, given the timing $\hat{t}$ of the last event *and* the input $I(t')$ for $\hat{t} < t' < t$.

Example: light bulb failure as a renewal system

A generic example of a (potentially input-dependent) renewal system is a light bulb. The event is the failure of the bulb and its subsequent exchange. Obviously, the state of the system only depends on the age of the current bulb, and not on that of any previous bulb that has already been exchanged. If the usage pattern of the bulbs is stationary (e.g., the bulb is switched on for 10 hours each night) then we have a stationary renewal process. If usage is irregular (higher usage in winter than in summer, no usage during vacation), the aging of the bulb will be more rapid or slower depending on how often it is switched on and off. We can use input-dependent renewal theory if we keep track of all the times we have turned the switch. The input in this case comprises the switching times. The aim of renewal theory is to calculate the probability of the next failure given the age of the bulb and the switching pattern.

5.2.2 *Interval distribution*

The estimation of interspike interval (ISI) distributions from experimental data is a common method for studying neuronal variability given a certain *stationary* input. In a typical experiment, the spike train of a single neuron (e.g., a neuron in the visual cortex) is recorded while driven by a constant stimulus. The stimulus might be an external input applied to the system (e.g., a visual contrast grating moving at constant speed); or it may be an intracellularly applied constant driving current. The spike train is analyzed and the distribution of intervals s_k between two subsequent spikes is plotted in a histogram. For a sufficiently long spike train, the histogram provides a good estimate of the ISI distribution which we denote as $P_0(s)$; cf. Fig. 5.1A. We will return to the special case of stationary input in subsection 5.2.4.

We now generalize the concept of interval distributions to time-dependent input. We concentrate on a single neuron which is stimulated by a known input current $I(t)$ and some unknown noise source. We suppose that the last spike occurred at time $\hat{t}$ and ask the following question. What is the probability that the next spike occurs between t and $t + \Delta t$, given the spike at $\hat{t}$ and the input $I(t')$ for $t' < t$? For $\Delta t \to 0$, the answer is given by the *probability density* of firing $P_I(t|\hat{t})$. Hence,

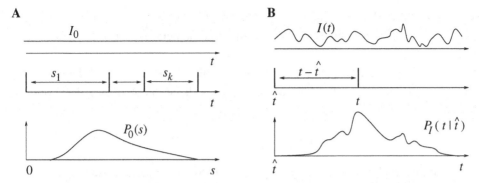

Fig. 5.1. **A**. Stationary interval distribution. A neuron is driven by a constant input (top). A histogram of the interspike intervals $s_1, s_2, \ldots$ can be used to estimate the interval distribution $P_0(s)$ (bottom). **B**. Input-dependent interval distribution. A neuron, stimulated by the current $I(t)$ (top), has emitted a first spike at $\hat{t}$. The interval distribution $P_I(t|\hat{t})$ (bottom) gives the probability density that the next spike occurs after an interval $t - \hat{t}$.

$\int_{t_1}^{t_2} P_I(t|\hat{t}) \, dt$ is the probability of finding a spike in the segment $[t_1, t_2]$, given that the last spike was at $\hat{t} < t_1$. The normalization of $P_I(t|\hat{t})$ is

$$\int_{\hat{t}}^{\infty} P_I(t \mid \hat{t}) \, dt = 1 - p_I^{\text{inact}} \tag{5.4}$$

where p_I^{inact} denotes the probability that the neuron stays inactive and will never fire again. For excitatory input and a sufficient amount of noise the neuron will always emit further spikes at some point. We therefore assume in the following that p_I^{inact} vanishes.

The lower index I of $P_I(t|\hat{t})$ is intended to remind us that the probability density $P_I(t|\hat{t})$ depends on the time course of the input $I(t')$ for $t' < t$. Since $P_I(t|\hat{t})$ is conditioned on the spike at $\hat{t}$, it can be called a spike-triggered spike density. We interpret $P_I(t \mid \hat{t})$ as the distribution of interspike intervals in the presence of an input current I. In the following, we will refer to P_I as the *input-dependent interval distribution*; see Fig. 5.1B. For renewal systems with stationary input $P_I(t|\hat{t})$ reduces to $P_0(t - \hat{t})$.

5.2.3 Survivor function and hazard

The interval distribution $P_I(t|\hat{t})$ as defined above is a probability *density*. Thus, integration of $P_I(t|\hat{t})$ over time yields a probability. For example, $\int_{\hat{t}}^{t} P_I(t'|\hat{t}) \, dt'$ is the probability that a neuron which has emitted a spike at $\hat{t}$ fires the next action potential between $\hat{t}$ and t. Thus

$$S_I(t|\hat{t}) = 1 - \int_{\hat{t}}^{t} P_I(t'|\hat{t}) \, dt' \tag{5.5}$$

is the probability that the neuron stays quiescent between $\hat{t}$ and t. $S_I(t|\hat{t})$ is called the *survivor function*: it gives the probability that the neuron "survives" from $\hat{t}$ to t without firing.

The survivor function $S_I(t|\hat{t})$ has an initial value $S_I(\hat{t}|\hat{t}) = 1$ and decreases to zero for $t \to \infty$. The rate of decay of $S_I(t|\hat{t})$ will be denoted by $\rho_I(t|\hat{t})$ and is defined by

$$\rho_I(t|\hat{t}) = -\frac{d}{dt}S_I(t|\hat{t}) / S_I(t|\hat{t}). \tag{5.6}$$

In the language of renewal theory, $\rho_I(t|\hat{t})$ is called the "age-dependent death rate" or "hazard" (Cox, 1962; Cox and Lewis, 1966).

Integration of Eq. (5.6) yields the survivor function

$$S_I(t|\hat{t}) = \exp\left[-\int_{\hat{t}}^{t} \rho_I(t'|\hat{t})\, dt'\right]. \tag{5.7}$$

According to the definition of the survivor function in Eq. (5.5), the interval distribution is given by

$$P_I(t|\hat{t}) = -\frac{d}{dt}S_I(t|\hat{t}) = \rho_I(t|\hat{t})\, S_I(t|\hat{t}), \tag{5.8}$$

which has a nice intuitive interpretation: in order to emit its *next* spike at t, the neuron has to survive the interval $(\hat{t}, t)$ without firing and then fire at t. The survival probability is $S_I(t|\hat{t})$ and the hazard of firing a spike at time t is $\rho_I(t|\hat{t})$ which explains the two factors on the right-hand side of Eq. (5.8). Inserting Eq. (5.7) in Eq. (5.8), we obtain an explicit expression for the interval distribution in terms of the hazard:

$$P_I(t|\hat{t}) = \rho_I(t|\hat{t}) \exp\left[-\int_{\hat{t}}^{t} \rho_I(t'|\hat{t})\, dt'\right]. \tag{5.9}$$

On the other hand, given the interval distribution we can derive the hazard from

$$\rho_I(t|\hat{t}) = -\frac{P_I(t|\hat{t})}{S_I(t|\hat{t})} = -\frac{P_I(t|\hat{t})}{1 - \int_{\hat{t}}^{t} P_I(t'|\hat{t})\, dt'}. \tag{5.10}$$

Thus, each of the three quantities $\rho_I(t|\hat{t})$, $P_I(t|\hat{t})$, and $S_I(t|\hat{t})$ is sufficient to describe the statistical properties of an input-dependent renewal system. For stationary renewal systems, Eqs. (5.5)–(5.10) hold with the replacement

$$P_I(t|\hat{t}) \quad\longrightarrow\quad P_0(t - \hat{t}), \tag{5.11}$$

$$S_I(t|\hat{t}) \quad\longrightarrow\quad S_0(t - \hat{t}), \tag{5.12}$$

$$\rho_I(t|\hat{t}) \quad\longrightarrow\quad \rho_0(t - \hat{t}). \tag{5.13}$$

Equations (5.5)–(5.10) are standard results of renewal theory (Cox, 1962; Cox and Lewis, 1966; Perkel et al., 1967a,b; Gerstein and Perkel, 1972).

Example: from interval distribution to hazard function

Let us suppose that we have found under stationary experimental conditions an interval distribution that can be approximated as

$$
P_0(s) = \begin{cases} 0 & \text{for} \quad s \le \Delta^{\text{abs}} \\ a_0 \, (s - \Delta^{\text{abs}}) \, e^{-\frac{1}{2} a_0 (s - \Delta^{\text{abs}})^2} & \text{for} \quad s > \Delta^{\text{abs}} \end{cases} \tag{5.14}
$$

with a constant $a_0 > 0$; cf. Fig. 5.2A. From Eq. (5.10), the hazard is found to be

$$
\rho_0(s) = \begin{cases} 0 & \text{for} \quad s \le \Delta^{\text{abs}} \\ a_0 \, (s - \Delta^{\text{abs}}) & \text{for} \quad s > \Delta^{\text{abs}}. \end{cases} \tag{5.15}
$$

Thus, during an interval Δ^{abs} after each spike the hazard vanishes. We may interpret Δ^{abs} as the absolute refractory time of the neuron. For $s > \Delta^{\text{abs}}$ the hazard increases linearly, i.e., the longer the neuron waits the higher its probability of firing. In Section 5.3, the hazard (5.15) will be motivated by a nonleaky integrate-and-fire neuron subject to noise.

Example: from hazard functions to interval distributions

Interval distributions and hazard functions have been measured in many experiments. For example, in auditory neurons of the cat driven by stationary stimuli, the hazard function $\rho_0(t - \hat{t})$ increases, after an absolute refractory time, to a constant level (Goldberg et al., 1964). We approximate the time course of the hazard function as

$$
\rho_0(s) = \begin{cases} 0 & \text{for} \quad s \le \Delta^{\text{abs}} \\ \nu \, [1 - e^{-\lambda (s - \Delta^{\text{abs}})}] & \text{for} \quad s > \Delta^{\text{abs}} \end{cases} \tag{5.16}
$$

with parameters Δ^{abs}, λ, and ν; Fig. 5.2B. In Section 5.3 we will see how the hazard (5.16) can be related to neuronal dynamics. Given the hazard function, we can calculate the survivor function and interval distributions. Application of Eq. (5.7) yields

$$
S_0(s) = \begin{cases} 1 & \text{for} \quad s < \Delta^{\text{abs}} \\ e^{-\nu (s - \Delta^{\text{abs}})} \, e^{\nu \rho_0(s)/\lambda} & \text{for} \quad s > \Delta^{\text{abs}}. \end{cases} \tag{5.17}
$$

The interval distribution is given by $P_0(s) = \rho_0(s) \, S_0(s)$. Interval distribution, survivor function, and hazard are shown in Fig. 5.2B.

Example: Poisson process

Let us compare the hazard functions of the two previous examples to the hazard of a homogeneous Poisson process that generates spikes stochastically at a fixed rate ν. Since different spikes are independent, the hazard of a Poisson process is constant $\rho_0(s) \equiv \nu$. In particular, there is no dependence of the hazard upon the last or any

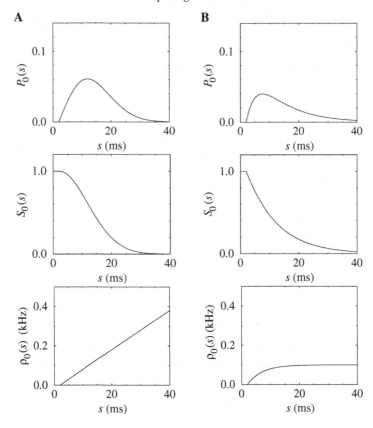

Fig. 5.2. **A**. Interval distribution $P_0(s)$ (top), survivor function $S_0(s)$ (middle) for a hazard function (bottom) defined by $\rho_0(s) = a_0\,(s - \Delta^{\text{abs}})\,\Theta(s - \Delta^{\text{abs}})$ with $a_0 = 0.01$ ms^{-2} and $\Delta^{\text{abs}} = 2$ ms, where Θ is the Heaviside function. **B**. Similar plots as in A but for a hazard function defined by $\rho_0(s) = \nu\{1 - \exp[-\lambda\,(s - \Delta^{\text{abs}})]\}\,\Theta(s - \Delta^{\text{abs}})$ with $\nu = 0.1$ kHz, $\lambda = 0.2$ kHz, and $\Delta^{\text{abs}} = 2$ ms.

earlier spike. From Eq. (5.8) we find the survivor function $S_0(s) = \exp[-\nu\,s]$. The interval distribution is exponential

$$P_0(s) = \nu\,e^{-\nu s} \quad \text{for } s > 0. \tag{5.18}$$

Interval distribution and survivor function of a Poisson neuron with constant rate ν are plotted in Fig. 5.3A. The most striking feature of Fig. 5.3A is that the interval distribution has its maximum at $s = 0$ so that extremely short intervals are most likely. In contrast to a Poisson process, real neurons show refractoriness so that the interval distribution $P_0(s)$ vanishes for $s \to 0$.

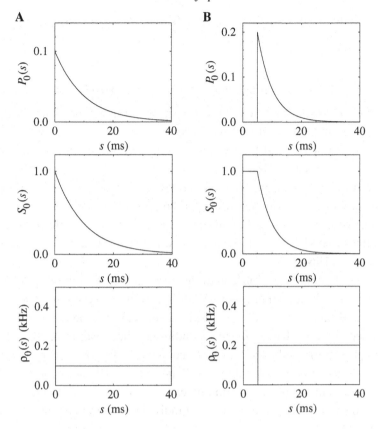

Fig. 5.3. Interval distribution $P_0(s)$ (top), survivor function $S_0(s)$ (middle), and hazard function (bottom) for a Poisson neuron (**A**) and a Poisson neuron with absolute refractoriness ($\Delta^{abs} = 5$ ms) (**B**).

A simple modification of the Poisson process allows us to incorporate absolute refractoriness. We define a hazard function

$$\rho_0(s) = \begin{cases} 0 & \text{for} & s < \Delta^{abs} \\ \nu & \text{for} & s > \Delta^{abs}. \end{cases} \tag{5.19}$$

We call a process with hazard function (5.19) a Poisson neuron with absolute refractoriness. It generates a spike train with an interval distribution

$$P_0(s) = \begin{cases} 0 & \text{for} & s < \Delta^{abs} \\ \nu \exp\left[-\nu\left(s - \Delta^{abs}\right)\right] & \text{for} & s > \Delta^{abs}; \end{cases} \tag{5.20}$$

see Fig. 5.3B. We may compare the hazard function of the Poisson neuron with absolute refractoriness with the more realistic hazard of Eq. (5.16). The main difference is that the hazard in Eq. (5.19) jumps from the state of absolute refractoriness to a constant firing rate, whereas in Eq. (5.16) the transition is smooth.

5.2.4 Stationary renewal theory and experiments

Renewal theory is usually associated with stationary input conditions. The interval distribution P_0 can then be estimated experimentally from a single long spike train. The applicability of renewal theory relies on the hypothesis that a memory back to the last spike suffices to describe the spike statistics. In particular, there should be no correlation between one interval and the next. In experiments, the renewal hypothesis can be tested by measuring the correlation between subsequent intervals. Under some experimental conditions, correlations are small, indicating that a description of spiking as a stationary renewal process is a good approximation (Goldberg et al., 1964).

The notion of stationary input conditions is a mathematical concept that cannot be easily translated into experiments. With intracellular recordings under *in vitro* conditions, constant input current can be imposed and thus the renewal hypothesis can be tested directly. Under *in vivo* conditions, the assumption that the input current to a neuron embedded in a large neural system is constant (or has stationary statistics) is questionable; see Perkel et al. (1967a,b) for a discussion. While the externally controlled stimulus can be made stationary (e.g., a grating drifting at constant speed), the input to an individual neuron cannot be controlled experimentally.

Let us suppose that, for a given experiment, we have checked that the renewal hypothesis holds to a reasonable degree of accuracy. From the experimental interval distribution P_0 we can then calculate the survivor function S_0 and the hazard ρ_0 via Eqs. (5.5) and (5.10); see the examples in subsection 5.2.2. If some additional assumptions regarding the nature of the noise are made, the form of the hazard $\rho_0(t|\hat{t})$ can be interpreted in terms of neuronal dynamics. In particular, a reduced hazard immediately after a spike is a signature of neuronal refractoriness (Goldberg et al., 1964; Berry and Meister, 1998).

For a stationary renewal process, the interval distribution P_0 contains *all* the statistical information, in particular mean firing rate, autocorrelation function and noise spectrum can be derived.

Mean firing rate

To arrive at an expression for the mean firing rate, we start with the definition of the mean interval,

$$\langle s \rangle = \int_0^\infty s\, P_0(s)\, ds \,. \tag{5.21}$$

The mean firing rate has been defined in Section 1.4 as $\nu = 1/\langle s \rangle$. Hence,

$$\nu = \left[\int_0^\infty s\, P_0(s)\, ds \right]^{-1} = \left[\int_0^\infty S_0(s)\, ds \right]^{-1}. \tag{5.22}$$

The second equality sign follows from integration by parts using $P_0(s) = -dS_0(s)/ds$; cf. Eq. (5.5).

Autocorrelation function

Let us consider a spike train $S_i(t) = \sum_f \delta(t - t_i^{(f)})$ of length T. The firing times $t_i^{(f)}$ might have been measured in an experiment or generated by a neuron model. We suppose that T is sufficiently long so that we can formally consider the limit $T \to \infty$. The autocorrelation function $C_{ii}(s)$ of the spike train is a measure of the probability of finding two spikes at a time interval s, i.e.,

$$C_{ii}(s) = \langle S_i(t)\, S_i(t+s) \rangle_t, \tag{5.23}$$

where $\langle \rangle_t$ denotes an average over time t,

$$\langle f(t) \rangle_t = \lim_{T \to \infty} \frac{1}{T} \int_{-T/2}^{T/2} f(t)\, dt. \tag{5.24}$$

We note that the right-hand side of Eq. (5.23) is symmetric so that $C_{ii}(-s) = C_{ii}(s)$ holds.

The calculation of the autocorrelation function for a stationary renewal process is the topic of the next section.

Noise spectrum

The power spectrum (or power spectral density) of a spike train is defined as $\mathcal{P}(\omega) = \lim_{T \to \infty} \mathcal{P}_T(\omega)$, where $\mathcal{P}_T$ is the power of a segment of length T of the spike train,

$$\mathcal{P}_T(\omega) = \frac{1}{T} \left| \int_{-T/2}^{T/2} S_i(t)\, e^{-i\omega t}\, dt \right|^2. \tag{5.25}$$

The power spectrum $\mathcal{P}(\omega)$ of a spike train is equal to the Fourier transform $\hat{C}_{ii}(\omega)$ of its autocorrelation function (Wiener–Khinchin theorem). To see this, we use the definition of the autocorrelation function

$$\hat{C}_{ii}(\omega) = \int_{-\infty}^{\infty} \langle S_i(t)\, S_i(t+s)\rangle\, e^{-i\omega s}\, ds$$

$$= \lim_{T\to\infty} \frac{1}{T} \int_{-T/2}^{T/2} S_i(t) \int_{-\infty}^{\infty} S_i(t+s)\, e^{-i\omega s}\, ds\, dt$$

$$= \lim_{T\to\infty} \frac{1}{T} \int_{-T/2}^{T/2} S_i(t)\, e^{+i\omega t}\, dt \int_{-\infty}^{\infty} S_i(s')\, e^{-i\omega s'}\, ds'. \tag{5.26}$$

In the limit of $T \to \infty$, Eq. (5.25) becomes identical to Eq. (5.26) so that the assertion follows. The power spectral density of a spike train during spontaneous activity is called the noise spectrum of the neuron (Edwards and Wakefield, 1993; Bair et al., 1994). As we will see in the next subsection, the noise spectrum of a stationary renewal process is intimately related to the interval distribution $P_0(s)$.

5.2.5 Autocorrelation of a stationary renewal process

Noise is a limiting factor to all forms of information transmission and in particular to information transmission by neurons. An important concept of the theory of signal transmission is the signal-to-noise ratio. A signal that is transmitted at a certain frequency ω should be stronger than (or at least of the same order of magnitude as) the noise at the same frequency. For this reason, the noise spectrum $\mathcal{P}(\omega)$ of the transmission channel is of interest. In this section we calculate the noise spectrum of a stationary renewal process. As we have seen above, the noise spectrum of a neuron is directly related to the autocorrelation function of its spike train. Both noise spectrum and autocorrelation function are experimentally accessible (Edwards and Wakefield, 1993; Bair et al., 1994).

Let $v_i = \langle S_i \rangle$ denote the mean firing rate (expected number of spikes per unit time) of the spike train. Thus the probability of finding a spike in a short segment $[t, t + \Delta t]$ of the spike train is $v\,\Delta t$. For large intervals s, firing at time $t + s$ is independent from whether or not there was a spike at time t. Therefore, the expectation of finding a spike at t and another spike at $t+s$ approaches for $s \to \infty$ a limiting value $\lim_{s\to\infty}\langle S_i(t)\,S_i(t+s)\rangle = \lim_{s\to\infty} C_{ii}(s) = v_i^2$. It is convenient to subtract the baseline value and introduce a "normalized" autocorrelation,

$$C_{ii}^0(s) = C_{ii}(s) - v_i^2, \tag{5.27}$$

with $\lim_{s\to\infty} C_{ii}^0(s) = 0$. Fourier transform of Eq. (5.27) yields

$$\hat{C}_{ii}(\omega) = \hat{C}_{ii}^0(\omega) + 2\pi v_i^2\, \delta(\omega). \tag{5.28}$$

Thus $\hat{C}_{ii}(\omega)$ diverges at $\omega = 0$; the divergence is removed by switching to the normalized autocorrelation. In the following we will calculate $\hat{C}_{ii}(\omega)$ for $\omega \neq 0$.

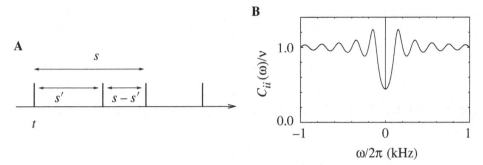

Fig. 5.4. **A**. The autocorrelation of a spike train describes the chance of finding two spikes at a distance s, independent of the number of spikes that occur in between. **B**. Fourier transform of the autocorrelation function C_{ii} of a Poisson neuron with absolute refractoriness ($\Delta^{ax} = 5$ ms) and constant stimulation ($\nu = 100$ Hz).

In the case of a stationary renewal process, the autocorrelation function is closely related to the interval distribution $P_0(s)$. This relation will now be derived. Let us suppose that we have found a first spike at t. To calculate the autocorrelation we need the probability density for a spike at $t + s$. Let us construct an expression for $C_{ii}(s)$ for $s > 0$. The correlation function for positive s will be denoted by $\nu_i \, C_+(s)$ or

$$C_+(s) = \frac{1}{\nu_i} C_{ii}(s) \, \Theta(s) . \tag{5.29}$$

The factor ν_i in Eq. (5.29) takes care of the fact that we expect a first spike at t with rate ν_i. $C_+(s)$ gives the *conditional* probability density that, given a spike at t, we will find another spike at $t + s > t$. The spike at $t + s$ can be the first spike after t, or the second one, or the nth one; see Fig. 5.4. Thus for $s > 0$

$$
\begin{aligned}
C_+(s) \;=\; & P_0(s) + \int_0^\infty P_0(s') \, P_0(s - s') \, ds' \\
& + \int_0^\infty \int_0^\infty P_0(s') \, P_0(s'') \, P_0(s - s' - s'') \, ds' \, ds'' + \cdots
\end{aligned} \tag{5.30}
$$

or

$$C_+(s) = P_0(s) + \int_0^\infty P_0(s') \, C_+(s - s') \, ds' , \tag{5.31}$$

as can be seen by inserting Eq. (5.30) on the right-hand side of Eq. (5.31).

Due to the symmetry of C_{ii}, we have $C_{ii}(s) = \nu \, C_+(-s)$ for $s < 0$. Finally, for $s = 0$, the autocorrelation has a δ peak reflecting the trivial autocorrelation of each spike with itself. Hence,

$$C_{ii}(s) = \nu_i \, [\delta(s) + C_+(s) + C_+(-s)] . \tag{5.32}$$

In order to solve Eq. (5.31) for C_+ we take the Fourier transform of Eq. (5.31) and find

$$\hat{C}_+(\omega) = \frac{\hat{P}_0(\omega)}{1 - \hat{P}_0(\omega)} , \qquad (5.33)$$

Together with the Fourier transform of Eq. (5.32), $\hat{C}_{ii} = \nu_i [1 + 2\,\mathrm{Re}\{C_+(\omega)\}]$, we obtain

$$\hat{C}_{ii}(\omega) = \nu_i\,\mathrm{Re}\left\{ \frac{1 + \hat{P}_0(\omega)}{1 - \hat{P}_0(\omega)} \right\} \qquad \text{for}\quad \omega \neq 0. \qquad (5.34)$$

Here $\mathrm{Re}\{\ \}$ refers to the real part of the expression in curly braces. For $\omega = 0$, the Fourier integral over the right-hand side of Eq. (5.30) diverges, since $\int_0^\infty P_0(s)ds = 1$. If we add the diverging term from Eq. (5.28), we arrive at

$$\hat{C}_{ii}(\omega) = \nu_i\,\mathrm{Re}\left\{ \frac{1 + \hat{P}_0(\omega)}{1 - \hat{P}_0(\omega)} \right\} + 2\pi\,\nu_i^2\delta(\omega). \qquad (5.35)$$

This is a standard result of stationary renewal theory (Cox and Lewis, 1966) which has been repeatedly applied to neuronal spike trains (Edwards and Wakefield, 1993; Bair et al., 1994).

Example: stationary Poisson process

In Section 5.2.3 we have defined the Poisson process as a stationary renewal process with constant hazard $\rho_0(t - \hat{t}) = \nu$. In the literature, a Poisson process is often defined via its autocorrelation

$$C_{ii}(s) = \nu\,\delta(s) + \nu^2. \qquad (5.36)$$

We want to show that Eq. (5.36) follows from Eq. (5.30).

Since the interval distribution of a Poisson process is exponential (cf. Eq. (5.18)), we can evaluate the integrals on the right-hand side of Eq. (5.30) in a straightforward manner. The result is

$$C_+(s) = \nu\,e^{-\nu s}\left[1 + \nu s + \frac{1}{2}(\nu s)^2 + \cdots \right] = \nu. \qquad (5.37)$$

Hence, with Eq. (5.32), we obtain the autocorrelation function (5.36) of a homogeneous Poisson process. The Fourier transform of Eq. (5.36) yields a flat spectrum with a δ peak at zero:

$$\hat{C}_{ii}(\omega) = \nu + 2\pi\,\nu^2\,\delta(\omega) . \qquad (5.38)$$

The result could have also been obtained by evaluating Eq. (5.35).

Example: Poisson process with absolute refractoriness

We return to the Poisson neuron with absolute refractoriness defined in Eq. (5.19). Apart from an absolute refractory time Δ^{abs}, the neuron fires with rate r. For $\omega \neq 0$, Eq. (5.35) yields the autocorrelation function

$$\hat{C}_{ii}(\omega) = v \left\{ 1 + 2 \frac{v^2}{\omega^2} [1 - \cos(\omega \, \Delta^{\mathrm{abs}})] + 2 \frac{v}{\omega} \sin(\omega \, \Delta^{\mathrm{abs}}) \right\}^{-1}, \tag{5.39}$$

cf. Fig. 5.4B. In contrast to the stationary Poisson process Eq. (5.36), the noise spectrum of a neuron with absolute refractoriness $\Delta^{\mathrm{abs}} > 0$ is no longer flat. In particular, for $\omega \to 0$ the noise level is *decreased* by a factor $[1 + 2(v \, \Delta^{\mathrm{abs}}) + (v \, \Delta^{\mathrm{abs}})^2]^{-1}$. Equation (5.39) and generalizations thereof have been used to fit the power spectrum of, e.g., auditory neurons (Edwards and Wakefield, 1993) and MT neurons (Bair et al., 1994).

Can we understand the decrease in the noise spectrum for $\omega \to 0$? The mean interval of a Poisson neuron with absolute refractoriness is $\langle s \rangle = \Delta^{\mathrm{abs}} + r^{-1}$. Hence the mean firing rate is

$$v = \frac{r}{1 + \Delta^{\mathrm{abs}} r}. \tag{5.40}$$

For $\Delta^{\mathrm{abs}} = 0$ we retrieve the stationary Poisson process Section 5.2.3, with $v = r$. For finite Δ^{abs} the firing is more regular than that of a Poisson process with the same mean rate v. We note that for finite $\Delta^{\mathrm{abs}} > 0$, the mean firing rate remains bounded even if $r \to \infty$. The neuron then fires regularly with period Δ^{abs}. Because the spike train of a neuron with refractoriness is more regular than that of a Poisson neuron with the same mean rate, the spike count over a long interval, and hence the spectrum for $\omega \to 0$, is less noisy. This means that Poisson neurons with absolute refractoriness can transmit slow signals more reliably than a simple Poisson process.

5.3 Escape noise

There are various ways to introduce noise in formal spiking neuron models. In this section we focus on a "noisy threshold" (also called escape or hazard model). In Section 5.5 we will discuss "noisy integration" (also called the stochastic spike arrival or diffusion model). In both cases, we are interested in the effect of the noise on the distribution of interspike intervals.

In the escape model, we imagine that the neuron can fire even though the formal threshold ϑ has not been reached or may stay quiescent even though the formal threshold has been passed. To do this consistently, we introduce an "escape rate" or "firing intensity" which depends on the momentary state of the neuron.

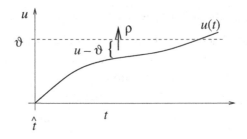

Fig. 5.5. Noisy threshold. A neuron can fire at time t with probability density $\rho[u(t) - \vartheta]$ even though the membrane potential u has not yet reached the threshold ϑ.

5.3.1 Escape rate and hazard function

Given the input I and the firing time $\hat{t}$ of the last spike, we can calculate the membrane potential of the Spike Response Model or the integrate-and-fire neuron from Eqs. (5.1) or (5.2), respectively. In the deterministic model the next spike occurs when u reaches the threshold ϑ. In order to introduce some variability into the neuronal spike generator, we replace the strict threshold by a stochastic firing criterion. In the noisy threshold model, spikes can occur at any time with a probability density,

$$\rho = f(u - \vartheta), \tag{5.41}$$

that depends on the momentary distance between the (noiseless) membrane potential and the threshold; see Fig. 5.5. We can think of f as an escape rate similar to the one encountered in models of chemical reactions (van Kampen, 1992). In the mathematical theory of point processes, the quantity ρ is called a "stochastic intensity". Since we use ρ in the context of neuron models we will refer to it as a firing intensity.

Since u on the right-hand side of Eq. (5.41) is a function of time, the firing intensity ρ is time-dependent as well. In view of Eqs. (5.1) and (5.2), we write

$$\rho_I(t|\hat{t}) = f[u(t|\hat{t}) - \vartheta], \tag{5.42}$$

where $\rho_I(t|\hat{t})$ is the hazard introduced in Eq. (5.10). In other words, the escape rate f allows us to translate the membrane potential $u(t|\hat{t})$ into a hazard $\rho_I(t|\hat{t})$.

Is Eq. (5.42) a sufficiently general noise model? We have seen in Section 2.2 that the concept of a pure voltage threshold is questionable. More generally, the spike trigger process could, for example, also depend on the slope $\dot{u} = du/dt$ with which the "threshold" is approached. In the noisy threshold model, we may therefore also consider an escape rate (or hazard) which depends not only on u but also on its derivative $\dot{u}$

$$\rho_I(t|\hat{t}) = f[u(t|\hat{t}), \dot{u}(t|\hat{t})]. \tag{5.43}$$

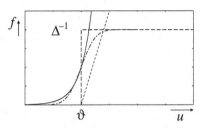

Fig. 5.6. Soft threshold escape rates. Exponential function (solid), piecewise linear function (dotted), step function (dashed), and error function (dot-dashed). The step function and error function saturate at a maximum rate of Δ^{-1}. The threshold is ϑ.

The choice of the escape function f in Eq. (5.42) or (5.43) is arbitrary. A reasonable condition is to require $f \to 0$ for $u \to -\infty$. Below we discuss some simple examples of Eq. (5.42). We will return to Eq. (5.43) in Section 5.7.

Note that the hazard ρ in Eq. (5.43) is *implicitly* time-dependent, via the membrane potential $u(t|\hat{t})$. In an even more general model, we could in addition include an *explicit* time dependence, e.g., to account for a reduced spiking probability immediately after the spike at $\hat{t}$. In the following examples we will stick to the hazard function as defined by Eq. (5.42).

Example: hard and soft threshold

We have motivated the escape model by a noisy version of the threshold process. In order to explore the relation between noisy and deterministic threshold models, we consider an escape function f defined as

$$f(u - \vartheta) = \begin{cases} 0 & \text{for} & u < \vartheta \\ \Delta^{-1} & \text{for} & u \geq \vartheta. \end{cases} \tag{5.44}$$

Thus, the neuron never fires if $u < \vartheta$. On the other hand, if the mean escape time Δ goes to zero, the neuron fires immediately when it crosses the threshold.

How can we "soften" the sharp threshold? A simple choice for a soft threshold is an exponential dependence,

$$f(u - \vartheta) = \frac{1}{\tau_0} \exp[\beta (u - \vartheta)], \tag{5.45}$$

where β and τ_0 are parameters. For $\beta \to \infty$, we return to the noiseless model of Eq. (5.44). Alternatively, we could introduce a piecewise linear escape rate,

$$f(u - \vartheta) = \beta [u - \vartheta]_+ = \begin{cases} 0 & \text{for} & u < \vartheta \\ \beta (u - \vartheta) & \text{for} & u \geq \vartheta \end{cases} \tag{5.46}$$

with slope β for $u > \vartheta$. For $u > \vartheta$, the firing intensity is proportional to $u - \vartheta$; cf. Fig. 5.6. This corresponds to the intuitive idea that instantaneous firing rates increase with the membrane potential. Variants of the linear escape-rate model are commonly used to describe spike generation in, e.g., auditory nerve fibers (Siebert and Gray, 1963; Miller and Mark, 1992).

Finally, we can also use a sigmoidal escape rate (Wilson and Cowan, 1972; Abeles, 1982),

$$f(u - \vartheta) = \frac{1}{2\Delta} \left[1 + \mathrm{erf} \left(\frac{u - \vartheta}{\sqrt{2}\sigma} \right) \right],$$ (5.47)

with time constant Δ and noise parameter σ. The error function "erf" is defined as

$$\mathrm{erf}(x) = \frac{2}{\sqrt{\pi}} \int_0^x \exp(-y^2) \, dy$$ (5.48)

with $\mathrm{erf}(-x) = -\mathrm{erf}(x)$. For $u \to \infty$, the escape rate in Eq. (5.47) saturates at a value $f = \Delta^{-1}$ independent of the noise parameter σ; cf. Fig. 5.7B. For $\sigma \to 0$, we retrieve the step function $f(u - \vartheta) = \Delta^{-1} \Theta(u - \vartheta)$.

Example: motivating a sigmoidal escape rate

We want to motivate the sigmoidal escape rate by a model with stochastic threshold in *discrete* time $t_n = n\,\Delta$. After each time step of length Δ, a new value of the threshold is chosen from a Gaussian distribution of threshold values ϑ' with mean ϑ,

$$P(\vartheta') = \frac{1}{\sqrt{2\pi}\sigma} \exp \left[-\frac{(\vartheta' - \vartheta)^2}{2\sigma^2} \right].$$ (5.49)

The probability of firing at time step t_n is equal to the probability that the momentary value ϑ' of the threshold is below the membrane potential $u(t_n)$

$$\mathrm{Prob}\,\{\text{spike at } t_n\} = \mathrm{Prob}\,\{u(t_n) > \vartheta'\} = \int_{-\infty}^{u(t_n)} P(\vartheta') \, d\vartheta';$$ (5.50)

cf. Fig. 5.7A. The firing probability divided by the step size Δ can be interpreted as a firing intensity (Wilson and Cowan, 1972),

$$f(u - \vartheta) = \frac{1}{\Delta} \int_{-\infty}^{(u-\vartheta)} \frac{1}{\sqrt{2\pi}\sigma} \exp \left(-\frac{x^2}{2\sigma^2} \right) \, dx = \frac{1}{2\Delta} \left[1 + \mathrm{erf} \left(\frac{u - \vartheta}{\sqrt{2}\sigma} \right) \right],$$ (5.51)

which is the sigmoidal escape rate introduced in Eq. (5.47).

Instead of considering a model with stochastic threshold and deterministic membrane potential, we can also study a model with fixed threshold and stochastic membrane potential. The total membrane potential at time step t_n is $u(t_n) + \Delta u(t_n)$, where u is the deterministic and Δu the stochastic contribution. If Δu is chosen at each time step independently from a Gaussian distribution with variance σ and

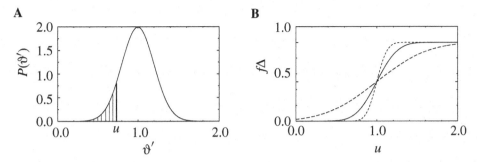

Fig. 5.7. **A**. Gaussian distribution of thresholds $P(\vartheta')$ with mean $\vartheta = 1$ and variance $\sigma = 0.2$. The shaded area gives the probability that u is above threshold. **B**. Escape rate according to Eq. (5.51) with $\vartheta = 1$ for different noise levels $\sigma = 0.1$ (dotted line), $\sigma = 0.2$ (solid line), and $\sigma = 0.5$ (dashed line).

vanishing mean, we arrive again at formula (5.47) (Geisler and Goldberg, 1966; Weiss, 1966; Abeles, 1982).

The sigmoidal escape rate (5.51) has been motivated here for models in *discrete* time. There are two potential problems. Firstly, if we keep Δ fixed and take $\sigma \to 0$ we do not recover the deterministic threshold model. Thus the low-noise limit is problematic. Secondly, since the firing intensity diverges for $\Delta \to 0$, simulations will necessarily depend on the discretization Δ. This is due to the fact that the bandwidth of the noise is limited by Δ^{-1} because a new value of ϑ' or Δu is chosen at intervals Δ. For $\Delta \to 0$, the bandwidth and hence the noise power diverge. Despite its problems, the sigmoidal escape rate is also used in neuronal models in continuous time and either motivated by a Gaussian distribution of threshold values (Wilson and Cowan, 1972) or else for fixed threshold ϑ by a Gaussian distribution of membrane potentials with *band-limited* noise (Weiss, 1966; Abeles, 1982). If we use Eq. (5.47) in continuous time, the time scale Δ becomes a free parameter and should be taken proportional to the correlation time τ_{corr} of the noise Δu in the membrane potential (i.e., proportional to the inverse of the noise bandwidth). If the correlation time is short, the model becomes closely related to continuous-time escape rate models (Weiss, 1966). A "natural" correlation time of the membrane potential will be calculated in Section 5.5 in the context of stochastic spike arrival.

Example: transition from continuous to discrete time

In the previous example, we started from a model in discrete time and found that the limit of continuous time is not without problems. Here we want to start from a model in continuous time and discretize time as it is often done in simulations. In a straightforward discretization scheme, we calculate the probability of firing during a time step Δt of a neuron that has fired the last time at $\hat{t}$ as $\int_{t}^{t+\Delta t} \rho_I(t'|\hat{t}) \, dt' \approx$

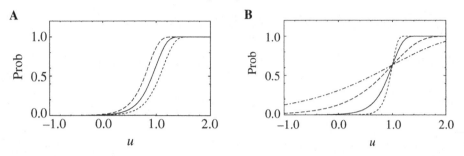

Fig. 5.8. **A.** Probability of firing in a discrete time interval Δt as a function of the membrane potential u for different discretizations $\Delta t = 0.5$ ms (dashed line), $\Delta t = 1$ ms (solid line), and $\Delta t = 2$ ms (dotted line) with $\beta = 5$. **B.** Similar plot as in **A** but for different noise levels $\beta = 10$ (dotted line), $\beta = 5$ (solid line), $\beta = 2$ (dashed line), and $\beta = 1$ (dot-dashed line) with $\Delta t = 1$ ms. The escape rate is given by Eq. (5.45) with parameters $\vartheta = 1$ and $\tau_0 = 1$ ms.

$\rho_I(t|\hat{t})\,\Delta t$. For $u \gg \vartheta$, the hazard $\rho_I(t|\hat{t}) = f[u(t|\hat{t}) - \vartheta]$ can take large values; see, e.g., Eq. (5.45). Thus Δt must be extremely short so as to guarantee $\rho_I(t|\hat{t})\,\Delta t < 1$.

In order to arrive at an improved discretization scheme, we calculate the probability that a neuron does *not* fire in a time step Δt. Since the integration of Eq. (5.6) over a *finite* time Δt yields an exponential factor analogous to Eq. (5.7), we arrive at a firing probability

$$\text{Prob}\left\{\text{spike in } [t, t + \Delta t] \,|\, u(t|\hat{t})\right\} \approx 1 - \exp\left\{-\Delta t\, f[u(t|\hat{t}) - \vartheta]\right\}. \qquad (5.52)$$

Even if f diverges for $u \to \infty$, the probability remains bounded between zero and one. We see from Fig. 5.8A that an increase in the discretization Δt mainly shifts the firing curve to the left while the form remains roughly the same. An increase of the noise level makes the curve flatter; cf. Fig. 5.8B.

5.3.2 *Interval distribution and mean firing rate*

In this section, we combine the escape rate model with the concepts of renewal theory and calculate the input-dependent interval distribution $P_I(t|\hat{t})$ for escape rate models.

We recall Eq. (5.9) and express the interval distribution in terms of the hazard ρ,

$$P_I(t|\hat{t}) = \rho_I(t|\hat{t}) \exp\left[-\int_{\hat{t}}^{t} \rho_I(t'|\hat{t})\,dt'\right]. \qquad (5.53)$$

This expression can be compared to the interval distribution of the stationary Poisson process in Eq. (5.18). The main difference to the simple Poisson model is that the hazard $\rho_I(t|\hat{t})$ depends on both the last firing time $\hat{t}$ and the (potentially

A

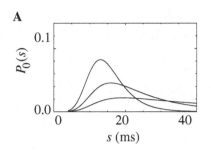

B

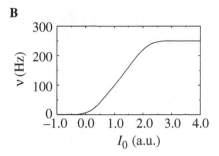

Fig. 5.9. **A**. Interval distribution $P_0(s)$ for a SRM$_0$ neuron with absolute refractory period $\Delta^{\text{abs}} = 4$ ms followed by an exponentially decreasing afterpotential as in Eq. (5.63) with $\eta_0 = 1$ and $\tau = 4$ ms. The model neuron is stimulated by a constant current $I_0 = 0.7, 0.5, 0.3$ (from top to bottom, arbitrary units). **B**. Output rate ν as a function of I_0 (gain function). The escape rate is given by Eq. (5.45) with $\vartheta = 1$, $\beta = 5$, and $\tau_0 = 1$ ms.

time-dependent) input. We know that immediately after firing a neuron is refractory and therefore not very likely to fire. Thus refractoriness strongly shapes the interval distribution of neurons; cf., e.g., Berry and Meister (1998). Escape models allow us to show the relation between the hazard $\rho_I(t|\hat{t})$ and refractoriness.

To do so, we express ρ_I by the escape rate. In order to keep the notation simple, we suppose that the escape rate f is a function of u only. We insert Eq. (5.42) into Eq. (5.53) and obtain

$$P_I(t|\hat{t}) = f[u(t|\hat{t}) - \vartheta] \exp\left[-\int_{\hat{t}}^{t} f[u(t'|\hat{t}) - \vartheta]\,dt'\right]. \qquad (5.54)$$

In order to make the role of refractoriness explicit, we consider the version SRM$_0$ of the Spike Response Model. The membrane potential is

$$u(t|\hat{t}) = \eta(t - \hat{t}) + h(t) \qquad (5.55)$$

with $h(t) = \int_0^\infty \kappa(s)\,I(t-s)\,ds$; cf. Eq. (4.42). We insert Eq. (5.55) into Eq. (5.54) and find

$$P_I(t|\hat{t}) = f[\eta(t-\hat{t}) + h(t) - \vartheta] \exp\left[-\int_{\hat{t}}^{t} f[\eta(t'-\hat{t}) + h(t') - \vartheta]\,ds'\right]. \qquad (5.56)$$

Figure 5.9 shows the interval distribution Eq. (5.56) for constant input current I_0 as a function of $s = t - \hat{t}$. With the normalization $\int_0^\infty \kappa(s)ds = 1$, we have $h_0 = I_0$. Due to the refractory term η, extremely short intervals are impossible and the maximum of the interval distribution occurs at some finite value of s. If I_0 is increased, the maximum is shifted to the left. The interval distributions of

Fig. 5.9A have qualitatively the same shape as those found for cortical neurons. The gain function $v = g(I_0)$ of a noisy SRM$_0$ neuron is shown in Fig. 5.9B.

Example: SRM$_0$ with absolute refractoriness

We study the model SRM$_0$ defined in Eq. (5.55) for absolute refractoriness

$$\eta(s) = \begin{cases} -\infty & \text{for} \quad s < \Delta^{\text{abs}} \\ 0 & \text{for} \quad s > \Delta^{\text{abs}}. \end{cases} \tag{5.57}$$

The hazard is $\rho_I(t|\hat{t}) = f[h(t) - \vartheta]$ for $t - \hat{t} > \Delta^{\text{abs}}$ and $\rho_I(t|\hat{t}) = 0$ for $t - \hat{t} < \Delta^{\text{abs}}$ since $f \to 0$ for $u \to -\infty$. Hence, with $r(t) = f[h(t) - \vartheta]$

$$P_I(t|\hat{t}) = r(t) \exp\left[-\int_{\hat{t}+\Delta^{\text{abs}}}^{t} r(t')\, dt' \right] \Theta(t - \hat{t} - \Delta^{\text{abs}}). \tag{5.58}$$

For stationary input $h(t) = h_0$, we are led back to the Poisson process with absolute refractoriness; see Eq. (5.20). For $\Delta^{\text{abs}} \to 0$, Eq. (5.58) is the interval distribution of an inhomogeneous Poisson process with rate $r(t)$.

Example: linear escape rates

In this example we show that interval distributions are particularly simple if a linear escape rate is adopted. We start with the nonleaky integrate-and-fire model. In the limit of $\tau_m \to \infty$, the membrane potential of an integrate-and-fire neuron is

$$u(t|\hat{t}) = u_r + \frac{1}{C} \int_{\hat{t}}^{t} I(t')\, dt'\, ; \tag{5.59}$$

cf. Eq. (5.2). Let us set $u_r = 0$ and consider a linear escape rate,

$$\rho_I(t|\hat{t}) = \beta\, [u(t|\hat{t}) - \vartheta]_+\, . \tag{5.60}$$

For constant input current I_0 and $\vartheta = 0$ the hazard is $\rho(t|\hat{t}) = a_0 (t - \hat{t} - \Delta^{\text{abs}})$ with $a_0 = \beta I_0/C$ and $\Delta^{\text{abs}} = \vartheta C/I_0$. The interval distribution for this hazard function has already been given in Eq. (5.14); see Fig. 5.2.

For a leaky integrate-and-fire neuron with constant input I_0, the membrane potential is

$$u(t|\hat{t}) = R I_0 \left[1 - e^{(-t-\hat{t})/\tau_m} \right], \tag{5.61}$$

where we have assumed $u_r = 0$. If we adopt Eq. (5.60) with $\vartheta = 0$, then the hazard is

$$\rho_0(t - \hat{t}) = v \left[1 - e^{-\lambda(t-\hat{t})} \right], \tag{5.62}$$

with $v = \beta R I_0$ and $\lambda = \tau_m^{-1}$. The interval distribution for this hazard function has been discussed in Section 5.2.3; cf. Eq. (5.17) and Fig. 5.2B. An absolute refractory

A

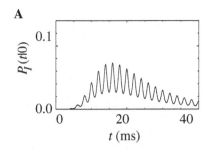

B

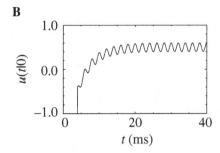

Fig. 5.10. **A**. Input-dependent interval distribution $P_I(t|0)$ for a SRM$_0$ neuron as in Fig. 5.9 stimulated by a periodically modulated input field $h(t) = h_0 + h_1 \cos(2\pi f t)$ with $h_0 = 0.5$, $h_1 = 0.1$ and frequency $f = 500$ Hz. **B**. The membrane potential $u(t|0) = \eta(t) + h(t)$ during stimulation as in **A**.

time Δ^{abs} as in the hazard Eq. (5.16) could be the result of a positive threshold $\vartheta > 0$.

Example: periodic input

We study the model SRM$_0$ as defined in Eq. (5.55) with periodic input $I(t) = I_0 + I_1 \cos(\Omega t)$, where Ω is the modulation frequency. This leads to an input potential $h(t) = h_0 + h_1 \cos(\Omega t + \varphi_1)$ with bias $h_0 = I_0$ and a periodic component with a certain amplitude h_1 and phase φ_1. We choose a refractory kernel with absolute and relative refractoriness defined as

$$\eta(s) = \begin{cases} -\infty & \text{for} \quad s < \Delta^{\text{abs}} \\ -\eta_0 \exp\left(-\dfrac{s - \Delta^{\text{abs}}}{\tau}\right) & \text{for} \quad s > \Delta^{\text{abs}} \end{cases} \tag{5.63}$$

and adopt the exponential escape rate given by Eq. (5.45).

Suppose that a spike has occurred at $\hat{t} = 0$. The probability density that the next spike occurs at time t is given by $P_I(t|\hat{t})$ and can be calculated from Eq. (5.53). The result is shown in Fig. 5.10. We note that the periodic component of the input is well represented in the response of the neuron. This example illustrates how neurons in the auditory system can transmit stimuli of frequencies higher than the mean firing rate of the neuron; see Section 12.5. We emphasize that the threshold in Fig. 5.10 is at $\vartheta = 1$. Without noise there would be no output spike. On the other hand, at very high noise levels, the modulation of the interval distribution would be much weaker. Thus a certain amount of noise is beneficial for signal transmission. The existence of a optimal noise level is a phenomenon called stochastic resonance and will be discussed in Section 5.8.

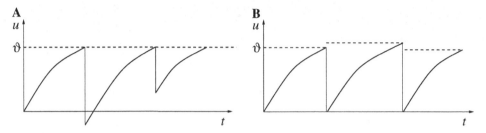

Fig. 5.11. Slow noise in the parameters. After each spike either the reset value (**A**) or the firing threshold (**B**) is set to a new randomly chosen value.

5.4 Slow noise in the parameters

In one of the previous examples ("Motivating a sigmoidal escape rate" in Section 5.3.1), a new value of the threshold was chosen at each time step; cf. Eq. (5.49). If time steps are short enough, such an approach is closely related to escape rate models. A completely different class of noise models can be constructed if the value of a parameter is changed *after each spike*. Thus between two spikes the noise is "frozen" so that the value of the fluctuating parameter does not change. In other words, the noise is slow compared to the fast neuronal dynamics. In principle, any of the neuronal parameters such as threshold, membrane time constant, or length of the refractory period can be subject to this type of noise (Knight, 1972a; Gestri, 1978; Lansky and Smith, 1989; Gerstner, 2000). In this section we want to show how to analyze such slow variations and calculate the interval distribution. We emphasize that these "slow" noise models cannot be mapped onto an escape rate formalism.

To keep the arguments simple, we will concentrate on noise in the formulation of reset and refractoriness. We assume an exponential refractory kernel,

$$\eta(s) = \eta_0 \, e^{-s/\tau} \,, \tag{5.64}$$

with time constant τ. In order to introduce noise, we suppose that the amount η_0 of the reset depends on a stochastic variable r,

$$\eta_0(r) = \tilde{\eta}_0 \, e^{r/\tau} \,, \tag{5.65}$$

where $\tilde{\eta}_0 < 0$ is a fixed parameter and r is a random variable with zero mean. In the language of the integrate-and-fire neuron, we can describe the effect of r as a stochastic component in the value of the reset potential.

In the "noisy reset" model, firing is given by the threshold condition

$$\vartheta = u(t|\hat{t}, r) = \eta_r(t - \hat{t}) + \int_0^\infty \kappa(t - \hat{t}, s) \, I(t - s) \, ds \,, \tag{5.66}$$

where $\eta_r(t - \hat{t}) = \eta_0(r) \exp[-(t - \hat{t})/\tau]$. Since u depends on the current value of r, we have written $u(t|\hat{t}, r)$ instead of $u(t|\hat{t})$. Let us write $T(\hat{t}, r)$ for the next interval of a neuron which has fired at $\hat{t}$ and was reset with a stochastic value r, i.e.,

$$T(\hat{t}, r) = \min \left\{ t - \hat{t} \mid u(t|\hat{t}, r) = \vartheta \right\} . \tag{5.67}$$

If r is drawn from a Gaussian distribution $\mathcal{G}_\sigma(r)$ with variance $\sigma \ll \tau$, the interval distribution is

$$P_I(t \mid \hat{t}) = \int dr \, \delta[t - \hat{t} - T(\hat{t}, r)] \, \mathcal{G}_\sigma(r) . \tag{5.68}$$

Let us now evaluate the interval distribution (5.68) for the variant SRM_0 of the Spike Response Model,

$$u(t|\hat{t}, r) = \eta_r(t - \hat{t}) + h(t) , \tag{5.69}$$

with constant input potential $h(t) = h_0$. Firstly, we show that a stochastic reset according to Eq. (5.65) with $r \neq 0$ shifts the refractory kernel horizontally along the time axis. To see this, let us consider a neuron that has fired its last spike at $\hat{t}$ and has been reset with a certain value r. The refractory term is

$$\eta_r(t - \hat{t}) = \tilde{\eta}_0 \exp[-(t - \hat{t} - r)/\tau] , \tag{5.70}$$

which is identical to that of a noiseless neuron that has fired its last spike at $t' = \hat{t} + r$. Given the constant input potential h_0, a noise-free SRM_0 neuron would fire regularly with period T_0. A noisy neuron that was reset with value r is delayed by a time r and fires therefore after an interval $T(\hat{t}, r) = T_0 + r$. Integration of Eq. (5.68) yields the interval distribution

$$P_0(t - \hat{t}) = \mathcal{G}_\sigma(t - \hat{t} - T_0) . \tag{5.71}$$

Thus, the Gaussian distribution $\mathcal{G}_\sigma(r)$ of the noise variable r maps directly to a Gaussian distribution of the intervals around the mean T_0. For a detailed discussion of the relation between the distribution of reset values and the interval distribution $P_0(t - \hat{t})$ of leaky integrate-and-fire neurons, see Lansky and Smith (1989).

Even though stochastic reset is not a realistic noise model for individual neurons, noise in the parameter values can approximate *inhomogeneous* populations of neurons where parameters vary from one neuron to the next (Knight, 1972a; Wilson and Cowan, 1972). Similarly, a fluctuating background input that changes slowly compared to the typical interspike interval can be considered as a slow change in the value of the firing threshold. More generally, noise with a cut-off frequency smaller than the typical firing rate can be described as slow noise in the parameters.

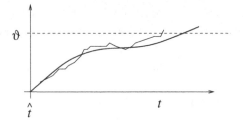

Fig. 5.12. Noisy integration. A stochastic contribution in the input current of an integrate-and-fire neuron causes the membrane potential to drift away from the reference trajectory (thick solid line). The neuron fires if the noisy trajectory (thin line) hits the threshold ϑ (schematic figure).

5.5 Diffusive noise

The integrate-and-fire model is, in its simplest form, defined by a differential equation $\tau_m \, du/dt = -u + R \, I(t)$ where τ_m is the membrane time constant, R the input resistance, and I the input current. The standard procedure of implementing noise in such a differential equation is to add a "noise term", $\xi(t)$, on the right-hand side. The noise term ξ is a stochastic process called "Gaussian white noise" characterized by its expectation value, $\langle \xi(t) \rangle = 0$, and the autocorrelation

$$\langle \xi(t) \, \xi(t') \rangle = \sigma^2 \, \tau_m \, \delta(t - t') \,, \tag{5.72}$$

where σ is the amplitude of the noise and τ_m the membrane time constant of the neuron. The result is a *stochastic differential equation*,

$$\tau_m \frac{d}{dt} u(t) = -u(t) + R \, I(t) + \xi(t) \,, \tag{5.73}$$

i.e., an equation for a stochastic process (Ornstein–Uhlenbeck process); cf. van Kampen (1992).

The neuron is said to fire an action potential whenever the membrane potential u reaches the threshold ϑ; cf. Fig. 5.12. We will refer to Eq. (5.73) as the Langevin equation of the noisy integrate-and-fire model. The analysis of Eq. (5.73) in the presence of the threshold ϑ is the topic of this section. Before we start with the discussion of Eq. (5.73), we indicate how the noise term $\xi(t)$ can be motivated by stochastic spike arrival.

5.5.1 Stochastic spike arrival

A typical neuron, e.g., a pyramidal cell in the vertebrate cortex, receives input spikes from thousands of other neurons, which in turn receive input from their presynaptic neurons and so forth; see Fig. 5.13. It is obviously impossible to

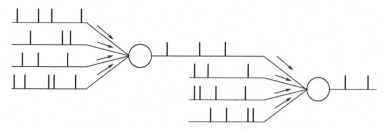

Fig. 5.13. Each neuron receives input spikes from a large number of presynaptic neurons. Only a small portion of the input comes from neurons within the model network; other input is described as stochastic spike arrival.

incorporate all neurons in the brain into one huge network model. Instead, it is reasonable to focus on a specific subset of neurons, e.g., a column in the visual cortex, and describe input from other parts of the brain as a stochastic background activity.

Let us consider an integrate-and-fire neuron that is part of a large network. Its input consists of (i) an external input $I^{\text{ext}}(t)$; (ii) input spikes $t_j^{(f)}$ from other neurons j of the network; and (iii) stochastic spike arrival $t_k^{(f)}$ due to the background activity in other parts of the brain. The membrane potential u evolves according to

$$\frac{\mathrm{d}}{\mathrm{d}t}u = -\frac{u}{\tau_m} + \frac{1}{C}I^{\text{ext}}(t) + \sum_j \sum_{t_j^{(f)}>\hat{t}} w_j\,\delta(t-t_j^{(f)}) + \sum_k \sum_{t_k^{(f)}>\hat{t}} w_k\,\delta(t-t_k^{(f)})\,, \quad (5.74)$$

where δ is the Dirac δ function and w_j is the coupling to other presynaptic neurons j in the network. Input from background neurons is weighted by the factor w_k. Firing times $t_k^{(f)}$ of a background neuron k are generated by a Poisson process with mean rate ν_k. Equation (5.74) is called Stein's model (Stein, 1965, 1967b).

In Stein's model, each input spike generates a postsynaptic potential $\Delta u(t) = w_j\epsilon(t-t_j^{(f)})$ with $\epsilon(s) = \mathrm{e}^{-s/\tau_m}\,\Theta(s)$, i.e., the potential jumps upon spike arrival by an amount w_j and decays exponentially thereafter. It is straightforward to generalize the model so as to include a synaptic time constant and work with arbitrary postsynaptic potentials $\epsilon(s)$ that are generated by stochastic spike arrival; cf. Fig. 5.14A.

Example: membrane potential fluctuations

We consider stochastic spike arrival at rate ν. Each input spike evokes a postsynaptic potential $w_0\,\epsilon(s)$. The input statistics is assumed to be Poisson, i.e., firing

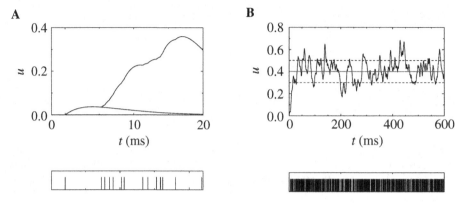

Fig. 5.14. Input spikes arrive stochastically (lower panel) at a mean rate of 1 kHz. **A**. Each input spike evokes an excitatory postsynaptic potential (EPSP) $\epsilon(s) \propto s \exp(-s/\tau)$ with $\tau = 4$ ms. The first EPSP (the one generated by the spike at $t = 0$) is plotted. The EPSPs of all spikes sum up and result in a fluctuating membrane potential $u(t)$. **B**. Continuation of the simulation shown in **A**. The horizontal lines indicate the mean (dotted line) and the standard deviation (dashed lines) of the membrane potential.

times are independent. Thus, the input spike train,

$$S(t) = \sum_{k=1}^{N} \sum_{t_k^{(f)}} \delta(t - t_k^{(f)}) , \tag{5.75}$$

that arrives at neuron i is a random process with expectation

$$\langle S(t) \rangle = \nu_0 \tag{5.76}$$

and autocorrelation

$$\langle S(t) \, S(t') \rangle - \nu_0^2 = N \, \nu_0 \, \delta(t - t') ; \tag{5.77}$$

cf. Eq. (5.36).

We suppose that the input is weak so that the neuron does not reach its firing threshold. Hence, we can safely neglect both threshold and reset. Using the definition of the random process S we find for the membrane potential

$$u(t) = w_0 \int_0^{\infty} \epsilon_0(s) \, S(t - s) \, ds . \tag{5.78}$$

We are interested in the mean potential $u_0 = \langle u(t) \rangle$ and the variance $\langle \Delta u^2 \rangle = \langle [u(t) - u_0]^2 \rangle$. Using Eqs. (5.76) and (5.77) we find

$$u_0 = w_0 \, \nu_0 \int_0^{\infty} \epsilon_0(s) \, ds \tag{5.79}$$

and

$$\langle \Delta u^2 \rangle = w_0^2 \int_0^\infty \int_0^\infty \epsilon_0(s) \, \epsilon_0(s') \, \langle S(t) \, S(t') \rangle \, ds \, ds' - u_0^2$$

$$= w_0^2 \, v_0 \int_0^\infty \epsilon_0^2(s) \, ds \, . \tag{5.80}$$

In Fig. 5.14 we have simulated a neuron which receives input from $N = 100$ background neurons with rate $v_j = 10$ Hz. The total spike arrival rate is therefore $v_0 = 1$ kHz. Each spike evokes an EPSP $w_0 \, \epsilon_0(s) = 0.1 \, (s/\tau) \, \exp(-s/\tau)$ with $\tau = 4$ ms. The evaluation of Eqs. (5.79) and (5.80) yields $u_0 = 0.4$ and $\sqrt{\langle \Delta u^2 \rangle} = 0.1$.

Mean and fluctuations for Stein's model can be derived by evaluation of Eqs. (5.79) and (5.80) with $\epsilon(s) = e^{-s/\tau_m}$. The result is

$$u_0 = w_0 \, v_0 \, \tau_m \tag{5.81}$$

$$\langle \Delta u^2 \rangle = 0.5 \, w_0^2 \, v_0 \, \tau_m \, . \tag{5.82}$$

Note that with excitation alone, as considered here, mean and variance cannot be changed independently. As we will see in the next example, a combination of excitation and inhibition allows us to increase the variance while keeping the mean of the potential fixed.

Example: balanced excitation and inhibition

Let us suppose that an integrate-and-fire neuron defined by Eq. (5.74) with $\tau_m = 10$ ms receives input from 100 excitatory neurons ($w_k = +0.1$) and 100 inhibitory neurons ($w_k = -0.1$). Each background neuron k fires at a rate of $v_k = 10$ Hz. Thus, in each millisecond, the neuron receives on average one excitatory and one inhibitory input spike. Each spike leads to a jump of the membrane potential of ± 0.1. The trajectory of the membrane potential is therefore similar to that of a random walk; cf. Fig. 5.15A. If, in addition, a constant stimulus $I^{\text{ext}} = I_0 > 0$ is applied so that the mean membrane potential (in the absence of the background spikes) is just below threshold, then the presence of random background spikes may drive u towards the firing threshold. Whenever $u \geq \vartheta$, the membrane potential is reset to $u_r = 0$.

We note that the mean of the stochastic background input vanishes since $\sum_k w_k \, v_k = 0$. Using the same arguments as in the previous example, we can convince ourselves that the stochastic arrival of background spikes generates fluctuations of the voltage with variance

$$\langle \Delta u^2 \rangle = 0.5 \, \tau_m \sum_k w_k^2 \, v_k = 0.1 \, ; \tag{5.83}$$

cf. Section 5.5.2 for a different derivation. Let us now increase all rates by a factor

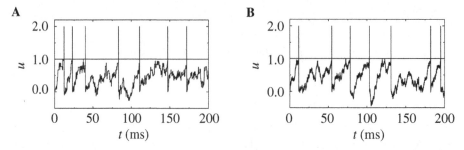

Fig. 5.15. **A**. Voltage trajectory of an integrate-and-fire neuron ($\tau_m = 10$ ms, $u_r = 0$) driven by stochastic excitatory and inhibitory spike input at $\nu_+ = \nu_- = 1$ kHz. Each input spike causes a jump of the membrane potential by $w_\pm = \pm 0.1$. The neuron is biased by a constant current $I_0 = 0.8$ which drives the membrane potential to a value just below the threshold of $\vartheta = 1$ (horizontal line). Spikes are marked by vertical lines. **B**. Similar plot as in **A** except that the jumps are smaller ($w_\pm = \pm 0.025$) while rates are higher ($\nu_\pm = 16$ kHz).

of $a > 1$ and multiply at the same time the synaptic efficacies by a factor $1/\sqrt{a}$. Then both the mean and variance of the stochastic background input are the same as before, but the size w_k of the jumps is decreased; cf. Fig. 5.15B. In the limit of $a \to \infty$ the jump process turns into a diffusion process and we arrive at the stochastic model of Eq. (5.73). A systematic discussion of the diffusion limit is the topic of the next subsection.

Since firing is driven by the fluctuations of the membrane potential, the interspike intervals vary considerably; cf. Fig. 5.15. Balanced excitatory and inhibitory spike input could thus contribute to the large variability of interspike intervals in cortical neurons (Shadlen and Newsome, 1994; Tsodyks and Sejnowski, 1995; van Vreeswijk and Sompolinsky, 1996; Amit and Brunel, 1997; Shadlen and Newsome, 1998; Brunel and Hakim, 1999); see Section 5.6.

5.5.2 Diffusion limit (*)

In this section we analyze the model of stochastic spike arrival defined in Eq. (5.74) and show how to map it to the diffusion model defined in Eq. (5.73) (Gluss, 1967; Johannesma, 1968; Capocelli and Ricciardi, 1971). Suppose that the neuron has fired its last spike at time $\hat{t}$. Immediately after the firing the membrane potential was reset to u_r. Because of the stochastic spike arrival, we cannot predict the membrane potential for $t > \hat{t}$, but we can calculate its probability density, $p(u, t)$.

For the sake of simplicity, we set for the time being $I^{\text{ext}} = 0$ in Eq. (5.74). The input spikes at synapse k are generated by a Poisson process and arrive stochastically with rate $\nu_k(t)$. The probability that no spike arrives in a short time interval Δt is therefore

$$\text{Prob}\{\text{no spike in } [t, t + \Delta t]\} = 1 - \sum_k v_k(t) \, \Delta t \, . \tag{5.84}$$

If no spike arrives in $[t, t + \Delta t]$, the membrane potential changes from $u(t) = u'$ to $u(t + \Delta t) = u' \exp(-\Delta t / \tau_m)$. On the other hand, if a spike arrives at synapse k, the membrane potential changes from u' to $u' \exp(-\Delta t / \tau_m) + w_k$. Given a value of u' at time t, the probability density of finding a membrane potential u at time $t + \Delta t$ is therefore given by

$$\begin{aligned} P^{\text{trans}}(u, t + \Delta t | u', t) &= \left[1 - \Delta t \sum_k v_k(t) \right] \delta \left(u - u' \, e^{-\Delta t / \tau_m} \right) \\ &\quad + \Delta t \sum_k v_k(t) \delta \left(u - u' \, e^{-\Delta t / \tau_m} - w_k \right) . \end{aligned} \tag{5.85}$$

We will refer to P^{trans} as the transition law. Since the membrane potential is given by the differential equation (5.74) with input spikes generated by a Poisson distribution, the evolution of the membrane potential is a Markov Process (i.e., a process without memory) and can be described by (van Kampen, 1992)

$$p(u, t + \Delta t) = \int P^{\text{trans}}(u, t + \Delta t | u', t) \, p(u', t) \, du' \, . \tag{5.86}$$

We put Eq. (5.85) in Eq. (5.86). To perform the integration, we have to recall the rules for δ functions, viz., $\delta(a \, u) = a^{-1} \delta(u)$. The result of the integration is

$$\begin{aligned} p(u, t + \Delta t) &= \left[1 - \Delta t \sum_k v_k(t) \right] e^{\Delta t / \tau_m} p \left(e^{\Delta t / \tau_m} u, t \right) \\ &\quad + \Delta t \sum_k v_k(t) \, e^{\Delta t / \tau_m} p \left(e^{\Delta t / \tau_m} u - w_k, t \right) . \end{aligned} \tag{5.87}$$

Since Δt is assumed to be small, we expand Eq. (5.87) about $\Delta t = 0$ and find to first order in Δt

$$\begin{aligned} \frac{p(u, t + \Delta t) - p(u, t)}{\Delta t} &= \frac{1}{\tau_m} p(u, t) + \frac{1}{\tau_m} u \frac{\partial}{\partial u} p(u, t) \\ &\quad + \sum_k v_k(t) \, [p(u - w_k, t) - p(u, t)] \, . \end{aligned} \tag{5.88}$$

For $\Delta t \to 0$, the left-hand side of Eq. (5.88) turns into a partial derivative $\partial p(u, t) / \partial t$. Furthermore, if the jump amplitudes w_k are small, we can expand the right-hand side of Eq. (5.88) with respect to u about $p(u, t)$:

$$\tau_m \frac{\partial}{\partial t} p(u, t) = -\frac{\partial}{\partial u} \left[-u + \tau_m \sum_k \nu_k(t)\, w_k \right] p(u, t)$$

$$+ \frac{1}{2} \left[\tau_m \sum_k \nu_k(t)\, w_k^2 \right] \frac{\partial^2}{\partial u^2} p(u, t), \qquad (5.89)$$

where we have neglected terms of order w_k^3 and higher. The expansion in w_k is called the Kramers–Moyal expansion. Equation (5.89) is an example of a Fokker–Planck equation(van Kampen, 1992), i.e., a partial differential equation that describes the temporal evolution of a probability distribution. The right-hand side of Eq. (5.89) has a clear interpretation. The first term in rectangular brackets describes the systematic drift of the membrane potential due to leakage ($\propto -u$) and *mean* background input ($\propto \sum_k \nu_k(t)\, w_k$). The second term in rectangular brackets corresponds to a "diffusion constant" and accounts for the fluctuations of the membrane potential. The Fokker–Planck Eq. (5.89) is equivalent to the Langevin equation (5.73) with $R\, I(t) = \tau_m \sum_k \nu_k(t)\, w_k$ and time-dependent noise amplitude

$$\sigma^2(t) = \tau_m \sum_k \nu_k(t)\, w_k^2. \qquad (5.90)$$

The specific process generated by the Langevin-equation (5.73) with *constant* noise amplitude σ is called the Ornstein–Uhlenbeck process (Uhlenbeck and Ornstein, 1930).

For the transition from Eq. (5.88) to (5.89) we have suppressed higher-order terms in the expansion. The missing terms are

$$\sum_{n=3}^{\infty} \frac{(-1)^n}{n!} A_n(t) \frac{\partial^n}{\partial u^n} p(u, t) \qquad (5.91)$$

with $A_n = \sum_k \nu_k(t)\, w_k^n$. Under what conditions do these terms vanish? As in the example of Figs. 5.15A and B, we consider a sequence of models where the size of the weights w_k decreases so that $A_n \to 0$ for $n \geq 3$ while the mean $\sum_k \nu_k(t)\, w_k$ and the second moment $\sum_k \nu_k(t)\, w_k^2$ remain constant. It turns out that, given both excitatory and inhibitory input, it is always possible to find an appropriate sequence of models (Lansky, 1984, 1997). For $w_k \to 0$, the diffusion limit is attained and Eq. (5.89) is exact. For excitatory input alone, however, such a sequence of models does not exist (Plesser, 1999).

The Fokker–Planck equation (5.89) and the Langevin equation (5.73) are equivalent descriptions of drift and diffusion of the membrane potential. Neither of these describes spike firing. To turn the Langevin equation (5.73) into a sensible neuron model, we have to incorporate a threshold condition. In the Fokker–Planck equation (5.89), the firing threshold is incorporated as a boundary condition

$$p(\vartheta, t) \equiv 0 \quad \text{for all } t .\tag{5.92}$$

Before we continue the discussion of the diffusion model in the presence of a threshold, let us study the solution of Eq. (5.89) without threshold.

Example: free distribution

In the absence of a threshold ($\vartheta \to \infty$), both the Langevin equation (5.73) and the Fokker–Planck equation (5.89) can be solved. Let us consider Eq. (5.73) for constant σ. At $t = \hat{t}$ the membrane potential starts at a value $u = u_r = 0$. Since Eq. (5.73) is a linear equation, its solution is

$$u(t|\hat{t}) = \frac{R}{\tau_m} \int_0^{t-\hat{t}} e^{-s/\tau_m} I(t-s) \, ds + \frac{1}{\tau_m} \int_0^{t-\hat{t}} e^{-s/\tau_m} \xi(t-s) \, ds .\tag{5.93}$$

Since $\langle \xi(t) \rangle = 0$, the expected trajectory of the membrane potential is

$$u_0(t) = \langle u(t|\hat{t}) \rangle = \frac{R}{\tau_m} \int_0^{t-\hat{t}} e^{-s/\tau_m} I(t-s) \, ds .\tag{5.94}$$

In particular, for constant input current $I(t) \equiv I_0$ we have

$$u_0(t) = u_\infty \left[1 - e^{-(t-\hat{t})/\tau_m} \right]\tag{5.95}$$

with $u_\infty = R I_0$. Note that the expected trajectory is that of the noiseless model.

The fluctuations of the membrane potential have variance $\langle \Delta u^2 \rangle = \langle [u(t|\hat{t}) - u_0(t)]^2 \rangle$ with $u_0(t)$ given by Eq. (5.94). The variance can be evaluated with the help of Eq. (5.93), i.e.,

$$\langle \Delta u^2(t) \rangle = \frac{1}{\tau_m^2} \int_0^{t-\hat{t}} ds \int_0^{t-\hat{t}} ds' \, e^{-s/\tau_m} e^{-s'/\tau_m} \langle \xi(t-s) \xi(t-s') \rangle .\tag{5.96}$$

We use $\langle \xi(t-s) \xi(t-s') \rangle = \sigma^2 \tau_m \delta(s-s')$ and perform the integration. The result is

$$\langle \Delta u^2(t) \rangle = \frac{1}{2} \sigma^2 \left[1 - e^{-2(t-\hat{t})/\tau_m} \right] .\tag{5.97}$$

Hence, noise causes the actual membrane trajectory to drift away from the noiseless reference trajectory $u_0(t)$. The typical distance between the actual trajectory and the mean trajectory approaches with time constant $\tau_m/2$ a limiting value

$$\sqrt{\langle \Delta u_\infty^2 \rangle} = \frac{1}{\sqrt{2}} \sigma .\tag{5.98}$$

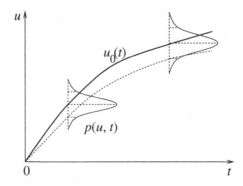

Fig. 5.16. In the absence of a threshold the membrane potential follows a Gaussian distribution around the noise-free reference trajectory $u_0(t)$ (schematic figure).

The solution of the Fokker–Planck equation (5.89) with initial condition $p(u, \hat{t}) = \delta(u - u_r)$ is a Gaussian with mean $u_0(t)$ and variance $\langle \Delta u^2(t) \rangle$, i.e.,

$$p(u, t) = \frac{1}{\sqrt{2\pi \langle \Delta u^2(t) \rangle}} \exp\left\{ -\frac{[u(t|\hat{t}) - u_0(t)]^2}{2 \langle \Delta u^2(t) \rangle} \right\} \tag{5.99}$$

as can be verified by inserting Eq. (5.99) into Eq. (5.89); see Fig. 5.16. In particular, the stationary distribution that is approached in the limit of $t \to \infty$ for constant input I_0 is

$$p(u, \infty) = \frac{1}{\sqrt{\pi}} \frac{1}{\sigma} \exp\left\{ \frac{[u - R\, I_0]^2}{\sigma^2} \right\}, \tag{5.100}$$

which describes a Gaussian distribution with mean $u_\infty = R\, I_0$ and variance $\sigma/\sqrt{2}$.

5.5.3 Interval distribution

Let us consider a neuron that starts at time $\hat{t}$ with a membrane potential u_r and is driven for $t > \hat{t}$ by a known input $I(t)$. Because of the diffusive noise generated by stochastic spike arrival, we cannot predict the exact value of the neuronal membrane potential $u(t)$ at a later time $t > \hat{t}$, but only the probability that the membrane potential is in a certain interval $[u_0, u_1]$. Specifically, we have

$$\text{Prob}\left\{ u_0 < u(t) < u_1 \mid u(\hat{t}) = u_r \right\} = \int_{u_0}^{u_1} p(u, t)\, du, \tag{5.101}$$

where $p(u, t)$ is the distribution of the membrane potential at time t. In the diffusion limit, $p(u, t)$ can be found by solution of the Fokker–Planck equation Eq. (5.89) with initial condition $p(u, \hat{t}) = \delta(u - u_r)$ and boundary condition

$p(\vartheta, t) = 0$. At any time $t > \hat{t}$, the survivor function,

$$S_I(t|\hat{t}) = \int_{-\infty}^{\vartheta} p(u, t)\, du, \tag{5.102}$$

is the probability that the membrane potential has not reached the threshold. In view of Eq. (5.5), the input-dependent interval distribution is therefore

$$P_I(t|\hat{t}) = -\frac{d}{dt} \int_{-\infty}^{\vartheta} p(u, t)\, du. \tag{5.103}$$

We recall that $P_I(t|\hat{t})\, \Delta t$ for $\Delta t \to 0$ is the probability that a neuron fires its next spike between t and $t + \Delta t$ given a spike at $\hat{t}$ and input I. In the context of noisy integrate-and-fire neurons $P_I(t|\hat{t})$ is called the distribution of "first passage times". The name is motivated by the fact that firing occurs when the membrane potential crosses ϑ for the first time. Unfortunately, no general solution is known for the first passage time problem of the Ornstein–Uhlenbeck process. For constant input $I(t) = I_0$, however, it is at least possible to give a moment expansion of the first passage time distribution. In particular, the mean of the first passage time can be calculated in closed form.

Example: mean interval for constant input

For constant input I_0 the mean interspike interval is $\langle s \rangle = \int_0^\infty s\, P_{I_0}(s|0)\, ds = \int_0^\infty s\, P_0(s)\, ds$; cf. Eq. (5.21). For the diffusion model Eq. (5.73) with threshold ϑ, reset potential u_r, and membrane time constant τ_m, the mean interval is

$$\langle s \rangle = \tau_m \sqrt{\pi} \int_{(u_r - h_0)/\sigma}^{(\vartheta - h_0)/\sigma} du\, \exp\left(u^2\right) \left[1 + \mathrm{erf}(u)\right], \tag{5.104}$$

where $h_0 = R\, I_0$ is the input potential caused by the constant current I_0 (Johannesma, 1968). This expression can be derived by several methods (for reviews see, e.g., Tuckwell 1988 and van Kampen 1992). We will return to Eq. (5.104) in Chapter 6.2.1 in the context of populations of spiking neurons.

Example: numerical evaluation of $P_I(t|\hat{t})$

We have seen that, in the absence of a threshold, the Fokker–Planck equation (5.89) can be solved; cf. Eq. (5.99). The transition probability from an arbitrary starting value u' at time t' to a new value u at time t is

$$P^{\mathrm{trans}}(u, t|u', t') = \frac{1}{\sqrt{2\pi\, \langle \Delta u^2(t) \rangle}} \exp\left\{-\frac{[u - u_0(t)]^2}{2\, \langle \Delta u^2(t) \rangle}\right\} \tag{5.105}$$

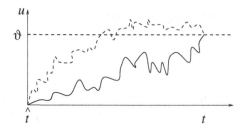

Fig. 5.17. Without a threshold, several trajectories can reach at time t the same value $u = \vartheta$ from above or below.

with

$$u_0(t) \;=\; u' \, e^{-(t-t')/\tau_m} + \int_0^{t-t'} e^{-s'/\tau_m} \, I(t-s') \, ds \qquad (5.106)$$

$$\langle \Delta u^2(t) \rangle \;=\; \frac{\sigma^2}{2} \left[1 - e^{-2(t-s)/\tau_m} \right] . \qquad (5.107)$$

A method due to Schrödinger uses the solution of the unbounded problem in order to calculate the input-dependent interval distribution $P_I(t|\hat{t})$ of the diffusion model with threshold (Schrödinger, 1915; Plesser and Tanaka, 1997; Burkitt and Clark, 1999). The idea of the solution method is illustrated in Fig. 5.17. Because of the Markov property, the probability density of crossing the threshold (not necessarily for the first time) at a time t is equal to the probability of crossing it for the first time at $t' < t$ and returning back to ϑ at time t, that is,

$$P^{\text{trans}}(\vartheta, t | u_r, \hat{t}) = \int_{\hat{t}}^t P_I(t' | \hat{t}) \, P^{\text{trans}}(\vartheta, t | \vartheta, t') \, dt' . \qquad (5.108)$$

This integral equation can be solved numerically for the distribution $P_I(t'|\hat{t})$ for arbitrary input current $I(t)$ (Plesser, 2000). An example is shown in Fig. 5.18.

5.6 The subthreshold regime

One of the aims of noisy neuron models is to mimic the large variability of interspike intervals found, e.g., in vertebrate cortex. To arrive at broad interval distributions, it is not enough to introduce noise into a neuron model. Apart from the noise level, other neuronal parameters such as the firing threshold or a bias current have to be tuned so as to make the neuron sensitive to noise. In this section we introduce a distinction between super- and subthreshold stimulation (Abeles, 1991; Shadlen and Newsome, 1994; König et al., 1996; Bugmann et al., 1997; Troyer and Miller, 1997). In Section 5.7 we will show that, in the subthreshold regime, there is a close relation between the two different noise models discussed

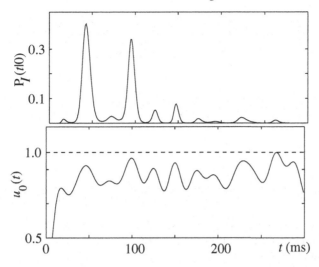

Fig. 5.18. A time-dependent input current $I(t)$ generates a noise-free membrane potential $u_0(t)$ shown in the lower part of the figure. In the presence of diffusive noise, spikes can be triggered although the reference trajectory stays below the threshold (dashed line). This gives rise to an input-dependent interval distribution $P_I(t|0)$ shown in the upper panel. Taken from Plesser and Gerstner (2000).

above, viz., escape noise (cf. Section 5.3) and diffusive noise (cf. Section 5.5). Finally, in Section 5.8 we turn to the phenomenon of stochastic resonance and discuss signal transmission in the subthreshold regime.

5.6.1 Sub- and superthreshold stimulation

An arbitrary time-dependent stimulus $I(t)$ is called subthreshold if it generates a membrane potential that stays – in the absence of noise – below the firing threshold. Due to noise, however, even subthreshold stimuli can induce action potentials. Stimuli that induce spikes even in a noise-free neuron are called superthreshold.

The distinction between sub- and superthreshold stimuli has important consequences for the firing behavior of neurons in the presence of noise. To see why, let us consider an integrate-and-fire neuron with constant input I_0 for $t > 0$. Starting from $u(t = 0) = u_r$, the trajectory of the membrane potential is

$$u_0(t) = u_\infty \left[1 - e^{-t/\tau_m}\right] + u_r\, e^{-t/\tau_m}. \qquad (5.109)$$

In the absence of a threshold, the membrane potential approaches the value $u_\infty = R\,I_0$ for $t \to \infty$. If we take the threshold ϑ into account, two cases may be distinguished. Firstly, if $u_\infty < \vartheta$ (subthreshold stimulation), the neuron does not fire at all. Secondly, if $u_\infty > \vartheta$ (superthreshold stimulation), the neuron fires

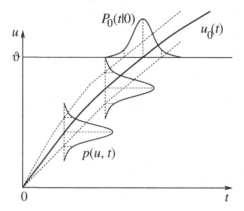

Fig. 5.19. Interval distribution $P_0(t|0)$ for superthreshold stimuli. The membrane potential distribution $p(u, t)$ is shifted across the threshold and generates an interval distribution $P_0(t|0)$ (schematic figure).

regularly. The interspike interval is s_0 derived from $u_0(s_0) = \vartheta$. Thus

$$s_0 = \tau \ln \frac{u_\infty - u_r}{u_\infty - \vartheta} . \tag{5.110}$$

We now add diffusive noise. In the superthreshold regime, noise has little influence except that it broadens the interspike interval distribution. Thus, in the superthreshold regime, the spike train in the presence of diffusive noise is simply a noisy version of the regular spike train of the noise-free neuron.

On the other hand, in the subthreshold regime, the spike train changes qualitatively if noise is switched on; see König et al. (1996) for a review. Stochastic background input turns the quiescent neuron into a spiking one. In the subthreshold regime, spikes are generated by the *fluctuations* of the membrane potential, rather than by its mean (Abeles, 1991; Shadlen and Newsome, 1994; Bugmann et al., 1997; Troyer and Miller, 1997; Feng, 2001). The interspike interval distribution is therefore broad; see Fig. 5.20.

Example: interval distribution in the superthreshold regime

For small noise amplitude $0 < \sigma \ll u_\infty - \vartheta$, the interval distribution is centered at s_0. Its width can be estimated from the width of the fluctuations $\langle \Delta u_\infty^2 \rangle$ of the free membrane potential; cf. Eq. (5.99). Since the membrane potential crosses the threshold with slope u_0', there is a scaling factor $u_0' = du_0(t)/dt$ evaluated at $t = s_0$; cf. Fig. 5.19. The interval distribution is therefore approximately given by a Gaussian with mean s_0 and width $\sigma/\sqrt{2}\, u_0'$ (Tuckwell, 1988), i.e.,

$$P_0(t|0) = \frac{1}{\sqrt{\pi}} \frac{u_0'}{\sigma} \exp\left[-\frac{(u_0')^2 (t - s_0)^2}{\sigma^2} \right] . \tag{5.111}$$

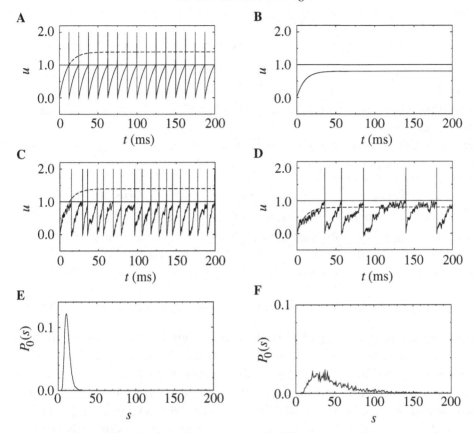

Fig. 5.20. Integrate-and-fire neuron ($\tau_m = 10$ ms) with superthreshold (left column) and subthreshold (right column) stimulation. **A**. Without noise, a neuron with superthreshold stimulus I_a fires regularly. Spikes are marked by vertical lines. The threshold is indicated by a horizontal line. The dashed line shows the evolution of the membrane potential in the absence of the threshold. **B**. The same neuron with subthreshold stimulation I_b does not fire. **C**. If we add stochastic excitatory and inhibitory spike input ($w_\pm = 0.05$ at $\nu_\pm = 1.6$ kHz) to the constant input I_a, the membrane potential drifts away from the noise-free reference trajectory, but firing remains fairly regular. **D**. The same sequence of input spikes added to the subthreshold current I_b generates irregular spiking. **E** and **F**. Histogram of interspike intervals in **C** and **D**, respectively, as an estimator of the interval distribution $P_0(s)$ in the super- and subthreshold regimes. The mean interval $\langle s \rangle$ is 12 ms (**E**) and 50 ms (**F**); the C_V values are 0.30 and 0.63, respectively.

5.6.2 Coefficient of variation C_V

Figures 5.20E and 5.20F show that interval distributions in the super- and subthreshold regime look quite different. To quantify the width of the interval distribution, neuroscientists often evaluate the coefficient of variation, or C_V, defined as the ratio of the variance and the mean squared,

$$C_V^2 = \frac{\langle \Delta s^2 \rangle}{\langle s \rangle^2},$$ (5.112)

where $\langle s \rangle = \int_0^\infty P_0(s)\,ds$ and $\langle \Delta s^2 \rangle = \int_0^\infty s^2 P_0(s)\,ds - \langle s \rangle^2$. A Poisson distribution has a value of $C_V = 1$. A value of $C_V > 1$ implies that a given distribution is broader than a Poisson distribution with the same mean. If $C_V < 1$, then the spike train is more regular than that generated by a Poisson neuron of the same rate. A long refractory period and low noise level decrease the C_V value.

Example: Poisson neuron with absolute refractoriness

We study a Poisson neuron with absolute refractory period Δ^{abs}. For $t - \hat{t} > \Delta^{abs}$, the neuron is supposed to fire stochastically with rate r. The interval distribution is given in Eq. (5.20) with mean $\langle s \rangle = \Delta^{abs} + 1/r$ and variance $\langle \Delta s^2 \rangle = 1/r^2$. The coefficient of variation is therefore

$$C_V = 1 - \frac{\Delta^{abs}}{\langle s \rangle}.$$ (5.113)

Let us compare the C_V of Eq. (5.113) with that of a homogeneous Poisson process of the same mean rate $\nu = \langle s \rangle^{-1}$. As we have seen, a Poisson process has $C_V = 1$. A refractory period $\Delta^{abs} > 0$ lowers the C_V, because a neuron with absolute refractoriness fires more regularly than a Poisson neuron. If we increase Δ^{abs}, we must increase the instantaneous rate r in order to keep the same mean rate ν. In the limit of $\Delta^{abs} \to \langle s \rangle$, the C_V approaches zero, since the only possible spike train is regular firing with period $\langle s \rangle$.

5.7 From diffusive noise to escape noise

In the subthreshold regime, the integrate-and-fire model with stochastic input (diffusive noise) can be mapped approximately onto an escape noise model with a certain escape rate f (Plesser and Gerstner, 2000). In this section, we motivate the mapping and the choice of f.

In the absence of a threshold, the membrane potential of an integrate-and-fire model has a Gaussian probability distribution, around the noise-free reference trajectory $u_0(t)$. If we take the threshold into account, the probability density at $u = \vartheta$ of the exact solution vanishes, since the threshold acts as an absorbing boundary; see Eq. (5.92). Nevertheless, in a phenomenological model, we can approximate the probability density near $u = \vartheta$ by the "free" distribution (i.e., without the threshold)

$$\text{Prob}\{u \text{ reaches } \vartheta \text{ in } [t, t + \Delta t]\} \propto \Delta t \, \exp\left\{-\frac{[u_0(t) - \vartheta]^2}{2\langle \Delta u^2(t) \rangle}\right\},$$ (5.114)

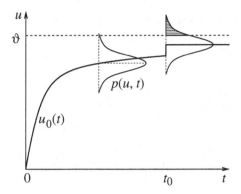

Fig. 5.21. The distribution of the membrane potential around the noise free reference trajectory $u_0(t)$ is given by $p(u, t)$. At $t = t_0$, where the reference trajectory has a discontinuity, the distribution of the membrane potential is shifted instantaneously across the threshold. The probability of firing at t_0 is given by the shaded surface under the distribution.

where $u_0(t)$ is the noise-free reference trajectory. The idea is illustrated in Fig. 5.21.

We have seen in Eq. (5.97) that the variance $\langle \Delta u^2(t) \rangle$ of the free distribution rapidly approaches a constant value $\sigma^2/2$. We therefore replace the time-dependent variance $2\langle \Delta u(t)^2 \rangle$ by its stationary value σ^2. The right-hand side of Eq. (5.114) is then a function of the noise-free reference trajectory only. In order to transform the left-hand side of Eq. (5.114) into an escape rate, we divide both sides by Δt. The firing intensity is thus

$$f(u_0 - \vartheta) = \frac{c_1}{\tau_m} \exp \left\{ -\frac{[u_0(t) - \vartheta]^2}{\sigma^2} \right\} . \tag{5.115}$$

The factor in front of the exponential has been split into a constant parameter $c_1 > 0$ and the time constant τ_m of the neuron in order to show that the escape rate has units of one over time. Equation (5.115) is the well-known Arrhenius formula for escape across a barrier of height $(\vartheta - u_0)^2$ in the presence of thermal energy σ^2 (van Kampen, 1992).

Let us now suppose that the neuron receives, at $t = t_0$, an input current pulse which causes a jump of the membrane trajectory by an amount $\Delta u > 0$; see Fig. 5.21. In this case the Gaussian distribution of membrane potentials is shifted *instantaneously* across the threshold so that there is a nonzero probability that the neuron fires exactly at t_0. To say it differently, the firing intensity $\rho(t) = f[u_0(t) - \vartheta]$ has a δ peak at $t = t_0$. The escape rate of Eq. (5.115), however, cannot reproduce this δ peak. More generally, whenever the noise-free reference trajectory increases with slope $\dot{u}_0 > 0$, we expect an increase of the instantaneous rate proportional to $\dot{u}_0$, because the tail of the Gaussian distribution drifts across the threshold; cf. Eq. (5.111). In order to take the drift into account, we generalize Eq. (5.115) and study

$$f(u_0, \dot{u}_0) = \left(\frac{c_1}{\tau_m} + \frac{c_2}{\sigma}[\dot{u}_0]_+ \right) \exp\left\{ -\frac{[u_0(t) - \vartheta]^2}{\sigma^2} \right\}, \qquad (5.116)$$

where $\dot{u}_0 = du_0/dt$ and $[x]_+ = x$ for $x > 0$ and zero otherwise. We call Eq. (5.116) the Arrhenius&Current model (Plesser and Gerstner, 2000).

We emphasize that the right-hand side of Eq. (5.116) depends only on the dimensionless variable

$$x(t) = \frac{u_0(t) - \vartheta}{\sigma}, \qquad (5.117)$$

and its derivative $\dot{x}$. Thus the amplitude of the fluctuations σ define a "natural" voltage scale. The only relevant variable is the momentary distance of the noise-free trajectory from the threshold in units of the noise amplitude σ. A value of $x = -1$ implies that the membrane potential is one σ below threshold. A distance of $u - \vartheta = -10$ mV at high noise (e.g., $\sigma = 10$ mV) is as effective in firing a cell as a distance of 1 mV at low noise ($\sigma = 1$ mV).

Example: comparison of diffusion model and Arrhenius&Current escape rate

To check the validity of the arguments that led to Eq. (5.116), let us compare the interval distribution generated by the diffusion model with that generated by the Arrhenius&Current escape model. We use the same input potential $u_0(t)$ as in Fig. 5.18. We find that the interval distributions P_I^{diff} for the diffusive noise model and $P_I^{\text{A\&C}}$ for the Arrhenius&Current escape model are nearly identical; cf. Fig. 5.22. Thus the Arrhenius&Current escape model yields an excellent approximation to the diffusive noise model. We quantify the error of the approximation by the measure

$$E = \frac{\int_0^\infty \left[P_I^{\text{diff}}(t|0) - P_I^{\text{A\&C}}(t|0) \right]^2 dt}{\int_0^\infty \left[P_I^{\text{diff}}(t|0) \right]^2 dt}. \qquad (5.118)$$

For the example shown in Fig. 5.22 we find $E = 0.026$. Over a large set of subthreshold stimuli, the difference between the diffusive noise and the Arrhenius&Current model is typically in the range of $E = 0.02$; the best choice of parameters is $c_1 \approx 0.72$ and $c_2 \approx \pi^{-1/2}$ (Plesser and Gerstner, 2000). The simple Arrhenius model of Eq. (5.115) or the sigmoidal model of Eq. (5.51) have errors which are larger by a factor of 3–5.

Even though the Arrhenius&Current model has been designed for subthreshold stimuli, it also works remarkably well for superthreshold stimuli with typical errors around $E = 0.04$. An obvious shortcoming of the escape rate in Eq. (5.116) is that

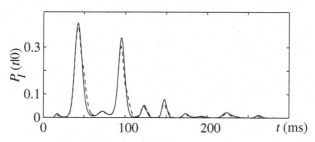

Fig. 5.22. The interval distributions $P_I(t|0)$ for diffusive noise (solid line) and Arrhenius&Current escape noise (dashed line) are nearly identical. The input potential is the same as in Fig. 5.18. Taken from Plesser and Gerstner (2000).

the instantaneous rate decreases with u for $u > \vartheta$. The superthreshold behavior can be corrected if we replace the Gaussian $\exp(-x^2)$ by $2 \exp(-x^2)/[1 + \mathrm{erf}(-x)]$ (Herrmann and Gerstner, 2001a). The subthreshold behavior remains unchanged compared to Eq. (5.116) but the superthreshold behavior of the escape rate f becomes linear. With this new escape rate the typical error E in the superthreshold regime is as small as that in the subthreshold regime.

5.8 Stochastic resonance

Noise can – under certain circumstances – improve the signal-transmission properties of neuronal systems. In most cases there is an optimum for the noise amplitude which has motivated the name *stochastic resonance* for this rather counterintuitive phenomenon. In this section we discuss stochastic resonance in the context of noisy spiking neurons.

We study the relation between an input $I(t)$ to a neuron and the corresponding output spike train $S(t) = \sum_f \delta(t - t^{(f)})$. In the absence of noise, a subthreshold stimulus $I(t)$ does not generate action potentials so that no information on the temporal structure of the stimulus can be transmitted. In the presence of noise, however, spikes do occur. As we have seen in Eq. (5.116), spike firing is most likely at moments when the normalized distance $|x| = |(u - \vartheta)/\sigma|$ between the membrane potential and the threshold is small. Since the escape rate in Eq. (5.116) depends exponentially on x^2, any variation in the membrane potential $u_0(t)$ that is generated by the temporal structure of the input is enhanced; cf. Fig. 5.10. On the other hand, for very large noise ($\sigma \to \infty$), we have $x^2 \to 0$, and spike firing occurs at a constant rate, irrespective of the temporal structure of the input. We conclude that there is some intermediate noise level where signal transmission is optimal.

The optimal noise level can be found by plotting the signal-to-noise ratio as a function of noise (McNamara and Wiesenfeld, 1989; Douglass et al., 1993; Longtin, 1993; Collins et al., 1996; Cordo et al., 1996; Levin and Miller, 1996;

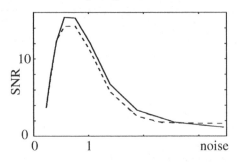

Fig. 5.23. Signal-to-noise ratio (SNR) for the transmission of a periodic signal as a function of the noise level $\sigma/(\vartheta - u_0)$. Solid line: diffusion model. Dashed line: Arrhenius&Current escape model. Taken from Plesser and Gerstner (2000).

Stemmler, 1996; Wiesenfeld and Jaramillo, 1998); for a review see Gammaitoni et al. (1998). Even though stochastic resonance does not require periodicity (see, e.g., Collins et al. (1996)), it is typically studied with a periodic input signal such as

$$I(t) = I_0 + I_1 \cos(\Omega t).\tag{5.119}$$

For $t - \hat{t} \gg \tau_m$, the membrane potential of the noise-free reference trajectory has the form

$$u_0(t) = u_\infty + u_1 \cos(\Omega t + \varphi_1),\tag{5.120}$$

where u_1 and φ_1 are the amplitude and phase of its periodic component. To quantify the signal-transmission properties, a long spike train is studied and the signal-to-noise ratio (SNR) is computed. The signal S is measured as the amplitude of the power spectral density of the spike train evaluated at frequency Ω, i.e., $S = \mathcal{P}(\Omega)$. The noise level $\mathcal{N}$ is usually estimated from the noise power $\mathcal{P}_{\text{Poisson}}$ of a Poisson process with the same number of spikes as the measured spike train, i.e., $\mathcal{N} = \mathcal{P}_{\text{Poisson}}$. Figure 5.23 shows the signal-to-noise ratio $S/\mathcal{N}$ of a periodically stimulated integrate-and-fire neuron as a function of the noise level σ. Two models are shown, viz., diffusive noise (solid line) and escape noise with the Arrhenius&Current escape rate (dashed line). The two curves are rather similar and exhibit a peak at

$$\sigma^{\text{opt}} \approx \frac{2}{3}(\vartheta - u_\infty).\tag{5.121}$$

Since $\sigma^2 = 2\langle \Delta u^2 \rangle$, signal transmission is optimal if the stochastic fluctuations of the membrane potential have an amplitude

$$2\sqrt{\langle \Delta u^2 \rangle} \approx \vartheta - u_\infty.\tag{5.122}$$

An optimality condition similar to Eq. (5.121) holds over a wide variety of stimulation parameters (Plesser, 1999). We will come back to the signal transmission properties of noisy spiking neurons in Section 7.3.

Example: extracting oscillations

The optimality condition Eq. (5.121) can be fulfilled by adapting either the left-hand side or the right-hand side of the equation. Even though it cannot be excluded that a neuron changes its noise level so as to optimize the left-hand side of Eq. (5.121) this does not seem very likely. On the other hand, it is easy to imagine a mechanism that optimizes the right-hand side of Eq. (5.121). For example, an adaptation current could change the value of ϑ, or synaptic weights could be increased or decreased so that the mean potential u_∞ is in the appropriate regime.

We apply the idea of an optimal threshold to a problem of neural coding. More specifically, we study the question of whether an integrate-and-fire or Spike Response Model neuron is only sensitive to the total number of spikes that arrive in some time window T, or also to the relative timing of the input spikes. In contrast to Section 4.5 where we have discussed this question in the deterministic case, we will explore it here in the context of stochastic spike arrival. We consider two different scenarios of stimulation. In the first scenario input spikes arrive with a periodically modulated rate,

$$\nu^{\text{in}}(t) = \nu_0 + \nu_1 \cos(\Omega t) \tag{5.123}$$

with $0 < \nu_1 < \nu_0$. Thus, even though input spikes arrive stochastically, they have some inherent temporal structure, since they are generated by an *inhomogeneous* Poisson process. In the second scenario input spikes are generated by a homogeneous (that is, stationary) Poisson process with constant rate ν_0. In a large interval $T \gg \Omega^{-1}$, however, we expect in both cases a total number of $\nu_0 T$ input spikes.

Stochastic spike arrival leads to a fluctuating membrane potential with variance $\Delta^2 = \langle \Delta u^2 \rangle$. If the membrane potential hits the threshold an output spike is emitted. If stimulus 1 is applied during the time T, the neuron emits a certain number of action potentials, say $n^{(1)}$. If stimulus 2 is applied it emits $n^{(2)}$ spikes. It is found that the spike count numbers $n^{(1)}$ and $n^{(2)}$ are significantly different if the threshold is in the range

$$u_\infty + \sqrt{\langle \Delta u^2 \rangle} < \vartheta < u_\infty + 3\sqrt{\langle \Delta u^2 \rangle}. \tag{5.124}$$

We conclude that a neuron in the subthreshold regime is capable of transforming a temporal code (amplitude ν_1 of the variations in the input) into a spike count code. Such a transformation plays an important role in the auditory pathway; see Section 12.5.

5.9 Stochastic firing and rate models

All neuron models considered up to now emit spikes, either explicit action potentials that are generated by ionic processes as in Chapter 2, or formal spikes that are generated by a threshold process as in Chapter 4. On the other hand, if we take the point of view of rate coding, single spikes of individual neurons do not play an important role; cf. Section 1.4. The essential quantity to be transmitted from one group of neurons to the next is the firing rate, defined as a temporal or as a population average. If this is true, models formulated at the level of firing rates would be sufficient.

As we have seen in Section 1.4, there are several ways to define the firing rate of a neuron. Consequently, rate-based models differ with respect to their notion of "firing rate". Here we focus on three different rate models, viz., analog neurons (averaging over time), stochastic rate models (averaging over a stochastic ensemble), and population rate models (averaging over a population of neurons).

5.9.1 Analog neurons

If rate coding is understood in the sense of a spike count, then the essential information is carried by the *mean firing rate*, defined by the number $n_{\text{sp}}(T)$ of spikes that occur in a given time interval T divided by T

$$\nu = \frac{n_{\text{sp}}(T)}{T}. \tag{5.125}$$

In the limit of a large interval T, many spikes occur within T and we can approximate the empirical rate by a continuous variable ν.

We have seen in the previous chapters that a neuron that is driven by a constant intracellular current I_0 emits a regular spike train. The rate ν is then simply the inverse of the constant interspike interval s. If the drive current I_0 is increased, the mean firing rate increases as well until it saturates at a maximum rate ν^{max}. The relation g between the output rate and the input,

$$\nu = g(I_0), \tag{5.126}$$

is called the *gain function* of the neuron. Examples of gain functions of detailed neuron models are given in Fig. 2.5B and Fig. 2.11A. Simplified gain functions used in formal neuron models are given in Fig. 5.24. In fact, for stationary input any regularly firing (i.e., nonbursting) neuron is fully characterized by its gain function.

In a network of neurons in rate description, the input I_i to a neuron i is generated by the rates ν_j of other neurons j. Typically it is assumed that I_i is just a weighted

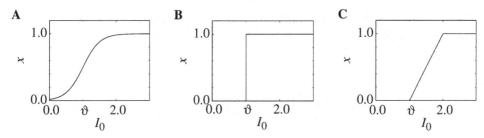

Fig. 5.24. Frequently used gain functions for rate models. The normalized output rate $x = \nu/\nu_{max}$ is plotted as a function of the total input I_0. **A**. Sigmoidal function; cf. Eq. (5.129) with $\beta = 2$ and $\vartheta = 1$. **B**. Step function. **C**. Piecewise linear function.

sum,

$$I_i = \sum_{j \in \Gamma_i} w_{ij} \nu_j , \qquad (5.127)$$

where the weighting factor w_{ij} is the synaptic efficacy. This implies that dendritic integration is a linear operation. A combination of Eqs. (5.127) and (5.126) yields

$$\nu_i = g\left(\sum_j w_{ij} \nu_j\right) , \qquad (5.128)$$

which gives the output rate ν_i of neuron i as a function of its inputs ν_j. This equation plays a central role in the theory of neural networks (Hertz et al., 1991; Haykin, 1994).

We refer to the variable ν_i as the firing rate or activation of neuron i. The interpretation of the input I_i is somewhat ambiguous. Some modelers think of it as a current, consistent with our notation in Eq. (5.127). Other researchers take I_i as a voltage and call it the postsynaptic potential. In the case of constant input, the interpretation is irrelevant, since Eq. (5.128) is only used as a phenomenological model of certain aspects of neural information processing. The neuron itself is essentially treated as a black box that transforms a set of input rates into an output rate.

Example: gain functions of formal neurons

In formal models the transfer function is often described by a hyperbolic tangent,

$$g(I_0) = \frac{\nu_{max}}{2} \{1 + \tanh[\beta (I_0 - \vartheta)]\} , \qquad (5.129)$$

with parameters ν_{max}, β, and ϑ. The gain function has slope $\nu_{max}\beta/2$ at its inflection point $I_0 = \vartheta$ and saturates at ν_{max} as $I_0 \to \infty$; cf. Fig. 5.24A.

For $\beta \to \infty$, the gain function (5.129) approaches a step function

$$g(I_0) = \nu_{max} \Theta(I_0 - \vartheta) ; \qquad (5.130)$$

cf. Fig. 5.24B. For the sake of simplicity, the sigmoidal transfer function (5.129) is often replaced by a piecewise linear transfer function

$$g(I_0) = \begin{cases} 0 & \text{for } I_0 \leq \vartheta \\ \nu_{\max}(I_0 - \vartheta) & \text{for } \vartheta < I_0 \leq \vartheta + 1 \\ \nu_{\max} & \text{for } \vartheta + 1 < I_0 \end{cases} \tag{5.131}$$

which is particularly convenient for a mathematical analysis; see, e.g., Sections 9.1.3 and 11.1.2.

5.9.2 Stochastic rate model

If we consider spike firing as a *stochastic* process we can think of the firing rate ν also as the probability density of finding a spike at a certain instance of time. In this picture, ν is the rate of the underlying Poisson process that generates the spikes; cf. Section 5.2.3. Stochastic rate models are therefore on the border line between analog rate models and noisy spiking neuron models. The main difference is that stochastic spiking neuron models such as the Spike Response Model with escape noise (cf. Section 5.3) allow us to include refractoriness whereas a Poisson model does not (Kistler and van Hemmen, 2000).

Example: inhomogeneous Poisson model

A stochastic rate model in continuous time is defined by an inhomogeneous Poisson process. Spikes are formal events characterized by their firing time $t_j^{(f)}$ where j is the index of the neuron and f counts the spikes. At each moment of time spikes are generated with rate $\nu_i(t)$ which depends on the input. It is no longer possible to calculate the input from a rate equation as in Eq. (5.127) since the input consists now of spikes that are point events in time. We set

$$\nu_i = g(h_i) \tag{5.132}$$

where g is the gain function of the neuron and

$$h_i(t) = \sum_j \sum_f w_{ij} \, \epsilon_0(t - t_j^{(f)}) \tag{5.133}$$

is the total input potential caused by presynaptic spike arrival. As in the model SRM$_0$, each presynaptic spike generates a postsynaptic potential with time course ϵ_0. The synaptic efficacy w_{ij} scales the amplitude of the response function. The postsynaptic potentials of all presynaptic spikes are added linearly. In contrast to the SRM$_0$, the stochastic rate model does not take into account refractoriness.

Example: stochastic model in discrete time

In order to illustrate the relation with the deterministic rate model of Eq. (5.128), we discretize time in steps of length $\Delta t = 1/\nu_{max}$ where ν_{max} is the maximum firing rate. In each time step the stochastic neuron is either active ($S_i = +1$) or quiescent ($S_i = 0$). The two states are taken stochastically with a probability that depends continuously upon the input h_i. The probability that a neuron is active at time $t + \Delta t$ given an input h_i at time t is

$$\text{Prob}\{S_i(t + \Delta t) = +1 \mid h_i(t)\} = \Delta t\, g(h_i), \tag{5.134}$$

where $g(\cdot)$ is the gain function. If we take $\epsilon(s) = 1/\Delta t$ for $0 < s < \Delta t$ and zero otherwise we find

$$h_i(t) = \sum_{ij} w_{ij}\, S_j(t). \tag{5.135}$$

5.9.3 Population rate model

Closely related to the stochastic point of view is the notion of the rate as the average activity of a population of equivalent neurons. "Equivalent" means that all neurons have identical connectivity and receive the same type of input. Noise, however, is considered to be independent for each pair of neurons so that their response to the input can be different. We have seen in Section 1.5 that we can define a "rate" if we take a short time window Δt, count the number of spikes (summed over all neurons in the group) that occur in an interval $t \dots t + \Delta t$ and divide by the number of neurons and Δt. In the limit of $N \to \infty$ and $\Delta t \to 0$ (in this order), the activity A is an analog variable that varies in continuous time,

$$A(t) = \lim_{\Delta t \to 0} \lim_{N \to \infty} \frac{1}{\Delta t} \frac{n_{\text{act}}(t; t + \Delta t)}{N}. \tag{5.136}$$

Let us assume that we have several groups of neurons. Each group l contains a large number of neurons and can be described by its activity A_l. A simple phenomenological model for the interaction between different groups is

$$A_k = g\left(\sum_l J_{kl} A_l\right), \tag{5.137}$$

where A_k is the population activity of group k which receives input from other groups l. Equation (5.137) is formally equivalent to Eq. (5.128) but the parameters J_{kl} are no longer the weights of synapses between two neurons but an effective interaction strength between groups of neurons.

We will see later in Chapter 6, that Eq. (5.137) is indeed a correct description of the fixed point of interacting populations of neurons, that is, if all activity values A_k are, apart from fluctuations, constant. As mentioned in Section 1.4, the interpretation of the rate as a population activity is not without problems. There are hardly ensembles that would be large enough to allow sensible averaging and, at the same time, consist of neurons that are strictly equivalent in the sense that the internal parameters and the input are identical for all the neurons belonging to the same ensemble. On the other hand, neurons in the cortex are often arranged in groups (columns) that are roughly dealing with the same type of signal and have similar response properties. We will come back to the interpretation of Eq. (5.137) as a population activity in Chapter 6.

Example: dynamic rate models

The population rate does not require temporal averaging and can, in principle, change on a rapid time scale. A time-dependent version of the population equation (5.137) is the so-called Wilson–Cowan equation (Wilson and Cowan, 1972)

$$\tau \frac{dA_k(t)}{dt} = -A_k(t) + g \left(\sum_l J_{kl} \int_0^\infty \alpha(s)\, A_l(t-s)\, ds \right). \qquad (5.138)$$

Here, A_k is the activity of a population k and the sum in the brackets runs over all other populations l which send signals to k. The signals cause postsynaptic currents with time course $\alpha(s)$ and are scaled by the coupling J_{kl}.

In order to derive Eq. (5.138), Wilson and Cowan had to make a couple of strong assumptions and we may wonder whether Eq. (5.138) can be considered a realistic description of the population dynamics. More specifically, what determines the time constant τ which limits the response time of the system? Is it given by the membrane time constant of a neuron? Is τ really constant or does it depend on the input or the activity of the system? We will see in Chapter 6 that the population activity of a group of spiking neurons can, in some cases, react instantaneously to changes in the input. This suggests that the "time constant" τ in Eq. (5.138) is, at least in some cases, extremely short. The theory of population dynamics developed in Chapter 6 does not make use of the differential equation (5.138), but uses a slightly different mathematical framework.

5.10 Summary

Variability of spike timing, quantified for example by the C_V values of interval distributions, is a common phenomenon in biological neurons. In models, noise is usually added *ad hoc* to account for this variability. There are at least two different ways of adding noise. Firstly, a noisy threshold can be defined by an instantaneous escape rate which depends on the distance of the membrane potential from the threshold. Escape rate models can be solved for arbitrary input currents in the context of renewal theory. Secondly, stochastic arrival of excitatory and inhibitory input pulses leads to a diffusion of the membrane potential. The interval distribution of an integrate-and-fire model with diffusive noise is equivalent to the first passage time problem of the Ornstein–Uhlenbeck process and difficult to solve. Both noise models are (approximately) equivalent in the subthreshold regime. The critical variable for firing is $x(t) = [u_0(t) - \vartheta]/\sigma$, that is the momentary distance between the noise-free membrane potential and the threshold in units of the membrane potential fluctuations, $\sigma = \sqrt{2\langle \Delta u^2 \rangle}$.

The subthreshold regime has several interesting properties. Firstly, constant input current plus noise leads to a distribution of interspike intervals with a large coefficient of variation, similar to what is found in cortical neurons. Secondly, in the subthreshold regime the neuron is most sensitive to temporal variations in the input. Stochastic resonance is an example of this phenomenon.

In rate models, the neuron is fully characterized by its nonlinear transfer function. If inputs are constant and all neurons are in a stationary state, then the static rate model provides a useful description. Dynamic versions of rate models are possible, but problematic. Stochastic rate models, finally, form the borderline to stochastic spiking neuron models.

Literature

Analysis of spike trains in terms of stochastic point processes has a long tradition (Perkel et al., 1967a; Gerstein and Perkel, 1972) and often involves concepts from renewal theory (Cox and Lewis, 1966). In formal spiking neuron models, stochasticity was introduced early on by adding a stochastic component to the membrane potential (Geisler and Goldberg, 1966; Weiss, 1966). If the correlation time of the noise is short, such an approach is closely related to an escape rate or hazard model (Weiss, 1966). Stochastic spike arrival as an important source of noise has been discussed by Stein in the context of integrate-and-fire models (Stein, 1965, 1967b). Some principles of spike-train analysis with an emphasis on modern results have been reviewed by Gabbiani and Koch (1998) and Rieke et al. (1996). For a discussion of the variability of interspike intervals see the debate of Shadlen and Newsome (1994), Softky (1995), and Bair and Koch (1996). In this context, the role of subthreshold versus superthreshold stimuli has been summarized in the review of König et al. (1996).

The intimate relation between stochastic spike arrival and diffusive noise has been known for a long time (Gluss, 1967; Johannesma, 1968). Mathematical results of diffusive noise in the integrate-and-fire neuron (i.e., the Ornstein–Uhlenbeck model) are reviewed in many texts (Tuckwell, 1988; van Kampen, 1992). The mathematical aspects of stochastic resonance have been reviewed by Gammaitoni et al. (1998); applications of stochastic resonance in biology have been summarized by Wiesenfeld and Jaramillo (1998).

Rate models are widely used in the formal theory of neural networks. Excellent introductions to the theory of neural networks are the books of Hertz et al. (1991) and Haykin (1994). The history of neural networks is highlighted in the nice collection of original papers by Anderson and Rosenfeld (1988) which contains for example a reprint of the seminal article of McCulloch and Pitts (1943).

Part two

Population models

6

Population equations

In many areas of the brain neurons are organized in populations of units with similar properties. Prominent examples are columns in the somatosensory and visual cortex (Mountcastle, 1957; Hubel and Wiesel, 1962) and pools of motor neurons (Kandel and Schwartz, 1991). Given the large number of neurons within such a column or pool it is sensible to describe the mean activity of the neuronal population rather than the spiking of individual neurons. The idea of a population activity has already been introduced in Section 1.4. In a population of N neurons, we calculate the proportion of active neurons by counting the number of spikes $n_{act}(t; t + \Delta t)$ in a small time interval Δt and dividing by N. Further division by Δt yields the *population activity*

$$A(t) = \lim_{\Delta t \to 0} \frac{1}{\Delta t} \frac{n_{act}(t; t + \Delta t)}{N} = \frac{1}{N} \sum_{j=1}^{N} \sum_{f} \delta(t - t_j^{(f)}), \qquad (6.1)$$

where δ denotes the Dirac δ function. The double sum runs over all firing times $t_j^{(f)}$ of all neurons in the population. In other words the activity A is defined by a population average. Even though the activity has units of a rate, the population activity is quite different from a mean firing rate defined by temporal average; cf. Section 1.4.

Theories of population activity have a long tradition (Knight, 1972a; Wilson and Cowan, 1972, 1973; Amari, 1974; Gerstner and van Hemmen, 1992; Abbott and van Vreeswijk, 1993; Treves, 1993; Gerstner, 1995; Amit and Brunel, 1997; Brunel and Hakim, 1999; Fusi and Mattia, 1999; Brunel, 2000; Gerstner, 2000; Nykamp and Tranchina, 2000; Omurtag et al., 2000; Eggert and van Hemmen, 2001). In this chapter we study the properties of a large and homogeneous population of spiking neurons. Why do we restrict ourselves to large populations? If we repeatedly conduct the same experiment on a population of, say, one hundred potentially noisy neurons, the observed activity $A(t)$ defined in Eq. (6.1) will vary from one trial to the next. Therefore we cannot expect a population theory to predict the activity measurements in a single trial. Rather all population activity equations that we discuss in this chapter predict the *expected* activity. For a large and homogeneous network, the observable activity is very close to the expected activity. For the sake of notational simplicity, we do not distinguish the observed activity from its expectation value and denote in the following the expected activity by $A(t)$.

After clarifying the notion of a homogeneous network in Section 6.1, we derive in Section 6.2 population density equations, i.e., partial differential equations that describe the probability that an arbitrary neuron in the population has a specific internal state. In some special cases, these density equations can be integrated and presented in the form of an integral equation. In Section 6.3 a general integral equation for the temporal evolution of the activity $A(t)$ that is exact in the limit of a large number of neurons is derived. In particular, we discuss its relation to the Wilson–Cowan equation, one of the standard models of population activity. In Section 6.4 we solve the population equation for the fixed points of the population activity and show that the neuronal gain function plays an important role. Finally, in Section 6.5 the approach is extended to multiple populations and its relation to neuronal field equations is discussed.

Most of the discussion in Part II of the present book will be based upon the population equations introduced in this chapter. The population activity equations will allow us to study signal transmission and coding (cf. Chapter 7), oscillations and synchronization (cf. Chapter 8), and the formation of activity patterns in populations with a spatial structure (cf. Chapter 9). The aim of the present chapter is twofold. Firstly, we want to provide the reader with the mathematical formalism necessary for a systematic study of spatial and temporal phenomena in large populations of neurons. Secondly, we want to show that various formulations of population dynamics that may appear quite different at a first glance are in fact closely related.

6.1 Fully connected homogeneous network

We study a large and homogeneous population of neurons; cf. Fig. 6.1. By homogeneous we mean that all neurons $1 \leq i \leq N$ are identical and receive the same external input $I_i^{\text{ext}}(t) = I^{\text{ext}}(t)$. Moreover, in a homogeneous population, the interaction strength between the neurons is taken to be uniform,

$$w_{ij} = \frac{J_0}{N}, \tag{6.2}$$

where J_0 is a parameter. For $J_0 = 0$ all neurons are independent; a value $J_0 > 0$ ($J_0 < 0$) implies excitatory (inhibitory) all-to-all coupling. The interaction strength

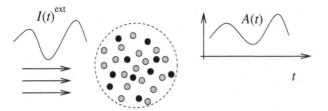

Fig. 6.1. Population of neurons (schematic). All neurons receive the same input $I^{ext}(t)$ (left) which results in a time-dependent population activity $A(t)$ (right). Taken from Gerstner (2000) with permission.

scales with one over the number of neurons so that the total synaptic input to each neuron remains finite in the limit of $N \to \infty$.

Model neurons are described by formal spiking neurons as introduced in Chapter 4. In the case of leaky integrate-and-fire neurons with

$$\tau_m \frac{\mathrm{d}}{\mathrm{d}t} u_i = -u_i + R\, I_i(t) \tag{6.3}$$

a homogeneous network implies that all neurons have the same input resistance R, the same membrane time constant τ_m, as well as identical threshold and reset values. The input current I_i takes care of both the external drive and synaptic coupling

$$I_i = \sum_{j=1}^{N} \sum_f w_{ij}\alpha(t - t_j^{(f)}) + I^{ext}(t)\,. \tag{6.4}$$

Here we have assumed that each input spike generates a postsynaptic current with some generic time course $\alpha(t - t_j^{(f)})$. The sum on the right-hand side of Eq. (6.4) runs over all firing times of all neurons. Because of the homogeneous all-to-all coupling, the total input current is identical for all neurons. To see this, we insert Eq. (6.2) and use the definition of the population activity, Eq. (6.1). We find a total input current,

$$I(t) = J_0 \int_0^\infty \alpha(s)\, A(t - s)\, \mathrm{d}s + I^{ext}(t)\,, \tag{6.5}$$

which is independent of the neuronal index i. As an aside we note that, for conductance-based synaptic input, the total input current would depend on the neuronal membrane potential which is different from one neuron to the next.

Instead of the integrate-and-fire neuron, we may also use the Spike Response Model (SRM) as the elementary unit of the population. The membrane potential of a SRM neuron is of the form

$$u_i(t) = \eta(t - \hat{t}_i) + h_{PSP}(t|\hat{t}_i)\,, \tag{6.6}$$

where $\hat{t}_i$ is the most recent firing time of neuron i. The kernel $\eta(.)$ describes the spike and the spike-afterpotential while

$$h_{\text{PSP}}(t|\hat{t}_i) = \sum_{j=1}^{N} \sum_{f} \frac{J_0}{N} \epsilon(t - \hat{t}_i, t - t_j^{(f)}) + \int_0^\infty \kappa(t - \hat{t}_i, s) \, I^{\text{ext}}(t - s) \, ds \quad (6.7)$$

is the postsynaptic potential caused by firings $t_j^{(f)}$ of presynaptic neurons j or by external input $I^{\text{ext}}(t)$. The kernel ϵ models the response of the neuron to a single presynaptic input spike while κ is the response to a unit current pulse. In Eq. (6.7) we have already exploited Eq. (6.2) and replaced the synaptic efficacies w_{ij} by J_0/N. The population theory developed in this chapter is valid for arbitrary response kernels ϵ and κ and for a broad variety of refractory kernels η. By an appropriate choice of the kernels, we recover the integrate-and-fire model; cf. Section 4.1. If we suppress the $t - \hat{t}_i$ dependency of ϵ and κ, we recover the simple model SRM$_0$ from Section 4.2.3.

Similarly to the approach that we used for the total input current of an integrate-and-fire neuron, we can rewrite Eq. (6.7) in terms of the population activity A,

$$h_{\text{PSP}}(t|\hat{t}) = J_0 \int_0^\infty \epsilon(t - \hat{t}, s) \, A(t - s) \, ds + \int_0^\infty \kappa(t - \hat{t}, s) \, I^{\text{ext}}(t - s) \, ds \,. \quad (6.8)$$

Thus, given the activity $A(t')$ and the external input I^{ext} for $t' < t$ we can determine the potential $h_{\text{PSP}}(t|\hat{t})$ of a neuron that has fired its last spike at $\hat{t}$. Note that we have suppressed the index i, since all neurons that have fired their last spike at $\hat{t}$ have the *same* postsynaptic potential h_{PSP}. As above, this is an immediate consequence of the assumption of a homogeneous network and does not require a limit of $N \to \infty$.

In the absence of noise, the next firing time of a spiking neuron i is found from the threshold condition,

$$u_i(t) = \vartheta \quad \text{and} \quad \frac{d}{dt} u_i > 0 \,. \quad (6.9)$$

In the presence of noise, the next firing time of a given neuron i cannot be predicted in a deterministic fashion. In the case of integrate-and-fire neurons with diffusive noise (stochastic spike arrival), a large noise level leads to a broad distribution of the membrane potential and indirectly to a large distribution of interspike intervals; cf. Chapter 5. In the case of spiking neurons with escape noise (noisy threshold), firing occurs probabilistically which results in a similar large distribution of interspike intervals. In the following sections, we formulate population equations for various types of spiking neuron and different types of noise. We start in the next section with a population of integrate-and-fire neurons with diffusive noise and turn then to Spike Response Model neurons.

6.2 Density equations

In a population of neurons, each neuron may be in a different internal state. In this section we derive partial differential equations that describe how the distribution of internal states evolves as a function of time. We start in Section 6.2.1 with a population of integrate-and-fire neurons. Since the state of an integrate-and-fire neuron is characterized by its membrane potential, we describe the dynamics of the population as the evolution of membrane potential densities. In Section 6.2.2 we turn to neurons described by the Spike Response Model. SRM neurons are characterized by their state of refractoriness so that we have to introduce refractory densities. We will see that the solution of the dynamics of refractory densities leads to a macroscopic population activity equation for escape noise models. In Section 6.2.3 we compare the two approaches (i.e. membrane potential densities and refractory densities) and show that they are equivalent in the low-noise limit. The formulation of the dynamics of a population of integrate-and-fire neurons at the level of membrane potential densities has been developed by Abbott and van Vreeswijk (1993), Brunel and Hakim (1999), Fusi and Mattia (1999), Nykamp and Tranchina (2000), and Omurtag et al. (2000). The closely related formulation in terms of refractory densities has been studied by Wilson and Cowan (1972), Gerstner and van Hemmen (1992), Bauer and Pawelzik (1993), and Gerstner and van Hemmen (1994). Generalized density equations have been discussed by Knight (2000).

6.2.1 Integrate-and-fire neurons with stochastic spike arrival

We study a homogeneous population of integrate-and-fire neurons. The internal state of a neuron i is determined by its membrane potential, which changes according to

$$\tau_m \frac{\mathrm{d}}{\mathrm{d}t} u_i = -u_i + R\, I_i(t)\,. \tag{6.10}$$

Here R is the input resistance, $\tau_m = RC$ the membrane time constant, and $I(t)$ the total input (external driving current and synaptic input). At $u_i = \vartheta$ the membrane potential is reset to $u_i = u_r < \vartheta$.

In a population of N integrate-and-fire neurons, we may ask how many of the neurons have at time t a given membrane potential. For $N \to \infty$ the fraction of neurons i with membrane potential $u_0 < u_i(t) \le u_0 + \Delta u$ is

$$\lim_{N \to \infty} \left(\frac{\text{neurons with } u_0 < u_i(t) \le u_0 + \Delta u}{N} \right) = \int_{u_0}^{u_0 + \Delta u} p(u, t)\, \mathrm{d}u\,, \tag{6.11}$$

where $p(u, t)$ is the *membrane potential density*; cf. Section 5.5. The aim of this section is to describe the evolution of the density $p(u, t)$ as a function of time. As we will see, the equation that describes the dynamics of $p(u, t)$ is nearly identical to that of a single integrate-and-fire neuron with diffusive noise; cf. Eqs. (5.88) and (5.89).

There are three subtle differences though. Firstly, while $p(u, t)$ was introduced in Section 5.5 as *probability* density for the membrane potential of a *single* neuron, it is now interpreted as the density of membrane potentials in a large population of neurons.

Secondly, the normalization is different. In Section 5.5 the integrated density $\int_{-\infty}^{\vartheta} p(u, t) \, du \leq 1$ was interpreted as the probability that the neuron under consideration has not yet fired since its last spike at $\hat{t}$. The value of the integral decreases therefore over time. On the other hand, if a neuron in the population fires, it remains part of the population. Apart from a reset of the membrane potential, nothing changes. Thus the integral over the density remains constant over time, i.e.,

$$\int_{-\infty}^{\vartheta} p(u, t) \, du = 1 . \tag{6.12}$$

The normalization to unity expresses the fact that all neurons have a membrane potential below or equal to threshold.

Thirdly, the fraction of neurons that "flow" across threshold per unit of time is the (expected value of) population activity $A(t)$. If we denote the flux across threshold as $J(\vartheta, t)$, we have

$$A(t) = J(\vartheta, t) . \tag{6.13}$$

Due to the reset, the neurons that "disappear" across threshold, "reenter" at the reset potential u_r. Hence, the membrane potential density at $u = u_r$ increases at a rate proportional to $A(t)$. More specifically, we have a "source" term $A(t) \, \delta(u - u_r)$ at the reset potential u_r that balances the loss that is due to the movement across the threshold. The value of $A(t)$ is given by Eq. (6.13).

We assume that all neurons in the population receive the same driving current I^{ext}. In addition each neuron receives stochastic background input. We allow for different types of synapse. An input spike at a synapse of type k causes a jump of the membrane potential by an amount w_k. The effective spike arrival rate (summed over all synapses of type k) is denoted as ν_k. While the mean spike arrival rates $\nu_k(t)$ are identical for all neurons, we assume that the actual input spike trains at different neurons and different synapses are independent.[1] With these assumptions,

---

[1] In a simulation, spike arrival could for example be simulated by independent Poisson processes.

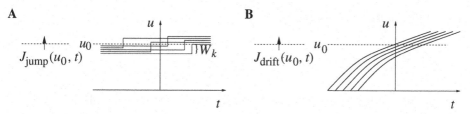

Fig. 6.2. **A.** All trajectory that are less than w_k below u_0 cross u_0 upon spike arrival. **B.** The drift $J_{\text{drift}}(u_0, t)$ depends on the density of trajectories and on the slope with which the trajectories cross the boundary u_0.

the dynamics for $u \leq \vartheta$ is in analogy to Eq. (5.88)

$$
\frac{\partial}{\partial t} p(u, t) = \frac{1}{\tau_m} p(u, t) - \frac{1}{\tau_m} \left[-u + R\, I^{\text{ext}}(t) \right] \frac{\partial}{\partial u} p(u, t) \qquad (6.14)
$$
$$
+ \sum_k v_k(t) \left[p(u - w_k, t) - p(u, t) \right] + A(t)\, \delta(u - u_r).
$$

The first two terms on the right-hand side describe the continuous drift, the third term the jumps caused by stochastic spike arrival, and the last term describes the reset. Because of the firing condition, we have $p(u, t) = 0$ for $u > \vartheta$.

In order to calculate the population activity $A(t)$, we need to determine the flux across threshold. To keep the argument slightly more general, we will consider the flux $J(u_0, t)$ across an arbitrary reference potential u_0,

$$
J(u_0, t) = J_{\text{drift}}(u_0, t) + J_{\text{jump}}(u_0, t), \qquad (6.15)
$$

where J_{drift} accounts for the continuous drift of the membrane potential during the time when no input spike arrives. J_{jump} is due to excitatory and inhibitory spike arrival.

To evaluate J_{jump}, let us consider excitatory input $w_k > 0$ first. All neurons that have a membrane potential u_i with $u_0 - w_k < u_i \leq u_0$ will jump across the reference potential u_0 upon spike arrival at synapse k; cf. Fig. 6.2A. Since the rate of spike arrival at synapse k is v_k, the total flux caused by input spikes at all synapses is

$$
J_{\text{jump}}(u_0, t) = \sum_k v_k \int_{u_0 - w_k}^{u_0} p(u, t)\, du. \qquad (6.16)
$$

The drift $J_{\text{drift}}(u_0, t)$ through the reference potential u_0 is given by the density $p(u_0, t)$ at the potential u_0 times the momentary "velocity" du/dt; cf. Fig. 6.2B. With $du/dt = [-u + R\, I^{\text{ext}}(t)]/\tau_m$ we have

$$
J_{\text{drift}}(u_0, t) = \frac{1}{\tau_m} \left[-u_0 + R\, I^{\text{ext}}(t) \right] p(u_0, t). \qquad (6.17)
$$

The total flux at the threshold $u_0 = \vartheta$ yields the population activity

$$A(t) = \frac{1}{\tau_m} [-\vartheta + R\, I^{\text{ext}}(t)]\, p(\vartheta, t) + \sum_k v_k \int_{\vartheta - w_k}^{\vartheta} p(u, t)\, du\,. \qquad (6.18)$$

Since the probability density vanishes for $u > \vartheta$, the sum over the synapses k can be restricted to all *excitatory* synapses. Equations (6.14) and (6.18) define the dynamics in a population of integrate-and-fire neurons with stochastic background input.

Continuity equation

In this subsection we aim at an interpretation of Eqs. (6.14)–(6.18). Let us consider the portion of neurons with a membrane potential between u_0 and u_1; cf. Fig. 6.3. The fraction of neurons with $u_0 < u < u_1$ increases if neurons enter from below through the boundary u_0 or from above through the boundary u_1. A positive flux $J(u, t) > 0$ is defined as a flux towards increasing values of u. Since trajectories cannot simply end, we have the conservation law

$$\frac{\partial}{\partial t} \int_{u_0}^{u_1} p(u', t)\, du' = J(u_0, t) - J(u_1, t)\,. \qquad (6.19)$$

Taking the derivative with respect to the upper boundary u_1 and changing the name of the variable from u_1 to u yields the continuity equation,

$$\frac{\partial}{\partial t} p(u, t) = -\frac{\partial}{\partial u} J(u, t) \quad \text{for } u \neq u_r \text{ and } u \neq \vartheta\,, \qquad (6.20)$$

which expresses the conservation of the number of trajectories. At $u = u_r$ and $u = \vartheta$ special care has to be taken because of the reset. For $u > \vartheta$ the flux vanishes because neurons that pass the threshold are reset. Since neurons that have fired start a new trajectory at u_r, we have a "source of new trajectories" at $u = u_r$, i.e., new trajectories appear in the interval $[u_r - \epsilon, u_r + \epsilon]$ that have not entered the interval through one of the borders. Adding a term $A(t)\, \delta(u - u_r)$ on the right-hand side of Eq. (6.20) accounts for this source of trajectories. If we insert the explicit form of the flux that we derived in Eqs. (6.16) and (6.17) into the continuity equation (6.20), we arrive once again at Eq. (6.14). For a numerical implementation of Eq. (6.20) we refer the reader to the literature (Nykamp and Tranchina, 2000; Omurtag et al., 2000).

Diffusion approximation

In the limit of small jump amplitudes w_k, the density dynamics given by Eq. (6.14) can be approximated by a diffusion equation. To show this we expand the right-

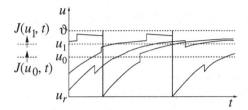

Fig. 6.3. The number of trajectories in the interval $[u_0, u_1]$ changes if one of the trajectories crosses the boundary u_0 or u_1. For a large number of neurons this fact is described by the continuity equation; cf. Eq. (6.20). Schematic figure where only three trajectories are shown.

hand side of Eq. (6.14) into a Taylor series up to second order in w_k. The result is the Fokker–Planck equation,

$$\tau_m \frac{\partial}{\partial t} p(u, t) = -\frac{\partial}{\partial u} \left\{ \left[-u + R\, I^{\text{ext}}(t) + \tau_m \sum_k v_k(t)\, w_k \right] p(u, t) \right\}$$

$$+ \frac{1}{2} \left[\tau_m \sum_k v_k(t)\, w_k^2 \right] \frac{\partial^2}{\partial u^2} p(u, t) \qquad (6.21)$$

$$+ \tau_m\, A(t)\, \delta(u - u_r) + \mathcal{O}(w_k^3)\,.$$

The term with the second derivative describes a "diffusion" in terms of the membrane potential. The firing threshold acts as an absorbing boundary so that the density at threshold vanishes,

$$p(\vartheta, t) = 0\,. \qquad (6.22)$$

In order to calculate the flux through the threshold we expand Eq. (6.18) in w_k about $u = \vartheta$ and obtain

$$A(t) = -\frac{\sigma^2(t)}{2\tau_m} \left. \frac{\partial p(u, t)}{\partial u} \right|_{u=\vartheta}\,, \qquad (6.23)$$

where we have defined

$$\sigma^2(t) = \tau_m \sum_k v_k(t)\, w_k^2\,. \qquad (6.24)$$

Equations (6.21)–(6.23) together with the normalization given by Eq. (6.12) define the dynamics of a homogeneous population of integrate-and-fire units with "diffusive" noise. For a more detailed discussion of the diffusion limit see Section 5.5, in particular Eqs. (5.89) and (5.91).

Example: stationary solution (*)

In this example, we derive the stationary solution $p(u, t) \equiv p(u)$ of the Fokker–Planck equation (6.21). The stationary distribution $p(u)$ of the membrane potential is of particular interest, since it is experimentally accessible (Calvin and Stevens, 1968; Destexhe and Pare, 1999; Ho and Destexhe, 2000).

We assume that the total input $h_0 = R I^{\text{ext}} + \tau_m \sum_k v_k w_k$ is constant. In the stationary state, the temporal derivative on the left-hand-side of Eq. (6.21) vanishes. The terms on the right-hand side can be transformed so that the stationary Fokker–Planck equation reads

$$0 = -\frac{\partial}{\partial u} J(u) + A_0 \delta(u - u_r),$$ (6.25)

where A_0 is the population activity (or mean firing rate) in the stationary state and

$$J(u) = \frac{-u + h_0}{\tau_m} p(u) - \frac{1}{2} \frac{\sigma^2}{\tau_m} \frac{\partial}{\partial u} p(u)$$ (6.26)

is the total flux; cf. Eq. (6.20). The meaning of Eq. (6.25) is that the flux is constant except at $u = u_r$ where it jumps by an amount A_0. Similarly, the boundary condition $p(\vartheta, t) = 0$ implies a second discontinuity of the flux at $u = \vartheta$.

With the results from Section 5.5 in mind, we expect that the stationary solution approaches a Gaussian distribution for $u \to -\infty$. In fact, we can check easily that for any constant c_1

$$p(u) = \frac{c_1}{\sigma} \exp\left[-\frac{(u - h_0)^2}{\sigma^2}\right] \quad \text{for } u \le u_r$$ (6.27)

is a solution of Eq. (6.25) with flux $J(u) = 0$. However, for $u > u_r$ a simple Gaussian distribution cannot be a solution since it does not respect the boundary condition $p(\vartheta) = 0$. Nevertheless, we can make an educated guess and try a modified Gaussian (Giorno et al., 1992; Tanabe et al., 1998b; Brunel and Hakim, 1999),

$$p(u) = \frac{c_2}{\sigma^2} \exp\left[-\frac{(u - h_0)^2}{\sigma^2}\right] \cdot \int_u^\vartheta \exp\left[\frac{(x - h_0)^2}{\sigma^2}\right] dx \quad \text{for } u_r < u \le \vartheta,$$ (6.28)

with some constant c_2. We have written the above expression as a product of two terms. The first factor on the right-hand side is a standard Gaussian while the second factor guarantees that $p(u) \to 0$ for $u \to \vartheta$. If we insert Eq. (6.28) in Eq. (6.25) we can check that it is indeed a solution. The constant c_2 is proportional to the flux,

$$c_2 = 2 \tau_m J(u) \quad \text{for } u_r < u \le \vartheta.$$ (6.29)

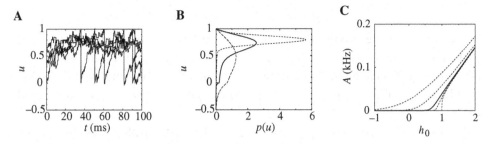

Fig. 6.4. **A.** Membrane potential trajectories of five neurons ($R = 1$ and $\tau_m = 10$ ms) driven by a constant background current $I_0 = 0.8$ and stochastic background input with $\nu_+ = \nu_- = 0.8$ kHz and $w_\pm = \pm 0.05$. These parameters correspond to $h_0 = 0.8$ and $\sigma = 0.2$ in the diffusive noise model. **B.** Stationary membrane potential distribution in the diffusion limit for $\sigma = 0.2$ (solid line), $\sigma = 0.1$ (short-dashed line), and $\sigma = 0.5$ (long-dashed line). (Threshold $\vartheta = 1$.) **C.** Mean activity of a population of integrate-and-fire neurons with diffusive noise as a function of h_0 for four different noise levels, viz. (from top to bottom) $\sigma = 1.0$, $\sigma = 0.5$, $\sigma = 0.2$ (solid line), $\sigma = 0.1$, $\sigma = 0.0$.

The solution defined by Eqs. (6.27) and (6.28) must be continuous at $u = u_r$. Hence

$$c_1 = \frac{c_2}{\sigma} \int_{u_r}^{\vartheta} \exp\left[\frac{(x - h_0)^2}{\sigma^2}\right] dx.\tag{6.30}$$

Finally, the constant c_2 is determined by the normalization condition (6.12). We use Eqs. (6.27), (6.28), and (6.30) in Eq. (6.12) and find

$$\frac{1}{c_2} = \int_{-\infty}^{u_r} \int_{u_r}^{\vartheta} f(x, u)\, dx\, du + \int_{u_r}^{\vartheta} \int_u^{\vartheta} f(x, u)\, dx\, du = \int_{u_r}^{\vartheta} \int_{-\infty}^{x} f(x, u)\, du\, dx,\tag{6.31}$$

with

$$f(x, u) = \frac{1}{\sigma^2} \exp\left[-\frac{(u - h_0)^2}{\sigma^2}\right] \exp\left[\frac{(x - h_0)^2}{\sigma^2}\right].\tag{6.32}$$

Figure 6.4B shows the stationary density $p(u)$ for different amplitudes of the noise.

The activity A_0 is identical to the flux $J(u)$ between u_r and ϑ and therefore proportional to the constant c_2; cf. Eq. (6.29). If we express the integral over u in Eq. (6.31) in terms of the error function, $\mathrm{erf}(x) = \frac{2}{\sqrt{\pi}} \int_0^x \exp(-u^2)\, du$, we obtain

$$A_0^{-1} = \tau_m \sqrt{\pi} \int_{\frac{u_r - h_0}{\sigma}}^{\frac{\vartheta - h_0}{\sigma}} \exp\left(x^2\right) [1 + \mathrm{erf}(x)]\, dx,\tag{6.33}$$

which is identical to expression (5.104) obtained in Section 5.5.

6.2.2 *Spike Response Model neurons with escape noise*

In this section we develop a density formalism for spike response neurons, similar to the membrane potential density approach for integrate-and-fire neurons that we have discussed in the preceding section. The main difference is that we replace the membrane potential density $p(u, t)$ by a refractory density $q(r, t)$, to be introduced below.

We study a homogeneous population of SRM neurons with escape noise. The membrane potential of the neurons,

$$u(t) = \eta(t - \hat{t}) + h_{\mathrm{PSP}}(t|\hat{t}), \tag{6.34}$$

depends on their refractory state,

$$r = t - \hat{t} \geq 0, \tag{6.35}$$

i.e., on the time that has passed since the last spike. If we know r and the total input current in the past, we can calculate the membrane potential,

$$u(t) = \eta(r) + h_{\mathrm{PSP}}(t|t - r). \tag{6.36}$$

Given the importance of the refractory variable r, we may wonder how many neurons in the population have a refractory state between r_0 and $r_0 + \Delta r$. For a large population ($N \to \infty$) the fraction of neurons with a momentary value of r in the interval $[r_0, r_0 + \Delta r]$ is given by

$$\lim_{N \to \infty} \left(\frac{\text{neurons with } r_0 < r(t) \leq r_0 + \Delta r}{N} \right) = \int_{r_0}^{r_0 + \Delta r} q(r, t) \, dr, \tag{6.37}$$

where $q(r, t)$ is the *refractory density*. The aim of this section is to describe the dynamics of a population of SRM neurons by the evolution of $q(r, t)$.

We start from the continuity equation,

$$\frac{\partial}{\partial t} q(r, t) = -\frac{\partial}{\partial r} J_{\mathrm{refr}}(r, t), \tag{6.38}$$

where we have introduce the flux J_{refr} along the axis of the refractory variable r. As long as the neuron does not fire, the variable $r = t - \hat{t}$ increases at a speed of $dr/dt = 1$. The flux is the density q times the velocity, hence

$$J_{\mathrm{refr}}(r, t) = q(r, t) \frac{dr}{dt} = q(r, t). \tag{6.39}$$

The continuity equation (6.38) expresses the fact that, as long as a neuron does not fire, its trajectories $r(t)$ can neither start nor end. On the other hand, if a neuron fires, the trajectory stops at the current value of r and "reappears" at $r = 0$. In the escape rate formalism, the instantaneous firing rate of a neuron with refractory variable r is given by the hazard

$$\rho(t|t-r) = f[\eta(r) + h_{\text{PSP}}(t|t-r)].\tag{6.40}$$

If we multiply the hazard ρ with the density $q(r, t)$, we get the loss per unit of time,

$$J_{\text{loss}} = -\rho(t|t-r)\,q(r, t).\tag{6.41}$$

The total number of trajectories that disappear at time t due to firing is equal to the population activity, i.e.,

$$A(t) = \int_0^\infty \rho(t|t-r)\,q(r, t)\mathrm{d}r.\tag{6.42}$$

The loss given by Eq. (6.41) has to be added as a "sink" term on the right-hand side of the continuity equation, while the activity $A(t)$ acts as a source at $r = 0$. The full dynamics is

$$\frac{\partial}{\partial t}q(r, t) = -\left[\frac{\partial}{\partial r}q(r, t)\right] - \rho(t|t-r)\,q(r, t) + \delta(r)\,A(t).\tag{6.43}$$

This partial differential equation is the analog of the Fokker–Planck equation (6.21) for the membrane potential density of integrate-and-fire neurons. The relation between the two equations will be discussed in Section 6.2.3.

Equation (6.43) can be rewritten in form of an integral equation for the population activity. The mathematical details of the integration will be presented below. The final result is

$$A(t) = \int_{-\infty}^t P_I(t|\hat{t})\,A(\hat{t})\,\mathrm{d}\hat{t},\tag{6.44}$$

where

$$P_I(t|\hat{t}) = \rho(t|\hat{t})\,\exp\left[-\int_{\hat{t}}^t \rho(t'|\hat{t})\,\mathrm{d}t'\right]\tag{6.45}$$

is the interval distribution of neurons with escape noise; cf. Eq. (5.9). Thus, neurons that have fired their last spike at time $\hat{t}$ contribute with weight $P_I(t|\hat{t})$ to the activity at time t. Integral equations of the form of Eq. (6.44) are the starting point for a formal theory of population activity; cf. Section 6.3. For a numerical implementation of population dynamics, it is more convenient to work directly at the level of the density equations (6.43). A simple discretization scheme for numerical implementations is discussed below.

Integrating the partial differential equation (*)

All neurons that have fired together at time $\hat{t}$ form a group that moves along the r-axis at constant speed. To solve Eq. (6.43) we turn to a frame of reference that moves along with the group. We replace the variable r by $t - r \equiv \hat{t}$ and define a new density

$$Q(\hat{t}, t) = q(t - \hat{t}, t),\tag{6.46}$$

with $\hat{t} \leq t$. The total derivative of Q with respect to t is

$$\frac{d}{dt}Q(\hat{t}, t) = \frac{\partial}{\partial r} q(r, t)|_{r=t-\hat{t}} \frac{dr}{dt} + \frac{\partial}{\partial t} q(r, t)|_{r=t-\hat{t}}\tag{6.47}$$

with $dr/dt = 1$. We insert Eq. (6.43) on the right-hand side of Eq. (6.47) and obtain

$$\frac{d}{dt}Q(\hat{t}, t) = -\rho(t|\hat{t})\, Q(\hat{t}, t).\tag{6.48}$$

The partial differential equation (6.43) has thus been transformed into an ordinary differential equation that is solved by

$$Q(\hat{t}, t) = Q(\hat{t}, t_0)\, \exp\left[-\int_{t_0}^{t} \rho(t'|\hat{t})\, dt'\right],\tag{6.49}$$

where $Q(\hat{t}, t_0)$ is the initial condition, which is still to be fixed.

From the definition of the refractory density $q(r, t)$ we conclude that $q(0, t)$ is the proportion of neurons at time t that have just fired, i.e., $q(0, t) = A(t)$ or, in terms of the new refractory density, $Q(t, t) = A(t)$. We can thus fix the initial condition in Eq. (6.49) at $t_0 = \hat{t}$ and find

$$Q(\hat{t}, t) = A(\hat{t})\, \exp\left[-\int_{\hat{t}}^{t} \rho(t'|\hat{t})\, dt'\right].\tag{6.50}$$

On the other hand, from Eq. (6.42) we have

$$A(t) = \int_{-\infty}^{t} \rho(t|\hat{t})\, Q(\hat{t}, t)\, d\hat{t}.\tag{6.51}$$

If we insert Eq. (6.50) into Eq. (6.51), we find

$$A(t) = \int_{-\infty}^{t} \rho(t|\hat{t})\, \exp\left[-\int_{\hat{t}}^{t} \rho(t'|\hat{t})\, dt'\right] A(\hat{t})\, d\hat{t},\tag{6.52}$$

which is the population equation (6.44) mentioned above (Gerstner and van Hemmen, 1992). See also the papers by Wilson and Cowan (1972) and Knight (1972a) for related approaches. If we insert Eq. (6.50) into the normalization condition $1 = \int_{-\infty}^{t} Q(\hat{t}, t)\, d\hat{t}$ we arrive at

$$1 = \int_{-\infty}^{t} \exp\left[-\int_{\hat{t}}^{t} \rho(t'|\hat{t})\, dt'\right] A(\hat{t})\, d\hat{t}.\tag{6.53}$$

Both the population equation (6.52) and the normalization condition (6.53) will play an important role below in Section 6.3.

Numerical implementation (*)

For a numerical implementation of Eq. (6.43) we discretize the refractory variable r in steps of Δt and define $n_k(t) = \int_0^{\Delta t} q(k\,\Delta t + s, t)\,ds$. The normalization is $\sum_k n_k(t) = 1$ for all t. The probability that a neuron with refractory state $r = k\,\Delta t$ fires in a time step Δt is

$$P_F(k) = 1 - \exp\{-f[\eta(k\,\Delta t) + h_{\text{PSP}}(t|t - k\,\Delta t)]\,\Delta t\}. \qquad (6.54)$$

Discretization of Eq. (6.43) yields

$$n_k(t + \Delta t) = n_{k-1}(t)[1 - P_F(k-1)] + \delta_{k,0} \sum_{k'=1}^{\infty} P_F(k')\,n_{k'}(t). \qquad (6.55)$$

If refractory effects are negligible for $r \geq \Delta^{\text{refr}}$, then we can truncate the summation at $k_{\max} \geq \Delta^{\text{refr}}/\Delta t$. All neurons with $k \geq k_{\max}$ have the same firing probability $P_F(k) \equiv P_{\text{free}}$. If we introduce the normalization $\sum_{k > k_{\max}} n_k = 1 - \sum_{k=1}^{k_{\max}}$ we arrive at the update rule

$$n_0(t + \Delta t) = P_{\text{free}} + \sum_{k=1}^{k_{\max}} [P_{\text{free}} - P_F(k)]\,n_k(t) \qquad (6.56)$$

and for $1 \leq k \leq k_{\max}$

$$n_k(t + \Delta t) = [1 - P_F(k-1)]\,n_{k-1}. \qquad (6.57)$$

Note that n_0 is the number of neurons that fire in the interval $[t, t + \Delta t]$. Hence we set $A(t + \Delta t) = n_0(t + \Delta t)/\Delta t$. The above algorithm allows for a rapid integration of the population density equation (6.43).

Example: time-dependent input

We simulate a population of integrate-and-fire neurons with escape rate given by Eq. (5.116). At $t = 100$ ms a time-dependent input is switched on. The population activity $A(t)$ calculated numerically by iterating Eqs. (6.56) and (6.57) responds to the input in a nonlinear fashion; cf. Fig. 6.5. The population activity of the model with escape noise can be compared to that of a model with diffusive noise. The results are strikingly similar. We note that even the rapid components of the input current are, at least partially, visible in the population activity.

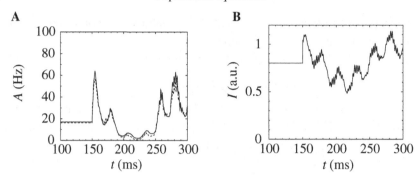

Fig. 6.5. **A**. Activity of a population of integrate-and-fire neurons with diffusive noise (solid line) or escape noise (dashed line). At $t = 150$ ms a time-dependent current is switched on. **B**. Time course of the input current. The current contains 5 randomly chosen frequencies components between 5 and 500 Hz. Parameters: $\vartheta = 1$, $R = 1$, $\tau_m = 10$ ms and $u_r = 0$; diffusive noise model with $\sigma = 0.2$; escape rate given by Eq. (5.116) with $\sigma = 0.2$; the diffusive noise model has been simulated using membrane potential densities while the escape noise model has been simulated using refractory densities.

6.2.3 Relation between the approaches

Density methods have proven to be a useful tool for the simulation and analysis of the behavior of large populations of neurons. The two approaches that we have discussed in this section, viz., membrane potential densities and refractory densities, are closely related. For noise-free neurons driven by a constant superthreshold stimulus, the two mathematical formulations are, in fact, equivalent and related by a simple change of variables. But even for noisy neurons with subthreshold stimulation the two approaches are comparable; cf. Fig. 6.5. Both methods are linear in the densities and amenable to efficient numerical implementations. The formal mathematical relation between the two approaches is shown at the end of this section.

What are the main differences between the two approaches? Both are *single-variable* density methods. In the refractory density method the relevant variable is the refractory variable r. The refractory method is therefore not compatible with diffusive noise since diffusive noise generates a distribution of membrane potentials so that we would need a description by two-dimensional densities. Diffusive noise can, to a certain degree, be replaced by a suitably chosen escape function f in a noisy threshold model. But while escape rate models can mimic the consequence of stochastic spike arrival for the population activity, escape rates cannot serve as a model for membrane potential fluctuations that are commonly seen in intracellular recordings.

On the other hand, refractory density methods combined with escape noise are well suited to describe neuronal refractoriness. It is, for example, straightforward to implement a spiking neuron model with two or more time scales, a slow one for the spike-afterpotential η and a fast one for the postsynaptic potential ϵ – as is typical for Hodgkin–Huxley-type neurons; cf. Sections 2.2 and 4.3. A finite rise time of the postsynaptic potential can be included in the analysis without any additional effort. While it is difficult to include reversal potentials and adaptation in the analysis of refractory density models, both effects can be incorporated phenomenologically in numerical implementations by a few additional macroscopic variables. An advantage of refractory densities combined with escape noise is that the density equations can be integrated formally. While the integral representation is not useful for numerical solutions, it is useful for an interpretation of the dynamics in terms of interspike interval distributions.

Membrane potential density methods work best for integrate-and-fire neurons. Since the membrane potential of an integrate-and-fire neuron is described by a single differential equation, the derivation of the density equation is straightforward. A numerical integration of the density equations causes no major problems if the threshold and reset mechanism as well as the "drift" and "jump" terms are carefully implemented (Nykamp and Tranchina, 2000). Reversal potential can be included at no extra cost – both in simulations and in the analysis (Abbott and van Vreeswijk, 1993; Nykamp and Tranchina, 2000; Omurtag et al., 2000). Stochastic spike arrival can be described explicitly and both the amplitude and the frequency spectrum of the fluctuations of the membrane potential can be predicted. While the formal approach can be extended to detailed neuron models, the implementation of high-dimensional density equations requires efficient numerical implementations (Knight, 2000). Most implementations, so far, have been restricted to integrate-and-fire neurons with or without reversal potentials.

From membrane potential densities to phase densities (*)

For *constant* input current I_0 it is possible to transform membrane potential densities into phase densities. A description by phase variables is interesting in itself; at the same time this section will introduce the methods that we will use below for the transformation from membrane potential densities to refractory densities.

We consider a population of noise-free integrate-and-fire neurons stimulated by a constant superthreshold current. To keep the arguments general, we consider a nonlinear integrate-and-fire neuron (cf. Section 4.1) defined by

$$\frac{\mathrm{d}}{\mathrm{d}t}u = F(u) = -\frac{u - h}{\tau(u)} + \frac{R(u)}{\tau(u)} I_0. \tag{6.58}$$

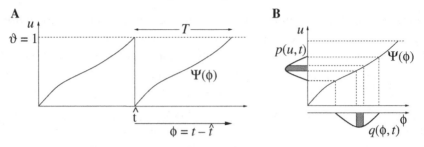

Fig. 6.6. **A**. With constant input, a noise-free (nonlinear) integrate-and-fire neuron fires regularly with period T. We define a phase variable by $\phi = t - \hat{t}$ and write the trajectory as $u = \psi(\phi)$. **B**. The membrane potential density $p(u, t)$ is related to the phase density $q(\phi, t)$ multiplied by $d\psi/d\phi$. The number of neurons with refractory variable between ϕ_0 and ϕ_1 (shaded region) is equal to the number of neurons with membrane potential between $u_0 = \psi(\phi_0)$ and $u_1 = \psi(\phi_1)$.

The voltage dependence of τ and r can account for voltage-dependent conductances and reversal potentials. For $\tau(u) = \tau_m$ and $R(u) = R$ we have the standard equation of an integrate-and-fire neuron.

For I_0 sufficiently large, the neuron will reach the firing threshold $\vartheta = 1$. After firing, the membrane potential is reset to $u_r = 0$. Integration of the differential equation (6.58) yields the membrane trajectory,

$$u(t) = \psi(t - \hat{t}),\tag{6.59}$$

with $d\psi/dt = F[\psi(t - \hat{t})]$. Here $\hat{t}$ denotes the last firing time of the neuron; cf. Fig. 6.6. For constant superthreshold input, the process of integration and reset repeats with a period T, i.e., $u(t + T) = u(t)$. We may therefore introduce a phase variable ϕ that increases from zero to T and is after each firing reset to zero, i.e., $\phi = t \bmod T$. This allows us to rewrite the membrane potential trajectory as $u(t) = \psi(\phi)$.

We can introduce a *phase density* $q(\phi, t)$ so that $\int_{\phi_0}^{\phi_1} q(\phi, t)\, d\phi$ is the fraction of neurons with phase variable in the interval $[\phi_0, \phi_1]$. The phase density q is related to the membrane potential density p by $q(\phi, t)\, d\phi = p(u, t)\, du$ (see Fig. 6.6B) so that

$$q(\phi, t) = p(u, t)|_{u=\psi(\phi)} \left. \frac{du}{dt} \right|_{u=\psi(\phi)} \frac{dt}{d\phi} = p[\psi(\phi), t]\, F[\psi(\phi)]\tag{6.60}$$

where we have used $d\phi/dt = 1$. The normalization is therefore

$$\int_0^T q(\phi, t)\, d\phi = \int_0^T p(\psi(\phi), t)\, F[\psi(r)]\, d\phi = \int_0^1 p(u, t)\, du = 1\tag{6.61}$$

as expected.

We now want to derive the continuity equation for the phase variable $q(\phi, t)$. We start from the continuity equation (6.20) of the membrane potential densities which reduces in the absence of noise to

$$\frac{\partial}{\partial t} p(u, t) = -\frac{\partial}{\partial u} [p(u, t) F(u)], \quad \text{for } 0 < u < 1. \tag{6.62}$$

The term in square brackets is the drift current with $F(u) = du/dt$. We use the product rule to evaluate the derivative on the right-hand side and multiply by $F(u)$. The result is

$$F(u) \frac{\partial}{\partial t} p(u, t) = -F^2(u) \frac{\partial}{\partial u} p(u, t) - F(u) p(u, t) \frac{\partial}{\partial u} F(u), \quad \text{for } 0 < u < 1. \tag{6.63}$$

The left-hand side is identical to $\frac{\partial}{\partial t} q(\phi, t)$; cf. Eq. (6.60). Taking the partial derivative of Eq. (6.60) with respect to ϕ yields the right-hand side of (6.63). Thus Eq. (6.63) can be rewritten as

$$\frac{\partial}{\partial t} q(\phi, t) = -\frac{\partial}{\partial \phi} q(\phi, t) \quad \text{for } 0 < \phi < T; \tag{6.64}$$

cf. (Abbott and van Vreeswijk, 1993). The phase variable ϕ plays a role similar to the refractory variable r. In fact, Eq. (6.64) is identical to the noise-free refractory density equation (6.43). We emphasize, however, that phase variables are restricted to periodic behavior and require therefore constant superthreshold input – in contrast to refractory densities.

From membrane potential densities to refractory densities (*)

In this paragraph we want to show the formal relation between the dynamics of $p(u, t)$ and the evolution of the refractory densities $q(r, t)$. We focus on a population of standard integrate-and-fire neurons with escape noise. The equation of the membrane potential

$$u(t | \hat{t}) = \eta_0 \exp\left(-\frac{t - \hat{t}}{\tau_m}\right) + \int_{\hat{t}}^{t} \exp\left(-\frac{t' - \hat{t}}{\tau_m}\right) I(t') \, dt' \tag{6.65}$$

can be used to define a transformation from voltage to refractory variables: $u \longrightarrow r = t - \hat{t}$. It turns out that the final equations are even simpler if we take $\hat{t}$ instead of r as our new variable. We therefore consider the transformation $u \longrightarrow \hat{t}$.

Before we start, we calculate the derivatives of Eq. (6.65). The derivative with respect to t yields $\partial u/\partial t = [-u + R I(t)]/\tau_m$ as expected for integrate-and-fire neurons. The derivative with respect to $\hat{t}$ is

$$\frac{\partial u}{\partial \hat{t}} = \frac{\eta_0 - R I(t)}{\tau_m} \exp\left(-\frac{t - \hat{t}}{\tau_m}\right) = F(t, \hat{t}), \tag{6.66}$$

where the function F is defined by Eq. (6.66).

The densities in the variable $\hat{t}$ are denoted as $Q(\hat{t}, t)$. From $Q(\hat{t}, t)\,d\hat{t} = p(u, t)\,du$ we have

$$Q(\hat{t}, t) = p[u(t|\hat{t}), t]\, F(t, \hat{t})\,. \tag{6.67}$$

We now want to show that the differential equation for the density $Q(\hat{t}, t)$ that we derived in (6.48),

$$\frac{\partial}{\partial t} Q(\hat{t}, t) = -\rho(t|\hat{t})\, Q(\hat{t}, t)\,, \quad \text{for } \hat{t} < t\,, \tag{6.68}$$

is equivalent to the partial differential equation for the membrane potential densities. If we insert Eq. (6.67) into Eq. (6.68) we find

$$\frac{\partial p}{\partial u} \frac{\partial u}{\partial t} F + \frac{\partial p}{\partial t} F + p \frac{\partial F}{\partial t} = -\rho\, p\, F\,. \tag{6.69}$$

For the linear integrate-and-fire neuron we have $\partial F/\partial t = -F/\tau_m$. Furthermore for $R\,I(t) > \eta_0$ we have $F \neq 0$. Thus we can divide Eq. (6.69) by F and rewrite it in the form

$$\frac{\partial p(u, t)}{\partial t} = -\frac{\partial}{\partial u} \left[\frac{-u + R\,I(t)}{\tau_m}\, p(u, t) \right] - f(u - \vartheta)\, p(u, t)\,, \quad \text{for } u_r < u < \vartheta\,, \tag{6.70}$$

where we have used the definition of the hazard via the escape function $\rho(t|\hat{t}) = f[u(t|\hat{t}) - \vartheta]$ and the definition of the reset potential $u_r = \eta_0$. If we compare Eq. (6.70) with the Fokker–Planck equation (6.21), we see that the main difference is the treatment of the noise. For noise-free integrate-and-fire neurons (i.e., $\rho(t|\hat{t}) = 0$ for $u \neq \vartheta$) the Eq. (6.21) for the membrane potential densities is therefore equivalent to the density equation $\partial Q(\hat{t}, t)/\partial t = 0$; cf. Eq. (6.68).

6.3 Integral equations for the population activity

In this section, we derive, starting from a small set of assumptions, an integral equation for the population activity. The essential idea of the mathematical formulation is that we work as much as possible at the macroscopic level without reference to a specific model of neuronal dynamics. We will see that the interval distribution $P_I(t|\hat{t})$ that has already been introduced in Chapter 5 plays a central role in the formulation of the population equation. Both the activity variable A and the interval distribution $P_I(t|\hat{t})$ are "macroscopic" spike-based quantities that could, in principle, be measured by extracellular electrodes. If we have access to the interval distribution $P_I(t|\hat{t})$ for arbitrary input $I(t)$, then this knowledge is enough to formulate the population equations. In particular, there is no need to know anything about the internal state of the neuron, e.g., the current values of the membrane potential of the neurons.

Integral formulations of the population dynamics have been developed (Knight, 1972a; Wilson and Cowan, 1972; Gerstner and van Hemmen, 1992; Gerstner, 1995, 2000). The integral equation Eq. (6.44) that we derived in Section 6.2 via integration of the density equations turns out to be a specific instance of the general framework presented in this section.

6.3.1 Assumptions

We consider a homogeneous and fully connected network of spiking neurons in the limit of $N \to \infty$. We aim for a dynamic equation that describes the evolution of the population activity $A(t)$ over time.

We have seen in Eq. (6.8) that, given the population activity $A(t')$ and the external input $I^{\text{ext}}(t')$ in the past, we can calculate the current input potential $h_{\text{PSP}}(t|\hat{t})$ of a neuron that has fired its last spike at $\hat{t}$, but we have no means yet to transform the potential h_{PSP} back into a population activity. What we need is therefore another equation that allows us to determine the present activity $A(t)$ given the past. The equation for the activity dynamics will be derived from three observations:

 (i) The total number of neurons in the population remains constant. We exploit this fact to derive a conservation law.
 (ii) The model neurons are supposed to show no adaptation. According to Eq. (6.6), the state of neuron i depends explicitly only on the most recent firing time $\hat{t}_i$ (and of course on the input h_{PSP}), but not on the firing times of earlier spikes of neuron i. This allows us to work in the framework of an input-dependent renewal theory; cf. Chapter 5. In particular, the probability density that neuron i fires again at time t given that its last spike was at time $\hat{t}$ and its input for $t' \leq t$ was $I(t')$ is given by the input-dependent interval distribution $P_I(t|\hat{t})$.
 (iii) On a time scale Δt that is shorter than the axonal transmission delay, all N neurons in the population can be considered as independent. The number of spikes $n_{\text{act}}(t; t + \Delta t)$ that the network emits in a short time window Δt is therefore the sum of independent random variables that, according to the law of large numbers, converges (in probability) to its expectation value. For a large network it is thus sufficient to calculate expectation values.

6.3.2 Integral equation for the dynamics

Because of observation (ii) we know that the input-dependent interval distribution $P_I(t \mid \hat{t})$ contains all relevant information. We recall that $P_I(t \mid \hat{t})$ gives the probability density that a neuron fires at time t given its last spike at $\hat{t}$ and an input $I(t')$

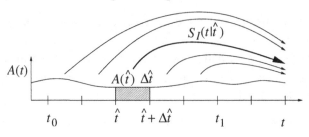

Fig. 6.7. Derivation of the population equation in discretized time. Of the $N\,A(\hat{t})\,\Delta\hat{t}$ neurons that have fired between $\hat{t}$ and $\hat{t} + \Delta\hat{t}$, a fraction $S_I(t|\hat{t})$ is expected to "survive" up to time t without firing another spike. Thus (with $t_1 = \hat{t}_0 + k^{\max}\Delta\hat{t}$) the Riemann sum $\sum_{k=0}^{k^{\max}} S_I(t|\hat{t}_0 + k\Delta\hat{t})\,A(\hat{t}_0 + k\Delta\hat{t})\,\Delta\hat{t} \approx \int_{t_0}^{t_1} S_I(t|\hat{t})\,A(\hat{t})\,d\hat{t}$ gives the expected fraction of neurons at time t that have fired their *last* spike between t_0 and t_1.

for $t' < t$. Integration of the probability density over time $\int_{\hat{t}}^{t} P_I(s \mid \hat{t})\,ds$ gives the probability that a neuron which has fired at $\hat{t}$ fires its next spike at some arbitrary time between $\hat{t}$ and t. Just as in Chapter 5, we can define a survival probability,

$$S_I(t \mid \hat{t}) = 1 - \int_{\hat{t}}^{t} P_I(s \mid \hat{t})\,ds\,, \qquad (6.71)$$

i.e., the probability that a neuron which has fired its last spike at $\hat{t}$ "survives" without firing up to time t.

We now return to the homogeneous population of neurons in the limit of $N \rightarrow \infty$ and use observation (iii). We consider the network state at time t and label all neurons by their last firing time $\hat{t}$. The proportion of neurons at time t which have fired their *last* spike between t_0 and $t_1 < t$ (and have not fired since) is expected to be

$$\left\langle \frac{\text{number of neurons at } t \text{ with last spike in } [t_0, t_1]}{\text{total number of neurons}} \right\rangle = \int_{t_0}^{t_1} S_I(t \mid \hat{t})\,A(\hat{t})\,d\hat{t}\,.$$

$$(6.72)$$

For an interpretation of the integral on the right-hand side of Eq. (6.72), we recall that $A(\hat{t})\Delta\hat{t}$ is the fraction of neurons that have fired in the interval $[\hat{t}, \hat{t} + \Delta\hat{t}]$. Of these a fraction $S_I(t|\hat{t})$ are expected to survive from $\hat{t}$ to t without firing. Thus among the neurons that we observe at time t the proportion of neurons that have fired their last spike between t_0 and t_1 is expected to be $\int_{t_0}^{t_1} S_I(t \mid \hat{t})\,A(\hat{t})\,d\hat{t}$; cf. Fig. 6.7.

Finally, we make use of observation (i). All neurons have fired at *some* point in the past.[2] Thus, if we extend the lower bound t_0 of the integral on the right-hand

---

[2] Neurons which have never fired before are assigned a formal firing time $\hat{t} = -\infty$.

side of Eq. (6.72) to $-\infty$ and the upper bound to t, the left-hand side becomes equal to one,

$$1 = \int_{-\infty}^{t} S_I(t\,|\,\hat{t})\,A(\hat{t})\,\mathrm{d}\hat{t}\,, \tag{6.73}$$

because all N neurons have fired their last spike in the interval $[-\infty, t]$. Since the number of neurons remains constant, the normalization Eq. (6.73) must hold at arbitrary times t. Equation (6.73) is an implicit equation for the population activity A. It is the starting point for the discussions in this and the following chapters.

Since Eq. (6.73) is rather abstract, we try to put it into a form that is easier to grasp intuitively. To do so, we take the derivative of Eq. (6.73) with respect to t. We find

$$0 = S_I(t|t)\,A(t) + \int_{-\infty}^{t} \frac{\mathrm{d}S(t|\hat{t})}{\mathrm{d}t}\,A(\hat{t})\,\mathrm{d}\hat{t}\,. \tag{6.74}$$

We now use $P_I(t|\hat{t}) = -\frac{\mathrm{d}}{\mathrm{d}t}S_I(t|\hat{t})$ and $S_I(t|t) = 1$ which is a direct consequence of Eq. (6.71). This yields the activity dynamics

$$A(t) = \int_{-\infty}^{t} P_I(t\,|\,\hat{t})\,A(\hat{t})\,\mathrm{d}\hat{t}\,. \tag{6.75}$$

A different derivation of Eq. (6.75) has been given in Section 6.2; cf. Eq. (6.44).

Equation (6.75) is easy to understand. The kernel $P_I(t\,|\,\hat{t})$ is the probability density that the next spike of a neuron which is under the influence of an input I occurs at time t given that its last spike was at $\hat{t}$. The number of neurons which have fired at $\hat{t}$ is proportional to $A(\hat{t})$ and the integral runs over all times in the past. The interval distribution $P_I(t|\hat{t})$ depends upon the total input (both external input and synaptic input from other neurons in the population) and hence upon the postsynaptic potential (6.8). Equations (6.8) and (6.75) together with an appropriate noise model yield a closed system of equations for the population dynamics. Equation (6.75) is exact in the limit of $N \to \infty$. Corrections for finite N have been discussed by Meyer and van Vreeswijk (2001) and Spiridon and Gerstner (1999).

An important remark concerns the proper normalization of the activity. Since Eq. (6.75) is defined as the *derivative* of Eq. (6.73), the integration constant on the left-hand side of Eq. (6.73) is lost. This is most easily seen for constant activity $A(t) \equiv A_0$. In this case the variable A_0 can be eliminated on both sides of Eq. (6.75) so that Eq. (6.75) yields the trivial statement that the interval distribution is normalized to unity. Equation (6.75) is therefore invariant under a rescaling of the activity $A_0 \longrightarrow c\,A_0$ with any constant c. To get the correct normalization of the activity A_0 we have to go back to Eq. (6.73).

We conclude this section with a final remark on the form of Eq. (6.75). Even though (6.75) looks linear, it is in fact a highly nonlinear equation because the kernel $P_I(t \mid \hat{t})$ depends nonlinearly on h_{PSP}, and h_{PSP} in turn depends on the activity via Eq. (6.8).

Absolute refractoriness and the Wilson–Cowan integral equation

Let us consider a population of Poisson neurons with an absolute refractory period Δ^{abs}. A neuron that is not refractory fires stochastically with a rate $f[h(t)]$ where $h(t)$ is the total input potential, viz., the sum of the postsynaptic potentials caused by presynaptic spike arrival. After firing, a neuron is inactive during the time Δ^{abs}. The population activity of a homogeneous group of Poisson neurons with absolute refractoriness is (Wilson and Cowan, 1972)

$$A(t) = f[h(t)] \left\{ 1 - \int_{t-\Delta^{abs}}^{t} A(t') \, dt' \right\}. \tag{6.76}$$

We will show below that Eq. (6.76) is a special case of the population activity equation (6.75).

The Wilson–Cowan integral equation (6.76) has a simple interpretation. Neurons stimulated by a total postsynaptic potential $h(t)$ fire with an instantaneous rate $f[h(t)]$. If there were no refractoriness, we would expect a population activity $A(t) = f[h(t)]$. However, not all neurons may fire, since some of the neurons are in the absolute refractory period. The fraction of neurons that participate in firing is $1 - \int_{t-\Delta^{abs}}^{t} A(t') \, dt'$ which explains the factor in curly brackets.

For constant input potential, $h(t) = h_0$, the population activity has a stationary solution,

$$A_0 = \frac{f(h_0)}{1 - \Delta^{abs} f(h_0)} = g(h_0). \tag{6.77}$$

For the last equality sign we have used the definition of the gain function of Poisson neurons with absolute refractoriness in Eq. (5.40). Equation (6.77) tells us that in a homogeneous population of neurons the population activity in a stationary state is equal to the firing rate of individual neurons. This is a rather important result since it allows us to calculate the stationary population activity from single-neuron properties. A generalization of Eq. (6.77) to neurons with relative refractoriness will be derived in Section 6.4.

The function f in Eq. (6.76) was motivated by an instantaneous "escape rate" due to a noisy threshold in a *homogeneous* population. In this interpretation, Eq. (6.76) is the exact equation for the population activity of neurons with absolute refractoriness. In their original paper, Wilson and Cowan motivated the function f by a distribution of threshold values ϑ in an *inhomogeneous* population. In this

A

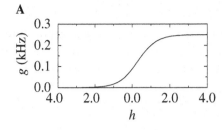

B

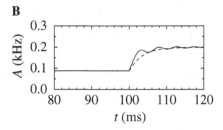

Fig. 6.8. Wilson–Cowan model. **A.** Gain function of neurons with absolute refractoriness of $\Delta^{\mathrm{abs}} = 4$ ms. **B.** The response of the population activity to an abrupt change of the input current shows an oscillatory behavior (solid line) in the approach to the new stationary state. The oscillations are neglected in the coarse-grained solution (dotted line). The input potential vanishes for $t_0 < 100$ ms and is $h(t) = 1 - \exp[-(t - t_0)/\tau_m]$ for $t > t_0$ with $\tau_m = 4$ ms. Exponential escape rate $f(h) = \tau_0^{-1} \exp[\beta(h - \vartheta)]$ with $\vartheta = 1, \tau_0 = 1$ ms, $\vartheta = 1$, and $\beta = 2$. No lateral coupling ($J_0 = 0$).

case, the population equation (6.76) is an approximation, since correlations are neglected (Wilson and Cowan, 1972).

Derivation of the Wilson–Cowan integral equation (*)

We apply the population equation (6.75) to SRM$_0$ neurons with escape noise; cf. Chapter 5. The escape rate $f(u - \vartheta)$ is a function of the distance between the membrane potential and the threshold. For the sake of notational convenience, we set $\vartheta = 0$. The neuron model is specified by a refractory function η as follows. During an absolute refractory period $0 < s \leq \Delta^{\mathrm{abs}}$, we set $\eta(s)$ to $-\infty$. For $s \geq \Delta^{\mathrm{abs}}$, we set $\eta(s) = 0$. Thus the neuron exhibits absolute refractoriness only; cf. Eq. (5.57). The total membrane potential is $u(t) = \eta(t - \hat{t}) + h(t)$ with

$$h(t) = J_0 \int_0^\infty \epsilon_0(s) A(t - s) \, ds + \int_0^\infty \kappa_0(s) I^{\mathrm{ext}}(t - s) \, ds \,. \tag{6.78}$$

Given η it seems natural to split the integral in the activity equation Eq. (6.75) into two parts

$$A(t) = \int_{-\infty}^{t - \Delta^{\mathrm{abs}}} P_I(t \mid \hat{t}) A(\hat{t}) \, d\hat{t} + \int_{t - \Delta^{\mathrm{abs}}}^{t} P_I(t \mid \hat{t}) A(\hat{t}) \, d\hat{t} \,. \tag{6.79}$$

The interval distribution $P_I(t \mid \hat{t})$ for the noisy threshold model has been derived in Chapter 5 and is repeated here for convenience

$$P_I(t \mid \hat{t}) = f[h(t) + \eta(t - \hat{t})] \exp\left\{-\int_{\hat{t}}^{t} f[h(t') + \eta(t' - \hat{t})] \, dt'\right\}. \tag{6.80}$$

Let us evaluate the two terms on the right-hand side of Eq. (6.79). Since spiking is impossible during the absolute refractory time, i.e., $f[-\infty] = 0$, the second term in Eq. (6.79) vanishes. In the first term we can move a factor $f[h(t) + \eta(t - \hat{t})] = f[h(t)]$ in front of the integral since η vanishes for $t - \hat{t} > \Delta^{\text{abs}}$. The exponential factor is the survivor function of neurons with escape noise as defined in Eq. (5.7); cf. Chapter 5. Therefore, Eq. (6.79) reduces to

$$A(t) = f[h(t)] \int_{-\infty}^{t - \Delta^{\text{abs}}} S_I(t \mid \hat{t}) \, A(\hat{t}) \, d\hat{t} \, . \tag{6.81}$$

Let us now recall the normalization of the population activity defined in Eq. (6.73), i.e.,

$$\int_{-\infty}^{t} S_I(t \mid \hat{t}) \, A(\hat{t}) \, d\hat{t} = 1 \, . \tag{6.82}$$

The integral in Eq. (6.81) can therefore be rewritten as

$$A(t) = f[h(t)] \left[1 - \int_{t - \Delta^{\text{abs}}}^{t} S_I(t \mid \hat{t}) \, A(\hat{t}) \, d\hat{t} \right] \, . \tag{6.83}$$

During the absolute refractory period we have a survival probability $S_I(t \mid \hat{t}) = 1$ since the neurons cannot fire. This yields

$$A(t) = f[h(t)] \left\{ 1 - \int_{t - \Delta^{\text{abs}}}^{t} A(t') \, dt' \right\} \, , \tag{6.84}$$

which is the Wilson–Cowan integral equation (6.76) for neurons with absolute refractoriness (Wilson and Cowan, 1972).

Quasi-stationary dynamics (*)

Integral equations are often difficult to handle. Wilson and Cowan aimed therefore at a transformation of their equation into a differential equation (Wilson and Cowan, 1972). To do so, they had to assume that the population activity changes slowly during the time Δ^{abs} and adopted a procedure of time coarse-graining. Here we present a slightly modified version of their argument (Gerstner, 1995; Pinto et al., 1996).

We start with the observation that the total postsynaptic potential,

$$h(t) = J_0 \int_0^{\infty} \epsilon_0(s) \, A(t - s) \, ds + \int_0^{\infty} \kappa_0(s) \, I^{\text{ext}}(t - s) \, ds \, , \tag{6.85}$$

contains the "low-pass filters" ϵ_0 and κ_0. If the postsynaptic potential ϵ_0 is broad, h changes only slowly. In particular the dynamics of h is limited by the membrane time constant τ_m. The activity $A(t)$, however, could still change rapidly. As a first, and essential, step in the procedure of "time coarse-graining", we simply *assume* that A changes only slowly over the time Δ^{abs}. In this case the integral

$\int_{t-\Delta^{\text{abs}}}^{t} A(t')\, dt'$ on the right-hand side of Eq. (6.76) can be approximated by $A(t)\, \Delta^{\text{abs}}$. With this approximation, we can solve Eq. (6.76) for A and find

$$A(t) = g[h(t)] \quad \text{with} \quad g[h] = \frac{f(h)}{1 + \Delta^{\text{abs}} f(h)}. \tag{6.86}$$

In other words, time coarse-graining implies that we replace the instantaneous activity $A(t)$ by its *stationary* value given by Eq. (6.77). As an aside we note that the activity A is given as a function of the input *potential* h rather than the input *current*.

As a second step, we transform Eq. (6.85) into a differential equation. If the response kernels are exponentials, i.e., $\epsilon_0(s) = \kappa_0(s) = \tau_m^{-1} \exp(-s/\tau_m)$, the derivative of Eq. (6.85) is

$$\tau_m \frac{dh}{dt} = -h(t) + J_0\, A(t) + I^{\text{ext}}(t). \tag{6.87}$$

The evolution of the activity A is given by Eq. (6.86) and follows the evolution of h as defined by Eq. (6.87). In particular, the coarse-grained activity $A(t)$ cannot be faster than the membrane potential h and is therefore limited by the membrane time constant τ_m. If the membrane time constant τ_m is much larger than the refractory time Δ^{abs}, the approximation in Eq. (6.86) is good. For $\tau_m \leq \Delta^{\text{abs}}$, the initial transient of the population activity after a change in the input I^{ext} can be faster than τ_m. The difference between the numerical solution of the Wilson–Cowan integral equation (6.76) and that of the coarse-grained equation (6.86) is shown in Fig. 6.8B for a step current input. Whereas the approximate solution approaches the new stationary solution asymptotically from below, the solution of the integral equation exhibits an oscillatory component. In particular, the initial response during the first 2 ms is faster than that of the approximate solution. In Chapter 7 we will study transient responses in more detail and show that in the limit of low noise, the population activity can respond much faster than the membrane potential.

Equation (6.87) is a differential equation for the membrane potential. Alternatively, the integral equation (6.76) can also be approximated by a differential equation for the activity A. We start from the observation that in a stationary state the activity A can be written as a function of the input *current*, i.e, $A_0 = g(I_0)$ where $I_0 = I^{\text{ext}} + J_0\, A_0$ is the sum of the external driving current and the postsynaptic current caused by lateral connections within the population. What happens if the input current changes? The population activity of neurons with a large amount of escape noise will not react to rapid changes in the input instantaneously, but follow slowly with a certain delay similar to the characteristics of a low-pass filter. An equation that qualitatively reproduces the low-pass behavior is

$$\tau \frac{dA(t)}{dt} = -A(t) + g\left[I^{\text{ext}} + J_0\, A(t)\right]. \tag{6.88}$$

This is the Wilson–Cowan differential equation. Note that, in contrast to Eq. (6.87) the sum $I^{\text{ext}} + J_0 A(t)$ appears *inside* the argument of the gain function g. If synaptic dynamics is slow, the term $J_0 A(t)$ should be replaced by $J_0 \int_0^\infty \alpha(s) A(t-s) \, ds$ where $\alpha(s)$ is the time course of the postsynaptic current; cf. Eq. (5.138). The time constant τ is arbitrary but is often identified with the membrane time constant τ_m.

Example: finite refractoriness and escape noise (*)

The Wilson–Cowan integral equation that has been discussed above is valid for neurons with absolute refractoriness only. We now generalize some of the arguments to a Spike Response Model with relative refractoriness. We suppose that refractoriness is over after a time Δ^{refr} so that $\eta(s) = 0$ for $s \geq \Delta^{\text{refr}}$. For $0 < s < \Delta^{\text{refr}}$, the refractory kernel may have any arbitrary shape. Furthermore we assume that for $t > \Delta^{\text{refr}}$ the kernels $\epsilon(t - \hat{t}, s)$ and $\kappa(t - \hat{t}, s)$ do not depend on $t - \hat{t}$. For $0 < t - \hat{t} < \Delta^{\text{refr}}$ we allow for an arbitrary time dependence. Thus, the postsynaptic potential is

$$\epsilon(t - \hat{t}, s) = \begin{cases} \epsilon(t - \hat{t}, s) & \text{for } 0 < t - \hat{t} \leq \Delta^{\text{refr}} \\ \epsilon_0(s) & \text{for } \Delta^{\text{refr}} < t - \hat{t}, \end{cases} \tag{6.89}$$

and similarly for κ. As a consequence, the input potential $h_{\text{PSP}}(t|\hat{t})$ defined in Eq. (6.8) depends on $\hat{t}$ for $t - \hat{t} \leq \Delta^{\text{refr}}$, but is independent of $\hat{t}$ for $t - \hat{t} > \Delta^{\text{refr}}$.

We start from the population equation (6.75) and split the integral into two parts

$$A(t) = \int_{t-\Delta^{\text{refr}}}^t P_I(t|\hat{t}) A(\hat{t}) \, d\hat{t} + \int_{-\infty}^{t-\Delta^{\text{refr}}} P_I(t|\hat{t}) A(\hat{t}) \, d\hat{t}. \tag{6.90}$$

Since $\eta(s)$ vanishes for $s \geq \Delta^{\text{refr}}$, refractoriness plays no role in the second term on the right-hand side of Eq. (6.90). We assume escape noise with an escape rate f and use the same arguments as with Eqs. (6.81)–(6.83). The result is

$$A(t) = \int_{t-\Delta^{\text{refr}}}^t P_I(t|\hat{t}) A(\hat{t}) \, d\hat{t} + f[h(t)] \left[1 - \int_{t-\Delta^{\text{refr}}}^t S_I(t|\hat{t}) A(\hat{t}) \, d\hat{t} \right]; \tag{6.91}$$

cf. Wilson and Cowan (1972) and Gerstner (2000). Here we have used $h_{\text{PSP}}(t|\hat{t}) = h(t)$ for $t - \hat{t} > \Delta^{\text{refr}}$. The term in square brackets is the fraction of neurons that are not refractory. These neurons form a homogeneous group and fire with instantaneous rate $f[h(t)]$. For $\Delta^{\text{refr}} \to \infty$ the term in square brackets vanishes and we retrieve the standard population equation (6.75).

The integrals on the right-hand side of Eq. (6.91) have finite support which makes Eq. (6.91) more convenient for numerical implementation than the standard formulation given in Eq. (6.75). For a rapid implementation scheme, it is convenient to introduce discretized refractory densities as discussed in Section 6.2; cf. Eq. (6.57).

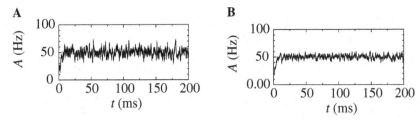

Fig. 6.9. Asynchronous firing. For a sufficient amount of noise, the population activity in a network of independent spiking neurons with constant external input approaches a stationary value A_0. **A.** The population activity of 1000 neurons has been filtered with a time window of 1 ms duration. **B.** Same parameters as before, but the size of the population has been increased to $N = 4000$. Fluctuations decrease with N and approach the value of $A_0 = 50$ Hz predicted by theory.

6.4 Asynchronous firing

We define asynchronous firing of a neuronal population as a macroscopic firing state with constant activity $A(t) = A_0$. In this section we use the population activity equations (6.73) and (6.75) to study the existence of asynchronous firing states in a homogeneous population of spiking neurons. We will see that the neuronal gain function plays an important role. More specifically, we will show that the knowledge of the single-neuron gain function $g(I_0)$ and the coupling parameter J_0 is sufficient to determine the activity A_0 during asynchronous firing.

6.4.1 Stationary activity and mean firing rate

In this section we will show that during asynchronous firing the population activity A_0 is equal to the mean firing rate of a single neuron in the population. To do so, we search for a stationary solution $A(t) = A_0$ of the population equation (6.73). Given constant activity A_0 and constant external input I_0^{ext}, the total input I_0 to each neuron is constant. In this case, the state of each neuron depends only on $t - \hat{t}$, i.e., the time since its last output spike. We are thus in the situation of *stationary* renewal theory.

In the stationary state, the survivor function and the interval distribution can not depend explicitly upon the absolute time, but only on the time difference $s = t - \hat{t}$. Hence we set

$$S_I(\hat{t} + s \,|\, \hat{t}) \longrightarrow S_0(s) \tag{6.92}$$

$$P_I(\hat{t} + s \,|\, \hat{t}) \longrightarrow P_0(s). \tag{6.93}$$

The value of the stationary activity A_0 follows now directly from the normalization

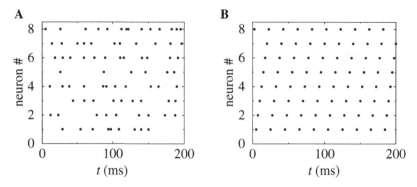

Fig. 6.10. Spike trains (black dots) of selected neurons as a function of time. **A**. Eight neurons out of the 1000 neurons in the simulation of Fig. 6.9A have been randomly chosen. If we sum vertically over the spikes of all 1000 neurons within time bins of 1 ms, we retrieve the plot of Fig. 6.9A. Note that intervals vary considerably, since the noise level is high. The mean interval is $\langle T \rangle = 20$ ms. **B**. Noise-free model network with the same mean firing rate. All neurons fire regularly with 50 Hz, but firing times of different neurons are shifted with respect to each other. Neuron numbers have been ordered in order to make the temporal structure visible.

equation (6.73),

$$1 = A_0 \int_0^\infty S_0(s) \, ds \, . \tag{6.94}$$

We use $dS_0(s)/ds = -P_0(s)$ and integrate by parts,

$$1 = A_0 \int_0^\infty 1 \, S_0(s) \, ds = A_0 \int_0^\infty s \, P_0(s) \, ds \, , \tag{6.95}$$

where we have exploited the fact that $s \, S_0(s)$ vanishes for $s = 0$ and for $s \to \infty$. We recall from Chapter 5 that

$$\int_0^\infty s \, P_0(s) \, ds = \langle T \rangle \tag{6.96}$$

is the mean interspike interval. Hence

$$A_0 = \frac{1}{\langle T \rangle} \, . \tag{6.97}$$

This equation has an intuitive interpretation: if everything is constant, then averaging over time (for a single neuron) is the same as averaging over a population of identical neurons.

Example: comparison with simulations

How can we compare the population activity A_0 calculated in Eq. (6.97) with simulation results? In a simulation of a population containing a finite number N

of spiking neurons, the observed activity fluctuates. Formally, the (observable) activity $A(t)$ has been defined in Eq. (6.1) as a sum over δ functions. The activity A_0 predicted by the theory is the *expectation* value of the observed activity. Mathematically speaking, the observed activity A converges for $N \to \infty$ in the weak topology to its expectation value. More practically this implies that we should convolve the observed activity with a continuous test function $\gamma(s)$ before comparing with A_0. We take a function γ with the normalization $\int_0^{s^{max}} \gamma(s)\, ds = 1$. For the sake of simplicity we assume furthermore that γ has finite support so that $\gamma(s) = 0$ for $s < 0$ or $s > s^{max}$. We define

$$\overline{A}(t) = \int_0^{s^{max}} \gamma(s)\, A(t-s)\, ds \, . \tag{6.98}$$

The firing is asynchronous if the averaged fluctuations $\langle |\overline{A}(t) - A_0|^2 \rangle$ decrease with increasing N; cf. Fig. 6.9.

For the purpose of illustration, we have plotted in Fig. 6.10A the spikes of eight neurons of the network simulation shown in Fig. 6.9. The mean interspike interval for a single neuron is $\langle T \rangle = 20$ ms which corresponds to a population activity of $A_0 = 50$ Hz.

6.4.2 Gain function and fixed points of the activity

The gain function of a neuron is the firing rate $\langle T \rangle^{-1}$ as a function of its input current I. In the previous subsection, we have seen that the firing rate is equivalent to the population activity A_0 in the state of asynchronous firing. We thus have

$$A_0 = g(I) \, . \tag{6.99}$$

Recall that the total input I to a neuron consists of the external input $I^{ext}(t)$ and a component that is due to the interaction of the neurons within the population. In the case of the simple Spike Response Model (SRM$_0$) the input is constant for stationary activity $A(t) = A_0$ and constant external input $I^{ext}(t) = I_0^{ext}$,

$$h(t) = J_0\, A_0 \int_0^{\infty} \epsilon_0(s)\, ds + I_0^{ext} \int_0^{\infty} \kappa_0(s)\, ds \equiv h_0 \, . \tag{6.100}$$

The constant factor $\int_0^{\infty} \epsilon_0(s)\, ds$ can be absorbed in the definition of J_0 and will be dropped in the following. The coupling to the external current is given by the input resistance $\int_0^{\infty} \kappa(s)\, ds = R$, so that

$$h_0 = J_0\, A_0 + R\, I_0^{ext} \, . \tag{6.101}$$

This, however, is rather an input *potential* than an input *current*. In order to be compatible with the definition of the gain function, we should divide the above

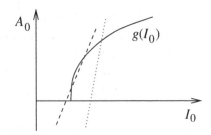

Fig. 6.11. Graphical solution for the fixed point A_0 of the activity in a population of SRM_0 neurons. The intersection of the gain function $A_0 = g(I_0)$ (solid line) with the straight line $A_0 = [I_0 - I_0^{ext}]/J_0$ (dotted) gives the value of the activity A_0. Depending on the parameters, several solutions may coexist (dashed line).

expression by R so as to obtain the total input current, but for the sake of simplicity we set $R = 1$ in the following. Together with Eq. (6.99) we thus find the following equation for the population activity A_0,

$$A_0 = g\left(J_0 A_0 + I_0^{ext}\right) . \tag{6.102}$$

This is the central result of this section, which is not only valid for SRM_0 neurons, but also holds for other spiking neuron models.

Figure 6.11 shows a graphical solution of Eq. (6.102) in terms of the mean interval $\langle T \rangle$ as a function of the input I_0 (i.e., the gain function) and the total input I_0 as a function of the activity A_0. The intersections of the two functions yield fixed points of the activity A_0.

As an aside we note that the graphical construction is identical to that of the Curie–Weiss theory of ferromagnetism, which can be found in any physics text-book. More generally, the structure of the equations corresponds to the mean-field solution of a system with feedback. As shown in Fig. 6.11, several solutions may coexist. We cannot conclude from the figure, whether one or several solutions are stable. In fact, it is possible that *all* solutions are unstable. In the latter case, the network leaves the state of asynchronous firing and evolves towards an oscillatory or quiescent state. The stability analysis of the asynchronous state is deferred to Chapter 8.

Example: SRM_0 neurons with escape noise

Consider a population of (noisy) SRM_0 neurons with escape rate f, e.g., $f(u - \vartheta) = \exp[\beta (u - \vartheta)]$; cf. Section 5.3. The stationary activity A_0 in the presence of a constant input potential $h_0 = R I_0$ is given by

$$
A_0 = \left[\int_0^\infty s\, P_0(s)\, ds \right]^{-1}
$$

$$
= \left[\int_0^\infty s\, f[u(s) - \vartheta]\, \exp\left\{ -\int_0^s f[u(s') - \vartheta] ds' \right\} ds \right]^{-1}, \quad (6.103)
$$

where $u(s) = \eta(s) + h_0$. Figure 6.12A shows the activity as a function of the total input current I_0. Note that the shape of the gain function depends on the noise level β. The stationary activity A_0 in a population with lateral coupling $J_0 \neq 0$ is given by the intersections of the gain function $g(I_0)$ with the straight line that gives the total input I_0 as a function of the activity A_0; cf. Fig. 6.12A.

Example: integrate-and-fire model with diffusive noise

In the limit of diffusive noise the stationary activity is

$$
A_0 = \left\{ \tau_m \sqrt{\pi} \int_{(u_r - h_0)/\sigma}^{(\vartheta - h_0)/\sigma} du\, \exp\left(u^2\right) [1 + \mathrm{erf}(u)] \right\}^{-1}, \quad (6.104)
$$

where σ^2 is the variance of the noise; cf. Eq. (6.33). In an asynchronously firing population of N integrate-and-fire neurons coupled by synapses with efficacy $w_{ij} = J_0/N$ and normalized postsynaptic currents ($\int_0^\infty \alpha(s) = 1$), the total input current is

$$
I_0 = I_0^{\mathrm{ext}} + J_0 A_0; \quad (6.105)
$$

cf. Eq. (6.5). The fixed points for the population activity are once more determined by the intersections of these two functions; cf. Fig. 6.12B.

6.4.3 Low-connectivity networks

In the preceding subsections we have studied the stationary state of a population of neurons for a given noise level. The noise was modeled either as diffusive noise mimicking stochastic spike arrival or as escape noise mimicking a noisy threshold. In both cases noise was added *explicitly* to the model. In this section we discuss how a network of *deterministic* neurons with fixed random connectivity can generate its own noise. In particular, we will focus on spontaneous activity and argue that there exist stationary states of asynchronous firing at low firing rates which have broad distributions of interspike intervals even though individual neurons are deterministic. This point has been emphasized by van Vreeswijk and Sompolinsky (1996, 1998) who used a network of binary neurons to demonstrate broad interval distribution in deterministic networks. Amit and Brunel (1997) where the first to analyze a network of integrate-and-fire neurons with

A **B**

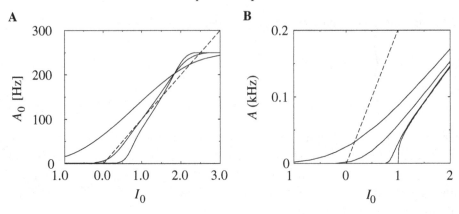

Fig. 6.12. **A**. Determination of the population activity A_0 for noisy SRM_0 neurons with exponential escape rate $f(u) = \exp[\beta\,(u - \vartheta)]$. Depending on the noise level, there are one or several intersections between the gain functions (solid lines) and the dashed line. Noise parameters are $\beta = 2$, 5, and 10. **B**. Similar construction for integrate-and-fire neurons with diffusive noise. The solid lines show the single-neuron firing rate as a function of the constant input current I_0 for four different noise levels, viz. $\sigma = 1.0$, $\sigma = 0.5$, $\sigma = 0.1$, $\sigma = 0.0$ (from top to bottom). The intersection with the dashed line with slope $1/J_0$ gives potential solutions for the stationary activity A_0 in a population with excitatory coupling J_0. Other parameters: $\vartheta = 1$, $R = 1$, $\tau = 10$ ms.

fixed random connectivity. While they allowed for an additional fluctuating input current, the major part of the fluctuations were in fact generated by the network itself. The theory of randomly connected integrate-and-fire neurons has been further developed by Brunel and Hakim (1999). In a recent study, Brunel (2000) confirmed that asynchronous highly irregular firing can be a stable solution of the network dynamics in a completely deterministic network consisting of excitatory and inhibitory integrate-and-fire neurons. The analysis of randomly connected networks of integrate-and-fire neurons is closely related to earlier theories for random nets of formal analog or binary neurons (Amari, 1972, 1974, 1977b; Crisanti and Sompolinsky, 1988; Kree and Zippelius, 1991; Nützel, 1991; Cessac et al., 1994).

The network structure plays a central role in the arguments. While we assume that all neurons in the population are of the same type, the connectivity between the neurons in the population is not homogeneous. Rather it is random, but fixed. Each neuron in the population of N neurons receives input from C randomly selected neurons in the population. Sparse connectivity means that the ratio

$$\frac{C}{N} \ll 1 \tag{6.106}$$

is a small number. Is this realistic? A typical pyramidal neuron in the cortex receives several thousand synapses from presynaptic neurons while the total number of neurons in the cortex is much higher. Thus globally the cortical connectivity C/N is low. On the other hand, we may concentrate on a single column in visual cortex and define, e.g., all excitatory neurons in that column as one population. We estimate that the number N of neurons in one column is below 10 000. Each neuron receives a large number of synapses from neurons within the same column. In order to have a connectivity ratio of 0.1, each neuron should have connections to about 1000 other neurons in the same column.

As a consequence of the sparse random network connectivity two neurons i and j share only a small number of common inputs. In the limit of $C/N \rightarrow 0$ the probability that neurons i and j have a common presynaptic neuron vanishes. Thus, *if* the presynaptic neurons fire stochastically, then the input spike trains that arrive at neuron i and j are independent (Derrida et al., 1987; Kree and Zippelius, 1991). In that case, the input of neuron i and j can be described as stochastic spike arrival which, as we have seen, can be described by a diffusive noise model.

The above reasoning, however, is based on the assumption that the presynaptic neurons (that are part of the population) fire stochastically. To make the argument self-consistent, we have to show that the firing of the postsynaptic neuron is, to a good approximation, also stochastic. The self-consistent argument will be outlined in the following.

We have seen in Chapter 5 that integrate-and-fire neurons with diffusive noise generate spike trains with a broad distribution of interspike intervals when they are driven in the subthreshold regime. We will use this observation to construct a self-consistent solution for the stationary states of asynchronous firing.

We consider two populations, an excitatory population with N_E neurons and an inhibitory population with N_I neurons. We assume that excitatory and inhibitory neurons have the same parameters ϑ, τ_m, R, and u_r. In addition all neurons are driven by a common external current I^{ext}. Each neuron in the population receives C_E synapses from excitatory neurons with weight $w_E > 0$ and C_I synapses from inhibitory neurons with weight $w_I < 0$. If an input spike arrives at the synapses of neuron i from a presynaptic neuron j, its membrane potential changes by an amount $\Delta u_i = w_j$ where $w_j = w_E$ if j is excitatory and $w_j = w_I$ if j is inhibitory. We set

$$\gamma = \frac{C_I}{C_E} \text{ and } g = -\frac{w_I}{w_E}. \tag{6.107}$$

Since excitatory and inhibitory neurons receive the same number of inputs in our model, we assume that they fire with a common firing rate v. The total input potential generated by the external current and by the lateral couplings is

$$h_0 = R I^{\text{ext}} + \tau_m \sum_j \nu_j w_j$$

$$= h_0^{\text{ext}} + \tau_m \nu w_E C_E (1 - \gamma g). \tag{6.108}$$

The variance of the input is given by Eq. (6.24), i.e.,

$$\sigma^2 = \tau_m \sum_j \nu_j w_j^2$$

$$= \tau_m \nu w_E^2 C_E (1 + \gamma g^2). \tag{6.109}$$

The stationary firing rate A_0 of the population with mean h_0 and variance σ is given by Eq. (6.33) which is repeated here for convenience

$$A_0 = \frac{1}{\tau_m} \left\{ \sqrt{\pi} \int_{(u_r - h_0)/\sigma}^{(\vartheta - h_0)/\sigma} \exp(x^2) [1 + \text{erf}(x)] \, dx \right\}^{-1}. \tag{6.110}$$

In a stationary state we must have $A_0 = \nu$. To get the value of A_0 we must therefore solve Eqs. (6.108)–(6.110) simultaneously for ν and σ. Since the gain function, i.e., the firing rate as a function of the input potential h_0, depends on the noise level σ, a simple graphical solution as in Section 6.4 is no longer possible. In the following paragraphs we give some examples of how to construct self-consistent solutions. Numerical solutions of Eqs. (6.108)–(6.110) have been obtained by Amit and Brunel (1997). For a mixed graphical-numerical approach see Mascaro and Amit (1999).

The arguments that have been developed above for low-connectivity networks can be generalized to fully connected networks with *asymmetric random* connectivity (Amari, 1972; Sompolinsky et al., 1988; Cessac et al., 1994; Ben Arous and Guionnet, 1995; van Vreeswijk and Sompolinsky, 1996).

Example: balanced excitation and inhibition

In the preceding sections, we have often considered neurons driven by a mean input potential $h_0 = 0.8$ and a variance $\sigma = 0.2$. Let us find connectivity parameters of our network so that $\sigma = 0.2$ is the result of stochastic spike arrivals from presynaptic neurons within the network. As always we set $R = \vartheta = 1$ and $\tau_m = 10$ ms.

Figure 6.13A shows that $h_0 = 0.8$ and $\sigma = 0.2$ correspond to a firing rate of $A_0 = \nu \approx 16$ Hz. We set $w_E = 0.025$, i.e., 40 simultaneous spikes are necessary to make a neuron fire. Inhibition has the same strength $w_I = -w_E$ so that $g = 1$. We constrain our search to solutions with $C_E = C_I$ so that $\gamma = 1$. Thus, on average, excitation and inhibition balance each other. To get an average input potential of $h_0 = 0.8$ we need therefore a constant driving current $I^{\text{ext}} = 0.8$.

A

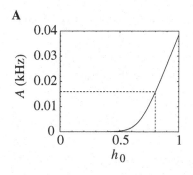

B

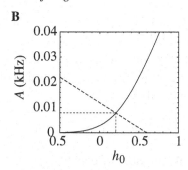

Fig. 6.13. **A**. Mean activity of a population of integrate-and-fire neurons with diffusive noise of $\sigma = 0.2$ as a function of $h_0 = R\,I_0$. For $h_0 = 0.8$ the population rate is $\nu \approx 16$ Hz (dotted line). **B**. Mean activity of a population of integrate-and-fire neurons with diffusive noise of $\sigma = 0.54$ as a function of $h_0 = R\,I_0$. For $h_0 = 0.2$ the population rate is $\nu = 8$ Hz (dotted line). The long-dashed line shows $A_0 = [h_0 - h_0^{\text{ext}}]/J^{\text{eff}}$ with an effective coupling $J^{\text{eff}} < 0$.

To arrive at $\sigma = 0.2$ we solve Eq. (6.109) for C_E and find $C_E = C_I = 200$. Thus for this choice of parameters the network generates enough noise to allow a stationary solution of asynchronous firing at 16 Hz.

Note that, for the same parameter, the inactive state where all neurons are silent is also a solution. Using the methods discussed in this section we cannot say anything about the stability of these states. For the stability analysis see (Brunel, 2000) and Chapter 7.

Example: spontaneous cortical activity

About 80% of the neurons in the cerebral cortex are excitatory and 20% inhibitory. Let us suppose that we have $N_E = 8000$ excitatory and $N_I = 2000$ inhibitory neurons in a cortical column. We assume random connectivity and take $C_E = 800$, $C_I = 200$ so that $\gamma = 1/4$. As before, excitatory synapses have a weight $w_E = 0.025$, i.e, an action potential can be triggered by the simultaneous arrival of 40 presynaptic spikes. If neurons are driven in the regime close to threshold, inhibition is rather strong and we take $w_I = -0.125$ so that $g = 5$. Even though we have fewer inhibitory than excitatory neurons, the mean feedback is then dominated by inhibition since $\gamma g > 1$. We search for a consistent solution of Eqs. (6.108)–(6.110) with a spontaneous activity of $\nu = 8$ Hz.

Given the above parameters, the variance is $\sigma \approx 0.54$; cf. Eq. (6.109). The gain function of integrate-and-fire neurons gives us for $\nu = 8$ Hz a corresponding total potential of $h_0 \approx 0.2$; cf. Fig. 6.13B. To attain h_0 we have to apply an external stimulus $h_0^{\text{ext}} = R\,I^{\text{ext}}$ which is slightly larger than h_0 since the net effect of the lateral coupling is inhibitory. Let us introduce the effective coupling

$J^{\text{eff}} = \tau\, C_E\, w_E\, (1 - \gamma\, g)$. Using the above parameters we find from Eq. (6.108) $h_0^{\text{ext}} = h_0 - J^{\text{eff}} A_0 \approx 0.6$.

The external input could, of course, be provided by (stochastic) spike arrival from other columns in the same or other areas of the brain. In this case Eq. (6.108) is to be replaced by

$$h_0 = \tau_m\, \nu\, w_E\, C_E\, [1 - \gamma\, g] + \tau_m\, \nu_{\text{ext}} w_{\text{ext}}\, C_{\text{ext}}, \tag{6.111}$$

with C_{ext} the number of connections that a neuron receives from neurons outside the population, w_{ext} their typical coupling strength, and ν_{ext} their spike arrival rate (Amit and Brunel, 1997). Due to the extra stochasticity in the input, the variance σ is larger and the total variance is

$$\sigma^2 = \tau_m\, \nu\, w_E^2\, C_E\, [1 + \gamma\, g^2] + \tau_m\, \nu_{\text{ext}} w_{\text{ext}}^2\, C_{\text{ext}}. \tag{6.112}$$

The equations (6.110), (6.111) and (6.112) can be solved numerically (Amit and Brunel, 1997). The analysis of the stability of the solution is slightly more involved but can be done (Brunel and Hakim, 1999; Brunel, 2000).

6.5 Interacting populations and continuum models

In this section we extend the population equations from a single homogeneous population to several populations. We start in Section 6.5.1 with interacting groups of neurons and then turn in Section 6.5.2 to a continuum description.

6.5.1 Several populations

Let us consider a network consisting of several populations; cf. Fig. 6.14. It is convenient to visualize the neurons as being arranged in spatially separate pools, but this is not necessary. All neurons could, for example, be physically localized in the same column of the visual cortex. Within the column we could define two pools, one for excitatory and one for inhibitory neurons, for example.

We assume that neurons are homogeneous within each pool. The activity of neurons in pool n is

$$A_n(t) = \frac{1}{N_n} \sum_{j \in \Gamma_n} \sum_f \delta(t - t_j^{(f)}) \tag{6.113}$$

where N_n is the number of neurons in pool n and Γ_n denotes the set of neurons that belong to pool n. We assume that each neuron i in pool n receives input from all neurons j in pool m with strength $w_{ij} = J_{nm}/N_m$; cf. Fig. 6.15. The input potential

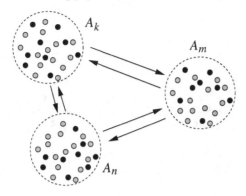

Fig. 6.14. Several interacting populations of neurons.

to a neuron i in group Γ_n is generated by the spikes of all neurons in the network,

$$
\begin{aligned}
h_i(t|\hat{t}_i) &= \sum_j \sum_f w_{ij}\,\epsilon(t - \hat{t}_i, t - t_j^{(f)}) \\
&= \sum_m J_{nm} \int_0^\infty \epsilon(t - \hat{t}_i, s) \sum_{j \in \Gamma_m} \sum_f \frac{\delta(t - t_j^{(f)} - s)}{N_m}\,.
\end{aligned}
\tag{6.114}
$$

We use Eq. (6.113) to replace the sum on the right-hand side of Eq. (6.114) and obtain

$$
h_n(t|\hat{t}) = \sum_m J_{nm} \int_0^\infty \epsilon(t - \hat{t}, s)\, A_m(t - s)\, \mathrm{d}s\,.
\tag{6.115}
$$

We have dropped the index i since the input potential is the same for all neurons in pool n that have fired their last spike at $\hat{t}$. Note that Eq. (6.115) is a straightforward generalization of Eq. (6.8) and could have been "guessed" immediately; external input I^{ext} could be added as in Eq. (6.8).

In the case of several populations, Eq. (6.75) for the population activity is to be applied to each pool activity separately, e.g., for pool n

$$
A_n(t) = \int_{-\infty}^t P_n(t|\hat{t})\, A_n(\hat{t})\, \mathrm{d}\hat{t}\,.
\tag{6.116}
$$

Equation (6.116) looks simple and we may wonder where the interactions between different pools come into play. In fact, pool n is coupled to other populations via the potential h_n which determines the kernel $P_n(t|\hat{t})$. For example, with the escape noise model, we have

$$
P_n(t|\hat{t}) = f[u_n(t|\hat{t}) - \vartheta]\, \exp\left\{ \int_{\hat{t}}^t f[u_n(t'|\hat{t}) - \vartheta]\, \mathrm{d}t' \right\}
\tag{6.117}
$$

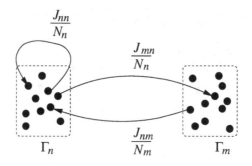

Fig. 6.15. All neurons in group Γ_n are coupled with synaptic efficacy $w_{ij} = J_{nn}/N_n$. Each pair of neurons i, j with the presynaptic j in groups Γ_m and the postsynaptic neuron i in Γ_n is coupled via $w_{ij} = J_{nm}/N_m$.

with $u_n(t|\hat{t}) = \eta(t - \hat{t}) + h_n(t|\hat{t})$, with $h_n(t|\hat{t})$ given by (6.115). Equations (6.115)–(6.117) determine the dynamics of interacting pools of Spike Response Model neurons with escape noise.

Example: stationary states

The fixed points of the activity in a network consisting of several populations can be found as in Section 6.4. Firstly we determine for each pool the activity as a function of the total input I_m

$$A_m = g_m(I_m), \tag{6.118}$$

where g_m is the gain function of neurons in pool m. Then we calculate the total input current to neurons in pool m,

$$I_m = \sum_n J_{mn} A_n. \tag{6.119}$$

Inserting Eq. (6.119) in Eq. (6.118) yields the standard formula of artificial neural networks,

$$A_m = g_m\left(\sum_n J_{mn} A_n\right), \tag{6.120}$$

derived here for interacting *populations* of neurons.

6.5.2 Spatial continuum limit

The physical location of a neuron in a population often reflects the task of a neuron. In the auditory system, for example, neurons are organized along an axis that reflects the neurons' preferred frequency. A neuron at one end of the

$w(nd, md)$

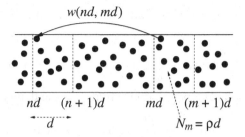

Fig. 6.16. In a spatially continuous ensemble of neurons, the number of neurons in a segment d is $N = \rho\, d$. The efficacy w_{ij} between two neurons depends on their location. The coupling strength between a presynaptic neuron j at position $x_j \approx md$ and a postsynaptic neuron i at location $x_i \approx nd$ is $w_{ij} \approx w(nd, md)$.

axis will respond maximally to low-frequency tones; a neuron at the other end to high frequencies. As we move along the axis the preferred frequency changes gradually. For neurons organized along a one-dimensional axis or, more generally in a spatially extended multidimensional network, a description by discrete pools does not seem appropriate. We will indicate in this section that a transition from discrete pools to a continuous population is possible. Here we give a short heuristic motivation of the equations. A thorough derivation along a slightly different line of arguments will be performed in Chapter 9.

To keep the notation simple, we consider a population of neurons that extends along a one-dimensional axis; cf. Fig. 6.16. We assume that the interaction between a pair of neurons i, j depends only on their location x or y on the line. If the location of the presynaptic neuron is y and that of the postsynaptic neuron is x, then $w_{ij} = w(x, y)$. In order to use Eq. (6.115), we discretize space in segments of size d. The number of neurons in the interval $[n\, d, (n + 1)\, d]$ is $N_n = \rho\, d$ where ρ is the spatial density. Neurons in that interval form the group Γ_n. We change our notation with respect to Eq.(6.115) and replace the subscript n in h_n and A_n by the spatial position

$$h_n(t|\hat{t}) \quad \longrightarrow \quad h(n\, d, t|\hat{t}) = h(x, t|\hat{t}) \tag{6.121}$$

$$A_n(t) \quad \longrightarrow \quad A(n\, d, t) = A(x, t). \tag{6.122}$$

Since the efficacy of a pair of neurons with $i \in \Gamma_n$ and $j \in \Gamma_m$ is by definition $w_{ij} = J_{nm}/N_m$ with $N_m = \rho\, d$, we have $J_{nm} = \rho\, d\, w(n\, d, m\, d)$. We use this in Eq. (6.115) and find

$$h(n\, d, t|\hat{t}) = \rho \sum_m d\, w(n\, d, m\, d) \int_0^\infty \epsilon(t - \hat{t}, s)\, A(m\, d, t - s)\, \mathrm{d}s. \tag{6.123}$$

For $d \rightarrow 0$, the summation on the right-hand side can be replaced by an integral and we arrive at

$$h(x, t|\hat{t}) = \rho \int w(x, y) \int_0^\infty \epsilon(t - \hat{t}, s) \, A(y, t - s) \, ds \, dy, \qquad (6.124)$$

which is the final result. The population activity has the dynamics

$$A(x, t) = \int_{-\infty}^t P_x(t \,|\hat{t}) \, A(x, \hat{t}) \, d\hat{t}, \qquad (6.125)$$

where P_x is the interval distribution for neurons with input potential $h(x, t|\hat{t})$.

If we are interested in stationary states of asynchronous firing, the activity $A(y, t) \equiv A_0(y)$ can be calculated as before with the help of the neuronal gain function g. The result is in analogy to Eqs. (6.118) and (6.120)

$$A_0(x) = g \left(\rho \int w(x, y) \, A_0(y) \, dy \right). \qquad (6.126)$$

Example: field equations for SRM$_0$ neurons

In the case of SRM$_0$ neurons, the input potential h does not depend on the last firing time $\hat{t}$ so that Eq. (6.124) reduces to

$$h(x, t) = \rho \int w(x, y) \int_0^\infty \epsilon_0(s) \, A(y, t - s) \, ds \, dy. \qquad (6.127)$$

We assume that the postsynaptic potential can be approximated by an exponential function with time constant τ_m, i.e., $\epsilon_0(s) = \tau_m^{-1} \exp(-s/\tau_m)$. Just as we did before in Eq. (6.87), we can now transform Eq. (6.127) into a differential equation,

$$\tau_m \frac{dh(x, t)}{dt} = -h(x, t) + \rho \int w(x, y) \, A(y, t) \, dy. \qquad (6.128)$$

If we make the additional assumption that the activity A changes only slowly over time, we may replace A by its stationary solution, i.e., $A(y, t) = g[h(y, t)]$. Here $g[h(y, t)]$ is the single neuron firing rate as a function of the total input *potential*. For constant input current I_0 and normalized input resistance $R = 1$ we have $h_0 = I_0$. In this case, we may identify $g(h_0)$ with the gain function $g(I_0)$ of the neuron – and knowing this we have chosen the same symbol g for both functions.

If we insert $A(y, t) = g[h(y, t)]$ in Eq. (6.128), we arrive at an integro-differential equation for the "field" $h(x, t)$

$$\tau_m \frac{dh(x, t)}{dt} = -h(x, t) + \rho \int w(x, y) \, g[h(y, t)] \, dy. \qquad (6.129)$$

We refer to Eq. (6.129) as the neuronal field equation (Wilson and Cowan, 1973; Ellias and Grossberg, 1975; Feldman and Cowan, 1975; Amari, 1977a). It will be studied in detail in Chapter 9.

6.6 Limitations

In this chapter we have studied an integral equation for population dynamics and discussed its relation to density methods. The validity of the population equations relies on three assumptions: (i) a *homogeneous* population of (ii) an *infinite* number of neurons which show (iii) *no adaptation*.

It is clear that there are no large and completely *homogeneous* populations in biology. The population equations may nevertheless be a useful starting point for a theory of heterogeneous populations (Tsodyks et al., 1993; Senn et al., 1996; Chow, 1998; Pham et al., 1998; Brunel and Hakim, 1999). We may distinguish between heterogeneity in the coupling weights w_{ij} and heterogeneity in the local parameters of the neurons, e.g., the threshold or reset value. The case of randomly chosen weights has been discussed in Section 6.4.3. In the stationary case, the population activity equations can be discussed by solving simultaneously for the mean activity A_0 and the noise amplitude σ. The form of the population activity is similar to that of a homogeneous network. In order to treat heterogeneity in local neuronal parameters, the variability of a parameter between one neuron and the next is often replaced by slow noise in the parameters. For example, a population of integrate-and-fire neurons whose reset value u_r is different for each neuron is replaced by a population whose reset values are randomly chosen after each firing (and not only once at the beginning). Such a noise model has been termed "noisy reset" in Section 5.4 and discussed as an example of slow noise in parameters. The replacement of heterogeneity by slow noise neglects, however, correlations that would be present in a truly heterogeneous model. To replace a heterogeneous model by a noisy version of a homogeneous model is somewhat *ad hoc*, but common practice in the literature.

The second condition is the limit of a *large network*. For $N \to \infty$ the population activity shows no fluctuations and this fact has been used for the derivation of the population equation. For systems of finite size fluctuations are important since they limit the amount of information that can be transmitted by the population activity. For a population without internal coupling ($J_0 = 0$), fluctuations can be calculated directly from the interval distribution $P_I(t \,|\, \hat{t})$; cf. Chapter 5. For networks with internal coupling, an exact treatment of finite size effects is difficult. For escape noise first attempts towards a description of the fluctuations have been made (Spiridon et al., 1998; Meyer and van Vreeswijk, 2001). For diffusive noise, finite size effects in the low-connectivity limit have been treated by Brunel and Hakim (1999).

The limit of *no adaptation* seems to be valid for fast-spiking neurons (Connors and Gutnick, 1990). Most cortical neurons, however, show adaptation. From the modeling point of view, all integrate-and-fire neurons that have been discussed in

Chapter 4 are in the class of nonadaptive neurons, since the membrane potential is reset (and the past forgotten) after each output spike. The condition of short memory (i.e. no adaptation) leads to the class of renewal models (Cox, 1962; Perkel et al., 1967a; Stein, 1967b) and this is where the population equation applies; cf. Gerstner (1995, 2000). A generalization of the population equation to neuron models with adaptation is not straightforward since the formalism assumes that only the last spike suffices. On the other hand, adaptation could be included phenomenologically by introducing a slow variable that integrates over the population activity in the past. A full treatment of adaptation would involve a density description in the high-dimensional space of the microscopic neuronal variables (Knight, 2000).

6.7 Summary

The dynamics of large populations of homogeneous neurons can efficiently be described by population equations. In the stationary state the population equations can be reduced to standard network equations with sigmoidal gain functions. In the limit of high noise or slowly changing stimulation, the description by the Wilson–Cowan differential equation or field equations is appropriate.

The formulation of the population dynamics on a *microscopic* level leads to partial differential equations for densities in the internal variables, e.g., refractory or membrane potential density. A description of the dynamics on the *macroscopic* level leads to an integral equation that is based on the input-dependent interval distributions. The relation between the macroscopic activity equations and the microscopic density equations can be most easily demonstrated for a population of Spike Response Model neurons with escape noise. Finally, we have seen that in a sparsely connected network of excitatory and inhibitory neurons noise-like fluctuations may arise even with deterministic dynamics.

Literature

The original paper of Wilson and Cowan (1972) can be recommended as the classical reference for population equations. It is worthwhile also to consult the papers of Knight (1972a) and Amari (1972) of the same year, because each takes a somewhat different approach to a derivation of population activity equations. Some standard references for field equations are Wilson and Cowan (1973), Ellias and Grossberg (1975), and Amari (1977a).

The study of randomly connected networks has a long tradition in the mathematical sciences. Random networks of formal neurons have been studied by numerous researchers, e.g., (Amari, 1972, 1974, 1977b; Sompolinsky et al., 1988;

Cessac et al., 1994; van Vreeswijk and Sompolinsky, 1996, 1998). The theory for integrate-and-fire neurons (Amit and Brunel, 1997; Brunel and Hakim, 1999; Brunel, 2000) builds upon this earlier work. Finally, as an introduction to the density equation formalism for neurons, we recommend, apart from Abbott and van Vreeswijk (1993) and Brunel and Hakim (1999), the recent paper by Nykamp and Tranchina (2000). For the general theory of Fokker–Planck equations see Risken (1984).

7

Signal transmission and neuronal coding

In the preceding chapters, a theoretical description of neurons and neuronal populations has been developed. We are now ready to apply the theoretical framework to one of the fundamental problems of neuroscience – the problem of neuronal coding and signal transmission. We will address the problem as three different questions, viz.,

(i) How does a population of neurons react to a fast change in the input? This question, which is particularly interesting in the context of reaction time experiments, is the topic of Section 7.2.

(ii) What is the response of an asynchronously firing population to an arbitrary time-dependent input current? This question points to the signal transfer properties as a function of stimulation frequency and noise. In Section 7.3 we calculate the signal transfer function for a large population as well as the signal-to-noise ratio in a finite population of, say, a few hundred neurons.

(iii) What is the "meaning" of a single spike? If a neuronal population receives one extra input spike, how does this affect the population activity? On the other hand, if a neuron emits a spike, what do we learn about the input? These questions, which are intimately related to the problem of neural coding, are discussed in Section 7.4.

The population integral equation of Section 6.3 allows us to discuss these questions from a unified point of view. We focus in this chapter on a system of identical and independent neurons, i.e., a homogeneous network without lateral coupling. In this case, the behavior of the population as a whole is identical to the averaged behavior of a single neuron. Thus the signal transfer function discussed in Section 7.3 or the coding characteristics discussed in Section 7.4 can also be interpreted as single-neuron properties. Before we dive into the main arguments we derive in Section 7.1 the *linearized* population equation that will be used throughout this chapter.

7.1 Linearized population equation

We consider a homogeneous population of independent neurons. All neurons receive the same current $I(t)$ fluctuating about the mean I_0. More specifically we set

$$I(t) = I_0 + \Delta I(t). \tag{7.1}$$

For small fluctuations, $|\Delta I| \ll I_0$, we expect that the population activity stays close to the value A_0 that it would have for a constant current I_0, i.e.,

$$A(t) = A_0 + \Delta A(t), \tag{7.2}$$

with $|\Delta A| \ll A_0$. In that case, we may expand the right-hand side of the population equation $A(t) = \int_{-\infty}^{t} P_I(t|\hat{t}) A(\hat{t}) \, d\hat{t}$ into a Taylor series about A_0 to linear order in ΔA. In this section, we want to show that for spiking neuron models (either integrate-and-fire or SRM_0 neurons) the linearized population equation can be written in the form

$$\Delta A(t) = \int_{-\infty}^{t} P_0(t - \hat{t}) \, \Delta A(\hat{t}) \, d\hat{t} + A_0 \frac{d}{dt} \int_0^{\infty} \mathcal{L}(x) \, \Delta h(t - x) \, dx, \tag{7.3}$$

where $P_0(t - \hat{t})$ is the interval distribution for constant input I_0, $\mathcal{L}(x)$ is a real-valued function that plays the role of an integral kernel, and

$$\Delta h(t) = \int_0^{\infty} \kappa(s) \, \Delta I(t - s) \, ds \tag{7.4}$$

is the input potential generated by the time-dependent part of the input current. The first term of the right-hand side of Eq. (7.3) takes into account that previous perturbations $\Delta A(\hat{t})$ with $\hat{t} < t$ have an after-effect one interspike interval later. The second term describes the immediate response to a change in the input potential. If we want to understand the response of the population to an input current $\Delta I(t)$, we need to know the characteristics of the kernel $\mathcal{L}(x)$. The main task of this section is therefore the calculation of $\mathcal{L}(x)$.

Here we give an overview of the main results that we will obtain in the present chapter; explicit expressions for the kernel $\mathcal{L}(x)$ are presented in Table 7.1.

(i) In the low-noise limit, the kernel $\mathcal{L}(x)$ is a Dirac δ function. Therefore, the dynamics of the population activity ΔA has a term proportional to the *derivative* of the input potential; cf. Eq. (7.3). We will see that this result implies a fast response ΔA to any change in the input.

(ii) For high noise, the kernel $\mathcal{L}(x)$ depends critically on the noise model. For noise that is slow compared to the intrinsic neuronal dynamics (e.g., noise in the reset or stochastic spike arrival in combination with a slow synaptic time constant), the kernel $\mathcal{L}(x)$ is similar to that in the noise-free case. Thus the

Table 7.1. *The function $\mathcal{L}(x)$ introduced in (7.3) for integrate-and-fire and SRM_0 neurons (upper index IF and SRM, respectively) in the general case ("Definition"), without noise, as well as for escape and reset noise. $S(x|0)$ is the survivor function for time-dependent input given that the last spike occurred at time zero, whereas $S_0(s)$ is the survivor function in the asynchronous state. Primes denote derivatives with respect to the argument. $\mathcal{G}_\sigma$ denotes a normalized Gaussian with width σ.*

Definition	$\mathcal{L}^{\mathrm{SRM}}(x)$	$= -\int_x^\infty d\xi\, \frac{\partial S(\xi|0)}{\partial \Delta h(\xi - x)}$
	$\mathcal{L}^{\mathrm{IF}}(x)$	$= \mathcal{L}^{\mathrm{SRM}}(x) + \int_0^x d\xi\, e^{-\xi/\tau}\, \frac{\partial S(x|0)}{\partial \Delta h(\xi)}$
No noise	$\mathcal{L}_0^{\mathrm{SRM}}(x)$	$= \delta(x)/\eta'$
	$\mathcal{L}_0^{\mathrm{IF}}(x)$	$= \left[\delta(x) - \delta(x - T_0)\, e^{-T_0/\tau}\right]/u'$
Escape noise	$\mathcal{L}^{\mathrm{SRM}}(x)$	$= \int_x^\infty d\xi\, f'[u(\xi - x)]\, S_0(\xi)$
	$\mathcal{L}^{\mathrm{IF}}(x)$	$= \mathcal{L}^{\mathrm{SRM}}(x) - S_0(x) \int_0^x d\xi\, e^{-\xi/\tau}\, f'[u(\xi)]$
Reset noise	$\mathcal{L}^{\mathrm{SRM}}(x)$	$= \delta(x)/\eta'$
	$\mathcal{L}^{\mathrm{IF}}(x)$	$= \left[\delta(x) - \mathcal{G}_\sigma(x - T_0)\, e^{-T_0/\tau}\right]/u'$

dynamics of ΔA is proportional to the *derivative* of the input potential and therefore fast.

(iii) For a large amount of "fast" noise (e.g., escape noise), the kernel $\mathcal{L}(x)$ is broad so that the dynamics of the population activity is proportional to the input potential rather than to its derivative; cf. Eq. (7.3). As we will see, this implies that the response to a change in the input is slow.

Results for escape noise and reset noise have been derived by Gerstner (2000) while results for diffusive noise have been presented by Brunel et al. (2001) based on a linearization of the membrane potential density equation (Brunel and Hakim, 1999). The effect of slow noise in parameters has already been discussed in Knight (1972a). Apart from the approach discussed in this section, a fast response of a population of integrate-and-fire neurons with diffusive noise can also be induced if the *variance* of the diffusive noise is changed (Lindner and Schimansky-Geier, 2001).

Before we turn to the general case, we will focus in Section 7.1.1 on a noise-free population. We will see why the dynamics of $\Delta A(t)$ has a contribution proportional

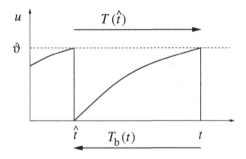

Fig. 7.1. A neuron that has fired at time $\hat{t}$ fires its next spike at $\hat{t} + T(\hat{t})$ where T is the "forward" interval. Looking backwards we find that a neuron that fires now at time t has fired its last spike at $t - T_{\mathrm{b}}(t)$ where T_{b} is the backward interval.

to the *derivative* of the input potential. In Section 7.1.2 we derive the general expression for the kernel $\mathcal{L}(x)$ and apply it to different situations. Readers not interested in the mathematical details may skip the remainder of this section and move directly to Section 7.2.

7.1.1 Noise-free population dynamics (*)

We start with a reduction of the population integral equation (6.75) to the noise-free case. In the limit of no noise, the input-dependent interval distribution $P_I(t \mid \hat{t})$ reduces to a Dirac δ function, i.e.,

$$P_I(t \mid \hat{t}) = \delta[t - \hat{t} - T(\hat{t})]. \qquad (7.5)$$

where $T(\hat{t})$ is the interspike interval of a neuron that has fired its last spike at time $\hat{t}$. If we insert Eq. (7.5) in the integral equation of the population activity, $A(t) = \int_{-\infty}^{t} P_I(t|\hat{t}) A(\hat{t}) \, d\hat{t}$, we find

$$A(t) = \int_{-\infty}^{t} \delta(t - \hat{t} - T(\hat{t})) A(\hat{t}) \, d\hat{t}. \qquad (7.6)$$

The interval $T(\hat{t})$ of a noise-free neuron is given implicitly by the threshold condition

$$T(\hat{t}) = \min\{(t - \hat{t}) \mid u(t) = \vartheta; \dot{u} > 0, t > \hat{t}\}. \qquad (7.7)$$

Note that $T(\hat{t})$ is the interval *starting* at $\hat{t}$ and looking *forward* toward the next spike; cf. Fig. 7.1. The integration over the δ function in Eq. (7.6) can be done, but since T in the argument of the δ function depends upon $\hat{t}$, the evaluation of the integral needs some care.

We recall from the rules for δ functions that

$$\int_a^b \delta[f(x)]\,g(x)\,dx = \frac{g(x_0)}{|f'(x_0)|} \qquad (7.8)$$

if f has a single zero-crossing $f(x_0) = 0$ in the interval $a < x_0 < b$ with $f'(x_0) \neq 0$. The prime denotes the derivative. If there is no solution $f(x_0) = 0$ in the interval $[a, b]$, the integral vanishes. In our case, x plays the role of the variable $\hat{t}$ with $f(\hat{t}) = t - \hat{t} - T(\hat{t})$. Hence $f'(\hat{t}) = -1 - T'(\hat{t})$ and

$$A(t) = \frac{1}{1 + T'(\hat{t})}\, A(\hat{t}), \qquad (7.9)$$

whenever a solution of $\hat{t} = t - T_b(t)$ exists. Here $T_b(t)$ is the *backward* interval of neurons that reach the threshold at time t. Equation (7.9) allows an intuitive interpretation. The activity at time t is proportional to the number of neurons that have fired one period earlier. The proportionality constant is called the *compression factor*. If the interspike intervals decrease ($T' < 0$), then neuronal firing times are "compressed" and the population activity increases. If interspike intervals become larger ($T' > 0$), the population activity decreases; cf. Fig. 7.2.

To evaluate $T'(\hat{t})$ we use the threshold condition (7.7). From $\vartheta = u[\hat{t} + T(\hat{t})] = \eta[T(\hat{t})] + h[\hat{t} + T(\hat{t})|\hat{t}]$ we find by taking the derivative with respect to $\hat{t}$

$$0 = \eta'[T(\hat{t})]\, T'(\hat{t}) + \partial_t h[\hat{t} + T(\hat{t})|\hat{t}]\,[1 + T'(\hat{t})] + \partial_{\hat{t}} h[\hat{t} + T(\hat{t})|\hat{t}]. \qquad (7.10)$$

The prime denotes the derivative with respect to the argument. We have introduced a short-hand notation for the partial derivatives, viz., $\partial_t h(t|\hat{t}) = \partial h(t|\hat{t})/\partial t$ and $\partial_{\hat{t}} h(t|\hat{t}) = \partial h(t|\hat{t})/\partial \hat{t}$. We solve for T' and find

$$T' = -\frac{\partial_{\hat{t}} h + \partial_t h}{\eta' + \partial_t h}, \qquad (7.11)$$

where we have suppressed the arguments for brevity. A simple algebraic transformation yields

$$\frac{1}{1 + T'} = 1 + \frac{\partial_t h + \partial_{\hat{t}} h}{\eta' - \partial_{\hat{t}} h}, \qquad (7.12)$$

which we insert into Eq. (7.9). The result is

$$A(t) = \left[1 + \frac{\partial_t h(t|\hat{t}) + \partial_{\hat{t}} h(t|\hat{t})}{\eta'(t - \hat{t}) - \partial_{\hat{t}} h(t|\hat{t})}\right] A(\hat{t}), \quad \text{with } \hat{t} = t - T_b(t), \qquad (7.13)$$

where $T_b(t)$ is the *backward* interval given a spike at time t. A solution $T_b(t)$ exists only if some neurons reach the threshold at time t. If this is not the case, the activity $A(t)$ vanishes. The partial derivatives in Eq. (7.13) are to be evaluated at $\hat{t} = t - T_b(t)$; the derivative $\eta' = d\eta(s)/ds$ is to be evaluated at $s = T_b(t)$.

We may summarize Eq. (7.13) by saying that the activity at time t depends on the activity one period earlier modulated by the factor in square brackets. Note that Eq. (7.13) is still exact.

Linearization

Let us consider a fluctuating input current that generates small perturbations in the population activity $\Delta A(t)$ and the input potential $\Delta h(t)$ as outlined at the beginning of this section. If we substitute $A(t) = A_0 + \Delta A(T)$ and $h(t|\hat{t}) = h_0 + \delta h(t|\hat{t})$ into Eq. (7.13) and linearize in ΔA and Δh, we obtain an expression of the form

$$\Delta A(t) = \Delta A(t - T) + A_0\, C(t)\,, \tag{7.14}$$

where $T = 1/A_0$ is the interval for constant input I_0 and C a time-dependent factor, called the compression factor. The activity at time t depends thus on the activity one interspike interval earlier and on the instantaneous value of the compression factor.

For SRM$_0$ neurons we have $h(t|\hat{t}) = h(t)$ so that the partial derivative with respect to $\hat{t}$ vanishes. The factor in square brackets in Eq. (7.13) reduces therefore to $[1 + (h'/\eta')]$. If we linearize Eq. (7.13) we find the compression factor

$$C^{\mathrm{SRM}}(t) = h'(t)/\eta'(T)\,. \tag{7.15}$$

For integrate-and-fire neurons we have a similar result. To evaluate the partial derivatives that we need in Eq. (7.13) we write $u(t) = \eta(t - \hat{t}) + h(t|\hat{t})$ with

$$
\begin{aligned}
\eta(t - \hat{t}) &= u_r\, e^{-(t-\hat{t})/\tau_m} \\
h(t|\hat{t}) &= h(t) - h(\hat{t})\, e^{-(t-\hat{t})/\tau_m}\,;
\end{aligned} \tag{7.16}
$$

cf. Eqs. (4.35) and (4.60). Here u_r is the reset potential of the integrate-and-fire neurons and $h(t) = \int_0^\infty \exp(-s/\tau_m)\, I(t - s)\, \mathrm{d}s$ is the input potential generated by the input current I.

Taking the derivative of η and the partial derivatives of h yields

$$\frac{\partial_t h + \partial_{\hat{t}} h}{\eta' - \partial_{\hat{t}} h} = \frac{h'(t) - h'(t - T_b)\, e^{-T_b/\tau_m}}{h'(t - T_b)\, e^{-T_b/\tau_m} - \tau_m^{-1}\, [u_r + h(t - T_b)]\, e^{-T_b/\tau_m}}\,, \tag{7.17}$$

which we now insert in Eq. (7.13). Since we are interested in the *linearized* activity equation, we replace $T_b(t)$ by the interval $T = 1/A_0$ for constant input and drop the term h' in the denominator. This yields Eq. (7.14) with a compression factor C^{IF} given by

$$C^{\mathrm{IF}}(t) = [h'(t) - h'(t - T)\, \exp(-T/\tau_m)]/u'\,. \tag{7.18}$$

Here u' is the derivative of the membrane potential for *constant* input current I_0,

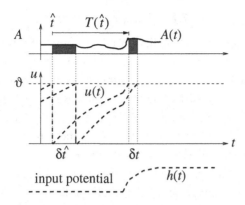

Fig. 7.2. A change in the input potential h with positive slope $h' > 0$ (dashed line, bottom) shifts neuronal firing times closer together (middle). As a result, the activity $A(t)$ (solid line, top) is higher at $t = \hat{t} + T(\hat{t})$ than it was at time $\hat{t}$ (schematic diagram); taken from Gerstner (2000).

i.e., $u' = -\tau_m^{-1} [u_r + h(t - T_b)] e^{-T_b/\tau_m}$. The label IF is short for integrate-and-fire neurons.

Example: compression of firing times for SRM$_0$ neurons

The variable C^{SRM} introduced in (7.15) has been called a "compression factor". In order to justify this name and to give an interpretation of Eq. (7.14) we consider SRM$_0$ neurons with an exponential refractory kernel $\eta(s) = -\eta_0 \exp(-s/\tau)$. We want to show graphically that the population activity ΔA has a contribution that is proportional to the *derivative* of the input potential.

We consider Fig. 7.2. A neuron which has fired at $\hat{t}$ will fire again at $t = \hat{t} + T(\hat{t})$. Another neuron which has fired slightly later at $\hat{t} + \delta\hat{t}$ fires its next spike at $t + \delta t$. If the input potential is constant between t and $t + \delta t$, then $\delta t = \delta\hat{t}$. If, however, h increases between t and $t + \delta t$ as is the case in Fig. 7.2, then the firing time difference is reduced. The compression of firing time differences is directly related to an increase in the activity A. To see this, we note that all neurons which fire between $\hat{t}$ and $\hat{t} + \delta\hat{t}$ must fire again between t and $t + \delta t$. This is because the network is homogeneous and the mapping $\hat{t} \to t = \hat{t} + T(\hat{t})$ is monotonous. If firing time differences are compressed, the population activity increases.

In order to establish the relation between Fig. 7.2 and Eq. (7.15), we note that the compression faction is equal to h'/η'. For a SRM$_0$ neuron with exponential refractory kernel, $\eta'(s) > 0$ holds for all $s > 0$. An input with $h' > 0$ implies then, because of Eq. (7.14), an increase of the activity:

$$h' > 0 \implies A(t) > A(t - T). \tag{7.19}$$

7.1.2 Escape noise (*)

In this section we focus on a population of neurons with escape noise. The aim of this section is twofold. Firstly, we want to show how to derive the linearized population equation Eq. (7.3) that has already been stated at the beginning of Section 7.1. Secondly, we will show that in the case of high noise the population activity follows the input potential $h(t)$, whereas for low noise the activity follows the derivative $h'(t)$. These results will be used in the following three sections for a discussion of signal transmission and coding properties.

In order to derive the linearized response ΔA of the population activity to a change in the input we start from the conservation law,

$$1 = \int_{-\infty}^{t} S_I(t \mid \hat{t}) \, A(\hat{t}) \, d\hat{t} \,, \tag{7.20}$$

cf. Eq. (6.73). As we have seen in Section 6.3 the population equation (6.75) can be obtained by taking the derivative of Eq. (7.20) with respect to t, i.e.,

$$0 = \frac{d}{dt} \int_{-\infty}^{t} S_I(t \mid \hat{t}) \, A(\hat{t}) \, d\hat{t} \,. \tag{7.21}$$

For constant input I_0, the population activity has a constant value A_0. We consider a small perturbation of the stationary state, $A(t) = A_0 + \Delta A(t)$, that is caused by a small change in the input current, $\Delta I(t)$. The time-dependent input generates a total postsynaptic potential,

$$h(t \mid \hat{t}) = h_0(t \mid \hat{t}) + \Delta h(t \mid \hat{t}) \,, \tag{7.22}$$

where $h_0(t \mid \hat{t})$ is the postsynaptic potential for constant input I_0 and

$$\Delta h(t \mid \hat{t}) = \int_0^{\infty} \kappa(t - \hat{t}, s) \, \Delta I(t - s) \, ds \tag{7.23}$$

is the change of the postsynaptic potential generated by ΔI. We expand Eq. (7.21) to linear order in ΔA and Δh and find

$$0 = \frac{d}{dt} \int_{-\infty}^{t} S_0(t - \hat{t}) \, \Delta A(\hat{t}) \, d\hat{t}$$
$$+ A_0 \frac{d}{dt} \left\{ \int_{-\infty}^{t} ds \int_{-\infty}^{t} d\hat{t} \, \Delta h(s \mid \hat{t}) \left. \frac{\partial S_I(t \mid \hat{t})}{\partial \Delta h(s \mid \hat{t})} \right|_{\Delta h = 0} \right\} . \tag{7.24}$$

We have used the notation $S_0(t - \hat{t}) = S_{I_0}(t \mid \hat{t})$ for the survivor function of the asynchronous firing state. To take the derivative of the first term in Eq. (7.24) we use $\mathrm{d}S_0(s)/\mathrm{d}s = -P_0(s)$ and $S_0(0) = 1$. This yields

$$\Delta A(t) = \int_{-\infty}^{t} P_0(t - \hat{t}) \, \Delta A(\hat{t}) \, \mathrm{d}\hat{t}$$
$$- A_0 \frac{\mathrm{d}}{\mathrm{d}t} \left\{ \int_{-\infty}^{t} \mathrm{d}s \int_{-\infty}^{t} \mathrm{d}\hat{t} \, \Delta h(s|\hat{t}) \left. \frac{\partial S_I(t \,|\, \hat{t})}{\partial \Delta h(s|\hat{t})} \right|_{\Delta h = 0} \right\} . \quad (7.25)$$

We note that the first term on the right-hand side of Eq. (7.25) has the same form as the population integral equation (6.75), except that P_0 is the interval distribution in the stationary state of asynchronous firing.

To make some progress in the treatment of the second term on the right-hand side of Eq. (7.25), we restrict the choice of neuron model and focus on SRM$_0$ or integrate-and-fire neurons. For SRM$_0$ neurons, we may drop the $\hat{t}$ dependence of the potential and set $\Delta h(t|\hat{t}) = \Delta h(t)$, where Δh is the input potential caused by the time-dependent current ΔI; compare Eqs. (7.4) and (7.23). This allows us to pull the variable $\Delta h(s)$ in front of the integral over $\hat{t}$ and write Eq. (7.25) in the form

$$\Delta A(t) = \int_{-\infty}^{t} P_0(t - \hat{t}) \, \Delta A(\hat{t}) \, \mathrm{d}\hat{t} + A_0 \frac{\mathrm{d}}{\mathrm{d}t} \left\{ \int_0^{\infty} \mathcal{L}(x) \, \Delta h(t - x) \, \mathrm{d}x \right\} , \quad (7.26)$$

with a kernel

$$\mathcal{L}(x) = -\int_x^{\infty} \mathrm{d}\xi \, \frac{\partial S(\xi|0)}{\partial \Delta h(\xi - x)} \equiv \mathcal{L}^{\mathrm{SRM}}(x) ; \quad (7.27)$$

cf. Table 7.1 and Fig. 7.3.

For integrate-and-fire neurons we set

$$\Delta h(t|\hat{t}) = \Delta h(t) - \Delta h(\hat{t}) \exp[-(t - \hat{t})/\tau];$$

cf. Eq. (7.16). After some rearrangements of the terms, Eq. (7.25) becomes identical to Eq. (7.26) with a kernel

$$\mathcal{L}(x) = -\int_x^{\infty} \mathrm{d}\xi \, \frac{\partial S(\xi|0)}{\partial \Delta h(\xi - x)} + \int_0^{x} \mathrm{d}\xi \, \mathrm{e}^{-\xi/\tau} \frac{\partial S(x|0)}{\partial \Delta h(\xi)} \equiv \mathcal{L}^{\mathrm{IF}}(x) ; \quad (7.28)$$

cf. Table 7.1 and Fig. 7.4.

Let us discuss Eq. (7.26). The first term on the right-hand side of Eq. (7.26) is of the same form as the dynamic equation (6.75) and describes how perturbations $\Delta A(\hat{t})$ in the past influence the present activity $\Delta A(t)$. The second term gives an additional contribution which is proportional to the derivative of a *filtered* version of the potential Δh.

We see from Fig. 7.3 that the width of the kernel $\mathcal{L}$ depends on the noise level. For low noise, it is significantly sharper than for high noise. For a further discussion

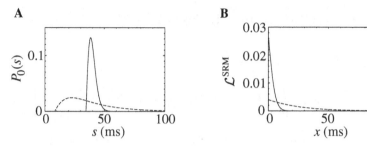

Fig. 7.3. Interval distribution (**A**) and the kernel $\mathcal{L}^{\mathrm{SRM}}(x)$ (**B**) for SRM_0 neurons with escape noise. The escape rate has been taken as piecewise linear $\rho = \rho_0 [u - \vartheta] \Theta(u - \vartheta)$. For low noise (solid lines in A and B) the interval distribution is sharply peaked and the kernel $\mathcal{L}^{\mathrm{SRM}}$ has a small width. For high noise (dashed line) both the interval distribution and the kernel $\mathcal{L}^{\mathrm{SRM}}$ are broad. The value of the bias current I_0 has been adjusted so that the mean interval is always 40 ms. The kernel has been normalized to $\int_0^\infty \mathcal{L}(x)\,dx = 1$.

of Eq. (7.26) we approximate the kernel by an exponential *low-pass* filter

$$\mathcal{L}^{\mathrm{SRM}}(x) = a\,\rho\,e^{-\rho x}\,\Theta(x)\,, \tag{7.29}$$

where a is a constant and ρ is a measure of the noise. It is shown in the examples below that Eq. (7.29) is exact for neurons with step-function escape noise and for neurons with absolute refractoriness.

The noise-free threshold process can be retrieved from Eq. (7.29) for $\rho \to \infty$. In this limit $\mathcal{L}^{\mathrm{SRM}}(x) = a\,\delta(x)$ and the initial transient is proportional to h' as discussed above. For small ρ, however, the behavior is different. We use Eq. (7.29) and rewrite the last term in Eq. (7.26) in the form

$$\frac{d}{dt}\int_0^\infty \mathcal{L}^{\mathrm{SRM}}(x)\,\Delta h(t - x)\,dx = a\rho\,[\Delta h(t) - \overline{\Delta h}(t)] \tag{7.30}$$

where $\overline{\Delta h}(t) = \int_0^\infty \rho\,\exp(-\rho x)\,\Delta h(t - x)\,dx$ is a running average. Thus the activity responds to the temporal contrast $\Delta h(t) - \overline{\Delta h}(t)$. At high noise levels ρ is small so that $\overline{\Delta h}$ is an average over a long time window; cf. Eq. (7.29). If the fluctuations ΔI have vanishing mean ($\langle\Delta I\rangle = 0$), we may set $\overline{\Delta h}(t) = 0$. Thus, we find that for escape noise in the large noise limit, $\Delta A(t) \propto h(t)$. This is exactly the result that would be expected for a simple rate model.

The kernel $\mathcal{L}(x)$ for escape noise (*)

In the escape noise model, the survivor function is given by

$$S_I(t\,|\,\hat{t}) = \exp\left\{ -\int_{\hat{t}}^t f[\eta(t' - \hat{t}) + h(t'|\hat{t})]\,dt' \right\} \tag{7.31}$$

where $f[u]$ is the instantaneous escape rate across the noisy threshold; cf. Chapter 5. We write $h(t|\hat{t}) = h_0(t - \hat{t}) + \Delta h(t|\hat{t})$. Taking the derivative with respect to

A

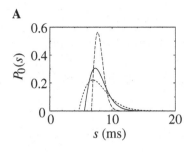

B

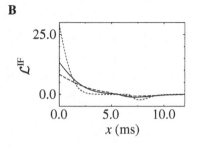

Fig. 7.4. Interval distribution (**A**) and the kernel $\mathcal{L}^{\text{IF}}(x)$ (**B**) for integrate-and-fire neurons with escape noise. The escape rate has been taken as piecewise linear $\rho = \rho_0 [u - \vartheta] \Theta(u - \vartheta)$. The value of the bias current I_0 has been adjusted so that the mean interval is always 8 ms. The dip in the kernel around $x = 8$ ms is typical for integrate-and-fire neurons. Low noise: sharply peaked interval distribution and kernel. High noise: broad interval distribution and kernel. Taken from Gerstner (2000) with permission.

Δh yields

$$\left. \frac{\partial S_I(t \mid \hat{t})}{\partial \Delta h(s \mid \hat{t})} \right|_{\Delta h=0} = -\Theta(s - \hat{t}) \, \Theta(t - s) \, f'[\eta(s - \hat{t}) + h_0(s - \hat{t})] \, S_0(t - \hat{t}), \quad (7.32)$$

where $S_0(t - \hat{t}) = S_{h_0}(t \mid \hat{t})$ and $f' = \mathrm{d}f(u)/\mathrm{d}u$. For SRM$_0$-neurons, we have $h_0(t - \hat{t}) \equiv h_0$ and $\Delta h(t \mid \hat{t}) = \Delta h(t)$, independent of $\hat{t}$. The kernel $\mathcal{L}$ is therefore

$$\mathcal{L}^{\text{SRM}}(t - s) = \Theta(t - s) \int_{-\infty}^{s} \mathrm{d}\hat{t} \, f'[\eta(s - \hat{t}) + h_0] \, S_0(t - \hat{t}), \quad (7.33)$$

as noted in Table 7.1.

Example: step-function escape rate (*)

We take $f(u) = \rho \, \Theta(u - \vartheta)$, i.e., a step-function escape rate. For $\rho \to \infty$ neurons fire immediately as soon as $u(t) > \vartheta$ and we are back to the noise-free sharp threshold. For finite ρ, neurons respond stochastically with time constant ρ^{-1}. We will show that the kernel $\mathcal{L}(x)$ for neurons with step-function escape rate is an exponential function; cf. Eq. (7.29).

Let us denote by T_0 the time between the last firing time $\hat{t}$ and the formal threshold crossing, $T_0 = \min \{s \mid \eta(s) + h_0 = \vartheta\}$. The derivative of f is a δ function,

$$f'[\eta(s) + h_0] = \rho \, \delta[\eta(s) + h_0 - \vartheta] = \frac{\rho}{\eta'} \delta(s - T_0) \quad (7.34)$$

where $\eta' = \frac{\mathrm{d}\eta(s)}{\mathrm{d}s}\big|_{s=T_0}$. The survivor function $S_0(s)$ is unity for $s < T_0$ and $S_0(s) = \exp[-\rho \, (s - T_0)]$ for $s > T_0$. Integration of Eq. (7.33) yields

$$\mathcal{L}(s) = \frac{1}{\eta'} \, \Theta(s) \, \rho \, \exp[-\rho \, (s)] \quad (7.35)$$

as claimed above.

Example: absolute refractoriness (*)

We take an arbitrary escape rate $f(u) \geq 0$ with $\lim_{u \to -\infty} f(u) = 0 = \lim_{u \to -\infty} f'(u)$. Absolute refractoriness is defined by a refractory kernel $\eta(s) = -\infty$ for $0 < s < \delta^{\mathrm{abs}}$ and zero otherwise. This yields $f[\eta(t - \hat{t}) + h_0] = f(h_0) \Theta(t - \hat{t} - \delta^{\mathrm{abs}})$ and hence

$$f'[\eta(t - \hat{t}) + h_0] = f'(h_0) \Theta(t - \hat{t} - \delta^{\mathrm{abs}}). \tag{7.36}$$

The survivor function $S_0(s)$ is unity for $s < \delta^{\mathrm{abs}}$ and decays as $\exp[-f(h_0)(s - \delta^{\mathrm{abs}})]$ for $s > \delta^{\mathrm{abs}}$. Integration of Eq. (7.33) yields

$$\mathcal{L}(t - t_1) = \Theta(t - t_1) \frac{f'(h_0)}{f(h_0)} \exp[-f(h_0)(t - t_1)]. \tag{7.37}$$

Note that for neurons with absolute refractoriness the transition to the noiseless case is not meaningful. We have seen in Chapter 6 that absolute refractoriness leads to the Wilson–Cowan integral equation (6.76). Thus $\mathcal{L}$ defined in Eq. (7.37) is the kernel relating to Eq. (6.76); it could have been derived directly from the linearization of the Wilson–Cowan integral equation. We note that it is a low-pass filter with cut-off frequency $f(h_0)$ which depends on the input potential h_0.

7.1.3 Noisy reset (*)

We consider SRM$_0$ neurons with noisy reset as introduced in Section 5.4. After each spike the membrane potential is reset to a randomly chosen value parameterized by the reset variable r. This is an example of a "slow" noise model, since a new value of the stochastic variable r is chosen only once per interspike interval. The interval distribution of the noisy reset model is

$$P_I(t|\hat{t}) = \int_{-\infty}^{\infty} dr \, \delta[t - \hat{t} - T(\hat{t}, r)] \mathcal{G}_\sigma(r), \tag{7.38}$$

where $\mathcal{G}_\sigma$ is a normalized Gaussian with width σ; cf. Eq. (5.68). The population equation (6.75) is thus

$$A(t) = \int_{-\infty}^{t} d\hat{t} \int_{-\infty}^{\infty} dr \, \delta[t - \hat{t} - T(\hat{t}, r)] \mathcal{G}_\sigma(r) A(\hat{t}). \tag{7.39}$$

A neuron that has been reset at time $\hat{t}$ with value r behaves identical to a noise-free neuron that has fired its last spike at $\hat{t} + r$. In particular we have the relation $T(\hat{t}, r) = r + T_0(\hat{t} + r)$ where $T_0(t')$ is the forward interval of a noiseless neuron that has fired its last spike at t'. The integration over $\hat{t}$ in Eq. (7.39) can therefore be done and yields

$$A(t) = \left[1 + \frac{h'}{\eta'}\right] \int_{-\infty}^{\infty} dr \, \mathcal{G}_{\sigma}(r) \, A[t - T_b(t) - r] \qquad (7.40)$$

where T_b is the backward interval. The factor $[1 + (h'/\eta')]$ arises due to the integration over the δ function just as in the noiseless case; cf. Eqs. (7.13) and (7.15).

To simplify the expression, we write $A(t) = A_0 + \Delta A(t)$ and expand Eq. (7.40) to first order in ΔA. The result is

$$\Delta A(t) = \int_{-\infty}^{\infty} \mathcal{G}_{\sigma}(r) \, \Delta A(t - T_0 - r) \, dr + \frac{h'(t)}{\eta'(T_0)} A_0 . \qquad (7.41)$$

A comparison of Eqs. (7.41) and (7.3) yields the kernel $\mathcal{L}(x) = \delta(x)/\eta'$ for the noisy-reset model. Note that it is identical to that of a population of noise-free neurons; cf. Table 7.1. The reason is that the effect of noise is limited to the moment of the reset. The approach of the membrane potential towards the threshold is noise-free.

7.2 Transients

How quickly can a population of neurons respond to a rapid change in the input? We know from reaction time experiments that the response of humans and animals to new stimuli can be very fast (Thorpe et al., 1996). We therefore expect that the elementary processing units, i.e., neurons or neuronal populations, should also show a rapid response. In this section we concentrate on one element of the problem of rapid reaction time and study the response of the population activity to a rapid change in the input. To keep the arguments as simple as possible, we consider an input that has a constant value I_0 for $t < t_0$ and changes then abruptly to a new value $I_0 + \Delta I$. Thus

$$I^{\text{ext}}(t) = \begin{cases} I_0 & \text{for} \quad t \le t_0 \\ I_0 + \Delta I & \text{for} \quad t > t_0. \end{cases} \qquad (7.42)$$

For the sake of simplicity, we consider a population of independent integrate-and-fire or SRM$_0$ neurons without lateral coupling. Given the current $I^{\text{ext}}(t)$, the input potential can be determined from $h(t) = \int_0^{\infty} \kappa_0(s) \, I^{\text{ext}}(t - s) \, ds$. For $t \le t_0$, the input potential then has a value $h_0 = R \, I_0$ where we have used $\int \kappa_0(s) ds = R$. For $t > t_0$, the input potential h changes due to the additional current ΔI so that

$$h(t) = \begin{cases} h_0 & \text{for} \quad t \le t_0 \\ h_0 + \Delta I \int_0^{t-t_0} \kappa_0(s) \, ds & \text{for} \quad t > t_0. \end{cases} \qquad (7.43)$$

Given the input potential $h(t)$ and the last firing time $\hat{t}$ we can calculate for any given neuron its momentary membrane potential $u(t)$ – but what is the time course of the population activity?

Let us suppose that for $t < t_0$ the network is in a state of *asynchronous* firing so that the population activity is constant, $A(t) = A_0$ for $t \leq t_0$; cf. Section 6.4. As soon as the input is switched on at time $t = t_0$, the population activity will change

$$A(t) = A_0 + \Delta A(t) \quad \text{for } t > t_0 . \tag{7.44}$$

In this section we will use the linear population equation,

$$\Delta A(t) = \int_{-\infty}^{t} P_0(t - \hat{t}) \, \Delta A(\hat{t}) \, d\hat{t} + A_0 \frac{d}{dt} \int_{0}^{\infty} \mathcal{L}(x) \, \Delta h(t - x) \, dx , \tag{7.45}$$

in order to calculate the linear response $\Delta A(t)$ to the change in the input; cf. Eq. (7.3). Here $P_0(t - \hat{t})$ is the interspike interval distribution in the stationary state and $\mathcal{L}(x)$ is the real-valued kernel given in Table 7.1. We are mainly interested in the *initial* phase of the transient, i.e., $0 < t - t_0 \ll T$ where $T = 1/A_0$ and is the mean interspike interval. During the initial phase of the transient, the first term on the right-hand side of Eq. (7.45) does not contribute, since $\Delta A(\hat{t}) = 0$ for $\hat{t} < t_0$. Therefore, Eq. (7.45) reduces to

$$\Delta A(t) = A_0 \frac{d}{dt} \int_{0}^{\infty} \mathcal{L}(x) \, \Delta h(t - x) \, dx , \quad \text{for } t - t_0 \ll T . \tag{7.46}$$

7.2.1 Transients in a noise-free network

In the noiseless case, neurons that receive a constant input I_0 fire regularly with some period T_0. For $t < t_0$, the mean activity is simply $A_0 = 1/T_0$. The reason is that, for a constant activity, averaging over time and averaging over the population are equivalent; cf. Section 6.4.

Let us consider a neuron which has fired exactly at t_0. Its next spike occurs at $t_0 + T$ where T is given by the threshold condition $u_i(t_0 + T) = \vartheta$. We focus on the initial phase of the transient and apply the noise-free kernel $\mathcal{L}(x) \propto \delta(x)$; cf. Table 7.1. If we insert the δ function into Eq. (7.46) we find

$$\Delta A(t) \propto \frac{d}{dt} h(t) \quad \text{for } t_0 < t < t_0 + T . \tag{7.47}$$

For both SRM_0 and integrate-and-fire neurons, the transient response is proportional to the *derivative* of the input potential h. Taking the derivative of Eq. (7.43) yields

$$\Delta A(t) = a \kappa_0(t - t_0) A_0 \quad \text{for } t_0 < t < t_0 + T , \tag{7.48}$$

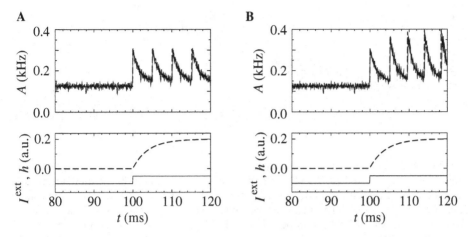

Fig. 7.5. Top: response of the population activity to a step current for very low noise. Solid line: simulation of a population of 1000 neurons. Dashed line: numerical integration of the population equation (6.75). **A.** Integrate-and-fire-neurons. **B.** SRM$_0$ neurons. Bottom: step current input I (solid line) and input potential $h(t)$ (dashed line). Note that the population responds instantaneously to the input switch at $t_0 = 100$ ms even though the membrane potential responds only slowly; taken from Gerstner (2000).

with a constant $a = R \Delta I / \eta'$ for SRM$_0$ neurons and $a = R \Delta I / u'$ for integrate-and-fire neurons. Thus, the time course of the initial transient reflects the time course of the response kernel κ_0. The initial transient of the neuronal response can therefore be extremely fast (Maršálek et al., 1997).

Example: initial transient of integrate-and-fire neurons

In this example we apply Eq. (7.48) to integrate-and-fire neurons. The response kernel is

$$\kappa_0(s) = \frac{1}{\tau_m} \exp\left(-\frac{s}{\tau_m}\right) \Theta(s). \qquad (7.49)$$

The response of the input *potential* to the step current in Eq. (7.42) is

$$h(t) = h_0 + R\Delta I \left[1 - \exp\left(-\frac{t - t_0}{\tau_m}\right)\right] \quad \text{for } t > t_0, \qquad (7.50)$$

which has the characteristics of a low-pass filter with time constant τ_m. The population activity, however, reacts *instantaneously* to the step current. We put the exponential kernel (7.49) in Eq. (7.48) and find

$$\Delta A(t) = \frac{a A_0}{\tau_m} \exp\left(-\frac{t - t_0}{\tau_m}\right) \Theta(t - t_0) \quad \text{for } t_0 < t < t_0 + T, \qquad (7.51)$$

where $\Theta(\cdot)$ is the Heaviside step function. Thus, there is an immediate response at $t = t_0$. The simulation in Fig. 7.5 clearly exhibits the rapid initial response of

A

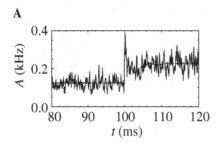

B

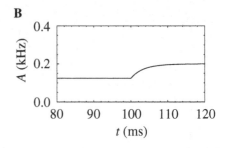

Fig. 7.6. **A**. Reset noise. Transients for SRM_0 neurons with noisy reset in response to the same step current as in Fig. 7.5. The results of a simulation of 1000 SRM_0 neurons (solid line) are compared with a numerical integration (dashed line) of the population integral equation; cf. Eq. (6.75). The instantaneous response is typical for "slow" noise models. Taken from Gerstner (2000) with permission. **B**. Transients in a standard rate model. The new stationary state is approached exponentially with the membrane time constant τ_m. The response to the input switch at $t_0 = 100$ ms is therefore comparatively slow.

the population. It is also confirmed by a numerical integration of the noise-free population equation; cf. Eq. (7.13).

A similar result holds for a population of SRM_0 neurons. The initial transient of SRM_0 is identical to that of integrate-and-fire neurons; cf. Fig. 7.5. A subtle difference, however, occurs during the late phase of the transient. For integrate-and-fire neurons the transient is over as soon as each neuron has fired once. After the next reset, all neurons fire periodically with a new period T that corresponds to the constant input $I_0 + \Delta I$. A population of SRM_0 neurons, however, reaches a periodic state only asymptotically. The reason is that the interspike interval T of SRM_0 neurons (which is given by the threshold condition $h(t) = \vartheta - \eta_0(T)$) depends on the momentary value of the input potential $h(t)$.

7.2.2 Transients with noise

So far, we have considered noiseless neurons. We have seen that after an initial sharp transient the population activity approaches a new periodic state where the activity oscillates with period T. In the presence of noise, we expect that the network approaches – after a transient – a new asynchronous state with stationary activity $A_0 = g(I_0 + \Delta I)$; cf. Section 6.4.

In Fig. 7.6A the response of a population of noisy neurons to a step current input is illustrated. The population activity responds instantaneously when the additional input is switched on. Can we understand the sharply peaked transient? Before the abrupt change the input was stationary and the population in a state of *asynchronous* firing. Asynchronous firing was defined as a state with constant activity so that at any point in time some of the neurons fire, others are in the refractory period, and again others approach the threshold. There is always a group of neurons whose potential is just below threshold. An increase in the input causes those neurons to fire immediately – and this accounts for the strong population response during the initial phase of the transient.

As we will see in the example below, the above consideration is strictly valid only for neurons with slow noise in the parameters, e.g., noisy reset as introduced in Section 5.4. In models based on the Wilson–Cowan differential equation the transient does not exhibit such a sharp initial peak; cf. Fig. 7.6B.

For diffusive noise models the picture is more complicated. A rapid response occurs if the current step is sufficiently large and the noise level not too high. On the other hand, for high noise and small current steps the response is slow. The question of whether neuronal populations react rapidly or slowly depends therefore on many aspects, in particular on the type of noise and the type of stimulation. It can be shown that for diffusive noise that is low-pass filtered by a slow synaptic time constant (i.e., cut-off frequency of the noise lower than the neuronal firing rate) the response is sharp, independent of the noise amplitude. On the other hand, for white noise the response depends on the noise amplitude and the membrane time constant (Brunel et al., 2001).

For a mathematical discussion of the transient behavior, it is sufficient to consider the equation that describes the initial phase of the linear response to a sudden onset of the input potential; cf. Eq. (7.46). Table 7.1 summarizes the kernel $\mathcal{L}(x)$ that is at the heart of Eq. (7.46) for several noise models. In the limit of low noise, the choice of noise model is irrelevant – the transient response is proportional to the *derivative* of the potential, $\Delta A \propto h'$. If the level of noise is increased, a population of neurons with slow noise (e.g., with noisy reset) retains its sharp transients since the kernel $\mathcal{L}$ is proportional to h'.

Neurons with escape noise turn in the high-noise limit to a different regime where the transients follow h rather than h'. To see why, we recall that the kernel $\mathcal{L}$ essentially describes a low-pass filter; cf. Fig. 7.3. The time constant of the filter increases with the noise level and hence the response switches from a behavior proportional to h' to a behavior proportional to h.

Example: response of neurons with escape noise

The width of the kernel $\mathcal{L}(x)$ in Eq. (7.46) depends on the noise level. For low noise, the kernel is sharply peaked at $x = 0$ and can be approximated by a Dirac δ function. The response ΔA of the population activity is sharp since it is proportional to the *derivative* of the input potential.

For high noise, the kernel is broad and the response becomes proportional to the input potential; cf. Fig. 7.7B.

A

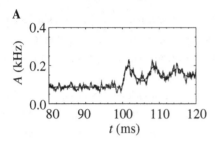

B

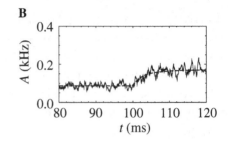

Fig. 7.7. *Escape noise.* Response of a network of 1000 SRM$_0$ neurons with exponential escape noise to step current input. The input is switched at $t = 100$ ms. Simulations (fluctuating solid line) are compared to the numerical integration of the population equation (thick dashed line). **A.** For low noise the transition is comparatively sharp. **B.** For high noise the response to the change in the input is rather smooth.

Example: slow response of standard rate model

In Section 6.3, we introduced Wilson–Cowan differential equations, which are summarized here for a population of independent neurons,

$$A(t) = g[h(t)],$$

$$\tau_m \frac{dh}{dt} = -h(t) + R\, I^{\text{ext}}(t); \tag{7.52}$$

cf. Eq. (6.87). A step current input causes a potential

$$h(t) = h_0 + R\,\Delta I \left[1 - \exp\left(-\frac{t - t_0}{\tau_m}\right)\right] \Theta(t - t_0). \tag{7.53}$$

The response of the population activity is therefore

$$\Delta A(t) = g'\, R\, \Delta I \left[1 - \exp\left(-\frac{t - t_0}{\tau_m}\right)\right] \Theta(t - t_0). \tag{7.54}$$

where $g' = dg/dh$ evaluated at h_0. Equation (7.54) describes a slow exponential response with time constant τ_m; cf. Fig. 7.6B. The Wilson–Cowan differential equation is a reasonable approximation for neurons with a large level of escape noise; compare Figs. 7.6B and 7.7B.

Example: rapid response of neurons with "slow" noise

For neurons with noisy reset, the kernel $\mathcal{L}$ is a Dirac δ function; cf. Table 7.1. As in the noiseless case, the initial transient is therefore proportional to the derivative of h. After this initial phase the reset noise leads to a smoothing of subsequent oscillations so that the population activity approaches rapidly a new asynchronous state; cf. Fig. 7.6A. The initial transient, however, is sharp.

A

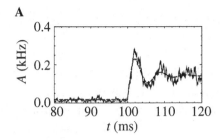

B

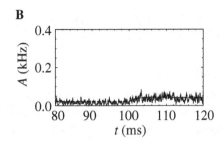

Fig. 7.8. *Diffusive noise.* Response of a network of 1000 integrate-and-fire neurons with diffusive noise to step current input. Simulations (fluctuating solid line) are compared to a numerical integration of the density equations (thick dashed line). **A.** For low noise and a big (superthreshold) current step the response is rapid. **B.** For high noise and a small current step the response is slow.

Example: diffusive noise

In this example, we present qualitative arguments to show that, in the limit of low noise, a population of spiking neurons with diffusive noise will exhibit an immediate response to a *strong* step current input. We have seen in the noise-free case that the rapid response is due the derivative h' in the compression factor. In order to understand why the derivative of h comes into play, let us consider, for the moment, a finite step in the input *potential* $h(t) = h_0 + \Delta h \, \Theta(t - t_0)$. All neurons i which are hovering below threshold so that their potential $u_i(t_0)$ is between $\vartheta - \Delta h$ and ϑ will be put above threshold and fire synchronously at t_0. Thus, a step in the potential causes a δ-pulse in the activity $\Delta A(t) \propto \delta(t - t_0) \propto h'(t_0)$. In Fig. 7.8A we have used a *current* step (7.42) (the same step current as in Fig. 7.5). The response at low noise (top) has roughly the form $\Delta A(t) \propto h'(t) \propto \kappa_0(t - t_0)$ as expected. The rapid transient is slightly less pronounced than for noisy reset, but nevertheless clearly visible; compare Figs. 7.6A and 7.8A. As the amplitude of the noise grows, the transient becomes less sharp. Thus there is a transition from a regime where the transient is proportional to h' (Fig. 7.8A) to another regime where the transient is proportional to h (Fig. 7.8B). What are the reasons for the change of behavior?

The simple argument from above based on a potential step $\Delta h > 0$ only holds for a *finite* step size which is at least of the order of the noise amplitude σ. With diffusive noise, the threshold acts as an absorbing boundary. Therefore the density of neurons with potential u_i vanishes for $u_i \to \vartheta$; cf. Section 6.2. Thence, for $\Delta h \to 0$ the proportion of neurons which are instantaneously put across threshold is 0. In a stationary state, the "boundary layer" with low density is of the order σ; e.g., cf. Eq. (6.28). A potential step $\Delta h > \sigma$ puts a significant proportion of neurons above threshold and leads to a δ-pulse in the activity. Thus the result that the response is proportional to the derivative of the potential is essentially valid in the low-noise regime.

On the other hand, we may also consider diffusive noise with large noise amplitude in the subthreshold regime. In the limit of high noise, a step in the potential raises the instantaneous rate of the neurons, but does not force them to fire immediately. The response to a *current* step is therefore smooth and follows the potential $h(t)$; cf. Fig. 7.8B. A comparison of Figs. 7.8 and 7.7 shows that the escape noise model exhibits a similar transition from sharp to smooth responses with increasing noise level. In fact, we have seen in Chapter 5 that diffusive noise can be well approximated by escape noise (Plesser and Gerstner, 2000). For the analysis of response properties with diffusive noise see Brunel et al. (2001).

7.3 Transfer function

Our considerations regarding step current input can be generalized to an arbitrary input current $I(t)$ that is fluctuating around a mean value of I_0. We study a population of independent integrate-and-fire or SRM$_0$ neurons. The input current $I(t) = I_0 + \Delta I(t)$ generates an input potential

$$h(t) = \int_0^\infty \kappa_0(s) \left[I_0 + \Delta I(t - s) \right] \mathrm{d}s = h_0 + \Delta h(t), \tag{7.55}$$

where $h_0 = R I_0$ with $R = \int_0^\infty \kappa_0(s) \, \mathrm{d}s$ is the mean input potential. In particular we want to know how well a periodic input current

$$I(t) = I_0 + I_1 \cos(\omega t) \tag{7.56}$$

can be transmitted by a population of neurons. The signal transfer function calculated in Section 7.3.1 characterizes the signal transmission properties as a function of the frequency ω. The signal-to-noise ratio is the topic of Section 7.3.2.

7.3.1 Signal term

We assume that the population is close to a state of asynchronous firing, viz., $A(t) = A_0 + \Delta A(t)$. The linear response of the population to the change in the input potential h is given by Eq. (7.3) which can be solved for ΔA by taking the Fourier transform. For $\omega \neq 0$ we find

$$\hat{A}(\omega) = i\omega \frac{A_0 \hat{\mathcal{L}}(\omega) \hat{\kappa}(\omega)}{1 - \hat{P}(\omega)} \hat{I}(\omega) = \hat{G}(\omega) \hat{I}(\omega). \tag{7.57}$$

Hats denote transformed quantities, i.e., $\hat{\kappa}(\omega) = \int \kappa_0(s) \exp(-i \omega s) \, \mathrm{d}s$ is the Fourier transform of the response kernel; $\hat{P}(\omega)$ is the Fourier transform of the interval distribution; and $\hat{\mathcal{L}}(\omega)$ is the transform of the kernel $\mathcal{L}$. Note that for $\omega \neq 0$ we have $A(\omega) = \Delta A(\omega)$ and $I(\omega) = \Delta I(\omega)$ since A_0 and I_0 are constant.

The function $\hat{G}(\omega)$, defined by Eq. (7.57), describes the (linear) response $\hat{A}(\omega)$ of a population of spiking neurons to a periodic signal $\hat{I}(\omega)$. It is also called the (frequency-dependent) gain of the system. Inverse Fourier transform of Eq. (7.57) yields

$$A(t) = A_0 + \int_0^\infty G(s) \, \Delta I (t - s) \, ds \qquad (7.58)$$

with

$$G(s) = \frac{1}{2\pi} \int_{-\infty}^\infty \hat{G}(\omega) \, e^{+i\omega s} \, d\omega . \qquad (7.59)$$

A_0 is the mean rate for constant drive I_0. Equation (7.58) allows us to calculate the linear response of the population to an *arbitrary* input current.

We can compare the amplitude of an input current at frequency ω with the amplitude of the response. The ratio

$$\hat{G}(\omega) = \frac{\hat{A}(\omega)}{\hat{I}(\omega)} \qquad (7.60)$$

as a function of ω characterizes the signal transmission properties of the system. If $|\hat{G}|$ decays for $\omega > \omega_0$ to zero, we say that $\hat{G}$ has a cut-off frequency ω_0. In this case, signal transmission at frequencies $\omega \gg \omega_0$ is difficult. On the other hand, if $|\hat{G}|$ approaches a positive value for $\omega \to \infty$, signal transmission is possible even at very high frequencies.

In the following examples, we will study the transmission properties of a population of neurons with different noise models. In particular, we will see that for slow noise in the parameters (e.g., noise in the reset) signal transmission is possible at very high frequencies (that is, there is no cut-off frequency) (Knight, 1972a; Gerstner, 2000). However, for escape noise models there is a cut-off frequency which depends on the noise level. For a large amount of escape noise, the cut-off frequency is given by the inverse of the membrane time constant (Gerstner, 2000). Finally, diffusive noise models have a cut-off frequency if the noise input is white (standard diffusion model), but do not have a cut-off frequency if the noise has a long correlation time (Brunel et al., 2001).

Even if there is no cut-off frequency for the transmission of fast input currents, we may not conclude that real neurons are infinitely fast. In fact, a finite time constant of synaptic channels leads to a frequency cut-off for the input *current* which may enter the cell. In this sense, it is the time constant of the synaptic current which determines the cut-off frequency of the population. The membrane time constant is of minor influence (Knight, 1972a; Treves, 1993; Gerstner, 2000).

A

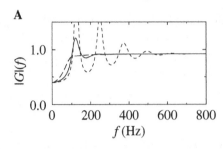

B

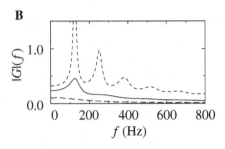

Fig. 7.9. Signal gain for integrate-and-fire neurons with noisy reset (**A**) and escape noise (**B**). For low noise (short-dashed line) the variance of the interval distribution is $\sigma = 0.75$ ms; for high noise (long-dashed line) the variance is $\sigma = 4$ ms. Solid line: variance $\sigma = 2$ ms. Note that for noisy reset (slow noise) the signal transfer function has no cut-off frequency, whatever the noise level. The value of the bias current has been adjusted so that the mean interval is always 8 ms. The escape rate in B is piecewise linear $\rho = \rho_0 [u - \vartheta]\Theta(u - \vartheta)$; taken from Gerstner (2000).

Example: slow noise in the parameters

In this example, we consider integrate-and-fire neurons with noisy reset; cf. Section 5.4. For noisy reset the interval distribution in the stationary state is a Gaussian $P_0(s) = \mathcal{G}_\sigma(s - T_0)$ with mean T_0 and width σ; cf. Eq. (7.38). Fourier transform of the interval distribution yields

$$\hat{P}(\omega) = \exp\left(-\frac{1}{2}\sigma^2\omega^2 - i\omega T_0\right) . \tag{7.61}$$

The kernel $\mathcal{L}$ may be read off from Eq. (7.41) or Table 7.1. Its Fourier transform is

$$\hat{\mathcal{L}}(\omega) = \frac{1}{u'}\left[1 - \exp\left(-\frac{1}{2}\sigma^2\omega^2 - i\omega T_0 - \frac{T_0}{\tau}\right)\right] \tag{7.62}$$

where u' is the slope of the noise-free membrane potential at the moment of threshold crossing.

We adjust the bias current I_0 so that the mean interspike interval of the neurons is $T_0 = 8$ ms. In Fig. 7.9A we have plotted the gain $|\hat{G}(\omega)| = |\hat{A}(\omega)/\hat{I}(\omega)|$ as a function of the stimulation frequency $f = \omega/(2\pi)$. For a medium noise level of $\sigma = 2$ ms, the signal gain has a single resonance at $f = 1/T_0 = 125$ Hz. For lower noise, further resonances at multiples of 125 Hz appear. For a variant of the noisy reset model, a result closely related to Eq. (7.57) has been derived by Knight (1972a).

Independently of the noise level, we obtain for integrate-and-fire neurons for $\omega \to 0$ the result $|\hat{G}(0)| = J_{\text{ext}}A_0[1 - \exp(-T_0/\tau)]/(u' T_0)$. Most interesting is the behavior in the high-frequency limit. For $\omega \to \infty$ we find $|\hat{G}(\omega)| \to RA_0/(u' \tau)$, hence

$$\left| \frac{\hat{G}(\infty)}{\hat{G}(0)} \right| = \frac{T_0}{\tau} \left[1 - e^{-T_0/\tau} \right]^{-1} . \qquad (7.63)$$

We emphasize that the high-frequency components of the current are not attenuated by the population activity – despite the integration at the level of the individual neurons. The reason is that the threshold process acts like a *differentiator* and reverses the low-pass filtering of the integration. In fact, Eq. (7.63) shows that high frequencies can be transmitted *more* effectively than low frequencies. The good transmission characteristics of spiking neurons at high frequencies have been studied by Knight (1972a), Gerstner (2000), and Brunel et al. (2001). They were also confirmed experimentally by Knight (1972b) and F. Chance (private communication).

So far we have discussed results of the *linearized* theory; viz., Eqs. (7.41) and (7.57). The behavior of the full nonlinear system is shown in Fig. 7.10. A population of unconnected SRM$_0$ neurons is stimulated by a time-dependent input current which was generated as a superposition of four sinusoidal components with frequencies at 9, 47, 111, and 1000 Hz which have been chosen arbitrarily. The activity equation $A(t) = \int_{-\infty}^{t} P_I(t|\hat{t}) A(\hat{t}) \, d\hat{t}$ been integrated with time steps of 0.05 ms and the results are compared with those of a simulation of a population of 4000 neurons. The 1 kHz component of the signal $I(t)$ is clearly reflected in the population $A(t)$. Theory and simulation are in excellent agreement.

Example: escape noise

We have seen in the preceding section that noisy reset is rather exceptional in the sense that the transient remains sharp even in the limit of high noise. To study the relevance of the noise model, we return to Eq. (7.57). The signal gain $\hat{G}(\omega) = |A(\omega)/I(\omega)|$ is proportional to $\hat{\mathcal{L}}(\omega)$. If the kernel $\mathcal{L}(x)$ is broad, its Fourier transform $\hat{\mathcal{L}}(\omega)$ will fall off to zero at high frequencies and so does the signal gain $\hat{G}(\omega)$. In Fig. 7.9B we have plotted the signal gain $\hat{G}(\omega)$ for integrate-and-fire neurons with escape noise at different noise levels. At low noise, the result for escape noise is similar to that of reset noise (compare Figs. 7.9A and B) except for a drop of the gain at high frequencies. Increasing the noise level, however, lowers the signal gain of the system. For high noise (long-dashed line in Fig. 7.9B) the signal gain at 1000 Hz is ten times lower than the gain at zero frequency. The cut-off frequency depends on the noise level. Note that for escape noise, the gain at zero frequency also changes with the level of noise.

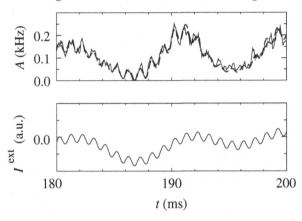

Fig. 7.10. Response of the population activity (top) of SRM_0 neurons with noisy reset to a time-dependent current (bottom). The current is a superposition of four sine waves at 9, 47, 111, and 1000 Hz. The simulation of a population of 4000 neurons (solid line, top) is compared with the numerical integration (dashed line) of the population equation (6.75). Note that even the 1 kHz component of the signal is well transmitted. Parameters: exponential response function with time constant $\tau = 4$ ms. Threshold is $\vartheta = -0.135$ so that the mean activity is $A = 125$ Hz; noise $\sigma = 2$ ms; $J_0 = 0$; taken from Gerstner (2000).

Example: diffusive noise (*)

It is possible to calculate the signal transmission properties of integrate-and-fire neurons with diffusive noise by a linearization of the population density equation (6.21) about the stationary membrane potential distribution $p_0(u)$. The resulting formula (Brunel et al., 2001) is rather complicated but can be evaluated numerically. It is found that in the standard diffusion model the gain $|\hat{G}(\omega)|$ decays as $1/\sqrt{\omega}$ for large ω. Thus the gain exhibits a cut-off frequency similar to that found in the escape noise model.

Standard diffusive noise corresponds to a drive by stochastic δ current pulses, which is used as a description of stochastic spike arrival; cf. Chapter 5. In a more realistic model of stochastic spike arrival, input spikes evoke a current pulse of *finite* width. The duration of the current pulse is characterized by the synaptic time constant τ_s. In that case, the effective noisy input current has correlations on the time scale of τ_s. If $\tau_s > 1/A_0$, the noise is "slow" compared to the intrinsic firing rate of the neuron. It is found that with such a slow noise, the $\hat{G}(\omega)$ has no cut-off frequency (Brunel et al., 2001). In this limit, the gain factor is therefore similar to that of the stochastic reset model. In other words, we have the generic result that for "fast" noise the gain factor has a cut-off frequency whereas for "slow" noise it has not.

7.3.2 Signal-to-noise ratio

So far we have considered the signal transmission properties of a large population in the limit $N \to \infty$. In this case the population activity can be considered as a continuous signal, even though individual neurons emit short pulse-like action potentials. For a finite number N of neurons, however, the population activity $A(t)$ will fluctuate around a time-dependent mean. In this section we want to estimate the amplitude of the fluctuations.

For independent neurons that are stimulated by a constant current I_0, we can calculate the noise spectrum of the population activity using the methods discussed in Chapter 5. In fact, the noise spectrum C_{AA} of the population activity is proportional to the Fourier transform of the autocorrelation function of a single neuron:

$$C_{AA}(\omega) = \frac{1}{N} C_{ii}(\omega). \tag{7.64}$$

The proportionality factor takes care of the fact that the amplitude of the fluctuations of $A(t)$ is inversely proportional to the number of neurons in the population. For constant input, we can calculate the single-neuron autocorrelation in the framework of stationary renewal theory. Its Fourier transform is given by Eq. (5.35) and is repeated here for convenience:

$$\hat{C}_{ii}(\omega) = v_i \, \mathrm{Re} \left[\frac{1 + \hat{P}_0(\omega)}{1 - \hat{P}_0(\omega)} \right] + 2\pi \, v_i^2 \delta(\omega). \tag{7.65}$$

Here $\hat{P}_0(\omega)$ is the Fourier transform of the interspike interval distribution in the stationary state.

If the amplitude of the periodic stimulation is small, the noise term of the population activity can be estimated from the *stationary* autocorrelation function. The signal-to-noise ratio at frequency ω is

$$\mathrm{SNR} = \frac{|\hat{G}(\omega)|^2}{\hat{C}_{AA}(\omega)} = N \, \frac{|\hat{G}(\omega)|^2}{\hat{C}_{ii}(\omega)} \tag{7.66}$$

where N is the number of neurons. The signal-to-noise ratio increases with N as expected.

7.4 The significance of a single spike

The above results derived for a *population* of spiking neurons have an intimate relation to experimental measurements of the input–output transforms of a *single* neuron as typically measured by a peri-stimulus-time histogram (PSTH) or by reverse correlations. This relation allows to give an interpretation of population

A **B**

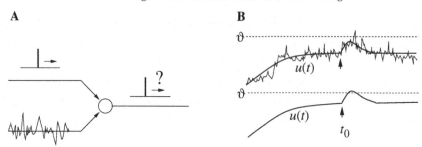

Fig. 7.11. **A**. A neuron which is driven by a noisy background input receives at time $t_0 = 0$ one extra input spike. Does this extra input trigger an output spike? **B**. Two hypothetic scenarios. Top: with noisy input an output spike is more likely the closer the mean membrane potential (thick solid line) is to the threshold (dashed line). The firing probability increases during the postsynaptic potential that is caused by the input pulse at $t_0 = 0$ (arrow). Bottom: without noise, the membrane potential can reach the threshold only during the rising phase of the postsynaptic potential. Adapted from Gerstner (2001).

results in the language of neural coding; see Section 1.4. In particular, we would like to understand the "meaning" of a spike. In Section 7.4.1 we focus on the typical effect of a single *presynaptic* spike on the firing probability of a postsynaptic neuron. In Section 7.4.2 we study how much we can learn from a single *postsynaptic* spike about the presynaptic input.

7.4.1 The effect of an input spike

What is the typical response of a neuron to a single presynaptic spike? An experimental approach to answer this question is to study the temporal response of a single neuron to current pulses (Fetz and Gustafsson, 1983; Poliakov et al., 1997). More precisely a neuron is driven by a constant background current I_0 plus a noise current I_{noise}. At time $t = 0$ an additional short current pulse is injected into the neuron that mimics the time course of an excitatory or inhibitory postsynaptic current. In order to test whether this extra input pulse can cause a postsynaptic action potential the experiment is repeated several times and a peri-stimulus-time histogram (PSTH) is compiled. The PSTH can be interpreted as the probability density of firing as a function of time t since the stimulus, here denoted $f_{PSTH}(t)$. Experiments show that the shape of the PSTH response to an input pulse is determined by the amount of synaptic noise and the time course of the postsynaptic potential (PSP) caused by the current pulse (Moore et al., 1970; Knox, 1974; Kirkwood and Sears, 1978; Fetz and Gustafsson, 1983; Poliakov et al., 1997).

How can we understand the relationship between PSP and PSTH? There are two different intuitive pictures; cf. Fig. 7.11. Firstly, consider a neuron driven by

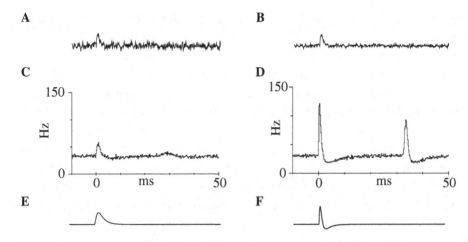

Fig. 7.12. Effect of noise on the PSTH. **A**. An integrate-and-fire neuron is stimulated by a current transient which consists of a deterministic pulse $I(t) = I_0 + \Delta I(t)$ plus a noise current I_{noise}. **B**. Same as in A, but reduced noise amplitude. **C**. The response of the neuron to repeated presentations of the stimulus is measured by the PSTH. For high noise the PSTH is similar to the PSP. **D**. For low noise, the PSTH resembles the derivative of the postsynaptic potential. **E**. Time course of the postsynaptic potential and **F** of its derivative; taken from Herrmann and Gerstner (2001a).

stochastic background input. If the input is not too strong, its membrane potential u hovers somewhere below threshold. The shorter the distance $\vartheta - u_0$ between the mean membrane potential u_0 and the threshold ϑ the higher the probability that the fluctuations drive the neuron to firing. Let us suppose that at $t = 0$ an additional excitatory input spike arrives. It causes an excitatory postsynaptic potential with time course $\epsilon_0(t)$ which drives the mean potential closer to threshold. We therefore expect (Moore et al., 1970) that the probability density of firing (and hence the PSTH) shows a time course similar to the time course of the PSP, i.e., $f_{\text{PSTH}}(t) \propto \epsilon_0(t)$; cf. Fig. 7.11B (top).

Let us now, consider a neuron driven by a constant superthreshold current I_0 without any noise. If an input spike arrives during the phase where the membrane potential $u_0(t)$ is just below threshold, it may trigger a spike. Since the threshold crossing can only occur during the rising phase of the PSP, we may expect (Kirkwood and Sears, 1978) that the PSTH is proportional to the *derivative* of the PSP, i.e., $f_{\text{PSTH}}(t) \propto \frac{d}{dt}\epsilon_0(t)$; cf. Fig. 7.11B (bottom).

Both regimes can be observed in simulations of integrate-and-fire neurons; cf. Fig. 7.12. An input pulse at $t = 0$ causes a PSTH. The shape of the PSTH depends on the noise level and is either similar to the postsynaptic potential or to its derivative. Closely related effects have been reported in the experimental literature cited above. In this section we show that the theory of signal transmission by a population of spiking neurons allows us to analyze these results from a systematic point of view.

In order to understand how the theory of population activity can be applied to single-neuron PSTHs, let us consider a homogeneous population of N unconnected, noisy neurons initialized with random initial conditions, all receiving the same input. Since the neurons are independent, the activity of the population as a whole in response to a given stimulus is equivalent to the PSTH compiled from the response of a single noisy neuron to N repeated presentations of the same stimulus. Hence, we can apply theoretical results for the activity of homogeneous populations to the PSTH of an individual neuron.

Since a presynaptic spike typically causes an input pulse of small amplitude, we may calculate the PSTH from the linearized population activity equation; cf. Eq. (7.3). During the *initial* phase of the response, the integral over $P_0(s) \, \Delta A(t-s)$ in Eq. (7.3) vanishes and the dominant term is

$$f_{\text{PSTH}}(t) = \frac{d}{dt} \int_0^\infty \mathcal{L}(x) \, \epsilon_0(t - x) \, dx \, , \quad \text{for } 0 < t \ll [A_0]^{-1} \tag{7.67}$$

where $\epsilon_0(t)$ is the PSP generated by the input pulse at $t = 0$. We have seen that for low noise the kernel $\mathcal{L}(x)$ approaches a δ function. Hence, in the low-noise limit, the PSTH is proportional to the derivative of the PSP. On the other hand, for high noise the kernel $\mathcal{L}(x)$ is rather broad. In this case, the derivative and the integration that are to be performed on the right-hand side of Eq. (7.67) cancel each other so that the PSTH is proportional to the PSP. Equation (7.67) can also be applied in the case of intermediate noise level, where the intuitive pictures outlined above are not sufficient.

Example: the input–output crosscorrelation of integrate-and-fire neurons

In this example we study integrate-and-fire neurons with escape noise. A bias current is applied so that we have a constant baseline firing rate of about 30 Hz. At $t = 0$ an excitatory (or inhibitory) current pulse is applied which increases (or decreases) the firing density as measured with the PSTH; cf. Fig. 7.13. At low noise the initial response is followed by a decaying oscillation with a period equal to the single-neuron firing rate. At high noise the response is proportional to the excitatory (or inhibitory) PSP. Note the asymmetry between excitation and inhibition, i.e., the response to an inhibitory current pulse is smaller than that to an excitatory one. The linear theory cannot reproduce this asymmetry. It is, however, possible to integrate the full nonlinear population equation (6.75) using the methods discussed in Chapter 6. The numerical integration reproduces nicely the nonlinearities found in the simulated PSTH; cf. Fig. 7.13A.

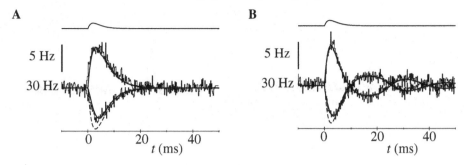

Fig. 7.13. Integrate-and-fire neurons with escape noise. Population activities in response to positive and negative current pulses at two different noise levels. Simulations (thin stepped lines) are compared to theoretical responses: the thick solid line shows the result of integrating the full nonlinear population equation (6.75) whereas the dashed line gives the approximation by the linear theory; cf. Eq. (7.3). **A.** High noise. **B.** Low noise. The bias current I_0 was adjusted to compensate for the change in mean activity resulting from the difference in noise levels so that in both cases $A_0 \approx 30$ Hz. The current pulse $\propto t \exp(-t/\tau_s)$ with $\tau_s = 2$ ms is indicated above the main figure. Input pulse amplitudes were chosen to produce peaks of comparable size, $\Delta A \approx 6$ Hz; taken from Herrmann and Gerstner (2001a).

Example: input–output measurements in motoneurons

In this example we compare theoretical results with experimental input–output measurements in motoneurons (Fetz and Gustafsson, 1983; Poliakov et al., 1996, 1997). In the study of Poliakov et al. (1997), PSTH responses to Poisson-distributed trains of current pulses were recorded. The pulses were injected into the soma of rat hypoglossal motoneurons during repetitive discharge. The time course of the pulses was chosen to mimic postsynaptic currents generated by presynaptic spike arrival. PSTHs of motoneuron discharge occurences were compiled when the pulse trains were delivered either with or without additional current noise which simulated noisy background input. Figure 7.14 shows examples of responses from a rat motoneuron taken from the work of Poliakov which is a continuation of earlier work (Moore et al., 1970; Knox, 1974; Kirkwood and Sears, 1978; Fetz and Gustafsson, 1983). The effect of adding noise can be seen clearly: the low-noise peak is followed by a marked trough, whereas the high-noise PSTH has a reduced amplitude and a much smaller trough. Thus, in the low-noise regime (where the type of noise model is irrelevant) the response to a synaptic input current pulse is similar to the *derivative* of the postsynaptic potential (Fetz and Gustafsson, 1983), as predicted by earlier theories (Knox, 1974), while for high noise it is similar to the postsynaptic potential itself.

Figure 7.14C and D shows PSTHs produced by a Spike Response Model of a motoneuron; cf. Section 4.2. The model neuron is stimulated by exactly the same

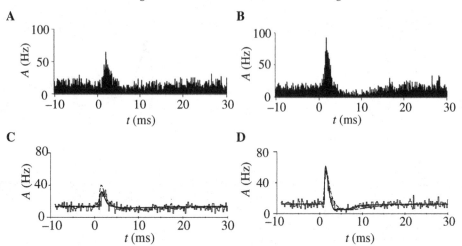

Fig. 7.14. Effect of noise on the PSTH response of a rat hypoglossal motoneuron. A Poisson train of excitatory alpha-shaped current pulses of amplitude 0.2 nA was injected into the soma of a rat hypoglossal motoneuron, superimposed on a long 1-nA current step inducing repetitive firing. In the "high" noise condition, this input was combined with an additional noise waveform. **A**. PSTH in the regime of "high" noise (noise power level 30 nA^2 μs). **B**. PSTH for "low" noise. **C**. Motoneuron model in the high-noise and **D** in the low-noise condition. Simulations (thin stepped line) are compared to the integration of the full nonlinear population equation (thick solid line) and to the prediction of the linear theory (thick dashed line). Experimental data from Poliakov et al. (1996), courtesy of M. Binder; model from Herrmann and Gerstner (2001b).

type of stimulus that was used in the above experiments on motoneurons. The simulations of the motoneuron model are compared with the PSTH response predicted from the theory. The linear response reproduces the general characteristics that we see in the simulations. The full nonlinear theory derived from the numerical solution of the population equation fits nicely with the simulation. The results are also in qualitative agreement with the experimental data.

7.4.2 Reverse correlation – the significance of an output spike

In a standard experimental protocol to characterize the coding properties of a single neuron, the neuron is driven by a time-dependent stimulus $I(t) = I_0 + \Delta I(t)$ that fluctuates around a mean value I_0. Each time the neuron emits a spike, the time-course of the input just before the spike is recorded. Averaging over many spikes yields the typical input that drives the neuron towards firing. This spike-triggered average is called the "reverse correlation" function; cf. Section 1.4. Formally, if neuronal firing times are denoted by $t^{(f)}$ and the stimulus before the spike by $I(t^{(f)} - s)$, we define the reverse correlation function as

$$C^{\text{rev}}(s) = \langle \Delta I(t^{(f)} - s) \rangle_f \qquad (7.68)$$

where the average is to be taken over all firing times $t^{(f)}$. In our definition the reverse correlation evaluated at a positive time $s > 0$ looks *backward* in time, i.e., describes the mean input that *precedes* a spike. If the type of allowed stimuli is appropriately constrained, it can be shown that, amongst all possible stimuli, a stimulus $\Delta I(t) \propto C^{\text{rev}}(-t)$ is in fact the optimal stimulus to trigger a spike; cf. the example at the end of this section.

In this section, we want to relate the reverse correlation function $C^{\text{rev}}(s)$ to the signal transfer properties of a single neuron (Bryant and Segundo, 1976). In Section 7.3, we have seen that, in the linear regime, signal transmission properties of a population of neuron are described by

$$\hat{A}(\omega) = \hat{G}(\omega) I(\omega), \qquad (7.69)$$

with a frequency-dependent gain $\hat{G}(\omega)$; see Eq. (7.57). We will use that, for independent neurons, the transfer characteristics of a population are identical to that of a single neuron. We therefore interpret $\hat{G}(\omega)$ as the single-neuron transfer function. Inverse Fourier transform of Eq. (7.69) yields

$$A(t) = A_0 + \int_0^\infty G(s)\, \Delta I(t - s)\, ds \qquad (7.70)$$

with a kernel defined in Eq. (7.59). A_0 is the mean rate for constant drive I_0. We want to show that the reverse correlation function $C^{\text{rev}}(s)$ is proportional to the kernel $G(s)$.

Equation (7.70) describes the relation between a known (deterministic) input $\Delta I(t)$ and the population activity. We now adopt a statistical point of view and assume that the input $\Delta I(t)$ is drawn from a statistical ensemble of stimuli with mean $\langle \Delta I(t) \rangle = 0$. Angular brackets denote averaging over the input ensemble or, equivalently, over an infinite input sequence. We are interested in the correlation

$$C_{AI}(s) = \lim_{T \to \infty} \frac{1}{T} \int_0^T A(t + s)\, \Delta I(t)\, dt = \langle A(t + s)\, \Delta I(t) \rangle \qquad (7.71)$$

between input ΔI and activity ΔA. If the input amplitude is small so that the linearized population equation (7.70) is applicable, we find

$$C_{AI}(s) = \int_0^\infty G(s) \langle \Delta I(t + s - s')\, \Delta I(t) \rangle\, ds'. \qquad (7.72)$$

where we have used $A_0 \langle \Delta I(t) \rangle = 0$. The correlation function C_{AI} depends on the kernel $G(s)$ as well as on the autocorrelation $\langle \Delta I(t')\, \Delta I(t) \rangle$ of the input ensemble.

For the sake of simplicity, we assume that the input consists of white noise,[1] i.e., the input has an autocorrelation

$$\langle \Delta I(t') \, \Delta I(t) \rangle = \sigma^2 \, \delta(t' - t) \,. \tag{7.73}$$

In this case Eq. (7.72) reduces to

$$C_{AI}(s) = \sigma^2 \, G(s) \,. \tag{7.74}$$

Thus the correlation function C_{AI} is proportional to $G(s)$.

In order to relate the correlation function C_{AI} to the reverse correlation C^{rev}, we recall the definition of the population activity

$$A(t) = \frac{1}{N} \sum_{i=1}^{N} \sum_{f} \delta(t - t_i^{(f)}) \,. \tag{7.75}$$

The correlation function Eq. (7.71) is therefore

$$C_{AI}(s) = \lim_{T \to \infty} \frac{1}{T} \left[\frac{1}{N} \sum_{i=1}^{N} \sum_{f} \Delta I(t_i^{(f)} - s) \right] \,. \tag{7.76}$$

Thus the value of the correlation function C_{AI} at, e.g., $s = 5$ ms, can be measured by observing the mean input 5 ms before each spike. The sum in the square brackets runs over all spikes of all neurons. With the neuronal firing rate $\nu = A_0$, the expected number of spikes of N identical and independent neurons is $\nu T N$ where T is the measurement time window. We now use the definition (7.68) of the reverse correlation function on the right-hand side of Eq. (7.76) and find

$$C_{AI}(s) = \nu \, C^{\mathrm{rev}}(s) \,. \tag{7.77}$$

Since we have focused on a population of independent neurons, the reverse correlation of the population is identical to that of a *single* neuron. The combination of Eqs. (7.74) and (7.77) yields

$$C^{\mathrm{rev}}(s) = \frac{\sigma^2}{\nu} \, G(s) \,. \tag{7.78}$$

This is an important result. For spiking neurons the transfer function $G(s)$ can be calculated from neuronal parameters while the reverse correlation function C^{rev} is easily measurable in single-neuron experiments. This allows an interpretation of

---

[1] It is called white noise because the power spectrum (i.e., the Fourier transform of the autocorrelation) is flat. A Poisson process is an example of a statistical process with autocorrelation (7.73); cf. Chapter 5.

A

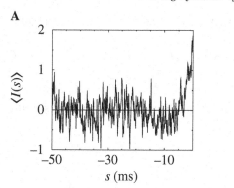

B

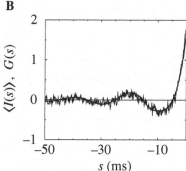

Fig. 7.15. Reverse correlations. A SRM_0 neuron is stimulated by a constant bias current plus a stochastic input current. Each time an output spike is triggered, the time course of the input current is recorded. **A**. Average input $\langle I(t - t^{(f)})\rangle_{t^{(f)}}$ as a function of $s = t - t^{(f)}$ averaged over 1000 output spikes $f = 1, \ldots, 1000$. **B**. The same, but averaged over 25 000 spikes. The simulation result is compared with the time-reversed impulse response $G(-s)$ predicted from the theory (smooth line). Adapted from Gerstner (2001).

reverse correlation results in terms of neuronal parameters such as membrane time constant, refractoriness, and noise.

Example: reverse correlation function for SRM_0 neurons

We consider a SRM_0 neuron $u(t) = \eta_0(t - \hat{t}) + \int_0^\infty \kappa_0(s) I(t - s)\, ds$ with piecewise linear escape noise. The response kernels are exponential with a time constant of $\tau = 4$ ms for the kernel κ and $\tau_{ref} = 20$ ms for the refractory kernel η. The neuron is driven by a current $I(t) = I_0 + \Delta I(t)$. The bias current I_0 was adjusted so that the neuron fires at a mean rate of 50 Hz. The noise current was generated by the following procedure. Every time step of 0.1 ms we apply with a probability of 0.5 an input pulse. The amplitude of the pulse is ± 1 with equal probability. To estimate the reverse correlation function, we build up a histogram of the average input $\langle I(t - t^{(f)})\rangle_{t^{(f)}}$ preceding a spike $t^{(f)}$. We see from Fig. 7.15A that the main characteristics of the reverse correlation function are already visible after 1000 spikes. After an average over 25 000 spikes, the time course is much cleaner and reproduces to a high degree of accuracy the time course of the time-reversed impulse response $G(-s)$ predicted by the theory; cf. Fig. 7.15B. The oscillation with a period of about 20 ms reflects the intrinsic firing period of the neuron.

Example: reverse correlation as the optimal stimulus (*)

In this example we want to show that the reverse correlation function $C^{\text{rev}}(s)$ can be interpreted as the optimal stimulus to trigger a spike. To do so, we assume that the amplitude of the stimulus is small and use the linearized population equation

$$A(t) = A_0 + \int_0^\infty G(s)\,\Delta I\,(t-s)\,\mathrm{d}s\,. \tag{7.79}$$

Suppose that we want to have a large response $\Delta A = A(0) - A_0$ at time $t = 0$. More precisely we ask the following question. Amongst all possible stimuli $I(t)$ for $t < 0$ with the same power

$$\int_{-\infty}^0 \Delta I^2(t)\,\mathrm{d}t = \mathrm{const}_P, \tag{7.80}$$

which one will give the maximal response ΔA? We claim that the optimal stimulus has the same time course as the linear kernel G apart from a reversal in time, i.e.,

$$\Delta I_{\mathrm{opt}}(t) \propto G(-t)\,. \tag{7.81}$$

To prove the assertion, we need to maximize $\Delta A = \int_0^\infty G(s)\,\Delta I(-s)\,\mathrm{d}s$ under the constraint (7.80). We insert the constraint by a Lagrange-multiplier λ and arrive at the condition

$$0 = \frac{\partial}{\partial I(t)}\left\{\int_0^\infty G(s)\,\Delta I(-s)\,\mathrm{d}s + \lambda\left[\mathrm{const}_P - \int_0^\infty \Delta I^2(-s)\,\mathrm{d}s\right]\right\} \tag{7.82}$$

which must hold at any arbitrary time t. Taking the derivative of the braced term with respect to $I(t)$ yields

$$G(t) = 2\lambda\,\Delta I_{\mathrm{opt}}(-t) \tag{7.83}$$

which proves the assertion (7.81). The exact value of λ could be determined from Eq. (7.80) but is not important for our arguments. Finally, from Eq. (7.78) we have $G(s) \propto C^{\mathrm{rev}}(s)$. Thus the result of reverse correlation measurements with white noise input can be interpreted as the optimal stimulus, as claimed in the text after Eq. (7.68).

7.5 Summary

In this chapter we have focused on the signal transmission properties of a population of identical and independent spiking neurons that are firing asynchronously. The state of asynchronous firing may be particularly interesting for information transmission, since the system can respond rapidly to changes in the input current. For slow noise such as noisy reset or correlated diffusive noise, the signal gain defined as the amplitude of the population activity divided by that of the input current shows no cut-off at high frequencies (Knight, 1972a; Gerstner, 2000; Brunel et al., 2001). The effective cut-off frequency of the system is therefore given by the input current. For real neurons, changes in the input current are of course limited by the opening and closing times of synaptic channels. The conclusion is that the response time of the system is determined by the time-course of the synaptic currents (Treves, 1993) and not by the membrane time constant.

These insights may have important implications for modeling as well as for interpretations of experiments. It is often thought that the response time of neurons is directly related to the membrane time constant τ_m. In neural network modeling, a description of the population activity by a differential equation of the form

$$\tau_m \frac{dA}{dt} = -A + g[h(t)] \qquad (7.84)$$

is common practice. The results presented in this chapter suggest that, in some cases, the population activity A can respond more rapidly than the input potential h. In particular, the response is faster than the time course of the membrane if either (i) noise is slow or (ii) the amplitude of the signal is larger than the noise amplitude.

We have used escape noise models to illustrate the differences between high and low levels of noise. In the high-noise limit, the activity follows during a transient the input *potential h*, i.e.,

$$A(t) = g[h(t)] . \qquad (7.85)$$

The transient is therefore slow. In the low-noise limit, however, the activity follows the derivative h' so that the transient is fast.

If neurons with either "low" noise or "slow" noise are in a state of asynchronous firing, the population activity responds immediately to an abrupt change in the input without integration delay. The reason is that there are always some neurons close to threshold. This property suggests that a population of neurons may transmit information fast and reliably. Fast information processing is a characteristic feature of biological nervous systems as shown by reaction time experiments.

The theoretical results on signal transmission properties of neuronal populations can be related to single-neuron experiments. Instead of observing a population of identical and independent neurons in a single trial, the spiking activity of a single neuron is measured in repeated trials. The experimental PSTH response to an input current pulse exhibits qualitatively the same type of noise dependence as predicted by the population theory. Furthermore, reverse correlation experiments can be related to the linear signal transmission function $\hat{G}(\omega)$ that can be calculated from population theories.

Literature

The signal transmission properties of single neurons and populations of neurons have been studied by numerous authors. We refer the interested reader to the early papers of Knight (1972a,b), Knox (1974), and Fetz and Gustafsson (1983) as well as the more recent discussions in Abeles (1991), Poliakov et al. (1997), Gerstner (2000), and Brunel et al. (2001).

8

Oscillations and synchrony

Oscillations are a prevalent phenomenon in biological neural networks and manifest themselves experimentally in electroencephalograms (EEG), recordings of local field potentials (LFP), and multiunit recordings. Oscillations of the spike activity are particularly interesting from a functional point of view. Synchronization of different populations of neurons has, for example, been proposed as a potential solution to the binding problem (Eckhorn et al., 1988; Gray et al., 1989; Wang et al., 1990; König and Schillen, 1991; Eckhorn et al., 1993; Singer, 1994). Oscillations play an important role in the coding of sensory information. In the olfactory system an ongoing oscillation of the population activity provides a temporal frame of reference for neurons coding information about the odorant (Laurent, 1996; Desmaison et al., 1999). Similarly, place cells in the hippocampus exhibit phase-dependent firing activity relative to a background oscillation (O'Keefe, 1993). Finally, rhythmic spike patterns in the inferior olive may be involved in various timing tasks and motor coordination (Llinás, 1991; Welsh et al., 1995; Kistler et al., 2000).

In this chapter we do not discuss all the interesting computational applications, but restrict ourselves to the analysis of mechanisms underlying oscillatory activity and synchronization. We start in Section 8.1 with a stability analysis of the state of asynchronous firing encountered in Section 6.4. In recurrent networks of spiking neurons we find that a state of asynchronous activity is unstable in the absence of noise. As a consequence, neurons tend to form clusters of cells that fire synchronously. In Section 8.2 we investigate network modes where neurons fire "in lockstep" and derive a stability criterion for synchronized activity. Finally, in Section 8.3 we explore the possibility that sparse recurrent networks exhibit an oscillatory population activity while generating irregular spike trains. Sparse networks producing irregular spike trains form a promising starting point for an understanding of the neuronal activity observed in various parts of the brain.

8.1 Instability of the asynchronous state

In Section 6.4 and throughout Chapter 7, we have assumed that the network is in a state of asynchronous firing. In this section, we study whether asynchronous firing can indeed be a stable state of a fully connected population of spiking neurons – or whether the connectivity drives the network towards oscillations. For the sake of simplicity, we restrict the analysis to SRM_0 neurons; the same methods can, however, be applied to integrate-and-fire neurons or general SRM neurons.

For SRM_0 neurons, the membrane potential is given by

$$u_i(t) = \eta(t - \hat{t}_i) + h(t) \tag{8.1}$$

where $\eta(t - \hat{t}_i)$ is the effect of the last firing of neuron i (i.e., the spike itself and its afterpotential) and $h(t)$ is the total postsynaptic potential caused by presynaptic firing. If all presynaptic spikes are generated within the homogeneous population under consideration, we have

$$h(t) = \sum_j w_{ij} \sum_f \epsilon_0(t - t_j^{(f)}) = J_0 \int_0^\infty \epsilon_0(s) \, A(t - s) \, ds . \tag{8.2}$$

Here $\epsilon_0(t - t_j^{(f)})$ is the time course of the postsynaptic potential generated by a spike of neuron j at time $t_j^{(f)}$ and $w_{ij} = J_0/N$ is the strength of lateral coupling within the population. The second equality sign follows from the definition of the population activity, i.e., $A(t) = N^{-1} \sum_j \sum_f \delta(t - t_j^{(f)})$; cf. Section 6.1. For the sake of simplicity, we have assumed in Eq. (8.2) that there is no external input.

The state of asynchronous firing corresponds to a fixed point $A(t) = A_0$ of the population activity. We have already seen in Section 6.4 how the fixed point A_0 can be determined either numerically or graphically. To analyze its stability we assume that for $t > 0$ the activity is subject to a small perturbation,

$$A(t) = A_0 + A_1 \, e^{i\omega t + \lambda t} \tag{8.3}$$

with $A_1 \ll A_0$. The perturbation in the activity induces a perturbation in the input potential,

$$h(t) = h_0 + h_1 \, e^{i\omega t + \lambda t} , \tag{8.4}$$

with $h_0 = J_0 \, \hat{\epsilon}(0) \, A_0$ and $h_1 = J_0 \, \hat{\epsilon}(\omega - i\lambda) \, A_1$, where

$$\hat{\epsilon}(\omega - i\lambda) = |\hat{\epsilon}(\omega - i\lambda)| \, e^{-i\psi(\omega - i\lambda)} = \int_0^\infty \epsilon_0(s) \, e^{-i(\omega - i\lambda)s} \, ds \tag{8.5}$$

is the Fourier transform of ϵ_0 and $\psi(\cdot)$ denotes the phase shift between h and A.

The perturbation of the potential causes some neurons to fire earlier (when the change in h is positive) and others to fire later (whenever the change is negative). The perturbation may therefore build up ($\lambda > 0$, the asynchronous state is unstable) or decay back to zero ($\lambda < 0$, the asynchronous state is stable). At the transition between the region of stability and instability the amplitude of the perturbation remains constant ($\lambda = 0$, marginal stability of the asynchronous state). These transition points, defined by $\lambda = 0$, are determined now.

We start from the population integral equation $A(t) = \int_{-\infty}^{t} P_I(t|\hat{t}) A(\hat{t}) \, d\hat{t}$ that was introduced in Section 6.3. Here $P_I(t|\hat{t})$ is the input-dependent interval distribution, i.e., the probability density of emitting a spike at time t given that the last spike occurred at time $\hat{t}$. We have seen in Chapter 7 that the linearized population activity equation can be written in the form

$$\Delta A(t) = \int_{-\infty}^{t} P_0(t - \hat{t}) \, \Delta A(\hat{t}) \, d\hat{t} + A_0 \frac{d}{dt} \int_{0}^{\infty} \mathcal{L}(x) \, \Delta h(t - x) \, dx \, ; \qquad (8.6)$$

cf. Eq. (7.3). Here $P_0(t - \hat{t})$ is the interval distribution during asynchronous firing and $\mathcal{L}$ is the kernel from Table 7.1. We use $\Delta A(t) = A_1 \, e^{i\omega t + \lambda t}$ and $\Delta h(t) = h_1 \, e^{i\omega t + \lambda t}$ in Eq. (8.6). After cancellation of a common factor $A_1 \exp(i\omega t)$, the result can be written in the form

$$1 = i\omega \, \frac{J_0 \, A_0 \, \hat{\epsilon}(\omega) \, \hat{\mathcal{L}}(\omega)}{1 - \hat{P}(\omega)} = S_f(\omega) \, \exp[i \, \Phi(\omega)] \, . \qquad (8.7)$$

$\hat{P}(\omega)$ and $\hat{\mathcal{L}}(\omega)$ are the Fourier transform of the interval distribution $P_0(t - \hat{t})$ and the kernel $\mathcal{L}$, respectively. The second equality sign defines the real-valued functions $S_f(\omega)$ and $\Phi(\omega)$. Equation (8.7) is thus equivalent to

$$S_f(\omega) = 1 \qquad \text{and} \qquad \Phi(\omega) \bmod 2\pi = 0 \, . \qquad (8.8)$$

Solutions of Eq. (8.8) yield bifurcation points where the asynchronous firing state loses its stability towards an oscillation with frequency ω.

We have written Eq. (8.8) as a combination of two requirements, i.e., an *amplitude* condition $S_f(\omega) = 1$ and a *phase* condition $\Phi(\omega) \bmod 2\pi = 0$. Let us discuss the general structure of the two conditions. Firstly, if $S_f(\omega) \le 1$ for all frequencies ω, an oscillatory perturbation cannot build up. All oscillations decay and the state of asynchronous firing is stable. We conclude from Eq. (8.7) that by increasing the absolute value $|J_0|$ of the coupling constant, it is always possible to increase $S_f(\omega)$. The amplitude condition can thus be met if the excitatory or inhibitory feedback from other neurons in the population is sufficiently strong. Secondly, for a bifurcation to occur we also need the phase condition to be met. Loosely speaking, the phase condition implies that the feedback from other neurons in the network must arrive just in time to keep the oscillation going. Thus the axonal signal transmission time and the rise time of the postsynaptic potential play a critical role during oscillatory activity (Abbott and van Vreeswijk, 1993; Gerstner and van Hemmen, 1993; Treves, 1993; Tsodyks et al., 1993; Ernst et al., 1995;

Gerstner, 1995; Brunel and Hakim, 1999; Brunel, 2000; Gerstner, 2000; Neltner et al., 2000; van Vreeswijk, 2000; Mattia and Del Giudice, 2002).

Example: phase diagram of instabilities

Let us apply the above results to SRM_0 neurons with noise in the reset. We assume that neurons are in a state of asynchronous firing with activity A_0. As we have seen in Chapter 5, the interval distribution for noisy reset is a Gaussian centered at $T_0 = 1/A_0$. The filter function $\mathcal{L}$ is a δ-function, $\mathcal{L}(x) = \delta(x)/\eta'$; cf. Table 7.1. Hence Eq. (8.7) is of the form

$$1 = \frac{i\omega}{\eta'} \frac{J_0 A_0 \hat{\epsilon}(\omega)}{1 - \hat{\mathcal{G}}_\sigma(\omega) e^{-i\omega T_0}} = S_f(\omega) \exp[i\,\Phi(\omega)], \qquad (8.9)$$

where $\hat{\mathcal{G}}_\sigma(\omega) = \exp(-\sigma^2\omega^2/2)$ is the Fourier transform of a Gaussian with width σ.

In order to analyze Eq. (8.9) numerically we have to specify the response kernel. For the sake of simplicity we choose a delayed alpha function,

$$\epsilon_0(s) = \frac{s - \Delta^{ax}}{\tau^2} \exp\left(-\frac{s - \Delta^{ax}}{\tau}\right) \Theta(s - \Delta^{ax}). \qquad (8.10)$$

The Fourier transform of ϵ as defined in Eq. (8.5) has an amplitude $|\hat{\epsilon}(\omega)| = (1 + \omega^2 \tau^2)^{-1}$ and a phase $\psi(\omega) = \omega\,\Delta^{ax} + 2\arctan(\omega\,\tau)$. Note that a change in the delay Δ^{ax} affects only the phase of the Fourier transform and not the amplitude.

Figure 8.1 shows S_f as a function of ωT_0. Since $S_f = 1$ is a necessary condition for a bifurcation, it is apparent that bifurcations can occur only for frequencies $\omega \approx \omega_n = n\,2\pi/T_0$ with integer n where $T_0 = 1/A_0$ is the typical interspike interval. We also see that higher harmonics are only relevant for low levels of noise. For $\sigma \to 0$ the absolute value of the denominator of (8.9) is $2|\sin(\omega T_0/2)|$ and bifurcations can occur for all higher harmonics. At a high noise level, however, the asynchronous state is stable even with respect to perturbations at $\omega \approx \omega_1$.

A bifurcation at $\omega \approx \omega_1$ implies that the period of the perturbation is identical to the firing period of individual neurons. Higher harmonics correspond to instabilities of the asynchronous state towards cluster states (Golomb et al., 1992; Gerstner and van Hemmen, 1993; Golomb and Rinzel, 1994; Ernst et al., 1995; Kistler and van Hemmen, 1999): each neuron fires with a mean period of T_0, but the population of neurons splits up into several groups that fire alternatingly so that the overall activity oscillates several times faster; cf. Section 8.2.3.

Figure 8.1 illustrates the amplitude condition for the solution of Eq. (8.9). The numerical solutions of the full equation (8.9) for different values of the delay Δ^{ax} and different levels of the noise σ are shown in the bifurcation diagram of Fig. 8.2.

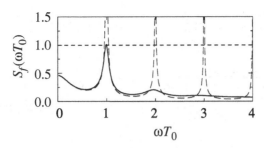

Fig. 8.1. Amplitude condition for instabilities in the asynchronous state. The amplitude S_f is plotted as a function of the normalized frequency $\omega\,T_0$ for two different values of the noise: $\sigma = 1$ ms (solid line) and $\sigma = 0.1$ ms (dashed line). Instabilities of the asynchronous firing state are possible at frequencies where $S_f > 1$. For low noise S_f crosses unity (dotted horizontal line) at frequencies $\omega \approx \omega_n = n\,2\pi/T_0$. For $\sigma = 1$ ms there is a single instability region for $\omega\,T_0 \approx 1$. For the plot we have set $T_0 = 2\tau$. Adapted from Gerstner (2000).

The insets show simulations that illustrate the behavior of the network at certain combinations of transmission delay and noise level.

Let us consider for example a network with transmission delay $\Delta^{\mathrm{ax}} = 2$ ms, corresponding to a x-value of $\Delta^{\mathrm{ax}}/T_0 = 0.25$ in Fig. 8.2. The phase diagram predicts that, at a noise level of $\sigma = 0.5$ ms, the network is in a state of asynchronous firing. The simulation shown in the inset in the upper right-hand corner confirms that the activity fluctuates around a constant value of $A_0 = 1/T_0 = 0.125$ kHz.

If the noise level of the network is significantly reduced, the system crosses the short-dashed line. This line is the boundary at which the constant activity state becomes unstable with respect to an oscillation with $\omega \approx 3\,(2\pi/T_0)$. Accordingly, a network simulation with a noise level of $\sigma = 0.1$ exhibits an oscillation of the population activity with period $T^{\mathrm{osc}} \approx T_0/3 \approx 2.6$ ms.

Keeping the noise level constant but reducing the transmission delay corresponds to a horizontal move across the phase diagram in Fig. 8.2. At some point, the system crosses the solid line that marks the transition to an instability with frequency $\omega_1 = 2\pi/T_0$. Again, this is confirmed by a simulation shown in the inset in the upper left corner. If we now decrease the noise level, the oscillation becomes even more pronounced (bottom left).

In the limit of low noise, the asynchronous network state is unstable for virtually all values of the delay. The region of the phase diagram in Fig. 8.2 around $\Delta^{\mathrm{ax}}/T_0 \approx 0.1$ which looks stable hides instabilities with respect to the higher harmonics ω_6 and ω_5 which are not shown. We emphasize that the specific location of the stability borders depends on the form of the postsynaptic response function

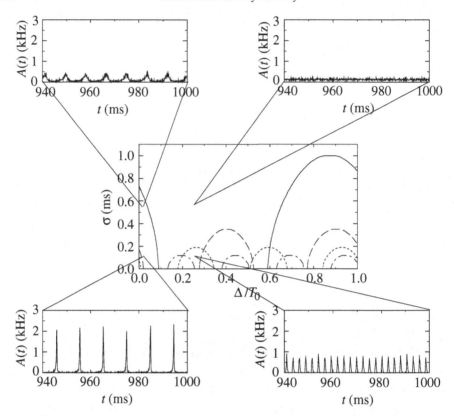

Fig. 8.2. Stability diagram (center) for the state of asynchronous firing in a SRM_0 network as a function of noise σ (y-axis) and delay Δ^{ax} (x-axis). Parameters are $J_0 = 1$ and $\tau = 4$ ms. The threshold ϑ was adjusted so that the mean interspike interval is $T_0 = 2\tau$. The diagram shows the borders of the stability region with respect to $\omega_1, \ldots, \omega_4$. For high values of the noise, the asynchronous firing state is always stable. If the noise is reduced, the asynchronous state becomes unstable with respect to an oscillation either with frequency ω_1 (solid border lines), or ω_2 (long-dashed border lines), ω_3 (short-dashed border lines), or ω_4 (long-short dashed border lines). Four insets show typical patterns of the activity as a function of time taken from a simulation with $N = 1000$ neurons. Parameters are $\sigma = 0.5$ ms and $\Delta^{ax} = 0.2$ ms (top left); $\sigma = 0.5$ ms and $\Delta^{ax} = 2.0$ ms (top right); $\sigma = 0.1$ ms and $\Delta^{ax} = 0.2$ ms (bottom left); $\sigma = 0.1$ ms and $\Delta^{ax} = 2.0$ ms (bottom right). Taken from Gerstner (2000).

ϵ. The qualitative features of the phase diagram in Fig. 8.2 are generic and hold for all kinds of response kernels.

The numerical results apply to the response kernel $\epsilon_0(s)$ defined in Eq. (8.10) which corresponds to a synaptic current $\alpha(s)$ with zero rise time; cf. Eq. (4.21). What happens if α is a double exponential with rise time τ_{rise} and decay time τ_{syn}? In this case, the right-hand side of Eq. (8.9) has an additional factor $[1 + i \omega \tau_{rise}]^{-1}$

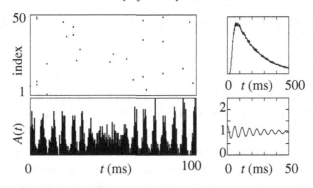

Fig. 8.3. Oscillations with irregular spike trains. The activity $A(t)$ (bottom left) of a population of 5000 integrate-and-fire neurons exhibits oscillations which are not evident in the spike trains of 50 individual neurons (top left), but which are confirmed by a significant oscillatory component in the autocorrelation function (bottom right). The spike trains have a broad distribution of interspike intervals (top right); adapted from Brunel and Hakim (1999).

which leads to two changes. Firstly, due to the reduced amplitude of the feedback, instabilities with frequencies $\omega > \tau_{\text{rise}}^{-1}$ are suppressed. The tongues for the higher harmonics are therefore smaller. Secondly, the phase of the feedback changes. Thus all tongues of frequency ω_n are moved horizontally along the x-axis by an amount $\Delta/T_0 = -\arctan(\omega_n \tau_{\text{rise}})/(n\,2\pi)$.

What happens if the excitatory interaction is replaced by inhibitory coupling? A change in the sign of the interaction corresponds to a phase shift of π. For each harmonic, the region along the delay axis where the asynchronous state is *unstable* for excitatory coupling (cf. Fig. 8.2) becomes *stable* for inhibition and vice versa. In other words, we simply have to shift the instability tongues for each frequency ω_n horizontally by an amount $\Delta/T_0 = 1/(2n)$. Apart from that the pattern remains the same.

Example: oscillations in random networks

Our discussion of random-connectivity networks in Section 6.4.3 has been focused on the stationary state of asynchronous firing. The stability analysis of the asynchronous state in such randomly connected networks is completely analogous to the approach sketched in Eqs. (8.3)–(8.6) except that the linearization is performed at the level of the density equations (Brunel and Hakim, 1999; Brunel, 2000). Close to the asynchronous state, the activity can be written as $A(t) = A_0 + A_1(t)$ and the membrane potential distribution as $p(u, t) = p_0(u) + p_1(u, t)$. Here $p_0(u)$ is the stationary distribution of membrane potential in the state of asynchronous firing (cf. Eqs. (6.27) and (6.28)) and $p_1(u, t)$ is a small time-dependent perturbation.

The stability analysis requires a linearization of the Fokker–Planck equation (6.21) with respect to p_1 and A_1.

For short transmission delays, the asynchronous state $A(t) \equiv A_0$ can lose its stability towards an oscillation with a frequency that is much faster than the single-neuron firing rate. Brunel (2000) distinguishes two different variants of such fast oscillations. Firstly, as in the previous example, there are cluster states where the neuronal population splits into a few subgroups. Each neuron fires nearly regularly and within a cluster neurons are almost fully synchronized; cf. Section 8.2.3. Secondly, there are synchronous irregular states where the global activity oscillates while individual neurons have a broad distribution of interspike intervals; cf. Fig. 8.3. We will come back to synchronous irregular states in Section 8.3.

8.2 Synchronized oscillations and locking

We have seen in the previous section that the state of asynchronous firing can lose stability towards certain oscillatory modes that are solutions of the *linearized* population equations. We are now going to investigate oscillatory modes in more detail and check whether a large-amplitude oscillation where all neurons are firing in "lockstep" can be a stable solution of the population equations.

8.2.1 Locking in noise-free populations

We consider a homogeneous population of SRM_0 or integrate-and-fire neurons which is nearly perfectly synchronized and fires almost regularly with period T. In order to analyze the existence and stability of a fully locked synchronous oscillation we approximate the population activity by a sequence of square pulses k, $k \in \{0, \pm 1, \pm 2, \ldots\}$, centered around $t = kT$. Each pulse k has a certain halfwidth δ_k and amplitude $(2\delta_k)^{-1}$ – since all neurons are supposed to fire once in each pulse. In order to check whether the fully synchronized state is a stable solution of the population equation (6.75), we assume that the population has already fired a couple of narrow pulses for $t < 0$ with widths $\delta_k \ll T$, $k \le 0$, and calculate the amplitude and width of subsequent pulses. If we find that the amplitude of subsequent pulses increases while their width decreases (i.e., $\lim_{k \to \infty} \delta_k = 0$), then we conclude that the fully locked state is stable.

To make the above outline more explicit, we use

$$A(t) = \sum_{k=-\infty}^{\infty} \frac{1}{2\delta_k} \Theta[t - (kT + \delta_k)] \, \Theta[(kT + \delta_k) - t] \qquad (8.11)$$

as a parameterization of the population activity; cf. Fig. 8.4. Here, Θ denotes the

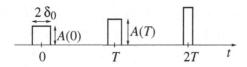

Fig. 8.4. Sequence of rectangular activity pulses. If the fully synchronized state is stable, the width δ of the pulses decreases while the amplitude A increases.

Heaviside step function with $\Theta(s) = 1$ for $s > 0$ and $\Theta(s) = 0$ for $s \le 0$. For stability, we need to show that the amplitude $A(0), A(T), A(2T), \ldots$ of the rectangular pulses increases while the width δ_k of subsequent pulses decreases.

As we will see below, the condition for stable locking of all neurons in the population can be stated as a condition on the *slope* of the input potential h at the moment of firing. More precisely, if the last population pulse occurred at about $t = 0$ with amplitude $A(0)$ the amplitude of the population pulse at $t = T$ increases if $h'(T) > 0$:

$$h'(T) > 0 \quad \Longleftrightarrow \quad A(T) > A(0) . \tag{8.12}$$

If the amplitude of subsequent pulses increases, their width decreases. In other words, we have the following *Locking Theorem*. In a spatially homogeneous network of SRM_0 or integrate-and-fire neurons, a necessary and, in the limit of a large number of presynaptic neurons ($N \to \infty$), also sufficient condition for a coherent oscillation to be asymptotically stable is that firing occurs when the postsynaptic potential arising from all previous spikes is increasing in time (Gerstner et al., 1996b).

The Locking Theorem is applicable for large populations that are already close to the fully synchronized state. A related but *global* locking argument has been presented by Mirollo and Strogatz (1990). The locking argument can be generalized to heterogeneous networks (Gerstner et al., 1993a; Chow, 1998) and to electrical coupling (Chow and Kopell, 2000). Synchronization in small networks is discussed elsewhere (Ernst et al., 1995; Hansel et al., 1995; van Vreeswijk et al., 1994; van Vreeswijk, 1996; Chow, 1998; Bose et al., 2000). For weak coupling, synchronization and locking can be systematically analyzed in the framework of phase models (Kuramoto, 1975; Ermentrout and Kopell, 1984; Kopell, 1986) or canonical neuron models (Hansel et al., 1995; Ermentrout, 1996; Hoppensteadt and Izhikevich, 1997; Izhikevich, 1999; Ermentrout et al., 2001).

Before we derive the locking condition for spiking neuron models, we illustrate the main idea by two examples.

Example: perfect synchrony in noiseless SRM$_0$ neurons

In this example we will show that locking in a population of spiking neurons can be understood by simple geometrical arguments: there is no need to use the abstract mathematical framework of the population equations. It will turn out that the results are – of course – consistent with those derived from the population equation.

We study a homogeneous network of N identical neurons which are mutually coupled with strength $w_{ij} = J_0/N$ where $J_0 > 0$ is a positive constant. In other words, the (excitatory) interaction is scaled with one over N so that the total input to a neuron i is of order one even if the number of neurons is large ($N \to \infty$). Since we are interested in synchrony we suppose that all neurons have fired simultaneously at $\hat{t} = 0$. When will the neurons fire again?

Since all neurons are identical we expect that the next firing time will also be synchronous. Let us calculate the period T between one synchronous pulse and the next. We start from the firing condition of SRM$_0$ neurons

$$\vartheta = u_i(t) = \eta(t - \hat{t}_i) + \sum_j w_{ij} \sum_f \epsilon(t - t_j^{(f)}), \tag{8.13}$$

where $\epsilon(t)$ is the postsynaptic potential. The axonal transmission delay Δ^{ax} is included in the definition of ϵ, i.e., $\epsilon(t) = 0$ for $t < \Delta^{\mathrm{ax}}$. Since all neurons have fired synchronously at $t = 0$, we set $\hat{t}_i = t_j^{(f)} = 0$. The result is a condition of the form

$$\vartheta - \eta(t) = J_0 \, \epsilon(t), \tag{8.14}$$

since $w_{ij} = J_0/N$ for $j = 1, \ldots, N$. Note that we have neglected the postsynaptic potentials that may have been caused by earlier spikes $t_j^{(f)} < 0$ back in the past. The graphical solution of Eq. (8.14) is presented in Fig. 8.5. The first crossing point of $\vartheta - \eta(t)$ and $J_0 \, \epsilon(t)$ defines the time T of the next synchronous pulse.

What happens if synchrony at $t = 0$ was not perfect? Let us assume that one of the neurons is slightly late compared to the others; Fig. 8.5B. It will receive the input $J_0 \, \epsilon(t)$ from the others, thus the right-hand side of Eq. (8.14) is the same. The left-hand side, however, is different since the last firing was at δ_0 instead of zero. The next firing time is at $t = T + \delta_1$ where δ_1 is found from

$$\vartheta - \eta(T + \delta_1 - \delta_0) = J_0 \, \epsilon(T + \delta_1). \tag{8.15}$$

Linearization with respect to δ_0 and δ_1 yields:

$$\delta_1 < \delta_0 \quad \Longleftrightarrow \quad \epsilon'(T) > 0. \tag{8.16}$$

Thus the neuron which has been late is "pulled back" into the synchronized pulse of the others if the postsynaptic potential ϵ is rising at the moment of firing at T. Equation (8.16) is a special case of the Locking Theorem.

A　　　　　　　　　　　　　　　　　**B**

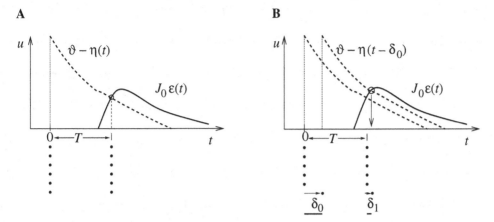

Fig. 8.5. **A**. Perfect synchrony. All neurons have fired at $\hat{t} = 0$. The next spike occurs when the summed postsynaptic potential $J_0\,\epsilon(t)$ reaches the dynamic threshold $\vartheta - \eta(t)$. **B**. Stability of perfect synchrony. The last neuron is out of tune. The firing time difference at $t = 0$ is δ_0. One period later the firing time difference is reduced ($\delta_1 < \delta_0$), since the threshold is reached at a point where $J_0\epsilon(t)$ is rising. Adapted from Gerstner et al. (1996b).

We see from Fig. 8.5B that, in the case of excitatory coupling, stable locking works nicely if the transmission delay Δ^{ax} is in the range of the firing period, but slightly shorter so that firing occurs during the rise time of the excitatory postsynaptic potential.

Example: SRM₀ neurons with inhibitory coupling

Locking can also occur in networks with purely inhibitory couplings (van Vreeswijk et al., 1994). In order to get a response at all in such a system, we need a constant stimulus I_0 or, equivalently, a negative firing threshold $\vartheta < 0$. The stability criterion, however, is equivalent to that of the previous example.

Figure 8.6 summarizes the stability arguments analogously to Fig. 8.5. In Fig. 8.6A all neurons have fired synchronously at $t = 0$ and do so again at $t = T$ when the inhibitory postsynaptic potential has decayed so that the threshold condition,

$$\vartheta - \eta(T) = J_0 \sum_k \epsilon(t - kT), \qquad (8.17)$$

is fulfilled. This state is stable if the synaptic contribution to the potential, $\sum_k \epsilon(t - kT)$, has positive slope at $t = T$. Figure 8.6 demonstrates that a single neuron firing at $t = \delta_0$ instead of $t = 0$ is triggered again at $t = T + \delta_1$ with $|\delta_1| < |\delta_0|$ for simple geometrical reasons.

A   **B**

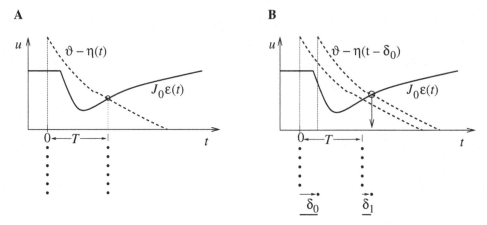

Fig. 8.6. Similar plot as in Fig. 8.5 but for purely inhibitory coupling. **A.** All neurons have fired synchronously at $\hat{t} = 0$. The next spike occurs when the summed inhibitory postsynaptic potential $J_0 \, \epsilon(t)$ has decayed back to the dynamic threshold $\vartheta - \eta(t)$. **B.** Stability of perfect synchrony. The last neuron is out of tune. The firing time difference at $t = 0$ is δ_0. One period later the firing time difference is reduced ($\delta_1 < \delta_0$), since the threshold is reached at a point where $J_0 \, \epsilon(t)$ is rising.

Derivation of the Locking Theorem (*)

We consider a homogeneous populations of SRM neurons that are close to a periodic state of synchronized activity. We assume that the population activity in the past consists of a sequence of rectangular pulses as specified in Eq. (8.11). We determine the period T and the sequence of halfwidths δ_k of the rectangular pulses in a self-consistent manner. In order to prove stability, we need to show that the amplitude $A(k\,T)$ increases while the halfwidth δ_k decreases as a function of k. To do so we start from the noise-free population equation (7.13) that we recall here for convenience

$$A(t) = \left[1 + \frac{\partial_t h + \partial_{\hat{t}} h}{\eta' - \partial_{\hat{t}} h} \right] A(t - T_{\mathrm{b}}(t)) \tag{8.18}$$

where $\partial_t h$ and $\partial_{\hat{t}} h$ are the partial derivatives of the total postsynaptic potential h_{PSP} and $T_{\mathrm{b}}(t)$ is the backward interval; cf. Fig. 7.1.

As a first step, we calculate the potential $h_{\mathrm{PSP}}(t|\hat{t})$. Given h_{PSP} we can find the period T from the threshold condition and also the derivatives $\partial_t h$ and $\partial_{\hat{t}} h$ required for Eq. (7.13). In order to obtain h_{PSP}, we substitute Eq. (8.11) in Eq. (6.8), assume $\delta_k \ll T$, and integrate. To first order in δ_k we obtain

$$h_{\mathrm{PSP}}(t|\hat{t}) = \sum_{k=0}^{k_{\max}} J_0 \, \epsilon(t - \hat{t}, t + k\,T) + \mathcal{O}\left[(\delta_k)^2 \right], \tag{8.19}$$

where $-\delta_0 \leq \hat{t} \leq \delta_0$ is the last firing time of the neuron under consideration. The sum runs over all pulses back in the past. Since $\epsilon(t - \hat{t}, s)$ as a function of s is rapidly decaying for $s \gg T$, it is usually sufficient to keep only a finite number of terms, e.g., $k_{max} = 1$ or 2.

In the second step we determine the period T. To do so, we consider a neuron in the *center* of the square pulse which has fired its last spike at $\hat{t} = 0$. Since we consider noiseless neurons the relative order of firing of the neurons cannot change. Consistency of Eq. (8.11) thus requires that the next spike of this neuron must occur at $t = T$, viz. in the center of the next square pulse. We use $\hat{t} = 0$ in the threshold condition for spike firing which yields

$$T = \min \left\{ t \mid \eta(t) + J_0 \sum_{k=0}^{k_{max}} \epsilon(t, t + k\,T) = \vartheta \right\}. \tag{8.20}$$

If a synchronized solution exists, (8.20) defines its period.

In the population equation (8.18) we need the derivative of h_{PSP},

$$\partial_t h + \partial_{\hat{t}} h = J_0 \sum_{k=0}^{k_{max}} \frac{\mathrm{d}}{\mathrm{d}s} \epsilon(x, s) \bigg|_{x=T, s=k\,T}. \tag{8.21}$$

According to Eq. (8.18), the new value of the activity at time $t = T$ is the old value multiplied by the factor in the square brackets. A necessary condition for an increase of the activity from one cycle to the next is that the derivative defined by the right-hand side of Eq. (8.21) is positive – which is the essence of the Locking Theorem.

We now apply Eq. (8.21) to a population of SRM$_0$ neurons. For SRM$_0$ neurons we have $\epsilon(x, s) = \epsilon_0(s)$, hence $\partial_{\hat{t}} h = 0$ and $h_{PSP}(t|\hat{t}) = h(t) = J_0 \sum_k \epsilon_0(t + k\,T)$. For a standard η kernel (e.g., an exponentially decaying function), we have $\eta'(T) > 0$ whatever T and thus

$$h'(T) = J_0 \sum_{k=1}^{k_{max}+1} \epsilon_0'(k\,T) > 0 \quad \Longleftrightarrow \quad A(T) > A(0), \tag{8.22}$$

which is identical to Eq. (8.12). For integrate-and-fire neurons we could go through an analogous argument to show that Eq. (8.12) holds. The amplitude of the synchronous pulse thus grows only if $h'(T) > 0$.

The growth of amplitude corresponds to a compression of the width of the pulse. It can be shown that the "corner neurons" which have fired at time $\pm\delta_0$ fire their next spike at $T \pm \delta_1$ where $\delta_1 = \delta_0 A(0)/A(T)$. Thus the square pulse remains normalized as it should be. By iteration of the argument for $t = k\,T$ with $k = 2, 3, 4, \ldots$ we see that the sequence δ_n converges to zero and the square pulses approach a Dirac δ-pulse under the condition that $h'(T) = \sum_k \epsilon_0'(k\,T) > 0$. In other words, the T-periodic synchronized solution with T given by Eq. (8.20) is

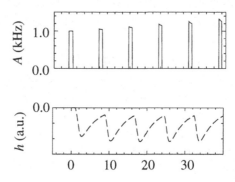

Fig. 8.7. A sequence of activity pulses (top) contracts to δ-pulses if firing occurs during the rising phase of the input potential h (dashed line, bottom). Numerical integration of the population equation (6.75) for SRM$_0$ neurons with inhibitory interaction $J = -0.1$ and kernel (8.10) with delay $\Delta^{\mathrm{ax}} = 2$ ms. There is no noise ($\sigma = 0$). The activity was initialized with a square pulse $A(t) = 1$ kHz for -1 ms $< t < 0$ and integrated with a step size of 0.05 ms. Adapted from Gerstner (2000).

stable if the input potential h at the moment of firing is rising (Gerstner et al., 1996b).

In order for the sequence of square pulses to be an exact solution of the population equation, we must require that the factor in the square brackets of Eq. (8.18) remains constant over the width of a pulse. The derivatives of Eq. (8.19), however, do depend on t. As a consequence, the form of the pulse changes over time as is visible in Fig. 8.7. The activity as a function of time was obtained by a numerical integration of the population equation with a square pulse as the initial condition for a network of SRM$_0$ neurons coupled via (8.10) with weak inhibitory coupling $J = -0.1$ and delay $\Delta^{\mathrm{ax}} = 2$ ms. For this set of parameters $h' > 0$ and locking is possible.

8.2.2 Locking in SRM$_0$ neurons with noisy reset (*)

The framework of the population equation allows us also to extend the locking argument to noisy SRM$_0$ neurons. At each cycle, the pulse of synchronous activity is compressed due to locking if $h'(T) > 0$. At the same time it is smeared out because of noise. To illustrate this idea we consider SRM$_0$ neurons with Gaussian noise in the reset.

In the case of noisy reset, the interval distribution can be written as $P_I(t|\hat{t}) = \int_{-\infty}^{\infty} dr\, \delta[t - \hat{t} - T(\hat{t}, r)]\, \mathcal{G}_\sigma(r)$; cf. Eq. (5.68). We insert the interval distribution

A

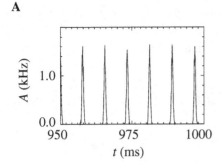

B

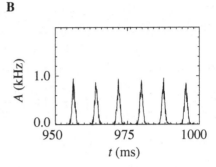

Fig. 8.8. Synchronous activity in the presence of noise. Simulation of a population of 1000 neurons with inhibitory coupling ($J = -1$, $\Delta^{\text{ax}} = 2$ ms) and noisy reset. **A**. Low noise level ($\sigma = 0.25$). **B**. For a high noise level ($\sigma = 0.5$), the periodic pulses become broader. Adapted from Gerstner (2000).

into the population equation $A(t) = \int_{-\infty}^{t} P_I(t|\hat{t}) \, A(\hat{t}) \, d\hat{t}$ and find

$$A(t) = \int_{-\infty}^{t} d\hat{t} \int_{-\infty}^{\infty} dr \, \delta[t - \hat{t} - T(\hat{t}, r)] \, \mathcal{G}_\sigma(r) \, A(\hat{t}). \tag{8.23}$$

The interspike interval of a neuron with reset parameter r is $T(\hat{t}, r) = r + T_0(\hat{t}+r)$ where $T_0(t')$ is the forward interval of a noiseless neuron that fired its last spike at t'. The integration over $\hat{t}$ in Eq. (8.23) can be done and yields

$$A(t) = \left[1 + \frac{h'}{\eta'}\right] \int_{-\infty}^{\infty} dr \, \mathcal{G}_\sigma(r) \, A[t - T_{\text{b}}(t) - r], \tag{8.24}$$

where T_{b} is the backward interval. The factor $[1 + (h'/\eta')]$ arises due to the integration over the δ function just as in the noiseless case; cf. Eqs. (7.13) and (7.15). The integral over r leads to a broadening, the factor $[1 + (h'/\eta')]$ to a compression of the pulse.

We now search for periodic solutions. As shown below, a limit cycle solution of Eq. (8.24) consisting of a sequence of Gaussian pulses exists if the noise amplitude σ is small and $(h'/\eta') > 0$. The width d of the activity pulses in the limit cycle is proportional to the noise level σ. A simulation of locking in the presence of noise is shown in Fig. 8.8. The network of SRM$_0$ neurons has inhibitory connections ($J_0 = -1$) and is coupled via the response kernel ϵ_0 in Eq. (8.10) with a transmission delay of $\Delta^{\text{ax}} = 2$ ms. Doubling the noise level σ leads to activity pulses with twice the width.

Pulse width in the presence of noise (*)

In order to calculate the width of the activity pulses in a locked state, we look for periodic pulse-type solutions of Eq. (8.24). We assume that the pulses are

Gaussians with width d and repeat with period T, viz., $A(t) = \sum_k \mathcal{G}_d(t - kT)$. The pulse width d will be determined self-consistently from Eq. (8.24). The integral over r in Eq. (8.24) can be performed and yields a Gaussian with width $\tilde{\sigma} = [d^2 + \sigma^2]^{1/2}$. Equation (8.24) becomes

$$\sum_k \mathcal{G}_d(t - kT) = \left[1 + \frac{h'(t)}{\eta'(T)}\right] \sum_k \mathcal{G}_{\tilde{\sigma}}[t - T_b(t) - kT], \qquad (8.25)$$

where $T_b(t) = \tau \ln\{\tilde{\eta}_0/[h(t) - \vartheta]\}$ is the interspike interval looking *backwards* in time.

Let us work out the self-consistency condition and focus on the pulse around $t \approx 0$. It corresponds to the $k = 0$ term on the left-hand side which must equal the $k = -1$ term on the right-hand side of Eq. (8.25). We assume that the pulse width is small, $d \ll T$, and expand $T_b(t)$ to linear order around $T_b(0) = T$. This yields

$$t - T_b(t) = t\left[1 + \frac{h'(0)}{\eta'(T)}\right] - T. \qquad (8.26)$$

The expansion is valid if $h'(t)$ varies slowly over the width d of the pulse. We use Eq. (8.26) in the argument of the Gaussian on the right-hand side of Eq. (8.25). Since we have assumed that h' varies slowly, the factor $h'(t)$ in Eq. (8.25) may be replaced by $h'(0)$. In the following we suppress the arguments and write simply h' and η'. The result is

$$\mathcal{G}_d(t) = \left(1 + \frac{h'}{\eta'}\right) \mathcal{G}_{\tilde{\sigma}}\left[t\left(1 + \frac{h'}{\eta'}\right)\right]. \qquad (8.27)$$

The Gaussian on the left-hand side of Eq. (8.27) must have the same width as the Gaussian on the right-hand side. The condition is $d = \tilde{\sigma}/[1 + h'/\eta']$ with $\tilde{\sigma} = [d^2 + \sigma^2]^{1/2}$. A simple algebraic transformation yields an explicit expression for the pulse width,

$$d = \sigma\left[2\left(h'/\eta'\right) + \left(h'/\eta'\right)^2\right]^{-1/2}, \qquad (8.28)$$

where d is the width of the pulse and σ is the strength of the noise.

8.2.3 Cluster states

We have seen that, on the one hand, the state of asynchronous firing is typically unstable for low levels of noise. On the other hand, the fully locked state may be unstable as well if transmission delay and the length of the refractory period do not allow spikes to be triggered during the rising phase of the input potential. The natural question is thus: what does the network activity look like if both the asynchronous and the fully locked state are unstable?

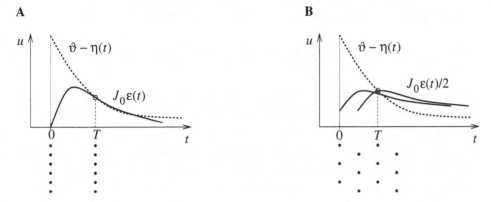

Fig. 8.9. Stability of cluster states. **A.** In an excitatory network with vanishing transmission delay the fully locked solution may be unstable. In this schematic drawing the next set of spikes at $t = T$ is triggered while the synaptic contribution to the potential is decaying. **B.** However, a cluster state where neurons split up into two groups that fire alternatingly can be stable. Here, the first group of neurons that have fired at $t = 0$ is triggered again at $t = T$ by the second group of neurons that fire with a phase shift of $T/2$ relative to the first group. This state is stable because spikes are triggered during the rising phase of the input potential.

Figure 8.9A shows an example of an excitatory network with vanishing transmission delay and a rather long refractory period as compared to the rising phase of the postsynaptic potential. As a consequence, the threshold condition is met when the postsynaptic potential has already passed its maximum. The fully locked state is thus unstable. This, however, does not mean that the network will switch into the asynchronous mode. Instead, the neurons may split into several subgroups ("cluster") that fire alternatingly. Neurons within each group stay synchronized. An example of such a cluster state with two subgroups is illustrated in Fig. 8.9B. Action potentials produced by neurons from group one trigger group two neurons and vice versa. The population activity thus oscillates with twice the frequency of an individual neuron.

In general, there is an infinite number of different cluster states that can be indexed by the number of subgroups. The length T of the interspike interval for a single neuron and the number of subgroups n in a cluster state are related by the threshold condition for spike triggering (Chow, 1998; Kistler and van Hemmen, 1999),

$$\vartheta - \eta(T) = \frac{J_0}{n} \sum_{k=0}^{\infty} \epsilon(k\,T/n) \,. \tag{8.29}$$

Stability is clarified by the Locking Theorem: a cluster state with n subgroups is stable if spikes are triggered during the rising flank of the input potential, i.e., if

$$\frac{d}{dt}\left[\frac{J_0}{n}\sum_{k=0}^{\infty}\epsilon(t+kT/n)\right]_{t=0} > 0. \qquad (8.30)$$

In Section 8.1 we have seen that the state of asynchronous firing in a SRM network is always unstable in the absence of noise. We now see that even if the fully locked state is unstable the network is not firing asynchronously but usually gets stuck in one of many possible cluster states. Asynchronous firing can only be reached asymptotically by increasing the number of subgroups so as to "distribute" the spike activity more evenly in time. Individual neurons, however, will always fire in a periodic manner. Nevertheless, increasing the number of subgroups will also reduce the amplitude of the oscillations in the input potential and the firing time of the neurons becomes more and more sensitive to noise. The above statement that asynchrony can only be reached asymptotically is therefore only valid in strictly noiseless networks.

A final remark on the stability of the clusters is in order. Depending on the form of the postsynaptic potential, the stability of the locked state may be asymmetric in the sense that neurons that fire too late are pulled back into their cluster; however, neurons that have fired to early are attracted by the cluster that has just fired before. If the noise level is not too low, there are always some neurons that drop out of their cluster and drift slowly towards an adjacent cluster (Ernst et al., 1995; van Vreeswijk, 1996).

Example: cluster states and harmonics

To illustrate the relationship between the instability of the state of asynchronous firing and cluster states, we return to the network of SRM_0 neurons with noisy reset that we studied in Section 8.1. For low noise ($\sigma = 0.04$), the asynchronous firing state is unstable whatever the axonal transmission delay; cf. Fig. 8.2. With an axonal delay of 2 ms, asynchronous firing is unstable with respect to an oscillation with ω_3. The population splits into three different groups of neurons that fire with a period of about 8 ms. The population activity, however, oscillates with a period of 2.7 ms; cf. Fig. 8.10A. With a delay of 1.2 ms, the asynchronous firing state has an instability with respect to ω_5 so that the population activity oscillates with a period of about 1.6 ms. The population splits into five diferent groups of neurons that fire with a period of about 8 ms; cf. Fig. 8.10B.

8.3 Oscillations in reverberating loops

In many areas of the brain synaptic projections form so-called *reverberating loops*. Neurons from one cortical area innervate an anatomically distinct nucleus that in

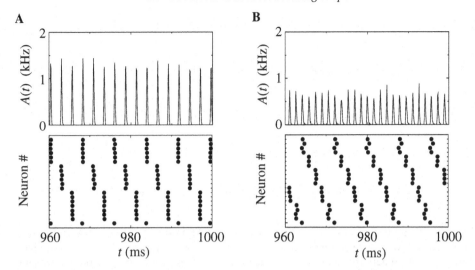

Fig. 8.10. Cluster states for SRM_0 neurons with stochastic reset. Population activity (top) and spike trains of 20 neurons (bottom). **A.** For an axonal delay of $\Delta^{ax} = 2$ ms, the population splits into three clusters. **B.** Same as in A, but with an axonal delay of $\Delta^{ax} = 1.2$ ms. The population splits into five clusters, because the asynchronous firing is unstable with respect to an oscillation with frequency ω_3; cf. Fig. 8.2. Very low noise ($\sigma = 0.04$ ms); all parameters as in Fig. 8.2.

turn projects back to the cortex in a topographically organized fashion. A prominent example is the olivo-cerebellar system. The inferior olive (IO) is a nucleus in the brainstem that is part of a reverberating loop formed by the cerebellar cortex and the deep cerebellar nuclei. A single round-trip from the IO to the cerebellar cortex, the deep cerebellar nuclei, and back to the olive takes about 100 ms – a rather long delay that is the result of slow synaptic processes, in particular of postinhibitory rebound firing; cf. Chapter 2.3.3. It is known that IO neurons tend to fire synchronously at about 10 Hz which is due to subthreshold oscillations of the membrane potential (Bell and Kawasaki, 1972; Sotelo et al., 1974; Llinás and Yarom, 1986; De Zeeuw et al., 1998) and an exceptionally high density of gap junctions. The delayed feedback can thus give rise to oscillations of the population activity in the olive. Analogously organized projections together with 10 Hz oscillations (the so-called theta rhythm) can also be observed in other areas of the brain including the olfactory system, hippocampus, and cortico-thalamic loops.

In the previous sections of this chapter we have dealt with networks that exhibit regular oscillations of the neuronal activity. On the other hand, experiments show that though oscillations are a common phenomenon, spike trains of individual neurons are often highly irregular. Here we investigate the question of whether these

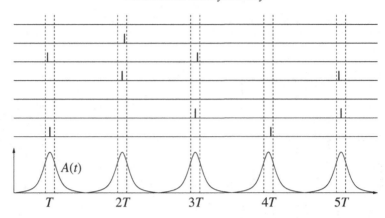

Fig. 8.11. Synchronous oscillation with irregular spike trains. Neurons tend to fire synchronously but with an average rate that is significantly lower than the oscillation frequency of the population activity (bottom). Each neuron is thus firing only in one out of, say, ten cycles, giving rise to highly irregular spike trains. Short vertical lines indicate the spikes of a set of six neurons (schematic figure).

observations can be reconciled: is it possible to have a periodic large-amplitude oscillation of the population activity and at the same time irregular spike trains? The answer is positive, provided that individual neurons fire with an average frequency that is significantly lower than the frequency of the population activity. Similarly to the cluster states discussed above, each neuron fires on average only in, say, one out of ten cycles of the population activity – the composition of the clusters of synchronously firing neurons, however, changes from cycle to cycle resulting in a broad distribution of interspike intervals; cf. Section 8.1. This is exactly what has been observed in the inferior olive. Individual neurons have a low firing rate of one spike per second; the population activity, however, oscillates at about 10 Hz; cf. Fig. 8.11.

We are particularly interested in the effect of feedback projections on the generated spike patterns. In keeping with experimental findings we assume that the feedback projections are *sparse*, i.e., that spikes from a given neuron in one cycle affect only a small portion of the whole population during the next cycle. Hence, we drop the assumption of an all-to-all connectivity and use randomly connected networks instead. It turns out that irregular spike trains can indeed be generated by the "frozen noise" of the network connectivity; cf. Chapter 6.4.3. Since the connectivity is random but fixed, the spike patterns of noiseless neurons are fully deterministic though they look irregular. Strong oscillations with irregular spike trains have interesting implications for short-term memory and timing tasks (Nützel et al., 1994; Billock, 1997; Kistler and De Zeeuw, 2002).

This section is dedicated to an investigation of the dynamic properties of neuronal networks that are part of a reverberating loop. We assume that the feedback is in resonance with a T-periodic oscillation of the population activity and that the neurons stay synchronized, i.e., fire only during narrow time windows every T milliseconds. We furthermore assume that the set of neurons that is active in each cycle depends only on the synaptic input that is due to the reverberating loop and thus depends only on the activity of the previous cycle. With these assumptions it is natural to employ a time-discrete description based on McCulloch–Pitts neurons. Each time step corresponds to one cycle of length T. The wiring of the reverberating loop is represented by a random coupling matrix. The statistical properties of the coupling matrix reflect the level of divergence and convergence within the reverberating network.

8.3.1 From oscillations with spiking neurons to binary neurons

We have seen that – depending on the noise level – a network can reach a state where all neurons are firing in lockstep. Such a large-amplitude oscillation implies that neurons only fire during short time windows around $t \approx n T$. Whether a neuron fires within the "allowed" time window depends on the input it receives from other neurons in the population.

The membrane potential for SRM$_0$ neurons is given by

$$u_i(t) = \eta(t - \hat{t}_i) + \sum_j w_{ij} \sum_f \epsilon(t - t_j^{(f)} - \Delta), \qquad (8.31)$$

where $\eta(t - \hat{t}_i)$ is the refractory effect of the last output spike of neuron i and $\epsilon(t - t_j^{(f)} - \Delta)$ is the postsynaptic potential caused by the firing of other neurons j with transmission delay Δ. A spike is triggered as soon as the threshold is reached. Here we assume that the network is in an oscillatory state so that spikes are fired only if $t \approx n T$. Due to refractoriness each neuron can fire at most on spike per cycle. Furthermore, we assume that the transmission delay Δ (and hence the period T) is long as compared to the characteristic time scale of ϵ and η. Therefore, $\epsilon(s)$ and $\eta(s)$ are negligible for $s \geq T$. Finally, we adjust the voltage scale so that $\epsilon(T - \Delta) = 1$.

With these assumptions, the dynamics of the spiking neuron model (8.31) reduces to a binary model in discrete time (McCulloch and Pitts, 1943). Let us set $t_n = n T$ and introduce binary variables $S_i \in \{0, 1\}$ for each neuron indicating whether neuron i is firing a spike at $t_i^{(f)} \approx t_n$ or not. Equation (8.31) can thus be rewritten as

$$u_i(t_{n+1}) = \sum_j w_{ij} S_j(t_n). \qquad (8.32)$$

The threshold condition $u_i(t_{n+1}) = \vartheta$ determines the state of the neuron in the next time step,

$$S_i(t_{n+1}) = \Theta[u_i(t_{n+1}) - \vartheta], \tag{8.33}$$

where Θ is the Heaviside step function with $\Theta(x) = 1$ if $x \geq 0$ and $\Theta(x) = 0$ for $x < 0$. The simple recursion defined by Eqs. (8.32) and (8.33) fully determines the sequence of spike patterns that is generated by the network given its coupling matrix w_{ij} and the initial firing pattern $S_i(0)$.

8.3.2 Mean field dynamics

The reduction of the spiking neuron model to discrete time and binary neurons allows us to study oscillations with irregular spike trains in a transparent manner. In a first step we derive mean field equations and discuss their macroscopic behavior. In a second step we look more closely into the microscopic dynamics. It will turn out that subtle changes in the density of excitatory and inhibitory projections can have dramatic effects on the microscopic dynamics that do not show up in a mean field description. Binary discrete-time models with irregular spike trains have been studied in various contexts by Kirkpatrick and Sherrington (1978), Derrida et al. (1987), Crisanti and Sompolinsky (1988), Nützel (1991), Kree and Zippelius (1991), van Vreeswijk and Sompolinsky (1996) to mention a few. As we have seen above, strong oscillations of the population activity provide a neuronal clocking mechanism and hence a justification of time discretization.

Purely excitatory projections

We consider a population of N McCulloch–Pitts neurons (McCulloch and Pitts, 1943) that is described by a state vector $S \in \{0, 1\}^N$. In each time step t_n any given neuron i is either active [$S_i(t_n) = 1$] or inactive [$S_i(t_n) = 0$]. Due to the reverberating loop, neurons receive (excitatory) synaptic input h that depends on the wiring of the loop – described by a coupling matrix w_{ij} – and on the activity during the previous cycle, i.e.,

$$u_i(t_n) = \sum_{j=1}^{N} w_{ij}\, S_j(t_{n-1}). \tag{8.34}$$

Since the wiring of the reverberating loop at the neuronal level is unknown we adopt a random coupling matrix with binary entries. More precisely, we take all entries w_{ij} to be identically and independently distributed (i.i.d.) with

$$\text{prob}\{w_{ij} = 1\} = \lambda/N. \tag{8.35}$$

We thus neglect possible differences in the synaptic coupling strength and content ourself with a description that accounts only for the presence or absence of a projection. In that sense, λ is the convergence and divergence ratio of the network, i.e., the averaged number of synapses that each neuron receives from and connects to other neurons, respectively.

The neurons are modeled as deterministic threshold elements. The dynamics is given by

$$S_i(t_n) = \Theta[u_i(t_n) - \vartheta] , \tag{8.36}$$

with ϑ being the firing threshold and Θ the Heaviside step function with $\Theta(x) = 1$ if $x \geq 1$ and $\Theta(x) = 0$ for $x < 0$.

Starting with a random initial firing pattern,

$$S_i(t_0) \in \{0, 1\} \text{ i.i.d. with } \text{prob}\{S_i(t_0) = 1\} = a_0 , \tag{8.37}$$

we can easily calculate the expectation value of the activity $a_1 = N^{-1} \sum_{i=1}^{N} S_i(t_1)$ in the next time step. According to Eq. (8.36) a neuron is active if it receives input from at least ϑ neurons that have been active during the last cycle. The initial firing pattern $S(t_0)$ and the coupling matrix w_{ij} are independent, so that the synaptic input h in Eq. (8.34) follows a binomial distribution. The probability a_1 of any given neuron to be active in the next cycle is thus

$$a_1 = \sum_{k=\vartheta}^{N} \binom{N}{k} (a_0 \, \lambda \, N^{-1})^k \, (1 - a_0 \, \lambda \, N^{-1})^{N-k} . \tag{8.38}$$

This equation gives the network activity a_1 as a function of the activity a_0 in the previous cycle. It is tempting to generalize this expression so as to relate the activity a_n in cycle n recursively to the activity in cycle $n - 1$,

$$a_{n+1} = 1 - \sum_{k=0}^{\vartheta-1} \binom{N}{k} (a_n \, \lambda \, N^{-1})^k \, (1 - a_n \, \lambda \, N^{-1})^{N-k} . \tag{8.39}$$

Unfortunately, this is in general not possible because the activity pattern S in cycle $n \geq 1$ and the coupling matrix w_{ij} are no longer independent and correlations in the firing patterns may occur. For sparse networks with $\lambda \ll N$, however, these correlations can be neglected and Eq. (8.39) can be used as an approximation (see Kree and Zippelius (1991) for a precise definition of "$\lambda \ll N$"). Fortunately, the case with $\lambda \ll N$ is the more interesting one anyway, because otherwise a_1 is a steep sigmoidal function of a_0 and the network activity either saturates ($a_1 \approx 1$) or dies out ($a_1 \approx 0$) after only one iteration. Furthermore, $\lambda \ll N$ may be a realistic assumption for certain biological reverberating loops such as the olivo-cerebellar system. In the following we thus assume that $\lambda \ll N$ so that the network activity

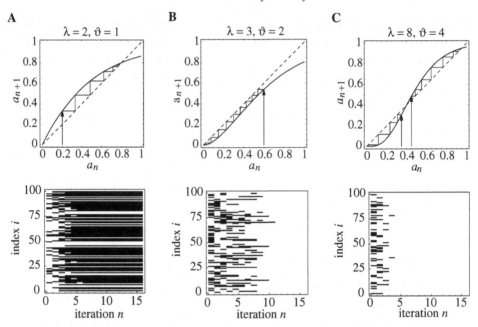

Fig. 8.12. Dynamics of a reverberating loop with purely excitatory projections. The upper row shows the mean field approximation of the population activity a_{n+1} as a function of the activity in the previous cycle a_n; cf. Eq. (8.40). The raster diagrams in the lower row give examples of the underlying microscopic dynamics in a simulation of $N = 100$ neurons. A horizontal bar indicates that the neuron is active. **A.** $\lambda = 2$, $\vartheta = 1$: Stable fixed point at $a \approx 0.8$. **B.** $\lambda = 3$, $\vartheta = 2$: Only $a_n = 0$ is stable. Note the long transient until the fixed point is reached. **C.** $\lambda = 8$, $\vartheta = 4$: Bistability of $a_n = 0$ and $a_n \approx 0.95$.

is given by Eq. (8.39), or – if we approximate the binomial distribution by the corresponding Poisson distribution – by the recursion

$$a_{n+1} = 1 - \sum_{k=0}^{\vartheta-1} \frac{(a_n \lambda)^k}{k!} \, \mathrm{e}^{-a_n \lambda} \,. \tag{8.40}$$

The dynamics of the population activity is completely characterized by the mean field equation (8.40). For instance, it can easily be shown that $a_n = 0$ is a stable fixed point except if $\vartheta = 1$ and $\lambda > 1$. Furthermore, a_n is a monotonously growing function of a_{n-1}. Therefore, no macroscopic oscillations can be expected. In summary, three different constellations can be discerned; cf. Fig. 8.12. Firstly, for $\vartheta = 1$ and $\lambda > 1$ there is a stable fixed point at high levels of a_n; the fixed point at $a_n = 0$ is unstable. Secondly, if the firing threshold ϑ is large as compared to the convergence λ only $a_n = 0$ is stable. Finally, if $\vartheta > 1$ and λ sufficiently large, bistability of $a_n = 0$ and $a_n > 0$ can be observed.

Balanced excitation and inhibition

In a network with purely excitatory interactions the nontrivial fixed point corresponds to a microscopic state where some neurons are active and others inactive. Since the active neurons fire at practically every cycle of the oscillation, we do not find the desired broad distribution of interspike intervals; cf. Fig. 8.12A. As we have already seen in Section 6.4.3, a random network with balanced excitation and inhibition is a good candidate for generating broad interval distributions. Reverberating projections are, in fact, not necessarily excitatory. Instead, they are often paralleled by an inhibitory pathway that may involve either another brain region or just inhibitory interneurons. Our previous model can easily be extended so as to account both for excitatory and inhibitory projections. The wiring of the excitatory loop is characterized, as before, by a random matrix $w_{ij}^{\text{exc}} \in \{0, 1\}$ with

$$\text{prob}\{w_{ij}^{\text{exc}} = 1\} = \lambda_{\text{exc}}/N \qquad \text{i.i.d.} \tag{8.41}$$

Similarly, the wiring of the inhibitory loop is given by a random matrix $w_{ij}^{\text{inh}} \in \{0, 1\}$ with

$$\text{prob}\{w_{ij}^{\text{inh}} = 1\} = \lambda_{\text{inh}}/N \qquad \text{i.i.d.} \tag{8.42}$$

The parameters λ_{exc} and λ_{inh} describe the divergence or convergence of excitatory and inhibitory projections, respectively.

Let us assume that a neuron is activated if the difference between excitatory and inhibitory input exceeds its firing threshold ϑ. The dynamics is thus given by

$$S_i(t_n) = \Theta\left[\sum_{j=1}^{N} w_{ij}^{\text{exc}} S_j(t_{n-1}) - \sum_{j=1}^{N} w_{ij}^{\text{inh}} S_j(t_{n-1}) - \vartheta \right]. \tag{8.43}$$

As in the previous section we can calculate the mean-field activity in cycle $n + 1$ as a function of the activity in the previous cycle. We obtain

$$a_{n+1} = \sum_{k=\vartheta}^{N} \sum_{l=0}^{k-\vartheta} \frac{a_n^{k+l} \lambda_{\text{exc}}^k \lambda_{\text{inh}}^l}{k!\, l!} e^{-a_n (\lambda_{\text{exc}} + \lambda_{\text{inh}})}. \tag{8.44}$$

The mean-field approximation is valid for sparse networks, i.e., if $\lambda_{\text{exc}} \ll N$ and $\lambda_{\text{inh}} \ll N$.

As compared to the situation with purely excitatory feedback Eq. (8.44) does not produce new modes of behavior. The only difference is that a_{n+1} is no longer a monotonous function of a_n; cf. Fig. 8.13.

8.3.3 Microscopic dynamics

As it is already apparent from the examples shown in Figs. 8.12 and 8.13 the irregularity of the spike trains produced by different reverberating loops can be

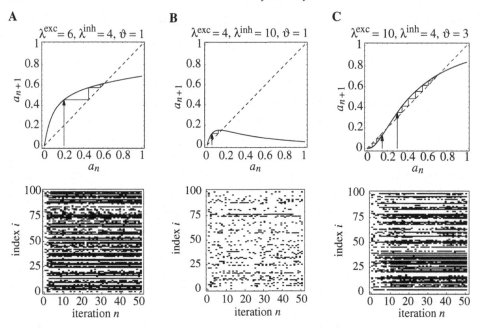

Fig. 8.13. Dynamics of a reverberating loop with excitatory and inhibitory projections (similar plots as in Fig. 8.12). **A.** $\lambda_{\mathrm{exc}} = 6$, $\lambda_{\mathrm{inh}} = 4$, $\vartheta = 1$: stable fixed point at $a_n \approx 0.6$. **B.** $\lambda_{\mathrm{exc}} = 4$, $\lambda_{\mathrm{inh}} = 10$, $\vartheta = 1$: stable fixed point at $a_n \approx 0.15$. **C.** $\lambda_{\mathrm{exc}} = 10$, $\lambda_{\mathrm{inh}} = 4$, $\vartheta = 3$: bistability between $a_n = 0$ and $a_n \approx 0.73$. Note the high level of irregularity in the raster diagrams. Although the mean field dynamics is characterized by a simple fixed point the corresponding limit cycle of the microscopic dynamics can have an extremely long period.

quite different. Numerical experiments show that in the case of purely excitatory projections fixed points of the mean field dynamics almost always correspond to a fixed point of the microscopic dynamics, or at least to a limit cycle with short period. As soon as inhibitory projections are introduced this situation changes dramatically. Fixed points in the mean field dynamics still correspond to limit cycles in the microscopic dynamics; the length of the periods, however, is substantially larger and grows rapidly with the network size; cf. Fig. 8.14 (Kirkpatrick and Sherrington, 1978; Nützel, 1991). The long limit cycles induce irregular spike trains that are reminiscent of those found in the asynchronous firing state of randomly connected integrate-and-fire network; cf. Section 6.4.3.

With respect to potential applications it is particularly interesting to see how information about the initial firing pattern is preserved in the sequence of patterns generated by the reverberating network. Figure 8.15A shows numerical results for the amount of information that is left after n iterations. At $t = 0$ firing is triggered in a subset of neurons. After n iterations, the patterns of active neurons

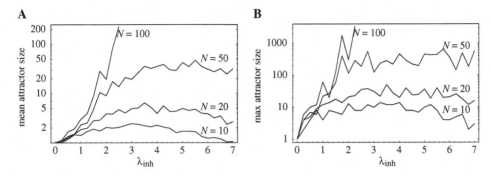

Fig. 8.14. Attractor length as a function of the inhibitory projection density λ_{inh} and the network size $N = 10, 20, 50, 100$. **A.** Length of the attractor averaged over 100 realizations of the coupling matrices and the initial pattern. The density of excitatory projections is kept constant at $\lambda_{exc} = 3$; the firing threshold is $\vartheta = 1$. The dynamics is given by Eq. (8.43). **B.** Maximal length of the attractor of 100 randomly chosen realizations of coupling matrices and initial patterns. Comparison of A and B shows that there is a large variability in the actual attractor length.

may be completely different. The measure I_n/I_0 is the normalized transinformation between the initial pattern and the pattern after n iterations. $I_n/I_0 = 1$ means that the initial pattern can be completely reconstructed from the activity pattern at iteration n; $I_n/I_0 = 0$ means that all the information is lost.

Once the state of the network has reached a limit cycle it will stay there forever due to the purely deterministic dynamics given by Eq. (8.36) or Eq. (8.43). In reality, however, the presence of noise leads to mixing in the phase space so that the information about the initial state will finally be lost. There are several sources of noise in a biological network – the most prominent are uncorrelated "noisy" synaptic inputs from other neurons and synaptic noise caused by synaptic transmission failures.

Figure 8.15B shows the amount of information about the initial pattern that is left after n iterations in the presence of synaptic noise in a small network with $N = 16$ neurons. As expected, unreliable synapses lead to a faster decay of the initial information. A failure probability of 5% already leads to a significantly reduced capacity. Nevertheless, a failure rate of 5% leaves after five iterations more than 10% of the information about the initial pattern; cf. Fig. 8.15B. This means that ten neurons are enough to discern two different events half a second – given a 10 Hz oscillation – after they actually occurred. Note that this is a form of "dynamic short-term memory" that does not require any form of synaptic plasticity. Information about the past is implicitly stored in the neuronal activity pattern. Superordinated neurons can use this information to react with a certain temporal relation to external events (Billock, 1997; Kistler et al., 2000; Kistler and De Zeeuw, 2002).

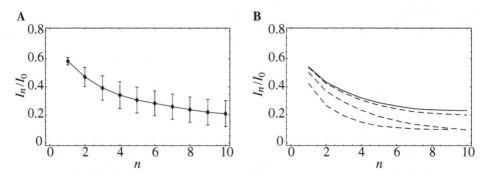

Fig. 8.15. **A**. Preservation of information about the initial firing pattern in a reverberating loop with $N = 16$. The transinformation $I(S_0, S_n)$ between the initial pattern and the pattern after n iterations is normalized by the maximum $I(S_0, S_0)$. Error bars give the standard deviation of ten different realizations of the coupling matrices ($\lambda_{exc} = 5$, $\lambda_{inh} = 5$, $\vartheta = 1$; cf. Eq. (8.43)). **B**. Similar plots as in A but with synaptic noise. The solid line is the noise-free reference ($N = 16$, $p_{fail} = 0$), the dashed lines correspond to $p_{fail} = 0.001$, $p_{fail} = 0.01$, and $p_{fail} = 0.05$ (from top to bottom).

Quantifying the information content (*)

Information theory (Shannon, 1948; Ash, 1990; Cover and Thomas, 1991) provides us with valuable tools to quantify the amount of "uncertainty" contained in a random variable and the amount of "information" that can be gained by measuring such a variable. Consider a random variable X that takes values x_i with probability $p(x_i)$. The entropy $H(X)$,

$$H(X) = -\sum_i p(x_i) \log_2 p(x_i), \qquad (8.45)$$

is a measure for the "uncertainty" of the outcome of the corresponding random experiment. If X takes only a single value x_1 with $p(x_1) = 1$ then the "uncertainty" $H(X)$ is zero since $\log_2 1 = 0$. On the other hand, if X takes two different values x_1 and x_2 with equal probability $p(x_{1,2}) = 0.5$ (e.g., tossing a coin) then the entropy $H(X)$ yields unity ("one bit").

If we have two random variables X and Y with joint probability $p(x_i, y_j)$ then we can define the conditioned entropy $H(Y|X)$ that gives the (remaining) uncertainty for Y given X,

$$H(Y|X) = -\sum_i \sum_j p(x_i, y_j) \log_2 \frac{p(x_i, y_j)}{p(x_j)}. \qquad (8.46)$$

For example, if Y gives the number of eyes obtained by throwing a dice while X is 0 if this number is odd and 1 if it is even, then the conditioned entropy yields $H(Y|X) \approx 1.58$ which is just 1 (bit) less than the full uncertainty of the dice experiment, $H(Y) \approx 2.58$. The difference between the full uncertainty and the conditioned uncertainty is the amount of information that we have "gained" through the observation of one of the variables. It is thus natural to define the transinformation $I(X, Y)$ between the random variables X and Y as

$$I(X, Y) = H(X) - H(X|Y). \tag{8.47}$$

Note that $I(X, Y)$ is symmetric, i.e., $I(X, Y) = I(Y, X)$.

In order to produce Fig. 8.15 we have generated random initial patterns S_0 together with the result of the iteration, S_n, and incremented the corresponding counters in a large ($2^{16} \times 2^{16}$) table so as to estimate the joint probability distribution of S_0 and S_n. Application of Eqs. (8.45)–(8.47) yields Fig. 8.15.

8.4 Summary

A linear stability analysis based on the population equations reveals that the asynchronous state in a homogeneous network of spiking neurons is unstable for low levels of noise. The asynchronous state is particularly vulnerable to oscillatory perturbations at the averaged firing frequency of the neurons or at harmonics thereof, which is a consequence of the tendency of the neurons to synchronize spontaneously. The axonal transmission delay plays an important role for the build-up of oscillations. However, asynchronous firing can be stabilized by a suitable choice of time constants and transmission delay if the noise level is sufficiently high.

The stability of perfectly synchronized oscillation is clarified by the Locking Theorem: a synchronous oscillation is stable if the spikes are triggered during the rising phase of the input potential which is the summed contribution of all presynaptic neurons. Stable synchronous oscillations can occur for a wide range of parameters and both for excitatory and inhibitory couplings.

Especially for short transmission delays in an excitatory network with pronounced refractory behavior, the fully synchronized state where all neurons are firing in "lock-step" is unstable. This, however, does not mean that the network switches into the asynchronous state, which may be unstable as well. Instead, the population of neurons splits up in several subgroups ("cluster") of neurons that fire alternatingly in a regular manner. Neurons within the same cluster stay synchronized over long times.

A replacement of the all-to-all connectivity by sparse random couplings can result in a network that generates highly irregular spike trains even without any additional source of noise. Neurons do not fire at every oscillation cycle, but *if* spike firing occurs it does so in phase with the global oscillation. The irregularity in the spike trains is due to the "frozen noise" of the connectivity and therefore purely deterministic. Restarting the population with the same initial condition thus leads to the very same sequence of spike patterns. Information on the initial condition is preserved in the spike patterns over several cycles even in the presence of synaptic transmission failures which suggests interesting applications for short-term memory and timing tasks.

Literature

Synchronization phenomena in pulse-coupled units have previously been studied in a nonneuronal context, such as the synchronous flashing of tropical fireflies (Buck and Buck, 1976), which triggered a whole series of theoretical papers on the synchronization of pulse-coupled oscillators. The most important one is probably the famous work of Mirollo and Strogatz (1990). Oscillations in the visual system and the role of synchrony for feature binding has been reviewed by Singer (1994) and Singer and Gray (1995). Oscillations in sensory systems have been reviewed by Ritz and Sejnowski (1997) and, specifically in the context of the olfactory system, by Laurent (1996), and the hippocampus by O'Keefe (1993).

9

Spatially structured networks

So far the discussion of network behavior in Chapters 6–8 has been restricted to *homogeneous* populations of neurons. In this chapter we turn to networks that have a spatial structure. In doing so we emphasize two characteristic features of the cerebral cortex, namely the high density of neurons and its virtually two-dimensional architecture.

Each cubic millimeter of cortical tissue contains about 10^5 neurons. This impressive number suggests that a description of neuronal dynamics in terms of an averaged *population activity* is more appropriate than a description at the single-neuron level. Furthermore, the cerebral cortex is huge. More precisely, the unfolded cerebral cortex of humans covers a surface of 2200–2400 cm^2, but its thickness amounts on average to only 2.5–3.0 mm^2. If we do not look too closely, the cerebral cortex can hence be treated as a continuous two-dimensional sheet of neurons. Neurons will no longer be labeled by discrete indices but by continuous variables that give their spatial position on the sheet. The coupling of two neurons i and j is replaced by the *average* coupling strength between neurons at position x and those at position y, or, even more radically simplified, by the average coupling strength of two neurons being separated by the distance $|x - y|$. Similar to the notion of an average coupling strength, we will also introduce the *average activity* of neurons located at position x and describe the dynamics of the network in terms of these averaged quantities only. The details of how these average quantities are defined are fairly involved and often disputable. In Section 9.1 we will – without a formal justification – introduce field equations for the spatial activity $A(x, t)$ in a spatially extended but otherwise homogeneous population of neurons. These field equations are particularly interesting because they have solutions in the form of complex stationary patterns of activity, traveling waves, and rotating spirals – a phenomenology that is closely related to pattern formation in certain nonlinear systems that are collectively termed *excitable media*. Some examples of these solutions are discussed in Section 9.1. In Section 9.2 we generalize the formalism so as to account for several distinct neuronal populations, such as those formed by excitatory and inhibitory neurons. The rest of this chapter is dedicated to models that describe neuronal activity in terms of individual action potentials. The propagation of spikes through a locally connected network of Spike Response Model (SRM) neurons is considered in Section 9.3. The last section, finally, deals with the transmission of a sharp pulse packet of action potentials in a layered feed-forward structure. It turns out that there is a stable wave form of the packet so that temporal information can be faithfully transmitted through several brain areas despite the presence of noise.

9.1 Stationary patterns of neuronal activity

We start with a generic example of pattern formation in a neural network with "Mexican-hat"-shaped lateral coupling, i.e., local excitation and long-range inhibition. In order to keep the notation as simple as possible, we will use the field equation derived in Chapter 6; cf. Eq. (6.129). As we have seen in Fig. 6.8, this equation neglects rapid transients and oscillations that could be captured by the full integral equations. On the other hand, in the limit of high noise and short refractoriness the approximation of population dynamics by differential equations is good; cf. Chapter 7. Exact solutions in the low-noise limit will be discussed in Section 9.3.

Consider a single sheet of densely packed neurons. We assume that all neurons are alike and that the connectivity is homogeneous and isotropic, i.e., that the coupling strength of two neurons is a function of their distance only. We loosely define a quantity $u(x, t)$ as the average membrane potential of the group of neurons located at position x at time t. We have seen in Chapter 6 that in the stationary state the "activity" of a population of neurons is strictly given by the single-neuron gain function $A_0(x) = g[u_0(x)]$; cf. Fig. 9.1. If we *assume* that changes of the input potential are slow enough so that the population always remains in a state of incoherent firing, then we can set

$$A(x, t) = g[u(x, t)],\qquad(9.1)$$

even for time-dependent situations. According to Eq. (9.1), the activity $A(x, t)$ of the population around location x is a function of the potential at that location.

The synaptic input current to a given neuron depends on the level of activity of its presynaptic neurons and on the strength of the synaptic couplings. We assume that the amplitude of the input current is simply the presynaptic activity scaled by the average coupling strength of these neurons. The total input current $I^{\text{syn}}(x, t)$ to

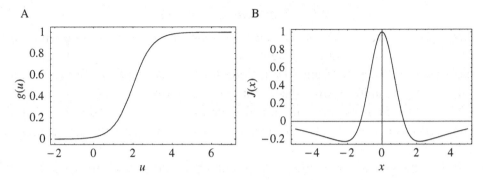

Fig. 9.1. **A.** Generic form of the sigmoidal gain function g of graded response neurons that describes the relationship between the potential u and the "activity" of the neural population. **B.** Typical "Mexican-hat"-shaped function that is used here as an ansatz for the coupling w of two neurons as a function of their distance x.

a neuron at position x is therefore

$$I^{\text{syn}}(x, t) = \int \mathrm{d}y \; w \,(|x - y|) \, A(y, t) . \tag{9.2}$$

Here, w is the average coupling strength of two neurons as a function of their distance. We consider a connectivity pattern that is excitatory for proximal neurons and predominantly inhibitory for distal neurons. Figure 9.1B shows the typical "Mexican-hat shape: of the corresponding coupling function. Equation (9.2) assumes that synaptic interaction is instantaneous. In a more detailed model we could include the axonal transmission delay and synaptic time constants. In that case, $A(y, t)$ on the right-hand side of Eq. (9.2), should be replaced by $\int \alpha(s) \, A(y, t - s) \, \mathrm{d}s$ where $\alpha(s)$ is the temporal interaction kernel.

In order to complete the definition of the model, we need to specify a relationship between the input current and the resulting membrane potential. In order to keep things simple we treat each neuron as a leaky integrator. The input potential is thus given by a differential equation of the form

$$\tau \, \frac{\partial u}{\partial t} = -u + I^{\text{syn}} + I^{\text{ext}} , \tag{9.3}$$

with τ being the time constant of the integrator and I^{ext} an additional external input. If we put things together we obtain the field equation

$$\tau \, \frac{\partial u(x, t)}{\partial t} = -u(x, t) + \int \mathrm{d}y \; w \,(|x - y|) \, g[u(y, t)] + I^{\text{ext}}(x, t) ; \tag{9.4}$$

cf. Wilson and Cowan (1973); Feldman and Cowan (1975); Amari (1977b); Kishimoto and Amari (1979). This is a nonlinear integro-differential equation for the average membrane potential $u(x, t)$.

9.1.1 Homogeneous solutions

Although we have kept the above model as simple as possible, the field equation (9.4) is complicated enough to prevent comprehensive analytical treatment. We therefore start our investigation by looking for a special type of solution, i.e., a solution that is uniform over space, but not necessarily constant over time. We call this the homogeneous solution and write $u(x, t) \equiv u(t)$. We expect that a homogeneous solution exists if the external input is homogeneous as well, i.e., if $I^{\text{ext}}(x, t) \equiv I^{\text{ext}}(t)$.

Substitution of the ansatz $u(x, t) \equiv u(t)$ into Eq. (9.4) yields

$$\tau \frac{du(t)}{dt} = -u(t) + \bar{w}\, g[u(t)] + I^{\text{ext}}(t) , \tag{9.5}$$

with $\bar{w} = \int dy\, w\, (|y|)$. This is a nonlinear ordinary differential equation for the average membrane potential $u(t)$. We note that the equation for the homogeneous solution is identical to that of a single population without spatial structure; cf. Eq. (6.87) in Chapter 6.3.

The fixed points of the above equation with $I^{\text{ext}} = 0$ are of particular interest because they correspond to a resting state of the network. More generally, we search for stationary solutions for a given constant external input $I^{\text{ext}}(x, t) \equiv I^{\text{ext}}$. The fixed points of Eq. (9.5) are solutions of

$$g(u) = \frac{u - I^{\text{ext}}}{\bar{w}} , \tag{9.6}$$

which is represented graphically in Fig. 9.2. Depending on the strength of the external input three qualitatively different situations can be observed. For low external stimulation there is a single fixed point at a very low level of neuronal activity. This corresponds to a quiescent state where the activity of the whole network has ceased. Large stimulation results in a fixed point at an almost saturated level of activity, which corresponds to a state where all neurons are firing at their maximum rate. Intermediate values of external stimulation, however, may result in a situation with more than one fixed point. Depending on the shape of the output function and the mean synaptic coupling strength $\bar{w}$, three fixed points may appear. Two of them correspond to the quiescent and the highly activated state, respectively, which are separated by the third fixed point at an intermediate level of activity.

Any potential physical relevance of fixed points clearly depends on their stability. Stability under the dynamics defined by the ordinary differential equation Eq. (9.5) is readily checked using standard analysis. Stability requires that at the intersection

$$g'(u) < \bar{w}^{-1} . \tag{9.7}$$

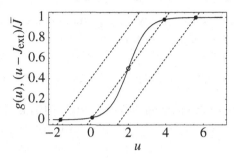

Fig. 9.2. Graphical representation of the fixed-point equation (9.6). The solid line corresponds to the neuronal gain function $g(u)$ and the dashed lines to $(u - I^{\text{ext}})/\bar{w}$ for different amounts of external stimulation I^{ext}. Depending on the amount of I^{ext} there is either a stable fixed point at low activity (leftmost black dot), a stable fixed point at high activity (rightmost black dot), or a bistable situation with stable fixed points (black dots on center line) separated by an unstable fixed point at intermediate level of activity (small circle).

Thus all fixed points corresponding to quiescent or highly activated states are stable whereas the middle fixed point in the case of multiple solutions is unstable; cf. Fig. 9.2. This, however, is only half of the truth because Eq. (9.5) only describes homogeneous solutions. Therefore, it may well be that the solutions are stable with respect to Eq. (9.5), but unstable with respect to *inhomogeneous* perturbations, i.e., to perturbations that do not have the same amplitude everywhere in the net.

9.1.2 Stability of homogeneous states

In the following we will perform a linear stability analysis of the homogeneous solutions found in the previous section. To this end we study the field equation (9.4) and consider small perturbations about the homogeneous solution. A linearization of the field equation will lead to a linear differential equation for the amplitude of the perturbation. The homogeneous solution is said to be stable if the amplitude of every small perturbation is *decreasing* whatever its shape.

Suppose $u(x, t) \equiv u_0$ is a homogeneous solution of Eq. (9.4), i.e.,

$$0 = -u_0 + \int dy \, w \, (|x - y|) \, g[u_0] + I^{\text{ext}}. \tag{9.8}$$

Consider a small perturbation $\delta u(x, t)$ with initial amplitude $|\delta u(x, 0)| \ll 1$. We substitute $u(x, t) = u_0 + \delta u(x, t)$ in Eq. (9.4) and linearize with respect to δu,

$$\tau \frac{\partial}{\partial t} \delta u(x, t) = -u_0 - \delta u(x, t)$$
$$+ \int dy \, w(|x - y|) \, [g(u_0) + g'(u_0) \, \delta u(y, t)] + I^{\text{ext}}(x, t) + \mathcal{O}(\delta u^2). \tag{9.9}$$

Here, a prime denotes the derivative with respect to the argument. Zero-order terms cancel each other because of Eq. (9.8). If we collect all terms linear in δu we find

$$\tau \frac{\partial}{\partial t} \delta u(x, t) = -\delta u(x, t) + g'(u_0) \int dy \, w(|x - y|) \, \delta u(y, t). \tag{9.10}$$

We make two important observations. Firstly, Eq. (9.10) is *linear* in the perturbations δu – simply because we have neglected terms of order $(\delta u)^n$ with $n \geq 2$. Secondly, the coupling between neurons at locations x and y is mediated by the coupling kernel $w(|x - y|)$ that depends only on the distance $|x - y|$. If we apply a Fourier transform over the spatial coordinates, the convolution integral turns into a simple multiplication. It suffices therefore to discuss a single (spatial) Fourier component of $\delta u(x, t)$. Any specific initial form of $\delta u(x, 0)$ can be created from its Fourier components by virtue of the superposition principle. We can therefore proceed without loss of generality by considering a single Fourier component, viz., $\delta u(x, t) = c(t) \, e^{ikx}$. If we substitute this ansatz in Eq. (9.10) we obtain

$$\tau \, c'(t) = -c(t) \left[1 - g'(u_0) \int dy \, w(|x - y|) \, e^{ik(y-x)} \right]$$

$$= -c(t) \left[1 - g'(u_0) \int dz \, w(|z|) \, e^{ikz} \right], \tag{9.11}$$

which is a *linear* differential equation for the amplitude c of a perturbation with wave number k. This equation is solved by

$$c(t) = c(0) \, e^{-\kappa(k) t}, \tag{9.12}$$

with

$$\kappa(k) = 1 - g'(u_0) \int dz \, w(|z|) \, e^{ikz}. \tag{9.13}$$

Stability of the solution u_0 with respect to a perturbation with wave number k depends on the sign of the real part of $\kappa(k)$. Note that – quite intuitively – only two quantities enter this expression, namely the slope of the activation function evaluated at u_0 and the Fourier transform of the coupling function w evaluated at k. If the real part of the Fourier transform of w stays below $1/g'(u_0)$, then u_0 is stable. Note that Eqs. (9.12) and (9.13) are valid for an arbitrary coupling function $w(|x - y|)$. In the following two examples we illustrate the typical behavior for two specific choices of the lateral coupling.

Example: purely excitatory coupling

We now apply Eq. (9.13) to a network with purely excitatory couplings. For the sake of simplicity we take a one-dimensional sheet of neurons and assume that the coupling function is bell-shaped, i.e.,

$$w(x) = \frac{\bar{w}}{\sqrt{2\pi\,\sigma^2}}\,e^{-x^2/(2\sigma^2)}, \tag{9.14}$$

with the mean strength $\int dx\, w(x) = \bar{w}$ and characteristic length scale σ. The Fourier transform of w is

$$\int dx\, w(x)\, e^{ikx} = \bar{w}\, e^{-k^2\sigma^2/2}, \tag{9.15}$$

with maximum $\bar{w}$ at $k = 0$. According to Eq. (9.13) a homogeneous solution u_0 is stable if $1 - \bar{w}\, g'(u_0) > 0$. This is precisely the result obtained by the simple stability analysis based on the *homogeneous* field equation; cf. Eq. (9.7). This result indicates that no particularly interesting phenomena will arise in networks with purely excitatory coupling.

Example: "Mexican-hat" coupling with zero mean

A more interesting example is provided by a combination of excitatory and inhibitory coupling described by the difference of two bell-shaped functions with different width. For the sake of simplicity we will again consider a one-dimensional sheet of neurons. For the lateral coupling we take

$$w(x) = \frac{\sigma_2\, e^{-x^2/(2\sigma_1^2)} - \sigma_1\, e^{-x^2/(2\sigma_2^2)}}{\sigma_2 - \sigma_1}, \tag{9.16}$$

with $\sigma_1 < \sigma_2$. The normalization of the coupling function has been chosen so that $w(0) = 1$ and $\int dx\, w(x) = \bar{w} = 0$; cf Fig. 9.3A.

As a first step we search for a homogeneous solution. If we substitute $u(x, t) = u(t)$ in Eq. (9.4) we find

$$\tau\frac{du(t)}{dt} = -u(t) + I^{\text{ext}}. \tag{9.17}$$

The term containing the integral drops out because of $\bar{w} = 0$. This differential equation has a single stable fixed point at $u_0 = I^{\text{ext}}$. This situation corresponds to the graphical solution of Fig. 9.2 with the dashed lines replaced by vertical lines ("infinite slope").

We still have to check the stability of the homogeneous solution $u(x, t) = u_0$ with respect to inhomogeneous perturbations. In the present case, the Fourier transform of w,

$$\int dx\, w(x)\, e^{ikx} = \frac{\sqrt{2\pi}\,\sigma_1\sigma_2}{\sigma_2 - \sigma_1}\left(e^{-k^2\sigma_1^2/2} - e^{-k^2\sigma_2^2/2}\right), \tag{9.18}$$

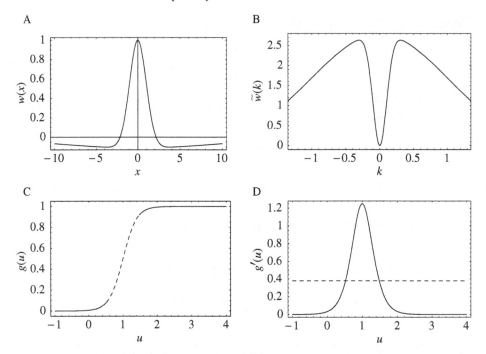

Fig. 9.3. **A**. Synaptic coupling function with zero mean as in Eq. (9.16) with $\sigma_1 = 1$ and $\sigma_2 = 10$. **B**. Fourier transform $\tilde{\omega}$ of the coupling function shown in A; cf. Eq. (9.18). **C**. Gain function $g(u) = \{1 + \exp[\beta(x - \theta)]\}^{-1}$ with $\beta = 5$ and $\theta = 1$. The dashing indicates that part of the graph where the slope exceeds the critical slope s^*. **D**. Derivative of the gain function shown in C (solid line) and critical slope s^* (dashed line).

vanishes at $k = 0$ and has its maxima at

$$k_m = \pm \left[\frac{2 \ln(\sigma_2^2/\sigma_1^2)}{\sigma_2^2 - \sigma_1^2} \right]^{1/2}. \qquad (9.19)$$

At the maximum, the amplitude of the Fourier transform has a value of

$$\hat{w}_m = \max_k \int dx\, w(x)\, e^{ikx} = \frac{\sqrt{2\pi}\,\sigma_1\,\sigma_2}{\sigma_2 - \sigma_1} \left[\left(\frac{\sigma_1^2}{\sigma_2^2} \right)^{\sigma_1^2/(\sigma_2^2 - \sigma_1^2)} - \left(\frac{\sigma_1^2}{\sigma_2^2} \right)^{\sigma_2^2/(\sigma_2^2 - \sigma_1^2)} \right], \qquad (9.20)$$

cf. Fig. 9.3B. We use this result in Eqs. (9.12) and (9.13) and conclude that stable homogeneous solutions can only be found for those parts of the graph of the output function $f(u)$ where the slope $s = g'(u)$ does not exceed the critical value $s^* = 1/\hat{w}_m$,

$$s^* = \frac{\sigma_2 - \sigma_1}{\sqrt{2\pi}\,\sigma_1\,\sigma_2} \left[\left(\frac{\sigma_1^2}{\sigma_2^2} \right)^{\sigma_1^2/(\sigma_2^2 - \sigma_1^2)} - \left(\frac{\sigma_1^2}{\sigma_2^2} \right)^{\sigma_2^2/(\sigma_2^2 - \sigma_1^2)} \right]^{-1}. \qquad (9.21)$$

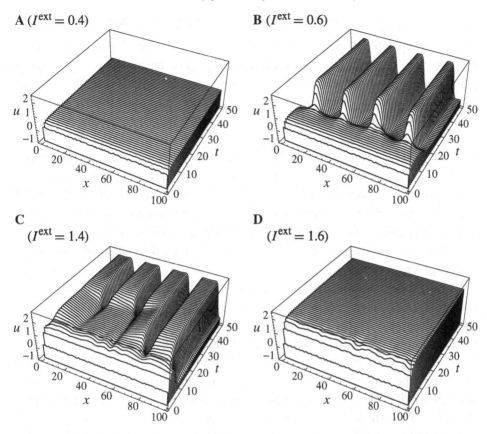

A ($I^{\text{ext}} = 0.4$)

B ($I^{\text{ext}} = 0.6$)

C ($I^{\text{ext}} = 1.4$)

D ($I^{\text{ext}} = 1.6$)

Fig. 9.4. Spontaneous pattern formation in a one-dimensional sheet of neurons with a "Mexican-hat" type of interaction and homogeneous external stimulation. The parameters for the coupling function and the output function are the same as in Fig. 9.3. The graphs show the evolution in time of the spatial distribution of the average membrane potential $u(x, t)$. **A**. For $I^{\text{ext}} = 0.4$ the homogeneous low-activity state is stable, but it loses stability at $I^{\text{ext}} = 0.6$ (**B**). Here, small initial fluctuations in the membrane potential grow exponentially and result in a global pattern of regions with high and low activity. **C**. Similar situation as in B, but with $I^{\text{ext}} = 1.4$. **D**. Finally, at $I^{\text{ext}} = 1.6$ the homogeneous high-activity mode is stable.

Figure Fig. 9.3 shows, that depending on the choice of coupling w and gain functions g a certain interval for the external input exists without a corresponding stable homogeneous solution. In this parameter domain a phenomenon called pattern formation can be observed: small fluctuations around the homogeneous state grow exponentially until a characteristic pattern of regions with low and high activity has developed; cf. Fig. 9.4.

9.1.3 "Blobs" of activity: inhomogeneous states

From a computational point of view, bistable systems are of particular interest because they can be used as "memory units". For example, a homogeneous population of neurons with all-to-all connections can exhibit bistable behavior where either all neurons are quiescent or all neurons are firing at their maximum rate. By switching between the inactive and the active state, the neuronal population would be able to represent, store, or retrieve one bit of information. The exciting question that arises now is whether a neuronal net with distance-dependent coupling $w(|x - y|)$ can store more than just a single bit of information, namely *spatial patterns* of activity. Sensory input, e.g., visual stimulation, could switch part of the network to its excited state whereas the unstimulated part would remain in its resting state. Due to bistability this pattern of activity could be preserved even if the stimulation is turned off again and thus provide a neuronal correlate of working memory.

Let us suppose we prepare the network in a state where neurons in one spatial domain are active and all remaining neurons are quiescent. Will the network stay in that configuration? In other words, we are looking for an "interesting" stationary solution $u(x)$ of the field equation Eq. (9.4). The borderline where quiescent and active domains of the network meet is obviously most critical to the function of the network as a memory device. To start with the simplest case with a single borderline, we consider a one-dimensional spatial pattern where the activity changes at $x = 0$ from the low-activity to the high-activity state. This pattern could be the result of inhomogeneous stimulation in the past, but since we are interested in a memory state we now assume that the external input is simply constant, i.e., $I^{\text{ext}}(x, t) = I^{\text{ext}}$. Substitution of the ansatz $u(x, t) = u(x)$ into the field equation yields

$$u(x) - I^{\text{ext}} = \int dy \; w(|x - y|) \, g[u(y)] \,. \tag{9.22}$$

This is a nonlinear integral equation for the unknown function $u(x)$.

We can find a particular solution of Eq. (9.22) if we replace the output function by a simple step function, e.g.,

$$g(u) = \begin{cases} 0, & u < \vartheta \\ 1, & u \geq \vartheta \,. \end{cases} \tag{9.23}$$

In this case $g[u(x)]$ is either zero or one and we can exploit translation invariance to define $g[u(x)] = 1$ for $x > 0$ and $g[u(x)] = 0$ for $x < 0$ without loss of generality. The right-hand side of Eq. (9.22) now no longer depends on u and we find

$$u(x) = I^{\text{ext}} + \int_{-\infty}^{x} dz \, w(|z|) \,, \tag{9.24}$$

and in particular

$$u(0) = I^{\text{ext}} + \frac{1}{2} \bar{w} \,. \tag{9.25}$$

with $\bar{w} = \int dy \, w(|y|)$. We have calculated this solution under the assumption that $g[u(x)] = 1$ for $x > 0$ and $g[u(x)] = 0$ for $x < 0$. This assumption imposes a self-consistency condition on the solution, namely that the membrane potential reaches the threshold ϑ at $x = 0$. A solution in the form of a stationary border between quiescent and active neurons can therefore only be found if

$$I^{\text{ext}} = \vartheta - \frac{1}{2} \bar{w} \,. \tag{9.26}$$

If the external stimulation is either smaller or greater than this critical value, then the border will propagate to the right or to the left.

Following the same line of reasoning, we can also look for a localized "blob" of activity. Assuming that $g[u(x)] = 1$ for $x \in [x_1, x_2]$ and $g[u(x)] = 0$ outside this interval leads to a self-consistency condition of the form

$$I^{\text{ext}} = \vartheta - \int_0^{\Delta} dx \, w(x) \,, \tag{9.27}$$

with $\Delta = x_2 - x_1$. The mathematical arguments are qualitatively the same if we replace the step function by a more realistic smooth gain function.

Figure 9.5 shows that solutions in the form of sharply localized excitations exist for a broad range of external stimulations. A simple argument also shows that the width Δ of the blob is stable if $w(\Delta) < 0$ (Amari, 1977a). In this case blobs of activity can be induced without the need of fine tuning the parameters in order to fulfill the self-consistency condition, because the width of the blob will adjust itself until stationarity is reached and Eq. (9.27) holds; cf. Fig. 9.5A.

Example: an application to orientation selectivity in the primary visual cortex

Stable localized blobs of activity may not only be related to memory states but also to the processing of sensory information. A nice example is the model of Ben-Yishai et al. (1995) (see also Hansel and Sompolinsky 1998) that aims at a description of orientation selectivity in the visual cortex.

It is found experimentally that cells from the primary visual cortex (V1) respond preferentially to lines or bars that have a certain orientation within the visual field. There are neurons that "prefer" vertical bars, and others that respond maximally to bars with a different orientation (Hubel, 1995). Up to now the origin of this

A

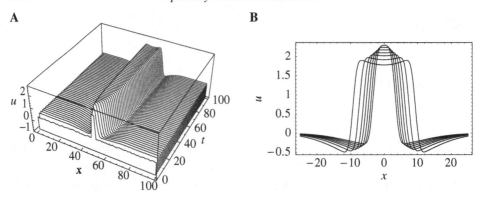

B

Fig. 9.5. Localized "blobs" of activity. **A**. A small initial perturbation develops into a stable blob of activity. **B**. Stationary profile of a localized excitation for various amounts of external stimulation ($I^{\text{ext}} = 0, 0.5, \ldots, 0.3$ in order of increasing width). Note that for strong stimuli neurons in the center of the activity blob are less active than those close to the edge of the blob.

orientation selectivity has remained controversial. It may be the result of the wiring of the input to the visual cortex, i.e., the wiring of the projections from the lateral geniculate nucleus (LGN) to V1, or it may result from intracortical connections, i.e., from the wiring of the neurons within V1, or both. Here we will investigate the extent to which intracortical projections can contribute to orientation selectivity.

We consider a network of neurons forming a so-called hypercolumn. These are neurons with receptive fields that correspond to roughly the same zone in the visual field but with different preferred orientations. The orientation of a bar at a given position within the visual field can thus be coded faithfully by the population activity of the neurons from the corresponding hypercolumn.

Instead of using spatial coordinates to identify a neuron in the cortex, we label the neurons in this section by their preferred orientation θ, which may vary from $-\pi/2$ to $+\pi/2$. In doing so we assume that the preferred orientation is indeed a good "name tag" for each neuron so that the synaptic coupling strength can be given in terms of the preferred orientations of pre- and postsynaptic neurons. Following the formalism developed in the previous sections, we assume that the synaptic coupling strength w of neurons with preferred orientation θ and θ' is a symmetrical function of the difference $\theta - \theta'$, i.e., $w = w(|\theta - \theta'|)$. Since we are dealing with angles from $[-\pi/2, +\pi/2]$ it is natural to assume that all functions are π-periodic, so we can use Fourier series to characterize them. Nontrivial results are obtained even if we retain only the first two Fourier components of the coupling function,

$$w(\theta - \theta') = w_0 + w_2 \cos[2(\theta - \theta')].$$ (9.28)

Similar to the intracortical projections we take the (stationary) external input from the LGN as a function of the difference of the preferred orientation θ and the orientation of the stimulus θ_0,

$$I^{\text{ext}}(\theta) = c_0 + c_2 \cos[2(\theta - \theta_0)] . \tag{9.29}$$

Here, c_0 is the mean of the input and c_2 describes the modulation of the input that arises from anisotropies in the projections from the LGN to V1.

In analogy to Eq. (9.4) the field equation for the present setup has thus the form

$$\tau \frac{\partial u(\theta, t)}{\partial t} = -u(\theta, t) + \int_{-\pi/2}^{+\pi/2} \frac{d\theta'}{\pi} w(|\theta - \theta'|) g[u(\theta', t)] + I^{\text{ext}}(\theta) . \tag{9.30}$$

We are interested in the distribution of the neuronal activity within the hyper-column as it arises from a stationary external stimulus with orientation θ_0. This will allow us to study the role of intracortical projections in sharpening orientation selectivity.

In order to obtain conclusive results we have to specify the form of the gain function g. A particularly simple case is the step-linear function,

$$g(u) = [u]_+ \equiv \begin{cases} u , & u \geq 0 \\ 0 , & u < 0 . \end{cases} \tag{9.31}$$

The idea behind this ansatz is that neuronal firing usually increases monotonously once the input exceeds a certain threshold. Within certain boundaries this increase in the firing rate is approximately linear. If we assume that the average membrane potential u stays within these boundaries and that, in addition, $u(\theta, t)$ is always above threshold, then we can replace the gain function g in Eq. (9.30) by the identity function. We are thus left with the following *linear* equation for the stationary distribution of the average membrane potential,

$$u(\theta) = \int_{-\pi/2}^{+\pi/2} \frac{d\theta'}{\pi} w(|\theta - \theta'|) u(\theta') + I^{\text{ext}}(\theta) . \tag{9.32}$$

This equation is solved by

$$u(\theta) = u_0 + u_2 \cos[2(\theta - \theta_0)] , \tag{9.33}$$

with

$$u_0 = \frac{c_0}{1 - w_0} \quad \text{and} \quad u_2 = \frac{2 c_2}{2 - w_2} . \tag{9.34}$$

As a result of the intracortical projections, the modulation u_2 of the response of the neurons from the hypercolumn is thus amplified by a factor $2/(2 - w_2)$ as compared to the modulation of the input c_2.

A

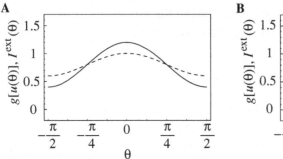

B

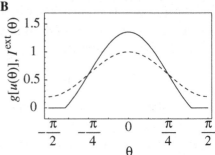

Fig. 9.6. Activity profiles (solid line) that result from stationary external stimulation (dashed line) in a model of orientation selectivity. **A**. Weak modulation ($c_0 = 0.8$, $c_2 = 0.2$) of the external input results in a broad activity profile; cf. Eq. (9.32). **B**. Strong modulation ($c_0 = 0.6$, $c_2 = 0.4$) produces a narrow profile; cf. Eq. (9.35). Other parameters are $\omega_0 = 0$, $\omega_2 = 1$, $\theta_0 = 0$.

In deriving Eq. (9.32) we have assumed that u always stays above threshold so that we have an additional condition, viz., $u_0 - |u_2| > 0$, in order to obtain a self-consistent solution. This condition may be violated depending on the stimulus. In that case the above solution is no longer valid and we have to take the nonlinearity of the gain function into account, i.e., we have to replace Eq. (9.32) by

$$u(\theta) = \int_{\theta_0-\theta_c}^{\theta_0+\theta_c} \frac{d\theta'}{\pi} \, w(|\theta - \theta'|) \, u(\theta') + I^{\text{ext}}(\theta) \,. \tag{9.35}$$

Here, $\theta_0 \pm \theta_c$ are the cutoff angles that define the interval where $u(\theta)$ is positive. If we insert Eq. (9.33) in the above equation, we obtain together with $u(\theta_0 \pm \theta_c) = 0$ a set of equations that can be solved for u_0, u_2, and θ_c. Figure 9.6 shows two examples of the resulting activity profiles $g[u(\theta)]$ for different modulation depths of the input.

Throughout this section we have described neuronal populations in terms of an averaged membrane potential and the corresponding firing rate. At least for stationary input and a high level of noise this is indeed a good approximation of the dynamics of spiking neurons. Figure 9.7 shows two examples of a simulation based on SRM_0 neurons with escape noise and a network architecture that is equivalent to what we have used above. The stationary activity profiles shown in Fig. 9.7 are qualitatively identical to those of Fig. 9.6; small deviations in the shape are due to a slightly different model (see Spiridon and Gerstner (2001) for more details). For low levels of noise, however, the description in terms of a firing rate is no longer valid, because the state of asynchronous firing becomes unstable (cf. Section 8.1) and neurons tend to synchronize. The arising temporal structure in the firing times leads to a destabilization of the stationary spatial structure (Laing and Chow, 2001).

A

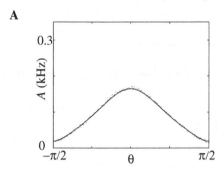

B

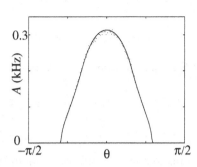

Fig. 9.7. Activity profiles in a model of orientation selectivity obtained by simulations based on SRM_0 neurons (dots) compared to the theoretical prediction (solid line). **A**. No modulation of the recurrent projections ($\omega_2 = 0$; cf. Eq. (9.28)) leads only to a weak modulation of the neuronal response. **B**. Excitatory coupling between iso-oriented cells ($\omega_2 = 10$) produces a sharp profile. (Taken from Spiridon and Gerstner (2001)).

In the low-noise limit localized "blobs" of activity are replaced by traveling waves of spike activity, as we will see in Section 9.3.

9.2 Dynamic patterns of neuronal activity

Up to now we have treated only a single sheet of neurons that were all of the same type. Excitatory and inhibitory couplings were lumped together in a single function w that gave the "average" coupling strength of two neurons as a function of their distance. "Real" neurons, however, are either excitatory *or* inhibitory, because they can use only one type of neurotransmitter (Dale's law). A coupling function that yields both positive and negative values for the synaptic couplings is therefore not realistic.

We can easily extend the previous model so as to account for different types of neuron or for several separate layers of neuronal tissue. To this end we embellish the variable u for the average membrane potential with an additional index k, $k = 1, \ldots, n$, that denotes the type of the neuron or its layer. Furthermore, we introduce coupling functions $w_{kl}(x, x')$ that describe the coupling strength of a neuron from layer l at position x' to a neuron located in layer k and position x. In analogy to Eq. (9.4) the field equations will be defined as

$$\tau_k \frac{\partial u_k(x, t)}{\partial t} = -u_k(x, t) + \sum_{l=1}^{n} \int dy\, w_{kl}(|x - y|)\, g[u_l(y, t)] + I^{\text{ext},k}(x, t),$$

$$(9.36)$$

with $k = 1, \ldots, n$. We will be particularly interested in systems made up of two different layers ($n = 2$) where layer 1 comprises all excitatory neurons and layer 2 all inhibitory neurons. Accordingly, the signs of the coupling functions are as follows

$$w_{11} \geq 0, \quad w_{21} \geq 0, \quad w_{12} \leq 0, \quad \text{and} \quad w_{22} \leq 0. \tag{9.37}$$

For the sake of simplicity we assume that all coupling functions are bell-shaped, e.g.,

$$w_{kl}(x) = \frac{\bar{w}_{kl}}{\sqrt{2\pi \sigma_{kl}^2}} \exp\left[-x^2/(2\sigma_{kl}^2)\right], \tag{9.38}$$

with mean coupling strength $\bar{w}_{kl}$ and spatial extension σ_{kl}.

9.2.1 Oscillations

As before, we start our analysis of the field equations by looking for homogeneous solutions. Substitution of $u_k(x, t) = u_k(t)$ into Eq. (9.36) yields

$$\tau_k \frac{du_k(t)}{dt} = -u_k(t) + \sum_{l=1}^{n} \bar{w}_{kl}\, g[u_l(t)] + I^{\text{ext},k}, \tag{9.39}$$

with $\bar{w}_{kl} = \int dx\, w_{kl}(|x|)$, as before.

We can gain an intuitive understanding of the underlying mechanism by means of phase plane analysis – a tool which we have already encountered in Chapter 3. Figure 9.8 shows the flow-field and nullclines of Eq. (9.39) with $\tau_1 = 1$, $\tau_2 = 5$, $\bar{w}_{11} = \bar{w}_{21} = 2$, $\bar{w}_{12} = -1$, and $\bar{w}_{22} = 0$. The gain function has a standard form, i.e., $g(u) = \{1 + \exp[\beta(u - \theta)]\}^{-1}$ with $\beta = 5$ and $\theta = 1$.

For zero external input Eq. (9.39) has only a single stable fixed point close to $(u_1, u_2) = (0, 0)$. This fixed point is attractive so that the system will return immediately to its resting position after a small perturbation; cf. Fig. 9.8A. If, for example, the external input to the excitatory layer is gradually increased, the behavior of the systems may change rather dramatically. Figure 9.8B shows that for $I^{\text{ext},1} = 0.3$ the system does not return immediately to its resting state after an initial perturbation but takes a large detour through phase space. In doing so, the activity of the network transiently increases before it finally settles down again at its resting point; cf. Fig. 9.8B. This behavior is qualitatively similar to the triggering of an action potential in a two-dimensional neuron model (cf. Chapter 3), though the interpretation in the present case is different. We will refer to this state of the network as an *excitable* state.

If the strength of the input is further increased the system undergoes a series of bifurcations so that the attractive $(0, 0)$ fixed point will finally be replaced by an unstable fixed point near $(1, 1)$ which is surrounded by a stable limit cycle; cf. Fig. 9.8C. This corresponds to an oscillatory state where excitatory and inhibitory neurons are activated alternatingly. Provided that the homogeneous solution is

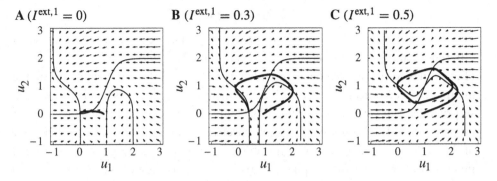

Fig. 9.8. Phase-space diagrams for homogeneous solutions of the field equation. The arrows indicate the flow-field of the differential equation (9.39), the thin lines are the nullclines for u_1 and u_2, and the thick lines, finally, give a sample trajectory with starting point $(u_1, u_2) = (0.9, 0)$. The existence and stability properties of the fixed points depend on the amount of external input to the layer of excitatory neurons ($I^{\text{ext},1}$). For $I^{\text{ext},1} < 0.35$ there is an attractive fixed point close to $(0, 0)$ (**A** and **B**). For $I^{\text{ext},1} = 0.5$ the fixed point at $(0, 0)$ is replaced by an unstable fixed point close to $(1, 1)$ which is surrounded by a stable limit cycle (**C**). In A the sample trajectory reaches the fixed point in the shortest possible way, but in B it takes a large detour which corresponds to a spike-like overshoot of neuronal activity.

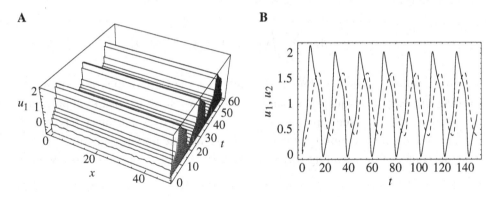

Fig. 9.9. Depending on the amount of external input homogeneous network oscillations can be observed. **A**. Average membrane potential $u_1(x, t)$ of the layer of excitatory neurons. **B**. Time course of the average membrane potential of the excitatory (solid line) and the inhibitory (dashed line) layer.

stable with respect to inhomogeneous perturbations, global network oscillations can be observed; cf. Fig. 9.9.

9.2.2 Traveling waves

Traveling waves are a well-known phenomenon and occur in a broad class of different systems that have collectively been termed *excitable media*. A large class of examples for these systems is provided by reaction-diffusion systems where the interplay of a chemical reaction with the diffusion of its reactants results in an often surprisingly rich variety of dynamical behavior. All these systems share a common property, namely "excitability". In the absence of an external input the behavior of the system is characterized by a stable fixed point, its resting state. Additional input, however, can evoke a spike-like rise in the activation of the system. Due to lateral interactions within the system such a pulse of activity can propagate through the medium without changing its form, and thus form a traveling wave.

In the previous section we have seen that the present system consisting of two separate layers of excitatory and inhibitory neurons can indeed exhibit an excitable state; cf. Fig. 9.8B. It is thus natural to look for a special solution of the field equations (9.36) in the form of a traveling wave. To this end we make an ansatz,

$$u_k(x, t) = \hat{u}_k(x - v t), \tag{9.40}$$

with an up to now unknown function $\hat{u}_k$ that describes the *form* of the traveling wave. We can substitute this ansatz into Eq. (9.36) and after a transformation into the moving frame of reference, i.e., with $z \equiv x - v t$, we find

$$-\tau_k v \frac{d\hat{u}_k(z)}{dz} = -\hat{u}_k(z) + \sum_{l=1}^{n} \int d\zeta \; w_{kl}(|z - \zeta|) \, g[\hat{u}_l(\zeta)] + I^{\text{ext},k} . \tag{9.41}$$

This is a nonlinear integro-differential equation for the form of the traveling wave. In order to obtain a uniquely determined solution we have to specify appropriate boundary conditions. Neurons cannot "feel" each other over a distance larger than the length scale of the coupling function. The average membrane potential far away from the center of the traveling wave will therefore remain at the low-activity fixed point $\bar{u}_k$, i.e.,

$$\lim_{z \to \pm\infty} \hat{u}_k(z) = \bar{u}_k , \tag{9.42}$$

with

$$0 = -\bar{u}_k + \sum_{l=1}^{n} \bar{w}_{kl} \, g[\bar{u}_l] + I^{\text{ext},k} . \tag{9.43}$$

This condition, however, still does not determine the solution uniquely because Eq. (9.41) is invariant with respect to translations. That is to say, with $\hat{u}_k(z)$ a solution of Eq. (9.41), $\hat{u}_k(z + \Delta z)$, is a solution as well for every $\Delta z \in \mathbb{R}$.

A   B

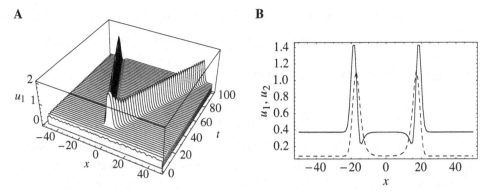

Fig. 9.10. Traveling wave in a network consisting of two separate layers for excitatory and inhibitory neurons. **A.** Average membrane potential of the excitatory neurons. An additional pulse of external input at $t = 10$ and $x = 0$ triggers two pulses of activity that propagate symmetrically to the left and to the right. **B.** Snapshot of the spatial distribution of the average membrane potential at time $t = 50$. The solid line corresponds to the excitatory neurons whereas the dashed line is for the inhibitory ones. Note that the activation of the inhibitory neurons is somewhat lagging behind.

Finding a solution of the integro-differential equation (9.41) analytically is obviously a hard problem unless a particularly simple form of the gain function g is employed. One possibility is to use a step function such as

$$g(u) = \begin{cases} 0, & u < \vartheta \\ 1, & u \geq \vartheta, \end{cases} \tag{9.44}$$

with $\vartheta \in \mathbb{R}$ being the threshold of the activation function. In this case we can use the translation invariance and look for solutions of Eq. (9.41) containing a single pulse of activation that exceeds threshold on a certain finite interval. Since $g(u_k)$ is equal to unity inside this interval and vanishes outside, the integral in Eq. (9.41) can be carried out and we are left with a system of ordinary differential equations. These differential equations are subject to boundary conditions at $z = \pm\infty$ (cf. Eq. (9.42)) and, for the sake of self-consistency, to $u_k(z) = \vartheta$ on the boundaries of the above-mentioned interval. In fact, this is too large a number of boundary conditions so as to find a solution in all cases. The differential equations together with its boundary conditions thus form an eigenvalue problem for the remaining parameters such as the propagation velocity, the width of the pulses of activity, and the time lag between the excitatory and the inhibitory pulse. We will not go further into details but refer the reader to the work of, e.g., Amari (1977a).

Figure 9.10 shows an example of a traveling wave in a network with excitatory (layer 1, $\tau_1 = 1$) and inhibitory (layer 2, $\tau_2 = 5$) neurons. The coupling functions are bell-shaped (cf. Eq. (9.38)) with $\sigma_{11} = \sigma_{12} = \sigma_{21} = 1$ and $\bar{w}_{11} = \bar{w}_{21} = 2,$

$\bar{w}_{12} = -1$, and $\bar{w}_{22} = 0$, as before. The excitatory neurons receive tonic input $I^{\text{ext},1} = 0.3$ in order to reach the excitable state (cf. Fig. 9.8B). A short pulse of additional excitatory input suffices to trigger a pair of pulses of activity that travel in opposite directions through the medium.

9.3 Patterns of spike activity

We have seen that the intricate interplay of excitation and inhibition in locally coupled neuronal nets can result in the formation of complex patterns of activity. Neurons have been described by a graded-response type formalism where the "firing rate" is given as a function of the "average membrane potential". This approach is clearly justified for a qualitative treatment of *slowly* varying neuronal activity. In the context of spatio-temporal patterns of neuronal activity, however, a slightly closer look is in order.

In the following we will dismiss the firing rate paradigm and use the Spike Response Model (SRM) instead in order to describe neuronal activity in terms of individual action potentials. We start with a large number of SRM neurons arranged on a two-dimensional grid. The synaptic coupling strength w of neurons located at r_i and r_j is, as hitherto, a function of their distance, i.e., $w = w(|r_i - r_j|)$. The response of a neuron to the firing of one of its presynaptic neurons is described by a response function ϵ and, finally, the afterpotential is given by a kernel named η, as customary. The membrane potential of a neuron located at r_i is thus

$$u(r_i, t) = \int_0^\infty ds\, \eta(s)\, S(r_i, t-s) + \sum_j w(|r_i - r_j|) \int_0^\infty ds\, \epsilon(s)\, S(r_j, t-s), \quad (9.45)$$

with $S(r_i, t) = \sum_f \delta(t - t_i^f)$ being the spike train of the neuron at r_i. Note that we have neglected distance-dependent propagation delays; constant (synaptic) delays, however, can be absorbed into the response function ϵ. Note also that for the sake of notational simplicity we have included the afterpotential of *all* spikes and not only the afterpotential of the last spike. This, however, will not affect the present discussion because we restrict ourselves to situations where each neuron is firing only once, or with long interspike intervals.

Spikes are triggered whenever the membrane potential reaches the firing threshold ϑ. This can be expressed in compact form as

$$S(r_i, t) = \delta[u(r_i, t) - \vartheta] \left[\frac{\partial u(r_i, t)}{\partial t} \right]_+ . \quad (9.46)$$

Here, $[\cdots]_+$ denotes the positive part of its argument. This factor is required in order to ensure that spikes are triggered only if the threshold is crossed with a positive slope and to normalize the Dirac δ functions to unity.

Figure 9.11 shows the result of a computer simulation of a network consisting of 1000×1000 SRM neurons. The coupling function is Mexican-hat shaped so that excitatory connections dominate small and inhibitory connections over large distances. In a certain parameter regime the network exhibits excitable behavior; cf. Section 9.2.2. Starting from a random initial configuration, a cloud of short stripes of neuronal activity evolves. These stripes propagate through the net and soon start to form rotating spirals with two, three or four arms. The spirals have slightly different rotation frequencies and in the end only a few large spirals with three arms will survive.

Let us try to gain an analytical understanding of some of the phenomena observed in the computer simulations. To this end we suppose that the coupling function w is slowly varying, i.e., that the distance between two neighboring neurons is small as compared to the characteristic length scale of w. In this case we can replace in Eq. (9.45) the sum over all presynaptic neurons by an integral over space. At the same time we drop the indices that label the neurons on the grid and replace both h and S by continuous functions of r and t that interpolate in a suitable way between the grid points for which they have been defined originally. This leads to field equations that describe the membrane potential $u(r, t)$ of neurons located at r,

$$u(r, t) = \int_0^\infty ds\, \eta(s)\, S(r, t - s) + \int dr'\, w(|r - r'|) \int_0^\infty ds\, \epsilon(s)\, S(r', t - s),$$
(9.47)

together with their spike activity $S(r, t)$,

$$S(r, t) = \delta[u(r, t) - \vartheta] \left[\frac{\partial u(r, t)}{\partial t} \right]_+,$$
(9.48)

as a function of time t. In the following sections we try to find particular solutions for this integral equation. In particular, we investigate solutions in the form of traveling fronts and waves. It turns out that the propagation velocity for fronts and the dispersion relation or waves can be calculated analytically; cf. Fig. 9.12. The stability of these solutions is determined in Section 9.3.2.

The approach sketched in Sections 9.3.1 and 9.3.2 (Kistler et al., 1998; Bressloff, 1999; Kistler, 2000) is presented for a network of a single population of neurons, but it can also be extended to coupled networks of excitatory and inhibitory neurons (Golomb and Ermentrout, 2001). In addition to the usual fast traveling waves that are found in purely excitatory networks, additional slow and noncontinuous "lurching" waves appear in an appropriate parameter regime (Rinzel et al., 1998; Golomb and Ermentrout, 2001).

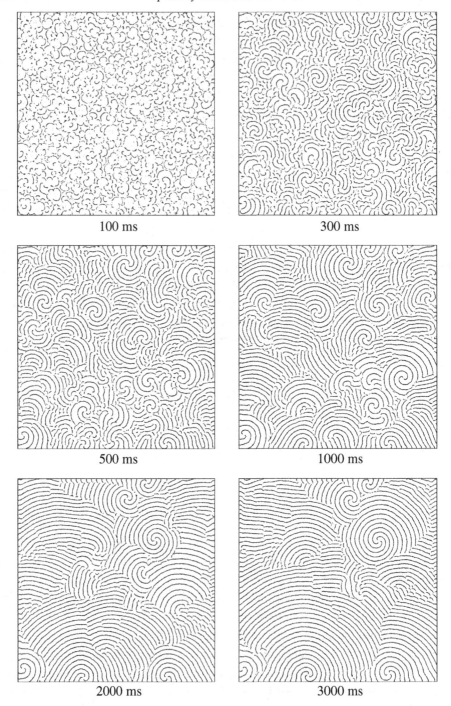

100 ms

300 ms

500 ms

1000 ms

2000 ms

3000 ms

Fig. 9.11. Snapshots from a simulation of a network of 1000×1000 neurons. (Taken from Kistler et al. (1998).)

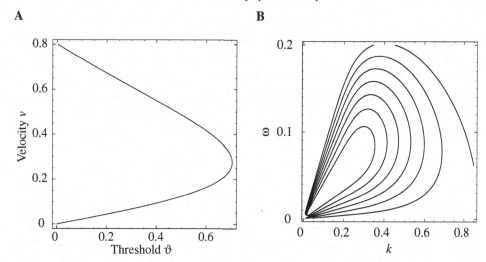

Fig. 9.12. **A.** Propagation velocity v of a single plane front versus the firing threshold ϑ. **B.** Dispersion relation of a traveling wave for different values of the firing threshold ($\vartheta = 0, 0.01, \ldots, 0.06$; $\vartheta = 0$ is the outermost curve, $\vartheta = 0.06$ corresponds to the curve in the center).

9.3.1 Traveling fronts and waves (*)

We start our analysis of the field equations (9.47) and (9.48) by looking for a particular solution in the form of a plane front of excitation in a two-dimensional network. To this end we make an ansatz for the spike activity

$$S(x, y, t) = \delta(t - x/v). \tag{9.49}$$

This is a plane front that extends from $y = -\infty$ to $y = +\infty$ and propagates in positive x-direction with velocity v. We substitute this ansatz into the expression for the membrane potential Eq. (9.47) and find

$$u(x, y, t) = \eta(t - x/v) + \iint \mathrm{d}x' \, \mathrm{d}y' \, w\left[\sqrt{(x - x')^2 + (y - y')^2}\right] \epsilon(t - x'/v). \tag{9.50}$$

Up to now the propagation velocity has been a free parameter. This parameter can be fixed by exploiting a self-consistency condition that states that the membrane potential along the wave front equals the firing threshold; cf. Eq. (9.48). This condition gives a relationship between the firing threshold ϑ and the propagation velocity v, i.e.,

$$u(vt, y, t) = \vartheta. \tag{9.51}$$

Note that the afterpotential η drops out because each neuron is firing only once. The propagation velocity as a function of the firing threshold is plotted in Fig. 9.12A.

Interestingly, there are two branches that correspond to two different velocities at the same threshold. We will see later on that not all velocities correspond to stable solutions.

The simulations show that the dynamics is dominated in large parts of the net by a regular pattern of stripes. These stripes are, apart from the centers of the spirals, formed by an arrangement of approximately plane fronts. We can use the same ideas as above to look for such a type of solution. We make an ansatz,

$$S(x, y, t) = \sum_{n=-\infty}^{\infty} \delta\left(t - \frac{x - n\lambda}{v}\right), \tag{9.52}$$

that describes a traveling wave, i.e., a periodic arrangement of plane fronts, with wavelength λ traveling in positive x direction with (phase) velocity v. Both the phase velocity and the wavelength are free parameters that have to be fixed by a self-consistency condition. We substitute this ansatz in Eq. (9.47) and find

$$u(x, y, t) = \sum_{n=-\infty}^{\infty} \eta\left(t - \frac{x - n\lambda}{v}\right) + u_{\text{front}}\left(x, y, t - \frac{x - n\lambda}{v}\right) \tag{9.53}$$

with

$$u_{\text{front}}(x, y, t) = \iint dx' \, dy' \, w\left[\sqrt{(x - x')^2 + (y - y')^2}\right] \epsilon(t - x'/v). \tag{9.54}$$

Using the fact that the membrane potential on each of the wave fronts equals the firing threshold, we find a relationship between the phase velocity and the wavelength. This relationship can be re-formulated as a *dispersion relation* for the wave number $k = 2\pi/\lambda$ and the frequency $\omega = 2\pi v/\lambda$. The dispersion relationship, which is shown in Fig. 9.12B for various values of the firing threshold, fully characterizes the behavior of the wave.

9.3.2 Stability (*)

A single front of excitation that travels through the net triggers a single action potential in each neuron. In order to investigate the stability of a traveling front of excitation we introduce the firing time $t(r)$ of a neuron located at r. The threshold condition for the triggering of spikes can be read as an implicit equation for the firing time as a function of space,

$$\vartheta = \int dr' \, w(r - r') \, \epsilon[t(r) - t(r')]. \tag{9.55}$$

In the previous section we have found that $t(x, y) = x/v$ can satisfy the above equation for certain combinations of the threshold parameter ϑ and the propagation velocity v.

We are aiming at a linear stability analysis in terms of the firing times (Bressloff, 1999). To this end we consider a small perturbation $\delta t(x, y)$, which will be added to the solution of a plane front of excitation traveling with velocity v in positive x-direction, i.e.,

$$t(x, y) = x/v + \delta t(x, y). \tag{9.56}$$

This ansatz will be substituted in Eq. (9.55) and after linearization we end up with a linear integral equation for δt, viz.

$$0 = \int d\mathbf{r}'\, w(\mathbf{r} - \mathbf{r}')\, \epsilon'[(x - x')/v]\, [\delta t(\mathbf{r}) - \delta t(\mathbf{r}')]. \tag{9.57}$$

Due to the superposition principle we can concentrate on a particular form of the perturbation, e.g., on a single Fourier component such as $\delta t(x, y) = e^{\lambda x} \cos \kappa y$. The above integral equation provides an implicit relationship between the wave number κ of the perturbation with the exponent λ that describes its growth or decay as the front propagates through the net. If there is for a certain κ a particular solution of

$$0 = \iint dx'\, dy'\, w\left[\sqrt{(x - x')^2 + (y - y')^2}\right] \epsilon'[(x - x')/v]$$
$$\times \, [e^{\lambda x} \cos(\kappa y) - e^{\lambda x'} \cos(\kappa y')] \tag{9.58}$$

with $\mathrm{Re}(\lambda) > 0$, then the front is unstable with respect to that perturbation.

Figure 9.13 shows the result of a numerical analysis of the stability equation (9.58). It turns out that the lower branch of the v–ϑ curve corresponds to unstable solutions that are susceptible to two types of perturbation, viz., a perturbation with $\mathrm{Im}(\lambda) = 0$ and an oscillatory perturbation with $\mathrm{Im}(\lambda) \neq 0$. In addition, fronts with a velocity larger than a certain critical velocity are unstable because of a form instability with $\mathrm{Im}(\lambda) = 0$ and $\kappa > 0$. Depending on the actual coupling function w, however, there may be a narrow interval for the propagation velocity where plane fronts are stable; cf. Fig. 9.13B.

The stability of plane waves can be treated in a similar way as that of a plane front: we only have to account for the fact that each neuron is not firing once but repetitively. We thus use the following ansatz for the firing times $\{t_n(x, y)|n = 0, \pm 1, \pm 2, \dots\}$ of a neuron located at (x, y),

$$t_n(x, y) = \frac{x - n\lambda}{v} + \delta t_n(x, y), \tag{9.59}$$

with $\delta t_n(x, y)$ being a "small" perturbation. If we substitute this ansatz into

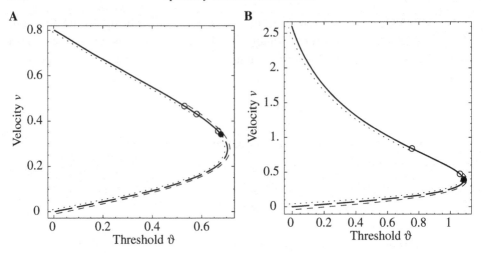

Fig. 9.13. Similar plots as in Fig. 9.12A showing the propagation velocity v as a function of the firing threshold ϑ (thick line). Dashes indicate solutions that are unstable with respect to instabilities with $\kappa = 0$. These instabilities could also be observed in a one-dimensional setup. Thin dotted lines mark the domain of instabilities that show up only in two dimensions, i.e., form instabilities with $\kappa > 0$. Wide dots correspond to perturbations with $\mathrm{Im}(\lambda) = 0$ and narrow dots to Hopf instabilities with $\mathrm{Im}(\lambda) > 0$. **A.** Coupling function $w(r) = \sum_{i=1}^{2} a_i \exp(-r^2/\lambda_i^2)$ with $\lambda_1^2 = 15$, $\lambda_2^2 = 100$, $a_1 = 1.2$ and $a_2 = -0.2$. **B.** Similar plot as in A, but with $a_1 = 1.1$ and $a_2 = -0.1$. Note that there is a small interval between $v = 0.475$ and $v = 0.840$ that corresponds to stable fronts. (Taken from Kistler (2000).)

Eq. (9.53) we obtain

$$0 = \sum_{n} \eta' \left[\frac{(n-m)\,\lambda}{v} \right] [\delta t_m(r) - \delta t_n(r)]$$

$$+ \int d\mathbf{r}'\, w(\mathbf{r} - \mathbf{r}')\,\epsilon' \left[\frac{x - x' + n\,\lambda - m\,\lambda}{v} \right] [\delta t_m(r) - \delta t_n(\mathbf{r}')] \quad (9.60)$$

in leading order of δt_n and with $\mathbf{r} = (x, y)$, $\mathbf{r}' = (x', y')$. Primes at η and ϵ denote derivation with respect to the argument. This equation has to be fulfilled for all $\mathbf{r} \in \mathbb{R}^2$ and all $m \in \{0, \pm 1, \pm 2, \dots\}$.

For the sake of simplicity we neglect the contribution of the afterpotential in Eq. (9.60), i.e., we assume that $\eta'[n\,\lambda/v] = 0$ for $n > 0$. This assumption is justified for short-lasting afterpotentials and a low firing frequency.

As before, we concentrate on a particular form of the perturbations $\delta t_n(x, y)$, namely $\delta t_n(x, y) = \exp[c\,(x - n\,\lambda)]\cos(\kappa_n\,n)\cos(\kappa_y\,y)$. This corresponds to a sinusoidal deformation of the fronts in the y-direction described by κ_y together with a modulation of their distance given by κ_n. If we substitute this ansatz for the perturbation in Eq. (9.60) we obtain a set of equations that can be reduced to

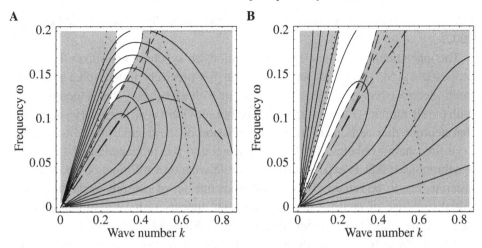

Fig. 9.14. **A.** Dispersion relation (solid lines) of periodic wave trains for various values of the threshold parameter $\vartheta = 0$ (uppermost trace), $0.1, \ldots, 0.6$ (center). Network parameters as in Fig. 9.13A. The shading indicates solutions that are unstable with respect to perturbations with $\kappa_n \in \{0, \pi\}$. The unshaded (white) region is bounded to the left by a form instability with $\kappa_n = 0$ and $\kappa_y > 0$ (dots). Its right border (dashes) is formed by a Hopf bifurcation with $\kappa_n = \pi$ and $\kappa_y > 0$. The right branch of this curve corresponds to the same type of bifurcation but with $\kappa_n = 0$. The remaining dotted lines to the left and to the right indicate form instabilities with $\kappa_n = \pi$. The long-dashed lines reflect bifurcations with $\kappa_y = 0$, i.e., bifurcations that would show up in the corresponding one-dimensional setup. **B.** Similar plot as in A but with a coupling function as in Fig. 9.12B. The firing threshold varies from $\vartheta = 0$ (leftmost trace) to $\vartheta = 1.0$ (center) in steps of 0.2. (Taken from Kistler (2000).)

two linearly independent equations for c, κ_n, and κ_y. The complex roots of this system of equations determines the stability of traveling waves, as is summarized in Fig. 9.14.

9.4 Robust transmission of temporal information

Any information processing scheme that relies on the precise timing of action potentials obviously requires a means to transmit spikes without destroying their temporal structure. A critical question is thus whether a packet of initially synchronous action potentials can be transmitted from one brain area to the next without losing the information. In this section we show that packets of (almost) synchronous spikes can propagate in a feed-forward structure from one layer to the next in such a way that their degree of synchrony is preserved – despite the presence of noise in the spike generating mechanism. Moreover, the temporal dispersion within such a packet can even be reduced during the transmission. This results in a stable wave form of the spike packet that can propagate – very much like a soliton –

through the network (Diesmann et al., 1999; Gewaltig, 2000; Kistler and Gerstner, 2002).

The phenomenon of a stable propagation of synchronous spikes has been proposed by M. Abeles as an explanation for precisely timed spike events in multi-electrode recordings that seem to occur with a frequency that is incompatible with purely random (Poisson) spike trains; but see Oram et al. (1999). He suggested that neurons that participate in the transmission of these spikes form a so-called "syn-fire chain" (Abeles, 1991). More generally, the propagation of (partially) synchronous spikes is expected to play a role whenever information about a new stimulus has to be reliably transmitted from one set of neurons to the next. The initial response of neurons to stimulus onset appears to have a similar form in different brain areas with remarkably low jitter (Maršálek et al., 1997).

The mechanisms that produce the low jitter in neuronal firing times during transmission from one "layer" of neurons to the next can be readily understood. Noise and broad postsynaptic potentials tend to smear out initially sharp spike packets. If, however, the synaptic coupling is strong enough, then postsynaptic neurons will start firing during the rising phase of their membrane potential. If, in addition, these neurons show pronounced refractory behavior, then firing will cease before the postsynaptic potentials have reached their maximum so that a sharp pulse of spike activity is generated. Refractoriness thus counteracts the effects of noise and synaptic transmission and helps to maintain precise timing.

In the following we show how the theory of population dynamics developed in Chapter 6 can be used to provide a quantitative description of the transmission of spike packets. We consider M pools containing N neurons each that are connected in a purely feed-forward manner, i.e., neurons from pool n project only to pool $n + 1$ and there are no synapses between neurons from the same pool. We assume all-to-all connectivity between two successive pools with uniform synaptic weights $\omega_{ij} = \omega/N$; cf. Fig. 9.15. In the framework of the Spike Response Model the membrane potential of a neuron $i \in \Gamma(n + 1)$ from pool $n + 1$ that has fired its last spike at $\hat{t}$ is given by

$$u_i(t, \hat{t}_i) = \frac{\omega}{N} \sum_{j \in \Gamma(n)} \int_0^\infty \epsilon(t') \, S_j(t - t') \, dt' + \eta(t_i - \hat{t}_i)$$

$$= \omega \int_0^\infty \epsilon(t') \, A_n(t - t') \, dt' + \eta(t_i - \hat{t}_i). \tag{9.61}$$

As usual, S_i denotes the spike train of neuron i, and ϵ and η are response kernels describing postsynaptic potential and afterpotential, respectively. $\Gamma(n)$ is the index set of all neurons that belong to pool n, and $A_n(t) = N^{-1} \sum_{j \in \Gamma(n)} S_j(t)$ is the *population activity* of pool n; cf. Eq. (6.1).

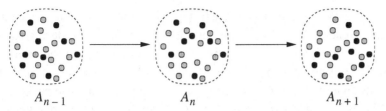

Fig. 9.15. Schematic representation of the network architecture. We investigate the transmission of spike packets in a linear chain of pools of neurons that are connected in a strictly feed-forward manner.

In contrast to the previous section, we explicitly take noise into account. To this end we adopt the "escape noise model" (Section 5.3) and replace the sharp firing threshold by a firing probability that is a function of the membrane potential. The probability of finding an action potential in the infinitesimal interval $[t, t + dt)$ provided that the last spike occurred at $\hat{t}$ is given by

$$\text{prob}\{\text{spike in } [t, t + dt) \mid \text{last spike at } \hat{t}\} = f[u(t, \hat{t})]. \qquad (9.62)$$

For the sake of simplicity we choose a semi-linear hazard function f, i.e.,

$$f(u) = \begin{cases} 0, & u \leq 0 \\ u, & u > 0. \end{cases} \qquad (9.63)$$

With this probabilistic criterion for triggering spikes both spike train and membrane potential become random variables. However, each pool is supposed to contain a large number of neurons ($N \gg 1$) so we can replace the population activity A_n in Eq. (9.61) by its expectation value, which is given by a normalization condition,

$$\int_{-\infty}^{t} S_n(t|\hat{t}) A_n(\hat{t}) \, d\hat{t} = 1 - s_n(t), \qquad (9.64)$$

cf. Eq. (6.73). The survivor function $S_n(t|\hat{t})$ for neurons of pool n is the probability that a neuron that has fired at $\hat{t}$ survives without firing until t. Here, $s_n(t) = S_n(t|-\infty)$ accounts for those neurons that have been quiescent in the past, i.e., have not fired at all up to time t. We have seen in Section 5.2 that

$$S_i(t|\hat{t}_i) = \exp\left\{ -\int_{\hat{t}_i}^{t} f[u_i(t', \hat{t}_i)] \, dt' \right\}. \qquad (9.65)$$

Simulation studies suggest that pronounced refractory behavior is required in order to obtain the stable propagation of a spike packet from one layer to the next (Diesmann et al., 1999; Gewaltig, 2000). If neurons were allowed to fire more than once within one spike packet, the number of spikes per packet and therewith the width of the packet would grow in each step. Therefore, we use a strong and long-lasting after potential η so that each neuron can fire only once during each pulse. The survivor function thus equals unity for the duration τ_{AP} of the afterpotential, i.e., $s_n(t, \hat{t}) = 1$ for $0 < t - \hat{t} < \tau_{AP}$ and τ_{AP} being large as compared to the typical pulse width. Let us denote by T_n the moment when a pulse packet arrives at pool n. We assume that for $t < T_n$, all neurons in layer n have been inactive, i.e., $A_n(t) = 0$ for $t < T_n$. Differentiation of Eq. (9.64) with respect to t leads to

$$A_n(t) = -\frac{\partial}{\partial t} s_n(t) = f[u_n(t)] \exp\left\{-\int_{-\infty}^{t} f[u_n(t')]\,dt'\right\}, \qquad (9.66)$$

with

$$u_n(t) = \omega \int_0^\infty \epsilon(t')\, A_{n-1}(t - t')\,dt'. \qquad (9.67)$$

Equation (9.66) provides an explicit expression for the firing-time distribution $A_n(t)$ in layer n as a function of the time course of the membrane potential. The membrane potential $u_n(t)$, in turn, depends on the time course of the activity $A_{n-1}(t)$ in the previous layer, as shown in Eq. (9.67). Both Eq. (9.66) and Eq. (9.67) can easily be integrated numerically; an analytic treatment, however, is difficult, even if a particularly simple form of the response kernel ϵ is chosen. Following Diesmann et al. (1999) we therefore concentrate on the first few moments of the firing-time distribution in order to characterize the transmission properties. More precisely, we approximate the firing-time distribution $A_{n-1}(t)$ by a gamma distribution and calculate – in step (i) – the zeroth, first, and second moment of the resulting membrane potential in the following layer n. In step (ii), we use these results to approximate the time course of the membrane potential by a gamma distribution and calculate the moments of the corresponding firing-time distribution in layer n. We thus obtain an analytical expression for the amplitude and the variance of the spike packet in layer n as a function of amplitude and variance of the spike packet in the previous layer.

Particularly interesting is the iteration that describes the amplitude of the spike packet. We will see below that the amplitude a_n in layer n as a function of the amplitude a_{n-1} in the previous layer is independent of the shape of the spike packet, viz.,

$$a_n = 1 - e^{-\omega a_{n-1}}. \qquad (9.68)$$

If $\omega \leq 1$, the mapping $a_{n-1} \to a_n$ has a single (globally attractive) fixed point at $a = 0$. In this case no stable propagation of spike packets is possible since any packet will finally die out.[1] For $\omega > 1$ a second fixed point at $a_\infty \in (0, 1)$ emerges through a pitchfork bifurcation. The new fixed point is stable and its basin

[1] The decay of the activity is exponential in n if $\omega < 1$; for $\omega = 1$ the decay is polynomial in n.

of attraction contains the open interval $(0, 1)$. This fixed point determines the wave form of a spike packet that propagates from one layer to the next without changing its form; cf. Fig. 9.16. The fact that the all-off state at $a = 0$ is unstable for $\omega > 1$ is related to the fact that there is no real firing threshold in our model.

Derivation of the spike packet transfer function (*)

In the following we calculate the form of the spike packet in layer n as a function of the form of the packet in layer $n - 1$. To this end we describe the spike packet in terms of the first few moments, as outlined above. In step (i) we assume that the activity $A_{n-1}(t)$ in layer $n - 1$ is given by a gamma distribution with parameters α_{n-1} and λ_{n-1}, i.e.,

$$A_{n-1}(t) = a_{n-1} \, \gamma_{\alpha_{n-1},\lambda_{n-1}}(t) \,. \tag{9.69}$$

Here, a_{n-1} is the portion of neurons of layer $n - 1$ that contribute to the spike packet, $\gamma_{\alpha,\lambda}(t) = t^{\alpha-1} e^{-t/\lambda} \Theta(t)/[\Gamma(\alpha)\lambda^\alpha]$ the density function of the gamma distribution, Γ the complete gamma function, and Θ the Heaviside step function with $\Theta(t) = 1$ for $t > 0$ and $\Theta(t) = 0$ elsewhere. The mean μ and the variance σ^2 of a gamma distribution with parameters α and λ are $\mu = \alpha \lambda$ and $\sigma^2 = \alpha \lambda^2$, respectively.

The membrane potential $u_n(t)$ in the next layer results from a convolution of A_{n-1} with the response kernel ϵ. This is the only point where we have to refer explicitly to the shape of the ϵ kernel. For the sake of simplicity we use a normalized α function,

$$\epsilon(t) = \frac{t}{\tau^2} e^{-t/\tau} \Theta(t) \equiv \gamma_{2,\tau}(t) \,, \tag{9.70}$$

with time constant τ. The precise form of ϵ is not important and similar results hold for a different choice of ϵ.

We want to approximate the time course of the membrane potential by a gamma distribution $\gamma_{\tilde{\alpha}_n,\tilde{\lambda}_n}$. The parameters[2] $\tilde{\alpha}_n$ and $\tilde{\lambda}_n$ are chosen so that the first few moments of the distribution are identical to those of the membrane potential, i.e.,

$$u_n(t) \approx \tilde{a}_n \, \gamma_{\tilde{\alpha}_n,\tilde{\lambda}_n}(t) \,, \tag{9.71}$$

with

$$\int_0^\infty t^n \, u_n(t) \, dt \stackrel{!}{=} \int_0^\infty t^n \, \tilde{a}_n \, \gamma_{\tilde{\alpha}_n,\tilde{\lambda}_n}(t) \, dt \,, \qquad n \in \{0, 1, 2\} \,. \tag{9.72}$$

As far as the first two moments are concerned, a convolution of two distributions

---

[2] We use a tilde in order to identify parameters that describe the time course of the membrane potential. Parameters without a tilde refer to the firing-time distribution.

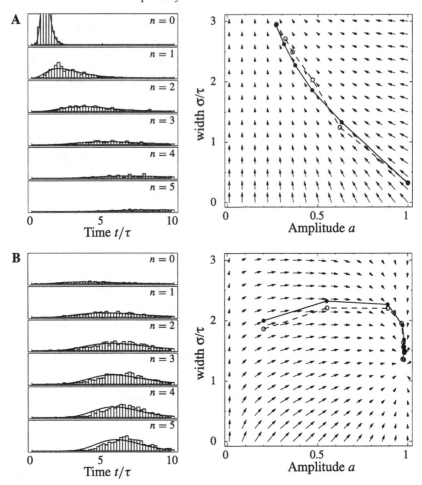

Fig. 9.16. Propagation of spike packets through a feed-forward network. **A.** Evolution of the firing-time distribution of a spike packet as it propagates from one layer to the next ($n = 0, 1, \ldots, 5$). Neurons between layers are only weakly coupled ($\omega = 1$) so that the packet will fade out. The neurons in layer $n = 0$ are driven by an external input that creates a sharp initial spike packet ($\alpha_0 = 10$, $\lambda_0 = 0.1$, $a_0 = 1$). The bars (bin width 0.2) represent the results of a simulation with $N = 1000$ neurons per layer; the solid line is the firing-time distribution as predicted by the theory; cf. Eqs. (9.73) and (9.75). The "flow-field" to the right characterizes the transmission function for spike packets in terms of their amplitude a_n and width $\sigma_n = \sqrt{\alpha_n}\,\lambda_n$. Open symbols connected by a dashed line represent the simulations shown to the left, filled symbols connected by solid lines represent the corresponding theoretical trajectories. Time is given in units of the membrane time constant τ. **B.** Same as in A but with increased coupling strength, $\omega = 4$. There is an attractive fixed point of the flow-field at $a = 0.98$ and $\sigma = 1.5$ that corresponds to the stable wave form of the spike packet. (Taken from Kistler and Gerstner (2002).)

reduces to a mere summation of their mean and variance. Therefore, the convolution of A_{n-1} with ϵ basically translates the center of mass by 2τ and increases the variance by $2\tau^2$. Altogether, amplitude, center of mass, and variance of the time course of the membrane potential in layer n are

$$\left. \begin{aligned} \tilde{a}_n &= \omega\, a_{n-1}\,, \\ \tilde{\mu}_n &= \mu_{n-1} + 2\tau\,, \\ \tilde{\sigma}_n^2 &= \sigma_{n-1}^2 + 2\tau^2\,, \end{aligned} \right\} \tag{9.73}$$

respectively. The parameters $\tilde{\alpha}_n$ and $\tilde{\lambda}_n$ of the gamma distribution are directly related to mean and variance, viz., $\tilde{\alpha}_n = \tilde{\mu}_n^2/\tilde{\sigma}_n^2$, $\tilde{\lambda}_n = \tilde{\sigma}_n^2/\tilde{\mu}_n$.

In step (ii) we calculate the firing-time distribution that results from a membrane potential with time course given by a gamma distribution as in Eq. (9.71). We use the same strategy as in step (i), that is, we calculate the first few moments of the firing-time distribution and approximate it by the corresponding gamma distribution,

$$A_n(t) \approx a_n\, \gamma_{\alpha_n, \lambda_n}(t)\,. \tag{9.74}$$

The zeroth moment of $A_n(t)$ (i.e., the portion of neurons in layer n that participate in the activity pulse) can be cast in a particularly simple form; the expressions for higher order moments, however, contain integrals that have to be evaluated numerically. For amplitude, center of mass, and variance of $A_n(t)$ we find

$$\left. \begin{aligned} a_n &= 1 - e^{-\tilde{a}_n}\,, \\ \mu_n &= m_n^{(1)}\,, \\ \sigma_n^2 &= m_n^{(2)} - \left[m_n^{(1)}\right]^2 \end{aligned} \right\}\,, \tag{9.75}$$

with

$$\begin{aligned} m_n^{(k)} &= \left(1 - e^{-\tilde{a}_n}\right)^{-1} \int_0^\infty u_n(t)\, \exp\!\left[-\int_{-\infty}^t u_n(t')\, dt'\right] t^k\, dt \\ &= \frac{\tilde{a}_n\, \tilde{\lambda}_n^k}{\left(1 - e^{-\tilde{a}_n}\right)\Gamma(\tilde{\alpha}_n)} \int_0^\infty \exp\!\left[-t - \tilde{a}_n\, \Gamma(\tilde{\alpha}_n, 0, t)/\Gamma(\tilde{\alpha}_n)\right] t^{k-1+\tilde{\alpha}_n}\, dt \end{aligned} \tag{9.76}$$

being the kth moment of the firing-time distribution Eq. (9.66) that results from a gamma-shaped time course of the membrane potential. $\Gamma(z, t_1, t_2) = \int_{t_1}^{t_2} t^{z-1}\, e^{-t}\, dt$ is the generalized incomplete gamma function. The last equality in Eq. (9.76) was obtained by substituting $\tilde{a}_n\, \gamma_{\tilde{\alpha}_n, \tilde{\lambda}_n}(t)$ for $u_n(t)$.

A combination of Eqs. (9.73) and (9.75) yields explicit expressions for the parameters (a_n, μ_n, σ_n) of the firing-time distribution in layer n as a function of the parameters in the previous layer. The mapping $(a_{n-1}, \mu_{n-1}, \sigma_{n-1}) \to (a_n, \mu_n, \sigma_n)$

is closely related to the neural transmission function for pulse packet input as discussed by Diesmann et al. (1999).

9.5 Summary

In this chapter we have investigated the dynamic properties of spatially structured networks with local interactions by means of two complementatory approaches. The first approach relies on a mean-field approximation that describes neuronal activity in terms of an averaged membrane potential and the corresponding mean firing rate; cf. Eq. (6.129). The second approach is directly related to the microscopic dynamics of the neurons. Equations for the firing time of single action potentials can be solved exactly in the framework of the Spike Response Model. In both cases, most of the observed phenomena – traveling waves, periodic wave trains, and rotating spirals – are very similar to those of chemical reaction-diffusion systems, though the underlying mathematical equations are rather different.

The last section deals with the reliable transmission of temporal information in a hierarchically organized network. We have seen that sharp packets of spike activity can propagate from one layer to the next without changing their shape. This effect, which is closely related to Abeles' synfire chain, has been analyzed in the framework of the population equation derived in Section 6.3.

Literature

There are several books that provide an in-depth introduction to wave propagation in excitable media, see, e.g., the standard reference for mathematical biology by Murray (1993) or the more recent book by Keener and Sneyd (1998). A text that is apart from the mathematics also very interesting from an asthetic point of view is the book by Meinhardt (1995) on pattern formation in sea shells. An interesting relationship between pattern formation in neuronal networks and visual hallucination patterns can be found in a paper by Ermentrout and Cowan (1979). The standard reference for information transmission with packets of precisely timed spikes is the book by Abeles (1991).

Part three

Models of synaptic plasticity

10

Hebbian models

In the neuron models discussed so far each synapse is characterized by a single constant parameter w_{ij} that determines the amplitude of the postsynaptic response to an incoming action potential. Electrophysiological experiments, however, show that the response amplitude is not fixed but can change over time. Appropriate stimulation paradigms can systematically induce changes of the postsynaptic response that last for hours or days. If the stimulation paradigm leads to a persistent *increase* of the synaptic transmission efficacy, the effect is called long-term potentiation of synapses, or LTP for short. If the result is a *decrease* of the synaptic efficacy, it is called long-term depression (LTD). These persistent changes are thought to be the neuronal correlate of "learning" and "memory".

In the formal theory of neural networks the weight w_{ij} of a connection from neuron j to i is considered as a parameter that can be adjusted so as to optimize the performance of a network for a given task. The process of parameter adaptation is called *learning* and the procedure for adjusting the weights is referred to as a *learning rule*. Here learning is meant in its widest sense. It may refer to synaptic changes during development just as well as to the specific changes necessary to memorize a visual pattern or to learn a motor task. There are so many different learning rules that we cannot cover them all in this book. In this chapter we consider the simplest set of rules, viz., synaptic changes that are driven by correlated activity of pre- and postsynaptic neurons. This class of learning rule can be motivated by Hebb's principle and is therefore often called "Hebbian learning".

10.1 Synaptic plasticity

Since the 1970s, a large body of experimental results on synaptic plasticity has been accumulated. Many of these experiments are inspired by Hebb's postulate (Hebb, 1949),

When an axon of cell A is near enough to excite cell B or repeatedly or persistently takes part in firing it, some growth process or metabolic change takes place in one or both cells such that A's efficiency, as one of the cells firing B, is increased.

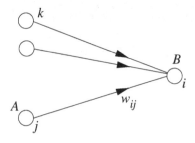

Fig. 10.1. The change at synapse w_{ij} depends on the state of the presynaptic neuron j and the postsynaptic neuron i and the present efficacy w_{ij}, but not on the state of other neurons k.

which describes how the connection from presynaptic neuron A to a postsynaptic neuron B should be modified.

Today, 50 years later, this famous postulate is often rephrased in the sense that modifications in the synaptic transmission efficacy are driven by correlations in the firing activity of pre- and postsynaptic neurons, cf. Fig. 10.1. Even though the idea of learning through correlations dates further back in the past (James, 1890), correlation-based learning is now generally called *Hebbian learning*.

Hebb formulated his principle on purely theoretical grounds. He realized that such a mechanism would help to stabilize specific neuronal activity patterns in the brain. If neuronal activity patterns correspond to behavior, then the stabilization of specific patterns implies the learning of specific types of behaviors (Hebb, 1949).

10.1.1 Long-term potentiation

When Hebb stated his principle in 1949, it was a mere postulate. More than 20 years later, long-lasting changes of synaptic efficacies were found experimentally (Bliss and Gardner-Medwin, 1973; Bliss and Lomo, 1973). These changes can be induced by the joint activity of presynaptic and postsynaptic neurons and resemble the mechanism that Hebb had in mind (Kelso et al., 1986). In this subsection we concentrate on long-term potentiation (LTP), viz., a persistent increase of synaptic efficacies. Long-term depression (LTD) is mentioned in passing.

The basic paradigm of LTP induction is, very schematically, the following (Brown et al., 1989; Bliss and Collingridge, 1993). A neuron is impaled by an intracellular electrode to record the membrane potential while presynaptic fibers are stimulated by means of a second extracellular electrode. Small pulses are applied to the presynaptic fibers in order measure the strength of the postsynaptic response (Fig. 10.2A). The amplitude of the test pulse is chosen

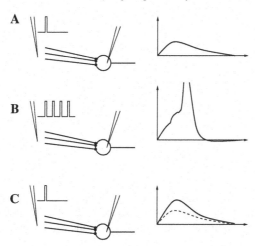

Fig. 10.2. Schematic drawing of a paradigm of long-term potentiation (LTP) induction. **A.** A weak test pulse (left) evokes the postsynaptic response sketched on the right-hand side of the figure. **B.** A strong stimulation sequence (left) triggers postsynaptic firing (right, the peak of the action potential is off scale). **C.** A test pulse applied some time later evokes a larger postsynaptic response (right; solid line) than the initial response. The dashed line is a copy of the initial response in **A** (schematic figure).

so that the stimulation evokes a postsynaptic potential, but no action potentials.

In a second step, the input fibers are strongly stimulated by a sequence of high-frequency pulses so as to evoke postsynaptic firing (Fig. 10.2B). After that the strength of the postsynaptic response to small pulses is tested again and a significantly increased amplitude of postsynaptic potentials is found (Fig. 10.2C). This change in the synaptic strength persists over many hours and is thus called *long-term potentiation.*

What can be learned from such an experiment? Obviously, the result is consistent with Hebb's postulate because the joint activity of pre- and postsynaptic units has apparently led to a strengthening of the synaptic efficacy. On the other hand, the above experiment would also be consistent with a purely postsynaptic explanation claiming that the strengthening is solely caused by postsynaptic spike activity. In order to exclude this possibility, a more complicated experiment has to be conducted (Brown et al., 1989; Bliss and Collingridge, 1993).

In an experiment as sketched in Fig. 10.3, a neuron is driven by two separate input pathways labeled S (strong) and W (weak), respectively. Each pathway projects to several synapses on the postsynaptic neuron i. Stimulating the S pathway excites postsynaptic firing but stimulation of the W channel alone does not evoke spikes. The response to the W input is monitored in order to detect

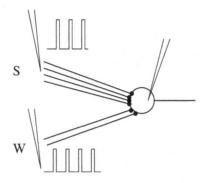

Fig. 10.3. Cooperativity in the induction of LTP. Synapses at the W channel are strengthened only if both the presynaptic site is stimulated via the W electrode and the postsynaptic neuron is active due to a simultaneous stimulation of the S pathway.

changes of the synaptic efficacy. A 100-Hz input over 600 ms at the W channel evokes no LTP at the W synapses. Similarly, a 100-Hz input (over 400 ms) at the S channel alone does not produce LTP at the W synapses (although it may evoke a change of the S synapses). However, if both stimulations occur simultaneously, then the W synapses are strengthened. This feature of LTP induction is known as cooperativity or associativity. It is consistent with the picture that both presynaptic *and* postsynaptic activity are required to induce LTP.

Experiments as the one sketched in Figs. 10.2 and 10.3 have shown that synaptic weights change as a function of pre- and postsynaptic activity. Many other paradigms of LTP induction have been studied over the last 20 years. For example, the state of the postsynaptic neuron can be manipulated by depolarizing or hyperpolarizing currents; synaptic channels can be blocked or activated pharmacologically, etc. Nevertheless, the underlying subcellular processes that lead to LTP are still not fully understood.

10.1.2 Temporal aspects

The essential aspect of the experiments described in the previous section is the AND condition that is at the heart of Hebb's postulate: both pre- and postsynaptic neurons have to be active in order to induce a strengthening of the synapse. However, such a summary neglects the temporal requirements for weight changes. When are two neurons considered as being active together?

In the experiment sketched in Fig. 10.3 inputs can be switched on and off with some arbitrary timing. A large increase of the synaptic efficacy can be induced by stimulating the W and the S pathways simultaneously. If there is a certain delay in the stimulation of W and S then the synaptic efficacy is only

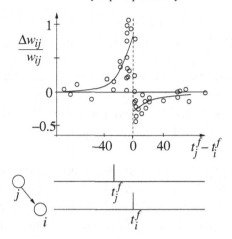

Fig. 10.4. Timing requirements between pre- and postsynaptic spikes. Synaptic changes Δw_{ij} occur only if presynaptic firing at $t_j^{(f)}$ and postsynaptic activity at $t_i^{(f)}$ occur sufficiently close to each other. Experimentally measured weight changes (circles) as a function of $t_j^{(f)} - t_i^{(f)}$ in milliseconds overlayed on a schematic two-phase learning window (solid line). A positive change (LTP) occurs if the presynaptic spike *precedes* the postsynaptic one; for reversed timing, synaptic weights are decreased. Data points redrawn after the experiments of Bi and Poo (1998).

slightly increased or even reduced. Stimulating W and S alternatively with a long interval in between does not result in any change at all (Levy and Stewart, 1983; Gustafsson et al., 1987; Debanne et al., 1994). With this setup, however, a precise measurement of the timing conditions for synaptic changes is difficult, because the pre- and postsynaptic activity are generated by extracellular electrodes. With modern patch-clamp techniques it is possible to stimulate or record from one or several neurons intracellularly. Multiple intracellular recordings in synaptically coupled neurons have enabled the study of synaptic plasticity at an excellent spatial and temporal resolution (Magee and Johnston, 1997; Markram et al., 1997; Bi and Poo, 1998, 1999; Debanne et al., 1998; Zhang et al., 1998); see Bi and Poo (2001) for a review.

Figure 10.4 illustrates a pairing experiment with cultured hippocampal neurons where the presynaptic neuron (j) and the postsynaptic neuron (i) are forced to fire spikes at time $t_j^{(f)}$ and $t_i^{(f)}$, respectively (Bi and Poo, 1998). The resulting change in the synaptic efficacy Δw_{ij} after several repetitions of the experiment turns out to be a function of the spike time differences $t_j^{(f)} - t_i^{(f)}$ ("spike-time-dependent synaptic plasticity"). Most notably, the direction of the change depends critically, i.e., on a millisecond time-scale, on the relative timing of pre- and postsynaptic spikes. The synapse is strengthened if the presynaptic spike occurs shortly before the postsynaptic neuron fires, but the synapse is weakened if the sequence of spikes is reversed; cf. Fig. 10.4. This observation is indeed in agreement with Hebb's postulate because presynaptic neurons that are active slightly *before* the postsynaptic neuron are those which "take part in firing it" whereas those that fire later obviously did not contribute to the postsynaptic action potential. An asymmetrical learning window such as the one in Fig. 10.4 is thus an implementation of the causality requirement that is implicit in Hebb's principle.

Similar results on spike-time-dependent synaptic plasticity have been found in various neuronal systems (Markram et al., 1997; Debanne et al., 1998; Bi and Poo, 1998, 1999; Zhang et al., 1998; Egger et al., 1999), but there are also characteristic differences. Synapses between parallel fibers and "Purkinje cells" in the cerebellar-like structure of electric fish, for example, show the opposite dependence on the relative timing of presynaptic input and the (so-called broad) postsynaptic spike. In this case the synapse is weakened if the presynaptic input arrives shortly before the postsynaptic spike (anti-Hebbian plasticity). If the timing is the other way round then the synapse is strengthened. A change in the timing of less than 10 ms can change the effect from depression to potentiation (Bell et al., 1997b).

10.2 Rate-based Hebbian learning

In order to prepare the ground for a thorough analysis of spike-based learning rules in Section 10.3 we will first review the basic concepts of correlation-based learning in a firing rate formalism.

10.2.1 A mathematical formulation of Hebb's rule

In order to find a mathematically formulated learning rule based on Hebb's postulate, we focus on a single synapse with efficacy w_{ij} that transmits signals from a presynaptic neuron j to a postsynaptic neuron i. For the time being we content ourselves with a description in terms of mean firing rates. In the following, the activity of the presynaptic neuron is denoted by ν_j and that of the postsynaptic neuron by ν_i.

There are two aspects in Hebb's postulate that are particularly important, viz. *locality* and *cooperativity*. Locality means that the change of the synaptic efficacy can only depend on local variables, i.e., on information that is available at the site of the synapse, such as pre- and postsynaptic firing rate, and the actual value of the synaptic efficacy, but not on the activity of other neurons. Based on the locality of Hebbian plasticity we can make a rather general ansatz for the change of the synaptic efficacy,

$$\frac{d}{dt} w_{ij} = F(w_{ij}; v_i, v_j) \,. \tag{10.1}$$

Here, dw_{ij}/dt is the rate of change of the synaptic coupling strength and F is a so far undetermined function (Sejnowski and Tesauro, 1989; Kohonen, 1984; Brown et al., 1991). We may wonder whether there are other local variables (e.g., the membrane potential u_i) that should be included as additional arguments of the function F. It turns out that in standard rate models this is not necessary, since the membrane potential u_i is uniquely determined by the postsynaptic firing rate, $v_i = g(u_i)$, with a monotone gain function g.

The second important aspect of Hebb's postulate, cooperativity, implies that pre- and postsynaptic neurons have to be active *simultaneously* for a synaptic weight change to occur. We can use this property to learn something about the function F. If F is sufficiently well-behaved, we can expand F in a Taylor series about $v_i = v_j = 0$,

$$\frac{d}{dt} w_{ij} = c_0(w_{ij}) + c_1^{\text{post}}(w_{ij}) v_i + c_1^{\text{pre}}(w_{ij}) v_j$$
$$+ c_2^{\text{pre}}(w_{ij}) v_j^2 + c_2^{\text{post}}(w_{ij}) v_i^2 + c_2^{\text{corr}}(w_{ij}) v_i v_j + \mathcal{O}(v^3) \,. \tag{10.2}$$

The factors c_0, c_1^{post}, etc. are expansion parameters, e.g., $c_0 = F(w_{ij}; 0, 0)$ and $c_1^{\text{post}} = dF/dv_i$ evaluated at $v_i = v_j = 0$. The term containing c_2^{corr} on the right-hand side of (10.2) is bilinear in pre- and postsynaptic activity. This term implements the AND condition for cooperativity which makes Hebbian learning a useful concept.

The simplest choice for our function F is to fix c_2^{corr} at a positive constant and to set all other terms in the Taylor expansion to zero. The result is the prototype of Hebbian learning,

$$\frac{d}{dt} w_{ij} = c_2^{\text{corr}} v_i v_j \,. \tag{10.3}$$

We note in passing that a learning rule with $c_2^{\text{corr}} < 0$ is usually called anti-Hebbian because it weakens the synapse if pre- and postsynaptic neurons are active simultaneously; a behavior that is just contrary to that postulated by Hebb. A learning rule with only first-order terms gives rise to so-called non-Hebbian plasticity, because pre- or postsynaptic activity alone induces a change of the synaptic efficacy. More complicated learning rules can be constructed if higher-order terms in the expansion of Eq. (10.2), such as $v_i v_j^2$, $v_i^2 v_j$, $v_i^2 v_j^2$, etc., are included.

The dependence of F on the synaptic efficacy w_{ij} is a natural consequence of the fact that w_{ij} is bounded. If F was independent of w_{ij} then the synaptic efficacy would grow without limit if the same potentiating stimulus was applied over and over again. A saturation of synaptic weights can be achieved, for example, if the parameter c_2^{corr} in Eq. (10.2) tends to zero as w_{ij} approaches its maximum value, say $w^{\text{max}} = 1$, e.g.,

$$c_2^{\text{corr}}(w_{ij}) = \gamma_2 (1 - w_{ij}) \tag{10.4}$$

with a positive constant γ_2.

Hebb's original proposal does not contain a rule for a decrease of synaptic weights. In a system where synapses can only be strengthened, all efficacies will finally saturate at their upper maximum value. An option of decreasing the weights (synaptic depression) is therefore a necessary requirement for any useful learning rule. This can, for example, be achieved by weight decay, which can be implemented in Eq. (10.2) by setting

$$c_0(w_{ij}) = -\gamma_0 w_{ij} . \tag{10.5}$$

Here, γ_0 is a (small) positive constant that describes the rate by which w_{ij} decays back to zero in the absence of stimulation. Our formulation (10.2) is hence sufficiently general to allow for a combination of synaptic potentiation and depression. If we combine Eq. (10.4) and Eq. (10.5) we obtain the learning rule

$$\frac{\mathrm{d}}{\mathrm{d}t} w_{ij} = \gamma_2 (1 - w_{ij}) v_i v_j - \gamma_0 w_{ij} . \tag{10.6}$$

The factors $(1 - w_{ij})$ and w_{ij} that lead to a saturation at $w_{ij} = 1$ for continued stimulation and an exponential decay to $w_{ij} = 0$ in the absence of stimulation, respectively, are one possibility for implementing "soft" bounds for the synaptic weight. In simulations, "hard" bounds are often used to restrict the synaptic weights to a finite interval, i.e., a learning rule with weight-independent parameters is only applied as long as the weight stays within its limits.

Another interesting aspect of learning rules is *competition*. The idea is that synaptic weights can only grow at the expense of others so that if a certain subgroup of synapses is strengthened, other synapses to the same postsynaptic neuron have to be weakened. Competition is essential for any form of self-organization and pattern formation. Practically, competition can be implemented in simulations by normalizing the sum of all weights converging onto the same postsynaptic neuron (Miller and MacKay, 1994); cf. Section 11.1.3. Though this can be motivated by a limitation of common synaptic resources, such a learning rule violates the locality of synaptic plasticity. On the other hand, competition of synaptic weight changes can also be achieved with purely local learning rules (Oja, 1982; Kistler and van Hemmen, 2000; Song et al., 2000; Kempter et al., 2001).

Example: postsynaptic gating versus *presynaptic gating*

Equation (10.6) is just one possibility for specifying the rules for the growth and decay of synaptic weights. In the framework of Eq. (10.2), other formulations are conceivable; cf. Table 10.1. For example, we can define a learning rule of the form

$$\frac{\mathrm{d}}{\mathrm{d}t} w_{ij} = \gamma \, v_i \left[v_j - v_\theta(w_{ij}) \right], \tag{10.7}$$

where γ is a positive constant and v_θ is some reference value that may depend on the current value of w_{ij}. A weight change occurs only if the postsynaptic neuron is active, $v_i > 0$. We say that weight changes are "gated" by the postsynaptic neuron. The direction of the weight change depends on the sign of the expression in the square brackets. Let us suppose that the postsynaptic neuron is driven by a subgroup of highly active presynaptic neurons ($v_i > 0$ and $v_j > v_\theta$). Synapses that connect the postsynaptic neuron and one of the highly active presynaptic neurons are strengthened while the efficacy of other synapses that have not been activated is decreased. Firing of the postsynaptic neuron thus leads to LTP at the active pathway ("homosynaptic LTP") and at the same time to LTD at the inactive synapses ("heterosynaptic LTD"); for reviews see Brown et al. (1991); Linden and Connor (1995); Bi and Poo (2001).

A particularly interesting case from a theoretical point of view is the choice $v_\theta(w_{ij}) = w_{ij}$, i.e.,

$$\frac{\mathrm{d}}{\mathrm{d}t} w_{ij} = v_i \left(v_j - w_{ij} \right). \tag{10.8}$$

The synaptic weights thus approach the fixed point $w_{ij} = v_j$ whenever the postsynaptic neuron is active. In the stationary state, the set of weight values w_{ij} reflects the presynaptic firing pattern v_j, $1 \leq j \leq N$. In other words, the presynaptic firing pattern is *stored* in the weights. This learning rule is an important ingredient of competitive unsupervised learning (Grossberg, 1976; Kohonen, 1984).

Let us now turn to a learning rule where synaptic changes are "gated" by the presynaptic activity v_j. The corresponding equation has the same form as Eq. (10.7) except that the roles of pre- and postsynaptic firing rate are exchanged,

$$\frac{\mathrm{d}}{\mathrm{d}t} w_{ij} = \gamma \left(v_i - v_\theta \right) v_j. \tag{10.9}$$

In this case, a change of synaptic weights can only occur if the presynaptic neuron is active ($v_j > 0$). The direction of the change is determined by the activity of the postsynaptic neuron. For $\gamma > 0$, the synapse is strengthened if the postsynaptic cell is highly active ($v_i > v_\theta$); otherwise it is weakened.

Table 10.1. *The change $\frac{d}{dt} w_{ij}$ of a synapse from j to i for various Hebb rules as a function of pre- and postsynaptic activity. "ON" indicates a neuron firing at high rate ($v > 0$), whereas "OFF" means an inactive neuron ($v = 0$). From left to right: standard Hebb rule, Hebb with decay, pre- and postsynaptic gating, covariance rule. The parameters are $0 < v_\theta < v_{\max}$ and $0 < c_0 < (v_{\max})^2$.*

post v_i	pre v_j	$dw_{ij}/dt \propto$ $v_i v_j$	$dw_{ij}/dt \propto$ $v_i v_j - c_0$	$dw_{ij}/dt \propto$ $(v_i - v_\theta) v_j$	$dw_{ij}/dt \propto$ $v_i (v_j - v_\theta)$	$dw_{ij}/dt \propto$ $(v_i - \langle v_i \rangle)(v_j - \langle v_j \rangle)$
ON	ON	+	+	+	+	+
ON	OFF	0	−	0	−	−
OFF	ON	0	−	−	0	−
OFF	OFF	0	−	0	0	+

For $\gamma < 0$, the correlation term has a negative sign and the learning rule (10.9) gives rise to anti-Hebbian plasticity, which has an interesting stabilizing effect on the postsynaptic firing rate. If the presynaptic firing rates are kept constant, the postsynaptic firing rate v_i will finally converge to the reference value v_θ. To see why, let us consider a simple rate neuron with output rate $v_i = g(\sum_j w_{ij} v_j)$. For $v_i < v_\theta$, *all* synapses are strengthened ($dw_{ij}/dt > 0$ for all j) and the overall input strength $h_i = \sum_j w_{ij} v_j$ is increasing. Since g is a monotonously growing function of h_i, the output rate tends to v_θ. On the other hand, if $v_i > v_\theta$, all synaptic efficacies decrease and so does v_i. Hence, $v_i = v_\theta$ is a globally attractive fixed point of the postsynaptic activity. Some of the detailed spike-based learning rule, to be discussed below, will show a similar stabilization of the postsynaptic activity.

Example: covariance rule

Sejnowski and Tesauro (1989) have suggested a learning rule of the form

$$\frac{d}{dt} w_{ij} = \gamma \, (v_i - \langle v_i \rangle) \, (v_j - \langle v_j \rangle) , \tag{10.10}$$

called the covariance rule. This rule is based on the idea that the rates $v_i(t)$ and $v_j(t)$ fluctuate around mean values $\langle v_i \rangle$, $\langle v_j \rangle$ that are taken as running averages over the recent firing history. To allow a mapping of the covariance rule to the general framework of Eq. (10.2), the mean firing rates $\langle v_i \rangle$ and $\langle v_j \rangle$ have to be constant in time. We will return to the covariance rule in Chapter 11.

Example: quadratic terms

All of the above learning rules had $c_2^{\text{pre}} = c_2^{\text{post}} = 0$. Let us now consider a nonzero quadratic term $c_2^{\text{post}} = -\gamma \, w_{ij}$. We take $c_2^{\text{corr}} = \gamma > 0$ and set all other parameters to zero. The learning rule

$$\frac{\mathrm{d}}{\mathrm{d}t} w_{ij} = \gamma \, (v_i \, v_j - w_{ij} \, v_i^2) \tag{10.11}$$

is called Oja's rule (Oja, 1982). As we will see in Section 1.3, Oja's rule converges asymptotically to synaptic weights that are normalized to $\sum_j w_{ij}^2 = 1$ while keeping the essential Hebbian properties of the standard rule of Eq. (10.3). We note that normalization of $\sum_j w_{ij}^2$ implies competition between the synapses that make connections to the same postsynaptic neuron, i.e., if some weights grow others must decrease.

Example: Bienenstock–Cooper–Munroe rule

Higher terms in the expansion on the right-hand side of Eq. (10.2) lead to more intricate plasticity schemes. As an example, let us consider a generalization of the presynaptic gating rule in Eq. (10.9)

$$\frac{\mathrm{d}}{\mathrm{d}t} w_{ij} = \eta \, \phi(v_i - v_\theta) \, v_j - \gamma \, w_{ij} \tag{10.12}$$

with a nonlinear function ϕ and a reference rate v_θ. If we replace v_θ by a running average of the output rate, $\langle v_i \rangle$, then we obtain the so-called Bienenstock–Cooper–Munroe (BCM) rule (Bienenstock et al., 1982).

Some experiments (Artola et al., 1990; Artola and Singer, 1993; Ngezahayo et al., 2000) suggest that the function ϕ should look similar to that sketched in Fig. 10.5. Synaptic weights do not change as long as the postsynaptic activity stays below a certain minimum rate, v_0. For moderate levels of postsynaptic excitation, the efficacy of synapses activated by presynaptic input is *decreased*. Weights are *increased* only if the level of postsynaptic activity exceeds a second threshold, v_θ. The change of weights is restricted to those synapses that are activated by presynaptic input, hence the "gating" factor v_j in Eq. (10.12). By arguments completely analogous to those made above for the presynaptically gated rule, we can convince ourselves that the postsynaptic rate has a fixed point at v_θ. For the form of the function shown in Fig.10.5 this fixed point is unstable. In order to prevent the postsynaptic firing rate from increasing rapidly or decaying to zero, it is therefore necessary to turn v_θ into an adaptive variable (Bienenstock et al., 1982). We will come back to the BCM rule towards the end of this chapter.

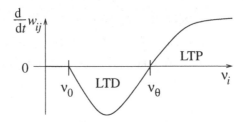

Fig. 10.5. Bidirectional learning rule. Synaptic plasticity is characterized by two thresholds for the postsynaptic activity (Bienenstock et al., 1982). Below v_0 no synaptic modification occurs, between v_0 and v_θ synapses are depressed, and for postsynaptic firing rates beyond v_θ synaptic potentiation can be observed. A similar dependence is found if weight changes are plotted as a function of the postsynaptic potential rather than the postsynaptic rate (Artola and Singer, 1993; Ngezahayo et al., 2000).

10.3 Spike-time-dependent plasticity

In this section we study synaptic plasticity at the level of individual spikes and focus on changes in the synaptic efficacy that are driven by temporal correlations between presynaptic spike arrival and postsynaptic firing.

We have seen in Section 1.4 that the neuronal code is still far from being fully understood. In particular, the relevance of precisely timed spikes in neuronal systems is a fundamental, yet unsolved question (Rieke et al., 1996). Nevertheless, there are neuronal systems for which the relevance of temporal information has been clearly shown. Prominent examples are the electro-sensory system of electric fish and the auditory system of barn owls (Konishi, 1986; Carr and Konishi, 1990; Heiligenberg, 1991; Carr, 1993; Konishi, 1993). If the timing of spikes is important then we have to deal with the following questions. How does the timing of spikes influence weight changes? How do weight changes influence the timing of spikes?

10.3.1 Phenomenological model

The experiments described in the Section 10.1 show that changes of the synaptic efficacy are driven by pre- and postsynaptic activity. The amplitude and even the direction of the change depend on the relative timing of presynaptic spike arrival and postsynaptic triggering of action potentials.

In the following we develop a phenomenological model for spike-time-dependent synaptic plasticity. We assume that apart from an activity-independent weight decay *all* changes are triggered by pre- or postsynaptic action potentials. For the sake of simplicity – and for want of detailed knowledge – we take weight changes to be instantaneous, i.e., the synaptic efficacy is a piecewise continuous function of time with steps whenever a spike occurs. The amplitude of each step depends on the relative timing of previous spikes; cf. Fig. 10.6.

Let us first concentrate on the effect of presynaptic spikes. Each spike that arrives at the presynaptic terminal can trigger a change in the synaptic efficacy even without additional postsynaptic action potentials. In the case of so-called (non-Hebbian) presynaptic LTP, the amplitude a_1^{pre} of these changes is positive; cf. Fig. 10.6B. In addition to this non-Hebbian effect there is also a contribution to the change that depends on the time since the last postsynaptic action potential(s). In analogy to the spike response formalism of Section 4.2 we use an integral kernel $a_2^{\text{pre,post}}$ to describe the amplitude of the change in the synaptic efficacy. Altogether we have

$$\frac{d}{dt} w_{ij}(t) = S_j(t) \left[a_1^{\text{pre}} + \int_0^\infty a_2^{\text{pre,post}}(s) \, S_i(t - s) \, ds \right], \tag{10.13}$$

where $S_j(t) = \sum_f \delta(t - t_j^{(f)})$ and $S_i(t) = \sum_f \delta(t - t_i^{(f)})$ are pre- and postsynaptic spike trains, respectively. The value of the kernel $a_2^{\text{pre,post}}(s)$ gives the weight change if a postsynaptic action potential is followed by presynaptic spike arrival with delay s. In pyramidal cells of the hippocampus, for example, this term is negative; cf. Fig. 10.4.

Changes in the synaptic efficacy can also be triggered by postsynaptic action potentials. Similarly to presynaptically triggered changes, the amplitude of the weight change consists of at least two contributions, viz., a non-Hebbian term a_1^{post} and the correlation term described by an integral kernel $a_2^{\text{post,pre}}$. Together with an activity-independent term a_0 the total change in the synaptic efficacy reads

$$\frac{d}{dt} w_{ij}(t) = a_0 + S_j(t) \left[a_1^{\text{pre}} + \int_0^\infty a_2^{\text{pre,post}}(s) \, S_i(t - s) \, ds \right]$$
$$+ S_i(t) \left[a_1^{\text{post}} + \int_0^\infty a_2^{\text{post,pre}}(s) \, S_j(t - s) \, ds \right], \tag{10.14}$$

cf. Kistler and van Hemmen (2000). Note that all parameters a_0, a_1^{pre}, a_1^{post} and both kernels $a_2^{\text{pre,post}}$, $a_2^{\text{post,pre}}$ may also depend upon the actual value of the synaptic efficacy. A possible consequence of this dependence, for example, is that it becomes increasingly difficult to strengthen a synapse that has already been potentiated and, vice versa, to weaken a depressed synapse (Ngezahayo et al., 2000). This can be exploited in a model in order to ensure that the weight w_{ij} stays bounded; cf. Section 10.2.1. Here and in the following we will suppress this dependence for the sake of brevity.

Equation (10.14) can easily be extended so as to include more complex dependencies between pre- and postsynaptic spikes or between different consecutive pre- or postsynaptic spikes. Analogously to Eq. (10.2) we can include higher-order terms such as $S_j(t) \int_0^\infty a_2^{\text{pre,pre}}(s) \, S_j(t - s) \, ds$ and $S_i(t) \int_0^\infty a_2^{\text{post,post}}(s) \, S_i(t - s) \, ds$ that are quadratic in pre- or postsynaptic spike trains. Nevertheless, the essence of

Hebbian synaptic plasticity is captured by the terms that are *bilinear* in the pre- and postsynaptic spike train. The terms containing $a_2^{\text{pre,post}}$ and $a_2^{\text{post,pre}}$ describe the form of the "learning window" such as the one shown in Fig. 10.4. The kernel $a_2^{\text{post,pre}}(s)$, which is usually positive, gives the amount of weight change when a presynaptic spike is followed by a postsynaptic action potential with delay s; cf. the left half of the graph shown in Fig. 10.4. The kernel $a_2^{\text{pre,post}}(s)$ describes the right half of the graph, i.e., the amount of change if the timing is the other way round. Since experimental results on spike-time-dependent plasticity are usually presented in graphical form such as in Fig. 10.4, we define a "learning window" W as

$$W(s) = \begin{cases} a_2^{\text{post,pre}}(-s) & \text{if } s < 0, \\ a_2^{\text{pre,post}}(s) & \text{if } s > 0, \end{cases} \tag{10.15}$$

where $s = t_j^{(f)} - t_i^{(f)}$ is the delay between presynaptic spike arrival and postsynaptic firing. Note that $s < 0$ refers to presynaptic spike arrival *before* postsynaptic firing.

Example: exponential learning windows

A simple choice for the learning window – and thus for the kernels $a_2^{\text{post,pre}}$ and $a_2^{\text{pre,post}}$ – inspired by Fig. 10.4 is

$$W(s) = \begin{cases} A_+ \exp[s/\tau_1] & \text{for } s < 0, \\ A_- \exp[-s/\tau_2] & \text{for } s > 0, \end{cases} \tag{10.16}$$

with some constants $A_\pm$ and $\tau_{1,2}$. If $A_+ > 0$ and $A_- < 0$ then the synaptic efficacy is increased if the presynaptic spike arrives slightly *before* the postsynaptic firing ($W(s) > 0$ for $s < 0$) and the synapse is weakened if presynaptic spikes arrive a few milliseconds *after* the output spike ($W(s) < 0$); cf. Fig. 10.7.

In order to obtain a realistic description of synaptic plasticity we have to make sure that the synaptic efficacy stays within certain bounds. Excitatory synapses, for example, should have a positive weight and must not exceed a maximum value of, say, $w_{ij} = 1$. We can implement these constraints in Eq. (10.16) by setting $A_- = w_{ij} a_-$ and $A_+ = (1 - w_{ij}) a_+$. The remaining terms in Eq. (10.14) can be treated analogously.[1] For each positive term (leading to a weight increase) we assume a weight dependence $\propto (1 - w_{ij})$, while for each negative term (leading to weight decrease) we assume a weight dependence $\propto w_{ij}$. The synapse is thus no longer strengthened (or weakened) if the weight reaches its upper (lower) bound (Kistler and van Hemmen, 2000; van Rossum et al., 2000).

---

[1] Note that w_{ij} is a step function of time with discontinuities whenever a presynaptic spike arrives or a postsynaptic action potential is triggered. In order to obtain a well-defined differential equation we specify that the amplitude of the step depends on the value of w_{ij} immediately *before* the spike. In mathematical terms, we impose the condition that $w_{ij}(t)$ is continuous from left, i.e., that $\lim_{s \to 0, s > 0} w_{ij}(t^{(f)} - s) = w_{ij}(t^{(f)})$.

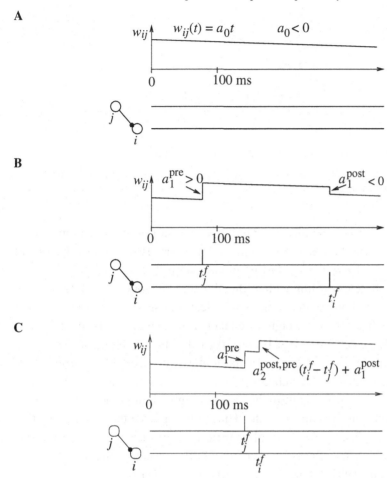

Fig. 10.6. The lower part of each graph shows presynaptic spikes (neuron j) and postsynaptic spikes (neuron i). The upper part shows the evolution of the weight w_{ij}. **A.** A zero-order term $a_0 < 0$ leads to a decrease of the synaptic weight w_{ij}. **B.** Linear order terms change the weight whenever a presynaptic spike arrives or a postsynaptic spike is fired. For $a_1^{\text{pre}} > 0$, presynaptic spike arrival at time $t_j^{(f)}$ leads to a positive weight change $\Delta w_{ij} = a_1^{\text{pre}}$. For $a_1^{\text{post}} < 0$, each postsynaptic spike leads to a negative weight change. **C.** We assume Hebbian plasticity with $a_2^{\text{post,pre}}(t_i^{(f)} - t_j^{(f)}) = W(t_j^{(f)} - t_i^{(f)}) > 0$ for $t_j^{(f)} < t_i^{(f)}$. Thus, if a postsynaptic spike $t_i^{(f)}$ is fired shortly after presynaptic spike arrival at $t_j^{(f)}$, the weight change $W(t_j^{(f)} - t_i^{(f)}) + a_1^{\text{post}}$ at the moment of the postsynaptic spike can be positive, even if $a_1^{\text{post}} < 0$.

10.3.2 Consolidation of synaptic efficacies

So far we have emphasized that the synaptic coupling strength is a dynamical variable that is subject to rapid changes dependent on pre- and postsynaptic activity.

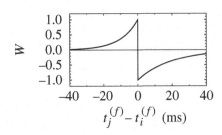

Fig. 10.7. Two-phase learning window W as a function of the time difference $s = t_j^{(f)} - t_i^{(f)}$ between presynaptic spike arrival and postsynaptic firing; cf. Eq. (10.16) with $A_+ = -A_- = 1$, $\tau_1 = 10$ ms, and $\tau_2 = 20$ ms (Zhang et al., 1998).

On the other hand, it is generally accepted that long-lasting modifications of the synaptic efficacy form the basis of learning and memory. How can fast dynamical properties be reconciled with long-lasting modifications?

Most learning theories dealing with artificial neural networks concentrate on the *induction* of weight changes. As soon as the "learning session" is over, synaptic plasticity is "switched off" and weights are taken as fixed parameters. In biological systems, a similar mechanism can be observed during development. There are critical periods in the early life time of an animal when certain synapses show a form of plasticity that is "switched off" after maturation (Crepel, 1982). The majority of synapses, especially those involved in higher brain functions, however, keep their plasticity throughout their life. Thus at first glance there is the risk that previously stored information is simply overwritten by new input ("palimpsest property"). Grossberg has coined the term "stability-plasticity dilemma" for this problem (Grossberg, 1987; Carpenter and Grossberg, 1987).

To address these questions, Fusi et al. (2000b) have studied the problem of the consolidation of synaptic weights. They argue that *bistability* of synaptic weights can solve the stability-plasticity dilemma. More specifically, the dynamics of synaptic efficacies is characterized by two stable fixed points at $w_{ij} = 0$ and $w_{ij} = 1$. In the absence of stimulation the synaptic weight will thus settle down at either one of these values. Pre- or postsynaptic activity can lead to a transition from one fixed point to the other, but only if the duration of the stimulus presentation or its amplitude exceeds a certain threshold. In other words, synapses can be switched on or off but this will happen only for those synapses where the learning threshold is exceeded. Learning thus affects only a few synapses so that previously stored information is mostly preserved.

In the framework of Eq. (10.14), such dynamics for synaptic weights can be implemented by setting

$$a_0(w_{ij}) = -\gamma\, w_{ij}\, (1 - w_{ij})\, (w_\theta - w_{ij}), \tag{10.17}$$

where $0 < w_\theta < 1$ and $\gamma > 0$. In the absence of stimulation, small weights ($w_{ij} < w_\theta$) decay to zero whereas large weights ($w_{ij} > w_\theta$) increase towards one. Spike activity thus has to drive the synaptic weight across the threshold w_θ before long-lasting changes take place. A combination of Eqs. (10.17) and (10.14) can therefore be considered as a model of induction and consolidation of synaptic plasticity.

10.3.3 General framework (*)

In Eq. (10.14) weight changes occur instantaneously at the moment of presynaptic spike arrival or postsynaptic firing. In this subsection we will develop a slightly more general equation for the evolution of synaptic weights. The approach taken in this section can be seen as a generalization of the Taylor expansion in the rate model of Section 10.2 to the case of spiking neurons.

We recall that we started our formulation of rate-based Hebbian learning from a general formula

$$\frac{\mathrm{d}}{\mathrm{d}t} w_{ij} = F(w_{ij}; v_i, v_j) \tag{10.18}$$

where weight changes are given as a function of the weight w_{ij} as well as of the pre- and postsynaptic rates v_j, v_i; cf. Eq. (10.1). The essential assumption was that neuronal activity is characterized by firing rates that change slowly enough to be considered stationary. Hebbian rules followed then from a Taylor expansion of Eq. (10.18). In the following, we keep the idea of an expansion, but drop the simplifications that are inherent to a description in terms of a mean firing rate.

The internal state of spiking neurons (e.g., integrate-and-fire or Spike Response Model neurons) is characterized by the membrane potential u which in turn depends on the input and the last output spike. The generalization of Eq. (10.18) to the case of spiking neurons is therefore

$$\frac{\mathrm{d}}{\mathrm{d}t} w_{ij}(t) = F\left[w_{ij}(t); \{u_i^{\mathrm{post}}(t' < t)\}, \{u_j^{\mathrm{pre}}(t'' < t)\} \right], \tag{10.19}$$

where F is now a *functional* of the time course of pre- and postsynaptic membrane potential *at the location of the synapse*. Our notation with t' and t'' is intended to indicate that the weight changes do not only depend on the momentary value of the pre- and postsynaptic potential, but also on their history $t' < t$ and $t'' < t$. The weight value w_{ij} and the local values of pre- and postsynaptic membrane potential are the essential variables that are available at the site of the synapse to control the up- and downregulation of synaptic weights. In detailed neuron models, F would depend not only on the weight w_{ij} and membrane potentials, but also on all other variables that are locally available at the site of the synapse. In particular, there could be a dependence upon the local calcium concentration; cf. Section 10.4.3.

In analogy to the approach taken in Section 10.2, we now expand the right-hand side of Eq. (10.19) about the resting state $u_i^{\text{post}} = u_j^{\text{pre}} = u_{\text{rest}}$ in a Volterra series (Volterra, 1959; Palm and Poggio, 1977; van Hemmen et al., 2000). For the sake of simplicity we shift the voltage scale so that $u_{\text{rest}} = 0$. We find

$$
\begin{aligned}
\frac{dw_{ij}}{dt} =\ & a_0(w_{ij}) + \int_0^\infty \alpha_1^{\text{pre}}(w_{ij}; s)\, u_j^{\text{pre}}(t-s)\, ds \\
& + \int_0^\infty \alpha_1^{\text{post}}(w_{ij}; s')\, u_i^{\text{post}}(t-s')\, ds' \\
& + \int_0^\infty \int_0^\infty \alpha_2^{\text{corr}}(w_{ij}; s, s')\, u_j^{\text{pre}}(t-s)\, u_i^{\text{post}}(t-s')\, ds'\, ds + \cdots .
\end{aligned}
$$
(10.20)

The next terms would be quadratic in u_i^{post} or u_j^{pre} and have been neglected. Equation (10.20) provides a framework for the formulation of spike-based learning rules and may be seen as the generalization of the general rate-based model that we derived in Section 10.2.

In order to establish a connection with various other formulations of spike-based learning rules, we consider the time course of the pre- and postsynaptic membrane potential in more detail. At the presynaptic terminal, the membrane potential is at rest most of the time, except when an action potential arrives. Since the duration of each action potential is short, the presynaptic membrane potential can be approximated by a train of δ functions

$$
u_j^{\text{pre}}(t) = \sum_f \delta(t - t_j^{(f)})
$$
(10.21)

where $t_j^{(f)}$ denotes the spike arrival times at the presynaptic terminal.

The situation at the postsynaptic site is somewhat more complicated. For the simple Spike Response Model SRM$_0$, the membrane potential can be written as

$$
u_i^{\text{post}}(t) = \eta(t - \hat{t}_i) + h_i(t),
$$
(10.22)

where $\hat{t}_i$ is the last postsynaptic firing time. In contrast to the usual interpretation of terms on the right-hand side of Eq. (10.22), the function η is now taken as the time course of the *back propagating* action potential at the location of the *synapse*. Similarly, $h_i(t)$ is the local postsynaptic potential at the synapse.

For a further simplification of Eq. (10.20), we need to make some approximations. Specifically we will explore two different approximation schemes. In the first scheme, we suppose that the dominating term on the right-hand side of Eq. (10.22) is the back propagating action potential, while in the second scheme we neglect η and consider h as the dominant term. Let us discuss both approximations in turn.

(i) Sharply peaked back propagating action potential

We assume that the back propagating action potential is sharply peaked, i.e., it has a large amplitude and short duration. In this case, the membrane potential of the postsynaptic neuron is dominated by the back propagating action potential and the term $h(t)$ in Eq. (10.22) can be neglected. Furthermore η can be approximated by a δ function. The membrane potential at the postsynaptic site reduces then to a train of pulses,

$$u_i^{\text{post}}(t) = \sum_f \delta(t - t_i^{(f)}), \qquad (10.23)$$

where $t_i^{(f)}$ denotes the postsynaptic firing times. Equation (10.23) is a sensible approximation for synapses that are located on or close to the soma so that the full somatic action potential is "felt" by the postsynaptic neuron. For neurons with active processes in the dendrite that keep the back propagating action potential well focused, Eq. (10.23) is also a reasonable approximation for synapses that are further away from the soma. A transmission delay for back propagation of the spike from the soma to the site of the synapse can be incorporated at no extra cost.

If we insert Eqs. (10.21) and (10.23) into Eq. (10.20) we find

$$\frac{dw_{ij}}{dt} = a_0 + \sum_f \alpha_1^{\text{pre}}(t - t_j^{(f)}) + \sum_f \alpha_1^{\text{post}}(t - t_i^{(f)})$$

$$+ \sum_f \sum_f \alpha_2^{\text{corr}}(t - t_i^{(f)}, t - t_j^{(f)}) + \cdots, \qquad (10.24)$$

where we have omitted the w_{ij} dependence of the right-hand side terms. In contrast to Eq. (10.14) weight changes are now continuous. A single presynaptic spike at time $t_j^{(f)}$, for example, will cause a weight change that builds up during some time after $t_j^{(f)}$. An example will be given below in Eq. (10.31).

In typical plasticity experiments, the synaptic weight is monitored every few hundred milliseconds so that the exact time course of the functions, α_1^{pre}, α_1^{post}, and α_2^{corr} is not measured. To establish the connection to Eq. (10.14), we now assume that the weight changes are rapid compared to the time scale of weight monitoring. In other words, we make the replacement

$$\alpha_1^{\text{pre}}(t - t_j^{(f)}) \quad \longrightarrow \quad a_1^{\text{pre}} \delta(t - t_j^{(f)}) \qquad (10.25)$$

$$\alpha_1^{\text{post}}(t - t_i^{(f)}) \quad \longrightarrow \quad a_1^{\text{post}} \delta(t - t_i^{(f)}) \qquad (10.26)$$

where $a_1^{\text{pre}} = \int_0^\infty \alpha_1^{\text{pre}}(s)\,ds$ and $a_1^{\text{post}} = \int_0^\infty \alpha_1^{\text{post}}(s)\,ds$. For the correlation term we exploit the invariance with respect to time translation, i.e., the final result only depends on the time difference $t_j^{(f)} - t_i^{(f)}$. The weight update occurs at the moment of the postsynaptic spike if $t_j^{(f)} < t_i^{(f)}$ and at the moment of the presynaptic spike if $t_j^{(f)} > t_i^{(f)}$. Hence, the assumption of instantaneous update yields two terms

$$
\alpha_2^{\text{corr}}(t - t_i^{(f)}, t - t_j^{(f)}) \longrightarrow \begin{cases} a_2^{\text{pre,post}}(t_j^{(f)} - t_i^{(f)})\,\delta(t - t_j^{(f)}) & \text{if } t_i^{(f)} < t_j^{(f)} \\ a_2^{\text{post,pre}}(t_i^{(f)} - t_j^{(f)})\,\delta(t - t_i^{(f)}) & \text{if } t_i^{(f)} > t_j^{(f)}. \end{cases}
$$
$$(10.27)$$

Thus, for sharply peaked back propagating action potentials and rapid weight changes, the general framework of Eq. (10.20) leads us back to Eq. (10.14).

(ii) No back propagating action potential

In the second approximation scheme, we assume that the membrane potential at the location of the synapse is dominated by the slowly varying potential $h_i(t)$. This is, for example, a valid assumption in voltage-clamp experiments where the postsynaptic neuron is artificially kept at a constant membrane potential h^{post}. This is also a good approximation for synapses that are located far away from the soma on a *passive* dendrite, so that the back propagation of somatic action potentials is negligible.

Let us consider a voltage-clamp experiment where $h_i(t)$ is kept at a constant level h^{post}. As before, we suppose that weight changes are rapid. If we insert $u_j^{\text{pre}}(t) = \sum_f \delta(t - t_j^{(f)})$ and $u_i^{\text{post}}(t) = h^{\text{post}}$ into Eq. (10.20), we find

$$
\begin{aligned}
\frac{dw_{ij}}{dt} &= a_0 + \sum_f a_1^{\text{pre}}\,\delta(t - t_j^{(f)}) \\
&\quad + a_1^{\text{post}}\,h^{\text{post}} + a_2^{\text{corr}}\,h^{\text{post}} \sum_f \delta(t - t_j^{(f)}) + \cdots,
\end{aligned}
\qquad (10.28)
$$

where $a_1^{\text{pre}} = \int_0^\infty \alpha_1^{\text{pre}}(s)\,ds$, $a_1^{\text{post}} = \int_0^\infty \alpha_1^{\text{post}}(s)\,ds$ and $a_2^{\text{corr}} = \int_0^\infty \int_0^\infty a_2^{\text{corr}}(s, s')\,ds\,ds'$. Equation (10.28) is the starting point of the theory of spike-based learning of Fusi et al. (2000b). Weight changes are triggered by presynaptic spikes. The direction and value of the weight update depends on the postsynaptic membrane potential. In our framework, Eq. (10.28) is a special case of the slightly more general Eq. (10.20).

10.4 Detailed models of synaptic plasticity

In the previous section we have introduced a purely phenomenological model for spike-time-dependent synaptic plasticity that is at least qualitatively in agreement with experimental results. In this section we take a slightly different approach and discuss how the core idea of this model, the learning window, arises from elementary kinetic processes. We start in Section 10.4.1 with a simple mechanistic model and turn then, in Section 10.4.2, to a more detailed model with saturation. A calcium-based model is the topic of Section 10.4.3. All three models give a qualitative explanation for the learning dynamics at the level of individual spikes.

10.4.1 A simple mechanistic model

The AND condition in Hebb's postulate suggests that two biochemical components are involved in the induction of LTP. We do not wish to speculate on the nature of these components, but simply call them a and b. We assume that the first component is generated by a chemical reaction chain triggered by presynaptic spike arrival. In the absence of further input, the concentration $[a]$ decays with a time constant τ_a back to its resting level $[a] = 0$. A simple way to describe this process is

$$\frac{d}{dt}[a] = -\frac{[a]}{\tau_a} + d_a \sum_f \delta(t - t_j^{(f)}),$$

(10.29)

where the sum runs over all *presynaptic* firing times $t_j^{(f)}$. Equation (10.29) states that $[a]$ is increased at each arrival of a presynaptic spike by an amount d_a. A high level of $[a]$ sets the synapse in a state where it is susceptible to changes in its weight. The variable $[a]$ by itself, however, does not trigger a weight change.

To generate the synaptic change, another substance b is needed. The production of b is controlled by a second process triggered by *postsynaptic* spikes,

$$\frac{d}{dt}[b] = -\frac{[b]}{\tau_b} + d_b \sum_f \delta(t - t_i^{(f)}),$$

(10.30)

where τ_b is another time constant. The sum runs over all postsynaptic spikes $t_i^{(f)}$. Note that the second variable $[b]$ does not need to be a biochemical quantity; it could, for example, be the electrical potential caused by the postsynaptic spike itself.

Hebbian learning needs both "substances" to be present at the same time, thus

$$\frac{d}{dt} w_{ij}^{\text{corr}} = \gamma [a(t)] [b(t)],$$

(10.31)

with some rate constant γ. The upper index corr is intended to remind us that we are dealing only with the correlation term on the right-hand side of Eq. (10.14) or Eq. (10.24).

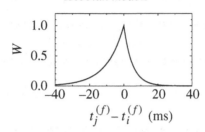

Fig. 10.8. Exponential learning window W as a function of the time difference $s = t_j^{(f)} - t_i^{(f)}$ between presynaptic spike arrival and postsynaptic firing. The time constants for exponential decay are $\tau_1 = 20$ ms for $s < 0$ and $\tau_2 = 10$ ms for $s > 0$.

Let us now consider the synaptic change caused by a single presynaptic spike at $t_j^{(f)} \geq 0$ and a postsynaptic spike at $t_i^{(f)} = t_j^{(f)} - s$. Integration of Eqs. (10.29) and (10.30) yields

$$[a(t)] = d_a \exp[-(t - t_j^{(f)})/\tau_a] \Theta(t - t_j^{(f)})$$
$$[b(t)] = d_b \exp[-(t - t_i^{(f)})/\tau_b] \Theta(t - t_i^{(f)}), \qquad (10.32)$$

where Θ denotes the Heaviside step function as usual. The change caused by the pair of pulses $(t_i^{(f)}, t_j^{(f)})$, measured after a time T, is

$$\int_0^T \left(\frac{d}{dt} w_{ij}^{\text{corr}}\right) dt = \gamma \, d_a \, d_b \int_{\max\{t_j^{(f)}, t_i^{(f)}\}}^T \exp\left[-\frac{t - t_j^{(f)}}{\tau_a} - \frac{t - t_i^{(f)}}{\tau_b}\right] dt . \qquad (10.33)$$

The integral over t can be calculated explicitly. The total weight change that is obtained for $T \gg \tau_a, \tau_b$ can be identified with the learning window. Thus we find

$$W(s) = \begin{cases} A \exp[s/\tau_a] & \text{for} \quad s < 0 \\ A \exp[-s/\tau_b] & \text{for} \quad s > 0 \end{cases} \qquad (10.34)$$

with $s = t_j^{(f)} - t_i^{(f)}$ and $A = \gamma \, d_a \, d_b \, \tau_a \tau_b / (\tau_a + \tau_b)$. As expected, the change of the synaptic efficacy depends only on the time difference between pre- and postsynaptic spikes (Gerstner et al., 1998); cf. Fig. 10.8.

Equation (10.34) describes the change caused by a single pair of spikes. Given a train of presynaptic input spikes and a set of postsynaptic output spikes, many combinations of firing times $(t_i^{(f)}, t_j^{(f)})$ exist. Due to the linearity of the learning equation (10.31), the total change is additive, which is consistent with Eq. (10.14).

The combination of two kinetic processes a and b thus yields an exponential learning window as in Eq. (10.16) but with $A_+ = A_-$. The learning window either describes LTP ($\gamma > 0$) or LTD ($\gamma < 0$), but not both. If we want to have an anti-symmetrical learning window with LTP and LTD we need additional processes as detailed below.

Example: LTP and LTD

For a learning window incorporating both LTP and LTD, we need more microscopic variables. Let us suppose that, as before, we have variables $[a]$ and $[b]$ that contribute to LTP according to (10.31), viz.,

$$\frac{\mathrm{d}}{\mathrm{d}t} w_{ij}^{\mathrm{LTP}} = \gamma^{\mathrm{LTP}} [a(t)] [b(t)] . \tag{10.35}$$

Similarly, we assume that there is a second set of variables $[c]$ and $[d]$, which initiate LTD according to

$$\frac{\mathrm{d}}{\mathrm{d}t} w_{ij}^{\mathrm{LTD}} = -\gamma^{\mathrm{LTD}} [c(t)] [d(t)] . \tag{10.36}$$

The variables $[c]$ and $[d]$ have dynamics analogous to Eq. (10.29) and Eq. (10.30) with amplitudes d_c and d_d, and time constants τ_c and τ_d. The total weight change is the sum of both contributions,

$$w_{ij}^{\mathrm{corr}} = w_{ij}^{\mathrm{LTP}} + w_{ij}^{\mathrm{LTD}} , \tag{10.37}$$

and so is the learning window, i.e.,

$$W(s) = \begin{cases} A_+ \exp[s/\tau_a] - A_- \exp[s/\tau_c] & \text{for} \quad s < 0 \\ A_+ \exp[-s/\tau_b] - A_- \exp[-s/\tau_d] & \text{for} \quad s > 0 \end{cases} \tag{10.38}$$

with $A_+ = \gamma^{\mathrm{LTP}} d_a d_b \tau_a \tau_b / (\tau_a + \tau_b)$ and $A_- = \gamma^{\mathrm{LTD}} d_c d_d \tau_c \tau_d / (\tau_c + \tau_d)$ (Gerstner et al., 1996a, 1998).

We now set $d_b = 1/\tau_b$ and $d_c = 1/\tau_c$. In the limit of $\tau_b \to 0$ and $\tau_c \to 0$, we find the asymmetrical two-phase learning window introduced in Eq. (10.16). Weight changes are now instantaneous. A postsynaptic spike that is triggered after a presynaptic spike arrival reads out the current value of $[a]$ and induces LTP by an amount

$$W(t_j^{(f)} - t_i^{(f)}) = \gamma^{\mathrm{LTP}} d_a \exp\left(-\frac{t_i^{(f)} - t_j^{(f)}}{\tau_a}\right) \qquad \text{for} \quad t_j^{(f)} < t_i^{(f)}. \tag{10.39}$$

A presynaptic spike $t_j^{(f)}$ that arrives *after* a postsynaptic spike reads out the current value of $[d]$ and induces LTD by an amount

$$W(t_j^{(f)} - t_i^{(f)}) = -\gamma^{\mathrm{LTD}} d_d \exp\left(-\frac{t_j^{(f)} - t_i^{(f)}}{\tau_d}\right) \qquad \text{for} \quad t_j^{(f)} > t_i^{(f)}. \tag{10.40}$$

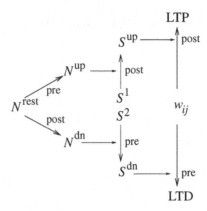

Fig. 10.9. Top: a presynaptic spike shifts NMDA receptors from the rest state N^{rest} to the up-regulated state N^{up}. If a postsynaptic spike arrives shortly afterwards, a second messenger S^1 will be activated (S^{up}). Depending on the amount of activated second messengers S^{up}, postsynaptic spikes lead to LTP. Bottom: postsynaptic spikes downregulate NMDA receptors (N^{dn}). In the presence of N^{dn}, presynaptic spikes activate another second messenger (S^{dn}) leading to LTD.

10.4.2 A kinetic model based on NMDA receptors

A model for LTP and LTD that is slightly more elaborate than the simplistic model discussed in the previous section has been developed by Senn et al. (1997, 2001). This model is based on the assumption that N-methyl-D-aspartate (NMDA) receptors can be in one of three different states, a resting state, an "up" and a "down" state. Transitions between these states are triggered by presynaptic spike arrival ("rest" → "up") and postsynaptic firing ("rest" → "down"). The actual induction of LTP or LTD, however, requires another step, namely the activation of so-called second messengers. The model assumes two types of second messenger, one for LTP and one for LTD. If a presynaptic spike arrives before a postsynaptic spike, the upregulation of the NMDA receptors in combination with the activitation $S_1 \rightarrow S^{\text{up}}$ of the first second-messenger triggers synaptic changes that lead to LTP. On the other hand, if the presynaptic spike arrives after postsynaptic firing, the NMDA receptors are downregulated and the activation $S_2 \rightarrow S^{\text{dn}}$ of the other second-messenger triggers LTD; cf. Fig. 10.9.

The variables N^{up}, N^{dn}, and N^{rest} describe the portion of NMDA receptors that are in one of the three possible states ($N^{\text{up}} + N^{\text{dn}} + N^{\text{rest}} = 1$). In the absence of pre- and postsynaptic spikes, all receptors return to the rest state,

$$\frac{\mathrm{d}}{\mathrm{d}t} N^{\text{rest}} = \frac{N^{\text{up}}}{\tau_{N^{\text{up}}}} + \frac{N^{\text{dn}}}{\tau_{N^{\text{dn}}}} . \tag{10.41}$$

N^{up} and N^{dn} decay with time constants $\tau_{N^{\text{up}}}$ and $\tau_{N^{\text{dn}}}$, respectively. Whenever a presynaptic spike arrives, NMDA receptors are up-regulated from rest to the "up" state according to

$$\frac{d}{dt} N^{\text{up}}(t) = r^{\text{up}} N^{\text{rest}}(t) \sum_f \delta(t - t_j^{(f)}) - \frac{N^{\text{up}}(t)}{\tau_{N^{\text{up}}}}, \tag{10.42}$$

where $t_j^{(f)}$ is the arrival time of a presynaptic spike and r^{up} is the proportion of receptors in the "rest" state that are up-regulated. Since presynaptic spike arrival triggers release of the neurotransmitter glutamate, which is then bound to the NMDA receptors, the "up" state can be identified with a state where the receptor is saturated with glutamate.

Firing of a postsynaptic spike at time $t_i^{(f)}$ leads to a down-regulation of NMDA receptors via

$$\frac{d}{dt} N^{\text{dn}}(t) = r^{\text{dn}} N^{\text{rest}}(t) \sum_f \delta(t - t_i^{(f)}) - \frac{N^{\text{dn}}(t)}{\tau_{N^{\text{dn}}}}. \tag{10.43}$$

Senn et al. (2001) suggest that down-regulation of the NMDA receptor is mediated by the intracellular calcium concentration, which changes with each postsynaptic spike. Note that, since $N^{\text{rest}} = 1 - N^{\text{up}} - N^{\text{dn}}$, Eqs. (10.42) and (10.43) account for saturation effects due to a limited number of NMDA receptors.

The secondary messenger S^{up}, which finally leads to LTP, is activated by postsynaptic spikes, but only if up-regulated NMDA channels are available. In the absence of postsynaptic spikes the concentration of second messengers decays with time constant $\tau_{S^{\text{up}}}$. Thus

$$\frac{d}{dt} S^{\text{up}}(t) = -\frac{S^{\text{up}}(t)}{\tau_{S^{\text{up}}}} + r_S N^{\text{up}}(t) [1 - S^{\text{up}}(t)] \sum_f \delta(t - t_i^{(f)}), \tag{10.44}$$

where r_S is a rate constant. Since $N^{\text{up}}(t) > 0$ requires that a presynaptic spike has occurred before t, the activation of S^{up} effectively depends on the specific timing of pre- and postsynaptic spikes ("first pre, then post").

Similarly, the other second messenger S^{dn} is activated by a presynaptic spike provided that there are receptors in their down-regulated state, i.e.,

$$\frac{d}{dt} S^{\text{dn}}(t) = -\frac{S^{\text{dn}}(t)}{\tau_{S^{\text{dn}}}} + r_S N^{\text{dn}}(t) [1 - S^{\text{dn}}(t)] \sum_f \delta(t - t_j^{(f)}), \tag{10.45}$$

where $\tau_{S^{\text{dn}}}$ is another decay time constant. The second messenger S^{dn} is therefore triggered by the sequence "first post, then pre". The factors $[1 - S^{\text{up}}]$ in Eq. (10.44) and $[1 - S^{\text{dn}}]$ in Eq. (10.45) account for the limited amount of second messengers available at the synapse.

LTP (weight increase) depends on the presence of S^{up}, LTD (weight decrease) on S^{dn}. This is described by

$$\frac{d}{dt}w_{ij} = \gamma_{LTP}(1 - w_{ij})[S^{up} - \theta^{up}]_+ \sum_f \delta(t - t_i^{(f)} - \Delta)$$

$$- \gamma_{LTD}\, w_{ij}[S^{dn} - \theta^{dn}]_+ \sum_f \delta(t - t_j^{(f)} - \Delta) \qquad (10.46)$$

with certain parameters $\gamma_{LTP/D}$ and $\theta^{up/dn}$. Here, $[x]_+ = x\,\Theta(x)$ denotes a piecewise linear function with $[x]_+ = x$ for $x > 0$ and zero otherwise. The delay $0 < \Delta \ll 1$ ensures that the actual weight change occurs *after* the update of S^{up}, S^{dn}. Note that this is a third-order model. The variable $S^{up} > 0$, for example, is already second-order, because it depends on presynaptic spikes followed by postsynaptic action potentials. In Eq. (10.46) the postsynaptic spike is then used again in order to trigger the weight change.

Example: low rates

For low pre- and postsynaptic firing rates, saturation effects can be neglected and Eq. (10.46) is equivalent to the elementary model discussed in Section 10.4.1. Let us assume that a single spike induces a small change (r^{dn}, $r^{up} \ll 1$) so that we can use $N^{rest} \approx 1$ in Eqs. (10.42) and (10.43). The equations for N^{up} and N^{dn} are then identical to those for the "substances" $[a]$ and $[d]$ in Eqs. (10.29), (10.35), and (10.36).

Let us furthermore assume that interspike intervals are long compared to the decay time constants $\tau_{S^{up}}$, $\tau_{S^{dn}}$ in Eqs. (10.44) and (10.45). Then S^{up} is negligible except during and shortly after a postsynaptic action potential. At the moment of postsynaptic firing, S^{up} "reads out" the current value of N^{up}; cf. Eq. (10.44). If this value is large than Θ_{up}, it triggers a positive weight change; cf. Eq. (10.46). Similarly, at the moment of presynaptic spike arrival S^{dn} "reads out" the value of N^{dn} and triggers a weight decrease. Thus, in this limit, the model of Senn et al. (2001) corresponds to an exponential time window

$$W(s) = \begin{cases} A_+(w_{ij})\,\exp[+s/\tau_{N^{up}}] & \text{for} \quad s < 0 \\ A_-(w_{ij})\,\exp[-s/\tau_{N^{dn}}] & \text{for} \quad s > 0 \end{cases} \qquad (10.47)$$

with $A_+(w_{ij}) = r^{up}\, r_S\,(1 - w_{ij})$ and $A_-(w_{ij}) = -r^{dn}\, r_S\, w_{ij}$.

Example: high rates

If we assume that all decay time constants are much longer than typical interspike intervals then the variables $N^{up/dn}$ and $S^{up/dn}$ will finally reach a steady state. If we neglect correlations between pre- and postsynaptic neurons by replacing spike trains by rates, we can solve for these stationary states,

$$N_\infty^{\text{up}} = \frac{\tau_{N^{\text{up}}} \, r^{\text{up}} \, \nu_j}{1 + \tau_{N^{\text{up}}} \, r^{\text{up}} \, \nu_j + \tau_{N^{\text{dn}}} r^{\text{dn}} \nu_i} \tag{10.48}$$

$$S_\infty^{\text{up}} = \frac{\tau_{S^{\text{up}}} \, r_S \, N^{\text{up}} \, \nu_i}{1 + \tau_{S^{\text{up}}} r_S \, N^{\text{up}} \, \nu_i} \tag{10.49}$$

and similar equations for N^{dn} and S^{dn}. Note that S_∞^{up} is a function of ν_i and ν_j. If we put the equations for S_∞^{up} and S_∞^{dn} in Eq. (10.46) we get an expression of the form

$$\frac{d}{dt} w_{ij} = \gamma_{\text{LTP}} \, (1 - w_{ij}) \, f_{\text{LTP}}(\nu_i, \nu_j) \, \nu_i - \gamma_{\text{LTD}} \, w_{ij} \, f_{\text{LTD}}(\nu_i, \nu_j) \, \nu_j \tag{10.50}$$

with functions f_{LTP} and f_{LTD}. We linearize f_{LTP} with respect to ν_j about a reference value $\bar{\nu} > 0$ and evaluate f_{LTD} at $\nu_j = \bar{\nu}$ in order to make the right-hand side of Eq. (10.50) linear in the input ν_j. The result is

$$\frac{d}{dt} w_{ij} = \phi(w_{ij}; \nu_i) \, \nu_j \tag{10.51}$$

with $\phi(w_{ij}; 0) = \phi(w_{ij}; \nu_\theta) = 0$ for some value ν_θ and $d\phi/d\nu_i < 0$ at $\nu_i = 0$. Equation (10.51) is a generalized Bienenstock–Cooper–Monroe rule where ϕ does not only depend on the postsynaptic rate ν_i but also on the individual synaptic weight; cf. Eq. (10.12). For details see Senn et al. (2001) and Bienenstock et al. (1982).

10.4.3 A calcium-based model

It has been recognized for a long time that calcium ions are an important second messenger for the induction of LTP and LTD in the hippocampus (Malenka et al., 1988; Lisman, 1989; Malinow et al., 1989) and cerebellum (Konnerth and Eilers, 1994; Lev-Ram et al., 1997). Particularly well investigated are "NMDA synapses" in the hippocampus (Collingridge et al., 1983; Bindman et al., 1991; Dudek and Bear, 1992; Bliss and Collingridge, 1993) where calcium ions can enter the cell through channels that are controlled by a glutamate receptor subtype called the NMDA receptor; cf. Section 2.4.2. These channels are involved in the transmission of action potentials in glutamatergic (excitatory) synapses. If an action potential arrives at the presynaptic terminal, glutamate, the most common excitatory neu-rotransmitter, is released into the synaptic cleft and diffuses to the postsynaptic membrane where it binds to NMDA and AMPA[2] receptors. The binding to AMPA receptors results in the opening of the associated ion channels and hence to a depolarization of the postsynaptic membrane. Channels controlled by NMDA

---

[2] AMPA is short for α-amino-3-hydroxy-5-methyl-4-isoxalone propionic acid.

receptors, however, are blocked by magnesium ions and do not open unless the membrane is sufficiently depolarized so as to remove the block. Therefore, calcium ions can enter the cell only if glutamate has been released by presynaptic activity *and* if the postsynaptic membrane is sufficiently depolarized. Calcium influx is the first step in a complex biochemical pathway that leads ultimately to a modification of the glutamate sensitivity of the postsynaptic membrane.

Biophysical models of Hebbian plasticity (Lisman, 1989; Holmes and Levy, 1990; Zador et al., 1990; Gold and Bear, 1994; Schiegg et al., 1995; Shouval et al., 2002) contain two essential components, viz. a description of intracellular calcium dynamics, in particular a model of calcium entry through NMDA synapses, and a hypothesis of how the concentration of intracellular calcium influences the change of synaptic efficacy. In this section we give a simplified account of both components. We start with a model of NMDA synapses and turn then to the so-called calcium control hypothesis of Shouval et al. (2002).

NMDA receptor as a coincidence detector

We have emphasized in Sections 10.1–10.3 that all Hebbian learning rules contain a term that depends on the *correlation* between the firings of pre- and postsynaptic neurons. The signaling chain that leads to a weight change therefore has to contain a nonlinear processing step that requires that pre- and postsynaptic neurons are active within some short time window. Synaptic channels controlled by NMDA receptors are an excellent candidate for a biophysical implementation of this condition of "coincidence" because the opening of the channel requires both the presence of glutamate, which reflects presynaptic activity, *and*, in order to remove the magnesium block, a depolarization of the postsynaptic membrane (Mayer et al., 1984; Nowak et al., 1984), cf. Fig. 10.10. A strong depolarization of the postsynaptic membrane does occur, for example, during the back propagation of an action potential into the dendritic tree (Stuart and Sakmann, 1994; Linden, 1999), which is a signature for *postsynaptic* activity.

In a simple model of NMDA-receptor-controlled channels, the calcium current through the channel is described by

$$I_{Ca}(t) = g_{Ca}\, \alpha(t - t_j^{(f)})\, [u(t) - E_{Ca}]\, B[u(t)]\,; \qquad (10.52)$$

cf. Section 2.4. Here g_{Ca} is the maximal conductance of the channel and E_{Ca} is the reversal potential of calcium. The time course of NMDA binding at the receptors is described by $\alpha(t - t_j^{(f)})$ where $t_j^{(f)}$ is the time of spike arrival at the presynaptic terminal. The function

$$B(u) = \frac{1}{1 + 0.28\, e^{-0.062\, u}} \qquad (10.53)$$

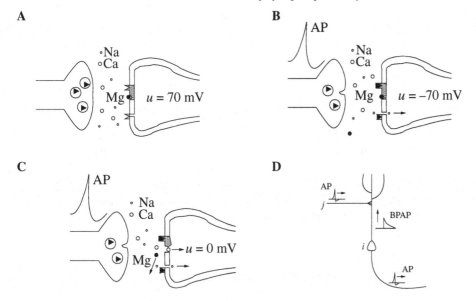

Fig. 10.10. NMDA synapse. **A**. Vesicles in the presynaptic terminal contain glutamate as a neurotransmitter (filled triangles). At resting potential, the NMDA-receptor-mediated channel (hatched) is blocked by magnesium (filled circle). **B**. If an action potential (AP) arrives at the presynaptic terminal the vesicle merges with the cell membrane, glutamate diffuses into the synaptic cleft, and binds to NMDA and nonNMDA receptors on the postsynaptic membrane. At the resting potential, the NMDA-receptor-mediated channel remains blocked by magnesium whereas the nonNMDA channel opens (bottom). **C**. If the membrane of the postsynaptic neuron is depolarized, the magnesium block is removed and calcium ions can enter the cell. **D**. The depolarization of the postsynaptic membrane can be caused by a back propagating action potential (BPAP).

describes the unblocking of the channel at depolarized levels of membrane potential.

The time course of α is taken as a sum of two exponentials with the time constant of the slow component in the range of 100 ms. If there are several presynaptic spikes within 100 ms, calcium accumulates inside the cell. The change of the intracellular calcium concentration $[Ca^{2+}]$ can be described by

$$\frac{d}{dt}[Ca^{2+}](t) = I_{Ca}(t) - \frac{[Ca^{2+}](t)}{\tau_{Ca}}, \tag{10.54}$$

where $\tau_{Ca} = 125$ ms is a phenomenological time constant of decay. Without any further presynaptic stimulus, the calcium concentration returns to a resting value of zero. More sophisticated models can take calcium buffers, calcium stores, and ion pumps into account (Gamble and Koch, 1987; Zador et al., 1990; Schiegg et al., 1995).

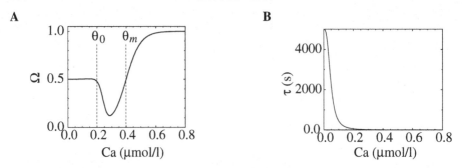

Fig. 10.11. Calcium control hypothesis. The asymptotic weight value $w_{ij} = \Omega([\mathrm{Ca}^{2+}])$ (**A**) and the time constant $\tau([\mathrm{Ca}^{2+}])$ (**B**) of weight changes as a function of the calcium concentration; cf. Eq. (10.55); adapted from Shouval et al. (2002).

The calcium control hypothesis

While the dynamics of NMDA synapses is fairly well understood in terms of the biophysical processes that control receptor binding and channel opening, much less is known about the complex signaling chain that is triggered by calcium and finally leads to a regulation of the synaptic efficacy (Lisman, 1989). Instead of a developing a detailed model, we adopt a phenomenological approach and assume that the change of the synaptic efficacy w_{ij} is fully determined by the intracellular calcium concentration $[\mathrm{Ca}^{2+}]$; an assumption that has been called "calcium control hypothesis" (Shouval et al., 2002). More specifically, we write the weight change as

$$\frac{\mathrm{d}}{\mathrm{d}t} w_{ij} = \frac{\Omega([\mathrm{Ca}^{2+}]) - w_{ij}}{\tau([\mathrm{Ca}^{2+}])} . \tag{10.55}$$

For constant calcium concentration, the weight w_{ij} reaches an asymptotic value $\Omega([\mathrm{Ca}^{2+}])$ with time constant $\tau([\mathrm{Ca}^{2+}])$.

Figure 10.11 shows the graph of the function $\Omega([\mathrm{Ca}^{2+}])$ as it is used in the model of Shouval et al. (2002). For a calcium concentration below θ_0, the weight assumes a resting value of $w_0 = 0.5$. For calcium concentrations in the range $\theta_0 < [\mathrm{Ca}^{2+}] < \theta_m$, the weight tends to decrease, for $[\mathrm{Ca}^{2+}] > \theta_m$ it increases. Qualitatively, the curve $\Omega([\mathrm{Ca}^{2+}])$ reproduces experimental results suggesting that a high level of calcium leads to an increase whereas an intermediate level of calcium leads to a decrease of synaptic weights. We will see below that the BCM rule of Eq. (10.12) is closely related to the function $\Omega([\mathrm{Ca}^{2+}])$.

The time constant $\tau([Ca^{2+}])$ in Eq. (10.55) decreases rapidly with increasing calcium concentration; cf. Fig. 10.11B. The specific dependence has been taken as

$$\tau([Ca^{2+}]) = \frac{\tau_0}{[Ca^{2+}]^3 + 10^{-4}} \tag{10.56}$$

where $\tau_0 = 500$ ms and $[Ca^{2+}]$ is the calcium concentration in μmol/l. At a low level of intracellular calcium ($[Ca^{2+}] \to 0$), the response time of the weight w_{ij} is in the range of hours while for $[Ca^{2+}] \to 1$ the weight changes rapidly with a time constant of 500 ms. In particular, the effective time constant for the induction of LTP is shorter than that for LTD.

Dynamics of the postsynaptic neuron

In order to complete the definition of the model, we need to introduce a description of the membrane potential u_i of the postsynaptic neuron. As in the simple spiking neuron model SRM$_0$ (cf. Chapter 4), the total membrane potential is described as

$$u_i(t) = \eta(t - \hat{t}_i) + \sum_f \epsilon(t - t_j^{(f)}). \tag{10.57}$$

Here $\epsilon(t - t_j^{(f)})$ is the time course of the postsynaptic potential generated by a presynaptic action potential at time $t_j^{(f)}$. It is modeled as a double exponential with a rise time of about 5 ms and a duration of about 50 ms. The action potential of the postsynaptic neuron is described as

$$\eta(s) = u_{AP} \left(0.75\, e^{-s/\tau_{fast}} + 0.25\, e^{-s/\tau_{slow}} \right). \tag{10.58}$$

Here $u_{AP} = 100$ mV is the amplitude of the action potential and $\hat{t}_i$ is the firing time of the last spike of the postsynaptic neuron. In contrast to the model SRM$_0$, η does not describe the reset of the membrane potential at the soma, but the form of the *back propagating* action potential (BPAP) at the site of the synapse. It is assumed that the BPAP has a slow component with a time constant $\tau_{slow} = 35$ ms. The fast component has the same rapid time constant (about 1 ms) as the somatic action potential. The somatic action potential is not described explicitly.

Results

Given the above components of the model, we can understand intuitively how calcium influx at NMDA synapses leads to spike-time-dependent plasticity. Let us analyze the behavior by comparing the calcium-based model with the elementary model of Section 10.4.1; cf. Eqs. (10.29)–(10.31). Binding of glutamate at NMDA receptors plays the role of the component a that is triggered by presynaptic firing; the back propagating action potential (BPAP) plays the role of the component b that is triggered by postsynaptic firing. As a result of the depolarization caused by

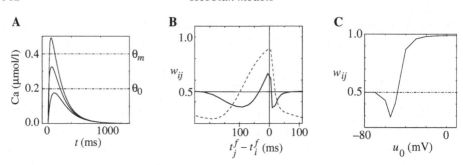

Fig. 10.12. Spike-timing-dependent plasticity in a calcium-based model. **A**. Calcium transient generated by a presynaptic spike in the absence of postsynaptic firing (bottom) and in the presence of a postsynaptic spike 10 ms before (middle) or 10 ms after (top) presynaptic spike arrival. Only for the sequence "pre-before-post" can the threshold θ_m for LTP be reached. **B**. The final weights obtained after several thousands of pre- and postsynaptic spikes that are generated at a rate of 1 Hz (solid line) or 3 Hz (dashed line). The weights are given as a function of the time difference between presynaptic spikes $t_j^{(f)}$ and postsynaptic spikes $t_i^{(f)}$. **C**. Pairing of presynaptic spikes with postsynaptic depolarization. The weights w_{ij} that are obtained after several hundreds of presynaptic spikes (at a rate of $\nu_j = 0.5$ Hz) as a function of the depolarization of the postsynaptic membrane; adapted from Shouval et al. (2002).

the BPAP, the magnesium block is removed and calcium ions enter the cell. The calcium influx is proportional to the product of the NMDA-binding, i.e., the factor α in Eq. (10.52), and the unblocking, i.e., the factor $B(u)$. Finally, the increase in calcium concentration leads to a weight change according to Eq. (10.55).

A single presynaptic spike (without a simultaneous postsynaptic action potential) leads to a calcium transient that stays below the induction threshold θ_0; cf. Fig. 10.12A. If a postsynaptic spike occurs 10 ms *before* the presynaptic spike arrival, the calcium transient has a somewhat larger amplitude that attains a level above θ_0. As a consequence, the weight w_{ij} is reduced. If, however, the postsynaptic spike occurs one or a few milliseconds *after* the presynaptic one, the calcium transient is much larger. The reason is that the blocking of the NMDA synapse is removed during the time when the NMDA receptors are almost completely saturated by glutamate. In this case, the calcium concentration is well above θ_m so that weights increase. Since the time constant $\tau([Ca^{2+}])$ is shorter in the regime of LTP induction than in the regime of LTD induction, the positive weight change is dominant even though the calcium concentration must necessarily pass through the regime of LTD in order to reach the threshold θ_m. The resulting time window of learning is shown in Fig. 10.12B. It exhibits LTP if the presynaptic spike precedes the postsynaptic one by less than 40 ms. If the order of spiking is inverted LTD occurs. LTD can also be induced by a sequence of "pre-before-post" if the spike time difference is larger than about 40 ms. The reason is that in this case the removal of the magnesium block (induced by the BPAP) occurs at a moment when the probability of glutamate binding is reduced; cf. the factor α in Eq. (10.52). As a consequence less calcium enters the cell – enough to surpass the threshold θ_0, but not sufficient to reach the threshold θ_1 of LTP. We emphasize that the form of the learning window is not fixed but depends on the frequency of pre- and postsynaptic spike firing; cf. Fig. 10.12B.

LTP and LTD can also be induced in the *absence* of postsynaptic spikes if the membrane potential of the postsynaptic neuron is clamped to a constant value. A pure spike-time-dependent learning rule defined by a learning window $W(t_j^{(f)} - t_i^{(f)})$ is obviously not a suitable description of such an experiment. The calcium-based model of Shouval et al. (2002), however, can reproduce voltage-clamp experiments; cf. Fig. 10.12C. Presynaptic spike arrival at low frequency ($v_j = 0.5$ Hz) is "paired" with a depolarization of the membrane potential of the postsynaptic neuron to a fixed value u_0. If u_0 is below -70 mV, no significant weight change occurs. For -70 mV $< u_0 < -50$ mV LTD is induced, while for $u_0 > -50$ mV LTP is triggered. These results are a direct consequence of the removal of the magnesium block at the NMDA synapses with increasing voltage. The mean calcium concentration – and hence the asymptotic weight value – is therefore a monotonously increasing function of u_0.

Finally, we would like to emphasize the close relation between Fig. 10.12C and the function ϕ of the BCM learning rule as illustrated in Fig. 10.5. In a simple rate model, the postsynaptic firing rate v_i is a sigmoidal function of the potential, i.e., $v_i = g(u_i)$. Thus, the mapping between the two figures is given by a nonlinear transformation of the horizontal axis.

10.5 Summary

Correlation-based learning is, as a whole, often called Hebbian learning. The Hebb rule of Eq. (10.2) is a special case of a *local* learning rule because it only depends on pre- and postsynaptic firing rates and the present state w_{ij} of the synapse, i.e., information that is easily "available" at the location of the synapse.

Recent experiments have shown that the relative timing of pre- and postsynaptic spikes critically determines the amplitude and even the direction of changes of synaptic efficacy. In order to account for these effects, learning rules at the level of individual spikes are formulated with a learning window that consists of two parts. If the presynaptic spike arrives before a postsynaptic output spike, the synaptic change is positive. If the timing is the other way round, the synaptic change is negative (Markram et al., 1997; Bi and Poo, 1998, 1999; Debanne et al., 1998;

Zhang et al., 1998). For some synapses, the learning window is reversed (Bell et al., 1997b), for others it contains only a single component (Egger et al., 1999).

Hebbian learning is considered to be a major principle of neuronal organization during development. The first modeling studies of cortical organization development (Willshaw and von der Malsburg, 1976; Swindale, 1982) have incited a long line of research, e.g., Kohonen (1984); Linsker (1986a,b,c); Miller et al. (1989); MacKay and Miller (1990); Obermayer et al. (1992). Most of these models use in some way or another an unsupervised correlation-based learning rule similar to the general Hebb rule of Eq. (10.2); see Erwin et al. (1995) for a recent review.

Literature

Correlation-based learning can be traced back to Aristoteles[3] and has been discussed extensively by James (1890) who formulated a learning principle on the level of "brain processes" rather than neurons:

When two elementary brain-processes have been active together or in immediate succession, one of them, on re-occurring, tends to propagate its excitement into the other.

A chapter of James' book is reprinted in volume 1 of Anderson and Rosenfeld's collection on neurocomputing (Anderson and Rosenfeld, 1988). More than 50 years later, Hebb's book (Hebb, 1949) of which two interesting sections are reprinted in the collection of Anderson and Rosenfeld (1988) was published. The historical context of Hebb's postulate is discussed in the review of Sejnowski (1999). In the reprint volume of Anderson and Rosenfeld (1988), articles of Grossberg (1976) and Bienenstock et al. (1982) illustrate the use of the rate-based learning rules discussed in Section 10.2. Kohonen's book gives an overview of some mathematical results for several generic rate-based learning rules (Kohonen, 1984).

For reviews on (hippocampal) LTP, see the book of Byrne and Berry (1989), in particular the articles of Sejnowski and Tesauro (1989) and Brown et al. (1989). Cerebellar LTD has been reviewed by Daniel et al. (1996, 1998) and Linden and Connor (1995). Further references and a classification of different forms of LTP and LTD can be found in the nice review of Bliss and Collingridge (1993). For the relation of LTP and LTD, consult Artola and Singer (1993). A modern and highly recommendable review with a focus on recent results, in particular on spike-time-dependent plasticity, has been written by Bi and Poo (2001). The

---

[3] Aristoteles, "De memoria et reminiscentia": There is no need to consider how we remember what is distant, but only what is neighboring, for clearly the method is the same. For the changes follow each other by habit, one after another. And thus, whenever someone wishes to recollect he will do the following: he will seek to get a starting point for a change after which will be the change in question.

theoretical context of the experiments on spike-time-dependent plasticity are discussed by Abbott (2000).

11

Learning equations

Neurons in the central nervous system form a complex network with a high degree of plasticity. In the previous chapter we have discussed synaptic plasticity from a phenomenological point of view. We now ask "what are the consequences for the connectivity between neurons if synapses are plastic?". To do so we consider a scenario known as unsupervised learning. We assume that some of the neurons in the network are stimulated by input with certain statistical properties. Synaptic plasticity generates changes in the connectivity pattern that reflect the statistical structure of the input. The relationship between the input statistics and the synaptic weights that evolve due to Hebbian plasticity is the topic of this chapter. We start in Section 11.1 with a review of unsupervised learning in a rate-coding paradigm. The extension of the analysis to spike-time-dependent synaptic plasticity is made in Section 11.2. We will see that spike-based learning naturally accounts for spatial *and* temporal correlations in the input and can overcome some of the problems of a simple rate-based learning rule.

11.1 Learning in rate models

We would like to understand how activity-dependent learning rules influence the formation of connections between neurons in the brain. We will see that plasticity is controlled by the statistical properties of the presynaptic input that is impinging on the postsynaptic neuron. Before we delve into the analysis of the elementary Hebb rule, we therefore need to recapitulate a few results from statistics and linear algebra.

11.1.1 Correlation matrix and principal components

A principal component analysis (PCA) is a standard technique to describe the statistical properties of a set of high-dimensional data points and is usually

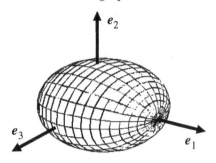

Fig. 11.1. Ellipsoid approximating the shape of a cloud of data points. The first principal component e_1 corresponds to the principal axis of the ellipsoid.

performed in order to find those components of the data that show the highest variability within the set. If we think of the input data set as of a cloud of points in a high-dimensional vector space centered around the origin, then the first principal component is the direction of the longest axis of the ellipsoid that encompasses the cloud; cf. Fig. 11.1. If the data points consisted of, say, two separate clouds then the first principal component would give the direction of the line that connects the center points of the two clouds. A PCA can thus be used to break a large data set into separate clusters. In the following, we will quickly explain the basic idea and show that the first principal component gives the direction where the variance of the data is maximal.

Let us consider an ensemble of data points $\{\boldsymbol{\xi}^1, \ldots, \boldsymbol{\xi}^P\}$ drawn from a (high-dimensional) vector space, for example $\boldsymbol{\xi}^\mu = (\xi_1^\mu, \ldots, \xi_N^\mu) \in \mathbb{R}^N$. For this set of data points we define the *correlation matrix* C_{ij} as

$$C_{ij} = \frac{1}{p} \sum_{\mu=1}^{p} \xi_i^\mu \xi_j^\mu = \left\langle \xi_i^\mu \xi_j^\mu \right\rangle_\mu . \tag{11.1}$$

Angular brackets $\langle\ \rangle_\mu$ denote an average over the whole set of data points. Similar to the variance of a single random variable we can also define the *covariance matrix* V_{ij} of our data set,

$$V_{ij} = \left\langle (\xi_i^\mu - \langle \xi_i^\mu \rangle_\mu)(\xi_j^\mu - \langle \xi_j^\mu \rangle_\mu) \right\rangle_\mu . \tag{11.2}$$

In the following we will assume that the coordinate system is chosen so that the center of mass of the set of data points is located at the origin, i.e., $\langle \xi_i \rangle_\mu = \langle \xi_j \rangle_\mu = 0$. In this case, correlation matrix and covariance matrix are identical.

The *principal components* of the set $\{\boldsymbol{\xi}^1, \ldots, \boldsymbol{\xi}^P\}$ are defined as the eigenvectors of the covariance matrix V. Note that V is symmetric, i.e., $V_{ij} = V_{ji}$. The eigenvalues of V are thus real-valued and different eigenvectors are orthogonal

(Horn and Johnson, 1985). Furthermore, V is positive semi-definite since

$$\mathbf{y}^{\mathrm{T}} V \mathbf{y} = \sum_{ij} y_i \left\langle \xi_i^\mu \xi_j^\mu \right\rangle_\mu y_j = \left\langle \left[\sum_i y_i \xi_i^\mu \right]^2 \right\rangle_\mu \geq 0 \qquad (11.3)$$

for any vector $\mathbf{y} \in \mathbb{R}^N$. Therefore, all eigenvalues of V are nonnegative.

We can sort the eigenvectors $\mathbf{e}_i$ according to the size of the corresponding eigenvalues $\lambda_1 \geq \lambda_2 \geq \cdots \geq 0$. The eigenvector with the largest eigenvalue is called the first principal component. It points in the direction where the variance of the data is maximal. To see this we calculate the variance of the projection of ξ^μ onto an arbitrary direction $\mathbf{y}$ that we write as $\mathbf{y} = \sum_i a_i \mathbf{e}_i$ with $\sum_i a_i^2 = 1$ so that $\|\mathbf{y}\| = 1$. The variance σ_y^2 along $\mathbf{y}$ is

$$\sigma_y^2 = \left\langle \left[\mathbf{x}^\mu \cdot \mathbf{y} \right]^2 \right\rangle_\mu = \mathbf{y}^{\mathrm{T}} V \mathbf{y} = \sum_i \lambda_i a_i^2 . \qquad (11.4)$$

The right-hand side is maximal under the constraint $\sum_i a_i^2 = 1$ if $a_1 = 1$ and $a_i = 0$ for $i = 2, 3, \ldots, N$, that is, if $\mathbf{y} = \mathbf{e}_1$.

11.1.2 Evolution of synaptic weights

In the following we analyze the evolution of synaptic weights using the Hebbian learning rules that have been described in Chapter 10. To do so, we consider a highly simplified scenario consisting of an analog neuron that receives input from N presynaptic neurons with firing rates v_i^{pre} via synapses with weights w_i; cf. Fig. 11.2A. We think of the presynaptic neurons as "input neurons", which, however, do not have to be sensory neurons. The input layer could, for example, consist of neurons in the lateral geniculate nucleus (LGN) that project to neurons in the visual cortex. We will see that the statistical properties of the input control the evolution of synaptic weights.

For the sake of simplicity, we model the presynaptic input as a set of static patterns. Let us suppose that we have a total of p patterns $\{\xi^\mu; 1 < \mu < p\}$. At each time step one of the patterns ξ^μ is selected at random and presented to the network by fixing the presynaptic rates at $v_i^{\mathrm{pre}} = \xi_i^\mu$. We call this the *static-pattern scenario*. The presynaptic activity drives the postsynaptic neuron and the joint activity of pre- and postsynaptic neurons triggers changes of the synaptic weights. The synaptic weights are modified according to a Hebbian learning rule, i.e., according to the correlation of pre- and postsynaptic activity; cf. Eq. (10.3). Before the next input pattern is chosen, the weights are changed by an amount

$$\Delta w_i = \gamma \, v^{\mathrm{post}} \, v_i^{\mathrm{pre}}. \qquad (11.5)$$

Here, $0 < \gamma \ll 1$ is a small constant called "learning rate". The learning rate

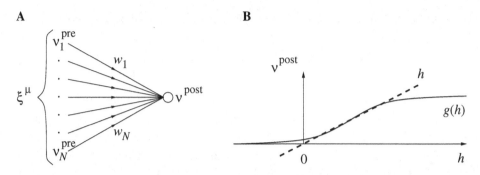

Fig. 11.2. Elementary model. **A.** Patterns $\boldsymbol{\xi}^{\mu}$ are applied as a set of presynaptic firing rates v_j, i.e., $\boldsymbol{\xi}_j^{\mu} = v_j^{\mathrm{pre}}$ for $1 \leq j \leq N$. **B.** The gain function of the postsynaptic neuron is taken as linear, i.e., $v^{\mathrm{post}} = h$. It can be seen as a linearization of the sigmoidal gain function $g(h)$.

in the static-pattern scenario is closely linked to the correlation coefficient c_2^{corr} in the continuous-time Hebb rule introduced in Eq. (10.3). In order to highlight the relationship, let us assume that each pattern $\boldsymbol{\xi}^{\mu}$ is applied during an interval Δt. For Δt sufficiently small, we have $\gamma = c_2^{\mathrm{corr}} \Delta t$.

In a general rate model, the firing rate v^{post} of the postsynaptic neuron is given by a nonlinear function of the total input

$$v^{\mathrm{post}} = g\left(\sum_i w_i\, v_i^{\mathrm{pre}} \right) ; \tag{11.6}$$

cf. Fig. 11.2B. For the sake of simplicity, we restrict our discussion in the following to a *linear* rate model with

$$v^{\mathrm{post}} = \sum_i w_i\, v_i^{\mathrm{pre}} . \tag{11.7}$$

Obviously, this is a highly simplified neuron model, but it will serve our purpose of gaining some insights in the evolution of synaptic weights.

If we combine the learning rule of Eq. (11.5) with the linear rate model of Eq. (11.7) we find after the presentation of pattern $\boldsymbol{\xi}^{\mu}$

$$\Delta w_i = \gamma \sum_j w_j\, v_j^{\mathrm{pre}}\, v_i^{\mathrm{pre}} = \gamma \sum_j w_j\, \xi_j^{\mu}\, \xi_i^{\mu} . \tag{11.8}$$

The evolution of the weight vector $\boldsymbol{w} = (w_1, \ldots, w_N)$ is thus determined by the iteration

$$w_i(n+1) = w_i(n) + \gamma \sum_j w_j\, \xi_j^{\mu_n}\, \xi_i^{\mu_n} , \tag{11.9}$$

where μ_n denotes the pattern that is presented during the nth time step.

We are interested in the long-term behavior of the synaptic weights. To this end we assume that the weight vector evolves along a more or less deterministic trajectory with only small stochastic deviations that result from the randomness at which new input patterns are chosen. This is, for example, the case if the learning rate is small so that a large number of patterns has to be presented in order to induce a substantial weight change. In such a situation it is sensible to consider the expectation value of the weight vector, i.e., the weight vector $\langle w(n) \rangle$ averaged over the sequence $(\xi^{\mu_1}, \xi^{\mu_2}, \ldots, \xi^{\mu_n})$ of all patterns that so far have been presented to the network. From Eq. (11.9) we find

$$
\begin{aligned}
\langle w_i(n+1) \rangle &= \langle w_i(n) \rangle + \gamma \sum_j \left\langle w_j(n)\, \xi_j^{\mu_{n+1}}\, \xi_i^{\mu_{n+1}} \right\rangle \\
&= \langle w_i(n) \rangle + \gamma \sum_j \langle w_j(n) \rangle \left\langle \xi_j^{\mu_{n+1}}\, \xi_i^{\mu_{n+1}} \right\rangle \\
&= \langle w_i(n) \rangle + \gamma \sum_j C_{ij} \langle w_j(n) \rangle .
\end{aligned}
\tag{11.10}
$$

The angular brackets denote an ensemble average over the whole sequence of input patterns $(\xi^{\mu_1}, \xi^{\mu_2}, \ldots)$. The second equality is due to the fact that input patterns are chosen *independently* in each time step, so that the average over $w_j(n)$ and $(\xi_j^{\mu_{n+1}} \xi_i^{\mu_{n+1}})$ can be factorized. In the final expression we have introduced the correlation matrix C_{ij},

$$
C_{ij} = \frac{1}{p} \sum_{\mu=1}^{p} \xi_i^{\mu} \xi_j^{\mu} = \left\langle \xi_i^{\mu} \xi_j^{\mu} \right\rangle_{\mu} .
\tag{11.11}
$$

Expression (11.10) can be written in a more compact form using matrix notation,

$$
\langle w(n+1) \rangle = (\mathbb{1} + \gamma\, C)\, \langle w(n) \rangle = (\mathbb{1} + \gamma\, C)^{n+1} \langle w(0) \rangle ,
\tag{11.12}
$$

where $w(n) = (w_1(n), \ldots, w_N(n))$ is the weight vector and $\mathbb{1}$ is the identity matrix.

If we express the weight vector in terms of the eigenvectors e_k of C,

$$
\langle w(n) \rangle = \sum_k a_k(n)\, e_k ,
\tag{11.13}
$$

we obtain an explicit expression for $\langle w(n) \rangle$ for any given initial condition $a_k(0)$, viz.,

$$
\langle w(n) \rangle = \sum_k (1 + \lambda_k)^n\, a_k(0)\, e_k .
\tag{11.14}
$$

Since the correlation matrix is positive semi-definite all eigenvalues λ_k are real and positive. Therefore, the weight vector is growing exponentially, but the growth

A

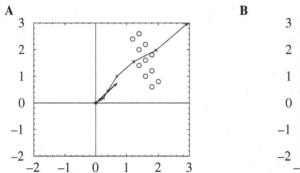

B

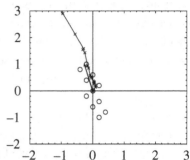

Fig. 11.3. Weight changes induced by the standard Hebb rule. Input patterns $\xi^\mu \in \mathbb{R}^2$ are marked as circles. The sequence of weight vectors $w(1)$, $w(2)$, ... , is indicated by crosses connected by a solid line. **A.** The weight vector evolves in the direction of the dominant eigenvector (arrow) of the correlation matrix. **B.** If the input patterns are normalized so that their center of mass is at the origin, then the dominant eigenvector of the correlation matrix coincides with the first principal component e_1 of the data set.

will soon be dominated by the eigenvector with the largest eigenvalue, i.e., the *first principal component*,

$$\langle w(n) \rangle \xrightarrow{n \to \infty} (1 + \lambda_1)^n \, a_1(0) \, e_1 ; \qquad (11.15)$$

cf. Section 11.1.1. Recall that the output of the linear neuron model of Eq. (11.7) is proportional to the projection of the current input pattern ξ^μ on the direction w. For $w \propto e_1$, the output is therefore proportional to the projection on the first principal component of the input distribution. A Hebbian learning rule such as Eq. (11.8) is thus able to extract the first principal component of the input data; cf Fig. 11.3.

From a data-processing point of view, the extraction of the first principle component of the input data set by a biologically inspired learning rule seems to be very compelling. There are, however, a few drawbacks and pitfalls. Firstly, the above statement about the Hebbian learning rule is limited to the *expectation value* of the weight vector. We will see below that, if the learning rate is sufficiently low, then the actual weight vector is in fact very close to the expected one.

Secondly, while the direction of the weight vector moves in the direction of the principal component, the *norm* of the weight vector grows without bounds. We will see below in Section 11.1.3 that suitable variants of Hebbian learning allow us to control the length of the weight vector without changing its direction.

Thirdly, principal components are only meaningful if the input data are normalized, i.e., distributed around the origin. This requirement is *not* consistent with a rate interpretation because rates are usually positive. This problem, however, can be overcome by learning rules such as the covariance rule of Eq. (10.10) that are based on the deviation of the rates from a certain mean firing rate. We will see in Section 11.2.4 that a spike-based learning rule can be devised that is sensitive only to deviations from the mean firing rate and can thus find the first principal component even if the input is not properly normalized.

Self-averaging (*)

So far, we have derived the behavior of the *expected* weight vector, $\langle w \rangle$. Here we show that explicit averaging is not necessary provided that learning is slow enough. In this case, the weight vector is the sum of a large number of small changes. The weight dynamics is thus "*self-averaging*" and the weight vector w can be well approximated by its expectation value $\langle w \rangle$.

We start from the formulation of Hebbian plasticity in continuous time,

$$\frac{\mathrm{d}}{\mathrm{d}t} w_i = c_2^{\mathrm{corr}} \, v^{\mathrm{post}} \, v_i^{\mathrm{pre}} ; \tag{11.16}$$

cf. Eq. (10.3). Each pattern ξ^μ is presented for a short period of duration Δt. We assume that the weights change during the presentation by a small amount only, i.e., $\int_t^{t+\Delta t} [\mathrm{d}w_j(t')/\mathrm{d}t'] \, \mathrm{d}t' \ll w_j(t)$. This condition can be met either by a short presentation time Δt or by a small learning coefficient c_2^{corr}. Under this condition, we can take the postsynaptic firing rate $v^{\mathrm{post}}(t) = \sum_j w_j(t) \, v_i^{\mathrm{pre}}$ as constant for the duration of one presentation. The total weight change induced by the presentation of pattern ξ^μ to first order in Δt is thus

$$\Delta w_i(t) = w_i(t + \Delta t) - w_i(t) = \gamma \sum_j w_j(t) \, \xi_j^\mu \, \xi_i^\mu + \mathcal{O}(\Delta t^2) . \tag{11.17}$$

with $\gamma = c_2^{\mathrm{corr}} \, \Delta t$; cf. Eq. (11.8).

In the next time step a new pattern ξ^ν is presented so that the weight is changed to

$$w_i(t + 2\Delta t) = w_i(t + \Delta t) + c_2^{\mathrm{corr}} \, \Delta t \sum_j w_j(t + \Delta t) \, \xi_j^\nu \, \xi_i^\nu + \mathcal{O}(\Delta t^2) . \tag{11.18}$$

Since we keep only terms to first order in Δt, we may set $w_j(t + \Delta t) = w_j(t)$ in the sum on the right-hand side of Eq. (11.18). Let us suppose that in the interval $[t, t + p\,\Delta t]$ each of the p patterns has been applied exactly once. Then, to first order in Δt,

$$w_i(t + p\,\Delta t) - w_i(t) = c_2^{\mathrm{corr}} \, \Delta t \sum_j w_j(t) \sum_{\mu=1}^{p} \xi_i^\mu \, \xi_j^\mu + \mathcal{O}(\Delta t^2) . \tag{11.19}$$

For $c_2^{\mathrm{corr}} \, \Delta t \ll 1$, all higher-order terms can be neglected. Division by $p\,\Delta t$ yields

$$\frac{w_i(t + p\,\Delta t) - w_i(t)}{p\,\Delta t} = c_2^{\mathrm{corr}} \sum_j w_j(t) \, C_{ij} . \tag{11.20}$$

A **B**

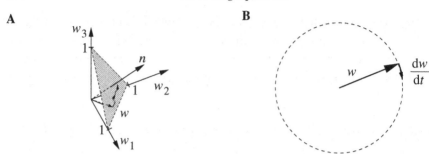

Fig. 11.4. Weight vector normalization. **A**. Normalization of the summed weights $\sum_j w_{ij} = 1$ constrains the weight vector w to a hyperplane perpendicular to the diagonal vector $n = (1, 1, \ldots, 1)^\mathsf{T}$. Hard bounds $0 \leq w_{ij} \leq 1$ force the weight vector to stay inside the shaded region. **B**. Normalization of the quadratic norm $\|w\|^2 = 1$. The weight change $\Delta w(n)$ is perpendicular to the current weight vector $w(n)$ so that the length of w remains constant (Oja's learning rule).

The left-hand side can be approximated by a differential operator dw/dt,

$$\frac{d}{dt} w_i(t) = c_2^{\text{corr}} \sum_j w_j(t) \, C_{ij} . \tag{11.21}$$

We thus recover our previous result that weights are driven by the correlations in the input but with the additional vantage that no explicit averaging step is necessary (Sanders and Verhulst, 1985).

11.1.3 Weight normalization

We have seen in Section 11.1.2 that the simple learning rule of Eq. (10.3) leads to exponentially growing weights. Since this is biologically not plausible, we must use a modified Hebbian learning rule that includes weight decrease and saturation; cf. Section 10.2. Particularly interesting are learning rules that lead to a normalized weight vector. Normalization is a desirable property since it leads to competition between synaptic weights w_{ij} that converge on the same postsynaptic neuron i. Competition means that if a synaptic efficacy increases, it does so at the expense of other synapses that must decrease.

For a discussion of weight vector normalization two aspects are important, namely *what* is normalized and *how* the normalization is achieved. Learning rules can be designed to normalize either the *sum* of weights, $\sum_j w_{ij}$, or the quadratic *norm*, $\|w\|^2 = \sum_j w_{ij}^2$ (or any other norm on $\mathbb{R}^N$). In the first case, the weight vector is constrained to a plane perpendicular to the diagonal vector $n = (1, \ldots, 1)$; in the second case it is constrained to a hypersphere; cf. Fig. 11.4.

Secondly, normalization of the weight vector can either be multiplicative or subtractive. In the former case all weights are multiplied by a common factor so that large weights w_{ij} are corrected by a larger amount than smaller ones. In the latter case a common constant is subtracted from each weight. Usually, subtractive normalization is combined with hard bounds $0 \leq w_{ij} \leq w^{\max}$ in order to avoid runaway of individual weights. Finally, learning rules may or may not fall into the class of *local* learning rules that we have considered in Section 10.2.

A systematic classification of various learning rules according to the above three criteria has been proposed by Miller and MacKay (1994). Here we restrict ourselves to two instances of learning with normalization properties which we illustrate in the examples below. We start with the subtractive normalization of the summed weights $\sum_j w_{ij}$ and turn then to a discussion of Oja's rule as an instance of a multiplicative normalization of $\sum_j w_{ij}^2$.

Example: subtractive normalization of $\sum_i w_i$

In a subtractive normalization scheme the sum over all weights, $\sum_i w_i$, can be kept constant by subtracting the average total weight change, $N^{-1} \sum_i \Delta \tilde{w}_i$, from each synapse after the weights have been updated according to a Hebbian learning rule with $\Delta \tilde{w}_i = \gamma \sum_j w_j \xi_j^\mu \xi_i^\mu$. Altogether, the learning rule is of the form

$$
\Delta w_i = \Delta \tilde{w}_i - N^{-1} \sum_j \Delta \tilde{w}_j
$$

$$
= \gamma \left(\sum_j w_j \xi_j^\mu \xi_i^\mu - N^{-1} \sum_k \sum_j w_j \xi_j^\mu \xi_k^\mu \right), \tag{11.22}
$$

where $\Delta \tilde{w}_i$ denotes the weight change that is due to the pure Hebbian learning rule without the normalization. It can easily be verified that $\sum_i \Delta w_i = 0$ so that $\sum_i w_i = $ const. The temporal evolution of the weight vector w is thus restricted to a hyperplane perpendicular to $(1, \dots, 1) \in \mathbb{R}^N$. Note that this learning rule is nonlocal because the change of weight depends on the activity of all presynaptic neurons.

In a similar way as in the previous section, we calculate the expectation of the weight vector $\langle w(n) \rangle$, averaged over the sequence of input patterns $(\xi^{\mu_1}, \xi^{\mu_2}, \dots)$,

$$
\langle w_i(n+1) \rangle = \langle w_i(n) \rangle + \gamma \left(\sum_j C_{ij} \langle w_j(n) \rangle - N^{-1} \sum_k \sum_j C_{kj} \langle w_j(n) \rangle \right), \tag{11.23}
$$

or explicitly, using matrix notation

$$
\langle w(n) \rangle = [1 + \gamma (C - \bar{C})]^n \langle w(0) \rangle, \tag{11.24}
$$

with $\bar{C}_{ij} = N^{-1} \sum_k C_{kj}$. The evolution of the weight vector is thus determined

A

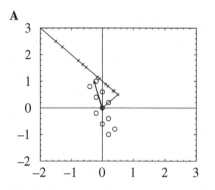

B

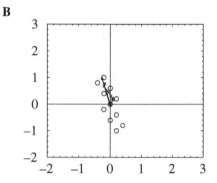

Fig. 11.5. Similar plots as in Fig. 11.3 but with weight vector normalization. **A**. With subtractive normalization, the weight vector evolves along a line that is perpendicular to the diagonal vector $(1, 1)$. Without additional constraints, the length of the weight vector grows without bounds. **B**. Oja's learning rule results in a quick convergence of the weight vector to the first principal component (arrow) of the data set.

by eigenvectors of the matrix $(C - \bar{C})$ that are in general different from those of the correlation matrix C. Hebbian learning with subtractive normalization is driven by the correlations of the input in the subspace orthogonal to the diagonal vector $(1, \ldots, 1)$. Though the sum of the weights stays constant individual weights keep growing. It is thus necessary to adopt an additional criterion to stop the learning process and to prevent components of the weight vector from growing beyond all bounds. A subtractive weight normalization is usually combined with hard boundaries for the weights; cf. Section 10.2.1. With these constraints, the weight vector converges to a final state where (almost) all weights are saturated at the upper or lower bound (Miller and MacKay, 1994); cf. Fig. 11.5A.

Example: multiplicative normalization of $\|w\|$

Normalization of the sum of the weights, $\sum_i w_i$, needs an additional criterion to prevent individual weights from perpetual growth. A more elegant way is to require that the sum of the squared weights, i.e., the length of the weight vector $\sum_i w_i^2$, remains constant. This restricts the evolution of the weight vector to a sphere in the N dimensional weight space. In addition, we can employ a multiplicative normalization scheme where all weights all multiplied by a common factor instead of subtracting a common constant. The advantage of multiplicative compared to subtractive normalization is that small weights will not change their sign during the normalization step.

In order to formalize the above idea we first calculate the "naïve" weight change $\tilde{w}(n)$ in time step n according to the common Hebbian learning rule,

$$\Delta\tilde{w}(n) = \gamma \left[w(n) \cdot \boldsymbol{\xi}^\mu \right] \boldsymbol{\xi}^\mu . \tag{11.25}$$

The update of the weights is accompanied by a normalization of the norm of the weight vector to unity, i.e.,

$$w(n + 1) = \frac{w(n) + \Delta \tilde{w}(n)}{\|w(n) + \Delta \tilde{w}(n)\|} . \tag{11.26}$$

If we assume that the weights are changed only by a very small amount during each step ($\gamma \ll 1$), we can calculate the new weights $w(n + 1)$ to first order in γ,

$$w(n + 1) = w(n) + \Delta \tilde{w}(n) - w(n) [w(n) \cdot \Delta \tilde{w}(n)] + \mathcal{O}(\gamma^2) . \tag{11.27}$$

The "effective" weight change $\Delta w(n)$ including normalization to leading order in γ is thus

$$\Delta w(n) = \Delta \tilde{w}(n) - w(n) [w(n) \cdot \Delta \tilde{w}(n)] , \tag{11.28}$$

which corresponds to the vector component of $\Delta \tilde{w}$ that is *orthogonal* to the current weight vector w. This is exactly what we would have expected because the length of the weight vector must stay constant; cf. Fig. 11.4B.

We may wonder whether Eq. (11.28) is a *local* learning rule. In order to answer this question, we recall that the "naïve" weight change $\Delta \tilde{w}_j = \gamma \, v^{\text{post}} \, v_j^{\text{pre}}$ uses only pre- and postsynaptic information. Hence, we can rewrite Eq. (11.28) in terms of the firing rates,

$$\Delta w_j = \gamma \, v^{\text{post}} \, v_j - \gamma \, w_j(n) \, \left(v^{\text{post}} \right)^2 . \tag{11.29}$$

In the second term on the right-hand side we have made use of the linear neuron model, i.e., $v^{\text{post}} = \sum_k w_k \, v_k^{\text{pre}}$. Since the weight change depends only on pre- and postsynaptic rates, Eq. (11.29), which is known as Oja's learning rule (Oja, 1982), is indeed local; cf. Eq. (10.11).

In order to see that Oja's learning rule selects the first principal component we show that the eigenvectors $\{e_1, \ldots, e_N\}$ of C are fixed points of the dynamics but that only the eigenvector e_1 with the largest eigenvalue is stable. For any fixed weight vector w we can calculate the expectation of the weight change in the next time step by averaging over the whole ensemble of input patterns $\{\xi^1, \xi^2, \ldots\}$. With $\langle \Delta \tilde{w}(n) \rangle = \gamma \, C \, w$ we find from Eq. (11.28)

$$\langle \Delta w \rangle = \gamma \, C \, w - \gamma \, w \, [w \cdot C \, w] . \tag{11.30}$$

We claim that any eigenvector e_i of the correlation matrix C is a fixed point of Eq. (11.30). Indeed, if we substitute $w = e_i$ in the above equation we find that $\langle \Delta w \rangle = 0$. In order to investigate the stability of this fixed point we consider a small perturbation $w = e_i + c \, e_j$ in the direction of e_j. Here, $|c| \ll 1$ is the amplitude of the perturbation. If we substitute $w = e_i + c \, e_j$ into Eq. (11.30) we find

$$\langle \Delta w \rangle = c \, \gamma \, (\lambda_j - \lambda_i) \, e_j + \mathcal{O}(c^2) . \tag{11.31}$$

The weight vector will thus evolve in the direction of the perturbation e_j if $\lambda_j > \lambda_i$ so that the initial perturbation will increase. In this case, e_i is unstable. On the other hand, if $\lambda_j < \lambda_i$ the averaged weight change tends to decrease the perturbation and e_i is stable. Consequently, the eigenvector of C with the largest eigenvalue, viz., the first principle component, is the sole stable fixed point of the dynamics generated by the learning rule of Eq. (11.26). Figure 11.5B shows a simple example.

11.1.4 Receptive field development

Most neurons of the visual system respond only to stimulation from a narrow region within the visual field. This region is called the *receptive field* of that neuron. Depending on the precise position of a narrow bright spot within the receptive field the corresponding neuron can either show an increase or a decrease of the firing rate relative to its spontaneous activity at rest. The receptive field is subdivided accordingly into "ON" and "OFF" regions in order to further characterize neuronal response properties. Bright spots in an ON region increase the firing rate whereas bright spots in an OFF region inhibit the neuron.

Different neurons have different receptive fields, but, as a general rule, neighboring neurons have receptive fields that "look" at about the same region of the visual field. This is what is usually called the *retinotopic organization* of the neuronal projections – neighboring points in the visual field are mapped to neighboring neurons of the visual system.

The visual system forms a complicated hierarchy of interconnected cortical areas where neurons show increasingly complex response properties from one layer to the next. Neurons from the lateral geniculate nucleus (LGN), which is the first neuronal relay of visual information after the retina, are characterized by so-called center-surround receptive fields. These are receptive fields that consist of two concentric parts, an ON region and an OFF region. LGN neurons come in two flavors, as ON-center and OFF-center cells. ON-center cells have a ON region in the center of their receptive field that is surrounded by a circular OFF region. In OFF-center cells the arrangement is the other way round; a central OFF region is surrounded by an ON region; cf. Fig. 11.6.

Neurons from the LGN project to the primary visual cortex (V1), which is the first cortical area involved in the processing of visual information. In this area neurons can be divided into "simple cells" and "complex cells". In contrast to LGN neurons, simple cells have *asymmetric* receptive fields which results in a selectivity with respect to the orientation of a visual stimulus. The optimal stimulus for a neuron with a receptive field such as that shown in Fig. 11.6D, for example, is a light bar tilted by about 45 degrees. Any other orientation would also stimulate the OFF region of the receptive field leading to a reduction of the neuronal response.

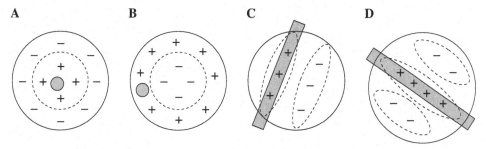

Fig. 11.6. Receptive fields (schematic). **A, B**. Circularly symmetric receptive field typical of neurons in the LGN. ON-center cells (A) are excited by light spots (gray) falling into the center of the receptive field. In OFF-center cells (B) the arrangement of excitatory and inhibitory regions in the receptive field is reversed. **C, D**. Two examples of asymmetric receptive fields of simple cells in the primary visual cortex. The cells are best stimulated by a light bar oriented as indicated by the gray rectangle.

Complex cells have even more intriguing properties and show responses that are, for example, selective for movements with a certain velocity and direction (Hubel, 1995).

It is still a matter of debate how the response properties of simple cells arise. The original proposal by Hubel and Wiesel (1962) was that orientation selectivity is a consequence of the specific wiring between LGN and V1. Several center-surround cells with slightly shifted receptive fields should converge on a single V1 neuron so as to produce the asymmetric receptive field of simple cells. Alternatively (or additionally), the intracortical dynamics can generate orientation selectivity by enhancing small asymmetries in neuronal responses; cf. Section 9.1.3. In the following, we pursue the first possibility and try to understand how activity-dependent processes during development can lead to the required fine-tuning of the synaptic organization of projections from the LGN to the primary visual cortex (Linsker, 1986a,b,c; Miller et al., 1989; MacKay and Miller, 1990; Miller, 1994, 1995; Wimbauer et al., 1997a,b).

Model architecture

We are studying a model that consists of a two-dimensional layer of cortical neurons (V1 cells) and two layers of LGN neurons, namely one layer of ON-center cells and one layer of OFF-center cells; cf. Fig. 11.7A. In each layer, neurons are labeled by their position and projections between the neurons are given as a function of their positions. Intracortical projections, i.e., projections between cortical neurons, are denoted by $w_{V1,V1}(x_1, x_2)$, where x_1 and x_2 are the position of the pre- and the postsynaptic neuron, respectively. Projections from ON-center and OFF-center LGN neurons to the cortex are denoted by $w_{V1,ON}(x_1, x_2)$ and $w_{V1,OFF}(x_1, x_2)$, respectively.

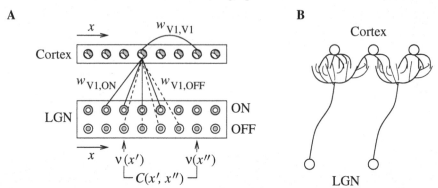

Fig. 11.7. **A.** Wiring diagram between LGN and cortex (schematic). **B.** Axons from LGN cells project only to a small region of cortex. Synaptic contacts are therefore limited to a localized cluster of cortical neurons.

In the following we are interested in the evolution of the weight distribution of projections from the LGN to the primary visual cortex. We thus take $w_{V1,ON}(x, x')$ and $w_{V1,OFF}(x, x')$ as the dynamic variables of the model. Intracortical projections are thought to be constant and dominated by short-range excitation, e.g.,

$$w_{V1,V1}(x_1, x_2) \propto \exp\left(-\frac{\|x_1 - x_2\|}{\sigma_{V1,V1}^2}\right). \tag{11.32}$$

As in the previous section we consider – for the sake of simplicity – neurons with a linear gain function. The firing rate $v_{V1}(x)$ of a cortical neuron at position x is thus given by

$$v_{V1}(x) = \sum_{x'} w_{V1,ON}(x, x')\, v_{ON}(x') + \sum_{x'} w_{V1,OFF}(x, x')\, v_{OFF}(x')$$

$$+ \sum_{\substack{x' \\ (x' \neq x)}} w_{V1,V1}(x, x')\, v_{V1}(x'), \tag{11.33}$$

where $v_{ON/OFF}(x')$ is the firing rate of a neuron in the ON/OFF layer of the LGN.

Due to the intracortical interaction the cortical activity v_{V1} shows up on both sides of the equation. Since this is a linear equation it can easily be solved for v_{V1}. To do so we write $v_{V1}(x) = \sum_{x'} \delta_{x,x'} v_{V1}(x')$, where $\delta_{x,x'}$ is the Kronecker δ that is unity for $x = x'$ and vanishes otherwise. Equation (11.33) can thus be rewritten as

$$\sum_{x'} [\delta_{x,x'} - w_{V1,V1}(x, x')]\, v_{V1}(x')$$

$$= \sum_{x'} w_{V1,ON}(x, x')\, v_{ON}(x') + \sum_{x'} w_{V1,OFF}(x, x')\, v_{OFF}(x'). \tag{11.34}$$

If we read the left-hand side as a multiplication of the matrix $M(x, x') \equiv [\delta_{x,x'} - w_{V1,V1}(x, x')]$ and the vector $v_{V1}(x')$ we can define the inverse I of M by

$$\sum_x I(x'', x) M(x, x') = \delta_{x'', x'} \tag{11.35}$$

and solve Eq. (11.34) for $v_{V1}(x')$. We find

$$v_{V1}(x'') = \sum_{x'} \bar{w}_{V1,ON}(x'', x') v_{ON}(x') + \sum_{x'} \bar{w}_{V1,OFF}(x'', x') v_{OFF}(x'), \tag{11.36}$$

which relates the input $v_{ON/OFF}$ to the output via the "effective" weights

$$\bar{w}_{V1,ON/OFF}(x'', x') \equiv \sum_x I(x'', x) w_{V1,ON/OFF}(x, x'). \tag{11.37}$$

Plasticity

We expect that the formation of synapses between LGN and V1 is driven by correlations in the input. In the present case, these correlations are due to the retinotopic organization of projections from the retina to the LGN. Neighboring LGN neurons receiving stimulation from similar regions of the visual field are thus correlated to a higher degree than neurons that are more separated. If we assume that the activity of individual photoreceptors on the retina is uncorrelated and that each LGN neuron integrates the input from many of these receptors, then the correlation of two LGN neurons can be calculated from the form of their receptive fields. For center-surround cells the correlation is a Mexican-hat-shaped function of their distance (Miller, 1994; Wimbauer et al., 1997a), e.g.,

$$C_{ON,ON}(x, x') = C_{ON,ON}(\|x - x'\|)$$
$$= \exp\left(-\frac{\|x - x'\|^2}{\sigma^2}\right) - \frac{1}{c^2} \exp\left(-\frac{\|x - x'\|^2}{c^2 \sigma^2}\right), \tag{11.38}$$

where c is a form factor that describes the depth of the modulation. $C_{ON,ON}$ is the correlation between two ON-center-type LGN neurons. For the sake of simplicity we assume that OFF-center cells have the same correlation, $C_{OFF,OFF} = C_{ON,ON}$. Correlations between ON-center and OFF-center cells, however, have the opposite sign, $C_{ON,OFF} = C_{OFF,ON} = -C_{ON,ON}$.

In the present formulation of the model each LGN cell can contact every neuron in the primary visual cortex. In reality, each LGN cell sends one axon to the cortex. Though this axon may split into several branches its synaptic contacts are restricted to small region of the cortex; cf. Fig. 11.7B. We take this limitation into account by defining an *arborization function* $A(x, x')$ that gives the *a priori* probability that a connection between an LGN cell at location x and a cortical cell at x' is formed

(Miller et al., 1989). The arborization is a rapidly decaying function of the distance, e.g.,

$$A(x, x') = \exp\left(-\frac{\|x - x'\|^2}{\sigma_{V1,LGN}^2}\right). \tag{11.39}$$

To describe the dynamics of the weight distribution we adopt a modified form of Hebb's learning rule that is completed by the arborization function,

$$\frac{d}{dt}w_{V1,ON/OFF}(x, x') = \gamma \, A(x, x') \, v_{V1}(x) \, v_{ON/OFF}(x'). \tag{11.40}$$

If we use Eq. (11.34) and assume that learning is slow enough so that we can rely on the correlation functions to describe the evolution of the weights, we find

$$\frac{d}{dt}w_{V1,ON}(x_1, x_2) = \gamma \, A(x_1, x_2) \sum_{x',x''} I(x_1, x')$$
$$\times \left[w_{V1,ON}(x', x'') - w_{V1,OFF}(x', x'')\right] C_{ON,ON}(x'', x_2) \tag{11.41}$$

and a similar equation for $w_{V1,OFF}$.

Expression (11.41) is still a linear equation for the weights and nothing exciting can be expected. A prerequisite for pattern formation is competition between the synaptic weights. Therefore, the above learning rule is extended by a term $w_{V1,ON/OFF}(x, x') \, v_{V1}(x)^2$ that leads to weight vector normalization and competition; cf. Oja's rule, Eq. (10.11).

Simulation results

Many of the standard techniques for nonlinear systems that we have already encountered in the context of neuronal pattern formation in Chapter 9 can also be applied to the present model (MacKay and Miller, 1990; Wimbauer et al., 1998). Here, however, we will just summarize some results from a computer simulation consisting of an array of 8×8 cortical neurons and two times 20×20 LGN neurons. Figure 11.8 shows a typical outcome of such a simulation. Each of the small rectangles shows the receptive field of the corresponding cortical neuron. A bright color means that the neuron responds with an increased firing rate to a bright spot at that particular position within its receptive field; dark colors indicate inhibition.

There are two interesting aspects. Firstly, the evolution of the synaptic weights has led to asymmetric receptive fields, which give rise to orientation selectivity. Secondly, the structure of the receptive fields of neighboring cortical neurons are similar; neuronal response properties thus vary continuously across the cortex. The neurons are said to form a *map* for, e.g., orientation.

The first observation, the breaking of the symmetry of LGN receptive fields, is

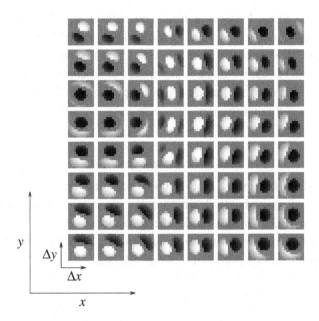

Fig. 11.8. Receptive fields (small squares) of 64 cortical neurons (large grid). Each small square shows the distribution of weights $w_{V1,ON}(x, x + \Delta x) - w_{V1,OFF}(x, x + \Delta x)$, where x is the position of the cortical neuron and Δx the position of the white or black spot within the small rectangle (adapted from Wimbauer et al. (1998)).

characteristic for all pattern formation phenomena. It results from the instability of the homogeneous initial state and the competition between individual synaptic weights. The second observation, the smooth variation of the receptive fields across the cortex, is a consequence of the excitatory intracortical couplings. During the development, neighboring cortical neurons tend to be either simultaneously active or quiescent and, due to the activity-dependent learning rule, similar receptive fields are formed.

11.2 Learning in spiking models

In the previous section we have seen that the evolution of synaptic weights under a rate-based learning rule depends on correlations in the input. What happens if the rate-based learning rule is replaced by a spike-time-dependent one?

In Section 11.2.1 we will derive an equation that relates the expectation value of the weight vector to the statistical properties of pre- and postsynaptic spike trains. We will see that spike-time-dependent plasticity is sensitive to spatial and *temporal* correlations in the input. In certain particularly simple cases spike–spike correlations can be calculated explicitly. This is demonstrated in Section 11.2.2

in the context of a linear Poisson neuron. This neuron model is also used in Section 11.2.3 for a comparison of spike-based and rate-based learning rules as well as in Section 11.2.4 where we revisit the static-pattern scenario of Section 11.1.2. Finally, in Section 11.2.5, we discuss the impact of stochastic spike arrival on the synaptic weights and derive a Fokker–Planck equation that describes the temporal evolution of the weight distribution.

11.2.1 Learning equation

We will generalize the analysis of Hebbian learning that has been developed in Section 11.1 to spike-based learning rules based on the phenomenological model of Section 10.3.1. In this model the synaptic weight $w_{ij}(t)$ is a piecewise continuous function of time with steps whenever a presynaptic spike arrives or when a postsynaptic action potential is triggered, i.e.,

$$\frac{\mathrm{d}}{\mathrm{d}t} w_{ij}(t) = a_0 + a_1^{\mathrm{pre}} S_j(t) + a_1^{\mathrm{post}} S_i(t)$$

$$+ S_j(t) \int_0^\infty W(s)\, S_i(t-s)\, \mathrm{d}s + S_i(t) \int_0^\infty W(-s)\, S_j(t-s)\, \mathrm{d}s, \quad (11.42)$$

cf. Eqs. (10.14) and 10.15. As before we want to relate the synaptic weight change to the statistical properties of the input. Given the increased level of complexity, a few remarks about the underlying statistical ensemble are in order.

In the previous section we have considered presynaptic firing rates ν_j as random variables drawn from an ensemble of input patterns ξ_j^μ. The output rate, however, was a deterministic function of the neuronal input. In the context of spike-time-dependent plasticity, we consider the set of presynaptic spike arrival times $(t_j^1, t_j^2, \dots)$ as a random variable. The underlying "randomness" may have several reasons. For example, different stimulation paradigms may be selected one by one in very much the same way as we have selected a new input pattern in the previous section. In contrast to the rate model, we do not want to restrict ourselves to deterministic neuron models. Hence, the randomness can also be produced by a stochastic neuron model that is used in order account for noise; cf. Chapter 5. In this case, the output spike train can be a random variable even if the input spike trains are fixed. A simple example is the Poisson neuron model that generates output spikes via an inhomogeneous Poisson process with an intensity that is a function of the membrane potential. In any case, we consider the set of spike trains $(S_1, \dots, S_i, S_j, \dots, S_N)$, i.e., pre- *and* postsynaptic trains, to be drawn from a stochastic ensemble. The specific properties of the chosen neuron model are thus implicitly described by the association of pre- and postsynaptic trains within the ensemble. Note that this formalism includes deterministic models as a special case if the ensemble contains only a single postsynaptic spike train for any given set of presynaptic spike trains. In the following, all averages denoted by $\langle \ \rangle_E$ are to be taken relative to this ensemble.

For the time being we are interested only in the long-term behavior of the synaptic weights and not in the fluctuations that are caused by individual spikes. As in Section 11.1.2 we therefore calculate the expectation value of the weight change over a certain interval of time,

$$\langle w_{ij}(t+T) - w_{ij}(t) \rangle_E = \left\langle \int_t^{t+T} \frac{\mathrm{d}}{\mathrm{d}t} w_{ij}(t') \mathrm{d}t' \right\rangle_E . \tag{11.43}$$

With the abbreviation

$$\langle f(t) \rangle_T \equiv T^{-1} \int_t^{t+T} f(t') \, \mathrm{d}t' \tag{11.44}$$

we obtain from Eq. (11.42)

$$\frac{\langle w_{ij}(t+T) - w_{ij}(t) \rangle_E}{T} = a_0 + a_1^{\mathrm{pre}} \langle\langle S_j(t) \rangle_T \rangle_E + a_1^{\mathrm{post}} \langle\langle S_i(t) \rangle_T \rangle_E$$

$$+ \int_0^\infty W(s) \langle\langle S_i(t-s) \, S_j(t) \rangle_T \rangle_E \, \mathrm{d}s$$

$$+ \int_{-\infty}^0 W(s) \langle\langle S_i(t) \, S_j(t+s) \rangle_T \rangle_E \, \mathrm{d}s . \tag{11.45}$$

If the time interval T is long as compared to typical interspike intervals then the time average is taken over many pre- or postsynaptic spikes. We can thus assume that the average $\langle\langle S_i(t) \, S_j(t+s) \rangle_T \rangle_E$ does not change if we replace t by $t-s$ as long as $s \ll T$. Furthermore, if $W(s)$ decays to zero sufficiently fast as $|s| \to \infty$ then the integration over s in the last term of Eq. (11.45) can be restricted to a finite interval determined by the width of the learning window W. In this case it is possible to replace $\langle\langle S_i(t) \, S_j(t+s) \rangle_T \rangle_E$ by $\langle\langle S_i(t-s) \, S_j(t) \rangle_T \rangle_E$ and to collect the last two terms of Eq. (11.45) into a single integral, provided that the width of learning window is small as compared to T. With this approximation we find

$$\frac{\langle w_{ij}(t+T) - w_{ij}(t) \rangle_E}{T} = a_0 + a_1^{\mathrm{pre}} \langle\langle S_j(t) \rangle_T \rangle_E + a_1^{\mathrm{post}} \langle\langle S_i(t) \rangle_T \rangle_E$$

$$+ \int_{-\infty}^\infty W(s) \langle\langle S_i(t-s) \, S_j(t) \rangle_T \rangle_E \, \mathrm{d}s . \tag{11.46}$$

The instantaneous firing rate $v_i(t)$ of neuron i is the ensemble average of its spike train,

$$v_i(t) \equiv \langle S_i(t) \rangle_E . \tag{11.47}$$

Similarly, we define the joint firing rate v_{ij} of neurons i and j as

$$v_{ij}(t, t') \equiv \langle S_i(t) \, S_j(t') \rangle_E \,, \tag{11.48}$$

which is the joint probability density of finding both a spike at time t and at time t' in neurons i and j, respectively. Note that $v_{ij}(t, t')$ is a probability density both in t and t' and thus has units of one over time squared.

Since averaging is a linear operation we can exchange ensemble average and time average. We obtain the following expression for the expected weight change in the interval from t to $t + T$ as a function of the statistical properties of the spike trains,

$$\frac{\langle w_{ij}(t + T) - w_{ij}(t) \rangle_E}{T} = a_0 + a_1^{\text{pre}} \langle v_j(t) \rangle_T + a_1^{\text{post}} \langle v_i(t) \rangle_T$$
$$+ \int_{-\infty}^{\infty} W(s) \langle v_{ij}(t - s, t) \rangle_T \, ds \,. \tag{11.49}$$

The time average $\langle v_{ij}(t - s, t) \rangle_T$ is the correlation function of pre- and post-synaptic spike train on the interval $[t, t + T]$. This function clearly depends on the actual value of the weight vector. In deriving Eq. (11.49) we had to assume that the correlations are a slowly varying function of time. For the sake of consistency we thus have the requirement that the weight vector itself is a slowly varying function of time. If this is the case then we can exploit the self-averaging property of the weight vector and argue that fluctuations around the expectation value are negligible and that Eq. (11.49) is a good approximation for the actual value of the weight vector. We thus drop the ensemble average on the left-hand side of Eq. (11.49) and find for the time-averaged change of the synaptic weight the following learning equation,

$$\frac{d}{dt} \langle w_{ij}(t) \rangle_T = a_0 + a_1^{\text{pre}} \langle v_j(t) \rangle_T + a_1^{\text{post}} \langle v_i(t) \rangle_T$$
$$+ \int_{-\infty}^{\infty} W(s) \langle v_{ij}(t - s, t) \rangle_T \, ds \,; \tag{11.50}$$

cf. Kempter et al. (1999) and Kistler and van Hemmen (2000). As expected, the long-term dynamics of the synaptic weights depends on the correlation of pre- and postsynaptic spike train on the time scale of the learning window. In the following we will always use the smooth time-averaged weight vector $\langle w_{ij}(t) \rangle_T$, but for the sake of brevity we shall drop the angular brackets.

11.2.2 Spike–spike correlations

It is tempting to rewrite the correlation term $\langle v_{ij}(t - s, t) \rangle_T$ that appears on the right-hand side of Eq. (11.50) in terms of the instantaneous firing rates $\langle v_i(t -$

s) $v_j(t)\rangle_T$. This, however, is only allowed if the spike trains of neuron i and j were independent, i.e., if $\langle S_i(t - s) \, S_j(t)\rangle_E = \langle S_i(t - s)\rangle_E \, \langle S_j(t)\rangle_E$. Such an approach would therefore neglect the specific spike–spike correlations that are induced by presynaptic action potentials.

Correlations between pre- and postsynaptic spike trains do not only depend on the input statistics but also on the dynamics of the neuron model and the way new output spikes are generated. The influence of a single presynaptic spike on the postsynaptic activity can be measured by a peri-stimulus-time histogram (PSTH) triggered at the time of presynaptic spike arrival; cf. Section 7.4.1. The form of the PSTH characterizes the spike–spike correlations between presynaptic spike arrival and the postsynaptic action potential. For high noise, the spike–spike correlations contain a term that is proportional to the time course of the postsynaptic potential ϵ, while for low noise this term is proportional to its derivative ϵ'; cf. Fig. 7.12.

In the following, we will calculate the spike–spike correlations in a particularly simple case, the linear Poisson neuron model. As we will see, the spike–spike correlations contain in this case a term proportional to the postsynaptic potential ϵ. The linear Poisson neuron model can therefore be considered as a reasonable approximation to spiking neuron models in the high-noise limit.

Example: linear Poisson neuron model

As a generalization of the analog neuron with linear gain function discussed in Section 11.1.2 we consider here a linear Poisson neuron. The input to the neuron consists of N Poisson spike trains with time-dependent intensities $v_j(t)$. Similar to the SRM$_0$ neuron the membrane potential u_i of neuron i is a superposition of postsynaptic potentials ϵ with $\int_0^\infty \epsilon(s) \, ds = 1$,

$$u_i(t) = \sum_j w_{ij} \int_0^\infty \epsilon(s) \, S_j(t - s) \, ds . \qquad (11.51)$$

In contrast to Section 4.2.3 we neglect refractoriness and external input.

Postsynaptic spikes are generated by an inhomogeneous Poisson process with an intensity v_i^{post} that is a (semi-)*linear* function of the membrane potential,

$$v_i^{\text{post}}(t|u) = [u_i(t)]_+ . \qquad (11.52)$$

Here, $[\cdot]_+$ denotes the positive part of the argument in order to avoid negative rates. In the following, however, we will always assume that $u_i(t) \geq 0$. The notation $v_i^{\text{post}}(t|u)$ indicates that the output rate depends on the actual value of the membrane potential.

We thus have a doubly stochastic process (Cox, 1955; Bartlett, 1963) in the sense that in a first step, a set of input spike trains is drawn from an ensemble characterized by Poisson rates v_j^{pre}. This realization of input spike trains then determines the membrane potential which produces in a second step a specific realization of the output spike train according to $v_i^{\text{post}}(t|u)$. It can be shown that, because of the finite duration of the postsynaptic potential ϵ, the output spike trains generated by this composite process are no longer Poisson spike trains; their expectation value $\langle S_i(t) \rangle_E \equiv v_i^{\text{post}}(t)$, however, is simply equivalent to the expectation value of the output rate, $v_i^{\text{post}}(t) = \langle v_i^{\text{post}}(t|u) \rangle_E$ (Kistler and van Hemmen, 2000). Due to the linearity of the neuron model the output rate is given by a convolution of the input rates with the response kernel ϵ,

$$v_i^{\text{post}}(t) = \sum_j w_{ij} \int_0^\infty \epsilon(s) \, v_j^{\text{pre}}(t-s) \, ds \,. \tag{11.53}$$

The joint firing rate $v_{ij}^{\text{post,pre}}(t, t') = \langle S_i(t) S_j(t') \rangle_E$ of pre- and postsynaptic neuron is the joint probability density of finding an input spike at synapse j at time t' and an output spike of neuron i at time t. According to Bayes' theorem this probability equals the probability of observing an input spike at time t' times the conditional probability of observing an output spike at time t given the input spike at time t', i.e.,

$$v_{ij}^{\text{post,pre}}(t, t') = \langle S_i(t) | \text{input spike at } t' \rangle_E \, \langle S_j(t') \rangle_E \,. \tag{11.54}$$

In the framework of a *linear* Poisson neuron, the term $\langle S_i(t) | \text{input spike at } t' \rangle_E$ equals the sum of the expected output rate (11.53) and the specific contribution $w_{ij} \epsilon(t - t')$ of a single (additional) input spike at time t'. Altogether we obtain

$$v_{ij}^{\text{post,pre}}(t, t') = v_i^{\text{post}}(t) \, v_j^{\text{pre}}(t') + w_{ij} \epsilon(t - t') \, v_j^{\text{pre}}(t') \,. \tag{11.55}$$

The first term on the right-hand side is the "chance level" of finding two spikes at t and t', respectively, if the neurons were firing independently at rates $v_i^{\text{post}}(t)$ and $v_j^{\text{pre}}(t')$. The second term describes the correlation that is due to synaptic coupling. If the presynaptic neuron has fired a spike at t' then the chance of the postsynaptic neuron firing a spike at time $t > t'$ is increased by $w_{ij} \epsilon(t - t')$. Note that this expression respects causality: the probability of finding first a postsynaptic spike and then a presynaptic spike is just chance level because $\epsilon(t - t') = 0$ for $t < t'$.

Example: learning equation for a linear Poisson neuron

If we use the result from Eq. (11.55) in the learning equation (11.50) we obtain

$$\frac{d}{dt} w_{ij}(t) = a_0 + a_1^{\text{pre}} \langle v_j^{\text{pre}}(t) \rangle_T + a_1^{\text{post}} \langle v_i^{\text{post}}(t) \rangle_T$$
$$+ \int_{-\infty}^\infty W(s) \langle v_i^{\text{post}}(t-s) \, v_j^{\text{pre}}(t) \rangle_T \, ds + w_{ij}(t) \langle v_j^{\text{pre}}(t) \rangle_T W_- \,, \tag{11.56}$$

with $W_- = \int_0^\infty W(-s) \, \epsilon(s) \, ds$.

In linear Poisson neurons, the correlation between pre- and postsynaptic activity that drives synaptic weight changes consists of two contributions. The integral over the learning window in Eq. (11.56) describes correlations in the instantaneous firing rate. The last term on the right-hand side of Eq. (11.56) finally accounts for spike–spike correlations of pre- and postsynaptic neurons.

If we express the instantaneous firing rates $v_i(t)$ in terms of their fluctuations $\Delta v_i(t)$ around the mean $\langle v_i(t) \rangle_T$,

$$v_i(t) = \Delta v_i(t) + \langle v_i(t) \rangle_T \,, \tag{11.57}$$

then we can rewrite Eq. (11.56) together with Eq. (11.53) as

$$\begin{aligned}
\frac{d}{dt} w_{ij}(t) = {} & a_0 + a_1^{\mathrm{pre}} \langle v_j^{\mathrm{pre}}(t) \rangle_T + a_1^{\mathrm{post}} \langle v_i^{\mathrm{post}}(t) \rangle_T \\
& + \bar{W} \langle v_j^{\mathrm{pre}}(t) \rangle_T \langle v_i^{\mathrm{post}}(t) \rangle_T + \sum_k w_{ik}\, Q_{kj}(t) + w_{ij}(t) \langle v_j^{\mathrm{pre}}(t) \rangle_T\, W_-
\end{aligned} \tag{11.58}$$

with

$$Q_{kj}(t) = \int_{-\infty}^{\infty} W(s) \int_0^{\infty} \epsilon(s') \langle \Delta v_k^{\mathrm{pre}}(t - s - s')\, \Delta v_j^{\mathrm{pre}}(t) \rangle_T \, ds'\, ds\,. \tag{11.59}$$

Here we have implicitly assumed that the temporal averaging interval T is much longer than the length of the learning window, the duration of a postsynaptic potential, or a typical interspike interval, so that $\langle v_i^{\mathrm{post}}(t - s) \rangle_T \approx \langle v_i^{\mathrm{post}}(t) \rangle_T$ and $\langle v_j^{\mathrm{pre}}(t - s') \rangle_T \approx \langle v_j^{\mathrm{pre}}(t) \rangle_T$.

The term containing $Q_{kj}(t)$ on the right-hand side of Eq. (11.58) shows how spatio-temporal correlations $\langle \Delta v_k^{\mathrm{post}}(t')\, \Delta v_j^{\mathrm{pre}}(t) \rangle_T$ in the input influence the evolution of synaptic weights. What matters are correlations on the time scale of the learning window and the postsynaptic potential.

11.2.3 Relation of spike-based to rate-based learning

In Section 11.1.2 we have investigated the weight dynamics in the context of an analog neuron where the postsynaptic firing rate is an instantaneous function of the input rates. We have seen that learning is driven by (spatial) correlations within the set of input patterns. The learning equation (11.56) goes one step further in the sense that it explicitly includes time. Consequently, learning is driven by *spatio-temporal* correlations in the input.

In order to compare the rate-based learning paradigm of Section 11.1.2 with the spike-based formulation of Eq. (11.56) we thus have to disregard temporal correlations for the time being. We thus consider a linear Poisson neuron with *stationary* input rates, $\langle v_j(t) \rangle_T = v_j(t) = v_j$, and assume that the synaptic weight is changing slowly as compared to the width of the learning window and the postsynaptic potential. The weight dynamics is given by Eq. (11.56),

$$\frac{\mathrm{d}}{\mathrm{d}t} w_{ij}(t) = a_0 + a_1^{\mathrm{pre}} v_j + a_1^{\mathrm{post}} v_i + \bar{W} v_i v_j + W_- w_{ij}(t) v_j , \qquad (11.60)$$

with $\bar{W} = \int_{-\infty}^{\infty} W(s)\,\mathrm{d}s$ and $W_- = \int_0^{\infty} W(-s)\,\epsilon(s)\,\mathrm{d}s$. If we identify

$$c_0(w_{ij}) = a_0 , \quad c_1^{\mathrm{pre}}(w_{ij}) = a_1^{\mathrm{pre}} + w_{ij}(t)\,W_- , \quad c_1^{\mathrm{post}}(w_{ij}) = a_1^{\mathrm{post}} , \quad (11.61)$$

and

$$c_2^{\mathrm{corr}}(w_{ij}) = \bar{W} , \qquad (11.62)$$

we recover the general expression for synaptic plasticity based on the rate description given in Eq. (10.2). The total area under the learning window thus plays the role of the correlation parameter c_2^{corr} that is responsible for Hebbian or anti-Hebbian plasticity in a rate formulation. The spike–spike correlations simply give rise to an additional weight-dependent term $w_{ij}(t)\,W_-$ in the parameter $c_1^{\mathrm{pre}}(w_{ij})$ that describes presynaptically triggered weight changes.

We may wonder what happens if we relax the requirement of strictly stationary rates. In the linear Poisson model, the output rate depends via Eq. (11.53) on the input rates and changes in the input rate translate into changes in the output rate. If the rate of change is small, we can expand the output rate

$$v_i^{\mathrm{post}}(t - s) \approx v_i^{\mathrm{post}}(t) - s\,\frac{\mathrm{d}}{\mathrm{d}t} v_i^{\mathrm{post}}(t) + \mathcal{O}(s^2) \qquad (11.63)$$

on the right-hand side of Eq. (11.56),

$$\frac{\mathrm{d}}{\mathrm{d}t} w_{ij}(t) = a_0 + a_1^{\mathrm{pre}} v_j^{\mathrm{pre}}(t) + a_1^{\mathrm{post}} v_i^{\mathrm{post}}(t) + \bar{W} v_i^{\mathrm{post}}(t) v_j^{\mathrm{pre}}(t)$$

$$+ W_- w_{ij}(t) v_j^{\mathrm{pre}}(t) - v_j^{\mathrm{pre}}(t) \frac{\mathrm{d}}{\mathrm{d}t} v_i^{\mathrm{post}}(t) \int_{-\infty}^{\infty} s\,W(s)\,\mathrm{d}s . \quad (11.64)$$

Here, we have dropped the temporal averages because rates are assumed to change slowly relative to T.

As compared to Eq. (11.60) we encounter an additional term that is proportional to the first moment $\int s\,W(s)\,\mathrm{d}s$ of the learning window. This term has been termed *differential* Hebbian (Roberts, 1999; Xie and Seung, 2000) and plays a certain role in the context of conditioning and reinforcement learning (Montague et al., 1995; Rao and Sejnowski, 2001).

Stabilization of postsynaptic rates

Another interesting property of a learning rule of the form of Eq. (10.2) or Eq. (11.60) is that it can lead to normalization of the postsynaptic firing rate and hence to normalization of the sum of the synaptic weights. This can be achieved even without including higher order terms in the learning equation or postulating a dependence of the parameters a_0, $a_1^{\text{pre/post}}$, etc., on the actual value of the synaptic efficacy.

Consider a linear Poisson neuron that receives input from N presynaptic neurons with spike activity described by independent Poisson processes with rate ν^{pre}. The postsynaptic neuron is thus firing at a rate $\nu_i^{\text{post}}(t) = \nu^{\text{pre}} \sum_{j=1}^{N} w_{ij}(t)$. From Eq. (11.56) we obtain the corresponding dynamics for the synaptic weights, i.e.,

$$\frac{d}{dt} w_{ij}(t) = a_0 + a_1^{\text{pre}} \nu^{\text{pre}} + a_1^{\text{post}} \nu^{\text{pre}} \sum_{k=1}^{N} w_{ik}(t)$$

$$+ (\nu^{\text{pre}})^2 \bar{W} \sum_{k=1}^{N} w_{ik}(t) + w_{ij}(t) \nu^{\text{pre}} W_- , \qquad (11.65)$$

with $\bar{W} = \int_{-\infty}^{\infty} W(s) \, ds$ and $W_- = \int_{0}^{\infty} \epsilon(s) W(-s) \, ds$. In this particularly simple case the weight dynamics is characterized by a fixed point for the sum of the synaptic weights, $\sum_j w_{ij}$, and, hence, for the postsynaptic firing rate, $\nu_i^{\text{post}} = \nu_{\text{FP}}$,

$$\nu_{\text{FP}} = -\frac{a_0 + a_1^{\text{pre}} \nu^{\text{pre}}}{a_1^{\text{post}} + \nu^{\text{pre}} \bar{W} + N^{-1} W_-} . \qquad (11.66)$$

This fixed point is attractive if the denominator is negative. Since ν_i^{post} is a firing rate we have the additional requirement that $\nu_{\text{FP}} \geq 0$. Altogether we thus have two conditions for the parameters of the learning rule, i.e., $a_1^{\text{post}} + \nu^{\text{pre}} \bar{W} + N^{-1} W_- < 0$ and $a_0 + a_1^{\text{pre}} \nu^{\text{pre}} \geq 0$. Note that, apart from the term $(N^{-1} W_-)$, we would obtain a completely analogous result from the rate formulation in Eq. (10.2) if we identify $c_2^{\text{corr}} = \bar{W}$; cf. Eq. (11.62). Note further, that the linearity is not essential for the stabilization of the postsynaptic rate. Any model where the output rate is a monotonous function of the sum of the synaptic weights yields qualitatively the same result.

11.2.4 Static-pattern scenario

In order to illustrate the above results with a concrete example we revisit the static-pattern scenario that we have already studied in the context of analog neurons in Section 11.1.2. We consider a set of static patterns $\{\xi^\mu; 1 < \mu < p\}$ that are presented to the network in a random sequence $(\mu_1, \mu_2, \dots)$ during time steps of length Δt. Presynaptic spike trains are described by an inhomogeneous Poisson process with a firing intensity that is determined by the pattern that is currently presented. Hence, the instantaneous presynaptic firing rates are piecewise constant functions of time,

$$v_j^{\text{pre}}(t) = \sum_k \xi_j^{\mu_k} \, \Theta[t - (k-1) \, \Delta t] \, \Theta[k \, \Delta t - t] \,. \tag{11.67}$$

Due to the randomness by which the patterns are presented the input does not contain any nontrivial temporal correlations. We thus expect to obtain the very same result as in Section 11.1.2, i.e., that the evolution of synaptic weights is determined by the correlation matrix of the input pattern set.

For linear Poisson neurons the joint firing rate of pre- and postsynaptic neurons is given by Eq. (11.55),

$$v_{ij}(t - s, t) = v_i^{\text{post}}(t - s) \, v_j^{\text{pre}}(t) + w_{ij}(t) \, \epsilon(-s) \, v_j^{\text{pre}}(t) \,. \tag{11.68}$$

The postsynaptic firing rate is

$$\begin{aligned}
v_i^{\text{post}}(t) &= \sum_j \int_0^\infty w_{ij}(t - s) \, \epsilon(s) \, v_j^{\text{pre}}(t - s) \, ds \\
&\approx \sum_j w_{ij}(t) \int_0^\infty \epsilon(s) \, v_j^{\text{pre}}(t - s) \, ds \,,
\end{aligned} \tag{11.69}$$

where we have assumed implicitly that the synaptic weights are approximately constant on the time scale defined by the duration of the postsynaptic potential ϵ so that we can pull w_{ij} in front of the integral.

As usual, we are interested in the long-term behavior of the synaptic weights given by Eq. (11.56). We thus need the time-average of $v_i(t - s) \, v_j(t)$ over the interval T,

$$\langle v_i^{\text{post}}(t - s) \, v_j^{\text{pre}}(t) \rangle_T = \sum_k w_{ik}(t) \int_0^\infty \epsilon(s') \, \langle v_k^{\text{pre}}(t - s - s') \, v_j^{\text{pre}}(t) \rangle_T \, ds' \,. \tag{11.70}$$

Due to the linearity of the neuron model, the correlation of input and output is a linear combination of the correlations $\langle v_k^{\text{pre}}(t - s) \, v_j^{\text{pre}}(t) \rangle_T$ in the input firing rates, which are independent of the specific neuron model. We assume that all patterns are presented once during the time interval T that defines the time scale at which we are investigating the weight dynamics. For $s = 0$ the time average corresponds to an ensemble average over the input patterns and the input correlation functions equals the correlation of the input pattern, $\langle v_k^{\text{pre}}(t) \, v_j^{\text{pre}}(t) \rangle_T = \langle \xi_k^\mu \, \xi_j^\mu \rangle_\mu$. Here, $\langle \, \rangle_\mu$ denotes an ensemble average over the set of input patterns. Since we have assumed that input patterns are presented randomly for time steps of length Δt the correlation $\langle v_k^{\text{pre}}(t - s) \, v_j^{\text{pre}}(t) \rangle_T$ will be computed from two independent input patterns if $|s| > \Delta t$, i.e., $\langle v_k^{\text{pre}}(t - s) \, v_j^{\text{pre}}(t) \rangle_T = \langle \xi_k^\mu \rangle_\mu \, \langle \xi_j^\mu \rangle_\mu$. For $0 < s < \Delta t$ the

A

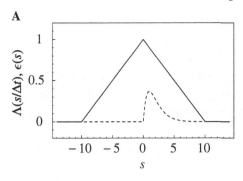

B

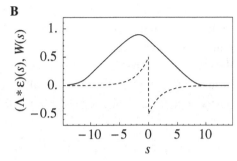

Fig. 11.9. Static-pattern scenario. **A**. Temporal correlations in the firing rate of presynaptic neurons have a triangular shape $\Lambda(s/\Delta t)$ (solid line). The correlation between pre- and postsynaptic neurons involves a convolution with the response kernel $\epsilon(s)$ (dashed line). **B**. The definition of the matrix Q_{kj} in Eq. (11.74) contains the overlap of the learning window $W(s)$ (dashed line) and the convolution $\int \epsilon(s') \Lambda[(s - s')/\Delta t]\, ds'$ (solid line). If the duration of one presentation is long as compared to the width of the learning window and the response kernel ϵ the overlap equals approximately the area below the learning window $\bar{W}$. If the presentation is short, as shown here, then the overlap may be different from zero, even if $\bar{W} = 0$.

input correlation is a linear function of s. Altogether we obtain

$$\left\langle v_k^{\text{pre}}(t - s)\, v_j^{\text{pre}}(t) \right\rangle_T = \langle \xi_k^\mu \rangle_\mu \langle \xi_j^\mu \rangle_\mu + \left(\langle \xi_k^\mu \xi_j^\mu \rangle_\mu - \langle \xi_k^\mu \rangle_\mu \langle \xi_j^\mu \rangle_\mu \right) \Lambda(s/\Delta t) . \tag{11.71}$$

Here, Λ is the triangular function

$$\Lambda(s) = (1 - |s|)\, \Theta(1 - |s|) ; \tag{11.72}$$

cf. Fig. 11.9A. If we use this result in the learning equation (11.56) we find

$$\frac{d}{dt} \bar{w}_{ij}(t) = \sum_k w_{ik}(t)\, \langle \xi_k^\mu \rangle_\mu \langle \xi_j^\mu \rangle_\mu\, \bar{W} + \sum_k w_{ik}(t)\, Q_{kj} + w_{ij}(t)\, \langle \xi_j^\mu \rangle_\mu\, W_- , \tag{11.73}$$

with $\bar{W} = \int_{-\infty}^{\infty} W(s)\, ds$, $W_- = \int_0^{\infty} \epsilon(s)\, W(-s)\, ds$, and

$$Q_{kj} = \left(\langle \xi_k^\mu \xi_j^\mu \rangle_\mu - \langle \xi_k^\mu \rangle_\mu \langle \xi_j^\mu \rangle_\mu \right) \int_{-\infty}^{\infty} W(s) \int_0^{\infty} \epsilon(s')\, \Lambda\left(\frac{s + s'}{\Delta t} \right) ds'\, ds . \tag{11.74}$$

Here we have used $\int_0^{\infty} \epsilon(s)\, ds = 1$ and dropped all non-Hebbian terms ($a_0 = a_1^{\text{pre}} = a_1^{\text{post}} = 0$).

In order to understand this result let us first consider the case where both the width of the learning window and the postsynaptic potential are small as compared to the duration Δt of one pattern presentation. The integral over s' in the definition of the matrix Q_{kj} is the convolution of ϵ with a triangular function centered around

$s = 0$ that has a maximum value of unity. Since ϵ is normalized, the convolution
yields a smoothed version of the originally triangular function that is approximately
equal to unity in a neighborhood of $s = 0$; cf. Fig. 11.9B. If the learning window is
different from zero only in this neighborhood, then the integral over s in Eq. (11.74)
is just $\bar{W}$, the area under the learning window. We can thus collect the first two
terms on the right-hand side of Eq. (11.73) and obtain

$$\frac{d}{dt} w_{ij}(t) = \sum_k w_{ik}(t) \, \langle \xi_k^\mu \xi_j^\mu \rangle_\mu \bar{W} + w_{ij}(t) \, \langle \xi_j^\mu \rangle_\mu \, W_- \,. \tag{11.75}$$

Apart from the non-Hebbian term $w_{ij}(t) \, \langle \xi_j^\mu \rangle_\mu \, W_-$ the weight dynamics is determined by the correlation matrix $\langle \xi_k^\mu \xi_j^\mu \rangle_\mu$ of the (unnormalized) input patterns.
This is exactly what we would have expected from the comparison of rate-based
and spike based learning; cf. Eq. (11.60).

More interesting is the case where the time scale of the learning window is of
the same order of magnitude as the presentation of an input pattern. In this case,
the integral over s in Eq. (11.74) is different from $\bar{W}$ and we can choose a time
window with $\bar{W} = 0$ so that the first term on the right-hand side of Eq. (11.73)
vanishes. In this case, the weight dynamics is no longer determined by $\langle \xi_k^\mu \xi_j^\mu \rangle_\mu$
but by the matrix Q_{jk},

$$\frac{d}{dt} w_{ij}(t) = \sum_k w_{ik}(t) \, Q_{kj} + w_{ij}(t) \, \langle \xi_j^\mu \rangle_\mu \, W_- \,, \tag{11.76}$$

which is proportional to the *properly normalized* covariance matrix of the input
patterns,

$$Q_{kj} \propto \langle \xi_k^\mu \xi_j^\mu \rangle_\mu - \langle \xi_k^\mu \rangle_\mu \, \langle \xi_j^\mu \rangle_\mu = \langle (\xi_k^\mu - \langle \xi_k^\mu \rangle_\mu) \, (\xi_j^\mu - \langle \xi_j^\mu \rangle_\mu) \rangle_\mu \,. \tag{11.77}$$

If we assume that all presynaptic neurons have the same mean activity, $\langle \xi_k^\mu \rangle_\mu = \langle \xi_j^\mu \rangle_\mu \equiv \langle \xi^\mu \rangle_\mu$ then we can rewrite Eq. (11.76) as

$$\frac{d}{dt} w_{ij}(t) = \sum_k w_{ik}(t) \, [Q_{kj} + \delta_{kj} \, \langle \xi^\mu \rangle_\mu \, W_-] \,. \tag{11.78}$$

The eigenvectors and the eigenvalues of the matrix in square brackets are (apart
from a common additive constant $\langle \xi^\mu \rangle_\mu \, W_-$ for the eigenvalues) the same as those
of the matrix Q. We have already seen that this matrix is proportional to the
properly normalized covariance matrix of the input patterns. If the proportionality
constant is positive, i.e., if the integral over s in Eq. (11.74) is positive, then the
dynamics of the weight vector is determined by the principal component of the set
of input patterns.

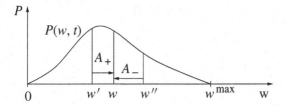

Fig. 11.10. Transitions of weight values due to synaptic plasticity. The probability density $P(w, t)$ increases if small weights increase, $w' \longrightarrow w' + A_+(w)$, or if large weights decrease, $w'' \longrightarrow w'' - A_-(w)$.

11.2.5 Distribution of synaptic weights

If spike arrival times are described as a stochastic process, the weight vector itself is also a random variable that evolves along a fluctuating trajectory. In Section 11.2.1, we have analyzed the expectation value of the synaptic weights smoothed over a certain interval of time. In the limit where the synaptic weights evolve much slower than typical pre- or postsynaptic interspike intervals, an approximation of the weight vector by its expectation values is justified. However, if the synaptic efficacy can be changed substantially by only a few pre- or postsynaptic spikes then the fluctuations of the weights have to be taken into account. Here, we are investigating the resulting distribution of synaptic weights in the framework of a Fokker–Planck equation (van Rossum et al., 2000; Rubin et al., 2001).

We consider a single neuron i that receives input from several hundreds of presynaptic neurons. All presynaptic neurons fire independently at a common constant rate ν^{pre}. We are interested in the probability density $P(w, t)$ for the synaptic weight of a given synapse. We assume that all weights are restricted to the interval $[0, w^{\mathrm{max}}]$ so that the normalization $\int_0^{w^{\mathrm{max}}} P(w, t)\,\mathrm{d}w = 1$ holds. Weight changes due to the potentiation or depression of synapses induce changes in the density function $P(w, t)$. The Fokker–Planck equation that we will derive below describes the evolution of the distribution $P(w, t)$ as a function of time; cf. Fig. 11.10.

For the sake of simplicity, we adopt a learning window with two rectangular phases, i.e.,

$$W(s) = \begin{cases} A_+(w_{ij}) & \text{for } -d < s < 0 \\ A_-(w_{ij}) & \text{for } 0 < s < d \\ 0 & \text{else} \end{cases} \qquad (11.79)$$

cf. Fig. 11.11A. Synapses are potentiated if the presynaptic spike shortly precedes the postsynaptic one. If the order of spike firing is reversed, the synapse is depressed.

A

B

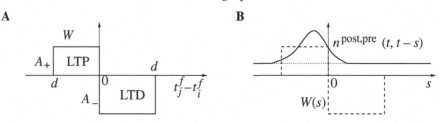

Fig. 11.11. **A.** Rectangular learning window $W(t_j^{(f)} - t_i^{(f)})$. Long-term potentiation (LTP) occurs if the presynaptic spike arrives before the postsynaptic one whereas long-term depression (LTD) occurs if the order of timing is reversed. **B.** Whether LTP or LTD is dominant depends on the overlap between the learning window $W(s)$ (dashed line) and the correlations (solid line) between pre- and postsynaptic spike firing. The correlations consist of a constant bias term and a time-dependent term with a peak at negative values of s; cf. Eq. (11.71).

There are basically two possibilities for restricting the synaptic weights to the interval $[0, w^{\text{max}}]$: we can either impose hard or soft bounds to the weight dynamics; cf. Section 10.2.1. Hard bounds means that the weights are simply no longer increased (decreased) if the upper (lower) bound is reached. Soft bounds, on the other hand, gradually slow down the evolution if the weight approaches one of its bounds. A simple way to implement soft bounds in our formalism is to define (Kistler and van Hemmen, 2000)

$$A_+(w_{ij}) = (w^{\text{max}} - w_{ij}) \, a_+ , \tag{11.80}$$

$$A_-(w_{ij}) = -w_{ij} \, a_- , \tag{11.81}$$

with constants a_+ and a_-. The choice of how the bounds are implemented turns out to have an important influence on the weight distribution $P(w, t)$ (van Rossum et al., 2000; Rubin et al., 2001).

In order to derive the evolution of the distribution $P(w, t)$ we consider transitions in the "weight space" induced by pre- and postsynaptic spike firing. The evolution is described by a master equation of the form

$$\frac{\partial}{\partial t} P(w, t) = -p_+(w) \, P(w, t) - p_-(w) \, P(w, t) \tag{11.82}$$

$$+ \int_0^{w^{\text{max}}} \delta[w - w' - A_+(w')] \, p_+(w', t) \, P(w', t) \, dw'$$

$$+ \int_0^{w^{\text{max}}} \delta[w - w' + A_-(w')] \, p_-(w', t) \, P(w', t) \, dw' ;$$

cf. Fig. 11.10. Here p_+ (or p_-) is the probability that a presynaptic spike falls in the positive (or negative) phase of the learning window. Using the definition of the

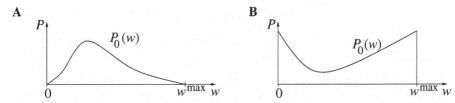

Fig. 11.12. Stationary distribution of synaptic weights. **A**. With soft bounds, the distribution of weights $P_0(w)$ has a single peak. **B**. With hard bounds, the distribution peaks at the two boundaries $w = 0$ and $w = w^{\max}$ (schematic figure).

joint firing rate of pre- and postsynaptic neuron

$$\nu^{\text{post,pre}}(t, t') = \langle S^{\text{post}}(t) \, S^{\text{pre}}(t') \rangle_E \qquad (11.83)$$

we have

$$p_+(w, t) = \int_{-d}^{0} \nu^{\text{post,pre}}(t, t - s) \, \mathrm{d}s \qquad (11.84)$$

$$p_-(w, t) = \int_{0}^{d} \nu^{\text{post,pre}}(t, t - s) \, \mathrm{d}s \, ; \qquad (11.85)$$

cf. Fig. 11.11B.

Equation (11.82) can be rewritten in the form of a Fokker–Planck equation if we expand the right-hand side to second order in the transition amplitudes A_+ and A_- (van Kampen, 1992),

$$\frac{\partial}{\partial t} P(w, t) = -\frac{\partial}{\partial w}[A(w) \, P(w, t)] + \frac{\partial^2}{\partial w^2}[B(w) \, P(w, t)] \qquad (11.86)$$

with

$$A(w, t) = p_+(w, t) \, A_+(w) - p_-(w, t) \, A_-(w) \,, \qquad (11.87)$$

$$B(w, t) = p_+(w, t) \, A_+^2(w) - p_-(w, t) \, A_-^2(w) \,. \qquad (11.88)$$

The Fokker–Planck equation (11.86) can be solved numerically to find stationary solutions. It turns out that the qualitative form of the distribution depends critically on how the bounds for the weights are implemented; cf. van Rossum et al. (2000) and Rubin et al. (2001) for details. With soft bounds the distribution is unimodal whereas with hard bounds it peaks at both borders of the interval; cf. Fig. 11.12. Experimental data suggest a unimodal distribution, consistent with soft bounds (van Rossum et al., 2000).

11.3 Summary

The synaptic weight dynamics can be studied analytically if weights are changing slowly as compared to the time scale of the neuronal activity. We have seen that weight changes are driven by correlations between pre- and postsynaptic activity. More specifically, simple Hebbian learning rules can find the first principal component of a normalized input data set. If non-Hebbian terms are included then both spike-based and rate-based learning rules can be constructed that are characterized by a stable fixed point for the sum of the synaptic weights. This fixed point leads to an intrinsic normalization of the output firing rate.

The interesting aspect of spike-time-dependent plasticity is that it naturally accounts for *temporal* correlations in the input by means of a learning window. Explicit expressions for temporal spike–spike correlations can be obtained for certain simple types of neuron model such as the linear Poisson model. In this case, correlations between pre- and postsynaptic neurons can be formulated in terms of the correlations in the input. It can be shown that, under certain circumstances, the weight vector evolves in the direction of the principal component of the input pattern set, even if the input is not normalized.

Spike-based and rate-based rules of plasticity are equivalent as long as *temporal* correlations are disregarded. The integral over the learning window $\int_{-\infty}^{\infty} W(s)\, ds$ plays the role of the Hebbian correlation term c_2^{corr}. If rates vary rapidly, i.e., on the time scale of the learning window, then spike-time-dependent plasticity is distinct from a rate-based formulation.

In addition to an analysis of the expectation value of the synaptic weight vector the distribution of weights can be described by means of a Fokker–Planck equation. The stationary distribution depends on the details of the learning rule.

Literature

More on the theory of unsupervised learning and principal component analysis can be found in the classical book by Hertz et al. (1991). Models of the development of receptive fields and cortical maps have a long tradition in the field of computational neuroscience; see, e.g., von der Malsburg (1973); Sejnowski (1977); Kohonen (1984); Linsker (1986c); Sejnowski and Tesauro (1989); Miller et al. (1989); MacKay and Miller (1990); Shouval and Perrone (1995); Miller (1994); for a review see, e.g., Erwin et al. (1995); Wiskott and Sejnowski (1998). The linear rate model discussed in Section 11.1 is reviewed in Miller (1995). The essential aspects of the weight dynamics in linear networks are discussed in Oja (1982); MacKay and Miller (1990); Miller and MacKay (1994).

The theory of spike-based Hebbian learning has been developed by Gerstner et al. (1996a); Häfliger et al. (1997); Ruf and Schmitt (1997); Eurich et al. (1999);

Kempter et al. (1999); Roberts (1999, 2000); Roberts and Bell (2000); Kistler and van Hemmen (2000); van Rossum et al. (2000); Xie and Seung (2000); Song et al. (2000); Senn et al. (2001); Rubin et al. (2001); and others. Spike-based learning rules are closely related to rules for sequence learning (Herz et al., 1988, 1989; van Hemmen et al., 1990; Gerstner et al., 1993b; Minai and Levy, 1993; Abbott and Blum, 1996; Gerstner and Abbott, 1997), where the idea of an asymmetric learning windows is exploited.

12

Plasticity and coding

In Chapters 10 and 11 we have explored the principle of Hebbian synaptic plasticity. In this final chapter we would like to close the chain of arguments that we have followed throughout the book and establish a link between synaptic plasticity and the problems of neuronal coding and signal transmission. We will start the chapter with the question of rapid and reliable signal transmission, a question that we have encountered on several occasions in this book. In Section 12.1 we will see that an asymmetric spike-time-dependent learning rule is capable of detecting early events that may serve as predictors for others. Such a mechanism can speed up signal processing and, hence, the reaction time. In Section 12.2 we show that spike-time-dependent plasticity can enhance signal transmission by selectively strengthening synaptic connections that transmit precisely timed spikes at the expense of those synapses that transmit poorly timed spikes. In Section 12.3 we turn to sequence learning and explore whether spike-time-dependent plasticity can support coding schemes that are based on spatio-temporal spike patterns with a millisecond resolution. The last two sections study the coding properties of specific neuronal systems. In Section 12.4 we will illustrate the role of an inverted (or anti-)Hebb rule for the subtraction of expectations – which has been hypothesized as an important component of signal processing in electric fish. Finally, in Section 12.5 we will see that a spike-time-dependent Hebbian rule can play an important role in the developmental tuning of signal transmission in the auditory system of barn owls.

12.1 Learning to be fast

In many real-world situations we must react rapidly to the earliest signs that could warn us about harmful stimuli. If an obstacle blocks our way, we want to avoid it before a painful contact occurs. If we ride a bicycle, we should make correcting steering movements even at small inclination angles of the bicycle, well before we

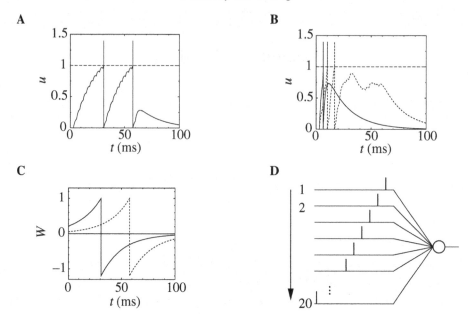

Fig. 12.1. **A**. A postsynaptic neuron receives inputs from 20 presynaptic cells at intervals of 3 ms. All synapses have the same weight. The neuron emits two output spikes at about 31 and 58 ms after stimulus onset. **B**. After five repetitions of the same stimulus the neuron fires after 10 ms (dashed line); after a total of 100 repetitions the neuron fires after about 5 ms (solid line). **C**. The reason is that synapses that have been active slightly before the postsynaptic spikes are strengthened while others are depressed. To illustrate this point, the learning window $W(t_j^{(f)} - t_i^{(f)})$ is shown twice, each time centered at the postsynaptic firing time $t_i^{(f)}$ of the first trial (shown in part A). **D**. The sequence of presynaptic spikes could be generated by a stimulus that moves from top to bottom.

are at risk of falling over. Spike-time-dependent learning rules with a temporally asymmetric learning window hint as to how a simple predictive coding could be implemented at the neuronal level.

   Let us consider a single neuron that receives inputs from, say, 20 presynaptic cells that are stimulated one after the other; cf. Fig. 12.1. Initially, all synapses w_{ij} have the same weight w_0. The postsynaptic neuron fires two spikes; cf. Fig. 12.1A. All synapses that have been activated *before* the postsynaptic spike are strengthened while synapses that have been activated immediately afterwards are depressed; cf. Fig. 12.1C. In subsequent trials the threshold is therefore reached earlier; cf. Fig. 12.1B. After many trials, those presynaptic neurons that fire first have developed strong connections while other connections are depressed. Thus a temporally asymmetric learning rule favors connections that can serve as "earliest predictors" of other spike events (Mehta et al., 2000; Song et al., 2000).

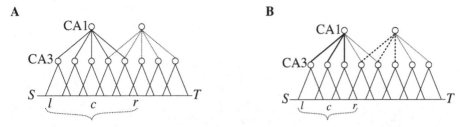

Fig. 12.2. **A**. The place fields of neurons in regions CA3 of hippocampus are indicated as cones along the track that extends from S to T. The place field of the neuron in CA1 shown with solid lines has its center at c and extends from l to r. **B**. After the rat has made several movements from left to right, some connections are increased (thick lines) others decreased (dotted lines). As a result, the place field center c has moved to the left.

This theoretical observation predicts a shift in so-called place fields of hippocampal neurons that seems to be in agreement with experiment observations (Mehta et al., 2000). More generally, early predictors play a central role in the theory of conditioning and reinforcement learning (Rescorla and Wagner, 1972; Sutton and Barto, 1981; Montague et al., 1995; Schultz et al., 1997).

Example: hippocampal place fields

Place cells are neurons in rodent hippocampus that are sensitive to the spatial location of the animal in an environment. The sensitive area is called the place field of the cell. If, for example, a rat runs on a linear track from a starting point S to a target point T, this movement would first activate cells with a place field close to S, then those with a place field in the middle of the track, and finally those with a place field close to T; cf. Fig. 12.2. In a simple feedforward model of the hippocampus (Mehta et al., 2000), a first set of place cells is identified with neurons in region CA3 of rat hippocampus. A cell further down the processing stream (i.e., a cell in hippocampal region CA1) receives input from several cells in CA1. If we assume that initially all connections have the same weight, the place field of a CA1 cell is therefore broader than that of a CA3 cell.

During the experiment, the rat moves repeatedly from left to right. During each movement, the same sequence of CA3 cells is activated. This has consequences for the connections from CA3 cells to CA1 cells. Hebbian plasticity with an asymmetric learning window strengthens those connections where the presynaptic neuron fires early in the sequence. Connections from neurons that fire later in the sequence are weakened. As a result the center of the place field of a cell in CA3 is shifted to the left; cf. Fig. 12.2B. The shift of place fields predicted by asymmetric Hebbian learning has been confirmed experimentally (Mehta et al., 2000).

A

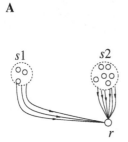

B

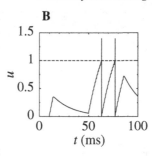

C

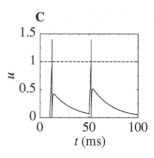

Fig. 12.3. **A.** Conditioning paradigm. A response neuron r can receive input from two neuronal populations, representing the stimuli $s1$ and $s2$. **B.** Membrane potential of the postsynaptic neuron. Before learning, stimulation of the presynaptic population $s1$ which occurs at about $t = 10$ ms leads to subthreshold excitation of the postsynaptic neuron whereas stimulation of group $s2$ 40 ms later evokes postsynaptic firing. **C.** After learning postsynaptic firing is triggered by the stimulus $s1$.

Example: conditioning

The shift of responses towards early predictors plays a central role in conditioning. The basic idea is best explained by the paradigm of Pavlovian conditioning (Pavlov, 1927). Tasting or smelling food (stimulus $s2$) evokes an immediate response r. During the conditioning experiment, a bell (stimulus $s1$) rings always at a fixed time interval ΔT *before* the food stimulus. After several repetitions of the experiment, it is found that the response now occurs after the first stimulus ($s1$). Thus the reaction has moved from stimulus $s2$ to stimulus $s1$ which reliably predicts $s2$.

Spike-time-dependent plasticity with an asymmetric learning window allows us to replicate this result if the time difference ΔT between the two stimuli is less than the width of the learning window. The mechanism is identical to that of the previous example with the only difference being that the input spikes are now clustered into two groups corresponding to the stimuli $s1$ and $s2$; cf. Fig. 12.3.

In behavioral experiments with monkeys, conditioning is possible with time intervals that span several seconds (Schultz et al., 1997) whereas typical learning windows extend over 50–100 ms (Magee and Johnston, 1997; Markram et al., 1997; Debanne et al., 1998; Bi and Poo, 1998, 1999; Zhang et al., 1998). In order to explain conditioning with time windows longer than 100 ms, additional assumptions regarding neuronal architecture and dynamics have to be made; see, e.g., Fiala et al. (1996); Brown et al. (1999); Suri and Schutz (2001). A potential solution could be provided by delayed reverberating loops; cf. Section 8.3. As an aside we note that, traditionally, conditioning experiments have been discussed at the level of rate coding. As we have seen in Chapter 11, spike-time-dependent learning rules can be mapped to rate-coded models in the limit of slowly changing firing rates. In this limit, a spike-time-dependent rule with an asymmetric learning window yield a differential Hebbian term (cf. Eq. (11.64)) that is proportional to the derivative of the postsynaptic rate, which is the starting point of models of conditioning (Montague et al., 1995; Schultz et al., 1997).

12.2 Learning to be precise

We have seen in Section 12.1 that learning rules with an asymmetric learning window can selectively strengthen those synapses that reliably transmit spikes at the earliest possible time before the postsynaptic neuron is activated by a volley of spikes from other presynaptic neurons. This mechanism may be relevant for speeding up information processing in networks that contain several hierarchically organized layers.

Here we are going to discuss a related phenomenon that may be equally important in networks that are based on a time-coding paradigm, i.e., in networks where information is coded in the precise firing time of individual action potentials. We show that an asymmetric learning window can selectively strengthen synapses that deliver precisely timed spikes at the expense of others that deliver spikes with a broad temporal jitter. This is obviously a way to reduce the noise level of the membrane potential and to increase the temporal precision of the postsynaptic response (Kistler and van Hemmen, 2000).

12.2.1 The model

We consider a neuron i that receives spike input from N presynaptic neurons via synapses with weights w_{ij}, $1 \leq j \leq N$. The membrane potential $u_i(t)$ is described by the usual SRM_0 formalism with response kernels ϵ and η, and the last postsynaptic firing time $\hat{t}_i$, i.e.,

$$u_i(t) = \eta(t - \hat{t}_i) + N^{-1} \sum_{\substack{j=1 \\ (j \neq i)}}^{N} \int_0^\infty w_{ij}(t - s)\,\epsilon(s)\,S_j(t - s)\,\mathrm{d}s \,. \tag{12.1}$$

Postsynaptic spikes are triggered according to the escape-noise model (Section 5.3) with a rate v that is a *nonlinear* function of the membrane potential,

$$v(u) = v_{\max}\,\Theta(u - \vartheta)\,. \tag{12.2}$$

If the membrane potential is below the firing threshold ϑ, the neuron is quiescent. If the membrane potential reaches the threshold, the neuron will respond with an action potential within a characteristic response time of $v_{\max}^{-1}$. Note that the output rate is determined by the shape of the η kernel rather than by $v(u)$. In particular,

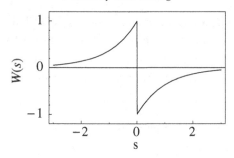

Fig. 12.4. Asymmetric exponential learning window W as a function of the time difference s between presynaptic spike arrival and postsynaptic firing with $A_+ = -A_- = 1$ and $\tau = 1$; cf. Eq. (12.4).

the constant ν_{max} is not the maximum firing rate but the reliability of the neuron. The larger ν_{max} the faster the neuron will fire after the firing threshold has been reached. For $\nu_{max} \to \infty$ we recover the sharp firing threshold of a noiseless neuron[a] model. We refer to this neuron model as the *nonlinear Poisson model*.

Presynaptic spike trains are described by inhomogeneous Poisson processes with a time-dependent firing intensity $\nu_i(t)$. More specifically, we consider a volley of spikes that reaches the postsynaptic neuron approximately at time t_0. The width of the volley is determined by the time course of the firing intensities ν_i. For the sake of simplicity we use bell-shaped intensities with a width σ_i centered around t_0. The width σ_i is a measure of the temporal precision of the spikes that are conveyed via synapse i. The intensities are normalized so that, on average, each presynaptic neuron contributes a single action potential to the volley.

Synaptic plasticity is implemented along the lines of Section 10.3.1. Synaptic weights change whenever presynaptic spikes arrive or when postsynaptic action potentials are triggered,

$$\frac{\mathrm{d}}{\mathrm{d}t} w_{ij}(t) = a_0 + a_1^{\mathrm{pre}} S_j(t) + a_1^{\mathrm{post}} S_i(t)$$
$$+ S_j(t) \int_0^\infty W(s) S_i(t-s) \, \mathrm{d}s + S_i(t) \int_0^\infty W(-s) S_j(t-s) \, \mathrm{d}s \, ; \quad (12.3)$$

cf. Eqs. (10.14) and (10.15). In order to describe Hebbian plasticity we choose an asymmetric exponential learning window W that is positive for $s < 0$ and negative for $s > 0$,

$$W(s) = \begin{cases} A_+ \exp(s/\tau), & \text{if } s < 0 \\ A_- \exp(-s/\tau), & \text{if } s > 0 \end{cases} \quad (12.4)$$

with $A_+ > 0$ and $A_- < 0$; cf. Fig. 12.4.

In addition to the Hebbian term we also take advantage of the non-Hebbian terms a_1^{pre} and a_1^{post} in order to ensure that the postsynaptic firing rate stays within certain bounds. More precisely, we use $0 < a_1^{\text{pre}} \ll 1$ and $-1 \ll a_1^{\text{post}} < 0$. A positive value for a_1^{pre} leads to growing synapses even if only the presynaptic neuron is active. This effect will bring the neuron back to threshold even if all synaptic weights were strongly depressed. A small negative value for a_1^{post}, on the other hand, leads to a depression of the synapse if the postsynaptic neuron is firing at an excessively high rate. Altogether, the non-Hebbian terms keep the neuron at its operating point.

Apart from the postsynaptic firing rate we also want to have individual synaptic weights restricted to a finite interval, e.g., to $[0, 1]$. We can achieve this by introducing a dependence of the parameters in Eqs. (12.3) and (12.4) on the actual value of the synaptic weight. All terms leading to potentiation should be proportional to $(1 - w_{ij})$ and all terms leading to depression to w_{ij}; cf. Section 10.3.1. Altogether we have

$$\frac{d}{dt} w_{ij}(t) = a_1^{\text{pre}} \left[1 - w_{ij}(t) \right] S_j(t) + a_1^{\text{post}} w_{ij}(t) S_i(t)$$

$$+ S_j(t) \int_0^\infty W(s) S_i(t-s) \, ds + S_i(t) \int_0^\infty W(-s) S_j(t-s) \, ds, \quad (12.5)$$

and $A_+ = a_+ [1 - w_{ij}(t)]$, $A_- = a_- w_{ij}(t)$ with constants $a_+ > 0$ and $a_- < 0$. The constant term a_0 describing weight decay has been discarded.

12.2.2 *Firing time distribution*

We have seen in Section 11.2.1 that the evolution of synaptic weights depends on correlations of pre- and postsynaptic spike trains at the time scale of the learning window. In order to calculate this correlation we need the joint probability density for pre- and postsynaptic spikes ("joint firing rate"), $v_{ij}(t, t')$; cf. Eq. (11.48). We have already calculated the joint firing rate for a particularly simple neuron model, the linear Poisson neuron, in Section 11.2.2. Here, however, we are interested in nonlinear effects due to the neuronal firing threshold. A straightforward calculation of spike–spike correlations is therefore no longer possible. Instead we argue that the spike correlation of the postsynaptic and a single presynaptic neuron can be neglected in neurons that receive synaptic input from many presynaptic cells. In this case, the joint firing rate is just the product of pre- and postsynaptic firing intensities,

$$v_{ij}(t, t') \approx v_i(t) \, v_j(t') \,. \quad (12.6)$$

It thus remains for us to determine the postsynaptic firing time distribution given the presynaptic spike statistics. As we have already discussed in Section 11.2.2 the output spike train is the result of a doubly stochastic process (Cox, 1955; Bartlett, 1963) in the sense that first the presynaptic spike trains are produced by inhomogeneous Poisson processes so that the membrane potential is in itself a stochastic process. In a second step the output spike train is generated from a firing intensity that is a function of the membrane potential. Though the composite process is not equivalent to an inhomogeneous Poisson process, the output spike train can be approximated by such a process with an intensity that is given by the expectation of the rate v with respect to the input statistics (Kistler and van Hemmen, 2000),

$$\bar{v}_i(t) = \langle v[u_i(t)] \rangle . \qquad (12.7)$$

The angular bracket denote an average over the ensemble of input spike trains.

Due to refractoriness, the neuron cannot fire two spikes directly one after the other; an effect that is clearly not accounted for by a description in terms of a firing intensity as in Eq. (12.7). A possible way out is to assume that the afterpotential is so strong that the neuron can fire only a single spike followed by a long period of silence. In this case we can focus on the probability density $p_{\text{first}}(t)$ of the *first* postsynaptic spike which is given by the probability density of finding a spike at t times the probability that there was no spike before, i.e.,

$$p_i^{\text{first}}(t) = \bar{v}_i(t) \exp\left[-\int_{\hat{t}}^{t} \bar{v}_i(t') \, dt'\right] , \qquad (12.8)$$

cf. the definition of the interval distribution in Eq. (5.9). The lower bound $\hat{t}$ is the time when the neuron has fired its last spike, from which time on we consider the next spike to be the "first" one.

Given the statistics of the presynaptic volley of action potentials we are now able to calculate the expected firing intensity $\bar{v}_i(t)$ of the postsynaptic neuron and hence the firing time distribution $p_{\text{first}}(t)$ of the first action potential that will be triggered by the presynaptic volley. In certain limiting cases, explicit expressions for $p_{\text{first}}(t)$ can be derived; cf. Fig. 12.5 (see Kistler and van Hemmen 2000 for details).

12.2.3 Stationary synaptic weights

In the limiting case of many presynaptic neurons and strong refractoriness the joint firing rate of pre- and postsynaptic neurons is given by

$$v_{ij}(t, t') = p_i^{\text{first}}(t) \, v_j(t') . \qquad (12.9)$$

A

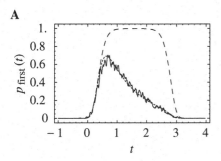

B

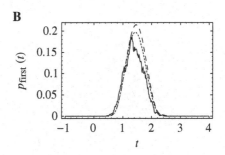

Fig. 12.5. Probability density of the postsynaptic firing time with (p_{first}, dotted line) and without refractoriness ($\bar{\nu}$, dashed line). The solid line shows a simulation of a neuron that receives input from $N = 100$ presynaptic neurons via synapses with strength $w_{ij} = 1/N$. Presynaptic spike rains are generated by an inhomogeneous Poisson process with rate function $\nu_j = (2\pi\sigma^2)^{-1/2}\exp\left[-t^2/2\sigma^2\right]$ and $\sigma = 1$. The ϵ kernel is an alpha function $t/\tau\exp(1-t/\tau)$ with time constant $\tau = 1$ so that the maximum of the membrane potential amounts to $u = 1$ if all spikes were to arrive simultaneously. The postsynaptic response is characterized by $\nu_{max} = 1$ and $\vartheta = 0.5$ in **A** and $\vartheta = 0.75$ in **B**. Increasing the threshold improves the temporal precision of the postsynaptic response, but the overall probability of a postsynaptic spike is decreased. Taken from Kistler and van Hemmen (2000).

We can use this result in Eq. (11.50) to calculate the change of the synaptic weight that is induced by the volley of presynaptic spikes and the postsynaptic action potential that may have been triggered by this volley. To this end we choose the length of the time interval T such that the time averages in learning equation (11.50) include all spikes within the volley and the postsynaptically triggered action potential.

A suitable combination of pre- and postsynaptic firing times will result in potentiation of the synaptic efficacy and the synaptic weight will be increased whenever this particular stimulus is applied. However, due to the soft bounds that we have imposed on the weight dynamics, the potentiating terms become less and less effective as the synaptic weight approaches its upper bound at $w_{ij} = 1$, because all terms leading to potentiation are proportional to $(1 - w_{ij})$. On the other hand, terms that lead to depression become increasingly effective due to their proportionality to w_{ij}. At some point potentiation and depression balance each other so that a fixed point for the synaptic weight is reached.

Figure 12.6 shows the stationary synaptic weight as a function of the firing time statistics given in terms of the temporal jitter σ of pre- and postsynaptic spikes and their relative firing time. For small values of σ, that is for precisely timed spikes, we recover the shape of the learning window. The synaptic weight saturates close to its maximum value if the presynaptic spikes arrive before the postsynaptic neuron is firing. If the timing is the other way round, the weight will be approximately zero. For increasing levels of noise in the firing times this relationship is smeared

A

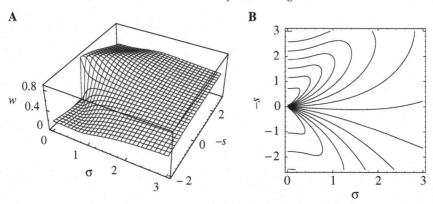

B

Fig. 12.6. Stationary synaptic weights. **A**. Three-dimensional plot of the stationary synaptic weight as a function of σ and s, where $\sigma^2 = \sigma^2_{\text{pre}} + \sigma^2_{\text{post}}$ is the sum of the variances of pre- and postsynaptic firing time, and s the mean time difference between the arrival of the presynaptic spike and the firing of the postsynaptic action potential. Note that the s-axis has been inverted for the sake of clarity. **B**. Contour plot of the same function as in A. The parameters used to describe synaptic plasticity are $a_1^{\text{post}} = -0.01$, $a_1^{\text{pre}} = 0.001$, $a_+ = -a_- = 0.1$, $\tau = 1$. Taken from Kistler and van Hemmen (2000).

out and the weight takes an intermediate value that is determined by non-Hebbian terms rather than by the learning window.

12.2.4 The role of the firing threshold

We have seen that the stationary value of the synaptic weight is a function of the statistical properties of pre- *and* postsynaptic spike train. The synaptic weights, on the other hand, determine the distribution of postsynaptic firing times. If we are interested in the synaptic weights that are produced by a given input statistics, we thus have to solve a self-consistency problem which can be done numerically by using explicit expressions for the firing time distributions derived along the lines sketched above.

Figure 12.7 shows an example of a neuron that receives spike input from two groups of presynaptic neurons. The first group is firing synchronously with a rather high temporal precision of $\sigma = 0.1$. The second group is also firing synchronously but with a much broader jitter of $\sigma = 1$. (All times are in units of the membrane time constant.) The spikes from both groups together form the spike volley that impinges on the postsynaptic neuron and induce changes in the synaptic weights. After a couple of these volleys have hit the neuron the synaptic weights will finally settle at their fixed point. Figure 12.7A shows the resulting weights for synapses that deliver precisely timed spikes together with those of the poorly timed group as a function of the neuronal firing threshold.

As is apparent from Fig. 12.7A there is a certain domain for the neuronal firing threshold ($\vartheta \approx 0.25$) at which synapses that convey precisely timed spikes are substantially stronger than synapses that deliver spikes with a broad temporal jitter. The key for an understanding of this result is the normalization of the postsynaptic firing rate by non-Hebbian terms in the learning equation.

The maximum value of the membrane potential if all presynaptic neurons deliver one precisely timed spike is $u_{\max} = 1$. The axis for the firing threshold in Fig. 12.7 therefore extends from 0 to 1. Let us consider high firing thresholds first. For $\vartheta \approx 1$ the postsynaptic neuron will reach its firing threshold only if all presynaptic spikes arrive almost simultaneously, which is rather unlikely given the high temporal jitter in the second group. The probability that the postsynaptic neuron is firing an action potential therefore tends to zero as $\vartheta \to 1$; cf. Fig. 12.7C. Every time the volley fails to trigger the neuron the weights are increased due to presynaptic potentiation described by $a_1^{\text{pre}} > 0$. Therefore, irrespective of their temporal precision, all synapses will finally reach an efficacy that is close to the maximum value.

On the other hand, if the firing threshold is very low, then a few presynaptic spikes suffice to trigger the postsynaptic neuron. Since the neuron can fire only a single action potential as a response to a volley of presynaptic spikes the neuron will be triggered by the earliest spikes; cf. Section 12.1. The early spikes however are mostly spikes from presynaptic neurons with a broad temporal jitter. The postsynaptic neuron has therefore already fired its action potential before the spikes from the precise neurons arrive. Synapses that deliver precisely timed spikes are hence depressed, whereas synapses that deliver early but poorly timed spikes are strengthened.

For some intermediate values of the firing threshold, synapses that deliver precisely timed spikes are strengthened at the expense of the other group. If the firing threshold is just high enough so that a few early spikes from the poorly timed group are not able to trigger an action potential then the neuron will be fired most of the time by spikes from the precise group. These synapses are consistently strengthened due to the Hebbian learning rule. Spikes from the other group, however, are likely to arrive either much earlier or after the neuron has fired so that the corresponding synapses are depressed.

A neuron that has synaptic input predominantly from neurons that fire with a high temporal precision will also show little temporal jitter in its firing time relative to its presynaptic neurons. This is illustrated in Fig. 12.7B, which gives the precision Δt of the postsynaptic firing time as a function of the firing threshold. The curve exhibits a clear peak for firing thresholds that favor "precise" synapses. The precision of the postsynaptic firing time shows similarly high values in the high firing threshold regime. Here, however, the overall probability $\bar{\nu}_{\text{post}}$ of the neuron reaching the threshold is very low (Fig. 12.7C). In terms of a "coding efficiency"

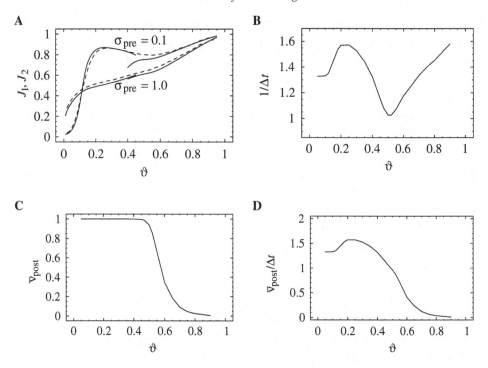

Fig. 12.7. **A.** Synaptic weights for a neuron receiving input from two groups of synapses – one group ($n_1 = 20$) delivers precisely timed spikes ($\sigma_1 = 0.1$) and the other one ($n_2 = 80$) spikes with a broad distribution of arrival times ($\sigma_2 = 1.0$). The upper trace shows the resulting stationary synaptic weight for the group of precise synapses; the lower trace corresponds to the second group. The solid lines give the analytical result obtained for two limiting cases; see Kistler and van Hemmen (2000) for details. The dashed lines show the results of a computer simulation. The parameters for the synaptic plasticity are the same as in Fig. 12.6. **B, C, D.** Precision Δt^{-1}, reliability $\bar{\nu}_{\text{post}}$, and "coding efficiency" $\bar{\nu}_{\text{post}}/\Delta t$ as a function of the threshold ϑ for the same neuron as in A. Reliability is defined as the overall firing probability $\bar{\nu}_{\text{post}} = \int \mathrm{d}t\, p_{\text{first}}(t)$. Precision is the inverse of the length of the interval containing 90% of the postsynaptic spikes, $\Delta t = t_2 - t_1$ with $\int_{-\infty}^{t_1} \mathrm{d}t\, p_{\text{first}}(t) = \int_{t_2}^{\infty} \mathrm{d}t\, p_{\text{first}}(t) = 0.05\, \bar{\nu}_{\text{post}}$. Taken from Kistler and van Hemmen (2000).

defined by $\nu_{\text{post}}/\Delta t$ there is thus a clear optimum for the firing threshold near $\vartheta = 0.25$ (Fig. 12.7D).

12.3 Sequence learning

It has been recognized for a long time that asymmetric Hebbian plasticity is well suited to store spatio-temporal patterns in a neuronal network (Sompolinsky and Kanter, 1986; Herz et al., 1989; Gerstner et al., 1993b; Minai and Levy, 1993; Hertz and Prugel-Bennet, 1996). In standard sequence learning models, where groups of

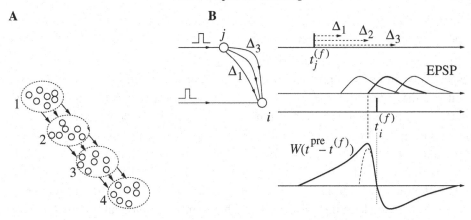

Fig. 12.8. Sequence learning. **A**. In a sequence, different groups of neurons (1,2,3,4) are activated one after the other. During learning the sequence is imposed by external stimuli. **B**. A presynaptic neuron j in one of the groups is connected to the postsynaptic neuron i in another group via several synapses with different axonal transmission delays $\Delta_1, \Delta_2, \Delta_3$. Initially, external stimulation by short current pulses (left) causes pre- and postsynaptic spikes (short vertical bars) at time $t_j^{(f)}$ and $t_i^{(f)}$, respectively. The presynaptic spike generates three excitatory postsynaptic potentials (EPSPs) with different delays (middle). If a Hebbian learning rule strengthens the connection with transmission delay Δ_2, a presynaptic spike $t_j^{(f)}$ can later cause a postsynaptic spike $t_i^{(f)}$ with approximately the same time difference $t_i^{(f)} - t_j^{(f)}$ as imposed during the initial stimulation. The bottom graph shows a hypothetical sharply peaked learning window (dashed line) and a more realistic window with two phases (solid line). The maximum of the learning window is so that the connection with transmission delay Δ_2 is maximally reinforced. t^{pre} indicates the presynaptic spike arrival time (schematic figure).

neurons are trained to fire one after the other, external input is used during an initial training period in order to induce neurons to fire in the desired spatio-temporal spike pattern. Let us suppose that neuron j fires shortly before neuron i. Hebbian synaptic plasticity with an asymmetric learning window will thus strengthen the synapse from neuron j to neuron i. After successful training, weights are kept fixed and the network is able to reproduce the learnt spatio-temporal spike pattern even in the *absence* of the external input because spikes of neuron j will stimulate neuron i and hence help to "recall" the sequence of firing. The resulting network architecture is equivalent to a synfire chain (Abeles, 1991) with feedforward connectivity; cf. Section 9.4.

The network should be able to recall the learnt sequence at the correct speed. This can most easily be achieved if each pair of neurons has several connections with a broad distribution of delays; cf. Fig. 12.8B. We assume that neuron i receives input from neuron j via three connections with different axonal transmission delays Δ_1, Δ_2, and Δ_3. A single presynaptic action potential that has been fired at time $t_j^{(f)}$ evokes therefore three excitatory postsynaptic potentials (EPSPs) which start after the presynaptic spike arrival time $t^{\text{pre}} = t_i^{(f)} + \Delta_1$, $t_i^{(f)} + \Delta_2$, and $t_i^{(f)} + \Delta_3$, respectively. In order to preserve the timing, Hebbian learning should maximally reinforce the connection that could have been causal for the postsynaptic spike at time $t_i^{(f)}$. A postsynaptic action potential is triggered in the low-noise limit most likely during the *rising* phase of the EPSP, while in the high-noise limit it occurs most likely at the time when the EPSP reaches its maximum; cf. Section 7.4.1, in particular Fig. 7.12. If we denote the rise time of the EPSP as δ^{rise} and the time difference between presynaptic spike arrival and postsynaptic firing by $s = t^{\text{pre}} - t_i^{(f)}$, then the learning window $W(s)$ should have its maximum s^* in the range $0.5\,\delta^{\text{rise}} < -s^* < \delta^{\text{rise}}$; (Herz et al., 1989; Gerstner et al., 1993b, 1996a; Senn et al., 2002). We call this the causality condition of Hebbian learning.

In early papers on sequence learning, it was assumed that the learning window is sharply peaked at s^*, so that only connections with the optimal delay are strengthened (Herz et al., 1989; Gerstner et al., 1993b). It is, however, also possible to achieve selective reinforcement of the optimal delay lines with a broader learning window, if a competition mechanism between different synapses leading onto the same postsynaptic neuron is implemented (Gerstner et al., 1996a; Senn et al., 2002). As we have seen in Section 11.2.3, synaptic competition in a stochastically firing network of spiking neurons can be induced by stabilization of the postsynaptic firing rate.

Example: coding by spatio-temporal spike patterns

A network of $N = 1000$ spiking neurons has been trained on three spatio-temporal patterns that are defined with a temporal resolution of 1 ms. Each pattern consists of a sequence of spikes from different neurons during a time window of $T = 40$ time steps, i.e., 40 ms. The sequence is then repeated. A spike pattern μ ($1 \le \mu \le 3$) is defined here by exactly one firing time $t_i^{(f)}(\mu)$ for each single neuron $1 \le i \le N$. The firing time is drawn from a random distribution with uniform probability $p = 0.025$ for all discrete time steps $t_i^{(f)} \in \{1, 2, \dots 40\}$. Thus, in an ideal and noiseless pattern all neurons fire regularly with a rate of 25 Hz, but the firing of different neurons is randomly correlated.

During the training session all spike patterns $1 \le \mu \le 3$ are impressed on the neurons and the synaptic efficacies are adjusted according to a Hebbian learning rule with a suitable time window. In order to check whether the patterns are now stable attractors of the neuronal dynamics, retrieval of the patterns has to be studied. A retrieval session is started by a short external stimulus of duration $t_{\text{init}} = 5$ ms. It consists of a spatio-temporal sequence of short pulses used to initialize the network for 5 ms in a state consistent with one of the learnt patterns. The pattern μ that is matched should be completed and cyclically retrieved afterwards.

The results of three retrieval sessions with different stimuli are shown in Fig. 12.9A–C. For each pattern, the ensemble activity (spatial average) during retrieval is plotted in (i), the spike pattern of a few selected neurons during the retrieval session is shown in (ii) and the mean firing rate in (iii).

Let us first turn to the spatio-temporal *spike pattern*, Fig. 12.9A(ii)–C(ii). We have selected 30 neurons whose label has been plotted along the y-axis. Time is plotted along the x-axis. The origin $t = 0$ marks the *end* of the stimulus, thus for all $t \geq 0$, the external input vanishes. All spikes of a given neuron i appear as black dots along a line parallel to the x-axis. For ease of visualization of the different spike patterns, we have used a little trick. Neurons with index $i = 1, \ldots, 10$ did not learn random patterns but "meaningful" objects such as diagonal stripes so that different spike patterns can be easily recognized.

If we analyze the series of Fig. 12.9A–C, a number of conclusions regarding potential neuronal coding schemes can be drawn. First of all, it is indeed possible to store and retrieve spatio-temporal spike patterns with a time resolution of 1 ms in a network of spiking neurons. This may seem remarkable in view of the typical duration of an EPSP (approximately 5–15 ms) which is much longer, but can easily be explained since (i) firing occurs, at least in the low-noise limit, during the *rise* time of the EPSP which is typically much shorter (1–5 ms) than the duration of the EPSP and (ii) after firing a neuron becomes refractory so that it cannot emit further spikes which would reduce the temporal precision; cf. Section 9.4.

Secondly, we see from Fig. 12.9 that several patterns can be stored in the same network. These patterns are defined by their spatio-temporal correlations and cannot be distinguished by mean firing rates or ensemble activity. To illustrate this point, let us count the number of spikes along a horizontal line and divide by the total recording time ($T = 200$ ms). This procedure allows us to determine the *mean firing rate* of the neuron plotted in subgraphs (iii) to the right of the spike pattern. We see that all neurons have approximately the same firing rate, 25 Hz. Thus, if we consider the mean firing rate only, we cannot detect any significant structure in the firing behavior of the neurons. Instead of averaging over time we could also average over space. If we count the number of spikes in every millisecond (along a vertical line in the spike raster) and divide by the total number of neurons, we find the *ensemble activity* plotted in (i). We see that immediately after the stimulus the ensemble activity is high ($\approx 5\%$), but then settles rapidly to an average of 2.5% and no significant structure is left. Nevertheless, if we look at the spike raster (ii), we see that the network remains in a regular firing state. The specific spike pattern has been induced by the stimulus and is different for Figs. 12.9A, B, and C. Data analysis methods that are based on mean firing rates or ensemble activities would

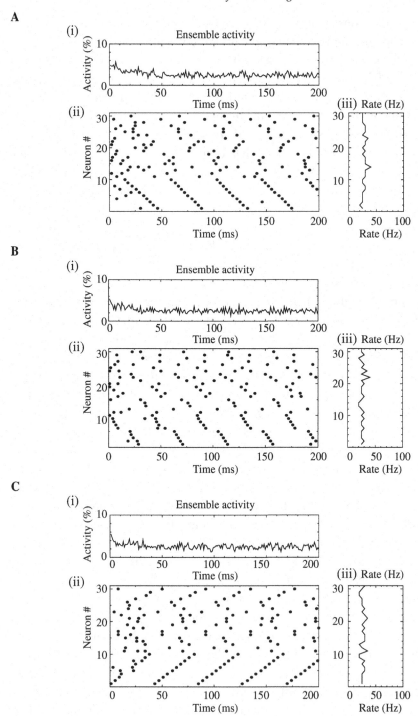

Fig. 12.9. Retrieval of spatio-temporal spike patterns. See text for details; taken from Gerstner et al. (1993b).

miss the information contained in the time-resolved spike raster. Indeed, the above examples clearly show that single spikes can carry important information.

Does this imply that the cortical spike activity is actually a huge spatio-temporal pattern that is stored in the synaptic connectivity? Do neurons use a temporal code at a millisecond time scale? Do different brain states correspond to different spatio-temporal patterns that are recalled from the storage? The answer is most likely negative – for a number of reasons. Simulations, for example, show that the spatio-temporal patterns that are presented during learning become stable attractors of the network dynamics. However, if we try to store in a network of 1000 neurons more than, say, 20 patterns the dynamics breaks down rapidly. Since a single spatio-temporal pattern of 40 ms duration contains 40 different spatial patterns that are retrieved one after another, a lot of information needs to be stored in the synaptic connections to cover a short interval of time.

On the other hand, specialized structures such as delayed reverberating loops in the olivo-cerebellar system that operate intrinsically at a time scale of 100 ms instead of 1 ms may actually rely on spatio-temporal spike patterns as a neuronal code; cf. Section 8.3.3. Furthermore, transient spatio-temporal spike activity *without* stable attractors could play a role in dynamic short-term memory and information processing (Kistler and De Zeeuw, 2002; Maass et al., 2002).

The final decision about whether the brain uses spatio-temporal spike patterns as a code has to come from experiments. The simulations shown in Fig. 12.9 suggest that during retrieval of a spatio-temporal spike pattern neuronal firing times are strongly correlated, a result which should clearly be visible in experimental data. However, recent analysis of experimental spike trains shows that correlations between the firing times of different neurons are rather weak and can be explained by stochastic models (Oram et al., 1999). Thus, spatio-temporal spike patterns with millisecond resolution are probably not a widely spread coding scheme in the brain.

12.4 Subtraction of expectations

In this and the following section we discuss temporal coding in specialized neuronal systems. We start in this section with the problem of electro-sensory signal processing in Mormoryd electric fish.

12.4.1 Electro-sensory system of Mormoryd electric fish

Mormoryd electric fish probe their environment with electric pulses. The electric organ of the fish emits a short electric discharge. The spatio-temporal electric field that is generated around the fish by the discharge depends on the location of objects in the surroundings. In order to reliably detect the location, size, or movement of

A

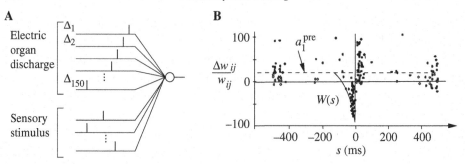

B

Fig. 12.10. **A**. Schematic view of ganglion cell input. Information about the timing of electric organ discharge is transmitted by a set of delayed spikes (top) while the sensory image is encoded in a second set of spikes (bottom). **B**. Synaptic plasticity as a function of the time difference $s = t_j^{(f)} - t_i^{(f)}$ between postsynaptic broad spikes and presynaptic spikes. The synapse is depressed if the presynaptic spike arrives slightly before the backpropagating action potential (-100 ms $< s < 0$) while it is strongly increased if the presynaptic spike arrives slightly after the postsynaptic one. This dependence is modeled by a learning window $W(s)$. The presynaptic term a_1^{pre} (horizontal dashed line) takes care of the fact that, for very large time differences, there is always a positive synaptic change. Experimental data points redrawn after Bell et al. (1997b).

objects the electro-sensory system must compare the momentary spatio-temporal electric field with the one that would occur in the absence of external objects. In other words, it must subtract the expected spatio-temporal image from the actual sensory input.

Experiments have shown that so-called medium ganglion cells in the electro-sensory lateral lobe (ELL) of electric fish can solve the task of subtracting expectations (Bell et al., 1997a). These cells receive two sets of input; cf. Fig. 12.10A. Information on the timing of a discharge pulse emitted by the electric organ is conveyed via a set of delay lines to the ganglion cells. The signal transmission delay Δ_j between the electric organ discharge and spike arrival at the ganglion cell changes from one connection to the next and varies between zero and 100 ms. A second set of input conveys the characteristics of the spatio-temporal electric field sensed by the fish's electro-receptors.

In experiments, electric organ discharges are triggered repetitively at intervals of $T = 150$ ms. If the sensory input has, after each discharge, the same spatio-temporal characteristics, the ganglion cell responds with stochastic activity at a constant rate. If the sensory input suddenly changes, the ganglion cell reacts strongly; cf. Fig. 12.11A. Thus the ganglion cell can be seen as a novelty detector. The predictable contribution of the sensory image is subtracted, and only unpredictable aspects of a sensory image evoke a response. In the following paragraph we will show that a spike-time-dependent learning rule with anti-Hebbian characteristics can solve the task of subtracting expectations (Bell et al., 1997b; Roberts and Bell, 2000).

12.4.2 Sensory image cancellation

In this section we review the model of Roberts and Bell (2000). We start with the model of the ganglion cell, turn then to the model of synaptic plasticity, and compare finally the model results with experimental results of ganglion cell activity.

Neuron model

We consider a single ganglion cell that receives two sets of inputs as indicated schematically in Fig. 12.10A. After each electric organ discharge, a volley of 150 input spikes arrives at different delays $\Delta_1, \Delta_2 \ldots \Delta_{150}$. Each spike evokes upon arrival an excitatory postsynaptic potential with time course $\epsilon(s)$. A second set of input carries the sensory stimulus. Instead of modeling the sequence of spike arrival times, the time course of the stimulus is summarized by a function $h^{\text{stim}}(s)$ where $s = 0$ is the moment of the electric organ discharge. The total membrane potential of the ganglion cell i is

$$u_i(t) = \sum_{n=1}^{n_{\max}} \left[\sum_j w_{ij}\, \epsilon(t - nT - \Delta_j) + h^{\text{stim}}(t - nT) \right] \qquad (12.10)$$

where w_{ij} is the synaptic efficacy, $T = 150$ ms the interval between electric organ discharges, and $n_{\max}$ the total number of repetitions of the stimulus h^{stim} up to time t.

A ganglion cell is described as a (semi-)linear Poisson model that emits spikes at a rate

$$\nu_i(t) = [u_i(t) - \vartheta]_+. \qquad (12.11)$$

There are two types of action potential, i.e., a narrow spike that travels along the axon and transmits information to other neurons; and a broad spike that back-propagates into the apical dendrite. It is therefore the broad spike that conveys information on postsynaptic spike firing to the site of the synapse. Both types of spike are generated by an inhomogeneous Poisson process with a rate given by Eq. (12.11) but the threshold ϑ of the broad spike is higher than that of the narrow spike.

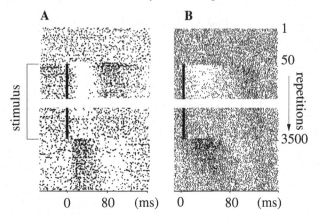

Fig. 12.11. Sensory image cancellation and negative after-image in experiments (**A**) and simulation (**B**). Each trial corresponds to one horizontal line. The electric organ discharge is elicited at time $t = 0$; spikes are denoted by black dots. For the first 50 trials no sensory input is given. After trial 50 a time-dependent stimulus is applied which is repeated in the following trials. The neuron adapts. After the stimulus is removed (trial 3500), the time course of the neuronal activity exhibits a negative after-image of the stimulus. The stimulus onset is denoted by a vertical bar; taken with slight adaptations from Roberts and Bell (2000), experiments of Bell et al. (1997a).

Synaptic plasticity

The synaptic efficacy w_{ij} changes according to a spike-time-dependent plasticity rule

$$\frac{\mathrm{d}}{\mathrm{d}t} w_{ij}(t) = S_j(t) \left[a_1^{\mathrm{pre}} + \int_0^\infty W(s)\, S_i(t - s)\, \mathrm{d}s \right]$$
$$+ S_i(t) \left[\int_0^\infty W(-s)\, S_j(t - s)\, \mathrm{d}s \right]; \qquad (12.12)$$

cf. Eq. (10.14). Here $a_1^{\mathrm{pre}} > 0$ is a non-Hebbian presynaptic term, $W(s)$ with $\bar{W} = \int_{-\infty}^\infty W(s)\, \mathrm{d}s < 0$ is the learning window, $S_j(t) = \sum_f \delta(t - t_j^{(f)})$ is the train of presynaptic spike arrivals, and $S_i(t) = \sum_f \delta(t - t_i^{(f)})$ is the train of postsynaptic broad spikes. The learning window $W(t_i^{(f)} - t_j^{(f)})$ as a function of the time difference between a back-propagating broad spike and a presynaptic spike has been measured experimentally (Bell et al., 1997b). It has two phases, one for long-term potentiation (LTP) and one for long-term depression (LTD), but the timing is reversed as compared to other spike-time-dependent plasticity rules (Markram et al., 1997; Bi and Poo, 1998; Debanne et al., 1998; Zhang et al., 1998). In particular, a presynaptic spike that arrives slightly *before* a postsynaptic broad spike leads to depression of the synapse; cf. Fig. 12.10B. It can thus be called anti-Hebbian. While Hebbian learning windows are apt to detect and reinforce temporal structure in the input, anti-Hebbian rules suppress any temporal structure, as we will see in the following paragraph.

Results

A simulation of the model introduced above is shown in Fig. 12.11B. During the first 50 trials, no stimulus was applied ($h^{\text{stim}} \equiv 0$). In all subsequent trials up to trial 3500, an inhibitory stimulus $h^{\text{stim}}(s)$ with triangular time course has been applied. While the activity is clearly suppressed in trial 51, it recovers after several hundred repetitions of the experiment. If the stimulus is removed thereafter, the neuronal activity exhibits a negative after-image of the stimulus, just as in the experiments shown in Fig. 12.11A.

Using the methods developed in Chapter 11, it is possible to show that, for $a_1^{\text{pre}} > 0$ and $\bar{W} < 0$, the learning rule stabilizes the mean output rate (of broad spikes) at a fixed point $\nu_{\text{FP}} = -a_1^{\text{pre}}/\bar{W}$. Moreover, weights w_{ij} are adjusted so that the membrane potential has minimal fluctuations about $u_{\text{FP}} = \nu_{\text{FP}} + \vartheta$. To achieve this, the weights must be tuned so that the term $\sum_j w_{ij} \epsilon(t - \Delta_j)$ cancels the sensory input $h^{\text{stim}}(t)$ – which is the essence of sensory image cancellation (Roberts and Bell, 2000).

12.5 Transmission of temporal codes

While the relevance of spike timing in the millisecond range in cortical areas is a topic of intense debate, there are a few specific systems where temporal coding is generally accepted. One of the most prominent examples is the auditory system of the barn owl (Konishi, 1986; Carr and Konishi, 1988, 1990; Carr, 1993, 1995), and this is the system we will focus on in this section. Owls hunt at night. From behavioral experiments it is known that owls can locate sound sources even in complete darkness with a remarkable precision. To do so, the signal processing in the auditory pathway must achieve a temporal precision in the microsecond range with elements that are noisy, unreliable and rather slow. In this section, we use the results of previous chapters and show that spiking neurons that are driven in the subthreshold regime are sensitive to temporal structure in the presynaptic input, in particular to synchronous spike arrival; cf. Sections 5.8 and 7.3. On the other hand, synchronous spike arrival is only possible if presynaptic transmission delays are appropriately tuned. A spike-time-dependent Hebbian learning rule can play the role of delay tuning or delay selection (Gerstner et al., 1996a, 1997; Hüning et al., 1998; Eurich et al., 1999; Kempter et al., 1999; Senn et al., 2002).

We start this section with an outline of the problem of sound source localization and a rough sketch of the barn owl auditory pathway. We turn then to the problem

Plasticity and coding

A   **B**

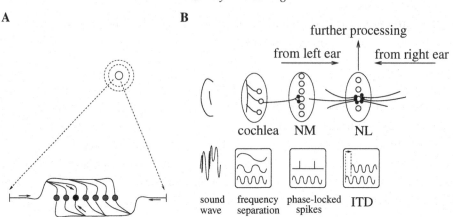

Fig. 12.12. **A**. Jeffress model. Sound waves (dashed circles) from a source located to the right of the owl's head arrive at the two ears where they excite neuronal activity. Neuronal signals travel along transmission lines to an array of coincidence detectors (gray filled circles). The coincidence-detecting neurons respond if signals from both sides arrive simultaneously. Due to transmission delays, the position of the coincidence detector activated by the signals (black filled circle) depends on the location of the external sound source. **B**. Auditory pathway (schematic). At the cochlea a sound wave is separated into its frequency components. Phase-locked spikes are transmitted along the auditory nerve to the nucleus magnocellularis (NM), an intermediate processing step. Action potentials at the output of the NM are phase locked as well. The signals from both ears meet in the nucleus laminaris (NL). Neurons in the NL are sensitive to the interaural time difference (ITD) and can be considered as the coincidence detectors of the Jeffress model. In further processing steps, the output of neurons with different frequencies is combined to resolve remaining ambiguities; taken from Gerstner et al. (1998).

of coincidence detection and the idea of delay selection by a spike-time-dependent learning rule.

12.5.1 Auditory pathway and sound source localization

Barn owls use interaural time differences (ITD) for sound source localization (Jeffress, 1948; Moiseff and Konishi, 1981; Carr and Konishi, 1990). Behavioral experiments show that barn owls can locate a sound source in the horizontal plane with a precision of about 1–2 degrees of angle (Knudsen et al., 1979). A simple calculation shows that this corresponds to a temporal difference of a few microseconds (< 5 μs) between the sound waves at the left and right ear. These small temporal differences must be detected and evaluated by the owl's auditory system; see Fig. 12.12.

The basic principle of how such a time-difference detector could be set up was discussed by Jeffress (1948) more than 50 years ago. It consists of delay lines and an array of coincidence detectors. If the sound source is on the right-hand side of the auditory space, the sound wave arrives first at the right ear and then at the left ear. The signals propagate from both ears along transmission lines towards the set of coincidence detectors. A signal originating from a source located to the right of the owl's head stimulates a coincidence detector on the left-hand side of the array. If the location of the signal source is shifted, a different coincidence detector responds. The "place" of a coincidence detector is therefore a signature for the location of the external sound source; cf. Fig. 12.12). Such a representation has been called "place" coding (Konishi, 1986; Carr and Konishi, 1990).

Remarkably enough, such a coincidence detector circuit was found four decades later by Carr and Konishi (1990) in the nucleus laminaris of the barn owl. The existence of the circuit confirms the general idea of temporal difference detection by delayed coincidence measurement. It gives, however, no indication of how the precision of a few microseconds is finally achieved.

In order to better understand how precise spike timing arises, we have to study signal processing in the auditory pathway. Three aspects are important: frequency separation, phase locking, and phase-correct averaging.

The first few processing steps along the auditory localization pathway are sketched in Fig. 12.12B. The figure represents, of course, a simplified picture of auditory information processing, but it captures some essential ingredients. At both ears the sound wave is separated into its frequency components. Signals then pass an intermediate processing area called nucleus magnocellularis (NM) and meet at the nucleus laminaris (NL). Neurons there are found to be sensitive to the interaural time difference (ITD). Due to the periodicity of a sinusoidal wave, the ITD of a single frequency channel is really a *phase* difference and leaves some ambiguities. In the next processing step further up in the auditory pathway, information on phase differences from different frequency channels is combined to retrieve the temporal difference and hence the location of the sound source in the horizontal plane. Reviews of the basic principles of auditory processing in the owl can be found in Konishi (1986, 1993).

Let us now discuss the first few processing steps in more detail. After cochlear filtering, different frequencies are processed by different neurons and stay separated up to the nucleus laminaris. In the following we may therefore focus on a single-frequency channel and consider a neuron which responds best to a frequency of, say, 5 kHz.

If the ear is stimulated with a 5-kHz tone, neurons in the 5-kHz channel are activated and fire action potentials. At first sight, the spike train looks noisy. A closer look, however, reveals that the pulses are phase locked to the stimulating tone: spikes occur preferentially around some phase φ_0 with respect to the periodic stimulus. Phase locking is, of course, not perfect, but subject to two types of noise;

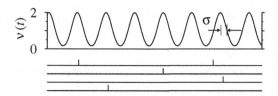

Fig. 12.13. Spike trains in the auditory pathway show phase locking and can be described by a time-dependent firing rate $v(t)$ (in kHz) which is modulated by the signal. Four samples of spike trains are shown at the bottom of the figure.

cf. Fig. 12.13. Firstly, spikes do not occur at every cycle of the 5-kHz tone. Often the neuron misses several cycles before it fires again. Secondly, spikes occur with a temporal jitter of about $\sigma = 40$ µs around the preferred phase (Sullivan and Konishi, 1984).

For the sake of simplicity we describe the spike train by a Poisson process with a periodically modulated rate

$$v_j(t) = p \sum_{m=-\infty}^{\infty} \mathcal{G}_\sigma(t - m T - \Delta_j) \tag{12.13}$$

where T is the period of the tone (e.g., $T = 0.2$ ms for our 5-kHz signal), $\mathcal{G}_\sigma$ is a Gaussian with variance σ, and $\Delta_j = \varphi_0 T / 2\pi$ is a delay associated with the preferred phase φ_0 of spikes of a given presynaptic neuron j. The amplitude p with $0 < p < 1$ is the probability of firing in one period. The temporally averaged mean firing rate is $\langle v_j \rangle = p/T$. Examples of spike trains generated from Eq. (12.13) are shown in Fig. 12.13.

Phase locking can be observed in the auditory nerve connecting the cochlea and the nucleus magnocellularis, in the nucleus magnocellularis, and also in the nucleus laminaris. The phase jitter σ even decreases from one processing step to the next so that the temporal precision of phase locking increases from around 40 µs in the nucleus magnocellularis to about 25 µs in the nucleus laminaris. The precision of phase locking is the topic of the following subsection.

12.5.2 *Phase locking and coincidence detection*

We focus on a single neuron i in the nucleus laminaris (NL). The neuron receives input from neurons in the nucleus magnocellularis through about 150 synapses. All input lines belong to the same frequency channel. The probability of spike arrival at one of the synapses is given by Eq. (12.13) where j labels the synapses and $T = 0.2$ ms is the period of the signal.

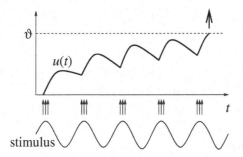

Fig. 12.14. Phase locking (schematic). Action potentials arrive periodically and are phase locked to the stimulus in bundles of spikes (bottom). The postsynaptic potentials evoked by presynaptic spike arrival are summed and yield the total postsynaptic potential $u(t)$ which shows a pronounced oscillatory structure. Firing occurs when $u(t)$ crosses the threshold. The output spike is phase locked to the external signal, since the threshold crossing is bound to occur during a *rising* phase of u; adapted from Gerstner et al. (1998).

As a neuron model for i we take an integrate-and-fire unit with membrane time constant τ_m and synaptic time constant τ_s. From experiments on chickens it is known that the duration of an excitatory postsynaptic potential (EPSP) in the NL is remarkably short (< 1 ms) (Reyes et al., 1994, 1996). Neurons of an auditory specialist like the barn owl may be even faster. In our model equations, we have set $\tau_m = \tau_s = 0.1$ ms. These values correspond to an EPSP with a duration of about 0.25 ms.

The short duration of EPSPs in neurons in the NL and NM is due to an outward rectifying current which sets in when the membrane potential exceeds the resting potential (Oertel, 1983; Manis and Marx, 1991). The purely *passive* membrane time constant is in the range of 2 ms (Reyes et al., 1994), but the outward rectifying current reduces the effective membrane resistance whenever the voltage is above the resting potential. In a conductance-based neuron model (cf. Chapter 2), all membrane currents would be described explicitly. In our integrate-and-fire model, the main effect of the outward rectifying current is taken into account by working with a short *effective* membrane time constant $\tau_m = 0.1$ ms. A membrane constant of 0.1 ms is much shorter than that found in cortical neurons where $\tau_m \approx 10$–50 ms seem to be typical values; see, e.g., Bernander et al. (1991). Note, however, that for temporal coding in the barn owl auditory system, $\tau_m = 0.1$ ms is quite long as compared to the precision of phase locking of 25 µs found in auditory neurons and necessary for successful sound source localization.

To get an intuitive understanding of how phase locking arises, let us study an idealized situation and take perfectly coherent spikes as input to our model neuron; cf. Fig. 12.14. Specifically, let us consider a situation where 100 input lines converge on the model neuron. On each line, spike arrival is given by Eq. (12.13) with $\sigma \to 0$ and $p = 0.2$. If the delays Δ_j are the same for all transmission lines ($\Delta_j = \Delta_0$), then in each cycle a volley of 20 ± 5 synchronized spikes arrive. The EPSPs evoked by those spikes are added as shown schematically in Fig. 12.14. The output spike occurs when the membrane potential crosses the threshold ϑ. Note that the threshold must be reached from below. It follows that the output spike must always occur during the *rise* time of the EPSPs generated by the last volley of spikes before firing.

Since the input spikes are phase locked to the stimulus, the output spike will also be phase locked to the acoustic waveform. The preferred phase of the output spike φ_i will, of course be slightly delayed with respect to the input phase $\varphi_0 = \Delta_0(2\pi/T)$. The typical delay will be less than the rise time τ_{rise} of an EPSP. Thus, $\varphi_i = (\Delta_0 + 0.5\,\tau_{\text{rise}})\,(2\pi/T)$ will be a reasonable estimate of the preferred output phase.

Can we transfer the above qualitative arguments to a more realistic scenario? We have simulated a neuron with 154 input lines. At each synapse spikes arrive at a time-dependent rate as in Eq. (12.13). The temporal jitter has been set to $\sigma = 40\,\mu$s. The delays Δ_j (and hence the preferred phases) have a jitter of 35 μs around some mean value Δ_0. As before, $p = 0.2$ for all inputs.

A short interval taken from a longer simulation run with these input parameters is shown in Fig. 12.15. Part A shows the membrane potential $u(t)$ as a function of time; Fig. 12.15B and C show the distribution of spike arrival times. Even though spike arrival is rather noisy, the trajectory of the membrane potential exhibits characteristic periodic modulations. Hence, following the same arguments as in Fig. 12.14, we expect the output spike to be phase locked. Figure 12.16A confirms our expectations: the distribution of output phases exhibits a pronounced peak. The width of the distribution corresponds to a temporal precision of $\sigma_{\text{out}} = 25\,\mu$s, a significant increase in precision compared to the input jitter $\sigma = 40\,\mu$s.

So far we have assumed that the delays Δ_j have a small variation of 35 μs only. Hence the preferred phases $\varphi_j = \Delta_j\,(2\pi/T)$ are nearly identical for all input lines. If the preferred phases are drawn stochastically from a uniform distribution over $[0, 2\pi]$, then spike arrival at the neuron is effectively *incoherent*, even though the spikes on each input line exhibit phase locking. If input spikes arrive incoherently, the temporal precision is lost and the output spikes have a flat phase distribution; see Fig. 12.16B.

We conclude that spiking neurons are capable of transmitting phase information if input spikes arrive with a high degree of coherence. If input spikes arrive incoherently, the temporal information is lost. As we will see in the following subsection, this observation implies that the reliable transmission of temporal codes requires a mechanism for delay-line tuning.

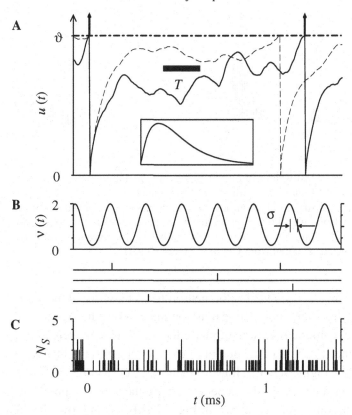

Fig. 12.15. **A.** Membrane potential $u(t)$ of an integrate-and-fire neuron as a function of time. **B.** Rate $v_j(t)$ of presynaptic firing during 5 kHz stimulation and four samples of input spike trains (vertical bars). The model neuron receives input from 154 presynaptic neurons (Carr, 1993; Carr and Konishi, 1990) in volleys of phase locked spikes with a jitter of $\sigma = 40$ μs driven by a 5-kHz tone. Spikes are generated by a stochastic process with periodically modulated rate (solid line in B). **C.** Histogram of spike arrival times (number of spikes N_s in bins of 5 μs) summed over all 154 synapses. Each input spike evokes an excitatory postsynaptic potential (EPSP) shown on an enlarged voltage scale (same time scale) in the inset of A. The EPSPs from all neurons are added linearly and yield the membrane voltage u (A, main figure). With the spike input shown in C the membrane voltage exhibits oscillations (solid line). The model neuron fires (arrow) if u reaches a threshold ϑ. Firing must always occur during the time when u increases so that, in the case of coherent input, output spikes are phase locked as well (see also Fig. 12.16A). If input spikes arrive incoherently, $u(t)$ follows a trajectory with stochastic fluctuations but no systematic oscillations (dashed line in A); see Fig. 12.16B. Voltage in A: arbitrary units; the threshold ϑ is 36 times the amplitude of a single EPSP. Rate in B in kHz. Adapted from Gerstner et al. (1996a).

12.5.3 Tuning of delay lines

Each neuron in the nucleus laminaris (NL) of the barn owl receives input from about 150 presynaptic neurons (Carr and Konishi, 1990; Carr, 1993). The high

A   **B**

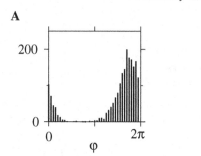
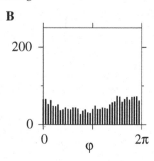

Fig. 12.16. Phase histograms of output spikes. **A.** The input spikes from the 154 presynaptic neurons arrive *coherently* with the spiking statistics as shown in Figs. 12.15B and C. In this case, the distribution of output spikes exhibits a pronounced maximum indicating a high degree of phase locking. The width of the peak corresponds to a temporal precision of 25 µs. **B.** If input spikes arrive incoherently, the histogram of output phases has no significant structure; taken from Gerstner et al. (1996a).

degree of convergence enables the neuron to increase the signal-to-noise ratio by averaging over many (noisy) transmission lines. As we have seen in the preceding section, the temporal precision of phase locking is indeed increased from 40 µs in the input lines to 25 µs in the output of our model neuron in the NL.

Such an averaging scheme, however, can work only if the preferred phases φ_j of all input lines are (nearly) the same. Otherwise the temporal precision is decreased or even lost completely as shown in Fig. 12.16B. To improve the signal-to-noise ratio, "phase-correct" averaging is needed. The question arises of how a neuron in the NL can perform correct averaging.

The total delay from the ear to the NL has been estimated to be in the range of 2–3 ms (Carr and Konishi, 1990). Even if the transmission delays vary by only 0.1–0.2 ms between one transmission line and the next, the phase information of a 5-kHz signal is completely lost when the signals arrive at the NL. Therefore, the delays must be precisely tuned so as to allow the neurons to perform phase-correct averaging.

Precise wiring of the auditory connections could be set up genetically. This is, however, rather unlikely since the owl's head grows considerably during development. Moreover, while neurons in the nucleus laminaris of the adult owl are sensitive to the interaural phase difference, no such sensitivity was found for young owls (Carr, 1995). This indicates that delay tuning arises only later during development. It is clear that there can be no external supervisor or controller that selects the appropriate delays. What the owl needs is an adaptive mechanism which can be implemented locally and which achieves a tuning of appropriate delays.

Tuning can be achieved either by selection of appropriate delay lines (Gerstner et al., 1996a) or by changes in axonal parameters that influence the transmission

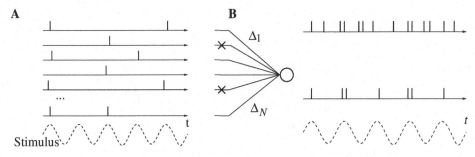

Fig. 12.17. Delay selection (schematic). **A**. When pulses are generated at the ear, they are phase locked to the periodic stimulus (dashed). **B**. Several transmission lines converge on a single coincidence detector neuron in the nucleus laminaris. In order to achieve a high temporal resolution, pulses should *arrive* synchronously at the coincidence detector neuron. With a broad distribution of delays, spike arrival is effectively asynchronous (spike train at top). Spike-timing-dependent Hebbian learning selects and reinforces some of the transmission lines and suppresses others (black crosses). After learning, pulses arrive with a high degree of coherence (spike train, middle). The periodic stimulus is represented for comparison (dashed line, bottom).

delay along the axon (Hüning et al., 1998; Eurich et al., 1999; Senn et al., 2002). We focus on learning by delay selection; cf. Fig. 12.17. Immediately after birth a large number of connections are formed. We suppose that during an early period of postnatal development a tuning process takes place which selectively reinforces transmission lines with similar preferred phase and eliminates others (Gerstner et al., 1996a). The selection process can be implemented by a spike-time-dependent Hebbian learning rule as introduced in Chapter 10.

In order to illustrate delay selection in a model study, we assume that both ears are stimulated by a pure 5-kHz tone with interaural time difference ITD = 0. The effect of stimulation is that spikes arrive at the synapses with a periodically modulated rate $\nu_j(t)$ as given by Eq. (12.13). During learning, synaptic weights are modified according to a spike-time-dependent Hebbian learning rule

$$\frac{\mathrm{d}}{\mathrm{d}t} w_{ij}(t) = S_j(t) \left[a_1^{\mathrm{pre}} + \int_0^\infty W(s)\, S_i(t-s)\, \mathrm{d}s \right] + S_i(t) \int_0^\infty W(-s)\, S_j(t-s)\, \mathrm{d}s\,,$$

(12.14)

cf. Eq. (10.14). Here $S_j(t) = \sum_f \delta(t - t_j^{(f)})$ is the presynaptic, and $S_i(t) = \sum_f \delta(t - t_i^{(f)})$ the postsynaptic spike train. The learning rule is not applied if the weights w_{ij} would become larger than an upper bound w_{max} or smaller than a lower bound $w = 0$.

The non-Hebbian term a_1^{pre} in Eq. (12.14) is taken as small but positive. The learning window $W(s)$ is the one shown in Fig. 12.18. It has a negative integral $\overline{W} = \int W(s)\, \mathrm{d}s < 0$ and a maximum at $s^* = -0.05$ ms. The choice $s^* =$

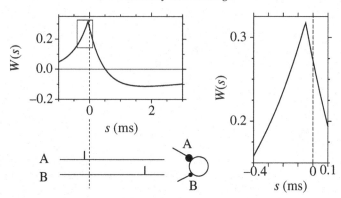

Fig. 12.18. Learning window W as a function of the delay s between postsynaptic firing and presynaptic spike arrival. The graph on the right-hand side shows the boxed region around the maximum on an expanded scale. If $W(s)$ is positive (negative) for some s, the synaptic efficacy is increased (decreased). The postsynaptic firing occurs at $s = 0$ (vertical dashed line). Learning is most efficient if presynaptic spikes arrive shortly before the postsynaptic neuron starts firing, as in synapse A. Another synapse B, which fires *after* the postsynaptic spike, is decreased. Taken from Gerstner et al. (1996a).

$-\tau_{\text{rise}}/2$ guarantees stable learning (Gerstner et al., 1996a). As we have seen in Section 11.2.3, the combination of a learning window with negative integral and a positive non-Hebbian term a_1^{pre} leads to a stabilization of the postsynaptic firing rate. Thus the postsynpatic neuron remains during learning in the subthreshold regime, where it is most sensitive to temporal coding; cf. Section 5.8. The rate stabilization induces in turn an effective competition between different synapses. Thus, we expect that some synapses grow at the expense of others that must decay.

The results of a simulation run are shown in Fig. 12.19. Before learning the neurons receive input over about 600 synapses from presynaptic neurons. Half of the input lines originate from the left, the other half from the right ear. The total transmission delays Δ_j are different between one line and the next and vary between 2 and 3 ms. At the beginning of learning all synaptic efficacies have the same strength $w_{ij} = 1$ for all j. The homogeneous weight distribution becomes unstable during learning (Fig. 12.19, middle). The instability can been confirmed analytically using the methods developed in Chapter 11 (Kempter, 1997). After learning the synaptic efficacies have approached either the upper bound $w_{\text{max}} = 3$ or they have decayed to zero. The transmission lines which remain after learning have either very similar delays, or delays differing by a full period (Fig. 12.19, bottom). Thus, the remaining delays form a consistent pattern that guarantees that spikes arrive with a high degree of coherence.

The sensitivity of the output firing rate to the interaural time difference (ITD) and the degree of phase locking were tested before, during, and after learning

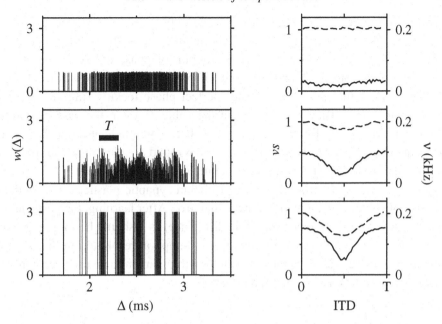

Fig. 12.19. Development of tuning to a 5-kHz tone. The left column shows the strength of synaptic efficacies w_{ij} of all synapses. Synapses are indexed according to the delay Δ_j of the corresponding transmission line and are plotted as $w_{ij} = w(\Delta)$. On the right, we show the vector strength (*vs*, solid line) and the output firing rate (ν, dashed) as a function of the interaural time delay (ITD). Top: before learning, there are 600 synapses (300 from each ear) with different delays, chosen randomly from a Gaussian distribution with mean 2.5 ms and variance 0.3 ms. All weights have unit value. The output is not phase locked ($vs \approx 0.1$) and shows no dependence upon the ITD. Middle: during learning, some synapses are strengthened, others decreased. Those synapses which increase have delays that are similar or that differ by multiples of the period $T = 0.2$ ms of the stimulating tone. The vector strength of the output increases and starts to depend on the ITD. Bottom: after learning, only about 150 synapses (≈ 75 from each ear) survive. Both the output firing rate ν and the vector strength vs show the characteristic dependence upon the ITD as seen in experiments with adult owls (Carr and Konishi, 1990). The neuron has the maximal response ($\nu = 200$ Hz) for ITD $= 0$, the stimulus used during the learning session of the model neuron. The vector strength at ITD $= 0$ is $vs \approx 0.8$ which corresponds to a temporal precision of 25 μs. Taken from Gerstner et al. (1997).

(right column in Fig. 12.19). Before learning, the neuron shows no sensitivity to the ITD. This means that the neuron is not a useful coincidence detector for the sound source localization task. During learning ITD sensitivity develops similar to that found in experiments (Carr, 1995). After learning the output rate is significantly modulated as a function of ITD. The response is maximal for ITD $= 0$, the ITD used during learning. The form of the ITD tuning curves corresponds to experimental measurements.

To test the degree of phase locking in the output we have plotted the vector strength, vs, as a function of ITD. By definition the vector strength is proportional to the first Fourier component of the histogram of phase distributions; cf. Fig. 12.16. It is therefore a suitable measure of phase locking. The vector strength is normalized so that $vs = 1$ indicates perfect phase locking (infinite temporal precision or $\sigma_{out} = 0$). Let us focus on the value of vs in the case of optimal stimulation (ITD $= 0$). Before learning $vs \approx 0.1$, which indicates that there is no significant phase locking. The value of $vs \approx 0.8$ found after learning confirms that, after the tuning of the synapses, phase locking is very pronounced.

To summarize, spike-time-dependent Hebbian synaptic plasticity selects delay lines so that spikes arrive with maximal coherence. After learning, the postsynaptic neuron is sensitive to the interaural time difference, as it should be for the neurons that are used for sound source localization. A temporal resolution in the range of a few microseconds can be achieved even though the membrane time constant and synaptic time constant are in the range of 100 ms.

12.6 Summary

Spike timing influences synaptic plasticity, and changes of synaptic efficacies induce variations in spike timing. In this chapter we have seen several examples of an interaction between plasticity and neuronal coding. Apart from some generic considerations regarding rapid and reliable signal transmission or sequence learning, we have also considered two specialized neuronal systems where the relevance of spike timing has clearly been shown. The example of subtraction of expectations in Mormoryd electric fish is noteworthy because it is one of the few cases where a direct link between measured synaptic properties and a clear computational paradigm has been established. The barn owl auditory system is remarkable because of the high temporal precision that the barn owl exhibits in in behavioral experiments of sound source localization. To achieve this precision a tuning mechanism such as a spike-time-dependent learning rule is necessary. It is tempting to speculate that future experiments will establish similar links between spike timing and synaptic plasticity in other neuronal systems.

Literature

For reviews of the coding principles and neural processing architecture in electric fish, see Heiligenberg (1991). The essential steps of sound source localization in the auditory system of the barn owl are reviewed in Konishi (1986, 1993). The paper of Carr (1993) provides a highly recommendable review of temporal processing in the brain with a special emphasis on the sensory systems of electric fish, bats, and owls.

References

Abbott, L. F. (1991). Realistic synaptic inputs for model neural networks. *Network*, **2**:245–258.

Abbott, L. F. (1994). Decoding neuronal firing and modeling neural networks. *Quart. Rev. Biophys.*, **27**:291–331.

Abbott, L. F. (2000). Synaptic plasticity – taming the beast. *Nature Neurosci.*, **3**:1178–1183.

Abbott, L. F. and Blum, K. I. (1996). Functional significance of long-term potentiation for sequence learning and prediction. *Cereb. Cortex*, **6**:406–416.

Abbott, L. F., Fahri, E. and Gutmann, S. (1991). The path integral for dendritic trees. *Biol. Cybern.*, **66**:49–60.

Abbott, L. F. and Kepler, T. B. (1990). Model neurons: from Hodgkin-Huxley to Hopfield. In Garrido, L., editor, *Statistical Mechanics of Neural Networks*. Springer-Verlag, Berlin.

Abbott, L. F. and van Vreeswijk, C. (1993). Asynchronous states in a network of pulse-coupled oscillators. *Phys. Rev. E*, **48**:1483–1490.

Abeles, M. (1982). *Local Cortical Circuits*. Springer-Verlag, Berlin.

Abeles, M. (1991). *Corticonics*. Cambridge University Press, Cambridge.

Abeles, M. (1994). Firing rates and well-timed events. In Domany, E., Schulten, K. and van Hemmen, J. L., editors, *Models of Neural Networks II*, chapter 3. Springer-Verlag, New York.

Abeles, M., Bergman, H., Margalit, E. and Vaadia, E. (1993). Spatiotemporal firing patterns in the frontal cortex of behaving monkeys. *J. Neurophysiol.*, **70**:1629–1638.

Adrian, E. D. (1926). The impulses produced by sensory nerve endings. *J. Physiol. (Lond.)*, **61**:49–72.

Adrian, E. D. (1928). *The Basis of Sensation*. W. W. Norton, New York.

Aertsen, A. and Arndt, M. (1993). Response synchronization in the visual cortex. *Curr. Opin. Neurobiol.*, **3**:586–594.

Aizenman, C. D. and Linden, D. J. (1999). Regulation of the rebound depolarization and spontaneous firing patterns of deep nuclear neurons in slices of rat cerebellum. *J. Neurophysiol.*, **82**:1697–1709.

Amari, S. (1972). Characteristics of random nets of analog neuron-like elements. *IEEE Trans. Syst. Man Cybern.*, **2**:643–657.

Amari, S. (1974). A method of statistical neurodynamics. *Kybernetik*, **14**:201–215.

Amari, S. (1977a). Dynamics of pattern formation in lateral-inhibition type neural fields. *Biol. Cybern.*, **27**:77–87.

Amari, S. I. (1977b). A mathematical foundation of statistical neurodynamics. *SIAM J. Appl. Math.*, **33**:95–126.

Amit, D. J. and Brunel, N. (1997). Model of global spontaneous activity and local structured activity during delay periods in the cerebral cortex. *Cereb. Cortex*, **7**:237–252.

Anderson, J. A. and Rosenfeld, E., editors (1988). *Neurocomputing: Foundations of research*. MIT Press, Cambridge, MA.

Artola, A., Bröcher, S. and Singer, W. (1990). Different voltage dependent thresholds for inducing long-term depression and long-term potentiation in slices of rat visual cortex. *Nature*, **347**:69–72.

Artola, A. and Singer, W. (1993). Long-term depression of excitatory synaptic transmission and its relationship to long-term potentiation. *Trends Neurosci.*, **16**(11):480–487.

Ash, R. (1990). *Information Theory*. Dover, New York.

Bair, W. and Koch, C. (1996). Temporal precision of spike trains in extrastriate cortex of the behaving macaque monkey. *Neural Comput.*, **8**:1185–1202.

Bair, W., Koch, C., Newsome, W. and Britten, K. (1994). Power spectrum analysis of MT neurons in the behaving monkey. *J. Neurosci.*, **14**:2870–2892.

Bartlett, M. S. (1963). The spectral analysis of point processes. *J. R. Statist. Soc. B*, **25**:264–296.

Bauer, H. U. and Pawelzik, K. (1993). Alternating oscillatory and stochastic dynamics in a model for a neuronal assembly. *Physica D*, **69**:380–393.

Bell, C., Bodznick, D., Montgomery, J. and Bastian, J. (1997a). The generation and subtraction of sensory expectations within cerebellar-like structures. *Brain. Behav. Evol.*, **50** [Suppl. I]:17–31.

Bell, C. C., Han, V., Sugawara, Y. and Grant, K. (1997b). Synaptic plasticity in a cerebellum-like structure depends on temporal order. *Nature*, **387**:278–281.

Bell, C. C. and Kawasaki, T. (1972). Relations among climbing fiber responses of nearby Purkinje cells. *J. Neurophysiol.*, **35**:155–169.

Ben Arous, G. and Guionnet, A. (1995). Large deviations for Langevin spin glass dynamics. *Prob. Theory Related Fields*, **102**:455–509.

Ben-Yishai, R., Lev Bar-Or, R. and Sompolinsky, H. (1995). Theory of orientation tuning in visual cortex. *Proc. Natl. Acad. Sci. USA*, **92**:3844–3848.

Bernander, Ö, Douglas, R. J., Martin, K. A. C. and Koch, C. (1991). Synaptic background activity influences spatiotemporal integration in single pyradimal cells. *Proc. Natl. Acad. Sci. USA*, **88**:11 569–11 573.

Berry, M. J. and Meister, M. (1998). Refractoriness and neural precision. *J. Neurosci.*, **18**:2200–2211.

Berry, M. J., Warland, D. K. and Meister, M. (1997). The structure and precision of retinal spike trains. *Proc. Natl. Acad. Sci. USA*, **94**:5411–5416.

Bi, G. and Poo, M. (1998). Synaptic modifications in cultured hippocampal neurons: dependence on spike timing, synaptic strength, and postsynaptic cell type. *J. Neurosci.*, **18**:10 464–10 472.

Bi, G. and Poo, M. (2001). Synaptic modification of correlated activity: Hebb's postulate revisited. *Annu. Rev. Neurosci.*, **24**:139–166.

Bi, G. Q. and Poo, M. M. (1999). Distributed synaptic modification in neural networks induced by patterned stimulation. *Nature*, **401**:792–796.

Bialek, W. and Rieke, F. (1992). Reliability and information transmission in spiking neurons. *Trends Neurosci.*, **15**(11):428–433.

Bialek, W., Rieke, F., de Ruyter van Stevenick, R. R. and Warland, D. (1991). Reading a neural code. *Science*, **252**:1854–1857.

Bienenstock, E. L., Cooper, L. N. and Munroe, P. W. (1982). Theory of the development of neuron selectivity: orientation specificity and binocular interaction in visual cortex. *J. Neurosci.*, **2**:32–48.

Billock, V. A. (1997). Very short-term visual memory via reverberation: a role for the cortico-thalamic excitatory circuit in temporal filling-in during blinks and saccades? *Vision Res.*, **37**:949–953.

Bindman, L., Christofi, G., Murphy, K. and Nowicky, A. (1991). Long-term potentiation (LTP) and depression (LTD) in the neocortex and hippocampus: an overview. In Stone, T. W., editor, *Aspects of Synaptic Transmission*, volume 1, pages 3–25. Taylor & Francis, London.

Bliss, T. V. P. and Collingridge, G. L. (1993). A synaptic model of memory: long-term potentiation in the hippocampus. *Nature*, **361**:31–39.

Bliss, T. V. P. and Gardner-Medwin, A. R. (1973). Long-lasting potentiation of synaptic transmission in the dendate area of unanaesthetized rabbit following stimulation of the perforant path. *J. Physiol. (Lond.)*, **232**:357–374.

Bliss, T. V. P. and Lomo, T. (1973). Long-lasting potentation of synaptic transmission in the dendate area of the anaesthetized rabbit following stimulation of the perforant path. *J. Physiol. (Lond.)*, **232**:331–356.

Bose, A., Kopell, N. and Terman, D. (2000). Almost-synchronous solutions for mutually coupled excitatory neurons. *Physica D*, **140**:69–94.

Bower, J. M. and Beeman, D. (1995). *The Book of GENESIS: Exploring Realistic Neural Models with the GEneral NEural SImulation System*. Springer-Verlag, New York.

Bressloff, P. C. (1999). Synaptically generated wave propagation in excitable neural media. *Phys. Rev. Lett.*, **82**:2979–2982.

Bressloff, P. C. and Taylor, J. G. (1994). Dynamics of compartmental model neurons. *Neural Netw.*, **7**:1153–1165.

Brillinger, D. R. (1988). Maximum likelihood analysis of spike trains of interacting nerve cells. *Biol. Cybern.*, **59**:189–200.

Brillinger, D. R. (1992). Nerve cell spike train data analysis: a progression of techniques. *J. Am. Statist. Assoc.*, **87**:260–271.

Brillinger, D. R. and Segundo, J. P. (1979). Empirical examination of the threshold model of neuronal firing. *Biol. Cybern.*, **35**:213–220.

Brown, J., Bullock, D. and Grossberg, S. (1999). How the basal ganglia use parallel excitatory and inhibitory learning pathways to selectively respond to unexpected rewarding cues. *J. Neurosci.*, **19**:10502–10511.

Brown, T. H., Ganong, A. H., Kairiss, E. W., Keenan, C. L. and Kelso, S. R. (1989). Long-term potentiation in two synaptic systems of the hippocampal brain slice. In Byrne, J. H. and Berry, W. O., editors, *Neural Models of Plasticity*, pages 266–306. Academic Press, San Diego, CA.

Brown, T. H., Zador, A. M., Mainen, Z. F. and Claiborne, B. J. (1991). Hebbian modifications in hippocampal neurons. In Baudry, M. and Davis, J. L., editors, *Long-Term Potentiation*, pages 357–389. MIT Press, Cambridge.

Brunel, N. (2000). Dynamics of sparsely connected networks of excitatory and inhibitory spiking neurons. *J. Comput. Neurosci.*, **8**:183–208.

Brunel, N., Chance, F., Fourcaud, N. and Abbott, L. F. (2001). Effects of synaptic noise and filtering on the frequency response of spiking neurons. *Phys. Rev. Lett.*, **86**:2186–2189.

Brunel, N. and Hakim, V. (1999). Fast global oscillations in networks of integrate-and-fire neurons with low firing rates. *Neural Comput.*, **11**:1621–1671.

Bryant, H. L. and Segundo, J. P. (1976). Spike initiation by transmembrane current: a white-noise analysis. *J. Physiol. (Lond.)*, **260**:279–314.

Buck, J. and Buck, E. (1976). Synchronous fireflies. *Sci. Am.*, **234**:74–85.

Bugmann, G., Christodoulou, C. and Taylor, J. G. (1997). Role of temporal integration and fluctuation detection in the highly irregular firing of leaky integrator neuron model with partial reset. *Neural Comput.*, **9**:985–1000.

Burkitt, A. N. and Clark, G. M. (1999). Analysis of integrate-and-fire neurons: synchronization of synaptic input and spike output. *Neural Comput.*, **11**:871–901.

Byrne, J. H. and Berry, W. O. (1989). *Neural Models of Plasticity*. Academic Press, San Diego, CA.

Calvin, W. and Stevens, C. F. (1968). Synaptic noise and other sources of randomness in motoneuron interspike intervals. *J. Neurophysiol.*, **31**:574–587.

Capocelli, R. M. and Ricciardi, L. M. (1971). Diffusion approximation and first passage time problem for a neuron model. *Kybernetik*, **8**:214–223.

Carpenter, G. and Grossberg, S. (1987). ART 2: self-organization of stable category recognition codes for analog input patterns. *Appl. Optics*, **26**:4919–4930.

Carr, C. E. (1993). Processing of temporal information in the brain. *Annu. Rev. Neurosci.*, **16**:223–243.

Carr, C. E. (1995). The development of nucleus laminaris in the barn owl. In Manley, G. A., Klump, G. M., Köppl, C., Fastl, H. and Oeckinghaus, H., editors, *Advances in Hearing Research*, pages 24–30. World Scientific, Singapore.

Carr, C. E. and Konishi, M. (1988). Axonal delay lines for time measurement in the owl's brainstem. *Proc. Natl. Acad. Sci. USA*, **85**:8311–8315.

Carr, C. E. and Konishi, M. (1990). A circuit for detection of interaural time differences in the brain stem of the barn owl. *J. Neurosci.*, **10**:3227–3246.

Cessac, B., Doyon, B., Quoy, M. and Samuelides, M. (1994). Mean-field equations, bifurcation map and route to chaos in discrete time neural networks. *Physica D*, **74**:24–44.

Chow, C. C. (1998). Phase-locking in weakly heterogeneous neuronal networks. *Physica D*, **118**:343–370.

Chow, C. C. and Kopell, N. (2000). Dynamics of spiking neurons with electrical coupling. *Neural Comput.*, **12**:1643–1678.

Chow, C. C. and White, J. (1996). Spontaneous action potential fluctuations due to channel fluctuations. *Biophys. J.*, **71**:3013–3021.

Collingridge, G. L., Kehl, S. J. and McLennan, H. (1983). Excitatory amino acids in synaptic transmission in the Schaffer collateral-commissural pathway of the rat hippocampus. *J. Physiol. (Lond.)*, **334**:33–46.

Collins, J. J., Chow, C. C., Capela, A. C. and Imhoff, T. T. (1996). Aperiodic stochastic resonance. *Phys. Rev. E*, **54**:5575–5584.

Connor, J. A., Walter, D. and McKown, R. (1977). Neural repetitive firing – modifications of the Hodgkin–Huxley axon suggested by experimental results from crustacean axons. *Biophys. J.*, **18**:81–102.

Connors, B. W. and Gutnick, M. J. (1990). Intrinsic firing patterns of diverse cortical neurons. *Trends Neurosci.*, **13**:99–104.

Cordo, P., Inglis, J. T., Verschueren, S. Collins, J. J., Merfield, D. H. and Rosenblum, S. (1996). Noise in human muscle spindels. *Nature*, **383**:769–770.

Cover, T. M. and Thomas, J. A. (1991). *Elements of Information Theory*. Wiley, New York.

Cox, D. R. (1955). Some statistical methods connected with series of events. *J. R. statist. Soc. B*, **17**:129–164.

Cox, D. R. (1962). *Renewal Theory*. Mathuen, London.

Cox, D. R. and Lewis, P. A. W. (1966). *The Statistical Analysis of Series of Events*. Methuen, London.

Crepel, F. (1982). Regression of functional synapses in the immature mammalian cerebellum. *Trends Neurosci.*, **5**:266–269.

Crisanti, A. and Sompolinsky, H. (1988). Dynamics of spin systems with randomly asymmetric bonds: Ising spins and Glauber dynamics. *Phys. Rev. A*, **37**:4865–4874.

Cronin, J. (1987). *Mathematical Aspects of Hodgkin–Huxley Theory*. Cambridge University Press, Cambridge.

Daniel, H., Blond, O., Jaillard, D. and Crepel, F. (1996). Synaptic plasticity in the cerebellum. In Fazeli, M. S. and Collingridge, G. L., editors, *Cortical Plasticity, LTP and LTD*, chapter 10. BIOS Scientific Publishers, Oxford.

Daniel, H., Levenes, C. and Crépel, F. (1998). Cellular mechanisms of cerebellar LTD. *Trends Neurosci.*, **21**:401–407.

de Boer, E. and Kuyper, P. (1968). Triggered correlation. *IEEE Trans. Biomed. Eng.*, **15**:169–179.

de Ruyter van Stevenick, R. R. and Bialek, W. (1988). Real-time performance of a movement-sensitive neuron in the blowfly visual system: coding and information transfer in short spike sequences. *Proc. R. Soc. B*, **234**:379–414.

de Ruyter van Steveninck, R. R., Lowen, G. D., Strong, S. P., Koberle, R., and Bialek, W. (1997). Reproducibility and variability in neural spike trains. *Science*, **275**:1805.

De Zeeuw, C. I., Simpson, J. I., Hoogenraad, C. C., Galjart, N., Koekkoek, S. K. E. and Ruigrok, T. J. H. (1998). Microcircuitry and function of the inferior olive. *Trends Neurosci.*, **21**:391–400.

DeAngelis, G. C., Ohzwaw, I. and Freeman, R. D. (1995). Receptive-field dynamics in the central visual pathways. *Trends Neurosci.*, **18**:451–458.

Debanne, D., Gähwiler, B. H. and Thompson, S. M. (1994). Asynchronous pre- and postsynaptic activity induces associative long-term depression in area CA1 of the rat hippocampus in vitro. *Proc. Natl. Acad. Sci. USA*, **91**:1148–1152.

Debanne, D., Gähwiler, B. H. and Thompson, S. M. (1998). Long-term synaptic plasticity between pairs of individual CA3 pyramidal cells in rat hippocampal slice cultures. *J. Physiol. (Lond.)*, **507**:237–247.

deCharms, R. C. and Merzenich, M. M. (1996). Primary cortical representation of sounds by the coordination of action-potential timing. *Nature*, **381**:610–613.

Derrida, B., Gardner, E. and Zippelius, A. (1987). An exactly solvable asymmetric neural network model. *Europhys. Lett.*, **2**:167–173.

Desmaison, D., Vincent, J.-D. and Lledo, P.-M. (1999). Control of action potential timing by intrinsic subthreshold oscillations in olfactory bulb output neurons. *J. Neurosci.*, **19**:10 727–10 737.

Destexhe, A. and Pare, D. (1999). Impact of network activity on the integrative properties of neocortical pyramidal neurons in vivo. *J. Neurophysiol.*, **81**:1531–1547.

Diesmann, M., Gewaltig, M.-O. and Aertsen, A. (1999). Stable propagation of synchronous spiking in cortical neural networks. *Nature*, **402**:529–533.

Douglass, J. K., Wilkens, L., Pantazelou, E. and Moss, F. (1993). Noise enhancement of information transfer in crayfish mechanoreceptors by stochastic resonance. *Nature*, **365**:337–340.

Dudek, S. M. and Bear, M. F. (1992). Homosynaptic long-term depression in area CA1 of hippocampus and effects of N-methyl-D-aspartate receptor blockade. *Proc. Natl. Acad. Sci. USA*, **89**:4363–4367.

Eckhorn, R., Bauer, R., Jordan, W., Brosch, M., Kruse, W., Munk, M. and Reitboeck,

H. J. (1988). Coherent oscillations: A mechanism of feature linking in the visual cortex? *Biol. Cybern.*, **60**:121–130.

Eckhorn, R., Frien, A., Bauer, R. Woelbern, T. and Kehr, H. (1993). High frequency (60–90 Hz) oscillations in primary visual cortex of awake monkey. *Neuroreport*, **4**:243–246.

Eckhorn, R., Krause, F. and Nelson, J. L. (1993). The RF-cinematogram: a cross-correlation technique for mapping several visual fields at once. *Biol. Cybern.*, **69**:37–55.

Eckhorn, R., Reitboeck, H. J., Arndt, M. and Dicke, P. (1990). Feature linking via synchronization among distributed assemblies: Simulations of results from cat visual cortex. *Neural Comput.*, **2**:293–307.

Edwards, B. E. and Wakefield, G. H. (1993). The spectral shaping of neural discharges by refractory effects. *J. Acoust. Soc. Am.*, **93**:3553–3564.

Egger, V., Feldmeyer, D. and Sakmann, B. (1999). Coincidence detection and changes of synaptic efficacy in spiny stellate neurons in barrel cortex. *Nature Neurosci.*, **2**:1098–1105.

Eggert, J. and van Hemmen, J. L. (2001). Modeling neuronal assemblies: theory and implementation. *Neural Comput.*, **13**:1923–1974.

Ekeberg, O., Wallen, P., Lansner, A., Traven, H., Brodin, L. and Grillner, S. (1991). A computer based model for realistic simulations of neural networks. *Biol. Cybern.*, **65**:81–90.

Ellias, S. A. and Grossberg, S. (1975). Pattern formation, contrast control, and oscillations in the short term memory of shunting on-center off-surround networks. *Biol. Cybern.*, **20**:69–98.

Engel, A. K., König, P., Kreiter, A. K. and Singer, W. (1991a). Interhemispheric synchronization of oscillatory neural responses in cat visual cortex. *Science*, **252**:1177–1179.

Engel, A. K., König, P. and Singer, W. (1991b). Direct physiological evidence for scene segmentation by temporal coding. *Proc. Natl. Acad. Sci. USA*, **88**:9136–9140.

Erisir, A., Lau, D., Rudy, B. and Leonard, C. S. (1999). Specific K^+ channels are required to sustain high frequency firing in fast-spiking neocortical interneurons. *J. Neurophysiol.*, **82**:2476–2489.

Ermentrout, G. B. (1996). Type I membranes, phase resetting curves, and synchrony. *Neural Comput.*, **8**:979–1001.

Ermentrout, G. B. and Cowan, J. D. (1979). A mathematical theory of visual hallucination patterns. *Biol. Cybern.*, **34**:137–150.

Ermentrout, G. B. and Kopell, N. (1984). Frequency plateaus in a chain of weakly coupled oscillators. *SIAM J. Math. Anal.*, **15**:215–237.

Ermentrout, G. B. and Kopell, N. (1986). Parabolic bursting in an excitable system coupled with a slow oscillation. *SIAM J. Appl. Math.*, **46**:233–253.

Ermentrout, G. B., Pascal, M. and Gutkin, B. (2001). The effects of spike frequency adaptation and negative feedback on the synchronization of neuronal oscillators. *Neural Comput.*, **13**:1285–1310.

Ernst, U., Pawelzik, K. and Geisel, T. (1995). Synchronization induced by temporal delays in pulse-coupled oscillators. *Phys. Rev. Lett.*, **74**:1570–1573.

Erwin, E., Obermayer, K. and Schulten, K. (1995). Models of orientation and ocular dominance columns in the visual cortex: a critcal comparison. *Neural Comput.*, **7**:425–468.

Eurich, C. W., Pawelzik, K., Ernst, U., Cowan, J. D. and Milton, J. G. (1999). Dynamics of self-organized delay adaption. *Phys. Rev. Lett.*, **82**:1594–1597.

Feldman, J. L. and Cowan, J. D. (1975). Large-scale activity in neural nets: I. Theory with application to motoneuron pool responses. *Biol. Cybern.*, **17**:29–38.

Feng, J. (2001). Is the integrate-and-fire model good enough – a review. *Neural Netw.*, **14**:1955–1975.

Fetz, E. E. and Gustafsson, B. (1983). Relation between shapes of post-synaptic potentials and changes in firing probability of cat motoneurones. *J. Physiol. (Lond.)*, **341**:387–410.

Fiala, J., Grossberg, S. and Bullock, D. (1996). Metabotropic glutamate receptor activation in cerebellar Purkinje cells as a substrate for adaptive timing of the classically conditioned eye-blink reflex. *J. Neurosci.*, **16**:3760–3774.

FitzHugh, R. (1961). Impulses and physiological states in models of nerve membrane. *Biophys. J.*, **1**:445–466.

French, A. S. and Stein, R. B. (1970). A flexible neural analog using integrated circuits. *IEEE Trans. Biomed. Eng.*, **17**(3):248–253.

Fuortes, M. G. F. and Mantegazzini, F. (1962). Interpretation of the repetitive firing of nerve cells. *J. Gen. Physiol.*, **45**:1163–1179.

Fusi, S., Del Giudice, P. and Amit, D. J. (2000a). Neurophysiology of a VLSI spiking neural network: LANN21. In Amari, S.-I., Giles, L., Gori, M. and Piuri, V., editors, International Joint Conference on Neural Networks, *Proceedings of IJCNN2000*, volume III, pages 121–126.

Fusi, S., Annunziato, M., Badoni, D., Salamon, A. and Amit, D. J. (2000b). Spike-driven synaptic plasticity: theory, simulation, VLSI implementation. *Neural Comput.*, **12**:227–2258.

Fusi, S. and Mattia, M. (1999). Collective behavior of networks with linear (VLSI) integrate and fire neurons. *Neural Comput.*, **11**:633–652.

Gabbiani, F. and Koch, C. (1998). Principles of spike train analysis. In Koch, C. and Segev, I., editors, 2nd edition, *Methods in Neuronal Modeling*, chapter 9, pages 312–360. MIT press, Cambridge, MA.

Gabbiani, F., Midtgaard, J. and Knoepfl, T. (1994). Synaptic integration in a model of cerebellar granule cells. *J. Neurophysiol.*, **72**:999–1009. Corrigenda have been published in *J. Neurophysiol.* (1996) **75**.

Gamble, E. and Koch, C. (1987). The dynamics of free calcium in dendritic spines in response to repetitive synaptic input. *Science*, **236**:1311–1315.

Gammaitoni, L., Hänggi, P., Jung, P. and Marchesoni, F. (1998). Stochastic resonance. *Rev. Mod. Phys.*, **70**:223–287.

Geisler, C. D. and Goldberg, J. M. (1966). A stochastic model of repetitive activity of neurons. *Biophys. J.*, **6**:53–69.

Georgopoulos, A. P., Schwartz, A. and Kettner, R. E. (1986). Neuronal populations coding of movement direction. *Science*, **233**:1416–1419.

Gerstein, G. L. and Perkel, D. H. (1972). Mutual temporal relations among neuronal spike trains. *Biophys. J.*, **12**:453–473.

Gerstner, W. (1995). Time structure of the activity in neural network models. *Phys. Rev. E*, **51**:738–758.

Gerstner, W. (1998). Spiking neurons. In Maass, W. and Bishop, C. M., editors, *Pulsed Neural Networks*, chapter 1, pages 3–53. MIT Press, Cambridge, MA.

Gerstner, W. (2000). Population dynamics of spiking neurons: fast transients, asynchronous states and locking. *Neural Comput.*, **12**:43–89.

Gerstner, W. (2001). Coding properties of spiking neurons: reverse- and cross-correlations. *Neural Netw.*, **14**:599–610.

Gerstner, W. and Abbott, L. F. (1997). Learning navigational maps through potentiation and modulation of hippocampal place cells. *J. Comput. Neurosci.*, **4**:79–94.

Gerstner, W., Kempter, R. and van Hemmen, J. L. (1998). Hebbian learning of pulse timing in the barn owl auditory system. In Maass, W. and Bishop, C. M., editors, *Pulsed Neural Networks*, chapter 14, pages 353–377. MIT Press, Cambridge, MA.

Gerstner, W., Kempter, R., van Hemmen, J. L. and Wagner, H. (1996a). A neuronal learning rule for sub-millisecond temporal coding. *Nature*, **386**:76–78.

Gerstner, W., Kempter, R., van Hemmen, J. L. and Wagner, H. (1997). A developmental learning rule for coincidence tuning in the barn owl auditory system. In Bower, J., editor, *Computational Neuroscience: Trends in Research 1997*, pages 665–669. Plenum Press, New York.

Gerstner, W., Ritz, R. and van Hemmen, J. L. (1993a). A biologically motivated and analytically soluble model of collective oscillations in the cortex: I. Theory of weak locking. *Biol. Cybern.*, **68**:363–374.

Gerstner, W., Ritz, R. and van Hemmen, J. L. (1993b). Why spikes? Hebbian learning and retrieval of time-resolved excitation patterns. *Biol. Cybern.*, **69**:503–515.

Gerstner, W. and van Hemmen, J. L. (1992). Associative memory in a network of 'spiking' neurons. *Network*, **3**:139–164.

Gerstner, W. and van Hemmen, J. L. (1993). Coherence and incoherence in a globally coupled ensemble of pulse emitting units. *Phys. Rev. Lett.*, **71**:312–315.

Gerstner, W. and van Hemmen, J. L. (1994). Coding and information processing in neural networks. In Domany, E., van Hemmen, J. L. and Schulten, K., editors, *Models of Neural Networks II*. Springer-Verlag, New York.

Gerstner, W., van Hemmen, J. L. and Cowan, J. D. (1996b). What matters in neuronal locking. *Neural Comput.*, **8**:1653–1676.

Gestri, G. (1978). Dynamics of a model for the variability of the interspike intervals in a retinal neuron. *Biol. Cybern.*, **31**:97–98.

Gewaltig, M.-O. (2000). *Evolution of Synchronous Spike Volleys in Cortical Networks – Network Simulations and Continuous Probabilistic Models*. Shaker Verlag, Aachen, Germany. PhD thesis.

Giorno, V., Nobile, A. G. and Ricciardi, L. (1992). Instantaneous return processes and neuronal firings. In Trappl, R., editor, *Cybernetics and Systems Research*, volume 1, pages 829–236. World Scientific Press, New York.

Gluss, B. (1967). A model of neuron firing with exponential decay of potential resulting in diffusion equations for the probability density. *Bull. Math. Biophys.*, **29**:233–243.

Gold, J. I. and Bear, M. F. (1994). A model of dendritic spike Ca^{2+} concentration exploring possible basis for sliding synaptic modification threshold. *Proc. Natl. Acad. Sci. USA*, **91**:3941–3945.

Goldberg, J. M., Adrian, H. O. and Smith, F. D. (1964). Response of neurons of the superior olivary complex of the cat to acoustic stimuli of long duration. *J. Neurophysiol.*, **27**:706–749.

Golomb, D. and Ermentrout, G. B. (2001). Bistability in pulse propagation in networks of excitatory and inhibitory populations. *Phys. Rev. Lett.*, **86**:4179–4182.

Golomb, D., Hansel, D., Shraiman, B. and Sompolinsky, H. (1992). Clustering in globally coupled phase oscillators. *Phys. Rev. A*, **45**:3516–3530.

Golomb, D. and Rinzel, J. (1994). Clustering in globally coupled inhibitory neurons. *Physica D*, **72**:259–282.

Gray, C. M., König, P., Engel, A. K. and Singer, W. (1989). Oscillatory responses in cat visual cortex exhibit inter-columnar synchronization which reflects global stimulus properties. *Nature*, **338**:334–337.

Gray, C. M. and Singer, W. (1989). Stimulus-specific neuronal oscillations in orientation columns of cat visual cortex. *Proc. Natl. Acad. Sci. USA*, **86**:1698–1702.

Grossberg, S. (1976). Adaptive pattern classification and universal recoding: I. Parallel development and coding of neuronal feature detectors. *Biol. Cybern.*, **23**:121–134.

Grossberg, S. (1987). *The Adaptive Brain I*. Elsevier, Amsterdam.

Gustafsson, B., Wigstrom, H., Abraham, W. C. and Huang, Y.-Y. (1987). Long-term potentiation in the hippocampus using depolarizing current pulses as the conditioning stimulus. *J. Neurosci.*, **7**:774–780.

Häfliger, P., Mahowald, M. and Watts, L. (1997). A spike based learning neuron in analog VLSI. In Mozer, M. C., Jordan, M. I. and Petsche, T., editors, *Advances in Neural Information Processing Systems*, volume 9, pages 692–698. MIT Press, Cambridge, MA.

Hale, J. and Koçak, H. (1991). *Dynamics and Bifurcations*. Springer-Verlag, New York.

Hansel, D. and Mato, G. (2001). Existence and stability of persistent states in large neuronal networks. *Phys. Rev. Lett.*, **86**:4175–4178.

Hansel, D., Mato, G. and Meunier, C. (1995). Synchrony in excitatory neural networks. *Neural Comput.*, **7**:307–337.

Hansel, D. and Sompolinsky, H. (1998). Modeling feature selectivity in local cortical circuits. In Koch, C. and Segev, I., editors, *Methods in Neuronal Modeling*. MIT Press, Cambridge MA.

Haykin, S. (1994). *Neural Networks*. Prentice Hall, Upper Saddle River, NJ.

Hebb, D. O. (1949). *The Organization of Behavior*. Wiley, New York.

Heiligenberg, W. (1991). *Neural Nets in Electric Fish*. MIT Press, Cambridge, CA.

Herrmann, A. and Gerstner, W. (2001a). Noise and the PSTH response to current transients: I. General theory and application to the integrate-and-fire neuron. *J. Comput. Neurosci.*, **11**:135–151.

Herrmann, A. and Gerstner, W. (2001b). Noise and the PSTH response to current transients: II. Integrate-and-fire model with slow recovery and application to motoneuron data. *J. Comput. Neurosci.*, **12**: (in press).

Hertz, J., Krogh, A. and Palmer, R. G. (1991). *Introduction to the Theory of Neural Computation*. Addison-Wesley, Redwood City, CA.

Hertz, J. and Prugel-Bennet, A. (1996). Learning short synfire chains by self-organization. *Network*, **7**:357–363.

Herz, A. V. M., Sulzer, B., Kühn, R. and van Hemmen, J. L. (1988). The Hebb rule: Representation of static and dynamic objects in neural nets. *Europhys. Lett.*, **7**:663–669.

Herz, A. V. M., Sulzer, B., Kühn, R. and van Hemmen, J. L. (1989). Hebbian learning reconsidered: representation of static and dynamic objects in associative neural nets. *Biol. Cybern.*, **60**:457–467.

Hessler, N. A., Shirke, A. M. and Malinow, R. (1993). The probability of transmitter release at a mammalian central synapse. *Nature*, **366**:569–572.

Hill, A. V. (1936). Excitation and accommodation in nerve. *Proc. R. Soc. B*, **119**:305–355.

Hille, B. (1992). *Ionic Channels of Excitable Membranes*, 2nd edition. Sinauer Associates, Sunderland, MA.

Ho, N. and Destexhe, A. (2000). Synaptic background activity enhances the responsiveness of neocortical pyramidal neurons. *J. Neurophysiol.*, **84**:1488–1496.

Hodgkin, A. L. and Huxley, A. F. (1952). A quantitative description of ion currents and its applications to conduction and excitation in nerve membranes. *J. Physiol. (Lond.)*, **117**:500–544.

Holden, A. V. (1976). *Models of the stochastic activity of neurons*, volume 12 of *Lecture notes in Biomathematics*. Springer-Verlag, Berlin.

Holmes, W. R. and Levy, W. B. (1990). Insights into associative long-term potentiation from computational models of NMDA receptor-mediated calcium influx and intracellular calcium concentration changes. *J. Neurophysiol.*, **63**:1148–1168.

Hopfield, J. J. (1995). Pattern recognition computation using action potential timing for stimulus representation. *Nature*, **376**:33–36.

Hopfield, J. J. and Herz, A. V. M. (1995). Rapid local synchronization of action potentials: towards computation with coupled integrate-and-fire networks. *Proc. Natl. Acad. Sci. USA*, **92**:6655–6662.

Hoppensteadt, F. C. and Izhikevich, E. M. (1997). *Weakly Connected Neural Networks*. Springer-Verlag, Berlin.

Horn, D. and Usher, M. (1989). Neural networks with dynamical thresholds. *Phys. Rev. A*, **40**:1036–1040.

Horn, R. A. and Johnson, C. R. (1985). *Matrix Analysis*. Cambridge University Press, Cambridge.

Hubel, D. H. (1988). *Eye, Brain, and Vision*. W. H. Freeman, New York.

Hubel, D. H. (1995). *Eye, Brain, and Vision*. Scientific American Library, New York; distributed by W. H. Freeman.

Hubel, D. H. and Wiesel, T. N. (1959). Receptive fields of single neurons in the cat's striate cortex. *J. Physiol. (Lond.)*, **148**:574–591.

Hubel, D. H. and Wiesel, T. N. (1962). Receptive fields, binocular interaction and functional architecture in the cat's visual cortex. *J. Physiol. (Lond.)*, **160**:106–154.

Hubel, D. H. and Wiesel, T. N. (1977). Functional architecture of macaque monkey visual cortex. *Proc. R. Soc. B*, **198**:1–59.

Huguenard, J. R. and McCormick, D. A. (1992). Simulation of the currents involved in rhythmic oscillations in thalamic relay neurons. *J. Neurophysiol.*, **68**:1373–1383.

Hüning, Glünder and Palm, G. (1998). Synaptic delay learning in pulse-coupled neurons. *Neural Comput.*, **10**:555–565.

Ito, M. (1984). *The Cerebellum and Neural Control*. Raven Press, New York.

Izhikevich, E. (1999). Class 1 neural excitability, conventional synapses, weakly connected networks, and mathematical foundations of pulse-coupled models. *IEEE Trans. Neural Netw.*, **10**:499–507.

Izhikevich, E. (2000). Neural excitability, spiking, and bursting. *Int. J. Bifurcat. Chaos*, **10**:1171–1266.

Izhikevich, E. (2001). Resonate-and-fire neurons. *Neural Netw.*, **14**:883–894.

Jackson, J. D. (1962). *Classical Electrodynamics*. Wiley, New York.

Jahnsen, H. (1986). Electrophysiological characteristics of neurones in the guinea-pig deep cerebellar nuclei in vitro. *J. Physiol. (Lond.)*, **372**:129–147.

James, W. (1890). *Psychology (Briefer Course)*, chapter 16. Holt, New York.

Jeffress, L. A. (1948). A place theory of sound localisation. *J. Comp. Physiol. Psychol.*, **41**:35–39.

Jensen, O. and Lisman, J. E. (1996). Hippocampal CA3 region predicts memory sequences: accounting for the phase precession of place cells. *Learn. Mem.*, **3**:279–287.

Johannesma, P. I. M. (1968). Diffusion models of the stochastic acticity of neurons. In *Neural Networks*, pages 116–144. Springer-Verlag, Berlin.

Kandel, E. C. and Schwartz, J. H. (1991). *Principles of Neural Science*, 3rd edition. Elsevier, New York.

Kass, R. E. and Ventura, V. (2001). A spike-train probability model. *Neural Comput.*, **13**:1713–1720.

Keener, J. and Sneyd, J. (1998). *Mathematical Physiology*, volume 8 of *Interdisciplinary*

Applied Mathematics. Springer-Verlag, New York.

Kelso, S. R., Ganong, A. H. and Brown, T. H. (1986). Hebbian synapses in hippocampus. *Proc. Natl. Acad. Sci. USA*, **83**:5326–5330.

Kempter, R. (1997). *Hebbsches Lernen zeitlicher Codierung: Theorie der Schallortung im Hörsystem der Schleiereule*, volume 17. Naturwissenschaftliche Reihe, Darmstadt.

Kempter, R., Gerstner, W. and van Hemmen, J. L. (1999). Hebbian learning and spiking neurons. *Phys. Rev. E*, **59**:4498–4514.

Kempter, R., Gerstner, W. and van Hemmen, J. L. (2001). Intrinsic stabilization of output rates by spike-based Hebbian learning. *Neural Comput.*, **13**:2709–2741.

Kepler, T. B., Abbott, L. F. and Marder, E. (1992). Reduction of conductance-based neuron models. *Biol. Cybern.*, **66**:381–387.

Keysers, C., Xiao, D. K., Foldiak, P. and Perrett, D. I. (2001). The speed of sight. *J. Cogn. Neurosci.*, **13**:90–101.

Kirkpatrick, S. and Sherrington, D. (1978). Infinite-ranged models of spin-glasses. *Phys. Rev. B*, **17**:4384–4403.

Kirkwood, P. A. and Sears, I. A. (1978). The synaptic connexions to intercostal motoneurones as revealed by the average common excitation potential. *J. Physiol. (Lond.)*, **275**:103–134.

Kishimoto, K. and Amari, S. (1979). Existence and stability of local excitations in homogeneous neural fields. *J. Math. Biol.*, **7**:303–318.

Kistler, W. M. (2000). Stability properties of solitary waves and periodic wave trains in a two-dimensional network of spiking neurons. *Phys. Rev. E*, **62**(6):8834–8837.

Kistler, W. M. and De Zeeuw, C. I. (2002). Dynamical working memory and timed responses: the role of reverberating loops in the olivo-cerebellar system. *Neural Comput.* (in press).

Kistler, W. M. and Gerstner, W. (2002). Stable propagation of activity pulses in populations of spiking neurons. *Neural Comput.*, **14**: (in press).

Kistler, W. M., Gerstner, W. and van Hemmen, J. L. (1997). Reduction of Hodgkin–Huxley equations to a single-variable threshold model. *Neural Comput.*, **9**:1015–1045.

Kistler, W. M., Seitz, R. and van Hemmen, J. L. (1998). Modeling collective excitations in cortical tissue. *Physica D*, **114**:273–295.

Kistler, W. M. and van Hemmen, J. L. (1999). Short-term synaptic plasticity and network behavior. *Neural Comput.*, **11**:1579–1594.

Kistler, W. M. and van Hemmen, J. L. (2000). Modeling synaptic plasticity in conjunction with the timing of pre- and postsynaptic action potentials. *Neural Comput.*, **12**:385–405.

Kistler, W. M., van Hemmen, J. L. and De Zeeuw, C. I. (2000). Time window control: A model for cerebellar function based on synchronization, reverberation, and time slicing. In Gerrits, N. M., Ruigrok, T. J. H. and De Zeeuw, C. I., editors, *Cerebellar Modules: Molecules, Morphology, and Function*, *Progress in Brain Research*, pages 275–297. Elsevier, Amsterdam.

Kjaer, T. W., Hertz, J. A. and Richmond, B. J. (1994). Decoding cortical neuronal signals: network models, information estimation and spatial tuning. *J. Comput. Neurosci.*, **1**:109–139.

Knight, B. W. (1972a). Dynamics of encoding in a population of neurons. *J. Gen. Physiol.*, **59**:734–766.

Knight, B. W. (1972b). The relationship between the firing rate of a single neuron and the level of activity in a population of neurons. *J. Gen. Physiol.*, **59**:767–778.

Knight, B. W. (2000). Dynamics of encoding in neuron populations: some general mathematical features. *Neural Comput.*, **12**:473–518.

Knox, C. K. (1974). Cross-correlation functions for a neuronal model. *Biophys. J.*, **14**:567–582.

Knudsen, E. I., Blasdel, G. G. and Konishi, M. (1979). Sound localization by the barn owl (*Tyto alba*) measured with the search coil technique. *J. Comp. Physiol.*, **133**:1–11.

Koch, C. (1999). *Biophysics of Computation.* Oxford University Press, New York.

Koch, C., Bernander, Ö. and Douglas, R. J. (1995). Do neurons have a voltage or a current threshold for action potential initiation? *J. Comput. Neurosci.*, **2**:63–82.

Koch, C. and Segev, I. (2000). The role of single neurons in information processing. *Nature Neurosci.*, *Suppl.* **3**:1160–1211.

Kohonen, T. (1984). *Self-organization and Associative Memory.* Springer-Verlag, Berlin.

Konishi, M. (1986). Centrally synthesized maps of sensory space. *Trends Neurosci.*, **9**:163–168.

Konishi, M. (1993). Listening with two ears. *Sci. Am.*, **268**:66–73.

Konnerth, A. and Eilers, J. (1994). Synaptic plasticity and calcium dynamics in cerebellar Purkinje neurons. *Biomed. Res.*, **15** [Suppl. 1]:73–77.

Kopell, N. (1986). Symmetry and phase locking in chains of weakly coupled oscillators. *Commun. Pure Appl. Math.*, **39**:623–660.

König, P., Engel, A. K. and Singer, W. (1996). Integrator or coincidence detector? The role of the cortical neuron revisited. *Trends Neurosci.*, **19**(4):130–137.

König, P. and Schillen, T. B. (1991). Stimulus-dependent assembly formation of oscillatory responses: I. synchronization. *Neural Comput.*, **3**:155–166.

Kree, R. and Zippelius, A. (1991). Asymmetrically diluted neural networks. In Domany, E., van Hemmen, J. L. and Schulten, K., editors, *Models of Neural Networks.* Springer-Verlag, Berlin.

Kreiter, A. K. and Singer, W. (1992). Oscillatory neuronal responses in the visual cortex of the awake macaque monkey. *Eur. J. Neurosci.*, **4**:369–375.

Krüger, J. and Aiple, F. (1988). Multimicroelectrode investigation of monkey striate cortex: spike train correlations in the infragranular layers. *J. Neurophysiol.*, **60**:798–828.

Kuffler, S. W., Nicholls, J. G. and Martin, A. R. (1984). *From Neuron to Brain*, 2nd edition. Sinauer, Sunderland, MA.

Kuramoto, Y. (1975). Self-entrainment of a population of coupled nonlinear oscillators. In Araki, H., editor, *International Symposium on Mathematical Problems in Theoretical Physics*, pages 420–422. Springer-Verlag, Berlin.

Laing, C. R. and Chow, C. C. (2001). Stationary bumps in networks of spiking neurons. *Neural Comput.*, **13**:1473–1494.

Lansky, P. (1984). On approximations of Stein's neuronal model. *J. Theor. Biol.*, **107**:631–647.

Lansky, P. (1997). Sources of periodical force in noisy integrate-and-fire models of neuronal dynamics. *Phys. Rev. E*, **55**:2040–2043.

Lansky, P. and Smith, C. (1989). The effect of random initial value in neural first-passage-time models. *Math. Biosci.*, **93**:191–215.

Lapicque, L. (1907). Recherches quantitatives sur l'excitation electrique des nerfs traitée comme une polarisation. *J. Physiol. Pathol. Gen.*, **9**:620–635.

Latham, P. E., Richmond, B. J., Nelson, P. G. and Nirenberg, S. (2000). Intrinsic dynamics in neuronal networks. I. Theory. *J. Neurophysiol.*, **83**:808–827.

Laurent, G. (1996). Dynamical representation of odors by oscillating and evolving neural assemblies. *Trends Neurosci.*, **19**:489–496.

Lestienne, R. (1996). Determination of the precision of spike timing in the visual cortex of anaesthetised cats. *Biol. Cybern.*, **74**:55–61.

Lev-Ram, V., Jiang, T., Wood, J., Lawrence, D. S. and Tsien, R. Y. (1997). Synergies and coincidence requirements between NO, cGMP, and Ca^{++} in the induction of cerebellar long-term depression. *Neuron*, **18**:1025–1038.

Levin, J. E. and Miller, J. P. (1996). Broadband neural encoding in the cricket cercal sensory system enhanced by stochastic resonance. *Nature*, **380**:165–168.

Levy, W. B. and Stewart, D. (1983). Temporal contiguity requirements for long-term associative potentiation/depression in hippocampus. *Neurosci,*, **8**:791–797.

Lewis, T. J. and Gerstner, W. (2001). Comparison of integrate-and-fire neurons: a case study. Internal Report.

Linden, D. J. (1999). The return of the spike: postsynaptic action potentials and the induction of LTP and LTD. *Neuron*, **22**:661–666.

Linden, D. J. and Connor, J. A. (1995). Long-term synaptic depression. *Annu. Rev. Neurosci.*, **18**:319–357.

Lindner, B. and Schimansky-Geier, L. (2001). Transmission of noise coded versus additive signals through a neuronal ensemble. *Phys. Rev. Lett.*, **86**:2934–2937.

Linsker, R. (1986a). From basic network principles to neural architecture: emergence of orientation columns. *Proc. Natl. Acad. Sci. USA*, **83**:8779–8783.

Linsker, R. (1986b). From basic network principles to neural architecture: emergence of orientation selective cells. *Proc. Natl. Acad. Sci. USA*, **83**:8390–8394.

Linsker, R. (1986c). From basic network principles to neural architecture: emergence of spatial-opponent cells. *Proc. Natl. Acad. Sci. USA*, **83**:7508–7512.

Lisman, J. (1989). A mechanism for Hebb and anti-Hebb processes underlying learning and memory. *Proc. Natl. Acad. Sci. USA*, **86**:9574–9578.

Llinás, R. (1988). The intrinsic electrophysiological properties of mammalian neurons: Insights into central nervous system function. *Science*, **242**:1654–1664.

Llinás, R. (1991). The noncontinuous nature of movement execution. In Humphrey, D. R. and Freund, H.-J., editors, *Motor Control: Concepts and Issues*, pages 223–242. Wiley, New York.

Llinás, R. and Mühlethaler, M. (1988). Electrophysiology of guinea-pig cerebellar nuclear cells in the in vitro brain stem-cerebellar preparation. *J. Physiol. (Lond.)*, **404**:241–258.

Llinás, R. and Yarom, Y. (1986). Oscillatory properties of guinea-pig inferior olivary neurones and their pharmacological modulation: an *in vitro* study. *J. Physiol. (Lond.)*, **376**:163–182.

Longtin, A. (1993). Stochastic resonance in neuron models. *J. Stat. Phys.*, **70**:309–327.

Maass, W. (1996). Lower bounds for the computational power of spiking neurons. *Neural Comput.*, **8**:1–40.

Maass, W. (1998). Computing with spiking neurons. In Maass, W. and Bishop, C. M., editors, *Pulsed Neural Networks*, chapter 2, pages 55–85. MIT Press, Cambridge, MA.

Maass, W. and Bishop, C. (1998). *Pulsed Neural Networks*. MIT Press, Cambridge, MA.

Maass, W., Natschläger, T. and Markram, H. (2002). Real-time computing without stable states: a new framework for neural computation based on perturbations. *Neural Comput.* (in press).

MacGregor, R. J. and Oliver, R. M. (1974). A model for repetitive firing in neurons. *Kybernetik*, **16**:53–64.

MacKay, D. J. C. and Miller, K. D. (1990). Analysis of Linsker's application of Hebbian rules to linear networks. *Network*, **1**:257–297.

Magee, J. C. and Johnston, D. (1997). A synaptically controlled associative signal for

Hebbian plastiticy in hippocampal neurons. *Science*, **275**:209–213.

Mainen, Z. F. and Sejnowski, T. J. (1995). Reliability of spike timing in neocortical neurons. *Science*, **268**:1503–1506.

Malenka, R. C., Kauer, J. A., Zucker, R. S. and Nicoll, R. A. (1988). Postsynaptic calcium is sufficient for potentiation of hippocampal synaptic transmission. *Science*, **242**:81–84.

Malinow, R., Schulman, H. and Tsien, R. W. (1989). Inhibition of postsynaptic PKC or CaMKII blocks induction but not expression of LTP. *Science*, **245**:862–866.

Manis, P. B. and Marx, S. O. (1991). Outward currents in isolated ventral cochlear nucleus neurons. *J. Neurosci.*, **11**:2865–2800.

Manwani, A. and Koch, C. (1999). Detecting and estimating signals in noisy cable structures, I: Neuronal noise sources. *Neural Comput.*, **11**:1797–1829.

Markram, H., Lübke, J., Frotscher, M. and Sakmann, B. (1997). Regulation of synaptic efficacy by coincidence of postsynaptic APs and EPSPs. *Science*, **275**:213–215.

Markram, H. and Tsodyks, M. (1996). Redistribution of synaptic efficacy between neocortical pyramidal neurons. *Nature*, **382**:807–810.

Maršálek, P., Koch, C. and Maunsell, J. (1997). On the relationship between synaptic input and spike output jitter in individual neurons. *Proc. Natl. Acad. Sci. USA*, **94**:735–740.

Mascaro, M. and Amit, D. J. (1999). Effective neural response function for collective population states. *Network*, **10**:351–373.

Mattia, M. and Del Giudice, P. (2002). On the population dynamics of interacting spiking neurons. *Phys. Rev. E*, (in press).

Mayer, M. L., Westbrook, G. L. and Guthrie, P. B. (1984). Voltage-dependent block by Mg^{2+} of NMDA responses in spinal cord neurones. *Nature*, **309**:261–263.

McCulloch, W. S. and Pitts, W. (1943). A logical calculus of ideas immanent in nervous activity. *Bull. Math. Biophys.*, **5**:115–133.

McNamara, B. and Wiesenfeld, K. (1989). Theory of stochastic resonance. *Phys. Rev. A*, **39**:4854–4869.

Mehta, M. R., Quirk, M. and Wilson, M. (2000). Experience-dependent asymmetric shap of hippocampal receptive fields. *Neuron*, **25**:707–715.

Meinhardt, H. (1995). *Algorithmic Beauty of Sea Shells*. Springer-Verlag, New York.

Mel, B. W. (1994). Information processing in dendritic trees. *Neural Comput.*, **6**:1031–1085.

Meyer, C. and van Vreeswijk, C. (2001). Temporal correlations in stochastic networks of spiking neurons. *Neural Comput.*, **14**:369–404.

Miller, K. D. (1994). A model for the development of simple cell receptive fields and the ordered arrangement of orientation columns through activity dependent competition between ON- and OFF-center inputs. *J. Neurosci.*, **14**:409–441.

Miller, K. D. (1995). Receptive fields and maps in the visual cortex: models of ocular dominance and orientation columns. In Domany, E., van Hemmen, J. L. and Schulten, K., editors, *Models of Neural Networks III*, pages 55–78. Springer-Verlag, New York.

Miller, K. D., Keller, J. B. and Stryker, M. P. (1989). Ocular dominance column development: analysis and simulation. *Science*, **245**:605–615.

Miller, K. D. and MacKay, D. J. C. (1994). The role of constraints in Hebbian learning. *Neural Comput.*, **6**:100–126.

Miller, M. I. and Mark, K. E. (1992). A statistical study of cochlear nerve discharge patterns in reponse to complex speech stimuli. *J. Acoust. Soc. Am.*, **92**:202–209.

Milner, P. M. (1974). A model for visual shape recognition. *Psychol. Rev.*, **81**:521–535.

Minai, A. A. and Levy, W. B. (1993). Sequence learning in a single trial. In *INNS World Congress on Neural Networks II*, pages 505–508. International Neural Network Society.

Mirollo, R. E. and Strogatz, S. H. (1990). Synchronization of pulse coupled biological oscillators. *SIAM J. Appl. Math.*, **50**:1645–1662.

Moiseff, A. and Konishi, M. (1981). The owl's interaural pathway is not involved in sound location. *J. Comp. Physiol.*, **144**:299–304.

Montague, P. R., Dayan, P., Person, C. and Sejnowski, T. J. (1995). Bee foraging in uncertain environments using predictive Hebbian learning. *Nature*, **377**:725–728.

Moore, G. P., Segundo, J. P., Perkel, D. H. and Levitan, H. (1970). Statistical signs of synaptic interaction in neurons. *Biophys. J.*, **10**:876–900.

Morris, C. and Lecar, H. (1981). Voltage oscillations in the barnacle giant muscle fiber. *Biophys. J.*, **35**:193–213.

Mountcastle, V. B. (1957). Modality and topographic properties of single neurons of cat's somatosensory cortex. *J. Neurophysiol.*, **20**:408–434.

Murray, J. D. (1993). *Mathematical Biology*. Springer-Verlag, Berlin.

Nagumo, J. S., Arimoto, S. and Yoshizawa, S. (1962). An active pulse transmission line simulating nerve axon. *Proc. IRE*, **50**:2061–2070.

Nelson, M. and Rinzel, J. (1995). The Hodgkin–Huxley model. In Bower, J. M. and Beeman, D., editors, *The Book of Genesis*, chapter 4, pages 27–51. Springer-Verlag, New York.

Neltner, L., Hansel, D., Mato, G. and Meunier, C. (2000). Synchrony in heterogeneous networks of spiking neurons. *Neural Comput.*, **12**:1607–1641.

Ngezahayo, A., Schachner, M. and Artola, A. (2000). Synaptic activity modulates the induction of bidirectional synaptic changes in adult mouse hippocampus. *J. Neurosci.*, **20**:2451–2458.

Nowak, L., Bregestovski, P., Asher, P., Herbet, A. and Prochiantz, A. (1984). Magnesium gates glutamate-activiated channels in mouse central neurons. *Nature*, **307**:462–465.

Nützel, K. (1991). The length of attractors in asymmetric random neural networks with deterministic dynamics. *J. Phys. A: Math. Gen.*, **24**:L151–L157.

Nützel, K., Kien, J., Bauer, K., Altman, J. S. and Krey, U. (1994). Dynamics of diluted attractor neural networks with delays. *Biol. Cybern.*, **70**:553–561.

Nykamp, D. and Tranchina, D. (2000). A population density approach that facilitates large-scale modeling of neural networks: Analysis and application to orientation tuning. *J. Comput. Neurosci.*, **8**:19–50.

Obermayer, K., Blasder, G. G. and Schulten, K. (1992). Statistical-mechanics analysis of self-organization and pattern formation during the development of visual maps. *Phys. Rev. E*, **45**:7568–7589.

Oertel, D. (1983). Synaptic responses and electrical properties of cells in brain slices of the mouse anteroventral cochlear nucleus. *J. Neurosci.*, **3**(10):2043–2053.

Oja, E. (1982). A simplified neuron model as a principal component analyzer. *J. Math. Biol.*, **15**:267–273.

O'Keefe, J. (1993). Hippocampus, theta, and spatial memory. *Curr. Opin. Neurobiol.*, **3**:917–924.

O'Keefe, J. and Recce, H. (1993). Phase relationship between hippocampal place units and the hippocampal theta rhythm. *Hippocampus*, **3**:317–330.

Omurtag, A., Knight, B. W. and Sirovich, L. (2000). On the simulation of a large population of neurons. *J. Comput. Neurosci.*, **8**:51–63.

Optican, L. M. and Richmond, B. J. (1987). Temporal encoding of two-dimensional patterns by single units in primate inferior temporal cortex. 3. Information theoretic analysis. *J. Neurophysiol.*, **57**:162–178.

Oram, M. W., Wiener, M. C., Lestienne, R. and Richmond, B. J. (1999). Stochastic nature of precisely timed spike patterns in visual system neuronal responses. *J. Neurophysiol.*, **81**:3021–3033.

Palm, G. and Poggio, T. (1977). The Volterra representation and the Wiener expansion: Validity and pitfalls. *SIAM J. Appl. Math.*, **33**:195–216.

Papoulis, A. (1991). *Probability, Random Variables, and Stochastic Processes.* McGraw-Hill, New York.

Pavlov, I. P. (1927). *Conditioned Reflexes.* Oxford University Press, Oxford.

Perkel, D. H., Gerstein, G. L. and Moore, G. P. (1967a). Neuronal spike trains and stochastic point processes. I: the single spike train. *Biophys. J.*, **7**:391–418.

Perkel, D. H., Gerstein, G. L. and Moore, G. P. (1967b). Neuronal spike trains and stochastic point processes. II: simultaneous spike trains. *Biophys. J.*, **7**:419–440.

Pham, J., Pakdaman, K., Champagnat, J. and Vibert, J.-F. (1998). Activity in sparsely connected excitatory neural networks: effect of connectivity. *Neural Netw.*, **11**:415–434.

Pinto, D. J., Brumberg, J. C., Simons, D. J. and Ermentrout, G. B. (1996). A quantitative population model of whiskers barrels: re-examining the Wilson–Cowan equations. *J. Comput. Neurosci.*, **3**:247–264.

Plesser, H. E. (1999). *Aspects of Signal Processing in Noisy Neurons.* Georg-August-Universität, Göttingen, PhD thesis.

Plesser, H. E. (2000). The ModUhl software collection. Technical report, MPI für Strömungsforschung, Göttingen. http://www.chaos.gwgd.de/~plesser/ModUhl.htm.

Plesser, H. E. and Gerstner, W. (2000). Noise in integrate-and-fire neurons: from stochastic input to escape rates. *Neural Comput.*, **12**:367–384.

Plesser, H. E. and Tanaka, S. (1997). Stochastic resonance in a model neuron with reset. *Phys. Lett. A*, **225**:228–234.

Poliakov, A. V., Powers, R. K. and Binder, M. C. (1997). Functional identification of input–output transforms of motoneurons in cat. *J. Physiol. (Lond.)*, **504**:401–424.

Poliakov, A. V., Powers, R. K., Sawczuk, A. and Binder, M. C. (1996). Effects of background noise on the response of rat and cat motoneurones to excitatory current transients. *J. Physiol. (Lond.)*, **495**:143–157.

Powers, R. K. D. B. and Binder, M. D. (1996). Experimental evaluation of input-output models of motoneuron discharges. *J. Neurophysiol.*, **75**:367–379.

Rall, W. (1989). Cable theory for dendritic neurons. In Koch, C. and Segev, I., editors, *Methods in Neuronal Modeling*, pages 9–62, MIT Press, Cambridge, MA.

Ramón y Cajal, S. (1909). *Histologie du Système Nerveux de l'Homme et des Vertébré.* A. Maloine, Paris.

Rao, R. P. N. and Sejnowski, T. J. (2001). Spike-timing dependent Hebbian plasticity as temporal difference learning. *Neural Comput.*, **13**:2221–2237.

Reich, D. S., Victor, J. D. and Knight, B. W. (1998). The power ratio and the interval map: spiking models and extracellular recordings. *J. Neurosci.*, **18**(23):10 090–10 104.

Rescorla, R. A. and Wagner, A. R. (1972). A theory of Pavlovian conditioning: variations in the effectiveness of reinforcement and nonreinforcement. In Black, A. H. and Prokasy, W. F., editors, *Classical Conditioning II: Current Research and Theory*, pages 64–99. Appleton Century Crofts, New York.

Reyes, A. D., Rubel, E. W. and Spain, W. J. (1994). Membrane properties underlying the firing of neurons in the avian cochlear nucleus. *J. Neurosci.*, **14**(9):5352–5364.

Reyes, A. D., Rubel, E. W. and Spain, W. J. (1996). *In vitro* analysis of optimal stimuli for phase-locking and time-delayed modulation of firing in avian nucleus laminaris neuron. *J. Neurosci.*, **16**:993–1007.

Rieke, F., Warland, D., de Ruyter van Steveninck, R. and Bialek, W. (1996). *Spikes – Exploring the neural code.* MIT Press, Cambridge, MA.

Rinzel, J. (1985). Excitation dynamics: insights from simplified membrane models. *Feder. Proc.*, **44**:2944–2946.

Rinzel, J. and Ermentrout, G. B. (1998). Analysis of neuronal excitability and oscillations. In Koch, C. and Segev, I., editors, *Methods in Neuronal Modeling*, 2nd edition. MIT Press, Cambridge, MA.

Rinzel, J., Terman, D., Wang, X. and Ermentrout, B. (1998). Propagating activity patterns in large-scale inhibitory neuronal networks. *Science*, **279**:1351–1355.

Risken, H. (1984). *The Fokker Planck Equation: Methods of Solution and Applications.* Springer-Verlag, Berlin.

Ritz, R., Gerstner, W. and van Hemmen, J. L. (1994). A biologically motivated and analytically soluble model of collective oscillations in the cortex: II. Application to binding and pattern segmentation. *Biol. Cybern.*, **71**:349–358.

Ritz, R. and Sejnowski, T. J. (1997). Synchronous oscillatory activity in sensory systems: new vistas on mechanisms. *Curr. Opin. Neurobiol.*, **7**:536–546.

Roberts, P. D. (1999). Computational consequences of temporally asymmetric learning rules: I. Differential Hebbian learning. *J. Comput. Neurosci.*, **7**:235–246.

Roberts, P. D. (2000). Dynamics of temporal learning rules. *Phys. Rev. E*, **62**:4077.

Roberts, P. D. and Bell, C. C. (2000). Computational consequences of temporally asymmetric learning rules: II. Sensory image cancellation. *J. Comput. Neurosci.*, **9**:67–83.

Rospars, J. P. and Lansky, P. (1993). Stochastic model neuron without resetting of dendritic potential: application to the olfactory system. *Biol. Cybern.*, **69**:283–294.

Rubin, J., Lee, D. D. and Sompolinsky, H. (2001). Equilibrium properties of temporally asymmetric Hebbian plasticity. *Phys. Rev. Lett.*, **86**:364–367.

Ruf, B. and Schmitt, M. (1997). Unsupervised learning in networks of spiking neurons using temporal coding. In Gerstner, W., Germond, A., Hasler, M. and Nicoud, J.-D., editors, *Artificial Neural Networks – ICANN'97.* Springer-Verlag, Heidelberg.

Sanders, J. A. and Verhulst, F. (1985). *Averaging Methods in Nonlinear Dynamical Systems.* Springer-Verlag, New York.

Schiegg, A., Gerstner, W. and van Hemmen, J. L. (1995). Intracellular Ca^{2+} stores can account for the time course of LTP induction: a model of Ca^{2+} dynamics in dendritic spines. *J. Neurophysiol.*, **74**:1046–1055.

Schillen, T. B. and König, P. (1991). Stimulus-dependent assembly formation of oscillatory responses: II. Desynchronization. *Neural Comput.*, **3**:167–178.

Schneidman, E., Freedman, B. and Segev, I. (1998). Ion channel stochasticity may be critical in determining the reliability and precision of spike timing. *Neural Comput.*, **10**:1679–1703.

Schrödinger, E. (1915). Zur Theorie der Fall- und Steigversuche an Teilchen mit Brownscher Bewegung. *Physikal. Zeitschrift*, **16**:289–295.

Schultz, W., Dayan, P. and Montague, R. R. (1997). A neural substrate for prediction and reward. *Science*, **275**:1593–1599.

Segundo, J. P., Moore, G. P., Stensaas, L. J. and Bullock, T. H. (1963). Sensitivity of neurons in Aplysia to temporal patterns of arriving impulses. *J. Exp. Biol.*, **40**:643–667.

Sejnowski, T. (1977). Storing covariance with nonlinearly interacting neurons. *J. Math. Biol.*, **4**:303–321.

Sejnowski, T. J. (1999). The book of Hebb. *Neuron*, **24**:773–776.

Sejnowski, T. J. and Tesauro, G. (1989). The Hebb rule for synaptic plasticity: algorithms and implementations. In Byrne, J. H. and Berry, W. O., editors, *Neural Models of Plasticity*, chapter 6, pages 94–103. Academic Press, New York.

Senn, W., Schneider, M. and Ruf, B. (2002). Activity-dependent development of axonal and dendritic delays or, why synaptic transmission should be unreliable. *Neural Comput.*, **14**:583–619.

Senn, W., Tsodyks, M. and Markram, H. (1997). An algorithm for synaptic modification based on exact timing of pre- and post-synaptic action potentials. In Gerstner, W., Germond, A., Hasler, M. and Nicoud, J.-D., editors, *Artificial Neural Networks – ICANN '97*, pages 121–126. Springer-Verlag, Berlin.

Senn, W., Tsodyks, M. and Markram, H. (2001). An algorithm for modifying neurotransmitter release probability based on pre- and postsynaptic spike timing. *Neural Comput.*, **13**:35–67.

Senn, W., Wyler, K., Streit, J., Larkum, M., Lüscher, H.-R., Merz, F., Mey, H., Müller, L., Steinhauser, D., Vogt, K. and Wannier, T. (1996). Dynamics of a random neural network with synaptic depression. *Neural Netw.*, **9**:575–588.

Shadlen, M. N. and Newsome, W. T. (1994). Noise, neural codes and cortical organization. *Curr. Opin. Neurobiol.*, **4**:569–579.

Shadlen, M. N. and Newsome, W. T. (1998). The variable discharge of cortical neurons: implications for connectivity, computation, and information coding. *J. Neurosci.*, **18**:3870–3896.

Shannon, C. E. (1948). A mathematical theory of communication. *Bell Sys. Tech. J.*, **27**:379–423. Reprinted in Shannon, C. E. and Weaver, W. (1949). *The Mathematical Theory of Communication*. University of Illinois Press, Urbana, IL, republished in paperback in 1963.

Shouval, H. Z., Bear, M. F. and Cooper, L. N. (2002). Rate, voltage, timing: what is the fundamental description of NMDA-receptor-dependent bidirectional synaptic plasticity (in press).

Shouval, H. Z. and Perrone, M. P. (1995). Post-Hebbian learning rules. In Arbib, M. A., editor, *The Handbook of Brain Theory and Neural Networks*, pages 645–748. MIT Press, Cambridge, MA.

Siebert, W. M. and Gray, P. R. (1963). Random process model for the firing pattern of single auditory nerve fibers. *Q. Prog. Rep. Lab. Elec. MIT*, **71**:241.

Singer, W. (1994). The role of synchrony in neocortical processing and synaptic plasticity. In Domany, E., van Hemmen, J. L. and Schulten, K., editors, *Models of Neural Networks II*, chapter 4. Springer-Verlag, Berlin.

Singer, W. and Gray, C. M. (1995). Visual feature integration and the temporal correlation hypothesis. *Annu. Rev. Neurosci.*, **18**:555–586.

Softky, W. and Koch, C. (1993). The highly irregular firing pattern of cortical cells is inconsistent with temporal integration of random EPSPS. *J. Neurosci.*, **13**:334–350.

Softky, W. R. (1995). Simple codes versus efficient codes. *Curr. Opin. Neurobiol.*, **5**:239–247.

Sompolinsky, H., Crisanti, A. and Sommers, H. J. (1988). Chaos in random neural networks. *Phys. Rev. Lett.*, **61**:259–262.

Sompolinsky, H. and Kanter, I. (1986). Temporal association in asymmetric neural networks. *Phys. Rev. Lett.*, **57**:2861–2864.

Song, S., Miller, K. D. and Abbott, L. F. (2000). Competitive Hebbian learning through spike-time-dependent synaptic plasticity. *Nature Neurosci.*, **3**:919–926.

Sotelo, C., Llinás, R. and Baker, R. (1974). Structural study of inferior olivary nucleus of the cat: morphological correlations of electrotonic coupling. *J. Neurophysiol.*,

37:541–559.

Spiridon, M., Chow, C. and Gerstner, W. (1998). Frequency spectrum of coupled stochstic neurons with refractoriness. In Niklasson, L., Bodén, M. and Ziemke, T., editors, *ICANN'98*, pages 337–342. Springer-Verlag, Berlin.

Spiridon, M. and Gerstner, W. (1999). Noise spectrum and signal transmission through a population of spiking neurons. *Network Comput. Neural Syst.*, **10**:257–272.

Spiridon, M. and Gerstner, W. (2001). Effect of lateral connections on the accuracy of the population code for a network of spiking neurons. *Network Comput. Neural Syst.*, **12**:409–421.

Stein, R. B. (1965). A theoretical analysis of neuronal variability. *Biophys. J.*, **5**:173–194.

Stein, R. B. (1967a). The information capacity of nerve cells using a frequency code. *Biophys. J.*, **7**:797–826.

Stein, R. B. (1967b). Some models of neuronal variability. *Biophys. J.*, **7**:37–68.

Steinmetz, P. N., Roy, A., Fitzgerald, P. J., Hsiao, S. S., Johnson, K. and Niebur, E. (2000). Attention modulates synchronized neuronal firing in primate somatosensory cortex. *Nature*, **404**:187–190.

Stemmler, M. (1996). A single spike suffices: the simplest form of stochastic resonance in model neurons. *Network*, **7**:687–716.

Stevens, C. F. and Zador, A. M. (1998). Novel integrate-and-fire like model of repetitive firing in cortical neurons. In *Proc. of the 5th Joint Symposium on Neural Computation*.

Strogatz, S. H. (1994). *Nonlinear dynamical systems and chaos*. Addison-Wesley, Reading MA.

Stuart, G. J. and Sakmann, B. (1994). Active propagation of somatic action potentials into neocortical pyramidal cell dendrites. *Nature*, **367**:69–72.

Sullivan, W. E. and Konishi, M. (1984). Segregation of stimulus phase and intensity coding in the cochlear nucleus of the barn owl. *J. Neurosci.*, **4**(7):1787–1799.

Suri, R. E. and Schutz, W. (2001). Temporal difference model reproduces anticipatory neural activity. *Neural Comput.*, **13**:841–862.

Sutton, R. S. and Barto, A. G. (1981). Towards a modern theory of adaptive networks: expectation and prediction. *Psychol. Rev.*, **88**:135–171.

Swindale, N. V. (1982). A model for the formation of orientation columns. *Proc. R. Soc. London B*, **215**:211–230.

Tanabe, M., Gäwiler, B. H. and Gerber, U. (1998a). L-type Ca^{2+} channels mediate the slow Ca^{2+}-dependent afterhyperpolarization current in rat CA3 pyramidal cells *in vitro*. *J. Neurophysiol.*, **80**:2268–2273.

Tanabe, S., Pakdaman, K., Nomura, T. and Sato, S. (1998b). Dynamics of an ensemble of leaky integrate-and-fire neuron models and its response to a pulse input. Technical Report of IEICE, NLP98-14.

Terman, D. and Wang, D. (1995). Global competition and local cooperation in a network of neural oscillators. *Physica D*, **81**:148–176.

Theunissen, F. and Miller, J. P. (1995). Temporal encoding in nervous systems: a rigorous definition. *J. Comput. Neurosci.*, **2**:149–162.

Thompson, R. F. (1993). *The Brain*, 2nd edition. W. H. Freeman, New York.

Thorpe, S., Fize, D. and Marlot, C. (1996). Speed of processing in the human visual system. *Nature*, **381**:520–522.

Tovee, M. J. and Rolls, E. T. (1995). Information encoding in short firing rate epochs by single neurons in the primate temporal visual cortex. *Vis. Cognit.*, **2**(1):35–58.

Tovee, M. J., Rolls, E. T., Treves, A. and Belles, R. P. (1993). Information encoding and the responses of single neurons in the primate visual cortex. *J. Neurophysiol.*,

70:640–654.

Traub, R. D., Wong, R. K. S., Miles, R. and Michelson, H. (1991). A model of a CA3 hippocampal pyramidal neuron incorporating voltage-clamp data on intrinsic conductances. *J. Neurophysiol.*, **66**:635–650.

Treves, A. (1993). Mean-field analysis of neuronal spike dynamics. *Network*, **4**:259–284.

Treves, A., Rolls, E. T. and Simmen, M. (1997). Time for retrieval in recurrent associative memories. *Physica D*, **107**:392–400.

Troyer, T. W. and Miller, K. D. (1997). Physiological gain leads to high ISI variability in a simple model of a cortical regular spiking cell. *Neural Comput.*, **9**:971–983.

Tsodyks, M., Mitkov, I. and Sompolinsky, H. (1993). Patterns of synchrony in inhomogeneous networks of oscillators with pulse interaction. *Phys. Rev. Lett.*, **71**:1281–1283.

Tsodyks, M. V. and Sejnowski, T. (1995). Rapid state switching in balanced cortical networks. *Network*, **6**:111–124.

Tuckwell, H. C. (1988). *Introduction to Theoretical Neurobiology*. Cambridge University Press, Cambridge.

Uhlenbeck, G. E. and Ornstein, L. S. (1930). On the theory of the Brownian motion. *Phys. Rev.*, **36**:823–841.

van Hemmen, J. L., Gerstner, W., Herz, A. V. M., Kühn, R., Sulzer, B. and Vaas, M. (1990). Encoding and decoding of patterns which are correlated in space and time. In Dorffner, G., editor, *Konnektionismus in Artificial Intelligence und Kognitionsforschung*, pages 153–162. Springer-Verlag, Berlin.

van Hemmen, J. L., Kistler, W. M. and Thomas, E. G. F. (2000). Calculation of Volterra kernels for solutions of nonlinear differential equations. *SIAM J. Appl. Math.*, **61**:1–21.

van Kampen, N. G. (1992). *Stochastic Processes in Physics and Chemistry*, 2nd edition. North-Holland, Amsterdam.

van Rossum, M. C. W., Bi, G. Q. and Turrigiano, G. G. (2000). Stable Hebbian learning from spike timing-dependent plasticity. *J. Neurosci.*, **20**:8812–8821.

van Vreeswijk, C. (1996). Partially synchronized states in networks of pulse-coupled neurons. *Phys. Rev. E*, **54**:5522–5537.

van Vreeswijk, C., Abbott, L. F. and Ermentrout, G. B. (1994). When inhibition not excitation synchronizes neural firing. *J. Comput. Neurosci.*, **1**:313–321.

van Vreeswijk, C. and Sompolinsky, H. (1996). Chaos in neuronal networks with balanced excitatory and inhibitory activity. *Science*, **274**:1724–1726.

van Vreeswijk, C. and Sompolinsky, H. (1997). Irregular firing in cortical circuits with inhibition/excitation balance. In Bower, J., editor, *Computational Neuroscience: Trends in Research, 1997*, pages 209–213. Plenum Press, New York.

van Vreeswijk, C. (2000). Stability of the asynchronous state in networks of non-linear oscillators. *Phys. Rev. Lett.*, **84**:5110–5113.

van Vreeswijk, C. and Sompolinsky, H. (1998). Chaotic balanced state in a model of cortical circuits. *Neural Comput.*, **10**:1321–1371.

Verhulst, F. (1996). *Nonlinear Differential Equations and Dynamical Systems*. Springer-Verlag, Berlin.

Volterra, V. (1959). *Theory of Functionals and of Integral and Integro-Differential Equations*. Dover, New York.

von der Malsburg, C. (1973). Self-organization of orientation selective cells in the striate cortex. *Kybernetik*, **14**:85–100.

von der Malsburg, C. (1981). The correlation theory of brain function. Internal Report 81–2, MPI für Biophysikalische Chemie, Göttingen. Reprinted in Models of Neural

Networks II, Domany et al., editors. Springer-Verlag, Berlin, 1994.

von der Malsburg, C. and Buhmann, J. (1992). Sensory segmentation with coupled neural oscillators. *Biol. Cybern.*, **67**:233–242.

Wang, D. (1995). Emergent synchrony in locally coupled neural oscillators. *IEEE Trans. Neural Netw.*, **6**:941–948.

Wang, D., Buhmann, J. and von der Malsburg, C. (1990). Pattern segmentation in associative memory. *Neural Comput.*, **2**:94–106.

Wehmeier, U., Dong, D., Koch, C. and van Essen, D. (1989). Modeling the mammalian visual system. In Koch, C. and Seger, J., editors, *Methods in Neuronal Modeling*, pages 335–359. MIT Press, Cambridge, MA.

Weiss, T. F. (1966). A model of the peripheral auditory system. *Kybernetik*, **3**:153–175.

Welsh, J. P., Lang, E. J., Sugihara, I. and Llinás, R. (1995). Dynamic organization of motor control within the olivocerebellar system. *Nature*, **374**:453–457.

White, J. A., Rubinstein, J. T. and Kay, A. R. (2000). Channel noise in neurons. *Trends Neurosci.*, **23**:131–137.

Wiesenfeld, K. and Jaramillo, F. (1998). Minireview of stochastic resonance. *Chaos*, **8**:539–548.

Willshaw, D. J. and von der Malsburg, C. (1976). How patterned neuronal connections can be set up by self-organization. *Proc. R. Soc. London Ser. B*, **194**:431–445.

Wilson, H. R. and Cowan, J. D. (1972). Excitatory and inhibitory interactions in localized populations of model neurons. *Biophys. J.*, **12**:1–24.

Wilson, H. R. and Cowan, J. D. (1973). A mathematical theory of the functional dynamics of cortical and thalamic nervous tissue. *Kybernetik*, **13**:55–80.

Wilson, M. A. and McNaughton, B. L. (1993). Dynamics of the hippocampal ensemble code for space. *Science*, **261**:1055–1058.

Wimbauer, S., Gerstner, W. and van Hemmen, J. L. (1998). Analysis of a correlation-based model for the development of orientation-selective receptive fields in the visual cortex. *Network*, **9**:449–466.

Wimbauer, S., Wenisch, O. G., Miller, K. D. and van Hemmen, J. L. (1997a). Development of spatiotemporal receptive fields of simple cells: I. Model formulation. *Biol. Cybern.*, **77**:453–461.

Wimbauer, S., Wenisch, O. G., van Hemmen, J. L. and Miller, K. D. (1997b). Development of spatiotemporal receptive fields of simple cells: II. Simulation and analysis. *Biol. Cybern.*, **77**:463–477.

Wiskott, L. and Sejnowski, T. (1998). Constraint optimization for neural map formation: a unifying framework for weight growth and normalization. *Neural Comput.*, **10**:671–716.

Xie, X. and Seung, S. (2000). Spike-based learning rules and stabilization of persistent neural activity. In Solla, S. A., Leen, T. K. and Müller, K.-R., editors, *Advances in Neural Information Processing Systems 12*. MIT Press, Cambridge, MA.

Yamada, W. M., Koch, C. and Adams, P. R. (1989). Multiple channels and calcium dynamics. In Koch, C. and Segev, I., editors, *Methods in Neuronal Modeling: From Synapses to Networks*, chapter 4. MIT Press, Cambridge, MA.

Zador, A., Koch, C. and Brown, T. H. (1990). Biophysical model of a Hebbian synapse. *Proc. Natl. Acad. Sci. USA*, **87**:6718–6722.

Zador, A. M. (1998). Impact of synaptic unreliability on the information transmitted by spiking neuron. *J. Neurophysiol.*, **79**:1219–1229.

Zhang, L. I., Tao, H. W., Holt, C. E., Harris, W. A. and Poo, M.-M. (1998). A critical window for cooperation and competition among developing retinotectal synapses. *Nature*, **395**:37–44.

Index

Printed in the United States
By Bookmasters